Understanding
ICD-10-CM & ICD-10-PCS
A Worktext

2021

Mary Jo Bowie
MS, BS, AAS, RHIA, RHIT

Australia • Brazil • Canada • Mexico • Singapore • United Kingdom • United States

Understanding ICD-10-CM and ICD-10-PCS: A Worktext, 2021 edition
Mary Jo Bowie

SVP, Higher Education & Skills Product:
Erin Joyner

Product Director: Matthew Seeley

Product Team Manager: Stephen G. Smith

Director, Learning Design: Rebecca von Gillern

Senior Manager, Learning Design:
Leigh Hefferon

Learning Designer: Kaitlin Schlicht

Product Assistant: Dallas Wilkes

Marketing Manager: Courtney Cozzy

Director, Content Creation: Juliet Steiner

Senior Manager, Content Creation: Patty Stephan

Content Manager: Mark Peplowski

Digital Delivery Lead: Lisa Christopher

Designer: Angela Sheehan

Cover image: antishock/Shutterstock.com

For product information and technology assistance, contact us at
Cengage Customer & Sales Support, 1-800-354-9706 or support.cengage.com

For permission to use material from this text or product, submit all requests online at **www.cengage.com/permissions**

Library of Congress Control Number: 2020919518

ISBN: 978-0-357-51684-3

Cengage
200 Pier 4 Boulevard
Boston, MA 02210
USA

Cengage is a leading provider of customized learning solutions with employees residing in nearly 40 different countries and sales in more than 125 countries around the world. Find your local representative at **www.cengage.com**

Cengage is committed to creating inclusive and diverse products, including perspectives that represent the diversity of people across all backgrounds, identities, opinions, and experiences. If you have any feedback related to this, please contact us at **Cengage Customer & Sales Support, 1-800-354-9706 or support.cengage.com.**

To learn more about Cengage platforms and services, register or access your online learning solution, or purchase materials for your course, visit **www.cengage.com.**

Notice to the Reader

Publisher does not warrant or guarantee any of the products described herein or perform any independent analysis in connection with any of the product information contained herein. Publisher does not assume, and expressly disclaims, any obligation to obtain and include information other than that provided to it by the manufacturer. The reader is expressly warned to consider and adopt all safety precautions that might be indicated by the activities described herein and to avoid all potential hazards. By following the instructions contained herein, the reader willingly assumes all risks in connection with such instructions. The publisher makes no representations or warranties of any kind, including but not limited to, the warranties of fitness for particular purpose or merchantability, nor are any such representations implied with respect to the material set forth herein, and the publisher takes no responsibility with respect to such material. The publisher shall not be liable for any special, consequential, or exemplary damages resulting, in whole or part, from the readers' use of, or reliance upon, this material.

Printed at CLDPC, USA, 09-21

To my husband, Bill, who is my encouragement and who finally is driving his sports car!

To my daughters and son-in-law and my granddaughters and grandsons, may you all find God's will for your lifes. Thanks for all you do to allow me the time to write. To my parents for making sure that you gave me all the opportunities to become who I am today.

To Stephen Smith, Kaitlin Schlicht, and Mark Peplowski, who provide a vision for the book. To all of my Cengage family, who work to make my books happen. A special thanks to Mark Peplowski for all he does that goes above and beyond his job. A special thanks to Lou Ann Decker for her expertise reviewing this book.

—*Mary Jo Bowie*

To my husband, Bill, who is my encouragement and who finally is driving his sports car.

To my daughters and son-in-law and my granddaughters and grandsons, may you all find God's will for your lives. Thanks for all you do to allow me the time to write. To my parents for making sure that you gave me all the opportunities to become who I am today.

To Stephen Smith, Keith Schilling, and Mark Pacifico, who provide a vision for the book. To all of my Cengage family, who work to make my books happen. A special thanks to Mark Pacifico for all he does that goes above and beyond his job. A special thanks to Lori Ann Decker for her expertise reviewing this book.

—Mary Jo Bowie

TABLE OF CONTENTS

Chapter 24: Injury, Poisoning, and Certain Other Consequences of External Causes   408

Chapter 25: External Causes of Morbidity   433

Understanding ICD-10-CM and ICD-10-PCS: A Worktext, 2021 Edition, provides a comprehensive textbook to learn and master ICD-10-CM and ICD-10-PCS coding. This book can be used to instruct learners in both academic and clinical settings. Its design helps coders transition to the new coding system.

The *ICD-10-CM Official Guidelines for Coding and Reporting* are highlighted in various book chapters, and the complete guidelines are contained in the appendix which is found in MindTap. Numerous clinical examples and case studies are used throughout the book to provide opportunities for learners to practice with real-life scenarios. Frequently encountered diseases are highlighted to enable the learner to become familiar with common disease signs and symptoms, clinical testing, and treatments.

Organization of the Worktext

Several features are incorporated into the chapters to facilitate learning:

- A **chapter outline** gives a brief overview of chapter content.
- **Learning objectives** familiarize the learner with chapter objectives.
- **Key terms** are listed at the start of each chapter and then highlighted and defined within the chapter.
- Many clinical **examples** are used throughout the text.
- **Illustrations** of human anatomy appear, based on the concept that learning is enhanced through visual tools.
- **Coding assignments** and **case studies** are used to determine comprehension of the material and to provide real-world practice.
- **Chapter summaries** review the main ideas for review purposes.
- **Internet links** provide additional reference materials for the learner and take learning beyond the textbook.
- **Chapter reviews** contain questions to reinforce content presented.

New to the 2021 Edition

- The most current code sets available at the time of publication
- Updated information from the 2021 ICD-10-CM and ICD-10-PCS Official Guidelines for Coding and Reporting
- Content added for the new ICD-10-CM chapter entitled "Codes for Special Purposes"
- Additional Coding Assignments in many chapters

Teaching Package for the Instructor

The following supplements are available online to enhance the use of *Understanding ICD-10-CM and ICD-10-PCS: A Worktext*, 2021 Edition. All instructor resources can be accessed by going to **www.cengage.com** to create a unique user login. Contact your sales representative for more information. Online instructor resources at the Companion Site are password-protected and include the following:

Instructor Resources

Spend less time planning and more time teaching with Cengage Learning's Instructor Resources to Accompany the 2021 Edition of *Understanding ICD-10-CM and ICD-10-PCS*. As an instructor, you will find these materials offer invaluable assistance by giving you access to all of your resources, anywhere, at any time.

Features of the Instructor Resources include:

- A downloadable, customizable *Instructor Manual* containing a complete list of chapter activities and assessments, additional activities and assignments, and a list of additional resources.
- A downloadable, customizable *Solution and Answer Guide* containing the answers for all textbook questions.
- A *Test Bank* with several hundred questions and answers for use in instructor-created quizzes and tests.
- Chapter slides created in *PowerPoint*® to use for in-class lecture material and as handouts for students.

Computerized Test Bank

Cengage Learning Testing Powered by Cognero is a flexible, online system that allows you to:

- author, edit, and manage test bank content from multiple Cengage Learning solutions
- create multiple test versions in an instant
- deliver tests from your LMS, your classroom, or wherever you want.

Cengage Learning Testing Powered by Cognero works on any operating system or browser.

- No special installs or downloads needed.
- Create tests from school, home, the coffee shop—anywhere with Internet access.
- Simplicity at every step. A desktop-inspired interface features drop-down menus and familiar, intuitive tools that take you through content creation and management with ease.
- Full-featured test generator. Create ideal assessments with your choice of 15 question types (including true/false, multiple choice, opinion scale/Likert, and essay). Multi-language support, an equation editor, and unlimited metadata help ensure your tests are complete and compliant.
- Cross-compatible capability. Import and export content into other systems.

MindTap: Empower Your Students

MindTap is a platform that propels students from memorization to mastery. It gives you complete control of your course, so you can provide engaging content, challenge every learner, and build student confidence. Customize interactive syllabi to emphasize priority topics, then add your own material or notes to the eBook as desired. This outcomes-driven application gives you the tools needed to empower students and boost both understanding and performance.

Access Everything You Need in One Place

Cut down on prep with the preloaded and organized MindTap course materials. Teach more efficiently with interactive multimedia, assignments, quizzes, and more. Give your students the power to read, listen, and study on their phones, so they can learn on their terms.

Empower Students to Reach their Potential

Twelve distinct metrics give you actionable insights into student engagement. Identify topics troubling your entire class and instantly communicate with those struggling. Students can track their scores to stay motivated towards their goals. Together, you can be unstoppable.

Control Your Course—and Your Content

Get the flexibility to reorder textbook chapters, add your own notes, and embed a variety of content including Open Educational Resources (OER). Personalize course content to your students' needs. They can even read your notes, add their own, and highlight key text to aid their learning.

Get a Dedicated Team, Whenever You Need Them

MindTap isn't just a tool, it's backed by a personalized team eager to support you. We can help set up your course and tailor it to your specific objectives, so you'll be ready to make an impact from day one. Know we'll be standing by to help you and your students until the final day of the term.

Learning Package for the Student

Companion Site

Additional textbook resources for students can be found online by creating an account at http://login.cengage.com. All resources located on the Companion Site to accompany *Understanding ICD-10-CM and ICD-10-PCS: A Worktext*, 2021 Edition, are free to textbook users.

MindTap

ISBN: 978-0-357-51689-8 (electronic access code)/ 978-0-357-51690-4 (printed access card)

MindTap is the first of its kind in an entirely new category: the Personalized Learning Experience (PLE). This personalized program of digital products and services uses interactivity and customization to engage students, while offering a range of choice in content, platforms, devices, and learning tools. MindTap is device agnostic, meaning that it will work with any platform or learning management system, and will be accessible anytime, anywhere: on desktops, laptops, tablets, mobile phones, and other Internet-enabled devices. *Understanding ICD-10-CM and ICD-10-PCS: A Worktext*, 2021 Edition, on MindTap includes:

- An interactive eBook with highlighting, note-taking functions, and more
- Flashcards for practicing chapter terms
- Computer-graded activities and exercises
- Case studies
- Medical Coding Trainer

Optum360® EncoderPro.com

Enhance your course with Cengage learning materials and online coding tools from Optum360®. *EncoderPro.com Expert* is an online coding and reference tool designed to enhance your coding capabilities.

- Using online coding tools can help by: saving you time and money;
- increasing accuracy, reducing denials, and ensuring you receive complete reimbursement; and
- reducing required storage space and paper.

Features of EncoderPro.com Expert include:

- ICD-10-CM code content search
- ICD-10 mapping tools
- Coders' Desk Reference
- Complete code history
- Local Coverage Determinations (LCDs) and Medicare Pub. 100 access
- Medicare CCI edits
- Modifier crosswalk
- Enhanced compliance editor
- Enhanced LCD/NCD policy searching
- Cross-coder relationships from seven coding and billing specialty reference books

To make the switch and start saving on coding materials with Cengage and Optum360®, contact your Cengage Learning Consultant today at cengage.com/repfinder.

ACKNOWLEDGMENTS

A special thank-you is extended to the reviewers who have provided recommendations to enhance the content of this work.

Dr. Tammie Bolling
Associate Professor
Pellissippi State Community
College
Knoxville, Tennessee

Lindsey Klimek, CPC, CIMC
Instructor
Alexandria Technical and
Community College
Alexandria, Minnesota

Keita Kornegay, CEHRS, CMAA, CMRS
Professor
Wilson Community College
Wilson, North Carolina

Natasha Johnson, RHIT
Health Information Management
Clinical Coordinator
Midlands Technical College
Columbia, South Carolina

Technical Reviewer

Both Mary Jo and the Cengage team offer their profound thanks to Lou Ann Decker for her significant technical review efforts. Your efforts were invaluable on this revision. Many thanks for all that you do!

Lou Ann Decker, AAS, RHIT

Mary Jo Bowie, MS, BS, AAS, RHIA, RHIT

Mary Jo has worked in the health information field for more than 40 years as a consultant, HIM department director, and college HIM and medical coding program director and associate professor, and instructor and medical transcriptionist. As consultant and owner of Health Information Professional Services in Binghamton, New York, she has consulted nationally in various levels of care, including inpatient hospital settings, ambulatory care settings, skilled nursing facilities, physician offices, and clinics. She is an active member of the American Health Information Management Association (AHIMA). She has held the following positions in the New York Health Information Management Association: education director and a member of the board of directors, and Ambulatory Care Coding Guidelines Committee chairperson. At the collegiate level, teaching both in the classroom and in an Internet-based format, she has taught numerous health information technology and coding and reimbursement courses. Mary Jo also conducts professional coding workshops for coders as well as for physicians and clinical staff. She is also an AHIMA-approved ICD-10-CM and ICD-10-PCS Train the Trainer. She has led more than 60 workshops for Cengage on ICD-10-CM and ICD-10-PCS.

Introduction to Coding and Coding Professions

Chapter Outline

Chapter Objectives

At the conclusion of this chapter, you should be able to:

1. Describe the purpose of coding.
2. Explain the development of the ICD classification system.
3. Discuss the standards mandated by the Health Insurance Portability and Accountability Act of 1996.
4. Describe professional associations with reference to their certifications, requirements, and purpose.
5. Identify the employment opportunities for coders.

Key Terms

Accrediting Bureau
  of Health Education
  Schools (ABHES)

Administrative
  Simplification

American Academy of
  Professional Coders
  (AAPC)

American Association
  of Medical Assistants
  (AAMA)

American Health
  Information
  Management
  Association
  (AHIMA)

American Medical
  Billing Association
  (AMBA)

American Medical
  Technologists
  (AMT)

Centers for Medicare
  and Medicaid Services
  (CMS)

Certified Coding
  Associate (CCA)

Certified Coding
  Specialist (CCS)

Certified Coding
  Specialist, Physician-
  Based (CCS-P)

Certified Documentation
  Improvement
  Practitioner
  (CDIP)

Certified Health Data
  Analyst (CHDA)

Certified in Healthcare
  Privacy and Security
  (CHPS)

Certified Inpatient Coder
  (CIC)

(continues)

Key Terms (*continued*)

Certified Medical Assistant (CMA)

Certified Medical Billing Specialist (CMBS)

Certified Medical Record Technician (CMRT)

Certified Medical Reimbursement Specialist (CMRS)

Certified Outpatient Coder (COC)

Certified Professional Coder (CPC)

Certified Risk Adjustment Coder (CRC)

Coding Commission on Accreditation of Allied Health Education Programs (CAAHEP)

Health Insurance Portability and Accountability Act of 1996 (HIPAA), Public Law 104-191

ICD-10-CM

ICD-10-PCS

ICD-10 Procedure Coding System

International Classification of Diseases, Tenth Revision, Clinical Modification (ICD-10-CM)

International Classification of Diseases, Tenth Revision (ICD-10)

Medical Association of Billers (MAB)

Morbidity

Mortality

National Center for Health Statistics (NCHS)

Registered Health Information Administrator (RHIA)

Registered Health Information Technician (RHIT)

Registered Medical Assistant (RMA)

World Health Organization (WHO)

Introduction

Medical **coding** is the assignment of numeric or alphanumeric digits and characters to specific diagnostic and procedural phrases. This coding, like any other language, needs to be translated to be understood, and each combination of numbers or of numbers and letters represents a diagnostic or procedural phrase.

> **EXAMPLE:** The diagnostic phrase "appendicitis" is translated into diagnostic code K37 in the ICD-10-CM coding system. The procedural phrase "open total appendectomy" is translated into procedure code 0DTJ0ZZ in ICD-10-PCS.

By using ICD-10-CM and ICD-10-PCS codes, health care professionals can effectively collect, process, and analyze diagnostic and procedural information.

Professional Coding

Coding is the language used by insurance companies and health care providers to describe what brought a person to a facility for treatment and what services were performed. The ability of health care professionals to communicate and translate these codes is vital to the care and treatment rendered to the patient. These codes are also communicated to the insurance company, which is required to make payment for the patient's care. All involved parties must be able to understand and fluently "speak" the coding language to convey the essence of the patient's visit and treatment.

In the chapters that follow, the student will gain a greater knowledge of the language of coding, specifically ICD-10-CM and ICD-10-PCS. By the completion of this book, the learner will have the knowledge base needed to become fluent in the language of ICD-10-CM and ICD-10-PCS coding, which is an ever-increasingly used tool in the health care industry.

ICD-10-CM and ICD-10-PCS codes are also used to collect information that is used for various purposes by hospitals, health departments and governmental organizations. For example, hospitals code diagnostic information and report that information to state health departments that in turn report the information to federal organizations such as the Centers for Disease Control and Prevention (CDC). The CDC then reports information to the World Health Organization. During 2020 the world has faced the COVID-19 pandemic and has collected and used information on the frequency of the disease and complications. This information was originally coded and generated by coders in hospitals and healthcare facilities.

History of Coding

ICD-10-CM, an abbreviation for the *International Classification of Diseases,* **Tenth Revision, Clinical Modification**, is an arrangement of classes or groups of diagnoses by systematic division that is used in the United States. ICD-10-CM is based on the official version of the *International Classification of Diseases,* **Tenth Revision (ICD-10)**, which was developed by the **World Health Organization (WHO)** in Geneva, Switzerland. ICD-10 is used throughout the world as a standard diagnostic tool for epidemiology, health management, and clinical purposes. In 1948, the WHO assumed responsibility for preparing and publishing the revisions to the ICD every 10 years. Thus, with every 10-year revision, the name of the current ICD changes.

EXAMPLE: ICD-8 was revised to become ICD-9; ICD-9 was revised to become ICD-10. An ICD-11 version for preparing implementation in Member States, including translations, was released on June 18 2018. During 2019 ICD-11 was presented at the Seventy-second Work Health Assembly. At this current time it is anticipated that the Member States of the World Health Organization will begin reporting health data using ICD-11 in January of 2022. For the most up-to-date information on ICD-11, visit *http://www.who.int/classifications/icd/revision/en/.* This website contains a wealth of information about ICD-11.

The ICD classification system was designed to compile and present statistical data on **morbidity** (the rate or frequency of disease) and **mortality** (the rate or frequency of deaths). Hospitals first used this form of classification to track, store, and retrieve statistical information. However, a more efficient basis for the storage and retrieval of diagnostic data was needed. In 1950, the Veterans Administration and the U.S. Public Health Service began independent studies of the use of the ICD for hospital indexing purposes. By 1956, the American Hospital Association and the American Association of Medical Record Librarians (now the American Health Information Management Association) felt that the ICD form of classification provided an efficient and useful vehicle for indexing hospital records.

With hospital indexing in mind, the WHO international conference published its eighth revision of the ICD in 1966. Health care professionals in some countries found that ICD-8 lacked the detail needed for diagnostic indexing. In the United States, consultants were asked to study ICD-8 for its applicability to various users. In 1968, the Advisory Committee to the Central Office on ICD published the *International Classification of Diseases, Eighth Revision,* adapted for use in the United States. It became known as ICDA-8 and was used for coding diagnostic data for both morbidity and mortality statistics in the United States.

In 1979, ICD-9-CM replaced earlier, less-specific versions of the classification system. ICD-9-CM streamlined the other versions of ICD classification into a single system that was intended for use primarily in U.S. hospitals. Please note that there is a difference between ICD-9 and ICD-9-CM. ICD-9 was developed by the WHO, and in the United States we take the ICD-9 version and modify codes to create the clinical modification of ICD-9 that will be used within the United States. The ICD-9-CM provided a more complete classification system for morbidity data to be used for indexing and reviewing patient records and medical care.

In 1992, the WHO published ICD-10, which is currently being used in many countries. In 1997, the National Center for Health Statistics (NCHS) began testing the ICD-10 system for implementation of the diagnostic codes in the United States. In the United States, the ICD codes are further developed into ICD-10-CM codes, which is the clinical modification of ICD codes. This modification allows for the ICD-10-CM codes to be more effectively used in clinical settings to capture diseases and signs and symptoms that patients display. In the United States, the **National Center for Health Statistics (NCHS)** is responsible for maintaining the ICD-10-CM diagnostic codes.

As the NCHS was testing ICD-10-CM, the draft and the preliminary crossfunctionality between ICD-9-CM and ICD-10-CM were made available on the NCHS website for public review and comment. In the summer of 2003, the American Hospital Association and the American Health Information Management Association conducted a field test for ICD-10-CM and reported the findings. Modifications were then made to the tenth revision.

In 2001, the Centers for Medicare and Medicaid Services funded a project to design a replacement system for the procedural codes of ICD-9-CM. The contract to redesign the procedural codes was awarded to 3M Health Information Systems. The new system is known as **ICD-10 Procedure Coding System** or **ICD-10-PCS**. The **Centers for Medicare and Medicaid Services (CMS)** is responsible for maintaining the procedure codes of ICD-10-PCS.

ICD-10-CM and ICD-10-PCS, when compared to ICD-9-CM, has additional information relevant to:

- Ambulatory and managed-care encounters.
- Expanded injury codes.
- More combination diagnosis-symptom codes to reduce the number of codes needed to fully describe a condition.
- Expanded use of sixth and seventh characters.
- Laterality and greater specificity in code assignment.

On August 22, 2008, the U.S. Department of Health and Human Services (HHS) published a proposed rule to adopt ICD-10-CM and ICD-10-PCS to replace ICD-9-CM. On January 16, 2009, the final rule on adoption of ICD-10-CM and ICD-10-PCS was published with an implementation date of October 1, 2013. During 2012 the implementation date of October 1, 2013 was reviewed and extended to October 1, 2014. And again in 2014, the implementation date was changed to October 1, 2015.

This system has become the key storyteller to the insurance companies, explaining what brought the patient into the office or facility (by means of a diagnostic code), as well as what services the facility provided (by means of a procedural code). Because coding plays such a critical role in the reimbursement for services rendered, *correct coding practices are essential.*

Health Insurance Portability and Accountability Act of 1996

The **Health Insurance Portability and Accountability Act of 1996 (HIPAA), Public Law 104-191**, was passed by Congress to improve the portability and continuity of health care coverage. The **Administrative Simplification** aspect of this legislation developed standards for the electronic exchange of health care data for administrative and financial transactions. The final rule on transactions and code sets mandated the use of standardized code sets for the electronic submission of health care data.

HIPAA mandated that ICD-9-CM diagnostic codes must be reported for diagnoses for all levels of care, including all hospital services, clinic services, long-term care, and physician offices. ICD-9-CM procedural codes were to be reported for inpatient hospital services. Health care providers used ICD-9-CM codes to accurately report diagnoses and services provided on submitted insurance claims. The codes are used to determine not only payment, but also the medical necessity of care, which is defined by Medicare as "the determination that a service or procedure rendered is reasonable and necessary for the diagnosis or treatment of an illness or injury." Thus, coders perform a vital role in the health care system.

ICD-10-CM and ICD-10-PCS codes replaced ICD-9-CM for use by inpatient facilities starting on October 1, 2015. Also on that date, ambulatory services and physician services started using ICD-10-CM codes for diagnosis and continued to use CPT codes for procedures.

Professional Coding Associations

To assist and promote correct coding and reimbursement, several organizations educate, train, and credential coders. Credentialing ensures the proper training and education of coders. As the transition was made from ICD-9-CM to ICD-10-CM and ICD-10-PCS, many professional organizations offered educational materials to assist in the transition. These organizations also continue to support ongoing training and continuing education that apply to coding and other aspects of the health information management field.

American Health Information Management Association (AHIMA)

The **American Health Information Management Association (AHIMA)** represents health information professionals who manage, organize, process, and manipulate patient data. Health-information professionals have knowledge of electronic and paper medical record systems, as well as of coding, reimbursement, and research methodologies. The information that these professionals manage directly impacts patient care and financial decisions made in the health care industry. Members of AHIMA feel that the quality of patient care is directly related to the effectiveness of the information available.

Health care providers, insurance companies, and institutional administrators depend on the accuracy and quality of that information. For this reason, AHIMA members are trained to provide a level of service that maintains the quality and accuracy of the medical information they come into contact with.

AHIMA offers a number of certifications and credentials to ensure that its members meet the level of proficiency needed by educated professionals to manage health care information. Members receive the following certifications or credentials through a combination of education, experience, and performance on national certification examinations:

- CCA—**Certified Coding Associate**
- CCS—**Certified Coding Specialist**
- CCS-P—**Certified Coding Specialist, Physician-Based**
- CDIP—**Certified Documentation Improvement Practitioner**
- CHDA—**Certified Health Data Analyst**
- CHPS—**Certified in Healthcare Privacy and Security**
- RHIA—**Registered Health Information Administrator**
- RHIT—**Registered Health Information Technician**

Once the certifications have been obtained, continuing education credits are required to maintain them. These credits can be obtained through conferences, seminars, classes, or other avenues of career development that AHIMA publishes and makes available to its members.

American Academy of Professional Coders (AAPC)

The **American Academy of Professional Coders (AAPC)** was founded to elevate the standards of medical coding. The AAPC provides networking opportunities through local chapter memberships and conferences. It also provides ongoing educational opportunities for members. AHIMA deals with all aspects of health information, whereas AAPC focuses on coding and reimbursement.

Like AHIMA, AAPC offers certifications for professional proficiency. The **Certified Professional Coder (CPC)** certification validates a coder's proficiency in the physician office setting, the **Certified Inpatient Coder, (CIC)** certification validates proficiency in the inpatient hospital setting, and the **Certified Outpatient Coder (COC)** certification validates coding proficiency in outpatient hospital and outpatient facility coding. The AAPC also offers specialty credentials for experienced coders. To understand the various specialty coding examinations and credentials review the following website: https://www.aapc.com/certification/specialty-credentials.aspx.

AAPC also offers the **Certified Risk Adjustment Coder (CRC)** certification that validates that a coder can read a medical chart and assign the correct diagnosis (ICD-10-CM) codes for a wide variety of clinical cases and services for risk adjustment models. AAPC also offers specialty coding certifications. Information about these and other certifications from AAPC can be found at ***https://www.aapc.com/certification/.***

Continuing education credits are also required to maintain AAPC certification.

American Association of Medical Assistants (AAMA)

The **American Association of Medical Assistants (AAMA)** represents individuals trained in performing routine administrative and clinical jobs, including coding, that keep medical offices and clinics running efficiently and smoothly. Credentialing is voluntary in most states; a medical assistant is not required to be certified or registered. However, the AAMA offers the national credential of **Certified Medical Assistant (CMA)** certification for medical assistants. The **Commission on Accreditation of Allied Health Education Programs (CAAHEP)** collaborates with the Curriculum Review Board of the AAMA Endowment to accredit medical assisting programs in both public and private postsecondary institutions throughout the United States.

This accreditation prepares candidates for entry in the medical assisting field. Students who have graduated from a medical assisting program accredited by the CAAHEP or the **Accrediting Bureau of Health Education Schools (ABHES)** are eligible to take the CMA examination, which tests candidates on tasks performed in the workplace. Recertification is required every five years, either by continuing education or by examination.

American Medical Technologists (AMT)

American Medical Technologists (AMT) offers professional credentials, such as **Registered Medical Assistant (RMA)**. These professionals perform the same tasks as those of a CMA but are credentialed by AMT. Students who have completed a college-level program approved by the U.S. Department of Education may voluntarily take the examination that credentials them as RMAs.

American Medical Billing Association (AMBA)

The **American Medical Billing Association's (AMBA)** mission is to provide education and networking opportunities for medical billers. The AMBA offers the **Certified Medical Reimbursement Specialist (CMRS)** credential and also provides continuing education and ongoing research related to medical billing.

Medical Association of Billers (MAB)

The **Medical Association of Billers (MAB)** was founded in 1995 and is approved and licensed by the Commission for Post Secondary Education. The MAB offers the following credentials:

- CMBS—**Certified Medical Billing Specialist**
- CMRT—**Certified Medical Record Technician**

Employment Opportunities for Coders

Regardless of the credentialing path that an individual takes, career opportunities are numerous. Coders work in all aspects of health care, including hospitals, physicians' offices, clinics, long-term care facilities, insurance companies, and billing agencies. With the evolution of the electronic health record, more coders will be needed to review the generated information for its accuracy and compliance. The Bureau of Labor Statistics calculates that the number of coding jobs in the United States will grow faster through 2028 than the average of all occupations. As the population of the United States ages, more individuals will use health care services and at a greater rate, thus increasing the need for additional services and for coded health care data, therefore also increasing the demand for additional medical coders.

Summary

- Coding is the assignment of numeric or alphanumeric digits and characters to diagnostic and procedural phrases.
- ICD-10-CM and ICD-10-PCS was implemented in the United States to code diagnoses and procedures on October 1, 2015.
- The National Center for Health Statistics coordinates the modifications to disease classifications.
- The Centers for Medicare and Medicaid Services coordinates the procedural classification updates.
- The American Health Information Management Association offers the following credentials: Certified Coding Associate; Certified Coding Specialist; Certified Coding Specialist, Physician-Based; Certified Documentation Improvement Practitioner; Certified Health Data Analyst; Certified in Healthcare Privacy and Security; Registered Health Information Administrator; and Registered Health Information Technician.
- The American Academy of Professional Coders offers the following credentials: Certified Professional Coder; Certified Inpatient Coder; Certified Outpatient Coder; Certified Risk Adjustment Coder; and various specialty coding certifications.

- The American Association of Medical Assistants offers the Certified Medical Assistant credential.
- American Medical Technologists offers professional credentials, such as a Registered Medical Assistant.
- The American Medical Billing Association offers the Certified Medical Reimbursement Specialist credential.
- The Medical Association of Billers offer the Certified Medical Billing Specialist, Certified Medical Billing Specialist for Chiropractic Assistants, Certified Medical Billing Specialist for Hospitals, Certified Medical Billing Specialist for Instructors, and Certified Medical Record Technician certifications.

Internet Links

To obtain information about ICD-10-CM, visit ***www.cdc.gov/nchs/icd/icd10cm.htm***. On this site you will find information about ICD-10-CM. Review the section entitled "ICD-10-CM."

To obtain information on the AAMA, visit ***www.aama-ntl.org***.

To obtain information on the AAPC, visit ***www.aapc.com***.

To obtain information on the AHIMA, visit ***www.ahima.org***.

To obtain information on AMT, visit ***www.americanmedtech.org***.

To obtain information on the AMBA, visit ***www.ambanet.net***.

To obtain information on the MAB, visit ***https://mabillers.com/***.

To obtain information on career statistics and opportunities, visit the Bureau of Labor Statistics at ***www.bls.gov***.

Chapter Review

True/False

Indicate whether each statement is true (T) or false (F).

1. _____ The CPC credential is offered by the American Health Information Management Association.

2. _____ AHIMA requires credentialed professionals to obtain continuing education credits to maintain their credentials.

3. _____ CMAs must be licensed to practice in the United States.

4. _____ The final rule on transactions and code sets mandated the use of ICD-9-CM for the electronic submission of health care data.

5. _____ The Centers for Medicare and Medicaid Services coordinates the procedural classification updates of ICD-10-PCS.

Fill-in-the-Blank

Enter the appropriate term(s) to complete each statement.

6. The rate or frequency of a disease is known as _____.

7. ICD-9 was developed by the _____.

8. ICD-10-CM is an abbreviation for the *International Classification of Diseases, Tenth Revision,* _____.

9. Modifications of the ICD-10-CM disease classification is coordinated by _____.

10. Public Law 104-191, known as _____, was passed by Congress to improve the portability and continuity of health care coverage.

Short Answer

Define each abbreviation and acronym.

11. AHIMA

_____

_____

_____

12. RHIA

_____

_____

_____

13. CIC

_____

_____

_____

_____

14. RHIT

_____

_____

_____

_____

15. CPC

_____

_____

_____

_____

16. AAMA

_____

_____

_____

_____

17. RMA

_____

_____

_____

18. CMA

_____

_____

_____

19. CCS

_____

_____

_____

20. CCS-P

_____

_____

21. COC

_____

_____

_____

22. CRC

_____

_____

_____

23. AAPC

_____

_____

24. Molly RHIT has been asked by the medical staff director to prepare a presentation for the medical staff describing the purpose of coding. Briefly describe what should be included in the presentation.

_____

_____

_____

25. Identify the employment opportunities for coders.

_____

_____

_____

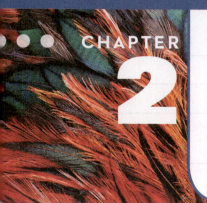

An Overview of ICD-10-CM

Chapter Outline

Chapter Objectives

At the conclusion of this chapter, you should be able to:

1. Explain the basic structure and components of the ICD-10-CM coding book.
2. Distinguish between the two ways chapters are organized in the Tabular List of Diseases and Injuries.
3. Identify the chapters of the Tabular List of Diseases and Injuries to which a code corresponds.

Key Terms

Index to Diseases
and Injuries

Index to External
Causes of Injury

Tabular List of Diseases
and Injuries (Tabular)

> **REMINDER:** As you work through this chapter and the remaining chapters, you will need to have a copy of the ICD-10-CM coding book to reference.

Introduction

The ICD-10-CM coding system allows health care providers and facilities to answer the question, "What brought the patient to my office/facility?" This information is needed for statistical purposes, reimbursement, and continuity of patient care. To accurately convey this information, the coder must become familiar with all aspects of the ICD-10-CM coding book. This chapter presents an overview of ICD-10-CM.

ICD-10-CM Coding Book Format

ICD-10-CM is used by the U.S. government for morbidity coding. ICD-10-CM is compatible with ICD-10, which is used for cause of death coding in the United States. Compared to the past editions, ICD-10-CM has a greater number of codes and has been expanded to include health-related conditions and to provide greater specificity in code assignment.

ICD-10-CM has two parts:

- The Index
- The Tabular List of Diseases and Injuries

The Index to Diseases and Injuries is an alphabetic listing of terms and corresponding codes. The two sections of the index are:

- **Index to Diseases and Injuries**
- **Index to External Causes of Injury**

A Neoplasm Table and a Table of Drugs and Chemicals are also included in the Index.

The **Tabular List of Diseases and Injuries** is an alphanumerical list of codes, commonly referred to as the *Tabular*. The Tabular is divided into chapters based on body system (anatomical site) or condition (etiology). The specific organization of the chapters is discussed throughout this book and overviewed in the next section.

ICD-10-CM Tabular List of Diseases and Injuries

The Tabular List of Diseases and Injuries is an alphanumerical list of the diseases and injuries found in ICD-10-CM. The Tabular consists of the following chapters:

1. Certain Infectious and Parasitic Diseases
2. Neoplasms
3. Diseases of the Blood and Blood-Forming Organs and Certain Disorders Involving the Immune Mechanism
4. Endocrine, Nutritional, and Metabolic Diseases
5. Mental, Behavioral, and Neurodevelopmental Disorders
6. Diseases of the Nervous System
7. Diseases of the Eye and Adnexa
8. Diseases of the Ear and Mastoid Process
9. Diseases of the Circulatory System
10. Diseases of the Respiratory System
11. Diseases of the Digestive System
12. Diseases of the Skin and Subcutaneous Tissue
13. Diseases of the Musculoskeletal System and Connective Tissue
14. Diseases of the Genitourinary System
15. Pregnancy, Childbirth, and the Puerperium
16. Certain Conditions Originating in the Perinatal Period
17. Congenital Malformations, Deformations, and Chromosomal Abnormalities
18. Symptoms, Signs, and Abnormal Clinical and Laboratory Findings, not elsewhere classified

19. Injury, Poisoning, and Certain Other Consequences of External Causes
20. External Causes of Morbidity
21. Factors Influencing Health Status and Contact with Health Services
22. Codes for Special Purposes

Exercise 2.1—Identifying Chapters

For each chapter title, indicate whether the chapter is organized by etiology or by anatomical site. Example: Diseases of the Musculoskeletal System and Connective Tissue. Answer: anatomical site

1. Congenital Malformations, Deformations, and Chromosomal Abnormalities _____

2. Diseases of the Circulatory System _____

3. Diseases of the Digestive System _____

4. Endocrine, Nutritional, and Metabolic Diseases _____

5. Certain Infectious and Parasitic Diseases _____

6. Diseases of Skin and Subcutaneous Tissue _____

7. Mental, Behavioral, and Neurodevelopmental Disorders _____

8. Diseases of the Nervous System _____

9. Diseases of the Genitourinary System _____

10. Diseases of the Respiratory System _____

Chapters of the Tabular List of Diseases and Injuries

The Tabular contains the following chapters.

Chapter 1—Certain Infectious and Parasitic Diseases (Code Range A00–B99)

This chapter includes diseases generally recognized as communicable or transmissible.

EXAMPLE: Using the Tabular section of your ICD-10-CM book, locate the start of Chapter 1. Here you will find the code listing for infectious and parasitic diseases. Reference the following codes to familiarize yourself with this chapter.

Diagnostic Code	Diagnostic Description
A01.00	Typhoid fever, unspecified
A06.0	Acute amebic dysentery
A59.09	Other urogenital trichomoniasis
B36.2	White piedra
B86	Scabies

Chapter 2—Neoplasms (Code Range C00–D49)

This chapter contains code assignments for malignant, benign, carcinoma in situ, and neoplasms of uncertain and unspecified behavior.

> **EXAMPLE:** Using the Tabular section of your ICD-10-CM book, locate the start of Chapter 2. Here you will find the code listing for neoplasms. Reference the following codes to familiarize yourself with this chapter.
>
> | Diagnostic Code | Diagnostic Description |
> |---|---|
> | C02.4 | Malignant neoplasm of lingual tonsil |
> | C46.9 | Kaposi's sarcoma, unspecified |
> | C94.02 | Acute erythoid leukemia, in relapse |
> | D37.1 | Neoplasm of uncertain behavior of stomach |
> | D38.4 | Neoplasm of uncertain behavior of thymus |

Chapter 3—Diseases of the Blood and Blood-Forming Organs and Certain Disorders Involving the Immune Mechanism (Code Range D50–D89)

Contained within this chapter are:

- Types of anemias.
- Coagulation defects.
- Hemorrhagic conditions.
- Diseases of the white blood cells and other components of the blood.
- Some diseases of the spleen and lymphatic system.

> **EXAMPLE:** Using the Tabular section of your ICD-10-CM book, locate the start of Chapter 3. Here you will find the code listing for diseases of the blood and blood-forming organs. Reference the following codes to familiarize yourself with this chapter.
>
> | Diagnostic Code | Diagnostic Description |
> |---|---|
> | D56.0 | Alpha thalassemia |
> | D67 | Hereditary factor IX deficiency |
> | D73.0 | Hyposplenism |
> | D73.4 | Cyst of spleen |
> | D86.0 | Sarcoidosis of lung |

Chapter 4—Endocrine, Nutritional, and Metabolic Diseases (Code Range E00–E89)

In this chapter are:

- Disorders and diseases of the thyroid and other endocrine glands.
- Nutritional deficiencies.
- Metabolic disorders.
- Disorders of the immune mechanism and immunity deficiencies.

EXAMPLE: Using the Tabular section of your ICD-10-CM book, locate the start of Chapter 4. Here you will find the code listing for diseases of the endocrine system, as well as nutritional and metabolic diseases. Reference the following codes to familiarize yourself with this chapter.

Diagnostic Code	Diagnostic Description
E04.0	Nontoxic diffuse goiter
E30.0	Delayed puberty
E55.0	Rickets, active
E61.2	Magnesium deficiency
E67.3	Hypervitaminosis D

Chapter 5—Mental, Behavioral, and Neurodevelopmental Disorders (Code Range F01–F99)

This chapter contains:

- Mental disorders, including psychotic, personality, neurotic, and nonpsychotic disorders.
- Chemical dependencies, such as alcoholism and drug dependence.
- Mental retardation and developmental disorders.
- Psychopathic symptoms that are not part of an organic illness.

EXAMPLE: Using the Tabular section of your ICD-10-CM book, locate the start of Chapter 5. Here you will find the code listing for mental and behavioral disorders. Reference the following codes to familiarize yourself with this chapter.

Diagnostic Code	Diagnostic Description
F01.50	Vascular dementia without behavioral disturbance
F20.0	Paranoid schizophrenia
F41.9	Anxiety disorder, unspecified
F60.6	Avoidant personality disorder
F84.0	Autistic disorder

Chapter 6—Diseases of the Nervous System (Code Range G00–G99)

This chapter contains diseases of the central and peripheral nervous systems that include the brain, spinal cord, meninges, and nerves.

EXAMPLE: Using the Tabular section of your ICD-10-CM book, locate the start of Chapter 6. Here you will find the code listing for diseases of the nervous system. Reference the following codes to familiarize yourself with this chapter.

Diagnostic Code	Diagnostic Description
G00.0	Hemophilus meningitis
G35	Multiple sclerosis
G43.011	Migraine without aura, intractable, with status migrainosus
G80.2	Spastic hemiplegic cerebral palsy
G91.9	Hydrocephalus, unspecified

Chapter 7—Diseases of the Eye and Adnexa (Code Range H00–H59)

This chapter includes diseases of the eye and adnexa.

> **EXAMPLE:** Using the Tabular section of your ICD-10-CM book, locate the start of Chapter 7. Here you will find the code listing for diseases of the eye and adnexa. Reference the following codes to familiarize yourself with this chapter.
>
> | Diagnostic Code | Diagnostic Description |
> | --- | --- |
> | H04.131 | Lacrimal cyst, right lacrimal gland |
> | H11.151 | Pinguecula, right eye |
> | H16.149 | Punctate keratitis, unspecified eye |
> | H17.9 | Unspecified corneal scar and opacity |
> | H27.00 | Aphakia, unspecified eye |

Chapter 8—Diseases of the Ear and Mastoid Process (Code Range H60–H95)

This chapter includes diseases of the ear and mastoid process.

> **EXAMPLE:** Using the Tabular section of your ICD-10-CM book, locate the start of Chapter 8. Here you will find the code listing for diseases of the ear and mastoid process. Reference the following codes to familiarize yourself with this chapter.
>
> | Diagnostic Code | Diagnostic Description |
> | --- | --- |
> | H61.21 | Impacted cerumen, right ear |
> | H65.22 | Chronic serous otitis media, left ear |
> | H81.311 | Aural vertigo, right ear |
> | H83.02 | Labyrinthitis, left ear |
> | H92.09 | Otalgia, unspecified ear |

Chapter 9—Diseases of the Circulatory System (Code Range I00–I99)

The circulatory system includes the heart, arteries, veins, and lymphatic system. Therefore, this chapter contains:

- Cardiac disorders.
- Arterial, venous, and some lymphatic diseases.

> **EXAMPLE:** Using the Tabular section of your ICD-10-CM book, locate the start of Chapter 9. Here you will find the code listing for diseases of the heart, arteries, arterioles, capillaries, veins, and lymphatic system. Reference the following codes to familiarize yourself with this chapter.
>
> | Diagnostic Code | Diagnostic Description |
> | --- | --- |
> | I05.0 | Rheumatic mitral stenosis |
> | I38 | Endocarditis, valve unspecified |
> | I51.0 | Cardiac septal defect, acquired |
> | I82.0 | Budd-Chiari syndrome |
> | I89.1 | Lymphangitis |

Chapter 10—Diseases of the Respiratory System (Code Range J00–J99)

In this chapter are diseases of the:

- Pharynx.
- Larynx.
- Trachea.
- Bronchus.
- Vocal cords.
- Sinuses.
- Nose.
- Tonsils and adenoids.
- Parts of the lung.

EXAMPLE: Using the Tabular section of your ICD-10-CM book, locate the start of Chapter 10. Here you will find the code listing for diseases of the respiratory system. Reference the following codes to familiarize yourself with this chapter.

Diagnostic Code	Diagnostic Description
J12.89	Other viral pneumonia
J35.1	Hypertrophy of tonsils
J43.1	Panlobular emphysema
J86.0	Pyothorax with fistula
J94.0	Chylous effusion

Chapter 11—Diseases of the Digestive System (Code Range K00–K95)

This chapter deals with diseases of the:

- Oral cavity.
- Salivary glands.
- Jaws.
- Esophagus.
- Stomach.
- Duodenum.
- Appendix.
- Abdominal cavity.
- Small and large intestines.
- Peritoneum.
- Anus.
- Liver.
- Gallbladder.
- Biliary tract.
- Pancreas.

EXAMPLE: Using the Tabular section of your ICD-10-CM book, locate the start of Chapter 11. Here you will find the code listing for diseases of the digestive system. Reference the following codes to familiarize yourself with this chapter.

Diagnostic Code	Diagnostic Description
K11.9	Disease of salivary gland, unspecified
K22.0	Achalasis of cardia
K59.00	Constipation, unspecified
K65.0	Generalized (acute) peritonitis
K81.0	Acute cholecystitis

Chapter 12—Diseases of the Skin and Subcutaneous Tissue (Code Range L00–L99)

This chapter includes:

- Inflammatory and infectious conditions of the skin and subcutaneous tissue.
- Diseases of the nail, hair and hair follicles, sweat, and sebaceous glands.

EXAMPLE: Using the Tabular section of your ICD-10-CM book, locate the start of Chapter 12. Here you will find the code listing for diseases of the subcutaneous tissue and skin. Reference the following codes to familiarize yourself with this chapter.

Diagnostic Code	Diagnostic Description
L03.012	Cellulitis of left finger
L55.0	Sunburn of first degree
L85.0	Acquired ichthyosis
L89.514	Pressure ulcer of right ankle, stage 4
L94.1	Linear scleroderma

Chapter 13—Diseases of the Musculoskeletal System and Connective Tissue (Code Range M00–M99)

This chapter includes diseases of the:

- Bones.
- Joints.
- Bursa.
- Muscles.
- Ligaments.
- Tendons.
- Soft tissues.

EXAMPLE: Using the Tabular section of your ICD-10-CM book, locate the start of Chapter 13. Here you will find the code listing for diseases of the musculoskeletal system and connective tissue. Reference the following codes to familiarize yourself with this chapter.

Diagnostic Code	Diagnostic Description
M06.9	Rheumatoid arthritis, unspecified
M21.531	Acquired clawfoot, right foot
M24.232	Disorder of ligament, left wrist
M24.569	Contracture, unspecified knee
M91.0	Juvenile osteochondrosis of pelvis

Chapter 14—Diseases of the Genitourinary System (Code Range N00–N99)

Coded from this chapter are diseases of the:

- Kidney.
- Ureter.
- Urinary bladder.
- Urethra.
- Male genital organs.
- Male and female breast, and female genital organs (not related to pregnancy, childbirth, and the postpartum period).

> **EXAMPLE:** Using the Tabular section of your ICD-10-CM book, locate the start of Chapter 14. Here you will find the code listing for diseases of the genitourinary system. Reference the following codes to familiarize yourself with this chapter.
>
> | Diagnostic Code | Diagnostic Description |
> |---|---|
> | N17.0 | Acute kidney failure with tubular necrosis |
> | N34.1 | Nonspecific urethritis |
> | N48.1 | Balanitis |
> | N75.0 | Cyst of Bartholin's gland |
> | N89.0 | Mild vaginal dysplasia |

Chapter 15—Pregnancy, Childbirth, and the Puerperium (Code Range O00–O9A)

This chapter includes:

- Ectopic and molar pregnancies.
- Spontaneous abortions.
- Legally and illegally induced abortions.
- Complications of pregnancy, abortions, labor and delivery, and the postpartum period.

> **EXAMPLE:** Using the Tabular section of your ICD-10-CM book, locate the start of Chapter 15. Here you will find the code listing for complications of pregnancy, childbirth, and the puerperium. Reference the following codes to familiarize yourself with this chapter.
>
> | Diagnostic Code | Diagnostic Description |
> |---|---|
> | O02.9 | Abnormal product of conception, unspecified |
> | O23.02 | Infections of kidney in pregnancy, second trimester |
> | O92.4 | Hypogalactia |
> | O99.011 | Anemia complicating pregnancy, first trimester |
> | O9A.53 | Psychological abuse complicating the puerperium |

Chapter 16—Certain Conditions Originating in the Perinatal Period (Code Range P00–P96)

This chapter includes conditions that have their origin in the perinatal period, a period of time before birth through the first 28 days after birth.

EXAMPLE: Using the Tabular section of your ICD-10-CM book, locate the start of Chapter 16. Here you will find the code listing for conditions originating in the perinatal period. Reference the following codes to familiarize yourself with this chapter.

Diagnostic Code	Diagnostic Description
P03.82	Meconium passage during delivery
P15.5	Birth injury to external genitalia
P28.3	Primary sleep apnea of newborn
P76.0	Meconium plug syndrome
P93.0	Grey baby syndrome

Chapter 17—Congenital Malformations, Deformations, and Chromosomal Abnormalities (Code Range Q00–Q99)

This chapter contains any congenital anomaly or malformation, regardless of the body system involved. A congenital anomaly is an anomaly present at or existing from the time of birth.

EXAMPLE: Using the Tabular section of your ICD-10-CM book, locate the start of Chapter 17. Here you will find the code listing for congenital anomalies. Reference the following codes to familiarize yourself with this chapter.

Diagnostic Code	Diagnostic Description
Q01.0	Frontal encephalocele
Q06.0	Amyelia
Q21.3	Tetralogy of Fallot
Q36.0	Cleft lip, bilateral
Q52.0	Congenital absence of vagina

Chapter 18—Symptoms, Signs, and Abnormal Clinical and Laboratory Findings, Not Elsewhere Classified (Code Range R00–R99)

This chapter includes symptoms, signs, abnormal results of laboratory tests and investigative procedures, as well as ill-defined conditions.

EXAMPLE: Using the Tabular section of your ICD-10-CM book, locate the start of Chapter 18. Here you will find the code listing for symptoms, signs, and ill-defined conditions. Reference the following codes to familiarize yourself with this chapter.

Diagnostic Code	Diagnostic Description
R10.0	Acute abdomen
R25.0	Abnormal head movements
R43.0	Anosmia
R57.0	Cardiogenic shock
R94.2	Abnormal results of pulmonary function studies

Chapter 19—Injury and Poisoning and Certain Other Consequences of External Causes (Code Range S00–T88)

This chapter includes:

- Fractures, dislocations, sprains, and strains of joints and muscles.
- Intracranial injuries.

- Internal injuries to the chest, abdomen, and pelvis.
- Open wounds.
- Superficial injuries.
- Contusions.
- Burns.
- Poisonings by drugs and by medicinal and biological substances.
- Effects of external cause.

EXAMPLE: Using the Tabular section of your ICD-10-CM book, locate the start of Chapter 19. Here you will find the code listing for injuries and poisonings. Reference the following codes to familiarize yourself with this chapter.

Diagnostic Code	Diagnostic Description
S00.211A	Abrasion of right eyelid and periocular area, initial encounter
S09.91xA	Unspecified injury of ear, initial encounter
S68.721A	Partial traumatic transmetacarpal amputation of right hand, initial encounter
S76.212D	Strain of adductor muscle, fascia and tendon of left thigh, subsequent encounter
S81.841A	Puncture wound with foreign body, right lower leg, initial encounter
T14.91	Suicide attempt

Chapter 20—External Causes of Morbidity (Code Range V00–Y99)

This chapter includes the classification of environmental events and circumstances as the cause of injury and other adverse effects. These codes are intended to be secondary codes to accompany those from other chapters.

EXAMPLE: Using the Tabular section of your ICD-10-CM book, locate the start of Chapter 20. Here you will find the code listings for external causes of morbidity. Reference the following codes to familiarize yourself with this chapter.

Diagnostic Code	Diagnostic Description
V00.131A	Fall from skateboard, initial encounter
W00.0xxA	Fall on same level due to ice and snow, initial encounter
W17.0xxA	Fall into well, initial encounter
W20.1xxA	Struck by object due to collapse of building, initial encounter
Y35.211A	Legal intervention involving injury by tear gas, law enforcement official injured, initial encounter

Chapter 21—Factors Influencing Health Status and Contact with Health Services (Z00–Z99)

This chapter codes reasons for encounters when a person may or may not be sick and when some circumstance or problem influences the person's health status but is not in itself a current illness or injury.

EXAMPLE: Using the Tabular section of your ICD-10-CM book, locate the start of Chapter 21. Here you will find the code listing for factors influencing health status and contact with health services. Reference the following codes to familiarize yourself with this chapter.

Diagnostic Code	Diagnostic Description
Z00.00	Encounter for general adult medical examination without abnormal findings
Z01.110	Encounter for hearing examination following failed hearing screening
Z04.42	Encounter for examination and observation following alleged child rape
Z17.0	Estrogen receptor positive status [ER+]
Z20.3	Contact with and (suspected) exposure to rabies

Chapter 22—Codes for Special Purposes (U00-U85)

This chapter was added in October of 2020 to report codes for special purposes. At this time the chapter only contained one block of codes.

EXAMPLE: Using the Tabular section of your ICD-10-CM book, locate the start of Chapter 22. Here you will find the code listing for codes for special purposes. Reference the following codes to familiarize yourself with this chapter.

Diagnostic Code	Diagnostic Description
U07.0	Vaping-related disorder
U07.1	COVID-19

Summary

- ICD-10-CM consists of an Index to Diseases and Injuries and a Tabular Listing of Diseases and Injuries.
- The Tabular List of Diseases and Injuries is divided into 22 chapters.
- The Index to Diseases and Injuries contains a Neoplasm Table and Table of Drugs and Chemicals.

Internet Link

The National Center for Health Statistics (NCHS) maintains information about ICD-10-CM. For a wealth of information, explore **www.cdc.gov/nchs/icd.htm**.

Chapter Review

For each of the following ICD-10-CM Tabular chapters, list the related category code range.

Chapter   *Code Range*

1. Neoplasms   _____

2. Endocrine, Nutritional, and Metabolic Diseases   _____

3. Diseases of the Circulatory System   _____

4. Diseases of the Digestive System   _____

5. Congenital Malformations, Deformations, and Chromosomal Abnormalities   _____

6. Diseases of the Nervous System   _____

7. External Causes of Morbidity   _____

8. Diseases of the Skin and Subcutaneous Tissue _____

9. Pregnancy, Childbirth, and the Puerperium _____

10. Mental, Behavioral, and Neurodevelopmental Disorders _____

11. Certain Infectious and Parasitic Diseases _____

12. Diseases of the Blood and Blood-Forming Organs and Certain Disorders Involving the Immune Mechanism _____

13. Diseases of the Eye and Adnexa _____

14. Diseases of the Ear and Mastoid Process _____

15. Diseases of the Respiratory System _____

16. Diseases of the Musculoskeletal System and Connective Tissue _____

17. Diseases of the Genitourinary System _____

18. Certain Conditions Originating in the Perinatal Period _____

19. Symptoms, Signs, and Abnormal Clinical and Laboratory Findings _____

20. Injury, Poisoning, and Certain Other Consequences of External Causes _____

21. Codes for special purposes _____

For each of the codes listed, state the chapter in which the code would be located.

22. Code D02.1 _____

23. Code F03.90 _____

24. Code E87.8 _____

25. Code A82.0 _____

26. Code M61.269 _____

27. Code P94.2 _____

28. Code K12.1 _____

29. Code H44.392 _____

30. Code G56.12 _____

31. Code I80.291 _____

32. Code U07.1 _____

33. Code Z96.9 _____

Short Answer

Briefly respond to each question.

34. List the two parts of ICD-10-CM.

_____

_____

35. Describe how the Tabular List of Diseases and Injuries is organized.

_____

_____

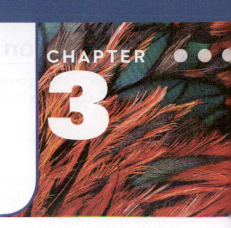

ICD-10-CM Coding Conventions

Chapter Outline

Chapter Objectives

Key Terms

Introduction

Convention Types

Coding Guidelines

Summary

Internet Link

Chapter Review

Chapter Objectives

At the conclusion of this chapter, you should be able to:

1. Explain the general purpose of the conventions used in ICD-10-CM.
2. Identify the abbreviations, symbols, and instructional notes used in ICD-10-CM.
3. Locate instructional notes in the ICD-10-CM code book.
4. Identify the difference between type 1 and type 2 Excludes notes.
5. Define the abbreviations NOS and NEC.
6. Define the punctuation used in the ICD-10-CM code book.
7. Define the symbols used in the ICD-10-CM code book.

Key Terms

Brackets

Code Also

Code First

Colon

Conventions

Excludes

Excludes1

Excludes2

In Diseases Classified Elsewhere

Includes

Instructional notes

NEC (not elsewhere classified)

Nonessential modifiers

NOS (not otherwise specified)

Parentheses

Point dash

See

See Also

Use Additional Code

REMINDER: As you work through this chapter, you will need to have a copy of the ICD-10-CM coding book to reference. For this chapter, you will also need to reference the ICD-10-CM Official Guidelines for Coding and Reporting. These guidelines can be found in Appendix A which are now available on the Student Companion site and MINDTAP From Cengage.

Introduction

This chapter highlights concepts that must be followed for coding to be accurate. Appendix A, Section 1, A, lists the ICD-10-CM Official Guidelines for Coding and Reporting that are relevant to this chapter.

Stop! When you see a stop sign while driving, you must stop and then proceed with caution. Similarly, ICD-10-CM uses the equivalent of "traffic signs" to guide coders: instructional notes, punctuation marks, abbreviations, and symbols, all of which are called **conventions**. To code accurately, a coder must understand what these conventions mean. You must follow these "traffic signs" to ensure accurate coding.

Convention Types

Conventions are used in both the ICD-10-CM Tabular List of Diseases and Injuries and the ICD-10-CM Index to Diseases and Injuries. Four types of conventions are used in ICD-10-CM to provide guidance to the coder:

- Instructional notes
- Punctuation marks
- Abbreviations
- Symbols

Some of the conventions are used in one volume and not in the other; other conventions are used in both the Tabular and Alphabetic volumes.

Instructional Notes

Instructional notes appear in both the Tabular List and Alphabetic Index of ICD-10-CM.

Includes Note

The **Includes** note is used to define, give examples, or both, of the content of a category of ICD-10-CM or of a block of category codes.

The location of the Includes note determines the category or block of category codes that the note governs.

When an Includes note appears in the Tabular List immediately *under a three-digit code title*, the note applies to the three-digit category. The word *Includes* is followed by examples of diagnostic terms that are included in that category.

> **EXAMPLE:** The category code A02, Other salmonella infections, appears as follows in ICD-10-CM:
>
> ```
> A02 Other salmonella infections
>
> Includes:  infection or foodborne intoxication due to any Salmonella species
>                  other than S. typhi and S. paratyphi
> ```

The Includes note signifies that infections or foodborne intoxication due to any Salmonella species other than *S. typhi* and *S. paratyphi* are included in this category.

When the Includes note appears *after the start of a chapter or block title*, the note governs the entire chapter or block of category codes.

EXAMPLE: The block of category codes A15–A19, Tuberculosis, appears as follows in the Tabular List of ICD-10-CM:

```
TUBERCULOSIS (A15-A19)
Includes:  infections due to Mycobacterium tuberculosis and Mycobacterium bovis
Excludes1: congenital tuberculosis (P37.0)
           nonspecific reaction to test for tuberculosis without active
               tuberculosis (R76.1-)
           pneumoconiosis associated with tuberculosis, any type in A15
           (J65)
           positive PPD (R76.11)
           positive tuberculin skin test without active tuberculosis
           (R76.11)
           sequelae of tuberculosis (B90.-)
           silicotuberculosis (J65)
```

When the Includes note appears at this level, the block of category codes is governed by the note. Therefore, in this example, code block A15–A19 is governed by the notes that follow the block title.

At times, the word *Includes* is not listed before the list of terms in the code; only the diagnostic terms are listed.

ICD-10-CM Official Coding Guidelines

Inclusion terms

List of terms is included under some codes. These terms are the conditions for which that code is to be used. The terms may be synonyms of the code title, or, in the case of "other specified" codes, the terms are a list of the various conditions assigned to that code. The inclusion terms are not necessarily exhaustive. Additional terms found only in the Alphabetic Index may also be assigned to a code. (See Appendix A, Section I.A.11.)

Courtesy of the Centers for Medicare & Medicaid Services, www.cms.gov

Exercise 3.1—Identifying Inclusion Notes

For each of the following items, list the diagnoses that are included as described by the inclusion note. The first one is completed for you.

1. category A06   infection due to *Entamoeba histolytica*
2. code A04.9
3. code N18.6
4. category R51
5. code R48.8
6. category F30
7. code D10.1
8. category K13
9. code J42
10. code L20.81

Excludes Instructional Notes

The **Excludes** notes are used to signify that the conditions listed are not assigned to the category or block of category codes. There are two types of Excludes notes in ICD-10-CM.

Excludes1 Note

The **Excludes1** note is easy to understand and apply. This note means that the diagnostic terms listed are *not* coded to the category or subcategory; therefore, the two conditions are mutually exclusive. The Official Coding Guidelines for Coding and Reporting define the Excludes1 note, as shown below.

ICD-10-CM Official Coding Guidelines

Excludes1

A type 1 Excludes note is a pure excludes note. It means "NOT CODED HERE!" An Excludes1 note indicates that the code excluded should never be used at the same time as the code above the Excludes1 note. An Excludes1 is used when two conditions cannot occur together, such as a congenital form versus an acquired form of the same condition. (See Appendix A, Section I.A.12.a for further information on this guideline.)

Category I00 is an example of the use of the Excludes1 note. The following appears for code I00.

EXAMPLE:

```
I00 Rheumatic fever without heart involvement
    Includes: arthritis, rheumatic, acute or subacute
    Excludes1: rheumatic fever with heart involvement (I01.0–I01.9)
```

Reading the category title and the diagnostic description following the Excludes1 note, you can see that the two are mutually exclusive because rheumatic fever would occur with or without heart involvement; therefore the two codes could not be used together.

Excludes2 Note

The **Excludes2** note is used to signify that the diagnostic terms listed after the note are *not* part of the condition(s) represented by the code or code block. This note also indicates that, at times, the assignment of more than one code should occur to fully represent the diagnostic statement being coded and to accurately record the patient's condition.

The Official Coding Guidelines define the Excludes2 note, as shown below.

ICD-10-CM Official Guidelines

Excludes2

A type 2 Excludes note represents "Not included here." An Excludes2 note indicates that the condition excluded is not part of the condition represented by the code, but a patient may have both conditions at the same time. When an Excludes2 note appears under a code, it is acceptable to use both the code and the excluded code together, when appropriate. (See Appendix A, Section I.A.12.b.)

An example of the use of the Excludes2 note appears for code C02.0. The code appears as follows in ICD-10-CM.

EXAMPLE:

```
C02.0 Malignant neoplasm of dorsal surface of tongue

        Malignant neoplasm of anterior two-thirds of tongue, dorsal
        surface

        Excludes2: malignant neoplasm of dorsal surface of base of tongue
        (C01)
```

The Excludes2 note means that code C02.0 does not code a malignant neoplasm of the dorsal surface of base of tongue. Code C01 is the appropriate code. Both code C02.0, malignant neoplasm of dorsal surface of tongue, and code C01, malignant neoplasm of base of tongue, would be selected if the patient had a neoplasm in both sites.

See Instructional Note

The **See** note is used in the Alphabetic Index of ICD-10-CM and instructs the coder to cross-reference the term or diagnosis that follows the notation.

EXAMPLE: In the Alphabetic Index, the following appears for the entry of Thromboarteritis:

```
Thromboarteritis—see Arteritis
```

This notation instructs the coder to cross-reference to the term *Arteritis* in the Alphabetic Index to obtain the correct code.

ICD-10-CM Official Coding Guidelines

The "see" instruction following a main term in the Alphabetic Index indicates that another term should be referenced. It is necessary to go to the main term referenced with the "see" note to locate the correct code. (See Appendix A, Section I.A.16.)

See Also Instructional Note

Another cross-reference note used in ICD-10-CM, the **See Also** note refers the coder to another location in the Alphabetic Index when the initial listing does not contain all the necessary information to accurately select a code.

EXAMPLE: When coding a diagnosis of altitude hypoxia, the coder first references the term *hypoxia* in the Alphabetic Index. Here the coder finds the following:

```
Hypoxia (see also Anoxia) R09.02

        cerebral, during a procedure NEC G97.81

          postprocedural NEC G97.82

        intrauterine P84

        myocardial—see Insufficiency, coronary

        newborn P84

        sleep related G47.34
```

Since the modifying term *altitude* does not appear in the entries under the main term of *hypoxia*, the coder references the term *anoxia* in the Alphabetic Index. The following appears at the start of the entry for Anoxia:

```
Anoxia (pathological) R09.02

         altitude T70.29

         cerebral G93.1

               complicating

                  anesthesia (general)
                  (local) or other
                  sedation T88.59

                  in labor and delivery
                  074.3
```

Since the modifying term *altitude* appears, the coder selects T70.29, from the ICD-10-CM Index to Diseases and Injuries, for the diagnostic statement of altitude hypoxia. To verify the code for the diagnosis, the coder must reference the ICD-10-CM Tabular List of Diseases and Injuries.

ICD-10-CM Official Guidelines

A "see also" instruction following a main term in the Alphabetic Index instructs that there is another main term that may also be referenced that may provide additional Alphabetic Index entries that may be useful. It is not necessary to follow the "see also" note when the original main term provides the necessary code. (See Appendix A, Section I.A.16.)

Courtesy of the Centers for Medicare & Medicaid Services, www.cms.gov

Use Additional Code and Code First Instructional Notes

The Use Additional Code and the Code First notes appear in the Tabular section of ICD-10-CM and must always be followed. These notes are used to signal that, when there is an underlying etiology and multiple body system manifestation due to the underlying etiology, two codes are needed. The **Use Additional Code** note instructs the coder to use an additional code to identify the manifestation that is present. The **Code First** note instructs the coder to select a code to represent the etiology that caused the manifestation. The two codes must appear in the correct order. The code that represents the etiology is sequenced first, followed by the code that represents the manifestation.

EXAMPLE: In coding the diagnostic statement of encephalitis in poliovirus, the coder references first the Alphabetic Index and then the Tabular List. In the Tabular List, the coder finds the following entry for the start of G05—Encephalitis, myelitis and encephalomyelitis in diseases classified elsewhere.

```
G05 Encephalitis, myelitis and encephalomyelitis in diseases classified
elsewhere

            Code first underlying disease, such as:

               human immunodeficieny virus [HIV] disease (B20)

               poliovirus (A80.-)

               suppurative otitis media (H66.01-H66.4)

               trichinellosis (B75)
```

The phrase "Code first underlying disease" signals to the coder that two codes are needed: code G05 and a code for the poliovirus from the A80.– subcategory, with the A80.– code listed first.

In addition to the notes found in the Tabular List, the coding for an etiology and manifestation has a unique Alphabetic Index entry structure. This is explained by the Official Coding Guidelines as follows:

ICD-10-CM Official Guidelines

In addition to the notes in the Tabular List, these conditions also have a specific Alphabetic Index entry structure. In the Alphabetic Index both conditions are listed together with the etiology code first followed by the manifestation codes in brackets. The code in brackets is always to be sequenced second. (See Appendix A, Section I.A.13.)

Courtesy of the Centers for Medicare & Medicaid Services, www.cms.gov

In Diseases Classified Elsewhere Note

A third note applies to the etiology/manifestation conventions: **In Diseases Classified Elsewhere**. The Official Coding Guidelines for Coding and Reporting explain the use of this note as follows:

ICD-10-CM Official Guidelines

In most cases the manifestation codes will have in the code title, "in diseases classified elsewhere." Codes with this title are a component of the etiology/manifestation convention. The code title indicates that it is a manifestation code. "In diseases classified elsewhere" codes are never permitted to be used as first listed or principal diagnosis codes. They must be used in conjunction with an underlying condition code and they must be listed following the underlying condition. See category F02, Dementia in other diseases classified elsewhere, for an example of this convention. There are manifestation codes that do not have "in diseases classified elsewhere" in the title. For such codes, there is a "use additional code" note at the etiology code and a "code first" note at the manifestation code and the rules for sequencing apply. (See Appendix A, Section I.A.13.)

Courtesy of the Centers for Medicare & Medicaid Services, www.cms.gov

Code Also Instructional Note

The **Code Also** note is used in ICD-10-CM to instruct the coder that two codes may be needed to fully code a diagnostic phrase. The note, however, does not provide sequencing direction. Code F80.4 provides an example of the Code Also note:

```
F80.4 Speech and language development delay due to hearing loss

Code also type of hearing loss (H90.-, H91.-)
```

Therefore, when both codes are assigned, the coder must determine the proper sequencing of the codes based on the case. The ICD-10-CM Official Guidelines state the following:

ICD-10-CM Official Guidelines

A "code also" note instructs that two codes may be required to fully describe a condition, but this note does not provide sequencing direction. The sequencing depends on the circumstances of the encounter. (See Appendix A, Section I.A.17.)

Courtesy of the Centers for Medicare & Medicaid Services, www.cms.gov

Default Codes

When a code is listed next to a main term in the Alphabetic Index, it is known as a default code. If no additional information, found in the medical record, modifies the main term, then the default code should be assigned.

ICD-10-CM Official Guidelines

A code listed next to a main term in the ICD-10-CM Alphabetic Index is referred to as a default code. The default code represents that condition that is most commonly associated with the main term, or is the unspecified code for the condition. If a condition is documented in a medical record (for example, appendicitis) without any additional information, such as acute or chronic, the default code should be assigned. (See Appendix A, Section I.A.18.)

Courtesy of the Centers for Medicare & Medicaid Services, www.cms.gov

Exercise 3.2—Identifying Notes

For each item listed, indicate the type of instructional note found. The first one is done for you.

1. Start of Chapter 3, Diseases of the Blood
   and Blood-Forming Organs and Certain Disorders
   Involving the Immune Mechanism   Excludes2 _____
2. Category D55   _____
3. Category F07   _____
4. Category K70   _____
5. Category K90   _____
6. Code R22.2   _____
7. Subcategory M10.1   _____
8. Category J05   _____
9. Category O02   _____
10. Category P00   _____

Punctuation Marks

Coders must understand the meaning of the punctuation marks used in the code book as ICD-10-CM defines them. Their definitions are unique to the coding system.

Parentheses: ( )

Parentheses are used in both the Tabular List and Alphabetic Index. Parentheses are used around terms that provide additional information about the main diagnostic term. The terms found within the parentheses are referred to as **nonessential modifiers**. The terms do not affect the code assignment for the diagnostic statement being coded.

EXAMPLE: In the Alphabetic Index, the term *dermatitis* is found as follows at the start of the entry:

```
Dermatitis (eczematous) L30.9

    ab igne L59.0

    acarine B88.0

    actinic (due to sun) L57.8
```

The parentheses are used around the nonessential modifying term of *eczematous*. If a coder is coding dermatitis or eczematous dermatitis, then code L30.9 is assigned.

ICD-10-CM Official Guidelines

( ) Parentheses are used in both the Alphabetic Index and Tabular List to enclose supplementary words that may be present or absent in the statement of a disease or procedure without affecting the code number to which it is assigned. The terms within the parentheses are referred to as nonessential modifiers. The nonessential modifiers in the Alphabetic Index to Diseases apply to subterms following a main term except when a nonessential modifier and a subentry are mutually exclusive, the subentry takes precedence. For example, in the ICD-10-CM Alphabetic Index under the main term Enteritis, "acute" is a nonessential modifier and "chronic" is a subentry. In this case, the nonessential modifier "acute" does not apply to the subentry "chronic". (See Appendix A, Section A.7.)

Courtesy of the Centers for Medicare & Medicaid Services, www.cms.gov

Brackets: [ ]

Brackets are used in the Tabular Listing and in the Alphabetic Index.

In the Tabular List, the brackets enclose synonyms, alternative wording, abbreviations, or explanatory phrases. The presence or absence of the phrase in the bracket does not affect code assignment.

> **EXAMPLE:** Category Code B01 appears in the Tabular List as follows:
>
> ```
> B01 Varicella [chickenpox]
> ```

Chickenpox is enclosed in brackets to provide an alternative word for *varicella*. Therefore, this category would be used to code the diagnoses chickenpox and varicella. Brackets are used in the Alphabetic Index to identify manifestation codes.

Colon: :

A **colon** is used in the Tabular listing after a term that is modified by one or more of the terms following the colon. The term to the left of the colon must be modified by a term to the right to be included in the code or instructional note being considered.

F20 Schizophrenia

```
     Excludes1: brief psychotic disorder (F23)

                 cyclic schizophrenia (F25.0)

                 mood [affective] disorders with psychotic symptoms (F30.2,
                     F31.2, F31.5, F31.64, F32.3, F33.3)

                 schizoaffective disorder (F25.-)

                 schizophrenic reaction NOS (F23)

     Excludes2: schizophrenic reaction in:

                 alcoholism (F10.15-, F10.25-, F10.95-)

                 brain disease (F06.2)

                 epilepsy (F06.2)

                 psychoactive drug use (F11-F19 with .15, .25, .95)

                 schizotypal disorder (F21)
```

The use of the colon after the phrase "schizophrenic reaction in:" means that the phrase must be followed by any of the diagnoses that follow to be validated for this Excludes2 note. If the diagnosis does not specify the terms to the right of the colon, the diagnosis is not valid for this Excludes2 note.

Abbreviations

Two abbreviations are consistently used in ICD-10-CM, NEC and NOS.

NEC: Not Elsewhere Classifiable

NEC means **not elsewhere classifiable**. This abbreviation is used in both the Tabular List and Alphabetic Index.

- In the Alphabetic Index, NEC represents "other specified." When a specific code is not available for a condition, the Alphabetic Index directs the coder to the "other specified" code in the Tabular List.

- In the Tabular List, NEC still means "not elsewhere classifiable" and can be read as "other specified." When a specific code is not available in the Tabular List for the condition being coded, the NEC entry under a code identifies it as the "other specified" code.

NOS: Not Otherwise Specified

NOS is the abbreviation for **not otherwise specified**. The note is used in both the Alphabetic Index and Tabular List and is interpreted to mean "unspecified." NOS codes are not specific and should be used only after the coder has clarified with the physician that a more specific diagnosis is not available. The coder should also reference the medical record to see if it contains documentation that can further specify the diagnosis.

> **EXAMPLE:** The physician makes a diagnosis of sinusitis, orders a series of sinus x-rays, and records sinusitis on the coding form for the order. The coder then references sinusitis in the Alphabetic Index and Tabular List and records code J32.9. However, after the reading of the x-ray, a diagnosis of chronic frontal sinusitis is established.
>
> The coder should then select code J32.1, which identifies chronic frontal sinusitis. If there were no further documentation or findings—in this case, no x-rays taken—to expand on the original diagnosis of sinusitis, then code J32.9 is correct. The entry in the Tabular appears as follows:
>
> ```
> J32.9 Chronic Sinusitis, unspecified
>         Sinusitis (chronic) NOS
> ```

The abbreviation *NOS* should signal to the coder to try to clarify the diagnosis more specifically prior to assigning the code.

Symbols

Symbols are used in ICD-10-CM to give direction to the coder.

Point Dash: . –

The **point dash** symbol (.–) tells the coder that the code contains a list of options at a level of specificity past the three-character category.

> **EXAMPLE:** In the Tabular List, at the start of the code block for mycoses, the following appears:
>
> ```
> MYCOSES     (B35–B49)
> Excludes2: hypersensitivity pneumonitis due to organic dust (J67.–)
>            Mycosis fungoides (C84.0–)
> ```

The point dash after J67 and the .0– after code C84 indicate that the codes are defined to a level of specificity higher than the three-character and four-character levels.

Coding Guidelines

The following ICD-10-CM Official Guidelines for Coding and Reporting apply to the conventions discussed in this chapter.

ICD-10-CM Official Coding Guidelines

Section I. Conventions, general coding guidelines and chapter specific guidelines

The conventions, general guidelines and chapter-specific guidelines are applicable to all health care settings unless otherwise indicated. The conventions and instructions of the classification take precedence over guidelines.

A. Conventions for the ICD-10-CM

The conventions for the ICD-10-CM are the general rules for use of the classification independent of the guidelines. These conventions are incorporated within the Alphabetic Index and Tabular List of ICD-10-CM as instructional notes.

1. The Alphabetic Index and Tabular List

The ICD-10-CM is divided into the Alphabetic Index, an alphabetical list of terms and their corresponding code, and the Tabular List, a structured list of codes divided into chapters based on body system or condition. The Alphabetic Index consists of the following parts: the Index of Diseases and Injury, the Index of External Causes of Injury, the Table of Neoplasms, and the Table of Drugs and Chemicals.

See Section I.C2. General guidelines

See Section I.C.19. Adverse effects, poisoning, underdosing and toxic effects

2. Format and Structure:

The ICD-10-CM Tabular List contains categories, subcategories and codes.

Characters for categories, subcategories and codes may be either a letter or a number. All categories are 3 characters. A three-character category that has no further subdivision is equivalent to a code. Subcategories are either 4 or 5 characters. Codes may be 3, 4, 5, 6, or 7 characters. That is, each level of subdivision after a category is a subcategory. The final level of subdivision is a code. Codes that have applicable 7th characters are still referred to as codes, not subcategories. A code that has an applicable 7th character is considered invalid without the 7th character.

The ICD-10-CM uses an indented format for ease in reference

3. Use of codes for reporting purposes

For reporting purposes only codes are permissible, not categories or subcategories, and any applicable 7th character is required.

4. Placeholder character

The ICD-10-CM utilizes a placeholder character "x". The "x" is used as a placeholder at certain codes to allow for future expansion. An example of this is at the poisoning, adverse effect and underdosing codes, categories T36–T50.

Where a placeholder exists, the x must be used in order for the code to be considered a valid code.

5. 7th Characters

Certain ICD-10-CM categories have applicable 7th characters. The applicable 7th character is required for all codes within the category, or as the notes in the Tabular List instruct. The 7th character must always be the 7th character in the data field. If a code that requires a 7th character is not 6 characters, a placeholder x must be used to fill in the empty characters.

6. Abbreviations

a. Alphabetic Index abbreviations

NEC "Not elsewhere classifiable"

This abbreviation in the Alphabetic Index represents "other specified". When a specific code is not available for a condition the Alphabetic Index directs the coder to the "other specified" code in the Tabular List.

NOS "Not otherwise specified"

This abbreviation is the equivalent of unspecified.

b. Tabular List abbreviations

NEC "Not elsewhere classifiable"

This abbreviation in the Tabular List represents "other specified". When a specific code is not available for a condition the Tabular List includes an NEC entry under a code to identify the code as the "other specified" code.

NOS "Not otherwise specified"

This abbreviation is the equivalent of unspecified.

7. Punctuation

[ ] Brackets are used in the Tabular List to enclose synonyms, alternative wording or explanatory phrases. Brackets are used in the Alphabetic Index to identify manifestation codes.

( ) Parentheses are used in both the Alphabetic Index and Tabular List to enclose supplementary words that may be present or absent in the statement of a disease or procedure without affecting the code number to which it is assigned. The terms within the parentheses are referred to as nonessential modifiers. The nonessential modifiers in the Alphabetic Index to Diseases apply to subterms following a main term except when a nonessential modifier and a subentry are mutually exclusive, the subentry takes precedence. For example, in the ICD-10-CM Alphabetic Index under the main term Enteritis, "acute" is a nonessential modifier and "chronic" is a subentry. In this case, the nonessential modifier "acute" does not apply to the subentry "chronic".

: Colons are used in the Tabular List after an incomplete term which needs one or more of the modifiers following the colon to make it assignable to a given category.

8. Use of "and"

See Section I.A.14. Use of the term "And"

9. Other and Unspecified codes

a. "Other" codes

Codes titled "other" or "other specified" are for use when the information in the medical record provides detail for which a specific code does not exist. Alphabetic Index entries with NEC in the line designate "other" codes in the Tabular List. These Alphabetic Index entries represent specific disease entities for which no specific code exists so the term is included within an "other" code.

b. "Unspecified" codes

Codes titled "unspecified" are for use when the information in the medical record is insufficient to assign a more specific code. For those categories for which an unspecified code is not provided, the "other specified" code may represent both other and unspecified.

See Section I.B.18 Use of Signs/Symptom/Unspecified Codes

10. Includes Notes

This note appears immediately under a three-character code title to further define, or give examples of, the content of the category.

11. Inclusion terms

List of terms is included under some codes. These terms are the conditions for which that code is to be used. The terms may be synonyms of the code title, or, in the case of "other specified" codes, the terms are a list of the various conditions assigned to that code. The inclusion terms are not necessarily exhaustive. Additional terms found only in the Alphabetic Index may also be assigned to a code.

12. Excludes Notes

The ICD-10-CM has two types of excludes notes. Each type of note has a different definition for use but they are all similar in that they indicate that codes excluded from each other are independent of each other.

a. Excludes1

A type 1 Excludes note is a pure excludes note. It means "NOT CODED HERE!" An Excludes1 note indicates that the code excluded should never be used at the same time as the code above the Excludes1 note. An Excludes1 is used when two conditions cannot occur together, such as a congenital form versus an acquired form of the same condition.

An exception to the Excludes1 definition is the circumstance when the two conditions are unrelated to each other. If it is not clear whether the two conditions involving an Excludes1 note are related or not, query the provider. For example, code F45.8, Other somatoform disorders, has an Excludes1 note for "sleep related teeth grinding (G47.63)," because "teeth grinding" is an inclusion term under F45.8. Only one of these two codes should be assigned for teeth grinding. However, psychogenic dysmenorrhea is also an inclusion term under F45.8, and a patient could have both this condition and sleep related teeth grinding. In this case, the two conditions are clearly unrelated to each other, and so it would be appropriate to report F45.8 and G47.63 together.

b. Excludes2

A type 2 excludes note represents "Not included here". An Excludes2 note indicates that the condition excluded is not part of the condition represented by the code, but a patient may have both conditions at the same time. When an Excludes2 note appears under a code, it is acceptable to use both the code and the excluded code together, when appropriate.

13. Etiology/manifestation convention ("code first", "use additional code" and "in diseases classified elsewhere" notes)

Certain conditions have both an underlying etiology and multiple body system manifestations due to the underlying etiology. For such conditions, the ICD-10-CM has a coding convention that requires the underlying condition be sequenced first, if applicable, followed by the manifestation. Wherever such a combination exists, there is a "use additional code" note at the etiology code, and a "code first" note at the manifestation code. These instructional notes indicate the proper sequencing order of the codes, etiology followed by manifestation.

In most cases the manifestation codes will have in the code title, "in diseases classified elsewhere." Codes with this title are a component of the etiology/manifestation convention. The code title indicates that it is a manifestation code. "In diseases classified elsewhere" codes are never permitted to be used as first listed or principal diagnosis codes. They must be used in conjunction with an underlying condition code and they must be listed following the underlying condition. See category F02, Dementia in other diseases classified elsewhere, for an example of this convention.

There are manifestation codes that do not have "in diseases classified elsewhere" in the title. For such codes, there is a "use additional code" note at the etiology code and a "code first" note at the manifestation code and the rules for sequencinig apply.

In addition to the notes in the Tabular List, these conditions also have a specific Alphabetic Index entry structure. In the Alphabetic Index both conditions are listed together with the etiology code first followed by the manifestation codes in brackets. The code in brackets is always to be sequenced second.

An example of the etiology/manifestation convention is dementia in Parkinson's disease. In the Alphabetic Index, code G20 is listed first, followed by code F02.80 or F02.81 in brackets. Code G20 presents the underlying etiology, Parkinson's disease, and must be sequenced first, whereas codes F02.80 and F02.81 represent the manifestation of dementia in diseases classified elsewhere, with or without behavioral disturbance.

"Code first" and "Use additional code" notes are also used as sequencing rules in the classification for certain codes that are not part of an etiology/manifestation combination.

See section I.B.7. Multiple coding for a single condition.

14. "And"

The word "and" should be interpreted to mean either "and" or "or" when it appears in a title. For example, cases of "tuberculosis of bones", "tuberculosis of joints" and "tuberculosis of bones and joints" are classified to subcategory A18.0, Tuberculosis of bones and joints.

15. "With"

The word "with" or "in" should be interpreted to mean "associated with" or "due to" when it appears in a code title, the Alphabetic Index (either under a main term or subterm), or an instructional note in the Tabular List. The classification presumes a causal relationship between the two conditions linked by these terms in the Alphabetic Index or Tabular List. These conditions should be coded as related even in the absence of provider documentation explicitly linking them, unless the documentation clearly states the conditions are unrelated or when another guideline exists that specifically requires a documented linkage between two conditions (e.g., sepsis guideline for "acute organ dysfunction that is not clearly associated with the sepsis").

For conditions not specifically linked by these relational terms in the classification or when a guideline requires that a linkage between two conditions be explicitly documented, provider documentation must link the conditions in order to code them as related.

The word "with" in the Alphabetic Index is sequenced immediately following the main term or subterm, not in alphabetic order.

16. "See" and "See Also"

The "see" instruction following a main term in the Alphabetic Index indicates that another term should be referenced. It is necessary to go to the main term referenced with the "see" note to locate the correct code.

A "see also" instruction following a main term in the Alphabetic Index instructs that there is another main term that may also be referenced that may provide additional Alphabetic Index entries that may be useful. It is not necessary to follow the "see also" note when the original main term provides the necessary code.

17. "Code also note"

A "code also" note instructs that two codes may be required to fully describe a condition, but this note does not provide sequencing direction. The sequencing depends on the circumstances of the encounter.

18. Default codes

A code listed next to a main term in the ICD-10-CM Alphabetic Index is referred to as a default code. The default code represents that condition that is most commonly associated with the main term, or is the unspecified code for the condition. If a condition is documented in a medical record (e.g., appendicitis) without any additional information, such as acute or chronic, the default code should be assigned.

19. Code assignment and Clinical Criteria

The assignment of a diagnosis code is based on the provider's diagnostic statement that the condition exists. The provider's statement that the patient has a particular condition is sufficient. Code assignment is not based on clinical criteria used by the provider to establish the diagnosis.

Courtesy of the Centers for Medicare & Medicaid Services, www.cms.gov

Summary

- ICD-10-CM uses a group of instructional notes, punctuation marks, abbreviations, and symbols to guide coders.
- The Includes notes found in ICD-10-CM give examples of the content of a section of the code book.
- Two types of Excludes notes are found in ICD-10-CM.
- *NEC* means "not elsewhere classifiable."

- *NOS* means "not otherwise specified."
- Brackets are used to enclose synonyms, alternative wording, and explanatory phrases.
- Parentheses are used to enclose nonessential modifiers.
- A colon is used after an incomplete term that needs one or more of the modifiers following the colon to make the modifier(s) assignable to a given category.
- Code First and Use Additional Code notes are used to identify the sequencing of codes.
- Coders should read all instructional notes that appear in the Alphabetic Index and the Tabular List and use them as a guide when selecting codes.

Internet Link

To review information about ICD-10-CM, go to **www.cdc.gov/nchs/icd/icd10cm.htm#10update**.

Chapter Review

True/False

Indicate whether each statement is true (T) or false (F).

1. _____ *NEC* means "not elsewhere coded."
2. _____ Terms that appear in parentheses must appear in the diagnostic statement being coded.
3. _____ *NOS* means "not otherwise specified."
4. _____ The placement of an Includes note signifies the section of the code book that the note governs.
5. _____ The See Also notation refers the coder to another location in the Tabular List.
6. _____ At times, two codes are used to code a diagnostic statement.
7. _____ The point dash symbol signifies that a code is not further specified.
8. _____ The abbreviation *NEC* is used only in the Alphabetic Index.
9. _____ A type 2 Excludes note represents "Not Coded Here."
10. _____ There are two types of Includes notes in ICD-10-CM.

Short Answer

Briefly respond to the following:

11. Differentiate between the abbreviations *NOS* and *NEC*.

_____

_____

_____

12. Explain why coders must reference both the Alphabetic Index and Tabular List.

_____

_____

_____

13. Compare and contrast the uses of the two types of Excludes notes.

_____

_____

_____

14. Give an example of a code that contains an instructional note. List the instructional note.

_____

_____

_____

15. List the purpose of the _See_ instruction.

_____

_____

_____

Steps in Diagnostic Code Selection

CHAPTER 4

Chapter Outline

Chapter Objectives

Key Terms

Introduction

ICD-10-CM Documentation Essentials

Steps in Coding

Coding Guideline References for Code
   Location

Summary

Chapter Review

Chapter Objectives

At the conclusion of this chapter, you should be able to:

1. Describe the medical documentation that must be present to select an ICD-10-CM code.
2. Identify and select main terms that are referenced in the Alphabetic Index.
3. Identify modifying terms in a diagnosis statement.
4. Summarize the steps in coding.
5. Identify the ICD-10-CM Official Guidelines for Coding and Reporting that impact the steps a coder follows when selecting diagnosis codes.

Key Terms

Granularity

Laterality

REMINDER: As you work through this chapter, you will need to have a copy of the ICD-10-CM coding book to reference. For this chapter, you will also need to reference the ICD-10-CM Official Guidelines for Coding and Reporting. These guidelines can be found in Appendix A which are now available on the Student Companion site and MINDTAP From Cengage.

Introduction

This chapter discusses the location of main terms in the Alphabetic Index of ICD-10-CM and the steps involved in the selection of diagnostic codes using ICD-10-CM.

ICD-10-CM Documentation Essentials

Equally important to understanding the conventions that ICD-10-CM uses to accurately assign codes is having specific written diagnoses and conditions to code. If the diagnoses and conditions are not specifically recorded or if they are recorded in more than one location in the record, the coder must review the complete record to select all the diagnoses and conditions to be coded. Even if the diagnoses and conditions are located on only one form in the record, coders should still review the whole record to obtain all the relevant information.

- For *inpatient* records, diagnoses are typically recorded on a face sheet.
- In the *outpatient* setting, various forms are used to record the diagnoses and conditions treated.
- In a *physician's office*, an encounter form or a problem list is used to record the diagnoses.

When reviewing the record, the coder should note any diagnoses based on findings from procedures or tests that had been ordered and whose results were not available at the time of the patient encounter. The test results could change the diagnosis, and therefore the coder should wait for the results of a test to determine the most accurate diagnosis to code. However, in some settings, such as a physician's office, coders do not wait for all test results. Organizations establish coding policies to address this issue.

Granularity and Laterality

For coders to select accurate codes using ICD-10-CM, medical documentation must be detailed. The increased number of codes in ICD-10-CM, makes for a greater level of detail, known as **granularity**. Because of the increase in the granularity, diagnoses can be recorded and retrieved in a more detailed and efficient manner. Thus, the reporting of diagnoses and statistics retrieved will be of greater use to the health care industry.

However, for the coder to be able to select codes at the highest level of detail, providers must document diseases to the level required by ICD-10-CM.

> **EXAMPLE:** In ICD-10-CM, the codes for a fracture of the femur are differentiated at the fifth-digit level among unspecified fracture of unspecified femur (S72.90), unspecified fracture of right femur (S72.91), and unspecified fracture of left femur (S72.92). Additional characters are needed at the sixth and seventh character levels for these codes. Reference the codes in an ICD-10-CM coding manual to review the meaning of the additional characters.

This level of specificity provides **laterality** in code assignment. In other words, for bilateral sites, ICD-10-CM indicates the specific site—in this example, the right or left femur.

Currently, most providers clearly define whether the left or right femur was fractured, but in other cases, when ICD-10-CM requires laterality, providers will have to be educated. Let's look at the Alphabetic Index (Figures 4-1a and 4-1b), and Tabular List (Figures 4-2a and 4-2b) entries for bursitis. Note in the Alphabetic Index (Figures 4-1a and 4-1b) that the term *bursitis* is further divided by means of many modifying terms. When coding the diagnostic phrase "bursitis of the right hand," the coder references the term *bursitis* and then the modifying term of *hand*. Here, the coder sees that code M70.1– appears in the Alphabetic Index. Then, referring to the Tabular List entry (Figure 4-2b), the coder notes that the code is further divided into the following codes:

- M70.10– bursitis, unspecified hand
- M70.11– bursitis, right hand
- M70.12– bursitis, left hand

Not until the coder references the Tabular List are the codes differentiated by laterality. After referencing the Tabular List, the coder selects M70.11 to report bursitis of the right hand.

- - - third degree T23.371
- - second degree T23.279
- - third degree T23.379
Burnett's syndrome E83.52
Burning
- feet syndrome E53.9
- sensation R20.8
- tongue K14.6
Burn-out (state) Z73.0
Burns' disease or osteochondrosis - see Osteochondrosis, juvenile, ulna
Bursa - see condition
Bursitis M71.9
- Achilles - see Tendinitis, Achilles
- adhesive - see Bursitis, specified NEC
- ankle - see Enthesopathy, lower limb, ankle, specified type NEC
- calcaneal - see Enthesopathy, foot, specified type NEC
- collateral ligament, tibial - see Bursitis, tibial collateral
- due to use, overuse, pressure - (see also Disorder, soft tissue, due to use, specified type NEC)
- - specified NEC - see Disorder, soft tissue, due to use, specified NEC
- Duplay's M75.0
- elbow NEC M70.3-
- - olecranon M70.2-
- finger - see Disorder, soft tissue, due to use, specified type NEC, hand
- foot - see Enthesopathy, foot, specified type NEC
- gonococcal A54.49
- gouty - see Gout
- hand M70.1-
- hip NEC M70.7-
- - trochanteric M70.6-
- infective NEC M71.10
- - abscess - see Abscess, bursa
- - ankle M71.17-
- - elbow M71.12-
- - foot M71.17-
- - hand M71.14-
- - hip M71.15-
- - knee M71.16-
- - multiple sites M71.19
- - shoulder M71.11-
- - specified site NEC M71.18
- - wrist M71.13-
- ischial - see Bursitis, hip
- knee NEC M70.5-
- - prepatellar M70.4-
- occupational NEC - (see also Disorder, soft tissue, due to, use)
- olecranon - see Bursitis, elbow, olecranon
- pharyngeal J39.1
- popliteal - see Bursitis, knee
- prepatellar M70.4-
- radiohumeral M77.8
- rheumatoid M06.20
- - ankle M06.27-
- - elbow M06.22-
- - foot joint M06.27-
- - hand joint M06.24-
- - hip M06.25-

FIGURE 4-1a ICD-10-CM Alphabetic Index pages for bursitis

- - knee M06.26-
- - multiple site M06.29
- - shoulder M06.21-
- - vertebra M06.28
- - wrist M06.23-
- scapulohumeral - see Bursitis, shoulder
- semimembranous muscle (knee) - see Bursitis, knee
- shoulder M75.5-
- - adhesive - see Capsulitis, adhesive
- specified NEC M71.50
- - ankle M71.57-
- - due to use, overuse or pressure - see Disorder, soft tissue, due to, use
- - elbow M71.52-
- - foot M71.57-
- - hand M71.54-
- - hip M71.55-
- - knee M71.56-
- - shoulder - see Bursitis, shoulder
- - specified site NEC M71.58
- - tibial collateral M76.4-
- - wrist M71.53-
- subacromial - see Bursitis, shoulder
- subcoracoid - see Bursitis, shoulder
- subdeltoid - see Bursitis, shoulder
- syphilitic A52.78
- Thornwaldt, Tornwaldt J39.2
- tibial collateral M76.4-
- toe - see Enthesopathy, foot, specified type NEC
- trochanteric (area) - see Bursitis, hip, trochanteric
- wrist - see Bursitis, hand
Bursopathy M71.9
- specified type NEC M71.80
- - ankle M71.87-
- - elbow M71.82-
- - foot M71.87-
- - hand M71.84-
- - hip M71.85-
- - knee M71.86-
- - multiple sites M71.89
- - shoulder M71.81-
- - specified site NEC M71.88
- - wrist M71.83-
Burst stitches or sutures (complication of surgery) T81.31
- external operation wound T81.31
- internal operation wound T81.32
Buruli ulcer A31.1
Bury's disease L95.1
Buschke's
- disease - see Cryptococcosis by site
- scleredema - see Sclerosis, systemic
Busse-Buschke disease see Cryptococcosis by site
Buttock - see condition
Button
- Biskra B55.1
- Delhi B55.1
- oriental B55.1

FIGURE 4-1b ICD-10-CM Alphabetic Index pages for bursitis

M67.95   Unspecified disorder of synovium and tendon, thigh

    M67.951 Unspecified disorder of synovium and tendon, right thigh

    M67.952 Unspecified disorder of synovium and tendon, left thigh

    M67.959 Unspecified disorder of synovium and tendon, unspecified thigh

M67.96   Unspecified disorder of synovium and tendon, lower leg

    M67.961 Unspecified disorder of synovium and tendon, right lower leg

    M67.962 Unspecified disorder of synovium and tendon, left lower leg

    M67.969 Unspecified disorder of synovium and tendon, unspecified lower leg

M67.97   Unspecified disorder of synovium and tendon, ankle and foot

    M67.971 Unspecified disorder of synovium and tendon, right ankle and foot

    M67.972 Unspecified disorder of synovium and tendon, left ankle and foot

    M67.979 Unspecified disorder of synovium and tendon, unspecified ankle and foot

M67.98   Unspecified disorder of synovium and tendon, other site

M67.99   Unspecified disorder of synovium and tendon, multiple sites

Other soft tissue disorders (M70-M79)

M70 Soft tissue disorders related to use, overuse and pressure
Includes: soft tissue disorders of occupational origin
Use additional external cause code to identify activity causing disorder (Y93.-)
Excludes1:bursitis NOS (M71.9-)
Excludes2:bursitis of shoulder (M75.5)
       enthesopathies (M76-M77)
       pressure ulcer (pressure area) (L89.-)

M70.0   Crepitant synovitis (acute) (chronic) of hand and wrist

FIGURE 4-2a ICD-10-CM Tabular List pages for bursitis

M70.03   Crepitant synovitis (acute) (chronic), wrist
    M70.031 Crepitant synovitis (acute) (chronic), right wrist
    M70.032 Crepitant synovitis (acute) (chronic), left wrist
    M70.039 Crepitant synovitis (acute) (chronic), unspecified wrist
M70.04   Crepitant synovitis (acute) (chronic), hand
    M70.041 Crepitant synovitis (acute) (chronic), right hand
    M70.042 Crepitant synovitis (acute) (chronic), left hand
    M70.049 Crepitant synovitis (acute) (chronic), unspecified hand
M70.1   Bursitis of hand
  M70.10   Bursitis, unspecified hand
  M70.11   Bursitis, right hand
  M70.12   Bursitis, left hand
M70.2   Olecranon bursitis
  M70.20   Olecranon bursitis, unspecified elbow
  M70.21   Olecranon bursitis, right elbow
  M70.22   Olecranon bursitis, left elbow
M70.3   Other bursitis of elbow
  M70.30   Other bursitis of elbow, unspecified elbow
  M70.31   Other bursitis of elbow, right elbow
  M70.32   Other bursitis of elbow, left elbow
M70.4   Prepatellar bursitis
  M70.40   Prepatellar bursitis, unspecified knee
  M70.41   Prepatellar bursitis, right knee
  M70.42   Prepatellar bursitis, left knee
M70.5   Other bursitis of knee
  M70.50   Other bursitis of knee, unspecified knee
  M70.51   Other bursitis of knee, right knee
  M70.52   Other bursitis of knee, left knee
M70.6   Trochanteric bursitis
Trochanteric tendinitis
  M70.60   Trochanteric bursitis, unspecified hip
  M70.61   Trochanteric bursitis, right hip
  M70.62   Trochanteric bursitis, left hip

FIGURE 4-2b ICD-10-CM Tabular List pages for bursitis

Documentation plays an important role in the coding process. Coders have to query providers for more specific information when it is missing as it has an impact on code selection. Increased dialogue between coders and providers is essential.

When the ICD-10-CM codes are used at their greatest level of granularity, they demonstrate the full degree of the patient's illness. Therefore, the processing of medical claims is enhanced because there is less need for payers to query providers for additional diagnostic information. Also, because patients' records have more accurate and detailed descriptions of the medical conditions and diseases treated, the quality of care is enhanced.

Steps in Coding

For accurate coding to occur, the coder should follow the following steps:

1. Locate the Main Term in the Alphabetic Index

To locate a main term in the Alphabetic Index, the coder must identify the term in the diagnostic phrase being coded. The main term is the condition that is present.

> **EXAMPLE:** When coding the diagnostic phrase "chronic allergic sinusitis due to pollen," the main term to be located in the Alphabetic Index is *sinusitis*. (This example is used to illustrate the steps in coding.)

Remember that, in the Alphabetic Index, for diagnoses, the primary arrangement of the terms is by condition.

2. Scan the Main Term Entry for Any Instructional Notations

After locating the main term in the Alphabetic Index, a coder should review the main term entry in the Alphabetic Index for any instructional notations. If a notation is present, follow it.

> **EXAMPLE:** No notations appear with the diagnosis of sinusitis.

3. In the Diagnostic Phrase Being Coded, Identify Any Terms That Modify the Main Term

Terms that serve as modifiers in this example are *chronic* and *allergic*.

> **EXAMPLE:** Following the main term of *sinusitis*, the term *allergic* appears as a subterm, indented under the main term.

4. Follow Any Cross-Reference Notes

Cross-references appear in the form of instructional notes such as *See*.

> **EXAMPLE:** Next to the term *allergic*, the instructional note of ("See Rhinitis, allergic") appears. The coder should follow this instruction. The coder should now reference "Rhinitis, allergic" in the Alphabetic Index. The entry of "Rhinitis, allergic" is further divided. The entry lists pollen as the allergen. Therefore, the coder should select the code J30.1.

5. Always Verify the Code in the Tabular List

After selecting a code from the Alphabetic List, the coder must always verify the code in the Tabular List. Additional instructional notations can appear in the Tabular that are not present in the Alphabetic List.

6. Follow Any Instructional Terms

After turning to the Tabular list, scan for any instructional terms that may be present. Coders should scan the following areas:

- *The start of the chapter*—Here, instructional notes appear that govern the entire chapter.

> **EXAMPLE:** In the case of sinusitis, the coder scans the start of Chapter 10, Diseases of the Respiratory System. Here, numerous notes appear that provide instruction to the coder. The notes for Chapter 10 do not impact the case in the example.

- *The beginning of the block range*—Instructional notations that govern the block range would appear here.

> **EXAMPLE:** The block range is titled "Other Diseases of the Upper Respiratory Tract (J30–J39)." No instructional notations appear at this level.

- *At the beginning of the category*—

> **EXAMPLE:** The following appears:
>
> ```
> J30 Vasomotor and allergic rhinitis
>       Includes: spasmodic rhinorrhea
>       Excludes1: allergic rhinitis with asthma (bronchial) (J45.909)
>             rhinitis NOS (J31.0)
> ```
>
> The presence of the notes does not impact this case.

7. Select the Code

After completing these steps, the coder can now select the code but should scan the code selected to ensure that the most specific one has been selected.

> **EXAMPLE:** The descriptions listed support selecting code J30.1. This is the most specific level that can be coded.

Coding Guideline References for Code Location

In Section I of the ICD-10-CM Official Guidelines for Coding and Reporting, coders are given the following direction for code location:

ICD-10-CM Official Coding Guidelines

To select a code in the classification that corresponds to a diagnosis or reason for visit documented in the medical record, first locate the term in the Alphabetic Index, and then verify the code in the Tabular List. Read and be guided by instructional notations that appear in both the Alphabetic Index and the Tabular List.

It is essential to use both the Alphabetic Index and the Tabular List when locating and assigning a code. The Alphabetic Index does not always provide the full code. Selection of the full code, including laterality and any applicable 7th character can only be done in the Tabular List. A dash (–) at the end of an Alphabetic Index entry indicates that additional characters are required. Even if a dash is not included at the Alphabetic Index entry, it is necessary to refer to the Tabular List to verify that no 7th character is required. (See Appendix A, Section I.B.1.)

Courtesy of the Centers for Medicare & Medicaid Services, www.cms.gov

This guideline will be further discussed in Chapter 5.

Summary

- The Alphabetic Index and the Tabular List must both be used when assigning codes.
- All instructional notations that appear in the Alphabetic Index and the Tabular List should be read and used as a guide when selecting codes because they can have an impact on code assignment.
- ICD-10-CM codes are very detailed, and medical documentation needs to be specific to justify the selection of codes.
- ICD-10-CM codes indicate laterality.
- The steps in coding need to be followed for accurate code selection.

Chapter Review

True/False

Indicate whether each statement is true (T) or false (F).

1. _____ To select a code in the classification that corresponds to a diagnosis or reason for visit documented in the medical record, first locate the term in the Tabular List.

2. _____ The Tabular Listing of ICD-10-CM provides great detail in code assignment, and therefore the coder does not have to reference the Alphabetic Index to assign codes.

3. _____ The instructional notes in the Alphabetic Index take precedence over the instructional notes in the Tabular List.

4. _____ Medical documentation should be detailed to support the granularity of the codes present in ICD-10-CM.

5. _____ The coder must follow the *See* note in the Alphabetic Index to review additional entries in the Index.

Short Answer

For each diagnostic statement, identify the main term that would be used in the Alphabetic Index of ICD-10-CM.

6. unstable angina

_____

7. congestive heart failure

_____

8. acute punctured eardrum

_____

9. fracture of mandible

_____

10. benign lesion of lip

_____

11. ulcerative chronic tonsillitis

_____

12. chronic left quadrant abdominal pain

_____

13. gastritis due to diet deficiency

_____

14. primary neoplasm of stomach

_____

15. abscess of vas deferens

_____

16. sepsis following immunization

_____

17. streptococcal peritonitis

_____

18. ileo-jejunal ulceration

_____

19. ulcer with gangrene

_____

20. dermatitis due to allergy

_____

21. abdominal wall gangrene

_____

22. congenital coronary fistula

_____

23. bilateral conductive and sensorineural deafness

_____

24. lateral condyle, lower end, fracture

_____

25. pelvic phlebitis following molar pregnancy

_____

26. chronic obstructive rhinitis

_____

27. extrinsic allergic alveolitis

_____

28. congenital retinal aneurysm

_____

29. amyloid cerebral angiopathy

_____

30. psychogenic atopic dermatitis

_____

For each of the following, identify the modifying term for the diagnostic statement listed.

31. chronic hepatitis

_____

32. lung mass

_____

33. atrial fibrillation

_____

Essay

Briefly respond to the following.

34. List the steps in coding.

_____

_____

_____

_____

_____

_____

_____

_____

35. Explain why it is important to use both the Alphabetic Index and Tabular List for code assignment.

_____

_____

_____

_____

_____

_____

_____

Chapter Outline

Chapter Objectives

At the conclusion of this chapter, you should be able to:

1. List the Cooperating Parties for ICD-10-CM.
2. Explain the purpose of the ICD-10-CM Official Guidelines for Coding and Reporting.
3. Identify the four sections of the ICD-10-CM Official Guidelines for Coding and Reporting.
4. Explain the differences between the guidelines for inpatient versus outpatient and physician office visits.
5. Summarize the guidelines for the sequencing of diagnostic codes.

Key Terms

Combination code	Principal diagnosis	Secondary diagnoses	Sequela (late effect)

REMINDER: As you work through this chapter, you will need to have a copy of the ICD-10-CM coding book to reference. For this chapter, you will also need to reference the ICD-10-CM Official Guidelines for Coding and Reporting. These guidelines can be found in Appendix A which are now available on the Student Companion site and MINDTAP From Cengage.

Introduction

To ensure accurate diagnostic and procedural information, ICD-10-CM will be used to capture information for third-party reimbursement, continuity of patient care, health care statistics, and other reporting functions.

To assist coders in consistently using ICD-10-CM, the Official Guidelines for Coding and Reporting were developed by the Centers for Medicare and Medicaid Services and the National Center for Health Statistics.

The Cooperating Parties for ICD-10-CM, which have cooperatively approved the ICD-10-CM Official Guidelines for Coding and Reporting, are the following organizations:

- American Hospital Association (AHA)
- American Health Information Management Association (AHIMA)
- Centers for Medicare and Medicaid Services (CMS)
- National Center for Health Statistics (NCHS)

The guidelines are used as a set of rules to guide in the selection of ICD-10-CM codes. They are organized into four sections with one appendix, as follows:

- *Section I—Conventions, General Coding Guidelines, and Chapter-Specific Guidelines*. In this section, the guidelines address the structure and conventions of ICD-10-CM and provide general guidelines that apply to the entire classification, as well as chapter-specific guidelines.

- *Section II—Selection of Principal Diagnosis*. This section includes guidelines for the selection of the principal diagnosis for non-outpatient settings. Non-outpatient settings include acute care, short-term care, long-term care, and psychiatric hospitals, home health agencies, rehab facilities, nursing homes, and the like.

- *Section III—Reporting Additional Diagnoses*. In this section, the guidelines cover the reporting of additional diagnoses that affect patient care in non-outpatient settings.

- *Section IV—Diagnostic Coding and Reporting Guidelines for Outpatient Services*. This section outlines the guidelines for outpatient coding and reporting. These guidelines for outpatient diagnoses have been approved for use by hospitals and providers in coding and reporting hospital-based outpatient services and provider-based office visits.

Section I—ICD-10-CM Conventions, General Coding Guidelines, and Chapter-Specific Guidelines

Section I provides guidelines for conventions, as well as general coding guidelines and chapter-specific guidelines. The general coding guidelines are reviewed in this chapter, and the chapter-specific guidelines are reviewed in the remaining chapters of this book. The chapter-specific guidelines are sequenced in the same order as the chapters appear in the ICD-10-CM Tabular List.

EXAMPLE: In the ICD-10-CM Tabular List, Chapter 1 is titled "Certain Infectious and Parasitic Diseases," and the first subsection in the chapter-specific guidelines is C1, titled "Chapter 1: Certain Infectious and Parasitic Diseases (A00–B99)."

Numerous guidelines have been used in the development of this textbook and appear in the highlighted Coding Guideline areas. However, coders need to read and become familiar with *all* of the Official Guidelines to enhance their coding accuracy. In fact, new coding students should read the Official Guidelines from front to back numerous times! The guidelines can be compared to the directions for baking. If you don't follow the directions when baking, your cake will not turn out as it should. If you don't follow the coding guidelines, you will not select the proper codes. Coding is also like baking in that the more you bake, the better baker you will become. The more you code, the better coder you will become!

General Coding Guidelines

The following general coding guidelines apply to the selection of ICD-10-CM diagnostic codes.

The first guidelines describe locating a code in ICD-10-CM, the level of detail in coding, and the codes from A00.0 through T88.9, Z00–Z99.8.

ICD-10-CM Official Coding Guidelines

1. Locating a code in the ICD-10-CM

To select a code in the classification that corresponds to a diagnosis or reason for visit documented in a medical record, first locate the term in the Alphabetic Index, and then verify the code in the Tabular List. Read and be guided by instructional notations that appear in both the Alphabetic Index and the Tabular List.

It is essential to use both the Alphabetic Index and Tabular List when locating and assigning a code. The Alphabetic Index does not always provide the full code. Selection of the full code, including laterality and any applicable 7th character can only be done in the Tabular list. A dash (-) at the end of an Alphabetic Index entry indicates that additional characters are required. Even if a dash is not included at the Alphabetic Index entry, it is necessary to refer to the Tabular list to verify that no 7th character is required.

2. Level of Detail in Coding

Diagnosis codes are to be used and reported at their highest number of characters available.

ICD-10-CM diagnosis codes are composed of codes with 3, 4, 5, 6 or 7 characters. Codes with three characters are included in ICD-10-CM as the heading of a category of codes that may be further subdivided by the use of fourth and/or fifth characters and/or sixth characters, which provide greater detail.

A three-character code is to be used only if it is not further subdivided. A code is invalid if it has not been coded to the full number of characters required for that code, including the 7th character, if applicable.

3. Code or codes from A00.0 through T88.9, Z00–Z99.8

The appropriate code or codes from A00.0 through T88.9, Z00–Z99.8 must be used to identify diagnoses, symptoms, conditions, problems, complaints or other reason(s) for the encounter/visit. (See Appendix A, Section I.B.1–3.)

EXAMPLE: The Alphabetic Index does not always provide the full code so the coder must reference the Tabular list. Reference the ICD-10-CM Alphabetic Index entry for Abrasion. Under the subheading of ankle note that S90.51- appears. The dash signals to the coder that additional characters are needed. This is telling the coder to reference the Tabular list to determine the full code.

Codes That Describe Symptoms and Signs

Codes that describe symptoms and signs, such as pain and fever, are acceptable for coding when a definitive diagnosis has not been established. For example, when a patient presents in a physician's office for abdominal pain and the cause has not been confirmed, the abdominal pain is coded.

ICD-10-CM Official Coding Guidelines

4. Signs and symptoms

Codes that describe symptoms and signs, as opposed to diagnoses, are acceptable for reporting purposes when a related definitive diagnosis has not been established (confirmed) by the provider. Chapter 18 of ICD-10-CM, Symptoms, Signs, and Abnormal Clinical and Laboratory Findings, Not Elsewhere Classified (codes R00.0–R99) contains many, but not all codes for symptoms. *See Section I.B.18 Use of Signs/Symptom/Unspecified Codes.* (See Appendix A, Section I.B.4.)

Conditions That Are an Integral Part of a Disease Process

When a definitive diagnosis is recorded, along with signs and symptoms, the coder should code the definitive diagnosis only if the signs and symptoms are integral to the disease process. Symptoms such as cough and fever are not recorded for a patient who has been diagnosed with a respiratory infection.

ICD-10-CM Official Coding Guidelines

5. Conditions that are an integral part of a disease process

Signs and symptoms that are associated routinely with a disease process should not be assigned as additional codes, unless otherwise instructed by the classification. (See Appendix A, Section I.B.5.)

Conditions That Are Not an Integral Part of a Disease Process

If signs and symptoms exist that are not routinely associated with a disease process, the signs and symptoms should be coded. If a patient presents for a sprained ankle and is also experiencing vomiting, both the ankle sprain and the symptom of vomiting are recorded.

ICD-10-CM Official Coding Guidelines

6. Conditions that are not an integral part of a disease process

Additional signs and symptoms that may not be associated routinely with a disease process should be coded when present. (See Appendix A, Section I.B.6.)

Multiple Coding for a Single Condition

Some conventions instruct coders to assign multiple codes to a single condition. These conventions include the instruction notations of Use Additional Code and Code First Underlying Condition.

ICD-10-CM Official Coding Guidelines

7. Multiple coding for a single condition

In addition to the etiology/manifestation convention that requires two codes to fully describe a single condition that affects multiple body systems, there are other single conditions that also require more than one code. "Use additional code" notes are found in the Tabular List at codes that are not part of an etiology/manifestation pair where a secondary code is useful to fully describe a condition. The sequencing rule is the same as the etiology/manifestation pair, "use additional code" indicates that a secondary code should be added, if known.

For example, for bacterial infections that are not included in Chapter 1, a secondary code from category B95, Streptococcus, Staphylococcus, and Enterococcus, as the cause of diseases classified elsewhere, or B96, Other bacterial agents as the cause of diseases classified elsewhere, may be required to identify the bacterial organism causing the infection. A "use additional code" note will normally be found at the infectious disease code, indicating a need for the organism code to be added as a secondary code.

"Code first" notes are also under certain codes that are not specifically manifestation codes but may be due to an underlying cause. When there is a "code first" note and an underlying condition is present, the underlying condition should be sequenced first, if known.

"Code, if applicable, any causal condition first", notes indicate that this code may be assigned as a principal diagnosis when the causal condition is unknown or not applicable. If a causal condition is known, then the code for that condition should be sequenced as the principal or first-listed diagnosis.

Multiple codes may be needed for sequela, complication codes, and obstetric codes to more fully describe a condition. See the specific guidelines for these conditions for further instruction. (See Appendix A, Section I.B.7.)

Acute and Chronic Conditions

This guideline instructs the coder to use multiple codes in the following situation.

ICD-10-CM Official Coding Guidelines

8. Acute and Chronic Conditions

If the same condition is described as both acute (subacute) and chronic, and separate subentries exist in the Alphabetic Index at the same indentation level, code both and sequence the acute (subacute) code first. (See Appendix A, Section I.B.8.)

Combination Code

A combination code is defined in the guidelines as follows:

ICD-10-CM Official Coding Guidelines

9. Combination Code

A combination code is a single code used to classify:

Two diagnoses, or

A diagnosis with an associated secondary process (manifestation)

A diagnosis with an associated complication

Combination codes are identified by referring to subterm entries in the Alphabetic Index and by reading the inclusion and exclusion notes in the Tabular List.

Assign only the combination code when that code fully identifies the diagnostic conditions involved or when the Alphabetic Index so directs. Multiple coding should not be used when the classification provides a combination code that clearly identifies all of the elements documented in the diagnosis. When the combination code lacks necessary specificity in describing the manifestation or complication, an additional code should be used as a secondary code.
(See Appendix A, Section I.B.9.)

Sequela (Late Effects)

The following guideline needs to be followed when coding sequelae (late effects):

ICD-10-CM Official Coding Guidelines

10. Sequela (Late Effects)

A sequela is the residual effect (condition produced) after the acute phase of an illness or injury has terminated. There is no time limit on when a sequela code can be used. The residual may be apparent early, such as in cerebral infarction, or it may occur months or years later, such as that due to a previous injury. Examples of sequela include: scar formation resulting from a burn, deviated septum due to a nasal fracture, and infertility due to tubal occlusion from old tuberculosis. Coding of sequela generally requires two codes sequenced in the following order: The condition or nature of the sequela is sequenced first. The sequela code is sequenced second.

An exception to the above guidelines are those instances where the code for the sequela is followed by a manifestation code identified in the Tabular List and title, or the sequela code has been expanded (at the 4th, 5th, or 6th character levels) to include the manifestation(s). The code for the acute phase of an illness or injury that led to the sequela is never used with a code for the late effect.

See Section I.C.9. Sequelae of cerebrovascular disease.

See Section I.C.15. Sequelae of complication of pregnancy, childbirth and the puerperium.

See Section I.C.19. Application of 7th characters for Chapter 19. (See Appendix A, Section I.B.10.)

Impending or Threatened Conditions

To accurately code a diagnosis that is modified by the terms *impending* or *threatened*, the coder must answer the question, "Did the condition actually occur?"

- If the condition occurred, then code the diagnosis as a confirmed diagnosis.
- If the condition did not occur, reference the Alphabetic Index to determine whether the condition has a subentry term for *impending* or *threatened*. Also reference main term entries for *impending* and *threatened*.

ICD-10-CM Official Coding Guidelines

11. Impending or Threatened Condition

Code any condition described at the time of discharge as "impending" or "threatened" as follows:

If it did occur, code as confirmed diagnosis.

If it did not occur, reference the Alphabetic Index to determine if the condition has a subentry term for "impending" or "threatened" and also reference main term entries for "Impending" and for "Threatened."

If the subterms are listed, assign the given code.

If the subterms are not listed, code the existing underlying condition(s) and not the condition described as impending or threatened. (See Appendix A, Section I.B.11.)

Reporting Same Diagnosis Code More Than Once

The guidelines give the following direction when reporting the same diagnosis code more than once:

ICD-10-CM Official Coding Guidelines

12. Reporting Same Diagnosis Code More Than Once

Each unique ICD-10-CM diagnosis code may be reported only once for an encounter. This applies to bilateral conditions when there are no distinct codes identifying laterality or two different conditions classified to the same ICD-10-CM diagnosis code. (See Appendix A, Section I.B.12.)

Laterality

The guidelines give the following direction when reporting the laterality of a condition:

ICD-10-CM Official Coding Guidelines

13. Laterality

Some ICD-10-CM codes indicate laterality, specifying whether the condition occurs on the left, right, or is bilateral. If no bilateral code is provided and the condition is bilateral, assign separate codes for both the left and right side. If the side is not identified in the medical record, assign the code for the unspecified side. When a patient has a bilateral condition and each side is treated during separate encounters, assign the "bilateral" code (as the condition still exists on both sides), including for the encounter to treat the first side. For the second encounter for treatment after one side has previously been treated and the condition no longer exists on that side, assign the appropriate unilateral code for the side where the condition still exists (e.g., cataract surgery performed on each eye in separate encounters). The bilateral code would not be assigned for the subsequent encounter, as the patient no longer has the condition in the previously-treated site. If the treatment on the first side did not completely resolve the condition, then the bilateral code would still be appropriate. (See Appendix A, Section I.B.13.)

Documentation for BMI Depth of Non-Pressure Ulcers, Pressure Ulcer Stages, Coma Scale, and NIH Stroke Scale

The coding guidelines give the following direction when reporting body mass index (BMI), depth of non-pressure ulcers, pressure ulcer stages, coma scale, and NIH stroke scale:

ICD-10-CM Official Coding Guidelines

14. Documentation by Clinicians Other Than the Patient's Provider

Code assignment is based on documentation by patient's provider (i.e., physician or other qualified health care practitioner legally accountable for establishing the patient's diagnosis). There are a few exceptions, such as codes for the Body Mass Index (BMI), depth of non-pressure chronic ulcers, pressure ulcer stage, coma scale, and NIH stroke scale (NIHSS) codes, code assignment may be based on medical record documentation from clinicians who are not the patient's provider (i.e., physician or other qualified health care practitioner legally accountable for establishing the patient's diagnosis), since this information is typically documented by other clinicians involved in the care of the patient (e.g., a dietitian often documents the BMI and nurses often document the pressure ulcer stages and an emergency medical technician often documents the coma scale). However, the associated diagnosis (such as overweight, obesity, acute stroke, or pressure ulcer) must be documented by the patient's provider. If there is conflicting medical record documentation, either from the same clinician or different clinicians, the patient's attending provider should be queried for clarification.

For social determinants of health, such as information found in categories Z55–Z65, Persons with potential health hazards related to socioeconomic and psychosocial circumstances, code assignment may be based on medical documentation from clinicians involved in the care of the patient who are not the patient's provider since this information represents social information, rather then medical diagnoses. Patient self-reported documentation may also be used to assign codes for social determinants of health, as long as the patient self-reported information is signed-off by and incorporated into the health record by either a clinician or provider.

The BMI, coma scale, and NIHSS codes and categories Z55–Z65 should only be reported as secondary diagnoses. (See Appendix A, Section I.B.14.)

Courtesy of the Centers for Medicare & Medicaid Services, www.cms.gov

Syndromes

When coding a condition listed as a syndrome, coders should be directed by the following coding guideline.

ICD-10-CM Official Coding Guidelines

15. Syndromes

Follow the Alphabetic Index guidance when coding syndromes. In the absence of Alphabetic Index guidance, assign codes for the documented manifestations of the syndrome. Additional codes for manifestations that are not an integral part of the disease process may also be assigned when the condition does not have a unique code. (See Appendix A, Section I.B.15.)

Courtesy of the Centers for Medicare & Medicaid Services, www.cms.gov

Documentation of Complications of Care

Coders should be directed by the following guideline to determine whether or not a condition is considered a complication of care.

ICD-10-CM Official Coding Guidelines

16. Documentation of Complications of Care

Code assignment is based on the provider's documentation of the relationship between the condition and the care or procedure unless otherwise instructed by the classification. The guideline extends to any complications of care, regardless of the chapter the code is located in. It is important to note that not all conditions that occur during or following medical care or surgery are classified as complications. There must be a cause-and-effect relationship between the care provided and the condition, and an indication in the documentation that it is a complication. Query the provider for clarification, if the complication is not clearly documented. (See Appendix A, Section I.B.16.)

Courtesy of the Centers for Medicare & Medicaid Services, www.cms.gov

Borderline Diagnosis

Coders should be directed by the following guideline to select codes for diagnoses reported as borderline.

ICD-10-CM Official Coding Guidelines

17. Borderline Diagnosis

If the provider documents a "borderline" diagnosis at the time of discharge, the diagnosis is coded as confirmed, unless the classification provides a specific entry (e.g., borderline diabetes). If a borderline condition has a specific index entry in

ICD-10-CM, it should be coded as such. Since borderline conditions are not uncertain diagnoses, no distinction is made between the care setting (inpatient versus outpatient). Whenever the documentation is unclear regarding a borderline condition, coders are encouraged to query for clarification. (See Appendix A, Section I.B.17.)

Signs, Symptoms, and Unspecified Codes

Coders should be directed by the following guideline for the reporting of signs, symptoms, and unspecified codes.

ICD-10-CM Official Coding Guidelines

18. Use of Sign/Symptom/Unspecified Codes

Sign/symptom and "unspecified" codes have acceptable, even necessary, uses. While specific diagnosis codes should be reported when they are supported by the available medical record documentation and clinical knowledge of the patient's health condition, there are instances when signs/symptoms or unspecified codes are the best choices for accurately reflecting the healthcare encounter. Each healthcare encounter should be coded to the level of certainty known for that encounter.

If a definitive diagnosis has not been established by the end of the encounter, it is appropriate to report codes for sign(s) and/or symptom(s) in lieu of a definitive diagnosis. When sufficient clinical information isn't known or available about a particular health condition to assign a more specific code, it is acceptable to report the appropriate "unspecified" code (e.g., a diagnosis of pneumonia has been determined, but not the specific type). Unspecified codes should be reported when they are the codes that most accurately reflect what is known about the patient's condition at the time of that particular encounter. It would be inappropriate to select a specific code that is not supported by the medical record documentation or conduct medically unnecessary diagnostic testing in order to determine a more specific code. (See Appendix A, Section I.B.18.)

Coding for Healthcare Encounters in Hurricane Aftermath

Coders should be directed by the following guidelines when coding health care encounters in a hurricane aftermath.

ICD-10-CM Official Coding Guidelines

19. Coding for Health care Encounters in Hurricane Aftermath

a. Use of External Cause of Morbidity Codes

An external cause of morbidity code should be assigned to identify the cause of the injury(ies) incurred as a result of the hurricane. The use of external cause of morbidity codes is supplemental to the application of ICD-10-CM codes. External cause of morbidity codes are never to be recorded as a principal diagnosis (first-listed in non-inpatient settings). The appropriate injury code should be sequenced before any external cause codes. The external cause of morbidity codes capture how the injury or health condition happened (cause), the intent (unintentional or accidental; or intentional, such as suicide or assault), the place where the event occurred, the activity of the patient at the time of the event, and the person's status (e.g., civilian, military). They should not be assigned for encounters to treat hurricane victims' medical conditions when no injury, adverse effect or poisoning is involved. External cause of morbidity codes should be assigned for each encounter for care and treatment of the injury. External cause of morbidity codes may be assigned in all health care settings. For the purpose of capturing complete and accurate ICD-10-CM data in the aftermath of the hurricane, a health care setting should be considered as any location where medical care is provided by licensed health care professionals.

b. Sequencing of External Causes of Morbidity Codes

Codes for cataclysmic events, such as a hurricane, take priority over all other external cause codes except child and adult abuse and terrorism and should be sequenced before other external cause of injury codes. Assign as many external cause of morbidity codes as necessary to fully explain each cause. For example, if an injury occurs as a result of a building collapse during the hurricane, external cause codes for both the hurricane and the building collapse should be assigned, with the external causes code for hurricane being sequenced as the first external cause code. For injuries incurred as a direct result of the hurricane, assign the appropriate code(s) for the injuries, followed by the code X37.0-, Hurricane (with the appropriate 7th character), and any other applicable external cause of injury codes. Code X37.0- also should be assigned when an injury is incurred as a result of flooding caused by a levee breaking related to the hurricane. Code X38.-, Flood (with the appropriate 7th character), should be assigned when an injury is from flooding resulting directly from the storm. Code X36.0.-, Collapse of dam or man-made structure, should not be assigned when the cause of the collapse is due to the hurricane. Use of code X36.0- is limited to collapses of man-made structures due to earth surface movements, not due to storm surges directly from a hurricane.

c. Other External Causes of Morbidity Code Issues

For injuries that are not a direct result of the hurricane, such as an evacuee that has incurred an injury as a result of a motor vehicle accident, assign the appropriate external cause of morbidity code(s) to describe the cause of the injury, but do not assign code X37.0-, Hurricane. If it is not clear whether the injury was a direct result of the hurricane, assume the injury is due to the hurricane and assign code X37.0-, Hurricane, as well as any other applicable external cause of morbidity codes. In addition to code X37.0-, Hurricane, other possible applicable external cause of morbidity codes include:

W54.0-, Bitten by dog

X30-, Exposure to excessive natural heat

X31-, Exposure to excessive natural cold

X38-, Flood

d. Use of Z codes

Z codes (other reasons for health care encounters) may be assigned as appropriate to further explain the reasons for presenting for healthcare services, including transfers between health care facilities. The ICD-10-CM Official Guidelines for Coding and Reporting identify which codes maybe assigned as principal or first-listed diagnosis only, secondary diagnosis only, or principal/first-listed or secondary (depending on the circumstances). Possible applicable Z codes include:

Z59.0, Homelessness

Z59.1, Inadequate housing

Z59.5, Extreme poverty

Z75.1, Person awaiting admission to adequate facility elsewhere

Z75.3, Unavailability and inaccessibility of health care facilities

Z75.4, Unavailability and inaccessibility of other helping agencies

Z76.2, Encounter for health supervision and care of other healthy infant and child

Z99.12, Encounter for respirator [ventilator] dependence during power failure

The external cause of morbidity codes and the Z codes listed above are not an all-inclusive list. Other codes may be applicable to the encounter based upon the documentation. Assign as many codes as necessary to fully explain each health care encounter. Since patient history information may be very limited, use any available documentation to assign the appropriate external cause of morbidity and Z codes. (See Appendix A, Section I.B.19.)

Chapter-Specific Coding Guidelines

The Official ICD-10-CM Guidelines for Coding and Reporting outline the chapter-specific coding guidelines in Section I, C. These guidelines are for specific diagnoses and complications found in ICD-10-CM, and they are discussed throughout the remaining chapters of this book.

Exercise 5.1—Section I

State whether each statement is true (T) or false (F) based on Section I of the ICD-10-CM Official Guidelines for Coding and Reporting.

1. A three-digit code is to be used only if it is not further subdivided. _____

2. If the same condition is described as both acute and chronic and if separate subentries exist in the Alphabetic Index at the same indentation level, code both, with the acute code first. _____

3. The Alphabetic Index provides the full code. _____

4. Each unique ICD-10-CM diagnosis code may be reported only once for an encounter. _____

5. A sequela is the residual effect after the acute phase of an illness or injury has terminated. _____

Section II—Selection of Principal Diagnosis

Section II of the guidelines is used to provide consistency in selecting the **principal diagnosis**, which is defined in the Uniform Hospital Discharge Data Set (UHDDS) as "that condition established after study to be chiefly responsible for occasioning the admission of the patient to the hospital for care." Hospitals use the UHDDS definitions to report inpatient data elements in a consistent, standardized manner. To review the definitions and the data elements that the definitions apply to, review the July 31, 1985, *Federal Register* (Vol. 50, No. 147, pp. 31038–31040).

Section II of the ICD-10-CM Official Guidelines state that when "determining principal diagnosis, coding conventions in the ICD-10-CM, the Tabular List and Alphabetic Index take precedence over these official coding guidelines. (See Section I.A, Conventions for the ICD-10-CM.) The importance of consistent, complete documentation in the medical record cannot be overemphasized. Without such documentation the application of all coding guidelines is a difficult, if not impossible, task."

The guidelines for coding and reporting outpatient services, which include hospital-based outpatient services and physician office visits, are outlined in Section IV of the ICD-10-CM Official Guidelines for Coding and Reporting.

 NOTE:

The guidelines in this section are for all non-outpatient settings (acute care; short-term care, long-term care, and psychiatric hospitals; home health agencies; rehab facilities; nursing homes; and the like).

Codes for Symptoms, Signs, and Ill-Defined Conditions

Codes from Chapter 18 of ICD-10-CM, "Symptoms, Signs, and Abnormal Clinical and Laboratory Findings, Not Elsewhere Classified (Codes R00.0-R99)," are not to be used as a principal diagnosis when a related definitive diagnosis has been established.

ICD-10-CM Official Coding Guideline

A. Codes for symptoms, signs and ill-defined conditions

Codes for symptoms, signs, and ill-defined conditions from Chapter 18 are not to be used as principal diagnosis when a related definitive diagnosis has been established. (See Appendix A, Section II.A.)

EXAMPLE: A patient is admitted because of severe abdominal pain. After diagnostic testing, it is determined that the patient has a gastric ulcer. The gastric ulcer is the principal diagnosis.

Two or More Interrelated Conditions, Each Potentially Meeting the Definition for Principal Diagnosis

The guidelines state that:

ICD-10-CM Official Coding Guidelines

B. Two or more interrelated conditions, each potentially meeting the definition for principal diagnosis

When there are two or more interrelated conditions (such as diseases in the same ICD-10-CM chapter or manifestations characteristically associated with a certain disease) potentially meeting the definition of principal diagnosis, either condition may be sequenced first, unless the circumstances of the admission, the therapy provided, the Tabular List or the Alphabetic Index indicate otherwise. (See Appendix A, Section II.B.)

Courtesy of the Centers for Medicare & Medicaid Services, www.cms.gov

EXAMPLE: Tom Pick is admitted due to severe vomiting, nausea, and abdominal pain. After study, it is determined that he has a gastric ulcer and diverticulitis. Treatment is directed equally at both diagnoses, and the physician documents that both conditions prompted the admission. Either condition could be listed as the principal diagnosis.

Two or More Diagnoses That Equally Meet the Definition for Principal Diagnosis

When two or more diagnoses equally meet the definition for principal diagnosis, the following coding guideline gives the coder direction.

ICD-10-CM Official Coding Guidelines

C. Two or more diagnoses that equally meet the definition for principal diagnosis

In the unusual instance when two or more diagnoses equally meet the criteria for principal diagnosis as determined by the circumstances of admission, diagnostic workup and/or therapy provided, and the Alphabetic Index, Tabular List, or another coding guideline does not provide sequencing direction, any one of the diagnoses may be sequenced first. (See Appendix A, Section II.C.)

Courtesy of the Centers for Medicare & Medicaid Services, www.cms.gov

Two or More Comparative or Contrasting Conditions

At times, physicians record comparative or contrasting diagnoses by using the terms *either* or *or*. The coding guidelines state that:

ICD-10-CM Official Coding Guidelines

D. Two or more comparative or contrasting conditions

In those rare instances when two or more contrasting or comparative diagnoses are documented as "either/or" (or similar terminology), they are coded as if the diagnoses were confirmed and the diagnoses are sequenced according to the circumstances of the admission. If no further determination can be made as to which diagnosis should be principal, either diagnosis may be sequenced first. (See Appendix A, Section II.D.)

Courtesy of the Centers for Medicare & Medicaid Services, www.cms.gov

Original Treatment Plan Not Carried Out

When treatment is not carried out, the coder must still answer the question, "What diagnosis, after study, occasioned the admission to the hospital?" The principal diagnosis remains the same even if the treatment is not carried out.

ICD-10-CM Official Coding Guidelines

F. Original treatment plan not carried out

Sequence as the principal diagnosis the condition, which after study occasioned the admission to the hospital, even though treatment may not have been carried out due to unforeseen circumstances. (See Appendix A, Section II.F.)

Courtesy of the Centers for Medicare & Medicaid Services, www.cms.gov

EXAMPLE: Denny Sams is an 80-year-old man with a past history of gastric ulcer. He is admitted because of severe abdominal pain and back pain. After diagnostic study, it is determined that he has kidney stones, and lithotripsy is planned. Before the lithotripsy, he is discharged at his request because he feels he needs to go home to care for his wife. The procedure is not performed.

In this example, the kidney stones are the reason for the admission and are therefore reported as the principal diagnosis.

The coding guidelines instruct coders how to sequence codes when the original treatment plan is not carried out.

Complications of Surgery and Other Medical Care

Complications may result after surgery or from other medical care. The coding guidelines give direction in the coding of complications of surgery and other medical care.

ICD-10-CM Official Coding Guidelines

G. Complications of surgery and other medical care

When the admission is for treatment of a complication resulting from surgery or other medical care, the complication code is sequenced as the principal diagnosis. If the complication is classified to the T80–T88 series and the code lacks the necessary specificity in describing the complication, an additional code for the specific complication should be assigned. (See Appendix A, Section II.G.)

Courtesy of the Centers for Medicare & Medicaid Services, www.cms.gov

Uncertain Diagnosis

At times, a physician does not have sufficient knowledge to make a definitive diagnosis at the time of discharge. In these cases, the physician commonly records the diagnosis as questionable or suspected. The relevant guideline applies only to the selection of a principal diagnosis for inpatient admissions to short-term, acute, or long-term care, and to psychiatric hospitals. The guidelines give direction in the coding of an uncertain diagnosis.

This guideline is not used for outpatient hospital records or physician office records. These settings are discussed later in this chapter under diagnostic coding and reporting guidelines for outpatient services.

ICD-10-CM Official Coding Guidelines

H. Uncertain Diagnosis

If the diagnosis documented at the time of discharge is qualified as "probable", "suspected", "likely", "questionable", "possible", or "still to be ruled out", "compatible with", "consistent with", or other similar terms indicating uncertainty, code the condition as if it existed or was established. The bases for these guidelines are the diagnostic workup, arrangements for further workup or observation, and initial therapeutic approach that correspond most closely with the established diagnosis.

Note: This guideline is applicable only to inpatient admissions to short-term, acute, long-term care and psychiatric hospitals. (See Appendix A, Section II.H.)

Courtesy of the Centers for Medicare & Medicaid Services, www.cms.gov

Admission from Observation Unit, Following Post-Operative Observation, or Outpatient Surgery

The following guidelines are used when coding an admission from an observation unit, following post-operative observation, or outpatient surgery. At times, patients are admitted as inpatients following medical observation, for postoperative observation following outpatient surgery, or for continuing inpatient care following outpatient surgery.

ICD-10-CM Official Coding Guidelines

I. Admission from Observation Unit

1. Admission Following Medical Observation

When a patient is admitted to an observation unit for a medical condition, which either worsens or does not improve, and is subsequently admitted as an inpatient of the same hospital for this same medical condition, the principal diagnosis would be the medical condition which led to the hospital admission.

2. Admission Following Post-Operative Observation

When a patient is admitted to an observation unit to monitor a condition (or complication) that develops following outpatient surgery, and then is subsequently admitted as an inpatient of the same hospital, hospitals should apply the Uniform Hospital Discharge Data Set (UHDDS) definition of principal diagnosis as "that condition established after study to be chiefly responsible for occasioning the admission of the patient to the hospital for care."

J. Admission from Outpatient Surgery

When a patient receives surgery in the hospital's outpatient surgery department and is subsequently admitted for continuing inpatient care at the same hospital, the following guidelines should be followed in selecting the principal diagnosis for the inpatient admission:

- If the reason for the inpatient admission is a complication, assign the complication as the principal diagnosis.

- If no complication, or other condition, is documented as the reason for the inpatient admission, assign the reason for the outpatient surgery as the principal diagnosis.

- If the reason for the inpatient admission is another condition unrelated to the surgery, assign the unrelated condition as the principal diagnosis. (See Appendix A, Section II. I1-2 and Section II.I-J.)

EXAMPLE: Tom Smith is placed in observation due to extreme renal colic. He is admitted because it is determined that he has kidney stones that are not going to pass. Surgery was completed to remove the kidney stones. The principal diagnosis for the admission is the kidney stones.

Admissions/Encounters for Rehabilitation

At times a patient is admitted or has an encounter with a health care provider for rehabilitation services. The following guideline directs the coder in these situations.

ICD-10-CM Official Coding Guidelines

K. Admissions/Encounters for Rehabilitation

When the purpose for the admission/encounter is rehabilitation, sequence first the code for the condition for which the service is being performed. For example, for an admission/encounter for rehabilitation for right-sided dominant hemiplegia following a cerebrovascular infarction, report code I69.351, Hemiplegia and hemiparesis following cerebral infarction affecting right dominant side, as the first-listed or principal diagnosis.

If the condition for which the rehabilitation service is being provided is no longer present, report the appropriate aftercare code as the first-listed or principal diagnosis, unless the rehabilitation service is being provided following an injury. For rehabilitation services following active treatment of an injury, assign the injury code with the appropriate seventh character for subsequent encounter as the first-listed or principal diagnosis. For example, if a patient with severe degenerative osteoarthritis of the hip underwent hip replacement and the current encounter/admission is for rehabilitation, report code Z47.1, Aftercare following joint replacement surgery, as the first-listed or principal diagnosis. If the patient requires rehabilitation post hip replacement for right intertrochanteric femur fracture, report code S72.141D, Displaced intertrochanteric fracture of right femur, subsequent encounter for closed fracture with routine healing, as the first-listed or principal diagnosis.

See Section I.C.21.c.7, Factors influencing health states and contact with health services, Aftercare.

See Section I.C.19.a for additional information about the use of 7th characters for injury codes. (See Appendix A, Section II, K.)

Exercise 5.2—Section II

State whether each statement is true (T) or false (F) based on the ICD-10-CM Official Guidelines for Coding and Reporting

1. When the purpose for the admission/encounter is rehabilitation, sequence first the code for the condition for which the service is being performed. _____

2. When the admission is for treatment of a complication resulting from surgery or other medical care, the complication code is sequenced as the secondary diagnosis. _____

3. If the diagnosis documented at the time of discharge is qualified with such terms as "probable," "suspected," "likely," "questionable," "possible," "still to be ruled out," or other phrases indicating uncertainty, code the condition as if it existed or is established. _____

4. When a patient is admitted to an observation unit for a medical condition, which either worsens or does not improve, and is subsequently admitted as an inpatient of the same hospital for the same medical condition, the principal diagnosis is the medical condition that led to the hospital admission. _____

5. Codes for symptoms, signs, and ill-defined conditions from Chapter 18 are not to be used as principal diagnosis when a related definitive diagnosis has been established. _____

Section III—Reporting Additional Diagnoses

In addition to the principal diagnosis, additional diagnoses are coded and reported. UHDDS defines other diagnoses, commonly called **secondary diagnoses**, as "all conditions that coexist at the time of admission, that develop subsequently, or that affect the treatment received and/or length of stay. Diagnoses that relate to an earlier episode which have no bearing on the current hospital stay are to be excluded." This definition is used to standardize reporting for inpatients in such facilities as:

- Acute care, short-term care, long-term care, and psychiatric hospitals
- Home health agencies
- Rehab facilities
- Nursing homes

The guidelines state the following:

ICD-10-CM Official Coding Guidelines

Section III. Reporting Additional Diagnoses

GENERAL RULES FOR OTHER (ADDITIONAL) DIAGNOSES

For reporting purposes the definition for "other diagnoses" is interpreted as additional conditions that affect patient care in terms of requiring:

> clinical evaluation; or
>
> therapeutic treatment; or

diagnostic procedures; or

extended length of hospital stay; or

increased nursing care and/or monitoring.

The UHDDS item #11-b defines Other Diagnoses as "all conditions that coexist at the time of admission, that develop subsequently, or that affect the treatment received and/or the length of stay. Diagnoses that relate to an earlier episode which have no bearing on the current hospital stay are to be excluded." UHDDS definitions apply to inpatients in acute care, short-term, long term care and psychiatric hospital setting. The UHDDS definitions are used by acute care short-term hospitals to report inpatient data elements in a standardized manner. These data elements and their definitions can be found in the July 31, 1985, Federal Register (Vol. 50, No. 147), pp. 31038-40.

Since that time the application of the UHDDS definitions has been expanded to include all non-outpatient settings (acute care, short term, long term care and psychiatric hospitals; home health agencies; rehab facilities; nursing homes, etc.). The UHDDS definitions also apply to hospice services (all levels of care).

The following guidelines are to be applied in designating "other diagnoses" when neither the Alphabetic Index nor the Tabular List in ICD-10-CM provide direction. The listing of the diagnoses in the patient record is the responsibility of the attending provider.

A. Previous conditions

If the provider has included a diagnosis in the final diagnostic statement, such as the discharge summary or the face sheet, it should ordinarily be coded. Some providers include in the diagnostic statement resolved conditions or diagnoses and status-post procedures from previous admission that have no bearing on the current stay. Such conditions are not to be reported and are coded only if required by hospital policy.

However, history codes (categories Z80–Z87) may be used as secondary codes if the historical condition or family history has an impact on current care or influences treatment.

B. Abnormal findings

Abnormal findings (laboratory, x-ray, pathologic, and other diagnostic results) are not coded and reported unless the provider indicates their clinical significance. If the findings are outside the normal range and the attending provider has ordered other tests to evaluate the condition or prescribed treatment, it is appropriate to ask the provider whether the abnormal finding should be added.

Please note: This differs from the coding practices in the outpatient setting for coding encounters for diagnostic tests that have been interpreted by a provider.

C. Uncertain Diagnosis

If the diagnosis documented at the time of discharge is qualified as "probable", "suspected", "likely", "questionable", "possible", "still to be ruled out", "compatible with", "consistent with", or other similar terms indicating uncertainty, code the condition as if it existed or was established. The bases for these guidelines are the diagnostic workup, arrangements for further workup or observation, and initial therapeutic approach that correspond most closely with the established diagnosis.

Note: This guideline is applicable only to inpatient admissions to short-term, acute, long-term care and psychiatric hospitals. (See Appendix A, Section III.A-C.)

Section IV—Diagnostic Coding and Reporting Guidelines for Outpatient Services

Section IV of the ICD-10-CM Official Guidelines for Coding and Reporting is approved for use by hospitals and by providers for reporting hospital-based outpatient services and provider-based office visits.

NOTE:

The guidelines in other sections can differ at times from the guidelines for outpatient and provider-based office visits.

In the outpatient or office setting, the definition of principal diagnosis does not apply. In the outpatient setting, the term *first-listed diagnosis* is used. The following guidelines are used in reporting outpatient services:

ICD-10-CM Official Coding Guidelines

Section IV. Diagnostic Coding and Reporting Guidelines for Outpatient Services

These coding guidelines for outpatient diagnoses have been approved for use by hospitals/providers in coding and reporting hospital-based outpatient services and provider-based office visits. Guidelines in Section I, Conventions, general coding guidelines and chapter-specific guidelines, should also be applied for outpatient services and office visits.

Information about the use of certain abbreviations, punctuation, symbols, and other conventions used in the ICD-10-CM Tabular List (code numbers and titles), can be found in Section IA of these guidelines, under "Conventions Used in the Tabular List." Section I.B. contains general guidelines that apply to the entire classification. Section I.C. contains chapter-specific guidelines that correspond to the chapters as they are arranged in the classification. Information about the correct sequence to use in finding a code is also described in Section I.

The terms encounter and visit are often used interchangeably in describing outpatient service contacts and, therefore, appear together in these guidelines without distinguishing one from the other.

Though the conventions and general guidelines apply to all settings, coding guidelines for outpatient and provider reporting of diagnoses will vary in a number of instances from those for inpatient diagnoses, recognizing that:

The Uniform Hospital Discharge Data Set (UHDDS) definition of principal diagnosis does not apply to hospital-based outpatient services and provider-based office visits.

Coding guidelines for inconclusive diagnoses (probable, suspected, rule out, etc.) were developed for inpatient reporting and do not apply to outpatients.

A. Selection of first-listed condition

In the outpatient setting, the term first-listed diagnosis is used in lieu of principal diagnosis.

In determining the first-listed diagnosis the coding conventions of ICD-10-CM, as well as the general and disease specific guidelines take precedence over the outpatient guidelines.

Diagnoses often are not established at the time of the initial encounter/visit. It may take two or more visits before the diagnosis is confirmed.

The most critical rule involves beginning the search for the correct code assignment through the Alphabetic Index. Never begin searching initially in the Tabular List as this will lead to coding errors.

1. Outpatient Surgery

When a patient presents for outpatient surgery (same day surgery), code the reason for the surgery as the first-listed diagnosis (reason for the encounter), even if the surgery is not performed due to a contraindication.

2. Observation Stay

When a patient is admitted for observation for a medical condition, assign a code for the medical condition as the-first-listed diagnosis.

When a patient presents for outpatient surgery and develops complications requiring admission to observation, code the reason for the surgery as the first reported diagnosis (reason for the encounter), followed by codes for the complications as secondary diagnoses.

B. Codes from A00.0 through T88.9, Z00–Z99

The appropriate code(s) from A00.0 through T88.9, Z00–Z99 must be used to identify diagnoses, symptoms, conditions, problems, complaints, or other reason(s) for the encounter/visit.

C. Accurate reporting of ICD-10-CM diagnosis codes

For accurate reporting of ICD-10-CM diagnosis codes, the documentation should describe the patient's condition, using terminology which includes specific diagnoses as well as symptoms, problems, or reasons for the encounter. There are ICD-10-CM codes to describe all of these.

D. Codes that describe symptoms and signs

Codes that describe symptoms and signs, as opposed to diagnoses, are acceptable for reporting purposes when a diagnosis has not been established (confirmed) by the provider. Chapter 18 of ICD-10-CM, Symptoms, Signs, and Abnormal Clinical and Laboratory Findings Not Elsewhere Classified (codes R00–R99) contain many, but not all codes for symptoms.

E. Encounters for circumstances other than a disease or injury

ICD-10-CM provides codes to deal with encounters for circumstances other than a disease or injury. The Factors Influencing Health Status and Contact with Health Services codes (Z00–Z99) are provided to deal with occasions when circumstances other than a disease or injury are recorded as diagnosis or problems.

See Section I.C.21. Factors influencing health status and contact with health services.

F. Level of Detail in Coding

1. ICD-10-CM codes with 3, 4, 5, 6 or 7 characters

ICD-10-CM is composed of codes with either 3, 4, 5, 6 or 7 characters. Codes with three characters are included in ICD-10-CM as the heading of a category of codes that may be further subdivided by the use of fourth, fifth, sixth or seventh characters which provide greater specificity.

2. Use of full number of characters required for a code

A three-character code is to be used only if it is not further subdivided. A code is invalid if it has not been coded to the full number of characters required for that code, including the 7th character extension, if applicable.

G. ICD-10-CM code for the diagnosis, condition, problem, or other reason for encounter/visit

List first the ICD-10-CM code for the diagnosis, condition, problem, or other reason for encounter/visit shown in the medical record to be chiefly responsible for the services provided. List additional codes that describe any coexisting conditions. In some cases the first-listed diagnosis may be a symptom when a diagnosis has not been established (confirmed) by the provider.

H. Uncertain diagnosis

Do not code diagnoses documented as "probable", "suspected", "questionable", "rule out", "compatible with", "consistent with", or "working diagnosis" or other similar terms indicating uncertainty. Rather, code the condition(s) to the highest degree of certainty for that encounter/visit, such as symptoms, signs, abnormal test results, or other reason for the visit.

Please note: This differs from the coding practices used by short-term, acute care, long-term care and psychiatric hospitals.

I. Chronic diseases

Chronic diseases treated on an ongoing basis may be coded and reported as many times as the patient receives treatment and care for the condition(s)

J. Code all documented conditions that coexist

Code all documented conditions that coexist at the time of the encounter/visit, and require or affect patient care treatment or management. Do not code conditions that were previously treated and no longer exist. However, history codes (categories Z80–Z87) may be used as secondary codes if the historical condition or family history has an impact on current care or influences treatment.

K. Patients receiving diagnostic services only

For patients receiving diagnostic services only during an encounter/visit, sequence first the diagnosis, condition, problem, or other reason for encounter/visit shown in the medical record to be chiefly responsible for the outpatient services provided during the encounter/visit. Codes for other diagnoses (e.g., chronic conditions) may be sequenced as additional diagnoses.

For encounters for routine laboratory/radiology testing in the absence of any signs, symptoms, or associated diagnosis, assign Z01.89, Encounter for other specified special examinations. If routine testing is performed during the same encounter as a test to evaluate a sign, symptom, or diagnosis, it is appropriate to assign both the Z code and the code describing the reason for the non-routine test.

For outpatient encounters for diagnostic tests that have been interpreted by a physician, and the final report is available at the time of coding, code any confirmed or definitive diagnosis(es) documented in the interpretation. Do not code related signs and symptoms as additional diagnoses.

Please note: This differs from the coding practice in the hospital inpatient setting regarding abnormal findings on test results.

L. Patients receiving therapeutic services only

For patients receiving therapeutic services only during an encounter/visit, sequence first the diagnosis, condition, problem, or other reason for encounter/visit shown in the medical record to be chiefly responsible for the outpatient services provided during the encounter/visit. Codes for other diagnoses (e.g., chronic conditions) may be sequenced as additional diagnoses.

The only exception to this rule is that when the primary reason for the admission/encounter is chemotherapy or radiation therapy, the appropriate Z code for the service is listed first, and the diagnosis or problem for which the service is being performed listed second.

M. Patients receiving preoperative evaluations only

For patients receiving preoperative evaluations only, sequence first a code from subcategory Z01.81, Encounter for pre-procedural examinations, to describe the pre-op consultations. Assign a code for the condition to describe the reason for the surgery as an additional diagnosis. Code also any findings related to the pre-op evaluation.

N. Ambulatory surgery

For ambulatory surgery, code the diagnosis for which the surgery was performed. If the postoperative diagnosis is known to be different from the preoperative diagnosis at the time the diagnosis is confirmed, select the postoperative diagnosis for coding, since it is the most definitive.

O. Routine outpatient prenatal visits

See Section I.C.15. Routine outpatient prenatal visits.

P. Encounters for general medical examinations with abnormal findings

The subcategories for encounters for general medical examinations, Z00.0- and encounter for routine child health examination, Z00.12-, provide codes for with and without abnormal findings. Should a general medical examination result in an abnormal finding, the code for general medical examination with abnormal finding should be assigned as the first listed diagnosis. An examination with abnormal findings refers to a condition/diagnosis that is newly identified or a change in severity of a chronic condition (such as uncontrolled hypertension, or an acute exacerbation of chronic obstructive pulmonary disease) during a routine physical examination. A secondary code for the abnormal finding should also be coded.

Q. Encounters for routine health screenings

See Section I.C.21. Factors influencing health status and contact with health services, Screening. (See Appendix A, Section IV.A-Q.)

Exercise 5.3—Sections III and IV

State whether each statement is true (T) or false (F) based on the ICD-10-CM Official Guidelines for Coding and Reporting.

1. In the coding of secondary diagnoses, if the provider has included a diagnosis in the final diagnostic statement, such as the discharge summary or the face sheet, that diagnosis should ordinarily be coded._____

2. Abnormal findings (laboratory, x-ray, pathologic, and other diagnostic results) are coded and reported. _____

3. When a general medical examination results in an abnormal finding, the code for general medical examination with abnormal finding should be assigned as the first listed diagnosis. _____

4. For patients receiving preoperative evaluations only, sequence first a code from subcategory Z01.81, Encounter for pre-procedural examinations, to describe the preop consultations. _____

5. For ambulatory surgery, code the diagnosis for which the surgery was performed. _____

Summary

- The ICD-10-CM Official Guidelines for Coding and Reporting were developed to provide coding consistency.
- The Cooperating Parties for ICD-10-CM are the American Hospital Association, the American Health Information Association, the Centers for Medicare and Medicaid Services, and the National Center for Health Statistics.
- The ICD-10-CM Official Guidelines for Coding and Reporting have four sections.
- Section I contains the ICD-10-CM Conventions, General Coding Guidelines, and Chapter-Specific Guidelines.
- Section II describes the Selection of Principal Diagnosis(es) for inpatient, short-term, acute care, and long-term care hospital records.
- Section III describes the Reporting of Additional Diagnoses for inpatient, short-term, acute care, and long-term care hospital records.
- Section IV describes the Diagnostic Coding and Reporting Guidelines for outpatient services.

Internet Link

The ICD-10-CM Official Guidelines for Coding and Reporting can be found online at **www.cdc.gov/nchs/icd/icd10cm.htm**. Click on the link at the bottom of the page titled "Guidelines."

Chapter Review

True/False

Indicate whether each statement is true (T) or false (F).

1. _____ The ICD-10-CM Official Guidelines for Coding and Reporting were developed by the American Health Information Management Association.

2. _____ For outpatient and physician office visits, the code that is listed first for coding and reporting purposes is the reason for the encounter.

3. _____ Codes that describe symptoms and signs are acceptable for coding when a definitive diagnosis has not been established in a physician's office.

4. _____ If signs and symptoms exist that are not routinely associated with a disease process, the signs and symptoms should not be coded.

5. _____ Sequela codes should be used only within six months after the initial injury or disease.

6. _____ The principal diagnosis is defined as "that condition established after study to be chiefly responsible for occasioning the outpatient visit of the patient to the hospital for care."

7. _____ If the diagnosis documented at the time of discharge is qualified as "probable" or "suspected," do not code the condition.

8. _____ Codes from Chapter 18 of ICD-10-CM, "Symptoms, Signs, and Abnormal Clinical and Laboratory Findings, Not Elsewhere Classified," are not to be used as a principal diagnosis when a related definitive diagnosis has been established.

9. _____ A patient is admitted because of severe abdominal pain. After diagnostic testing, it is determined that the patient has appendicitis. The abdominal pain is the principal diagnosis.

10. _____ In a physician's office, a chronic disease treated on an ongoing basis may be coded and reported as many times as the patient receives treatment and care for the condition.

Fill-in-the-Blank

Enter the appropriate term(s) to complete each statement.

11. A _____ is the residual effect (condition produced) after the acute phase of an illness or injury has terminated.

12. For ambulatory surgery, if the postoperative diagnosis is known to be different from the preoperative diagnosis at the time the diagnosis is confirmed, select the _____ diagnosis for coding.

13. In the _____ setting, the definition of principal diagnosis does not apply.

14. All conditions that coexist at the time of admission, that develop subsequently, or that affect the treatment received and length of stay, or both, are known as the _____.

15. Rule-out conditions are not coded in the _____ setting.

16. In the outpatient setting, do not code conditions that were previously _____ and no longer exist.

17. Abnormal findings are not coded and reported for unless the _____ indicates their clinical significance.

18. In the outpatient setting, the term _____ is used in lieu of *principal diagnosis*.

19. In most cases, when coding sequela, two codes are required, with the _____ sequenced first, followed by the sequela code.

20. Each unique ICD-10-CM code may be reported _____ for an encounter.

21. If the condition for which a rehabilitation service is no longer present, report the appropriate _____ code as the first-listed or principal diagnosis.

22. For reporting purposes, the definition for "other diagnoses" is interpreted as additional conditions that affect patient care in terms of requiring:

_____ evaluation; or

therapeutic treatment; or

diagnostic procedures; or

extended length of hospital stay; or

increased _____ care and/or monitoring.

23. Information about the use of certain abbreviations, punctuation, symbols, and other conventions used in the ICD-10-CM Tabular List (code numbers and titles) can be found in Section _____ of the ICD-10-CM Official Guidelines for Coding and Reporting.

24. In the ICD-10-CM Official Guidelines for Coding and Reporting, Section _____ contains general guidelines that apply to the entire classification.

25. In the ICD-10-CM Official Guidelines for Coding and Reporting, Section _____ contains chapter-specific guidelines that correspond to the chapters as they are arranged in the classification.

Short Answer

Briefly answer each of the following.

26. Discuss how to code a diagnosis recorded as "suspected" in both an inpatient and an outpatient record.

_____

_____

_____

27. List the Cooperating Parties that approved the ICD-10-CM Official Coding Guidelines.

_____

_____

_____

28. List the sections of the ICD-10-CM Official Guidelines for Coding and Reporting.

_____

_____

_____

29. Discuss the sequencing of codes for outpatients receiving diagnostic services only.

_____

_____

_____

30. Define principal diagnosis.

_____

_____

_____

31. Explain the purpose of the ICD-10-CM Official Guidelines for Coding and Reporting.

_____

_____

_____

Infectious and Parasitic Diseases

Chapter Outline

Chapter Objectives

Key Terms

Introduction

Abbreviations

Coding of Infectious and Parasitic Diseases

A Codes

B Codes

Summary

Internet Links

Chapter Review

Coding Assignments

Case Studies

Chapter Objectives

At the conclusion of this chapter, you should be able to:

1. Identify infectious and parasitic diseases.
2. Identify clinical tests used to diagnose diseases.
3. Explain single-code, combination-code, and dual-code assignment.
4. Summarize the coding of symptomatic and asymptomatic cases of HIV.
5. Identify and code the types of hepatitis.
6. Accurately code infectious and parasitic diseases.
7. Select and code diagnoses from case studies.

Key Terms

Acariasis

Acquired immunodeficiency syndrome (AIDS)

Arthropods

Bacteria

Candidiasis

Chlamydiae

Combination-code assignment

Culture and sensitivity (C&S)

Dual-code assignment

Escherichia coli (E. coli)

Fungi

Helminths

Host

Human immunodeficiency virus (HIV)

Infectious diseases

Molds

Moniliasis

Parasite

Parasitic diseases

Pathogen

Pediculosis

Protozoa

Rickettsioses

Sepsis

Septicemia

Severe sepsis

Single-code assignment

Spirochetal

Tuberculosis

Viruses

Yeast infection

REMINDER: As you work through this chapter, you will need to have a copy of the ICD-10-CM coding book to reference. For this chapter, you will also need to reference the ICD-10-CM Official Guidelines for Coding and Reporting. These guidelines can be found in Appendix A which are now available on the Student Companion site and MINDTAP From Cengage.

Introduction

Certain infectious and parasitic diseases are found in Chapter 1 of ICD-10-CM. The code range used to report these diseases is A00–B99. **Infectious diseases** are diseases that occur when a **pathogen**, a microorganism that can cause disease in humans, invades the body and causes disease. In **parasitic diseases**, a **parasite** lives within another organism, known as a **host**, and causes disease. In this relationship, the parasite benefits and the host is harmed.

An easy reference to the diseases discussed in this chapter can be found at the start of Chapter 1 in the Tabular List of the ICD-10-CM code book. It should be noted that at the start of each chapter in the ICD-10-CM code book, there appears a listing of the code blocks that are contained in each chapter. Use the listing of the code blocks to become familiar with the content of the chapter. The following table notes the blocks found in Chapter 1.

Block Title	Category Codes
Intestinal infectious diseases	A00–A09
Tuberculosis	A15–A19
Certain zoonotic bacterial diseases	A20–A28
Other bacterial diseases	A30–A49
Infections with a predominantly sexual mode of transmission	A50–A64
Other spirochetal diseases	A65–A69
Other diseases caused by chlamydiae	A70–A74
Rickettsioses	A75–A79
Viral and Prion infections of the central nervous system	A80–A89
Arthropod-borne viral fevers and viral hemorrhagic fevers	A90–A99
Viral infections characterized by skin and mucous membrane lesions	B00–B09
Other human herpesviruses	B10
Viral hepatitis	B15–B19
Human immunodeficiency virus [HIV] disease	B20
Other viral diseases	B25–B34
Mycoses	B35–B49
Protozoal diseases	B50–B64
Helminthiases	B65–B83
Pediculosis, acariasis, and other infestations	B85–B89
Sequelae of infectious and parasitic diseases	B90–B94
Bacterial and viral infectious agents	B95–B97
Other infectious diseases	B99

Several instructional notations are also at the start of the chapter, and they need to be referenced prior to code assignment.

Abbreviations

Abbreviations that are associated with this chapter of ICD-10-CM include:

AIDS	acquired immunodeficiency syndrome
C&S	culture and sensitivity (test)
EBV	Epstein-Barr virus
E. coli	Escherichia coli
hep	hepatitis
HAV	Hepatitis A
HBV	Hepatitis B
HCV	Hepatitis C
HDV-delta	Hepatitis D
HEV	Hepatitis E
HIV	human immunodeficiency virus
mono	mononucleosis
polio	poliomyelitis
staph	staphylococcal bacteria
strep	streptococcal bacteria
TB	tuberculosis

Organisms Found in Chapter

The various blocks in Chapter 1 identify the types of organisms that cause infections. In ICD-10-CM, the organisms are classified into the following groups:

- Bacteria
- Fungi
- Parasites
- Viruses

Bacteria

Bacteria are one-celled organisms named according to their shapes and arrangements. (See Figure 6-1.)

> **EXAMPLE:** Diplococci bacteria are round, spherical, or coffee bean-shaped bacteria that occur in pairs. (See Figure 6-2.)

Bacteria can live inside or outside the body. Outside the body, bacteria can be found on most surfaces, such as countertops, faucet handles, and doorknobs.

Singular Name of Bacterial Shape	Plural Form	Description
Coccus	Cocci	Spherical or round
Bacillus	Bacilli	Straight rod
Spirillum	Spirilla	Spiral, corkscrew, or slightly curved

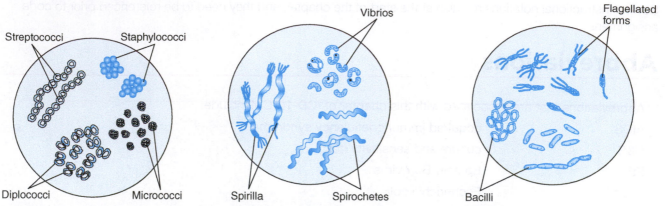

FIGURE 6-1 Forms of cocci, bacilli, and spirilla (From B Acello and B Hegner, *Nursing Assistant: A Nursing Process Approach*, 9th ed., Clifton Park, NY: Delmar Cengage Learning, 2003).

Arrangement	Medical Word Part
Single	There is no specific medical term.
Pairs	diplo-
Chains	strepto-
Clusters	staphylo-

FIGURE 6-2 Arrangements of bacteria

Inside the body, some common bacterial infection sites are the bloodstream, the skin, and the gastrointestinal, respiratory, and urinary tracts. Some organisms that are commonly found in the human body do not cause disease in one body site but can cause disease in another site.

Organisms enter a cell and begin poisoning the cell by producing toxins that cause disease. Because a specific organism can cause disease in different body sites, a coder must note the type of organism and body site when coding.

EXAMPLE: *Escherichia coli*, also known as *E. coli*, is a rod-shaped bacillus found in the large intestine of humans, where it is normally nonpathogenic. However, when *E. coli* is found outside the intestine, it can cause disease in the urinary tract or infections in pressure ulcers.

To accurately diagnose a specific bacterial infection that is affecting a patient, a physician orders a **culture and sensitivity** test, also known as a **C&S**. The *culture* identifies the type of organism causing the infection, and the *sensitivity* identifies the antibiotic that should be used to treat the infection. The coder has to reference the culture and sensitivity report to identify the specific bacteria causing the infection and the sensitivity identifying the antibiotic to be used. Common bacterial infections include the following:

Name of Infection	Common Pathogen
Pseudomembraneous colitis	*Clostridium difficile*
Salmonella food poisoning	*Salmonella*
Urinary tract infection	*E. coli*
	Pseudomonas aeruginosa
Tuberculosis	*Mycobacterium tuberculosis*
Impetigo	*Streptococci A*
Strep throat	*Streptococcus*

Fungi

Fungi are microscopic plant life that lack chlorophyll and must have a source of matter for nutrition because they cannot manufacture their own food. The two common forms of fungal infections that affect humans are molds and yeast. **Yeast infections** are caused by unicellular fungi that reproduce by budding; **molds** are caused by long filament-shaped fungi. Yeasts and molds that infect human tissues are known as opportunistic parasites; they cause opportunistic infections when a patient has a weakened immune system. Opportunistic infections commonly occur in the following types of individuals:

- Patients with chronic conditions, such as AIDS, diabetes, and cancer
- Infants and newborns
- Patients who are postsurgery
- Patients who have taken antibiotics
- Steroid users

Common Yeast and Molds That Affect Humans

Name of Infection	Common Pathogen
Athlete's foot	*Tinea pedis*
Thrush	*Candida albicans*
Ringworm	*Tinea capitis*
Chicago disease	*Blastomyces dermatitidis*

Parasites

Parasites are organisms that feed on other organisms to nourish themselves. Specific parasitic organisms are:

- **Protozoa**—one-celled organisms that live on living matter and are classified by the way they move.
- **Helminths**—organisms such as flatworms, roundworms, and flukes.
- **Arthropods**—organisms such as insects, ticks, spiders, and mites.

Parasitic infections are found in the intestinal tract, bloodstream, lymph nodes, central nervous system, and skin. Some parasitic infections multiply in the bloodstream and move into the tissue of body organs, such as the liver and spleen. Figure 6-3 shows malarial parasites in red blood cells. Other parasites, such as tapeworms, attach to body structures and cause disorders. A tapeworm uses hooks and suckers to attach to the intestinal wall of its host, causing weight loss (Figure 6-4).

Common Parasitic Infections

Name of Infection	Common Pathogen
African sleeping sickness	*Trypanosoma gambiense*
Chagas' disease	*Trypanosoma cruzi*
Malaria	*Plasmodium falciparum*
	Plasmodium vivax
	Plasmodium malariae
	Plasmodium ovale

(continues)

(continued)

Name of Infection	Common Pathogen
Pinworm	*Enterobius vermicularis*
Head lice	*Pediculus Capitis*
Scabies	*Sarcoptes*

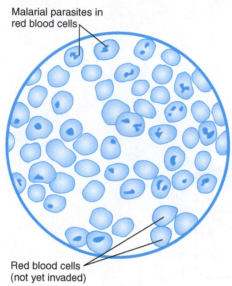

Malarial parasites in red blood cells

Red blood cells (not yet invaded)

FIGURE 6-3 Malarial parasites in red blood cells (From L.L. Grover-Lakomia and E. Fong, *Microbiology for Health Careers*, 6th ed. (Clifton Park, NY: Delmar Cengage Learning, 1991)).

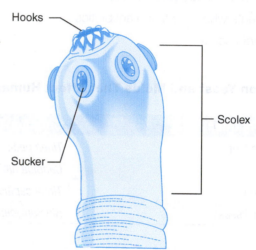

Hooks

Scolex

Sucker

FIGURE 6-4 Tapeworm (From L.L. Grover-Lakomia and E. Fong, *Microbiology for Health Careers*, 6th ed. (Clifton Park, NY: Delmar Cengage Learning, 1991)).

Viruses

Viruses are the smallest of infectious pathogens. They penetrate cells and release their DNA or RNA into the cell nucleus, causing damage to the cell. Viruses are completely dependent on the nutrients inside the cells for reproduction and metabolism, and they vary in their effects from a common cold to viral hepatitis and acquired immunodeficiency syndrome (AIDS).

Common Viral Infections

Name of Disease	Name of Pathogen
Shingles	*Herpes zoster*
Chickenpox	*Varicella*
AIDS	Human immunodeficiency virus
Genital herpes	*Herpes simplex*
German measles	RNA virus
West Nile fever	*Flavivirus*

Exercise 6.1—Code Assignments and Instructional Notations

For each of the conditions listed, identify any instructional notations and then assign an ICD-10-CM code. The first one is done for you.

Condition	Instructional Notation	Code Assignment
1. Shingles	Includes shingles, zona	B02.9
2. German measles	_____	_____
3. Hutchinson's teeth	_____	_____
4. Scarlet fever with otitis media	_____	_____
5. Amebic lung abscess	_____	_____

Coding of Infectious and Parasitic Diseases

Infectious and parasitic diseases are coded in ICD-10-CM in one of three ways: single-code assignment, combination-code assignment, or dual-code assignment.

Single-Code Assignment

Single-code assignment occurs when only one code is needed to code the diagnostic statement. The condition is referenced in the Alphabetic Index and the code selection is made from the Tabular List.

> **EXAMPLE:** Millie presents with an acute case of scarlet fever. To code this condition, the coder references the terms *fever* or *scarlet fever* in the Alphabetic Index. Assume the coder references the term *scarlet fever* in the alphabetic index. The coder finds:
>
> ```
> Scarlet fever (albuminuria) (angina) A38.9
> ```
>
> After referencing the Alphabetic Index, the coder now verifies the code in the Tabular List. Code A38.9 appears in the Tabular List:
>
> ```
> A38        Scarlet fever
>
>            Includes        scarlatina
>
>            Excludes2 streptococcal sore throat (J02.0)
>
>            A38.0 Scarlet fever with otitis media
>
>            A38.1 Scarlet fever with myocarditis
>
>            A38.8 Scarlet fever with other complications
>
>            A38.9 Scarlet fever, uncomplicated
>
>                  Scarlet fever NOS
> ```
>
> Referencing the Tabular Listing verifies the correct code assignment of A38.9.

Combination-Code Assignment

Combination-code assignment occurs when a single code is used to identify the organism and the condition caused by the organism. Here, only one code is needed to code the diagnostic statement.

EXAMPLE: A patient presents with lesions and fatigue. The patient is subsequently diagnosed with herpes simplex meningitis. To code this diagnostic statement, the coder references the term *meningitis* in the Alphabetic Index. The entry appears in the Alphabetic Index as shown:

```
Meningitis
        in (due to)
                adenovirus A87.1
                African trypanosomiasis B56.9 [G02]
                anthrax A22.8
                bacterial disease NEC A48.8 [G01]
                Chagas' disease (chronic) B57.41
                chickenpox B01.0
                coccidioidmycosis B38.4
                Diplococcus pneumonia G00.1
                enterovirus A87.0
                herpes (simplex) virus B00.3
                    zoster B02.1
                infectious mononucleosis B27.92
```

After referencing the Alphabetic Index, the coder notes the code B00.3. The coder needs to verify the code in the Tabular List. Only one code, B00.3, is needed to code the herpes simplex organism and the manifestation of the meningitis.

Dual-Code Assignment

Dual-code assignment occurs when two codes are needed to code a diagnostic statement. In these cases, the infectious and parasitic disease codes are sequenced before the code from another ICD-10-CM chapter. Due to the level of specificity of ICD-10-CM coding, there are less dual-assignment codes than combination codes.

EXAMPLE: A patient is diagnosed with late syphilitic anemia. To code this diagnostic statement, the coder references the term *anemia* and the subterm *syphilitic* in the Alphabetic Index:

```
Anemia
            Syphyilitic (acquired) (late) A52.79 [D63.8]
```

In the Alphabetic Index, two codes are listed: A52.79 and D63.8. Code A52.79 identifies the syphilis, and the D63.8 identifies the anemia. The code D63.8 is found within brackets in the Alphabetic Index to identify the manifestation code.

A Codes

The A codes include the various blocks as outlined at the start of this chapter. The various blocks are now discussed in greater detail.

Intestinal Infectious Diseases (Category Codes A00–A09)

This range of codes includes infections that include cholera, shigellosis, and other bacterial intestinal infections. Also found here are codes for food poisoning, cyclosporiasis, and viral intestinal infections.

Disease Highlight—Infectious Intestinal Diseases

Infectious intestinal diseases can be caused by a number of organisms. The provider will determine the organism that is causing the disease.

Signs and Symptoms:

> Nausea
> Vomiting
> Anorexia
> Abdominal pain
> Fever
> Muscular aches
> Malaise

Clinical Testing:

> Blood and stool cultures to identify the type of infectious organisms

Treatment:

> Patients are given an antiemetric drug to reduce the vomiting.
>
> Antimotility drugs are used to relieve the abdominal pain.
>
> To replace lost fluids, patients are encouraged to increase fluid intake.
>
> In severe cases, patients are given IV replacement therapy. Antibiotics are given to treat the organism present.

Tuberculosis (Category Codes A15–A19)

Tuberculosis is an infection caused by *Mycobacterium tuberculosis* that spreads throughout the body via lymph and blood vessels and that most commonly localizes in the lungs. At the start of the A15–A19 coding section of ICD-10-CM, an Includes note states that infections due to *Mycobacterium tuberculosis* and *Mycobacterium bovis* are coded from this section. An *Excludes1* note excludes from this code block:

- Congenital tuberculosis (P37.0)
- Nonspecific reaction to test for tuberculosis without active tuberculosis (R76.1–)
- Pneumoconiosis associated with tuberculosis, any type in A15 (J65)
- Positive PPD (R76.11)
- Positive tuberculin skin test without active tuberculosis (R76.11)
- Sequelae of tuberculosis (B90.–)
- Silicotuberculosis (J65)

An understanding of the symptoms of tuberculosis is important. Symptoms of the disease are:

- Fatigue and weakness
- Loss of appetite and weight
- Coughing
- Hemoptysis
- Night sweats
- Increased temperature late in the day and evening
- Pulmonary hemorrhage
- Dyspnea

Clinical tests used to diagnosis tuberculosis include:

- Chest x-rays
- Mantoux skin test
- Sputum culture

The tuberculosis codes are broken down by site, such as category A15. A15, Respiratory tuberculosis, further breaks down to identify tuberculosis of the lungs, the intrathoracic lymph nodes, the larynx, the trachea, and the bronchus. Coders must be able to identify the site of the disease for accurate coding. For example, tuberculosis of the larynx is coded with A15.5, while tuberculosis of the mediastinal lymph nodes is coded with A15.4.

Certain Zoonotic Bacterial Diseases (Category Codes A20–A28)

This section includes zoonotic bacterial diseases that are transmitted to humans after contact with infected animals, insects, fleas, ticks, or their discharges or products. Common symptoms of diseases in this range include fever, chills, headache, sweating, body aches, weakness, and fatigue. Blood specimens are used for diagnosis. Diseases in this section include:

- Anthrax
- Bubonic plague
- Glanders and melioidosis
- Leptospirosis

Other Bacterial Diseases (Category Codes A30–A49)

This range of codes classifies a wide range of bacterial diseases, including:

- Meningococcal meningitis
- Whooping cough
- Diphtheria

Septic infections are also coded to this category. Physicians commonly use the terms *septicemia* and *sepsis* synonymously; however, current medical practice makes a distinction between these terms and related conditions. The distinction is that **septicemia** is defined as bacteremia with sepsis.

Sepsis is a life-threatening bacterial infection that causes blood clots to form, which block blood flow to vital organs. For a diagnosis of sepsis, assign the appropriate code for the underlying systemic infection. If the type of infection or causal organism is not further specified, assign code A41.9, Sepsis, unspecified. ICD-10-CM guides the coder to R78.81 for the term bacteremia. The coder should review the medical documentation and query the provider to ensure the coder has a complete understanding of the infectious condition that is being treated during the episode of care.

Severe sepsis is a septic infection with associated acute organ dysfunction or failure. One or more organs may be affected, and coding accurately requires a minimum of two codes: first a code for the underlying systemic infection, followed by a code from subcategory R65.2, Severe sepsis. If the causal organism is not documented, assign code A41.9, Sepsis, unspecified, for the infection.

Whenever possible, identify the causal organism. If the patient is diagnosed with sepsis and an acute organ dysfunction, the documentation must clearly identify the relationship between the organ dysfunction and the sepsis. If the relationship is not clearly identified, then R65.2, Severe sepsis, is not assigned. If the documentation does not identify a causal relationship code, then A41.9, Sepsis, unspecified, is the correct code to assign.

EXAMPLE: Mr. Bahji is admitted to the hospital with low blood pressure. After admission testing is performed, it is determined that he has sepsis. The kidneys have begun to shut down, but Dr. Smyth is not ready to consider this as related to the sepsis infection because Mr. Bahji was having urinary problems prior to admission.

The diagnosis code A41.9 is used because the diagnosis documented is "sepsis" and not "severe sepsis." The kidney problem is not being associated with the sepsis at this time. So the additional code from the subcategory of R65.2 for the severe sepsis does not apply.

Coders need to be familiar with the following guidelines that direct code assignment for the reporting of sepsis and severe sepsis.

ICD-10-CM Official Coding Guidelines

d. Sepsis, Severe Sepsis, and Septic Shock

1) Coding of Sepsis and Severe Sepsis

(a) Sepsis

For a diagnosis of sepsis, assign the appropriate code for the underlying systemic infection. If the type of infection or causal organism is not further specified, assign code A41.9, Sepsis, unspecified organism.

A code from subcategory R65.2, Severe sepsis, should not be assigned unless severe sepsis or an associated acute organ dysfunction is documented.

(i) Negative or inconclusive blood cultures and sepsis

Negative or inconclusive blood cultures do not preclude a diagnosis of sepsis in patients with clinical evidence of the condition, however, the provider should be queried.

(ii) Urosepsis

The term urosepsis is a nonspecific term. It is not to be considered synonymous with sepsis. It has no default code in the Alphabetic Index. Should a provider use this term, he/she must be queried for clarification.

(iii) Sepsis with organ dysfunction

If a patient has sepsis and associated acute organ dysfunction or multiple organ dysfunction (MOD), follow the instructions for coding severe sepsis.

(iv) Acute organ dysfunction that is not clearly associated with the sepsis

If a patient has sepsis and an acute organ dysfunction, but the medical record documentation indicates that the acute organ dysfunction is related to a medical condition other than the sepsis, do not assign a code from subcategory R65.2, Severe sepsis. An acute organ dysfunction must be associated with the sepsis in order to assign the severe sepsis code. If the documentation is not clear as to whether an acute organ dysfunction is related to the sepsis or another medical condition, query the provider.

(b) Severe sepsis

The coding of severe sepsis requires a minimum of 2 codes: first a code for the underlying systemic infection, followed by a code from subcategory R65.2, Severe sepsis. If the causal organism is not documented, assign code A41.9, Sepsis, unspecified organism, for the infection. Additional code(s) for the associated acute organ dysfunction are also required.

Due to the complex nature of severe sepsis, some cases may require querying the provider prior to assignment of the codes.

2) Septic shock

(a) Septic shock generally refers to circulatory failure associated with severe sepsis, and therefore, it represents a type of acute organ dysfunction.

For cases of septic shock, the code for the systemic infection should be sequenced first, followed by code R65.21, Severe sepsis with septic shock or code T81.12, Postprocedural septic shock. Any additional codes for the other acute organ dysfunctions should also be assigned. As noted in the sequencing instructions in the Tabular List, the code for septic shock cannot be assigned as a principal diagnosis.

3) Sequencing of severe sepsis

If severe sepsis is present on admission, and meets the definition of principal diagnosis, the underlying systemic infection should be assigned as principal diagnosis followed by the appropriate code from subcategory R65.2 as required by the sequencing rules in the Tabular List. A code from subcategory R65.2 can never be assigned as a principal diagnosis.

When severe sepsis develops during an encounter (it was not present on admission) the underlying systemic infection and the appropriate code from subcategory R65.2 should be assigned as secondary diagnoses.

Severe sepsis may be present on admission but the diagnosis may not be confirmed until sometime after admission. If the documentation is not clear whether severe sepsis was present on admission, the provider should be queried.

4) Sepsis and severe sepsis with a localized infection

If the reason for admission is sepsis or severe sepsis and a localized infection, such as pneumonia or cellulitis, a code(s) for the underlying systemic infection should be assigned first and the code for the localized infection should be assigned as a secondary diagnosis. If the patient has severe sepsis, a code from subcategory R65.2 should also be assigned as a secondary diagnosis. If the patient is admitted with a localized infection, such as pneumonia, and sepsis/severe sepsis doesn't develop until after admission, the localized infection should be assigned first, followed by the appropriate sepsis/severe sepsis codes.

5) Sepsis due to a postprocedural infection

(a) Documentation of causal relationship

As with all postprocedural complications, code assignment is based on the provider's documentation of the relationship between the infection and the procedure.

(b) Sepsis due to a postprocedural infection

For infections following a procedure, a code from T81.40 to T81.43, Infection following a procedure, or a code from O86.00 to O86.03, Infection of obstetric surgical wound, that identifies the site of the infection should be coded first, if known. Assign an additional code for sepsis following a procedure (T81.44) or sepsis following an obstetrical procedure (O86.04). Use an additional code to identify the infectious agent. If the patient has severe sepsis, the appropriate code from subcategory R65.2 should also be assigned with the additional code(s) for any acute organ dysfunction.

For infections following infusion, transfusion, therapeutic injection, or immunization, a code from subcategory T80.2, Infections following infusion, transfusion, and therapeutic injection, or code T88.0–, Infection following immunization, should be coded first, followed by the code for the specific infection. If the patient has severe sepsis, the appropriate code from subcategory R65.2 should also be assigned, with the additional codes(s) for any acute organ dysfunction.

(c) Postprocedural infection and postprocedural septic shock

If a postprocedural infection has resulted in postprocedural septic shock, assign the codes indicated above for sepsis due to a postprocedural infection, followed by code T81.12–, Postprocedural septic shock. Do not assign code R65.21, Severe sepsis with septic shock. Additional code(s) should be assigned for any acute organ dysfunction.

6) Sepsis and severe sepsis associated with a noninfectious process (condition)

In some cases a noninfectious process (condition), such as trauma, may lead to an infection which can result in sepsis or severe sepsis. If sepsis or severe sepsis is documented as associated with a noninfectious condition, such as a burn or serious injury, and this condition meets the definition for principal diagnosis, the code for the noninfectious condition should be sequenced first, followed by the code for the resulting infection. If severe sepsis, is present a code from subcategory R65.2 should also be assigned with any associated organ dysfunction(s) codes. It is not necessary to assign a code from subcategory R65.1, Systemic inflammatory response syndrome (SIRS) of non-infectious origin, for these cases.

If the infection meets the definition of principal diagnosis it should be sequenced before the noninfectious condition. When both the associated noninfectious condition and the infection meet the definition of principal diagnosis either may be assigned as principal diagnosis.

Only one code from category R65, Symptoms and signs specifically associated with systemic inflammation and infection, should be assigned. Therefore, when a non-infectious condition leads to an infection resulting in severe sepsis, assign the appropriate code from subcategory R65.2, Severe sepsis. Do not additionally assign a code from subcategory R65.1, Systemic inflammatory response syndrome (SIRS) of noninfectious origin.

See Section I.C.18. SIRS due to noninfectious process

7) Sepsis and septic shock complicating abortion, pregnancy, childbirth, and the puerperium

See Section I.C.15. Sepsis and septic shock complicating abortion, pregnancy, childbirth and the puerperium

8) Newborn sepsis

See Section I.C.16. f. Bacterial sepsis of Newborn. (See Appendix A, Section I.C.1.d.1-8.)

Exercise 6.2—Guidelines for Sepsis

True/False: Indicate whether each statement is true (T) or false (F) based on the coding guidelines.

1. _____ A code from subcategory R65.2, Severe sepsis, should not be assigned unless severe sepsis or an associated acute organ dysfunction is documented.

2. _____ The coding of severe sepsis requires one code for the underlying systemic infection.

3. _____ When severe sepsis develops during an encounter and it was not present on admission, the underlying systemic infection and the appropriate code from subcategory R65.2 should be assigned as secondary diagnoses.

4. _____ Urosepsis is a synonymous term with sepsis.

5. _____ An acute organ dysfunction must be associated with sepsis in order to assign the severe sepsis code.

Infections with a Predominantly Sexual Mode of Transmission (Category Codes A50–A64)

The Excludes1 notation at the start of this subcategory acts as a guide to coding for human immunodeficiency virus (HIV) disease, Reiter's disease, and nonspecific and nongonococcal urethritis. These conditions are found in other categories of the code book.

This block of codes, A50–A64, does include such conditions as early congenital syphilitic pneumonia, gonococcal infections, and other sexually transmitted diseases. Careful attention to the documentation is necessary to properly assign a code from this section because the selection of codes from this range of codes is very specific. For example, category A51 reports early syphilis and is further differentiated as primary or secondary, in addition to the site of the syphilis. Code A51.0 reports primary genital syphilis, while code A51.44 reports secondary syphilitic nephritis.

Other Spirochetal Diseases (Category Codes A65–A69)

Spirochetal is a term for a gram-negative bacteria made up of spiral-shaped cells. This code block contains codes for nonvenereal syphilis, yaws, pinta, relapsing fevers, and other spirochetal infections, as well as Lyme disease. The Excludes2 note at the beginning of the code set excludes leptospirosis and syphilis, which are located in other areas of the chapter.

Other Diseases Caused by Chlamydiae (Category Codes A70–A74)

Chlamydiae is a type of bacteria that live inside host cells. This bacterium is usually dormant but at some point may become active in the disease process. Diseases reported from this block of codes include:

- Parrot Fever
- Trachoma
- Chlamydial diseases, such as chlamydial peritonitis and chlamydial conjunctivits

The Excludes1 note following the category A74 should be noted when reporting codes from this category. The Excludes1 note states that neonatal chlamydial conjunctivitis, neonatal chlamydial pneumonia, Reiter's disease, and sexually transmitted chlamydial diseases are excluded from this category.

Rickettsioses (Category Codes A75–A79)

Rickettsioses is a bacterial infection that is caused by a Richettsia organism. This code block includes the following diseases:

- Typhus fever
- Spotted fever
- Q fever
- Trench Fever
- Other specified and unspecified rickettsioses

Viral Infections of the Central Nervous System (Category Codes A80–A89) and Arthropod-borne Viral Fevers and Viral Hemorrhagic Fevers (A90–A99)

Viral infections found in this block of codes include:

- Acute poliomyelitis
- Rabies
- Mosquito-borne viral encephalitis
- Tick-borne viral meningitis

It is very important that the coder review the code descriptions found in the Tabular List because they involve many Include and Exclude notations. For example, referencing category A87, it should be noted that an Excludes1 notation appears that alerts the coder to various types of meningitis that are excluded from this category and are reported using codes from other categories.

Arthropod-borne viral fevers and viral hemorrhagic fevers include: dengue fever, mosquito-borne viral fever, West Nile virus infection, Rift Vally fever, Zika virus and Yellow fever. Reference category range A90–A99 for the complete list of fevers and viral diseases.

Exercise 6.3—Bacterial, Parasitic, and Infectious Diseases

Using an ICD-10-CM code book, assign codes to the following diagnostic statements.

1. campylobacter enteritis _____
2. acute amebic dysentery _____
3. meningitis due to anthrax _____
4. Kyasanur Forest disease _____
5. necrotizing ulcerative stomatitis _____
6. urban rabies _____
7. enteroviral meningitis _____
8. pasteurellosis _____
9. respiratory tuberculosis _____
10. anthrax sepsis _____
11. ameboma of intestine _____
12. generalized tularemia _____
13. tuberculous pleurisy _____
14. clostridial cellulitis _____
15. gonococcal arthritis _____

B Codes

B codes are used to report:

- Viral infections characterized by skin and mucous membrane lesions, categories B00–B09
- Other Human herpesviruses, category B10
- Viral hepatitis, categories B15–B19
- Human immunodeficiency virus (HIV) disease, category B20
- Other viral diseases, categories B25–B34
- Mycoses, categories B35–B49
- Protozoal diseases, categories B50–B64
- Helminthiases, categories B65–B83
- Pediculosis, acariasis, and other infestations, categories B85–B89
- Sequelae of infectious and parasitic diseases, categories B90–B94
- Bacterial and viral infectious agents, categories B95–B97
- Other infectious diseases, category B99

Viral Infections Characterized by Skin and Mucous Membrane Lesions (Category Codes B00–B09)

Many common viral infections are found in this block of codes. Viral infections that are included in this block of codes include:

- Herpes viral [herpes simplex] infections (category B00)
- Varicella, commonly known as chickenpox (category B01)
- Zoster [herpes zoster] (category B02)
- Smallpox (category B03)
- Monkeypox (category B04)
- Measles (category B05)
- Rubella [German measles] (category B06)
- Viral warts (category B07)
- Other viral infections characterized by skin and mucous membrane lesions, not elsewhere classified (category B08)
- Unspecified viral infection characterized by skin and mucous membrane lesions (category B09)

Please note that for many categories the codes are differentiated to identify the site that is impacted by the viral infection or the site of a complication. For example reference code B05.0, measles, complicated by encephalitis. The code identifies the disease, measles, and the complication from measles, encephalitis.

Other Human Herpesviruses (Category Code B10)

The B10 category is used to report other human herpesviruses. Coders need to read the Excludes2 note under the category heading for B10. Remember an Excludes2 note indicates that the condition excluded is not part of the condition represented by the code, but if a patient has both conditions at the same time it is acceptable to use both the code and the excluded code together. In category B10, varicella is an excluded condition listed in the Excludes2 note. Therefore, if a patient was diagnosed with Human herpesvirus 6 infection (B10.81) and varicella keratitis, both code B10.81 and code B01.81 would be reported.

Viral Hepatitis (Category Codes B15–B19)

In order to select the appropriate code for viral hepatitis, the coder has to be able to identify whether the hepatitis is acute or chronic, or unspecified, and the type of hepatitis. Complications are also indicated in codes such as code B15.0, acute hepatitis A with hepatic coma.

Disease Highlight—Viral Hepatitis (Category Codes B15–B19)

Viral hepatitis is an inflammatory condition of the liver caused by a virus.

Signs and Symptoms:

- Nausea
- Vomiting
- Fever
- Anorexia
- Malaise
- Enlarged and tender liver
- Jaundice
- Abdominal and gastric pain and discomfort
- Discolored stools, clay-colored
- Discolored urine, tea-colored

Clinical Testing:

- White blood cell count in the normal to low range
- Abnormal liver tests showing that especially markedly elevated aminotransferases are present early in the course of the disease
- Biopsy of the liver showing hepatocellular necrosis and mononuclear infiltrates
- Mild proteinuria and bilirubinuria

Treatment:

- Antiviral drug therapy
- Bed rest
- A gradual return to normal activity without overexertion

Human Immunodeficiency Virus (HIV) Disease (Category Code B20)

Human immunodeficiency virus (HIV) is the virus that leads to **AIDS**, or **acquired immunodeficiency syndrome**. AIDS is a condition in which the body's immune system deteriorates.

The ICD-10-CM Official Guidelines for Coding and Reporting give the coder guidance on the reporting of cases that involve HIV infections.

ICD-10-CM Official Coding Guidelines

a. Human Immunodeficiency Virus (HIV) Infections

1) Code only confirmed cases

Code only confirmed cases of HIV infection/illness. This is an exception to the hospital inpatient guideline Section II, H.

In this context, "confirmation" does not require documentation of positive serology or culture for HIV; the provider's diagnostic statement that the patient is HIV positive, or has an HIV-related illness is sufficient.

2) Selection and sequencing of HIV codes

(a) Patient admitted for HIV-related condition

If a patient is admitted for an HIV-related condition, the principal diagnosis should be B20, Human immunodeficiency virus [HIV] disease followed by additional diagnosis codes for all reported HIV-related conditions.

(b) Patient with HIV disease admitted for unrelated condition

If a patient with HIV disease is admitted for an unrelated condition (such as a traumatic injury), the code for the unrelated condition (e.g., the nature of injury code) should be the principal diagnosis. Other diagnoses would be B20 followed by additional diagnosis codes for all reported HIV-related conditions.

(c) Whether the patient is newly diagnosed

Whether the patient is newly diagnosed or has had previous admissions/encounters for HIV conditions is irrelevant to the sequencing decision.

(d) Asymptomatic human immunodeficiency virus

Z21, Asymptomatic human immunodeficiency virus [HIV] infection status, is to be applied when the patient without any documentation of symptoms is listed as being "HIV positive," "known HIV," "HIV test positive," or similar terminology. Do not use this code if the term "AIDS" is used or if the patient is treated for any HIV-related illness or is described as having any condition(s) resulting from his/her HIV positive status; use B20 in these cases.

(e) Patients with inconclusive HIV serology

Patients with inconclusive HIV serology, but no definitive diagnosis or manifestations of the illness, may be assigned code R75, Inconclusive laboratory evidence of human immunodeficiency virus [HIV].

(f) Previously diagnosed HIV-related illness

Patients with any known prior diagnosis of an HIV-related illness should be coded to B20. Once a patient has developed an HIV-related illness, the patient should always be assigned code B20 on every subsequent admission/encounter. Patients previously diagnosed with any HIV illness (B20) should never be assigned to R75 or Z21, Asymptomatic human immunodeficiency virus [HIV] infection status.

(g) HIV Infection in Pregnancy, Childbirth and the Puerperium

During pregnancy, childbirth or the puerperium, a patient admitted (or presenting for a health care encounter) because of an HIV-related illness should receive a principal diagnosis code of O98.7–, Human immunodeficiency [HIV] disease complicating pregnancy, childbirth and the puerperium, followed by B20 and the code(s) for the HIV-related illness(es). Codes from Chapter 15 always take sequencing priority.

Patients with asymptomatic HIV infection status admitted (or presenting for a health care encounter) during pregnancy, childbirth, or the puerperium should receive codes of O98.7– and Z21.

(h) Encounters for testing for HIV

If a patient is being seen to determine his/her HIV status, use code Z11.4, Encounter for screening for human immunodeficiency virus [HIV]. Use additional codes for any associated high risk behavior.

If a patient with signs or symptoms is being seen for HIV testing, code the signs and symptoms. An additional counseling code Z71.7, Human immunodeficiency virus [HIV] counseling, may be used if counseling is provided during the encounter for the test.

When a patient returns to be informed of his/her HIV test results and the test result is negative, use code Z71.7, Human immunodeficiency virus [HIV] counseling.

If the results are positive, see previous guidelines and assign codes as appropriate. (See Appendix A, Section I.C.1.a.1-2.)

Other Viral Diseases (Category Codes B25–B34)

Category Codes B25–B34 contains the following code categories:

- B25 Cytomegaloviral disease
- B26 Mumps
- B27 Infectious mononucleosis
- B30 Viral conjunctivitis
- B33 Other viral diseases, not elsewhere classified- such as epidemic myalgia, Ross River disease, viral carditis, retrovirus infections, not elsewhere classified, Hantavirus (cardio)-pulmonary syndrome [HPS] [HCPS], and other specified viral diseases.
- B34 Viral infection of unspecified site

The detail of the codes requires that the coder identify the site that the condition is impacting. For example, for mumps the code book is differentiated as follows:

- Mumps orchitis, B26.0
- Mumps meningitis, B26.1
- Mumps encephalitis, B26.2
- Mumps pancreatitis, B26.3
- Mumps with other complications, B26.81 to B26.89
- Mumps without complications, B26.9

When coding infectious mononucleosis, category B27, the coder needs to identify the type of mononucleosis and complications. Category B27 infectious mononucleosis includes glandular fever, monocytic angina and Pfeiffer's disease. Reference the ICD-10-CM tabular list for category B27. Note the detail found in the codes that identify the type of mononucleosis and the presence or lack of complications. For example code B27.00 reports Gammaherpesviral mononucleosis without complication while code B27.01 reports Gammaherpesviral mononucleosis with polyneuropathy and code B27.02 reports Gammaherpesviral mononucleosis with meningitis. Review the additional codes found in the ICD-10-CM coding manual and note the types of mononucleosis and the complications.

Disease Highlight—Infectious Mononucleosis

Infectious mononucleosis is an acute infection caused by the Epstein-Barr virus.

Signs and Symptoms:

- Enlarged lymph nodes
- Fever
- Sore throat
- Malaise and fatigue
- Anorexia
- Myalgia
- Splenomegaly and mild hepatomegaly

Clinical Testing:

- Elevated WBC and atypical lymphocytes
- A positive monospot test
- Abormal liver function tests

Treatment:

- Steroid therapy is common.
- Symptomatic treatment includes over-the-counter pain relievers and throat gargles using warm saline, adequate hydration, nonaspirin analgesics, and antipyretics.
- For severe anemia or thrombocytopenia, transfusions are given.
- For splenic rupture, a splenectomy is indicated.

Category B34 reports viral infections of unspecified site. An Excludes1 note appears for category B34 that identifies diseases that are reported elsewhere in ICD-10-CM. The Excludes1 note identifies the following:

anogenital human papillomavirus infection (A63.0)

cytomegaloviral disease NOS (B25.9)

herpesvirus [herpes simplex] infection NOS (B00.9)

retrovirus infection NOS (B33.3)

viral agents as the cause of diseases classified elsewhere (B97.–)

viral warts due to human papillomavirus infection (B07)

The Excludes1 note is directing the coder to the correct codes for the diseases identified.

Category B34 contains the following codes:

- B34.0 Adenovirus infection, unspecified.
- B34.1 Enterovirus infection, unspecified, including Coxsackievirus infection NOS and Echovirus infection NOS.
- B34.2 Coronavirus infection, unspecified. Reference the ICD-10-CM tabular listing for code B34.2. Note the Excludes1 note that reads as follows:

    Excludes1: COVID-19 (U07.1)

    pneumonia due to SARS-associated coronavirus (J12.81)

This is signaling to the coder that COVID-19 and pneumonia due to SARS-associated coronavirus is not reported with a code from category B34 and is reported with the codes listed.

- B34.3 Parvovirus infection, unspecified.
- B34.4 Papovavirus infection, unspecified.
- B34.8 Other viral infections of unspecified site.
- B34.9 Viral infection, unspecified.

Therefore when coding from category B34 the coder must identify the type of viral infection even though the site is not known. Code B34.8 is used for other viral infections that are not listed in the category but are identified by the provider while code B34.9 is used for a viral infection that is unspecified by the provider.

Mycoses (Category Codes B35–B49)

This section includes fungal infections that affect various body sites. The Excludes2 notation at the start of the section excludes hypersensitivity pneumonitis due to organic dust and mycosis fungoides. In this code range, a coder finds codes for *tinea pedis* and *tinea coporis*.

Candidiasis and **moniliasis** infections are fungal infections caused by the fungus *Candida*, which can affect various sites. Common sites are:

- Mouth (commonly called thrush), B37.0
- Skin and nails (commonly called candidial onychia), B37.2
- Vulva and vagina (commonly called candidial or monilial vulvovaginitis), B37.3

Additional B Codes

The additional B codes that are found in ICD-10-CM include:

Code	Description
B50–B64 Protozoal disease	This code block includes plasmodium malaria, other specified forms of malaria, leishmaniasis, African trypanosomiasis, Chagas' disease, and toxoplasmosis.
B65–B83 Helminthiasis	This code block includes locate echinococcosis, filariasis, trichinellosis, and other intestinal helminthiases.
B85–B89 Pediculosis, acariasis, and other infestations	**Pediculosis**, also known as lice, is coded to this code range, as are scabies, myiasis, and acariasis. **Acariasis** is an infestation with mites or acariads.
B90–B94 Sequelae of infectious and parasitic diseases	This code range is used to indicate conditions in categories A00–B89 as the cause of sequelae that are classified elsewhere. The "Note" and "Code first" instructional notations, that appears in the Tabular Listing of ICD-10-CM block heading B90–B94, need to be reviewed prior to code selection. Also included are residuals of diseases classifiable to the same categories (A00–B89) if there is documented evidence that the disease no longer exists.
B95–B97 Bacterial and viral infectious agents B99 other infectious diseases	Categories B95 to B97 are used as supplementary or additional codes to identify the infectious agent(s) in diseases classified elsewhere to identify the specific organism present. Category B99 reports other infectious diseases and unspecified infectious diseases.

Courtesy of the Centers for Medicare & Medicaid Services, www.cms.gov

Exercise 6.4—Selecting Codes

Assign a diagnosis code for each diagnostic phrase.

1. candidial pyelonephritis   _____
2. acute gonococcal vulvovaginitis   _____
3. latent early syphilis   _____
4. acute pulmonary blastomycosis   _____
5. fluke infection   _____
6. herpes simplex iridocyclitis   _____
7. acute hepatitis E   _____
8. candidial stomatitis   _____
9. syphilitic meningitis, late congenital   _____
10. *tinea cruris*   _____
11. cytomegaloviral hepatitis   _____
12. mumps pancreatitis   _____
13. hand ringworm   _____
14. tinea blanca   _____
15. candidal balanitis   _____

The coding guidelines direct coders in the reporting of infectious agents as the cause of diseases classified to other chapters.

ICD-10-CM Official Coding Guidelines

b. Infectious agents as the cause of diseases classified to other chapters

Certain infections are classified in chapters other than Chapter 1 and no organism is identified as part of the infection code. In these instances, it is necessary to use an additional code from Chapter 1 to identify the organism. A code from category B95, Streptococcus, Staphylococcus, and Enterococcus as the cause of diseases classified to other chapters, B96, Other bacterial agents as the cause of diseases classified to other chapters, or B97, Viral agents as the cause of diseases classified to other chapters, is to be used as an additional code to identify the organism. An instructional note will be found at the infection code advising that an additional organism code is required. (See Appendix A, Section I.C.1.b.)

Courtesy of the Centers for Medicare & Medicaid Services, www.cms.gov

For example, when coding urinary tract infection due to *E. coli*, codes N39.0 and B96.20 are reported to fully describe the case.

The coding guidelines also direct coders in the reporting of infections resistant to antibiotics.

ICD-10-CM Official Coding Guidelines

c. Infections resistant to antibiotics

Many bacterial infections are resistant to current antibiotics. It is necessary to identify all infections documented as antibiotic resistant. Assign a code from category Z16, Resistance to antimicrobial drugs, following the infection code only if the infection code does not identify drug resistance. (See Appendix A, Section C.1.c.)

Courtesy of the Centers for Medicare & Medicaid Services, www.cms.gov

The guidelines give further direction in the coding of methicillin-resistant *Staphylococcus aureus* (MRSA) conditions and Zika virus infections.

ICD-10-CM Official Coding Guidelines

e. Methicillin Resistant Staphylococcus aureus (MRSA) Conditions

(1) Selection and sequencing of MRSA codes

(a) Combination codes for MRSA infection

When a patient is diagnosed with an infection that is due to methicillin resistant Staphylococcus aureus (MRSA), and that infection has a combination code that includes the causal organism (e.g., sepsis, pneumonia) assign the appropriate combination code for the condition (e.g., code A41.02, Sepsis due to Methicillin resistant Staphylococcus aureus or code J15.212, Pneumonia due to Methicillin resistant Staphylococcus aureus). Do not assign code B95.62, Methicillin resistant Staphylococcus aureus infection as the cause of diseases classified elsewhere, as an additional code because the combination code includes the type of infection and the MRSA organism. Do not assign a code from subcategory Z16.11, Resistance to penicillins, as an additional diagnosis.

See Section C.1. for instructions on coding and sequencing of sepsis and severe sepsis.

(b) Other codes for MRSA infection

When there is documentation of a current infection (e.g., wound infection, stitch abscess, urinary tract infection) due to MRSA, and that infection does not have a combination code that includes the causal organism, assign the appropriate code to identify the condition along with code B95.62, Methicillin resistant Staphylococcus aureus infection as the cause of diseases classified elsewhere for the MRSA infection. Do not assign a code from subcategory Z16.11, Resistance to penicillins.

(c) Methicillin susceptible Staphylococcus aureus (MSSA) and MRSA colonization

The condition or state of being colonized or carrying MSSA or MRSA is called colonization or carriage, while an individual person is described as being colonized or being a carrier. Colonization means that MSSA or MSRA is present on or in the body without necessarily causing illness. A positive MRSA colonization test might be documented by the provider as "MRSA screen positive" or "MRSA nasal swab positive".

Assign code Z22.322, Carrier or suspected carrier of Methicillin resistant Staphylococcus aureus, for patients documented as having MRSA colonization. Assign code Z22.321, Carrier or suspected carrier of Methicillin susceptible Staphylococcus aureus, for patient documented as having MSSA colonization. Colonization is not necessarily indicative of a disease process or as the cause of a specific condition the patient may have unless documented as such by the provider.

(d) MRSA colonization and infection

If a patient is documented as having both MRSA colonization and infection during a hospital admission, code Z22.322, Carrier or suspected carrier of Methicillin resistant Staphylococcus aureus, and a code for the MRSA infection may both be assigned.

f. Zika virus infections

(1) Code only confirmed cases

Code only a confirmed diagnosis of Zika virus (A92.5, Zika virus disease) as documented by the provider. This is an exception to the hospital inpatient guideline Section II, H.

In this context, "confirmation" does not require documentation of the type of test performed; the provider's diagnostic statement that the condition is confirmed is sufficient. This code should be assigned regardless of the stated mode of transmission.

If the provider documents "suspected", "possible" or "probable" Zika, do not assign code A92.5. Assign a code(s) explaining the reason for encounter (such as fever, rash, or joint pain) or Z20.821, Contact with and (suspected) exposure to Zika virus. (See Appendix A, Section I.C.1.e-f.)

Courtesy of the Centers for Medicare & Medicaid Services, www.cms.gov

Exercise 6.5—Coding Guidelines for Infectious Agents as the Cause of Diseases Classified to Other Chapters and MRSA

True/False: Indicate whether each statement is true (T) or false (F) based on the coding guidelines.

1. _____ When there is documentation of a current wound infection due to MRSA and that infection does not have a combination code that includes the causal organism, assign a code from subcategory Z16.11, Resistance to penicillins.

2. _____ For patients documented as having MRSA colonization, assign code Z22.322, Carrier or suspected carrier of Methicillin resistant *Staphylococcus aureus*.

3. _____ If a patient is documented as having both MRSA colonization and infection during a hospital admission, code Z22.322, Carrier or suspected carrier of Methicillin resistant *Staphylococcus aureus*, and a code for the MRSA infection may both be assigned.

4. _____ Categories B95 to B97 are codes that are assigned to identify the cause of diseases classified to other chapters and are to be used as an additional code to identify an organism.

5. _____ Colonization means that MSSA or MSRA is present on or in the body without necessarily causing illness.

Coding COVID-19

COVID-19 is an infectious disease; however the code for COVID-19 is reported with code U07.1 which is not presented in chapter 1 of ICD-10-CM entitled Certain Infectious and Parasitic diseases. Code U07.1 is found in chapter 22 of ICD-10-CM. However in the Official ICD-10-CM Guidelines for Coding and Reporting the guidelines for reporting COVID-19 are found in various chapter specific guidelines. For example the chapter specific guidelines for chapter 1 of ICD-10-CM contain some of the COVID-19 guidelines. The ICD-10-CM Official Guidelines for Coding and Reporting are available in Appendix A on the Companion Site for this textbook. As you review Appendix A please note the COVID-19 specific guidelines found in section I within the chapter specific section entitled Chapter 1: Certain Infectious and Parasitic Diseases (A00-B99), U071. The COVID-19 guidelines are found under the heading of g. Coronavirus infections. All of the COVID-19 guidelines will be reviewed in chapter 26 of this textbook.

Summary

- ICD-10-CM Chapter 1 includes infectious and parasitic diseases.
- Organisms are classified into the following groups: bacteria, fungi, parasites, and viruses.
- Opportunistic infections occur when a patient has a weakened immune system.
- Single-code assignment, combination-code assignment, and dual-code assignment are used in ICD-10-CM Chapter 1.
- An underlying condition or infection code is sequenced first, followed by the manifestation code.
- Septicemia occurs when there is a systematic infection with the presence of organisms or their toxins in the blood.
- Coding HIV depends on the place of service.
- If a patient is admitted for an HIV-related condition, the principal diagnosis should be code B20, followed by additional diagnosis codes for all reported HIV-related conditions.
- Asymptomatic HIV cases are coded to code Z21.
- Viral hepatitis includes hepatitis A, B, C, D, and E.

Internet Links

For information on infectious and parasitic diseases, search the Centers for Disease Control and Prevention website at **www.cdc.gov** and the National Institutes of Health website at **www.nih.gov**.

For recent research on infectious diseases from the National Foundation for Infectious Diseases, go to **www.nfid.org**.

Chapter Review

True/False

Indicate whether each statement is true (T) or false (F).

1. _____ The terms *cocci*, *bacilli*, and *spirilla* describe fungal shapes.
2. _____ To describe clusters of bacteria, the medical word part *staphylo-* is used.
3. _____ A culture and sensitivity test is used to identify parasitic infections.
4. _____ Yeast infections are caused by fungi.
5. _____ Dual-code assignment is mandatory for all bacterial infections.

Fill-in-the-Blank

Enter the appropriate term(s) to complete each statement.

6. In dual-code assignment, two codes appear in the Alphabetic Index. This is to signal to the coder that the code in the brackets should be listed as the _____ code.

7. Clinical tests used to diagnose tuberculosis include chest x-rays, _____ skin tests, and sputum cultures.

8. Two forms of fungal infections that affect humans are yeasts and _____.

9. Thrush is a common infection of the mouth and is caused by _____.

10. Athlete's foot is caused by the pathogen _____.

Coding Guidelines True/False

Reference the ICD-10-CM Official Coding Guidelines to answer the following questions.

11. _____ Code only confirmed cases of HIV infection/illness.

12. _____ The term urosepsis is a specific term.

13. _____ If a patient with HIV disease is admitted for an unrelated condition, the code for the unrelated condition should be the principal diagnosis.

14. _____ Patients with inconclusive HIV serology, but no definitive diagnosis or manifestations of the illness, may be assigned code R75, Inconclusive laboratory evidence of human immunodeficiency virus (HIV).

15. _____ Patients with asymptomatic HIV infection status admitted (or presenting for a health care encounter) during pregnancy, childbirth, or the puerperium should receive only code O98.7–.

Coding Assignments

Using an ICD-10-CM coding book, select the code for each diagnostic statement.

1. botulism   _____

2. gonococcal keratitis   _____

3. scarlet fever   _____

4. amebic balanitis   _____

5. herpes simplex meningitis   _____

6. frambesioma   _____

7. warts, viral   _____

8. congential syphilis   _____

9. hyperkeratosis of pinta   _____

10. scabies   _____

11. internal hirudiniasis   _____

12. syphilitic bursitis   _____

13. malaria   _____

14. foot and mouth disease   _____

15. conjunctivitis, viral _____

16. chronic viral hepatitis _____

17. West Nile virus _____

18. rubella _____

19. shingles _____

20. genital herpes _____

21. mumps without mention of complications _____

22. tuberculosis of bronchus _____

23. tetanus neonatorum _____

24. shigellosis due to *Shigella sonnei* _____

25. oxyuriasis _____

26. viral endocarditis _____

27. candidal paronychia _____

28. vaginal thrush _____

29. verruca plantaris _____

30. zoster keratitis _____

31. cytomegaloviral mononucleosis with meningitis _____

32. mumps polyneuropathy _____

33. chronic viral hepatitis C _____

34. human herpesvirus 6 infection _____

35. hemorrhagic fever with renal syndrome _____

Case Studies

Instructions: Review each case study and select the correct ICD-10-CM diagnostic code.

Case 1

S: A 55-year-old male presents today with severe abdominal pain, nausea, and vomiting, persistent over the last 24 hours. Diarrhea has developed, and abdominal cramping is also present. The patient states that he cannot keep anything down. Upon questioning, he states that he attended a neighborhood clambake and ate at least a dozen raw clams. No over-the-counter (OTC) medications were tried because the patient cannot keep anything down.

O: Pleasant, alert gentleman who appears in mild discomfort. **Vital signs:** Temp—99, pulse—70, resp—22, BP—120/75. **Skin:** Warm and clammy.

HEENT: Unremarkable except for dryness around conjunctiva and the mouth. The patient appears slightly dehydrated.

Neck: No JVD; no thyromegaly or bruits.

(continues)

(continued)

Lungs: Clear to auscultation and percussion.

Heart: No murmurs.

Extremities: No edema.

A: Food poisoning due to *salmonella*

P: Will order a suppository to help with the nausea. Stressed the importance of forcing fluids once the suppository has had time to work. The patient will call in the morning if he does not feel better. If he is improving, he will follow up as needed.

ICD-10-CM Code Assignment: _____

Case 2

S: A 19-year-old woman presents today with slight fever, cough, and fatigue for 4 days. OTC medications were tried with little relief. No other family members are symptomatic. No nausea or vomiting, no shortness of breath.

O: **Vital Signs:** Temp—98.7, BP—100/72; Skin: warm and dry; **HEENT:** TM's normal; throat is slightly red; **Neck:** normal; **Lungs:** clear; **Heart:** RRR.

A: Viral Infection

P: I explained to the patient that I think this is a viral infection and could have come on in a variety of different ways. I suggested Advil for comfort and plenty of fluids. The patient requested an antibiotic. I explained that since this infection was viral in nature, an antibiotic would not be effective. She said she would try the Advil and notify us if she does not improve in 7–10 days.

ICD-10-CM Code Assignment: _____

Case 3

S: This is a 29-year-old female who presents today with fever and nausea for 3 days. The patient has tried over-the-counter cold and flu medicine with no results. No other family members are ill at this time. Temp. has been running between 99 and 102°F. When asked about any other symptoms, the patient states that she "feels like my heart is racing sometimes." The patient has not voided in 2 days.

O: **Respirations:** 31; **Pulse:** 100; **BP:** 150/90. She is alert, oriented, and in no acute distress.

Lungs: Clear, no rhonci or wheezing.

HEENT: WNL.

Skin: Clammy to touch.

Heart: RRR with no murmurs.

Abdomen: Soft and nontender.

Extremities: Ankle edema +12.

(continues)

A: Staphylococcus septicemia

P: The patient is admitted to the hospital and will follow staphylococcus septicemia protocol.

ICD-10-CM Code Assignment: _____

Case 4

Dr. Malik had just returned from a trip to overseas. He was providing free medical care to the people of a small village in a very desolate region of central Africa. Upon his return, he suddenly developed a severe headache, pain in his joints and back, and an extremely high fever. After extensive testing, combined with the fact that he had just returned from overseas, it was determined that Dr. Malik had contracted African tick typhus.

ICD-10-CM Code Assignment: _____

Case 5

Kaley presented today with an unsightly sore on the lower lip and onto the skin. The patient said this is extremely painful and occurs usually around the time of her period. After a brief examination, Dr. Snyder diagnosed Kaley with herpes simplex, at which time he prescribed medication that will help relieve her symptoms.

ICD-10-CM Code Assignment: _____

Case 6

Inpatient Progress Note

This 74-year-old patient was admitted 3 days ago with symptoms of nausea, vomiting, and abdominal pain. Diagnostic testing confirmed botulism food poisoning. Nursing has been instructed to follow appropriate protocol documented by myself at the time of admission.

ICD-10-CM Code Assignment: _____

Case 7

Discharge Summary Note

This 34-year-old male patient is being discharged to his home today following an admission for acute appendicitis. During this admission, it was also determined that the patient is HIV positive.

ICD-10-CM Code Assignment: _____

Case 8

Office Note

This 3-year-old male patient presented to my office today with numerous pruritic vesicular skin lesions and difficulty breathing. The mother reports that prior to the lesions, the child refused to eat. The child has had a fever of 100°F for 24 hours. Because of the patient's difficulty breathing, a chest x-ray was ordered. Assessment: chickenpox with complication of pneumonia. The mother was instructed to keep the child hydrated and follow-up with me in 3 days.

ICD-10-CM Code Assignment: _____

Case 9

Office Note

This 65-year-old female patient was seen today to remove a flat wart on her left finger. The wart was removed and a dressing was applied. She was instructed to return to me if the wound does not heal within the next 3 weeks.

ICD-10-CM Coding Assignment: _____

Case 10

Office Note

This 16-year-old male is a high-school wrestler and has developed a rash in his groin. The patient states that it is becoming bothersome and he would like treatment.

Assessment: tinea cruris

A prescription for a topical miconazole antifungal was written.

The patient was instructed to return if the rash reappears after treatment.

ICD-10-CM Coding Assignment: _____

Neoplasms

Chapter Outline

Chapter Objectives

At the conclusion of this chapter, you should be able to:

1. Identify the groups of neoplasms classified in ICD-10-CM.
2. Identify a neoplasm as benign or malignant based on the term used.
3. Apply coding guidelines that relate to neoplasms to select and/or sequence ICD-10-CM codes.
4. Select and code diagnoses from case studies.

Key Terms

Benign tumors

Biopsy

Ca in situ (CIS)

Cancer

Cancerous growths

Carcinoma

Carcinoma in situ (CIS)

Encapsulated

In situ neoplasms

Leukemia

Lipoma

Lymphoma

Malignant neoplasms

Malignant primary

Malignant secondary

Melanoma

Metastasize

Morphology

Neoplasms

Neoplasms of
  uncertain behavior

Neoplasms of
  unspecified behavior

Noninfiltrating carcinoma

Noninvasive carcinoma

Nonmalignant tumors

Preinvasive carcinoma

Sarcoma

Transitional cell
  carcinoma

Tumors

REMINDER: As you work through this chapter, you will need to have a copy of the ICD-10-CM coding book to reference. For this chapter, you will also need to reference the ICD-10-CM Official Guidelines for Coding and Reporting. These guidelines can be found in Appendix A which are now available on the Student Companion site and MINDTAP From Cengage.

Introduction

Chapter 2 of ICD-10-CM contains diagnostic codes for neoplasms. ICD-10 classifies neoplasms into the following blocks:

- C00–C14, Malignant neoplasms of lip, oral cavity, and pharynx
- C15–C26, Malignant neoplasms of digestive organs
- C30–C39, Malignant neoplasms of respiratory and intrathoracic organs
- C40–C41, Malignant neoplasms of bone and articular cartilage
- C43–C44, Melanoma and other malignant neoplasms of skin
- C45–C49, Malignant neoplasms of mesothelial and soft tissue
- C50, Malignant neoplasms of breast
- C51–C58, Malignant neoplasms of female genital organs
- C60–C63, Malignant neoplasms of male genital organs
- C64–C68, Malignant neoplasms of urinary tract
- C69–C72, Malignant neoplasms of eye, brain, and other parts of central nervous system
- C73–C75, Malignant neoplasms of thyroid and other endocrine glands
- C7A, Malignant neuroendocrine tumors
- C7B, Secondary neuroendocrine tumors
- C76–C80, Malignant neoplasms of ill-defined, other secondary, and unspecified sites
- C81–C96, Malignant neoplasms of lymphoid, hematopoietic, and related tissue
- D00–D09, In situ neoplasms
- D10–D36, Benign neoplasms, except benign neuroendocrine tumors
- D3A, Benign neuroendocrine tumors
- D37–D48, Neoplasms of uncertain behavior, polycythemia vera, and myelodysplastic syndromes
- D49, Neoplasms of unspecified behavior

Neoplasms, or **tumors**, are defined as uncontrolled abnormal growths of cells and are characterized as malignant or benign. **Malignant neoplasms**, called **cancerous growths**, are life-threatening, whereas **benign**, or **nonmalignant tumors**, are usually not life-threatening.

Abbreviations

The following abbreviations are commonly associated with neoplasms:

ALL	acute lymphoblastic leukemia
AML	acute myelogenous leukemia
BCE	basal cell epithelioma
BMA	bone marrow aspiration
BSE	breast self-exam
Bx	biopsy
Ca, CA	cancer, carcinoma
CA-125	ovarian carcinoma antigen (tumor marker-ovary)

CEA	carcinoembryonic antigen (tumor marker-colon, lung, breast, others)
Chemo	chemotherapy
PSA	prostate-specific antigen (tumor marker-prostate)
TNM	tumor, nodes, metastasis (refers to tumor staging)

Introduction to the Body System

To understand the organization of codes in ICD-10-CM, the coder must realize that neoplasms are described according to the form and structure of the neoplastic growth of the cell, known as the **morphology**, and the anatomical site. Neoplastic conditions are located in the Alphabetic Index by referring to the morphological term or to the Neoplasm Table. Coders must be familiar with the medical terms used to characterize neoplasms before attempting to locate the terms in ICD-10-CM.

Malignant Versus Benign Neoplasms

Malignant neoplasms, also called **cancer**, grow relatively rapidly and may **metastasize**, or spread, to other body parts. The malignant cells multiply excessively and can invade or infiltrate normal tissue, making the condition life-threatening if untreated. The cancerous cells interfere with normal cell growth (Figure 7-1) and draw nutrients away from body tissue. Compared with normal tissue, cancerous cells appear disorderly and do not look like the tissue of origin. Patients with malignant conditions may experience:

- Anorexia
- Abnormal bleeding or bruising
- Difficulty swallowing
- Indigestion
- Malaise
- Fever
- Sores that do not heal or that change to the appearance of a wart or mole
- Bladder and bowel habit changes
- Mass growth in the breast or other body site
- Persistent cough
- Weight loss

To determine whether a patient has a tumor, various laboratory tests and procedures, such as

FIGURE 7-1 Cellular growth patterns: (A) normal cells; (B) cancer cells.

endoscopies, magnetic resonance imaging (MRI), computed tomography (CT) scans, x-rays, and ultrasound, are used. A **biopsy**, or the removal of tissue for pathological examination, is completed to differentiate between malignant and benign tumors.

Benign neoplasms:

- Usually grow slowly
- Typically are **encapsulated** (surrounded by a capsule)
- Do not metastasize

Under a microscope, benign neoplastic cells appear similar to the tissue of origin. Benign tumors do not cause death unless they are located in vital organs. For example, if a patient has a benign tumor located in the spinal cord or brain, removal may be complicated because of the location of the tumor, thus causing death.

Both benign and malignant neoplasms are named and classified by the tissue of origin. Neoplasms are typically named by adding the suffix -*oma* to the name of the body part, such as in **lipoma**, a benign neoplasm of adipose tissue. Malignant tumors are called:

- **Carcinoma**—Cancer of the epithelial cells of connective tissue
- **Lymphoma**—Cancer of the lymph nodes and immune system
- **Melanoma**—Cancer of melanin-producing cells
- **Sarcoma**—Cancer of supportive tissue, such as blood vessels, bones, cartilage, and muscles

Disease Highlight—Basal Cell Carcinoma of Skin

Basal cell carcinoma of the skin is the most common form of skin cancer. The cancer forms at the skin's epidermal layer. The types of basal cell carcinoma are sclerosing, noduloulcerative, and superficial. The most common cause of basal cell carcinoma is prolonged sun exposure, but it can also be a result of radiation exposure, immunosuppression, or even arsenic ingestion.

Signs and Symptoms:

- Noduloulcerative type of basal cell carcinoma—Small, smooth, pinkish, or translucent lesions form in the early stages; ulcerations and tumors spread and become infected in later stages.

- Sclerosing basal cell carcinoma—Waxy looking growths that have yellowish plaques without any distinct borders.

- Superficial types of basal cell carcinoma—Irregularly shaped lesions, most often found on the chest and back, sometimes a scaly look with atrophic areas in the centers.

Clinical Testing:

- Biopsy and examination

Treatment:

- Excision
- Chemotherapy
- Radiotherapy
- Cryotherapy

Common benign and malignant neoplasms are listed in Table 7-1.

TABLE 7-1 Benign and Malignant Neoplasms

Tissue of Origin	Benign Neoplasms	Malignant Neoplasms
Adipose	Lipoma	Liposarcoma
Blood vessel	Hemangioma	Hemangiosarcoma
Bone	Osteoma	Osteogenic sarcoma Osteosarcoma

(continues)

TABLE 7-1 (*continued*)

Tissue of Origin	Benign Neoplasms	Malignant Neoplasms
Bone marrow		Ewing sarcoma Multiple myeloma **Leukemia**
Breast		Carcinoma of breast
Cartilage	Chondroma	Chondrosarcoma
Cervix		Epidermoid carcinoma of the cervix
Colon		Carcinoma of colon
Esophagus		Esophageal adenocarcinoma
Fibrous	Fibroma	Fibrosarcoma
Ganglion cells	Ganglioneuroma	Neuroblastoma
Kidney		Hypernephroma Wilm's tumor
Lung		Adenocarcinoma of the lung Oat cell carcinoma
Meninges	Meningioma	Malignant meningioma
Muscle tissue, smooth	Leiomyoma	Leiomyosarcoma
Muscle tissue, striated	Rhabdomyoma	Rhabdomyosarcoma
Nerve tissue	Neuroma Neurinoma Neurofibroma	Neurogenic sarcoma
Ovaries		Cystadenocarcinoma of the ovaries
Penis		Carcinoma of penis
Skin		Basal cell carcinoma
Stomach		Gastric adenocarcinoma Melanoma Squamous cell carcinoma
Testes		Seminoma
Uterus	Fibroid	Adenocarcinoma of the uterus

Exercise 7.1—Identifying Neoplasms

For each of the terms listed, determine whether the neoplasm is benign (B) or malignant (M).

1. choriocarcinoma   _____

2. reticulosarcoma   _____

3. uterine leiomyoma   _____

4. adenomatous polyp   _____

(*continues*)

Exercise 7.1—*continued*

5. giant-cell sarcoma

6. juxtacortical chondroma

7. fibromyxosarcoma of connective tissue

8. osteofibroma

9. psammocarcinoma

10. angiomyolipoma

11. squamous cell carcinoma

12. Wilm's tumor

13. leukemia

14. Kaposi's sarcoma

15. uterine fibroid

Coding of Neoplasms

ICD-10-CM groups neoplasms into the following behavior groups:

- Malignant neoplasms, C00–C96, C7A, and C7B—A malignant neoplasm that grows rapidly, can spread to other organs, and can be life-threatening if not treated.

- **In situ neoplasms**, also known as **carcinoma in situ**, **ca in situ**, or **CIS**, D00–D09—Neoplastic cells undergoing malignant changes that are confined to the original epithelium site without invading surrounding tissues. Common sites of in situ neoplasms include the breast, bladder, cervix, and vulva. Ca in situ is also referred to as **transitional cell carcinoma**, **noninfiltrating carcinoma**, **noninvasive carcinoma**, and **preinvasive carcinoma**.

- Benign neoplasms, D10–D36 and D3A—Characterized by slow growth, not spreading, and typically not life-threatening.

- **Neoplasms of uncertain behavior**, D37–D48—Neoplasms in which the cells are not histologically confirmed even after pathological investigation. The cells exhibit characteristics of both benign and malignant behavior, and further study is needed to arrive at a definitive diagnosis. To specify the purpose of this code range, the following note appears in the Tabular List after the heading D37–D48 (Figure 7-2).

- **Neoplasms of unspecified behavior**, D49—Neoplasms in which the morphology and behavior of the neoplasm is not specified in the patient's record. To specify the purpose of this category, a note is included in the Tabular List after the category heading D49, Neoplasms of unspecified behavior (Figure 7-3).

NEOPLASMS OF UNCERTAIN BEHAVIOR , POLYCYTHEMIA VERA AND MYELODYS-PLASTIC SYNDROME (D37–D48)

Note: Categories D37- D44, and D48 classify by site neoplasms of uncertain behavior, i.e., histologic confirmation whether the neoplasm is malignant or benign cannot be made.

Excludes1: neoplasms of unspecified behavior (D49.-)

FIGURE 7-2 Neoplasms of uncertain behavior.

D49 Neoplasms of unspecified behavior
Note: Category D49 classifies by site neoplasms of unspecified morphology and behavior. The term "mass," unless otherwise stated, is not to be regarded as a neoplastic growth.
Includes: "growth" NOS neoplasm NOS new growth NOS tumor NOS
Excludes1: neoplasms of uncertain behavior (D37–D44, D48)

FIGURE 7-3 Neoplasms of unspecified behavior.

General Neoplasm Guidelines

A coder needs to become familiar with the following general guidelines that relate to the coding of neoplasms:

ICD-10-CM Official Coding Guidelines

2. Chapter 2: Neoplasms (C00-D49)

General guidelines

Chapter 2 of the ICD-10-CM contains the codes for most benign and all malignant neoplasms. Certain benign neoplasms, such as prostatic adenomas, may be found in the specific body system chapters. To properly code a neoplasm it is necessary to determine from the record if the neoplasm is benign, in-situ, malignant, or of uncertain histologic behavior. If malignant, any secondary (metastatic) sites should also be determined.

Primary malignant neoplasms overlapping site boundaries

A primary malignant neoplasm that overlaps two or more contiguous (next to each other) sites should be classified to the subcategory/code .8 ('overlapping lesion'), unless the combination is specifically indexed elsewhere. For multiple neoplasms of the same site that are not contiguous such as tumors in different quadrants of the same breast, codes for each site should be assigned.

Malignant neoplasm of ectopic tissue

Malignant neoplasms of ectopic tissue are to be coded to the site of origin mentioned, i.e., ectopic pancreatic malignant neoplasms involving the stomach are coded to malignant neoplasm of pancreas, unspecified (C25.9).

The neoplasm table in the Alphabetic Index should be referenced first. However, if the histological term is documented, that term should be referenced first, rather than going immediately to the Neoplasm Table, in order to determine which column in the Neoplasm Table is appropriate. For example, if the documentation indicates "adenoma," refer to the term in the Alphabetic Index to review the entries under this term and the instructional note to "see also neoplasm, by site, benign." The table provides the proper code based on the type of neoplasm and the site. It is important to select the proper column in the table that corresponds to the type of neoplasm. The Tabular List should then be referenced to verify that the correct code has been selected from the table and that a more specific site code does not exist.

See Section I.C.21. Factors influencing health status and contact with health services, Status, for information regarding Z15.0, codes for genetic susceptibility to cancer. (See Appendix A, Section I, C2.)

Locating a Neoplasm Code

To locate a code for a neoplastic condition, a new coder needs to reference the Alphabetic Index to start.

EXAMPLE: To code the term primary *basal cell* carcinoma of the *chin*, the coder first references the term *carcinoma* in the Alphabetic Index and then *basal cell*. The entry appears as shown in Figure 7-4.

The Alphabetic Index instructs the coder to reference "Neoplasm, skin, malignant." This refers the coder to the Table of Neoplasms. The coder must follow that instruction to locate the site in the Table of Neoplasms.

Carcinoma (malignant) - (see also Neoplasm, by site, malignant)

    acidophil

        specified site - see Neoplasm, malignant, by site

        unspecified site C75.1

    acidophil-basophil, mixed

        specified site - See Neoplasm, malignant, by site

        unspecified site C75.1

    adnexal (skin) - see Neoplasm, skin, malignant

    adrenal cortical C74.0-

    alveolar - see Neoplasm, lung, malignant

        cell - see Neoplasm, lung, malignant

    ameloblastic C41.1

        upper jaw (bone) C41.0

    apocrine

        breast - see Neoplasm, breast, malignant

        specified site NEC - see Neoplasm, skin, malignant

        unspecified site C44.99

    basal cell (pigmented) (see also Neoplasm, skin, malignant) C44.91

        fibro-epithelial - see Neoplasm, skin, malignant

        morphea - see Neoplasm, skin, malignant

        multicentric - see Neoplasm, skin, malignant

    basaloid

FIGURE 7-4 Partial Alphabetical Listing for carcinoma.

The Table of Neoplasms alphabetically lists anatomical sites and then subterms. At the start of the Table of Neoplasms, notes appear (see Figure 7-5). These notes give the coder specific details about the Table of Neoplasms. This information must be considered when selecting codes.

The list below gives the code numbers for neoplasms by anatomical site. For each site there are six possible code numbers according to whether the neoplasm in question is malignant, benign, in situ, of uncertain behavior, or of unspecified nature. The description of the neoplasm will often indicate which of the six columns is appropriate; e.g. malignant melanoma of skin, benign fibroadenoma of breast, carcinoma in situ of cervix uteri.

Where such descriptors are not present, the remainder of the Index should be consulted where guidance is given to the appropriate column for each morphological (histological) variety listed; e.g. Mesonephroma- see Neoplasm, malignant; Embryoma- see also Neoplasm, uncertain behavior; Disease, Bowen's- see Neoplasm, skin, in situ. However, the guidance in the Index can be overridden if one of the descriptors mentioned above is present; e.g. malignant adenoma of colon is coded to C18.9 and not to D12.6 as the adjective "malignant" overrides the Index entry "Adenoma- (see also Neoplasm, benign.)"

Codes listed with a dash -, following the code have a required additional character for laterality. The tabular must be reviewed for the complete code.

FIGURE 7-5 Notes at the start of the Neoplasm Table.

To continue coding basal cell carcinoma of the chin, the coder searches the Neoplasm Table for the anatomical site of skin and then the subterm *chin*. See Figures 7-6A and 7-6B. Note that the coder is instructed to see also Neoplasm, skin, face. See Figure 7-6B. Columns to the right of the anatomical sites list the codes for each type of neoplasm. Remember, the case presently being coded referred the coder to *malignant* in the Table of Neoplasms. Malignant neoplasms are organized in three columns in the table: primary, secondary, and ca in situ.

	Malignant Primary	Malignant Secondary	Ca in situ	Benign	Uncertain Behavior	Unspecified Behavior
- - urethrovaginal	C57.9	C79.82	D07.30	D28.9	D39.9	D49.5
- - vesicovaginal	C57.9	C79.82	D07.30	D28.9	D39.9	D49.5
- shoulder NEC	C76.4-	C79.89	D04.6-	D36.7	D48.7	D49.89
- sigmoid flexure(lower)(upper)	C18.7	C78.5	D01.0	D12.5	D37.4	D49.0
- sinus(accessory)	C31.9	C78.39	D02.3	D14.0	D38.5	D49.1
- - bone(any)	C41.0	C79.51	-	D16.4-	D48.0	D49.2
- - ethmoidal	C31.1	C78.39	D02.3	D14.0	D38.5	D49.1
- - frontal	C31.2	C78.39	D02.3	D14.0	D38.5	D49.1
- - maxillary	C31.0	C78.39	D02.3	D14.0	D38.5	D49.1
- - nasal, paranasal NEC	C31.9	C78.39	D02.3	D14.0	D38.5	D49.1
- - overlapping lesion	C31.8	-	-	-	-	-
- - pyriform	C12	C79.89	D00.08	D10.7	D37.05	D49.0
- - sphenoid	C31.3	C78.39	D02.3	D14.0	D38.5	D49.1
- skeleton, skeletal NEC	C41.9	C79.51	-	D16.9-	D48.0	D49.2
- Skene's gland	C68.1	C79.19	D09.19	D30.8	D41.8	D49.59
- skin NOS	C44.90	C79.2	D04.9	D23.9	D48.5	D49.2
- - abdominal wall	C44.509	C79.2	D04.5	D23.5	D48.5	D49.2
- - basal cell carcinoma	C44.519	-		-	-	-
- - - specified type NEC	C44.599	-		-	-	-
- - - squamous cell carcinoma	C44.529	-				
- - ala nasi—*see also Neoplasm, nose, skin*	C44.301	C79.2	D04.39	D23.39	D48.5	D49.2
- - ankle—*see also Neoplasm, skin, limb, lower*	C44.70-	C79.2	D04.7-	D23.7-	D48.5	D49.2
- - antecubital space—*see also Neoplasm, skin, limb, upper*	C44.60-	C79.2	D04.6-	D23.6-	D48.5	D49.2
- - anus	C44.500	C79.2	D04.5	D23.5	D48.5	D49.2
- - - basal cell carcinoma	C44.510	-	-	-	-	-
- - - specified type NEC	C44.590	-	-	-	-	-
- - - squamous cell carcinoma	C44.520	-	-	-	-	-
- - arm—*see also Neoplasm, skin, limb, upper*	C44.60-	C79.2	D04.6-	D23.6-	D48.5	D49.2
- - auditory canal(external)—*see also Neoplasm, skin, ear*	C44.20-	C79.2	D04.2-	D23.2-	D48.5	D49.2
- - auricle(ear)—*see also Neoplasm, skin, ear*	C44.20-	C79.2	D04.2-	D23.2-	D48.5	D49.2
- - auricular canal(external)—*see also Neoplasm, skin, ear*	C44.20-	C79.2	D04.2-	D23.2-	D48.5	D49.2
- - axilla, axillary fold—*see also Neoplasm, skin, trunk*	C44.509	C79.2	D04.5	D23.5	D48.5	D49.2
- - back—*see also Neoplasm, skin, trunk*	C44.509	C79.2	D04.5	D23.5	D48.5	D49.2
- - basal cell carcinoma	C44.91					
- - breast	C44.501	C79.2	D04.5	D23.5	D48.5	D49.2
- - - basal cell carcinoma	C44.511	-	-	-	-	-
- - - specified type NEC	C44.591	-	-	-	-	-
- - - squamous cell carcinoma	C44.521	-	-	-	-	-
- - brow—*see also Neoplasm, skin, face*	C44.309	C79.2	D04.39	D23.39	D48.5	D49.2
- - buttock—*see also Neoplasm, skin, trunk*	C44.509	C79.2	D04.5	D23.5	D48.5	D49.2
- - calf—*see also Neoplasm, skin, limb, lower*	C44.70-	C79.2	D04.7-	D23.7-	D48.5	D49.2
- - canthus(eye) (inner) (outer)	C44.10-	C79.2	D04.1-	D23.1-	D48.5	D49.2
- - - basal cell carcinoma	C44.11-	-	-	-	-	-
- - - sebaceous cell	C44.13-	-	-	-	-	-
- - - specified type NEC	C44.19-	-	-	-	-	-
- - - squamous cell carcinoma	C44.12-	-	-	-	-	-

FIGURE 7-6A Alphabetic Index Entry for Neoplasm, skin, as it appears in the Table of Neoplasms.

	Malignant Primary	Malignant Secondary	Ca in situ	Benign	Uncertain Behavior	Unspecified Behavior
- - cervical region—*see also Neoplasm, skin, neck*	C44.40	C79.2	D04.4	D23.4	D48.5	D49.2
- - cheek(external)—*see also Neoplasm, skin, face*	C44.309	C79.2	D04.39	D23.39	D48.5	D49.2
- - chest(wall)—*see also Neoplasm, skin, trunk*	C44.509	C79.2	D04.5	D23.5	D48.5	D49.2
- - chin—*see also Neoplasm, skin, face*	C44.309	C79.2	D04.39	D23.39	D48.5	D49.2
- - clavicular area—*see also Neoplasm, skin, trunk*	C44.509	C79.2	D04.5	D23.5	D48.5	D49.2
- - clitoris	C51.2	C79.82	D07.1	D28.0	D39.8	D49.59
- - columnella—*see also Neoplasm, skin, face*	C44.309	C79.2	D04.39	D23.39	D48.5	D49.2
- - concha—*see also Neoplasm, skin, ear*	C44.20-	C79.2	D04.2-	D23.2-	D48.5	D49.2
- - ear(external)	C44.20-	C79.2	D04.2-	D23.2-	D48.5	D49.2
- - - basal cell carcinoma	C44.21-	-	-	-	-	-
- - - specified type NEC	C44.29-	-	-	-	-	-
- - - squamous cell carcinoma	C44.22-	-	-	-	-	-
- - elbow—*see also Neoplasm, skin, limb, upper*	C44.60-	C79.2	D04.6-	D23.6-	D48.5	D49.2
- - eyebrow—*see also Neoplasm, skin, face*	C44.309	C79.2	D04.39	D23.39	D48.5	D49.2
- - eyelid	C44.10-	C79.2	D04.1-	D23.1-	D48.5	D49.2
- - - basal cell carcinoma	C44.11-	-	-	-	-	-
- - - sebaceous cell	C44.13	-	-	-	-	-
- - - specified type NEC	C44.19-	-	-	-	-	-
- - - squamous cell carcinoma	C44.12-	-	-	-	-	-
- - face NOS	C44.300	C79.2	D04.30	D23.30	D48.5	D49.2
- - - basal cell carcinoma	C44.310	-	-	-	-	-
- - - specified type NEC	C44.390	-	-	-	-	-
- - - squamous cell carcinoma	C44.320	-	-	-	-	-
- - female genital organs(external)	C51.9	C79.82	D07.1	D28.0	D39.8	D49.59
- - - clitoris	C51.2	C79.82	D07.1	D28.0	D39.8	D49.59
- - - labium NEC	C51.9	C79.82	D07.1	D28.0	D39.8	D49.59
- - - - majus	C51.0	C79.82	D07.1	D28.0	D39.8	D49.59
- - - - minus	C51.1	C79.82	D07.1	D28.0	D39.8	D49.59
- - - pudendum	C51.9	C79.82	D07.1	D28.0	D39.8	D49.59
- - - vulva	C51.9	C79.82	D07.1	D28.0	D39.8	D49.59
- - finger—*see also Neoplasm, skin, limb, upper*	C44.60-	C79.2	D04.6-	D23.6-	D48.5	D49.2
- - flank—*see also Neoplasm, skin, trunk*	C44.509	C79.2	D04.5	D23.5	D48.5	D49.2
- - foot—*see also Neoplasm, skin, limb, lower*	C44.70-	C79.2	D04.7-	D23.7-	D48.5	D49.2
- - forearm—*see also Neoplasm, skin, limb, upper*	C44.60-	C79.2	D04.6-	D23.6-	D48.5	D49.2
- - forehead—*see also Neoplasm, skin, face*	C44.309	C79.2	D04.39	D23.39	D48.5	D49.2
- - glabella—*see also Neoplasm, skin, face*	C44.309	C79.2	D04.39	D23.39	D48.5	D49.2
- - gluteral region—*see also Neoplasm, skin, trunk*	C44.509	C79.2	D04.5	D23.5	D48.5	D49.2
- - groin—*see also Neoplasm, skin, trunk*	C44.509	C79.2	D04.5	D23.5	D48.5	D49.2
- - hand—*see also Neoplasm, skin, limb, upper*	C44.60-	C79.2	D04.6-	D23.6-	D48.5	D49.2
- - head NEC—*see also Neoplasm, skin, scalp*	C44.40	C79.2	D04.4	D23.4	D48.5	D49.2
- - heel—*see also Neoplasm, skin, limb, lower*	C44.70-	C79.2	D04.7-	D23.7-	D48.5	D49.2
- - helix—*see also Neoplasm, skin, ear*	C44.20-	C79.2	D04.2-	D23.2-	D48.5	D49.2
- - hip—*see also Neoplasm, skin, limb, lower*	C44.70-	C79.2	D04.7-	D23.7-	D48.5	D49.2
- - infraclavicular region—*see also Neoplasm, skin, trunk*	C44.509	C79.2	D04.5	D23.5	D48.5	D49.2

FIGURE 7-6B Alphabetic Index Entry for Neoplasm, skin, chin, as it appears in the Table of Neoplasms.

- The column for **malignant primary** is used when the neoplasm originated from the site being coded.

- The column for **malignant secondary** is used when the neoplasm metastasized or spread to the site being coded.

- Ca in situ is used when the pathological report or diagnostic statement records ca in situ.

From the Neoplasm Table, select the code listed for the entry of skin, face, basal cell carcinoma. Here, code C44.310 appears. Now the coder must reference the Tabular List to verify the code selected (see Figure 7-7).

C44.3 Other and unspecified malignant neoplasm of skin of other and unspecified parts of face

    C44.30 Unspecified malignant neoplasm of skin of other and unspecified parts of face

        C44.300 Unspecified malignant neoplasm of skin of unspecified part of face

        C44.301 Unspecified malignant neoplasm of skin of nose

        C44.309 Unspecified malignant neoplasm of skin of other parts of face

    C44.31 Basal cell carcinoma of skin of other and unspecified parts of face

        C44.310 Basal cell carcinoma of skin of unspecified parts of face

        C44.311 Basal cell carcinoma of skin of nose

        C44.319 Basal cell carcinoma of skin of other parts of face

FIGURE 7-7 Tabular List for Basal Cell Carcinoma.

Verifying the code of C44.310, the coder should note that this code is for an unspecified part of the face. Therefore, code C44.319 should be selected since the documentation has specified the part of the face.

Exercise 7.2—Coding for Neoplasms

For each diagnostic statement listed, select the appropriate code.

1. subependymal glioma _____
2. malignant neoplasm of skin of breast _____
3. ca of lung _____
4. ceruminous adenocarcinoma _____
5. metastatic carcinoma to lung _____
6. liposarcoma of the left shoulder _____
7. pheochromocytoma (benign) of the adrenal gland _____
8. metastatic tumor to the common bile duct _____
9. amelobastic odontoma _____
10. fibromyoma of the uterus _____
11. neoplasm, benign, of left lacrimal gland and duct _____
12. malignant neoplasm of retroperitoneum _____
13. tonsillar fossa neoplasm malignant _____
14. bronchial carcinoma (right lower lobe) _____
15. benign neoplasm of brain _____

Sequencing of Codes

When coding for the treatment of neoplasms, a coder must read the patient's record to determine the reason for the visit or admission. The coder must then sequence codes based on the ICD-10-CM Official Guidelines and the documentation found in the patient's record.

Malignancy as Principal Diagnosis

If the focus of the patient's visit is to treat the neoplasm, then the neoplasm is sequenced as the principal diagnosis, unless the treatment is solely for the administration of chemotherapy, immunotherapy or external beam radiation therapy. (The specific guidelines for coding encounters or admissions involving chemotherapy, immunotherapy or external beam radiation are discussed later in this chapter.) If a patient with cancer is seen for an acute or chronic condition and the treatment is focused on that condition, then the acute or chronic condition becomes the principal diagnosis.

ICD-10-CM Official Coding Guidelines

a. Treatment directed at a malignancy

If the treatment is directed at the malignancy, designate the malignancy as the principal diagnosis. The only exception to this guideline is if a patient admission/encounter is solely for the administration of chemotherapy, immunotherapy or external beam radiation therapy, assign the appropriate Z51.— code as the first-listed or principal diagnosis, and the diagnosis or problem for which the service is being performed as a secondary diagnosis. (See Appendix A, Section I, C2, a.)

Courtesy of the Centers for Medicare & Medicaid Services, www.cms.gov

EXAMPLE: On May 1, Sally Jones is admitted to Hill Top Hospital with a blood sugar level of 375. The following diagnoses are on the face sheet at admission: carcinoma of the breast, uncontrolled insulin-dependent diabetes, and hypertension. She is admitted to control the diabetes. For this admission, the diabetes is the principal diagnosis.

The same patient is admitted on September 1 for a mastectomy due to carcinoma of the breast. Although her medical condition also includes insulin-dependent diabetes and hypertension, on this admission the principal diagnosis is the carcinoma of the breast.

Eradication of Malignancy and Follow-Up Examinations

Cancer patients are monitored on a regular basis for recurrence or metastasis. Code selection is based on the status of the patient at the time of the encounter.

Treatment Followed by Recurrence

When a patient is treated for a malignancy, whether it is with chemotherapy, radiation, or surgery, and there is evidence that the cancer has recurred, the primary malignancy is the principal diagnosis.

Excised Malignancy Followed by Recurrence

When a previously excised malignancy recurs, the code for the malignancy is used for the principal diagnosis.

Follow-Up Visit with No Recurrence

Follow-up Z code category Z08, Encounter for follow-up examination after completed treatment for malignant neoplasm, is used when a patient is seen for follow-up after undergoing surgery, chemotherapy, radiation, or other treatment and when no evidence of a recurrence or metastasis exists. The follow-up Z codes are used to explain the continuing monitoring of the patient. This code implies that the neoplastic condition has been fully treated and no longer exists. The follow-up code explains the repeated visits. The Tabular List entry for Z08 is shown in Figure 7-8.

Z08 Encounter for follow-up examination after completed treatment for malignant neoplasm

Medical surveillance following completed treatment

Use additional code to identify any acquired absence of organs (Z90.-)

Use additional code to identify the personal history of malignant neoplasm (Z85.-)

Excludes1: aftercare following medical care (Z43-Z49, Z51)

FIGURE 7-8 Tabular List entry for Z08.

Two Primary Sites

In some malignant cancer cases, two primary sites are present. The coder must determine whether the treatment is directed at one site or at both.

- When the treatment is directed at one site, that site should be designated as the principal diagnosis.
- When the treatment is directed at both sites, either site can be designated as the principal diagnosis.

EXAMPLE: Tom Top has a diagnosis of primary carcinoma of the esophagus and primary carcinoma of the stomach. On February 1, he was admitted for partial removal of carcinogenic esophageal tissue. There was no treatment for the carcinoma of the stomach. In this case the principal diagnosis is the primary carcinoma of the esophagus (C15.9). On May 1, he was admitted for removal of the tissue of the esophagus and stomach due to carcinoma. Because the treatment was directed at two primary sites, either site can be used as the principal diagnosis (C15.9 or C16.9).

Primary and Secondary Malignancies

When a patient has both primary and secondary malignancies, the coder must determine the focus of treatment to ensure correct code sequencing. Patients with primary and secondary malignancies can be admitted or seen to:

- Address the primary malignancy only.
- Address the secondary malignancy only.
- Address both the primary and secondary malignancies.
- Address the secondary site when a primary site has been excised or eradicated.

Primary Malignancy Only

When the primary malignancy is the only condition treated, designate the primary malignancy as the principal diagnosis.

Secondary Malignancy Only

When treatment is directed only at the secondary, or metastatic malignancy, the secondary site is designated as the principal diagnosis, unless the admission is for chemotherapy, immunotherapy or radiotherapy. An additional code is assigned for the primary site.

ICD-10-CM Official Coding Guidelines

b. Treatment of secondary site

When a patient is admitted because of a primary neoplasm with metastasis and treatment is directed toward the secondary site only, the secondary neoplasm is designated as the principal diagnosis even though the primary malignancy is still present. (See Appendix A, Section I, C2, b.)

EXAMPLE: Bob Pint is admitted for removal of a metastatic tumor of the spinal cord that has metastasized from the lung. The secondary malignant tumor of the spinal cord is the principal diagnosis, and the primary malignant cancer of the lung is used as an additional code.

Primary and Secondary Malignancy

When the treatment is directed equally at both primary and secondary malignancies, the primary malignancy is sequenced as the principal diagnosis and the secondary malignancy is sequenced as an additional code.

> **EXAMPLE:** Nate Newman was admitted to the hospital for surgery on a malignant tumor of the pancreas and a malignant tumor of the spleen, which had been discovered with the latest CT scan done before admission. The tumor of the spleen is believed to have metastasized from the pancreas, but this will be confirmed when the pathology report comes back after surgery.
>
> In this case, the pancreatic tumor has already been diagnosed, making it the primary malignancy. The tumor in the spleen is a new tumor that is going to be removed during the same surgery and is coded as a secondary diagnosis.

Secondary Sites with Excision or Eradication of Primary Site

A patient may undergo treatment for a primary site that could include excision, chemotherapy, immunotherapy, or radiation therapy. After such treatment, the site may show no evidence of any existing primary malignancy, and therefore further treatment is not directed at the primary site. Treatment may then be directed at the secondary site. The secondary site is then used as the principal diagnosis, and the former primary site is assigned a code from category Z85, Personal history of malignant neoplasm. The start of category Z85 appears in the Tabular Listing, as shown in Figure 7-9.

> **EXAMPLE:** Steve Smith was treated for carcinoma of the gallbladder with metastasis to the lungs. In January, he underwent removal of the gallbladder, and currently there is no evidence of the carcinoma in the biliary area. He is now being admitted for removal of his left lung due to cancer. The secondary site of the lung cancer is coded and sequenced first, and the previous primary site is coded to Z85.09, Personal history of malignant neoplasm of other digestive organs.

Coders should be cautious when looking up "personal history of a malignant neoplasm" in the Alphabetic Index. Be sure to pay particular attention to the indentations, because there is also a category for family history of malignant neoplasms. Figures 7-10 and 7-11 compare the two Alphabetic Listing entries for family and personal history of malignant neoplasms.

Z85 Personal history of malignant neoplasm

Code first any follow-up examination after treatment of malignant neoplasm (Z08).
Use additional code to identify:

    alcohol use and dependence (F10.-)
    exposure to environmental tobacco smoke (Z77.22)
    history of tobacco dependence (Z87.891)
    occupational exposure to environmental tobacco smoke (Z57.31)
    tobacco dependence (F17.-)
    tobacco use (Z72.0)

Excludes2: personal history of benign neoplasm (Z86.01-)
          personal history of carcinoma-in-situ (Z86.00-)

Courtesy of the Centers for Medicare & Medicaid Services, www.cms.gov

FIGURE 7-9 Tabular Listing for Z85.

History

- family (of) - see also History, personal (of)

    alcohol abuse Z81.1

    allergy NEC Z84.89

    anemia Z83.2

    arthritis Z82.61

↓

    hearing loss Z82.2

    human immunodeficiency virus (HIV) infection Z83.0

    Huntington's chorea Z82.0

    hyperlipidemia, familial combined Z83.438

    intellectual disability Z81.0

    leukemia Z80.6

    malignant neoplasm (of) NOS Z80.9

        bladder Z80.52

        breast Z80.3

        bronchus Z80.1

        digestive organ Z80.0

        gastrointestinal tract Z80.0

        genital organ Z80.49

            ovary Z80.41

            prostate Z80.42

            specified organ NEC Z80.49

            testis Z80.43

        hematopoietic NEC Z80.7

        intrathoracic organ NEC Z80.2

        kidney Z80.51

        lung Z80.1

        lymphatic NEC Z80.7

        ovary Z80.41

        prostate Z80.42

        respiratory organ NEC Z80.2

        specified site NEC Z80.8

        testis Z80.43

        trachea Z80.1

        urinary organ or tract Z80.59

            bladder Z80.52

            kidney Z80.51

    mental

        disorder NEC Z81.8

FIGURE 7-10 Alphabetical Listing for family history.

History-continued
    personal (of)
        irradiation Z92.3
        kidney stones Z87.442
        latent tuberculosis infection Z86.15
        leukemia Z85.6
        lymphoma (non-Hodgkin's) Z85.72
        malignant melanoma (skin) Z85.820
        malignant neoplasm (of) Z85.9
            accessory sinuses Z85.22
            anus NEC Z85.048
                carcinoid Z85.040
            bladder Z85.51
            bone Z85.830
            brain Z85.841
            breast Z85.3
            bronchus Z85.118

FIGURE 7-11 Alphabetical Entry for personal history of malignant neoplasm.

ICD-10-CM Official Coding Guidelines

d. Primary malignancy previously excised

When a primary malignancy has been previously excised or eradicated from its site and there is no further treatment directed to that site, and there is no evidence of any existing primary malignancy at that site, a code from category Z85, Personal history of malignant neoplasm should be used to indicate the former site of the malignancy. Any mention of extension, invasion, or metastasis to another site is coded as a secondary malignant neoplasm to that site. The secondary site may be the principal or first-listed diagnosis with the Z85 code used as a secondary code. (See Appendix A, Section I, C2, d.)

Coders should also be guided by the following guidelines when coding current malignancy versus personal history of malignancy, aftercare and follow-up care, and malignant neoplasm associated with a transplanted organ.

ICD-10-CM Official Coding Guidelines

m. Current malignancy versus personal history of malignancy

When a primary malignancy has been excised, but further treatment, such as an additional surgery for the malignancy, radiation therapy or chemotherapy is directed to that site, the primary malignancy code should be used until treatment is completed.

When a primary malignancy has been previously excised or eradicated from its site, there is no further treatment (of the malignancy) directed to that site, and there is no evidence of any existing primary malignancy at that site, a code from category Z85, Personal history of malignant neoplasm, should be used to indicate the former site of the malignancy.

Codes from subcategories Z85.0 – Z85.85 should only be assigned for the former site of a primary malignancy, not the site of a secondary malignancy. Code Z85.89 may be assigned for the former site(s) of either a primary or secondary malignancy.

See Section I.C.21. Factors influencing health status and contact with health services, History (of)

n. Leukemia, Multiple Myeloma, and Malignant Plasma Cell Neoplasms in remission versus personal history

The categories for leukemia, and category C90, Multiple myeloma and malignant plasma cell neoplasms, have codes indicating whether or not the leukemia has achieved remission. There are also codes Z85.6, Personal history of leukemia, and Z85.79, Personal history of other malignant neoplasms of lymphoid, hematopoietic and related tissues. If the documentation is unclear, as to whether the leukemia has achieved remission, the provider should be queried.

See Section I.C.21. Factors influencing health status and contact with health services, History (of)

o. Aftercare following surgery for neoplasm

See Section I.C.21. Factors influencing health status and contact with health services, Aftercare

p. Follow-up care for completed treatment of a malignancy

See Section I.C.21. Factors influencing health status and contact with health services, Follow-up

q. Prophylactic organ removal for prevention of malignancy

See Section I.C. 21, Factors influencing health status and contact with health services, Prophylactic organ removal

r. Malignant neoplasm associated with transplanted organ

A malignant neoplasm of a transplanted organ should be coded as a transplant complication. Assign first the appropriate code from category T86.-, Complications of transplanted organs and tissue, followed by code C80.2, Malignant neoplasm associated with transplanted organ. Use an additional code for the specific malignancy.

(See Appendix A Section I, C2, m-r.)

Malignancy in Two or More Noncontiguous Sites

The following coding guideline should be followed when a patient has a malignancy in two or more noncontiguous sites:

ICD-10-CM Official Coding Guidelines

i. Malignancy in two or more noncontiguous sites

A patient may have more than one malignant tumor in the same organ. These tumors may represent different primaries or metastatic disease, depending on the site. Should the documentation be unclear, the provider should be queried as to the status of each tumor so that the correct codes can be assigned. (See Appendix A, Section I, C2, i.)

Unspecified Disseminated Malignant Neoplasm

In cases when a patient has advanced metastatic disease and no known primary or secondary sites are specified, the following coding guideline should be followed:

ICD-10-CM Official Coding Guidelines

j. Disseminated malignant neoplasm, unspecified

Code C80.0, Disseminated malignant neoplasm, unspecified, is for use only in those cases where the patient has advanced metastatic disease and no known primary or secondary sites are specified. It should not be used in place of assigning codes for the primary site and all known secondary sites. (See Appendix A, Section I, C2, j.)

Malignant Neoplasm Without Specification of Site

When the medical record of the patient does not designate the site of a malignant neoplasm, the following guideline gives direction to the coder:

ICD-10-CM Official Coding Guidelines

k. Malignant Neoplasm Without Specification of Site

Code C80.1, Malignant (primary) neoplasm, unspecified, equates to Cancer, unspecified. This code should only be used when no determination can be made as to the primary site of a malignancy. This code should rarely be used in the inpatient setting. (See Appendix A, Section I, C2, k.)

Additional Coding Guidelines for Sequencing of Neoplasm Codes

The following coding guidelines also appear in the Official ICD-10-CM Coding Guidelines for the sequencing of neoplasm codes and should be referenced before coding assignment is completed:

ICD-10-CM Official Coding Guidelines

l. Sequencing of neoplasm codes

1) Encounter for treatment of primary malignancy

If the reason for the encounter is for treatment of a primary malignancy, assign the malignancy as the principal/first listed diagnosis. The primary site is to be sequenced first, followed by any metastatic sites.

2) Encounter for treatment of secondary malignancy

When an encounter is for a primary malignancy with metastasis and treatment is directed toward the metastatic (secondary) site(s) only, the metastatic site(s) is designated as the principal/first listed diagnosis. The primary malignancy is coded as an additional code.

3) Malignant neoplasm in a pregnant patient

When a pregnant woman has a malignant neoplasm, a code from subcategory O9A.1- Malignant neoplasm complicating pregnancy, childbirth, and the puerperium, should be sequenced first, followed by the appropriate code from Chapter 2 to indicate the type of neoplasm.

4) Encounter for complication associated with a neoplasm

When an encounter is for management of a complication associated with a neoplasm, such as dehydration, and the treatment is only for the complication, the complication is coded first, followed by the appropriate code(s) for the neoplasm. The exception to this guideline is anemia. When the admission/encounter is for management of an anemia associated with the malignancy, and the treatment is only for anemia, the appropriate code for the malignancy is sequenced as the principal or first-listed diagnosis followed by code D63.0, Anemia in neoplastic disease.

5) Complication from surgical procedure for treatment of a neoplasm

When an encounter is for treatment of a complication resulting from a surgical procedure performed for the treatment of the neoplasm, designate the complication as the principal/first listed diagnosis. See the guideline regarding the coding of a current malignancy versus personal history to determine if the code for the neoplasm should also be assigned.

6) Pathologic fracture due to a neoplasm

When an encounter is for a pathological fracture due to a neoplasm, and the focus of treatment is the fracture, a code from subcategory M84.5, Pathological fracture in neoplastic disease, should be sequenced first, followed by the code for the neoplasm. If the focus of treatment is the neoplasm with an associated pathological fracture, the neoplasm code should be sequenced first, followed by a code from M84.5 for the pathological fracture. (See Appendix A, Section I, C2, l 1–6.)

Complications Associated with Neoplasms

Numerous complications are associated with malignant neoplasms and their treatment. Patients commonly seek health care that is directed at the treatment of the complications, not at the treatment of the neoplasm.

Anemia

Cancer patients can experience anemia, a deficiency of the red blood cells, caused by the malignancy or chemotherapy. When encounters or admissions occur for the management of the anemia, the following coding guidelines should be followed:

ICD-10-CM Official Coding Guidelines

1. Anemia associated with malignancy

When the admission/encounter is for management of an anemia associated with the malignancy and the treatment is only for anemia, the appropriate code for the malignancy is sequenced as the principal or first-listed diagnosis followed by the appropriate code for the anemia (such as code D63.0, Anemia in neoplastic disease).

2. Anemia associated with chemotherapy, immunotherapy and radiation therapy

When the admission/encounter is for management of an anemia associated with an adverse effect of the administration of chemotherapy or immunotherapy and the only treatment is for the anemia, the anemia code is sequenced first, followed by the appropriate codes for the neoplasm and the adverse effect (T45.1X5, Adverse effect of antineoplastic and immunosuppressive drugs).

When the admission/encounter is for management of an anemia associated with an adverse effect of radiotherapy, the anemia code should be sequenced first, followed by the appropriate neoplasm code and code Y84.2, Radiological procedure and radiotherapy as the cause of abnormal reaction of the patient, or of later complication, without mention of misadventure at the time of the procedure. (See Appendix A, Section I, C2, c, 1–2.)

EXAMPLE: Patty Pink is diagnosed with carcinoma of the breast and is undergoing chemotherapy. She has developed anemia associated with an adverse effect of the chemotherapy and is being admitted for treatment of the anemia only. Because she is being admitted for the management of the anemia associated with an adverse effect of the administration of the chemotherapy and the only treatment is for the anemia, the anemia code is sequenced first, followed by the appropriate codes for the neoplasm and the adverse effect (T45.1X5-, Adverse effect of antineoplastic and immunosuppressive drugs.)

Dehydration

Dehydration, the excess loss of fluids, is also a complication that can occur due to vomiting and diarrhea caused by the malignancy, chemotherapy, or radiation therapy. When a patient has experienced dehydration, an encounter or admission may be necessary to rehydrate the patient.

EXAMPLE: Sally Smith has been undergoing radiation therapy for leukemia on an outpatient basis. She has experienced diarrhea and vomiting, and she is now dehydrated. Her physician is admitting her to Sunny Hill Hospital to receive intravenous rehydration. In this case, the dehydration is sequenced as the principal diagnosis, followed by a code for the leukemia.

ICD-10-CM Official Coding Guidelines

3. Management of dehydration due to the malignancy

When the admission/encounter is for management of dehydration due to the malignancy and only the dehydration is being treated (intravenous rehydration), the dehydration is sequenced first, followed by the code(s) for the malignancy. (See Appendix A, Section I, C2, c, 3.)

Surgical Procedure Performed for Treatment of a Malignancy

Sometimes a malignancy requires surgical intervention. A complication that results from the surgery is coded as the primary diagnosis when an admission or encounter is needed.

EXAMPLE: Amanda Pan had surgery on a malignant tumor of the small intestine. One month after the surgery, Amanda developed an infection that required treatment with antibiotics as an inpatient. The infection is designated as the principal diagnosis.

ICD-10-CM Official Coding Guidelines

4. Treatment of a complication resulting from a surgical procedure

When the admission/encounter is for treatment of a complication resulting from a surgical procedure, designate the complication as the principal or first-listed diagnosis if treatment is directed at resolving the complication. (See Appendix A, Section I, C2, c, 4.)

Courtesy of the Centers for Medicare & Medicaid Services, www.cms.gov

Pain

As the malignancy progresses and as treatment occurs, cancer patients sometimes experience pain that can result in depression, anxiety, difficulty sleeping, and loss of appetite. Narcotic medications may be necessary to control the pain. If a patient seeks medical care for the management of a neoplasm and the pain is present, the neoplasm code is designated as the principal diagnosis. This coding guideline, found in Chapter 6 of the ICD-10-CM Official Guidelines for Coding and Reporting, should be followed when assigning codes:

ICD-10-CM Official Coding Guidelines

Neoplasm Related Pain

Code G89.3 is assigned to pain documented as being related, associated or due to cancer, primary or secondary malignancy, or tumor. This code is assigned regardless of whether the pain is acute or chronic.

This code may be assigned as the principal or first-listed code when the stated reason for the admission/encounter is documented as pain control/pain management. The underlying neoplasm should be reported as an additional diagnosis.

When the reason for the admission/encounter is management of the neoplasm and the pain associated with the neoplasm is also documented, code G89.3 may be assigned as an additional diagnosis. It is not necessary to assign an additional code for the site of the pain.

See Section I.C.2 for instructions on the sequencing of neoplasms for all other stated reasons for the admission/encounter (except for pain control/pain management). (See Appendix A, Section I, C6, b, 5.)

Courtesy of the Centers for Medicare & Medicaid Services, www.cms.gov

Admissions and Encounters Involving Surgery, Chemotherapy, Immunotherapy, and Radiation Therapy

After a patient has been diagnosed with a malignant condition, treatment options can include surgery, chemotherapy, immunotherapy, radiation therapy, or a combination of treatments. A coder must identify the treatment occurring during the current encounter or admission.

Surgery Followed by Chemotherapy or Radiation

In some cases, a patient will undergo surgery to remove the cancerous tissue and then undergo chemotherapy or radiation.

EXAMPLE: Sally Pink, who was diagnosed with carcinoma of the breast, is admitted for a total mastectomy followed by radiation therapy. In this case, the carcinoma of the breast is the principal diagnosis.

ICD-10-CM Official Coding Guidelines

1. Episode of care involves surgical removal of neoplasm

When an episode of care involves the surgical removal of a neoplasm, primary or secondary site, followed by adjunct chemotherapy or radiation treatment during the same episode of care, the code for the neoplasm should be assigned as principal or first-listed diagnosis. (See Appendix A, Section I, C2, e, 1.)

Courtesy of the Centers for Medicare & Medicaid Services, www.cms.gov

Encounter or Admission Solely for Administration of Chemotherapy, Immunotherapy, or Radiation

The Official Coding Guidelines provide instructions in selecting codes for encounters or admissions solely for the administration of chemotherapy, immunotherapy, and radiation therapy.

ICD-10-CM Official Coding Guidelines

2. Patient admission/encounter solely for administration of chemotherapy, immunotherapy and radiation therapy

If a patient admission/encounter is solely for the administration of chemotherapy, immunotherapy or external beam radiation therapy assign code Z51.0, Encounter for antineoplastic radiation therapy, or Z51.11, Encounter for antineoplastic chemotherapy, or Z51.12, Encounter for antineoplastic immunotherapy as the first-listed or principal diagnosis. If a patient receives more than one of these therapies during the same admission more than one of these codes may be assigned, in any sequence.

The malignancy for which the therapy is being administered should be assigned as a secondary diagnosis.

If a patient admission/encounter is for the insertion or implantation of radioactive elements (e.g., brachytherapy) the appropriate code for the malignancy is sequenced as the principal or first-listed diagnosis. Code Z51.0 should not be assigned. (See Appendix A, Section I, C2, e, 2.)

Courtesy of the Centers for Medicare & Medicaid Services, www.cms.gov

EXAMPLE: Mary Ann Jones is admitted for chemotherapy for plasma cell leukemia. The principal diagnostic code listed first is Z51.11, Encounter for antineoplastic chemotherapy. A code for the plasma cell leukemia is also assigned as an additional code.

EXAMPLE: Mary Ann Jones's physician decides not only to have her receive chemotherapy, but also, to follow up the treatment with radiation therapy. Codes Z51.0, Encounter for antineoplastic radiation therapy, and Z51.11, Encounter for antineoplastic chemotherapy, should be used. Either can be sequenced first.

Radiation Therapy, Chemotherapy, or Immunotherapy Followed by Complications

It is common for patients to experience nausea, vomiting, and dehydration after chemotherapy, immunotherapy, or radiation therapy. When a patient is admitted for the purpose of chemotherapy, immunotherapy, or radiation and subsequently develops a complication, the following coding guideline offers coding guidance:

ICD-10-CM Official Coding Guidelines

3. Patient admitted for radiation therapy, chemotherapy, or immunotherapy and develops complications

When a patient is admitted for the purpose of external beam radiotherapy, immunotherapy, or chemotherapy and develops complications such as uncontrolled nausea and vomiting or dehydration, the principal or first-listed diagnosis is Z51.0, Encounter for antineoplastic radiation therapy, or Z51.11, Encounter for antineoplastic chemotherapy, or Z51.12, Encounter for antineoplastic immunotherapy followed by any codes for the complications.

When a patient is admitted for the purpose of insertion or implantation of radioactive elements (e.g., brachytherapy) and develops complications such as uncontrolled nausea and vomiting or dehydration, the principal or first-listed diagnosis is the appropriate code for the malignancy followed by any codes for the complications. (See Appendix A, Section I, C2, e, 3.)

Courtesy of the Centers for Medicare & Medicaid Services, www.cms.gov

EXAMPLE: Sally Jones is admitted for radiation therapy for blast cell leukemia. Immediately after the treatment, she develops nausea and excessive vomiting, for which she is treated. Code Z51.0, Encounter for antineoplastic radiation therapy, is sequenced first, followed by C95.00 for the blast cell leukemia and R11.2, Nausea and vomiting.

Admission or Encounter to Determine Extent of Malignancy or to Perform a Procedure

When an admission or encounter occurs to determine the extent of malignancy or to perform a procedure, the following guideline should be followed:

ICD-10-CM Official Coding Guidelines

f. Admission/encounter to determine extent of malignancy

When the reason for the admission/encounter is to determine the extent of the malignancy, or for a procedure such as paracentesis or thoracentesis, the primary malignancy or appropriate metastatic site is designated as the principal or first-listed diagnosis, even though chemotherapy or radiotherapy is administered. (See Appendix A, Section I, C2, f.)

Courtesy of the Centers for Medicare & Medicaid Services, www.cms.gov

A paracentesis is a surgical puncture of the abdominal cavity for the aspiration of fluid. A thoracentesis is a surgical procedure for the aspiration of fluid from the chest wall.

Symptoms, Signs and Abnormal Findings Listed in Chapter 18 (of ICD-10-CM) Associated with Neoplasms, and Admission/Encounter for Pain Control/Management

The following ICD-CM Official guidelines govern the coding of symptoms, signs and abnormal findings associated with neoplasms and admission/encounters for pain control/management.

ICD-10-CM Official Coding Guidelines

g. Symptoms, signs, and abnormal findings listed in Chapter 18 associated with neoplasms.

Symptoms, signs, and ill-defined conditions listed in Chapter 18 (of ICD-10-CM) characteristic of, or associated with, an existing primary or secondary site malignancy cannot be used to replace the malignancy as principal or first-listed diagnosis, regardless of the number of admissions or encounters for treatment and care of the neoplasm.

See Section I.C.21, Factors influencing health status and contact with health services, Encounter for prophylactic organ removal.

h. Admission/encounter for pain control/management

See Section I.C.6 for information on coding admission/encounter for pain control/management.

The specific guideline for neoplasm related pain is found earlier in this chapter under the heading of Pain.

Summary

- ICD-10-CM codes neoplastic conditions to code range C00–D49.
- Neoplasms are classified as malignant, benign, cancer in situ, of uncertain behavior, or unspecified.
- A biopsy is completed to determine whether a neoplasm is malignant or benign.
- Carcinoma in situ is defined as neoplastic cells undergoing malignant changes that are confined to the original epithelium site without invading surrounding tissues.
- Neoplasms of uncertain behavior include cases in which the neoplasm exhibits characteristics of both benign and malignant behavior.
- Neoplasms of unspecified behavior include cases in which the behavior or morphology of the neoplasm is not specified in the patient's medical record.
- In the Alphabetic Index, codes for neoplasms are located by referencing the name of the neoplasm and by using the Neoplasm Table.
- Sequencing of codes for neoplasms depends on the reason for the encounter or admission.

Internet Links

For information about approved cancer drugs, go to **www.fda.gov/Drugs/default.htm** and search on the words "cancer drugs".

For information on cancer, visit the American Cancer Society website at **www.cancer.org**.

For information on cancer research, visit **www.cancer.gov/research**.

For information on types of cancer, treatments, and other information about the disease, visit **www.CancerCenter.com**.

Chapter Review

True/False

Indicate whether each statement is true (T) or false (F).

1. _____ There is no differentiation between malignant and benign neoplasms in ICD-10-CM.

2. _____ Lipoma and chondroma are malignant neoplasms.

3. _____ Carcinoma of the breast is malignant.

4. _____ Code block D10–D36 reports benign neoplasms except benign neuroendocrine tumors.

5. _____ In the Neoplasm Table, benign neoplasms are divided into primary and secondary sites.

6. _____ When a patient is seen for chemotherapy, the neoplasm is sequenced as the principal diagnosis.

7. _____ If treatment is directed at a malignancy and the patient is also treated for an acute condition, the malignancy is designated as the principal diagnosis.

8. _____ When an encounter is for management of a complication associated with a neoplasm, such as dehydration, and the treatment is only for the complication, the complication is coded first, followed by the appropriate code(s) for the neoplasm.

9. _____ Narcotic medications are used to control the pain of cancer patients.

10. _____ When an encounter is for treatment of a complication resulting from a surgical procedure performed for the treatment of the neoplasm, designate the complication as the principal, first-listed diagnosis.

Coding Assignments

Instructions: Using an ICD-10-CM code book, assign the proper diagnosis code to the following diagnostic statements.

1. carcinoma of mouth _____

2. adenocarcinoma of adrenal cortical _____

3. lipoma _____

4. leiomyoma of uterus _____

5. neoplasm of anterior wall of urinary bladder, malignant _____

6. plasma cell leukemia _____

7. B cell lymphoma; intrapelvic lymph nodes _____

8. acute promyelocytic leukemia _____

9. secondary malignant neoplasm of skin of the chin _____

10. carcinoma of uterine cervix _____

11. malignant neoplasm of orbital bone _____

12. carcinoma in situ of bladder _____

13. primary neoplasm of ovary _____

14. secondary cancer of islet cells of pancreas _____

15. cancer of prostate gland _____

16. neoplasm of uncertain behavior of renal pelvis _____

17. basal cell carcinoma of skin on scalp _____

18. plasma cell tumor _____

19. Wilm's nephroblastoma _____

20. benign neoplasm of abdomen _____

21. benign neoplasm of the bursa of the shoulder _____

22. CIS of the rectosigmoid junction _____

23. malignant neoplasm of the adrenal gland (left side) with
    metastasis to the kidney and renal pelvis   _____

24. metastatic cancer from the bladder dome to the ureter   _____

25. cancer of the stomach (fundus)   _____

26. endometrial sarcoma   _____

27. multiple myeloma   _____

28. lipoma of right kidney   _____

29. right lung cancer   _____

30. chronic myeloid leukemia   _____

Case Studies

Instructions: Review each case study and select the correct ICD-10-CM diagnostic code.

Case 1

Physician Office Note

4/25/XX Weight: 154 pounds, decrease from 2 weeks ago; weight then was 160.

CHIEF COMPLAINT: loss of weight, here for follow-up from breast biopsy.

Sally was seen 2 weeks ago, and I palpated a mass in her left breast. She was sent for a biopsy. She is here today for follow-up.

BREAST: Mass present in left breast; right breast has no masses present.

ABDOMEN: Normal, no masses or tenderness.

The patient is anxious about results of biopsy.

Pathology report reviewed with patient that confirmed cancer of central portion, left breast. The patient was referred to Dr. Smith at West Oncology.

ICD-10-CM Code Assignment: _____

Case 2

Inpatient Discharge Summary

HISTORY OF PRESENT ILLNESS: The patient is a 76-year-old with a known history of cancer of the lung with metastasis to the brain.

Cancer of lung was resected 6 months ago. The patient was admitted because his daughter noticed him getting weaker and because he was not eating or drinking well for the last 2 days. He has undergone chemotherapy and radiation in the past 5 months, and he has asked for the treatment to be stopped.

(continues)

(continued)

Upon examination at the time of admission, he was dehydrated and weak due to lack of eating.

HOSPITAL COURSE: The patient requested that he receive care only for his dehydration. He was given IV hydration and refused all other treatment.

MEDICATIONS AT DISCHARGE: The patient was discharged on Vicodin for pain management, 1 every 4 hours as needed for pain.

DISCHARGE DIAGNOSES: Dehydration, metastatic cancer to the brain; history of lung cancer

ICD-10-CM Code Assignment: _____

Case 3

Oncology Clinic Note

The patient was seen today to receive his first chemotherapy treatment for his diagnosis of acute lymphoid leukemia.

EXAM:

VITALS: Temperature 98.9, B/P 125/80. Pulse: regular.

LUNGS: Normal

ABDOMEN: Soft, no masses noted.

HEENT: Normal

HEART: Normal rate and rhythm

Chemotherapy schedule was reviewed, and side effects of treatment were discussed. Chemotherapy was given; the patient tolerated treatment well.

ICD-10-CM Code Assignment: _____

Case 4

Clinic Visit

Ellen is a 65-year-old female who presents today with severe headaches and blurred vision. She said these symptoms have been going on for approximately 2 weeks. She says that the pain is 10 out of 10 and that nothing seems to help relieve it. She has a history of breast cancer, which has been in remission for 1 year. A CT scan of the head and neck reveals a tumor in the temporal lobe of the brain.

A biopsy was performed and confirmed this to be a metastasis from the breast tumor.

ICD-10-CM Code Assignment: _____

Case 5

Clinic Visit

A 52-year-old female presented with a 1-year history of epiphora. During this year, the tears were not bloodstained but very much a nuisance to the patient. CT revealed a small tumor connected to the right lacrimal sac and duct. Incisional biopsy revealed a benign tumor of the right lacrimal sac. The patient was treated by removing the tumor.

ICD-10-CM Code Assignment: _____

Case 6

Emergency Department Visit

A 59-year-old male presented to the ED with dyspnea on exertion, fevers, and cough. A routine chest x-ray was completed to rule out pneumonia. The x-ray revealed a mass in the left lung. The patient was instructed to follow up with Dr. Ram in oncology.

Diagnosis: Probable neoplastic lung disease

ICD-10-CM Code Assignment: _____

Case 7

Inpatient Admission

A 40-year-old female was admitted with severe abdominal pain. She has a history of cervical cancer that was excised 4 years ago. An MRI showed possible metastasis to the left ovary, which was confirmed during this admission as ovarian carcinoma, malignant secondary site.

ICD-10-CM Code Assignment: _____

Case 8

Inpatient Admission

This 89-year-old female patient was transferred from a nursing home due to a suspected urinary bladder mass, after she underwent a series of diagnostic tests that concluded that she has malignant primary adenocarcinoma of the posterior wall of the urinary bladder. She has requested no treatment and was discharged to hospice care.

ICD-10-CM Code Assignment: _____

Case 9

Office Visit Note

This 65-year-old female patient will return to the office today for follow-up for her breast cancer. The cancer was treated 3 years ago, via a bilateral mastectomy, and at this time, she is showing no signs of recurrence or metastasis. Vital signs as recorded by nurse.

Heart: Normal rate and rhythm

Lungs: Clear

Abdomen: Soft, nontender, no masses

Assessment: status post mastectomy, no recurrence at this time.

Plan: Follow-up in 6 months.

ICD-10-CM Coding Assignment: _____

Case 10

Office Note

This 35-year-old female patient is being seen today because she has been experiencing abdominal pain for the last month. She is concerned because her mother died of stomach cancer when she was 40 years old.

Vitals: B/P 120/75 Weight: 165 pounds.

The patient reports no weight loss.

HEENT: Normal

Heart: Normal rate and rhythm

Lungs: Clear, no rales.

Abdomen: No masses, no hepatomegaly or splenomegaly noted. Bowel sounds normal.

Breast: Symmetrical, no masses noted.

Plan: Orders as written for diagnostic testing.

The patient should follow up with me following test results.

ICD-10-CM Coding Assignment: _____

Diseases of the Blood and Blood-Forming Organs

Chapter Outline

Chapter Objectives

At the conclusion of this chapter, you should be able to:

1. List the three types of blood cells.
2. Identify functions of the blood, blood composition, and blood test values.
3. Identify diseases of the blood and blood-forming organs.
4. Explain the various types of anemia and the codes for each.
5. Accurately code diseases of the blood and blood-forming organs.
6. Select and code diagnoses from case studies.

Key Terms

Agammaglobulinemia	Erythrocytes	Lupus	Purpura
Agranulocytes	Folate	Methemoglobinemia	Red blood cells (RBC)
Alpha thalassemia	Folate deficient anemia	Myelophthisis	Sickle-cell anemia
Anemia	Granulocytes	Neutropenia	Sickle-cell trait
Angiohemophilia	Hemoglobin (Hgb)	Pancytopenia	Sideropenic dysphagia
Aplastic anemia	Hemolytic anemia	Pernicious anemia	Spleen
Beta thalassemia	Hereditary factor VIII	Plasma	Thalassemia
Coagulation	Idiopathic aplastic anemia	Platelets	Thrombocytes
Constitutional aplastic anemia		Polymorphonuclear neutrophils	Thrombocytopenia
	Immune system		Thrombophilia
Eosinophilia	Leukocytes	Pure red cell aplasia	Transcobalamin II

Vitamin B$_{12}$ deficiency
    anemia

Von Willebrand's
    disease

White blood cells
    (WBC)

> **REMINDER:** As you work through this chapter, you will need to have a copy of the ICD-10-CM coding book to reference. Please note that there are no ICD-10-CM Official Guidelines for Coding and Reporting for Chapter 3 of ICD-10-CM: Diseases of the Blood and Blood-forming Organs and Certain Disorders Involving the Immune Mechanism.

Introduction

Chapter 3 of ICD-10-CM contains diagnoses codes for nutritional anemias, hemolytic anemias, aplastic anemias, bone marrow failure syndromes, coagulation defects, purpura and other hemorrhagic conditions, and other types of disorders of the blood and blood-forming organs such as the spleen. This chapter also contains disorders involving the immune mechanisms, such as deficiency of immunoglobulin A, G, and M.

Abbreviations

The following abbreviations are commonly associated with the blood and blood-forming organs:

CBC	complete blood count
ESR	erythrocyte sedimentation rate
Hct	hematocrit
Hgb	hemoglobin
MPV	mean platelet volume
RBC	red blood cells
sed rate	erythrocyte sedimentation rate
WBC	white blood cells

Introduction to the Body System

Blood performs many functions in the body. The blood transports oxygen from the lungs to the cells and then moves waste from the cells to organs that dispose of the waste. Blood transports various nutrients throughout the body. Different fluids and electrolyte balance are maintained by the flow of the blood through the body. The interior of the body is also protected from infection by ability of the blood to clot, thereby keeping out infection and also preventing death due to excessive blood loss.

Blood Composition

The liquid portion of the blood, without its cellular elements, is known as **plasma**. The cellular elements in blood are erythrocytes (red blood cells), leukocytes (white blood cells), and thrombocytes (platelets). Red bone marrow produces three types of blood cells, which all originate from a stem cell. A stem cell becomes a red blood cell, a white blood cell, or a platelet.

Erythrocytes, also known as **red blood cells (RBC)**, form in the bone marrow. Red blood cells are disc-shaped and contain hemoglobin. **Hemoglobin (Hgb)** absorbs oxygen and transports it to the tissues of the body.

Leukocytes, also known as **white blood cells (WBC)**, work to protect the body from disease. Leukocytes contain no hemoglobin and are less numerous than RBCs. These cells have an irregular ball-like shape. Leukocytes are classified into two major groups: **granulocytes** (cells with a granular appearance) and **agranulocytes** (cells that are not granular). The various types of granulocytes and agranulocytes are as follows:

Type of Leukocyte	Specific Type of Granulocyte or Agranulocyte
Granulocyte	Neutrophils
	Eosinophils
	Basophils
Agranulocytes	Lymphocytes
	Monocytes

Thrombocytes, also called **platelets**, are ovoid-shaped structures that initiate blood clotting, or **coagulation**. A so-called platelet plug is formed by the body to stop bleeding when a cut or injury occurs. The platelet plug slows or stops bleeding, which in the worst case keeps the person from bleeding to death. Figure 8-1 illustrates the formed elements of the blood.

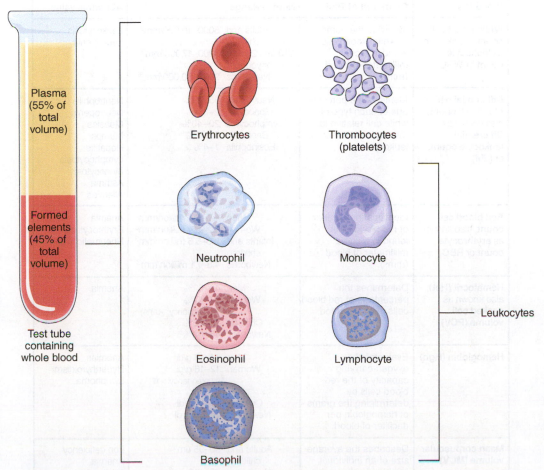

FIGURE 8-1 Formed elements of the blood (From Donald Rizzo, *Fundamentals of Anatomy and Physiology*, 2nd ed. (Clifton Park, NY: Delmar, 2003, Cengage Learning), p. 298.).

Coders should understand the components of blood and the terminology associated with it to be able to review blood-test reports and accurately substantiate the diagnosis code assigned. The reports provide the medical documentation to justify the medical necessity of the tests. Figure 8-2 provides a listing of normal ranges for blood tests.

Exercise 8.1—Blood Components

Match the term in the first column with the description in the second column.

_____ 1. granulocyte   a. protects the body from disease

_____ 2. plasma   b. ovoid-shaped cell, also called a platelet

_____ 3. bone marrow   c. neutrophil example of this type of leukocyte

_____ 4. thrombocyte   d. liquid portion of blood without cellular elements

_____ 5. white blood cell   e. where a RBC is formed

Blood Test	Definition of Test	Normal Range	Examples of Diseases Indicated by Abnormal Value
White blood cell count, also known as **leukocyte count** or **WBC**	Identifies the number of white blood cells found in a cubic millimeter of blood (mm³).	Adults and children 5000–10,000/mm³ Children 2 years or younger 6200–17,000/mm³ Newborns 9000–30,000/mm³	Leukocytosis Leukopenia
Differential white blood cell count, also known as **Differential leukocyte count**, or **(diff)**	Identifies the percentage of each type of white cell relative to the total number of leukocytes.	Neutrophils 55–70% Monocytes 2–8% Lymphocytes 20–40% Basophils 0.5–1% Eosinophils 1–4%	Neutrophilia Neutropenia Measles Mumps Hepatitis Lymphocytosis Monocytosis Asthma Allergies
Red blood cell count, also known as **erythrocyte count** or **RBC**	Identifies the number of red blood cells found in a cubic millimeter of blood (mm³).	Men 4.7–6.1 million/mm³ Women 4.2–5.4 million/mm³ Infants and children 3.8–5.5 million/mm³ Newborns 4.8–7.1 million/mm³	Anemia Erythrocytosis Rheumatic fever
Hematocrit (Hct) also known as **packed cell volume (PCV)**	Determines the percentage of red blood cells in whole blood.	Men 42–52% Women 37–47% (in pregnancy: >33%) Children 30–42% Newborns 44–64%	Anemia
Hemoglobin (Hgb)	Evaluates the oxygen-carrying capacity of the red blood cells by determining the grams of hemoglobin per deciliter of blood.	Men 14–18 g/dl Women 12–16 g/dl (in pregnancy: >11 g/dl) Children 11–16 g/dl Newborns 14–24 g/dl	Anemias Hyperthyroidism Lymphoma
Mean corpuscular volume (MCV)	Describes the average size of an individual red blood cell in cubic microns.	Adults and children 80–95 um³ Newborns 96–108 um³	Iron deficiency Anemia Thalassemia Pernicious anemia

FIGURE 8-2 Normal ranges for blood tests.

Mean corpuscular hemoglobin (MCH)	Identifies the average weight of hemoglobin in an average red blood cell reported in picograms (pg).	Adults and children 27–31 pg Newborns 32–38 pg	Macrocytic and Microcytic anemia
Mean corpuscular hemoglobin concentration (MCHC)	Measures the average concentration or percentage of hemoglobin within each red blood cell.	Adults and children 32–36% Newborns 32–33%	Hypochromic Anemia Spherocytosis
Erythrocyte sedimentation rate (ESR, sed rate)	Measures the rate at which red blood cells settle out of unclotted blood in an hour. Expressed as millimeters per hour (mm/hr).	Men <50 yrs 0–10 mm/hr Men >50 yrs 0–13 mm/hr Women <50 yrs 0–13 mm/hr Women >50 yrs 0–20 mm/hr Children 0–10 mm/hr	Polycythemia vera Sickle cell anemia
Platelet count	Measures the number of platelets per cubic millimeter of blood (mm^3).	Adults and children 150,000–400,00/mm^3	Thrombocytosis Thrombopenia
Mean platelet volume (MPV)	Measures the relative size of platelets expressed in micrometers.	Adults and children 2–4 um diameter	Systematic lupus Erythematosus Anemia

FIGURE 8-2 *(continued)*

Exercise 8.2—Blood Test Values

Using Figure 8-2, answer the following questions:

1. The normal range of a WBC for a child 2 years or younger is _____.
   a. 5,000–10,000/mm^3
   b. 6,200–17,000/mm^3
   c. 9,000–30,000/mm^3

2. A normal MCH in an adult is 27–31 pg. The *pg* stands for _____.
   a. picograms
   b. pecometers
   c. pacograms

3. When testing an Hgb level, a provider is determining _____.
   a. the number of platelets per cubic millimeter of blood
   b. the oxygen-carrying capacity of the red blood cells
   c. the rate at which red blood cells settle out of unclotted blood in an hour

4. If the mean corpuscular volume does not fall within normal limits, this can be an indication of _____.
   a. hyperthyroidism
   b. thrombocytopenia
   c. thalassemia

5. The test that gives an indication of the percentage of red blood cells in whole blood is the _____.
   a. MCV
   b. Hct
   c. differential leukocyte count

Coding of Diseases of the Blood and Blood-Forming Organs

This chapter of ICD-10-CM begins with an Excludes2 instructional note. This instructional note means that the conditions noted are not part of the conditions represented in the chapter. If the patient has the condition noted in the Excludes2 notation in addition to another condition coded to Chapter 3 of ICD-10-CM, both codes can be assigned provided there is not another instructional note at the code site.

> **EXAMPLE:** Mrs. Barton was diagnosed with vitamin B_{12} deficiency anemia due to selective vitamin B_{12} malabsorption with proteinuria. She also is a type II diabetic.

In this example, code D51.1 would reflect the vitamin B_{12} deficiency anemia due to selective vitamin B_{12} malabsorption with proteinuria. The Excludes2 note at the beginning of Chapter 3 contains "endocrine, nutritional and metabolic diseases (E00-E88)." Code E11.9 is also assigned to indicate the type II diabetes.

Anemia

ICD-10-CM breaks the conditions of anemia down into nutritional, hemolytic, and aplastic, among other types. Anemia is a condition marked by a decrease in red blood cells, hemoglobin, hematocrit, or a combination thereof. There are numerous causes and types of anemia. When anemia is coded, identifying the type of anemia is important. The correct code assignment is based on the documentation in the medical record.

Nutritional Anemias (D50–D53)

Nutritional anemias are conditions caused by decreased or nonexistent supplies of nutrients in the blood. Category D50, entitled Iron Deficiency Anemia, is summarized as follows.

Code	Description
D50.0	Iron deficiency anemia secondary to blood loss (chronic) is reported with this code. The term *posthemorrhagic anemia* also codes to this subcategory.
D50.1	Sideropenic dysphagia is a type of iron-deficiency anemia that becomes so severe that the patient has difficulty swallowing in addition to the other symptoms of anemia. Also known as Plummer-Vinson syndrome.
D50.8	Should the provider document that the patient is iron deficient due to lack of iron in the diet, this is the code assigned.
D50.9	This code is reported for other iron-deficiency anemias and is assigned when a more specific code cannot be used.

Courtesy of the Centers for Medicare & Medicaid Services, www.cms.gov

Vitamin B_{12} deficiency anemia is very detailed in ICD-10-CM and is coded with category code D51. This type of anemia is due to insufficient dietary intake of vitamin B_{12} or the inability of the body to absorb the vitamin B_{12} appropriately.

The types of vitamin B_{12} deficient anemias can be summarized as follows:

Code	Description
D51.0	This code reports vitamin B_{12} deficiency anemia due to intrinsic factor deficiency. Diseases coded here include Addison anemia, Biermer anemia, Pernicious (congenital) anemia, and congenital intrinsic factor deficiency. Vitamin B_{12} deficiency occurs when there is a lack of the protein necessary for the B_{12} to bond within the cell.
D51.1	This code reports vitamin B_{12} deficiency anemia due to selective vitamin B_{12} malabsorption with proteinuria.
D51.2	Transcobalamin II deficiency is a very rare autosomal recessive disease. Transcobalamin II is necessary to transport vitamin B_{12}.
D51.3–D51.9	This range of codes is used for other vitamin B_{12} deficiencies, such as dietary vitamin B_{12} deficiency anemia, vegan anemia, and unspecified vitamin B_{12} anemia.

Courtesy of the Centers for Medicare & Medicaid Services, www.cms.gov

Disease Highlight—Pernicious Anemia

Pernicious anemia is an autoimmune disorder in which the stomach is unable to produce the intrinsic factor, which is needed to absorb vitamin B_{12}. This type of anemia can be caused by gastritis, gastric surgery, or endocrine or metabolic disorders.

Signs and Symptoms:

- Anorexia
- Gastrointestinal symptoms that include diarrhea or intermittent constipation
- Nonlocalized abdominal pain
- Atrophic gastritis
- Fatigue
- Shortness of breath
- Pallor
- Positive Babinski's reflex

Clinical Testing:

Pernicious anemia is confirmed by a positive Schilling test. Additional laboratory testing would show:

- Increased MCV
- Increased serum LDH
- Increased bilirubin
- Decreased WBC and platelet count
- Decrease in vitamin B_{12} serum
- Abnormal bone marrow

Treatment:

Since intrinsic factor is not being produced, the patient's body inadequately absorbs vitamin B_{12}. Therefore, the patient receives monthly injections of vitamin B_{12} for his or her lifetime.

Folate deficient and other nutritional deficiency anemias are coded to the D52 and D53 categories. **Folate deficient anemia** is the result of insufficient amounts of folic acid, which is needed for proper cell reproduction and growth. **Folate** itself is a salt of the folic acid. Medical record documentation should be referenced for the specific type of nutritional anemia that needs to be reported. Providers should be encouraged to document as much detail as possible so that a proper code assignment can be made. Documentation should include whether the folate deficiency anemia is caused by a dietary deficiency, drug-induced folate deficiency, or other folate deficiency.

Exercise 8.3—Assigning Codes

Using an ICD-10-CM code book, assign the proper code for each diagnosis:

Diagnosis	Code
1. Kelly-Paterson syndrome	_____
2. folic acid deficiency anemia	_____
3. anemia associated with copper deficiency	_____
4. Addison anemia	_____
5. megaloblastic anemia	_____

Hemolytic Anemias (Category Codes D55–D59)

Hemolytic anemia occurs when red blood cells are broken down at a faster rate than bone marrow can produce them, leading to an abnormal reduction of red blood cells. This disease can be acquired or hereditary.

Category D55 is used to report anemia in enzyme disorders such as glucose-6-phosphate dehydrogenase deficiency (G6PD), glycolytic enzyme disorders, and nucleotide metabolism disorders. For code D55.0, anemia due to glucose-6-phosphate dehydrogenase (G6PD) deficiency, it should be noted that an EXCLUDES1 note for this code appears. The EXCLUDES 1 note states that glucose-6-phosphate dehydrogenase (G6PD) deficiency without anemia is to be coded using code D75.A. It should also be noted that for code D55.2, anemia due to disorders of glycolytic enzymes, an EXCLUDES1 note appears that states for disorders of glycolysis not associated with anemia use code E74.81-.

Category D56 is used to report thalassemia disorders. **Thalassemia** is a condition in which the red blood cells are not formed or are not functioning properly and the globulin gene arrangement is affected. Due to the different types of thalassemia, the malfunction of the cells varies. Codes from the category D56 can be summarized as follows:

Code	Description
D56.0	**Alpha thalassemia** is a condition in which there is a deficiency in the alpha protein being produced. There are four types of alpha thalassemia. The coder must read the diagnostic statement and the code description to be sure the correct code is assigned. It should also be noted that an Excludes1 notation and a notation that directs the coder to "Use additional code…" is found at this code level.
D56.1	**Beta thalassemia** is a condition in which there is a lack of the beta protein being produced. There are various types of beta thalassemia, and verification of the code description is necessary before a code assignment is made.
D56.2	Delta-beta thalassemia, as well as homozygous delta-beta thalassemia, is reported using this code. Code assignment is directed by the Excludes1 note.
D56.3	This code is used to report diseases such as thalassemia minor, alpha thalassemia trait, beta thalassemia minor, and delta-beta thalassemia minor. Review the code in the Tabular Listing for additional diagnoses reported with this code. The coder should note the Excludes1 note found in the code book for this code.
D56.4	Hereditary persistence of fetal hemoglobin (HPFH) is reported with this code.
D56.5	Hemoglobin E-beta thalassemia is reported with this code and coders should reference the Excludes1 note for guidance when assigning this code.
D56.8	Other thalassemias, including dominant thalassemia, Hemoglobin C thalassemia, mixed thalassemia and thalassemia with other hemoglobinopathy are reported with this code.
D56.9	This code reports Thalassemia, unspecified. Mediterranean anemia and Mediterranean anemia with other hemoglobinopathy are reported with this code.

Courtesy of the Centers for Medicare & Medicaid Services, www.cms.gov

Exercise 8.4—Code Block D55–D56

Complete the statements.

1. G6PD deficiency anemia is reported with code _____.
2. Cooley's anemia is reported using ICD-10-CM code _____.
3. _____ occurs when red blood cells are broken down at a faster rate than bone marrow can produce them.
4. The D56 category of codes excludes _____.
5. Alpha thalassemia trait is reported using ICD-10-CM code _____.

Sickle-cell disorders are coded to category D57. Sickle-cell anemia and sickle-cell trait are inherited conditions. **Sickle-cell trait** is an asymptomatic condition in which the patient receives the genetic trait from only one parent. **Sickle-cell anemia** occurs when a patient receives the genetic trait from both parents, thus developing an abnormal type of hemoglobin in the red blood cell that causes decreased oxygenation in the tissues. When a patient is in crisis—that is, experiencing painful symptoms—an additional code for the type of crisis may be needed if the category does not contain a combination code reflecting what is going on with the patient at the encounter, such as fever. At the start of the D57 category, in the code book, there is a notation that directs the coder to "Use additional code for any associated fever (R50.81)." Review category D57 and note that some of the codes denote associated conditions. For example code D57.03 codes Hb-SS disease with cerebral vascular involvement. There is also an "Code also, if applicable, cerebral infarction (I63.-)" notation at the code level, that is to be followed if applicable to the patient's condition.

Category D58, Other hereditary hemolytic anemias, and D59, Acquired hemolytic anemias, contain the remaining codes used to report the different types of hemolytic anemias. Autoimmune and nonautoimmune hemolytic anemias are also included in these categories.

Exercise 8.5—Category D57–D59

Answer the following questions using the ICD-10-CM coding book.

1. Code D58.8, Other specified hereditary hemolytic anemias, includes what condition?
   _____.

2. Chronic idiopathic hemolytic anemia is reported with code _____.

3. Familial acholuric jaundice is reported with code _____.

4. Hb-S trait is coded with code _____.

5. Paroxysmal nocturnal hemoglobinuria is coded with code _____.

Aplastic and Other Anemias and Other Bone Marrow Failure Syndromes (Category Codes D60–D64)

Aplastic anemia is caused by the failure of bone marrow to produce blood components. ICD-10-CM refers to acquired and constitutional aplastic anemias. Constitutional aplastic anemia is the same as congenital or hereditary anemia. ICD-10-CM offers more specific reportable diagnosis codes for aplastic anemia conditions. Code range D60–D64 is summarized as follows:

Code	Description
D60.0	Chronic acquired pure red cell aplasia. Pure red cell aplasia is a condition in which precursors to the red blood cells are affected in the bone marrow and eventually cease to be produced. White cells are not affected.
D60.1	This code is used to report transient acquired pure red cell aplasia.
D60.8	Other acquired pure red cell aplasias are reported using this code.
D60.9	This code is used to report acquired pure red cell aplasia in which the documentation does not specify the type of aplasia. Prior to code assignment, the coder should query the provider to see if the disease could be further defined to prevent the assignment of this unspecified code.
D61.01	This code is used to report constitutional (pure) red blood cell aplasia which includes Blackfan-Diamond syndrome, red cell (pure) aplasia of infants and primary (pure) red cell aplasia. The other types of red blood cell aplasia that are reported with this code are listed in the code book. It should also be noted that this code has an Excludes1 notation.
D61.09	Other constitutional aplastic anemias including Fanconi's anemia and pancytopenia with malformations are reported using code D61.09.
D61.1	Drug-induced aplastic anemia is reported with this code. An instructional note appears under the code that instructs the coder to "Use additional code for adverse effect, if applicable, to identify drug (T36-T50 with fifth or sixth character 5)."
D61.2	Aplastic anemia due to other external agents is reported using this code. The coder must also follow the note that instructs the coder to "Code first, if applicable, toxic effects of substances chiefly nonmedicinal as to source (T51-T65)."
D61.3	This code reports idiopathic aplastic anemia, which is a condition in which the bone marrow is not able to produce cells properly for unknown reasons.
D61.8	Within the D61.8 subcategory, other specified aplastic anemias and other bone marrow failure syndromes are differentiated at the fifth character level with the following codes:

(continues)

(continued)

Code	Description
D61.81	This subcategory reports **Pancytopenia**, a condition in which there is a decrease in the number of platelets, white blood cells, and red blood cells. An extensive Excludes1 note appears for this subcategory of codes. The subcategory is differentiated at the sixth character level to identify the various types of pancytopenia. Remember, codes must be reported to the greatest level of specificity. In this case, sixth characters must be reported.
D61.82	D61.82 reports **Myelophthisis**, a severe form of anemia in which certain bone marrow material shows up in the peripheral blood. Coders should be guided by the "Code also" and the Excludes1 notations that appear for this code.
D61.89	Other specified aplastic anemias and other bone marrow failure syndromes are reported with this code.
D61.9	Aplastic anemia in which the documentation is unspecified is assigned this code.
D62	This code is used to report acute posthemorrhagic anemia and is one of the few three-digit codes in ICD-10-CM. It should be noted that an Excludes1 notation is present for this code.
D63.0	Anemia in neoplastic disease is assigned this code. The coder is instructed to code first the neoplasm (C00–D49). Excludes1 and Excludes2 notes also appear for this code. Review the notes prior to code assignment.
D63.1	This code is used to report anemia in chronic kidney disease. Coders should be guided by the notation for this code that instructs the coder to "Code first underlying chronic kidney disease (CKD) (N18.-)."
D63.8	Anemia in other chronic diseases classified elsewhere is reported with this code. Coders need to be guided by the extensive "Code first" notation that appears in the code book for this code.
D64	This category is used to report other types of anemia. The category is further divided at the fourth and sometimes fifth character levels to further differentiate the codes. Coders should also note the various Excludes1 and other notations that appear at various codes.

Courtesy of the Centers for Medicare & Medicaid Services, www.cms.gov

Coagulation Defects, Purpura, and Other Hemorrhagic Conditions (Category Codes D65–D69)

Coagulation defects occur when there is a deficiency in one or more of the blood clotting factors, resulting in prolonged clotting time and possibly serious bleeding. The normal stages of blood clotting are summarized in Figure 8-3. A coagulation defect occurs when there is a disruption in the process because of heredity or acquired conditions. One disease that is coded within this block of codes is Von Willebrand's disease, code D68.0.

Code	Description
D65	Disseminated intravascular coagulation (defibrination syndrome) is reported with this code. It should be noted that there are extensive Includes and Excludes1 notes for this code.
D66	This code reports **hereditary factor VIII** deficiency, a form of hemophilia. The hereditary factor diseases noted in this block of codes involve clotting factor problems.
D67	This code reports hereditary factor IX deficiency, which includes Christmas disease, factor IX deficiency, hemophilia B, and plasma thromboplastin component deficiency.
D68.0	D68.0 reports **von Willebrand's disease** the most common of the hereditary bleeding disorders. When this disease occurs, the von Willebrand factor is missing from the blood or is not working properly. This factor is essential in the clotting process.
D68.1	Hereditary factor XI deficiency, hemophilia C, and Rosenthal's disease are reported with this code.
D68.2	Hereditary deficiencies of other clotting factors are reported with this code. The coder should note the extensive list of diseases included in the ICD-10-CM book under the heading for this code.
D68.3	This subcategory reports hemorrhagic disorder due to circulating anticoagulants and is divided as follows:
D68.31	Hemorrhagic disorder due to intrinsic circulating anticoagulants, antibodies, or inhibitors is reported with this subcategory. It should be noted that six characters are needed to code accurately for this subcategory. This subcategory includes hemorrhagic disorders due to intrinsic increase in antithrombin, anti-VIIIa, anti-IXa, anti-Xa, anti-XIa, and hyperheparinemia. Review ICD-10-CM coding manual for six characters of 1, 2, and 8.

(continues)

(continued)

Code	Description
D68.32	This code is used to report a hemorrhagic disorder due to extrinsic circulating anticoagulants. The coder must take note of the instructional notation that appears for this code that states "Use additional code for adverse effect, if applicable, to identify drug (T45.515, T45.525)."
D68.4	This code reports acquired coagulation factor deficiency, including deficiencies of coagulation factors due to liver disease and vitamin K deficiency. This code does not, however, include a vitamin K deficiency in a newborn. The coder has to reference code P53 for this condition.
D68.5	The D68.5 subcategory reports primary thrombophilia, a condition that can be genetic (primary) or acquired. **Thrombophilia** is a condition in which the patient is predisposed to develop thromboses. ICD-10-CM reports the following codes for the various types of primary thrombophilia:
D68.51	Activated protein C resistance
D68.52	Prothrombin gene mutation
D68.59	Other primary thrombophilia such as antithrombin III deficiency, hypercoagulable state, protein C deficiency, and protein S deficiency are reported using this code. Additional diseases are listed in the code book.
D68.61	Antiphospholipid syndrome and Anticardiolipin syndrome is reported with this code. Coders should note the Excludes1 note that appears in the code book for this code.
D68.62	Lupus anticoagulant syndrome is reported by using this code. **Lupus** is a disease in which the body produces too many antibodies, which begin to turn against the patient's own body attacking body organs, joints, and muscles.
D68.69	Other thrombophilia for which ICD-10-CM does not provide a specific code is assigned D68.69.
D68.8	Other specified coagulation defects for which ICD-10-CM does not report a specific code are assigned D68.8.
D68.9	Coagulation defect, unspecified, is coded with D68.9.
D69	Purpura and other hemorrhagic conditions are reported using this category of codes. **Purpura** is the accumulation of blood under the skin that forms multiple pinpoint hemorrhages. The following codes are used:
D69.0	Allergic purpura. An extensive listing of diseases that are coded using this code appears in the code book, as well as an Excludes1 note that governs this code.
D69.1	Qualitative platelet defects. An extensive listing of diseases that are coded using this code appears in the code book, as well as an Excludes1 note that governs this code.
D69.2	Other nonthrombocytopenic purpura including purpura, purpura simplex, and senile purpura are reported with this code.
D69.3	Immune thrombocytopenic purpura is reported by using this code. **Thrombocytopenia** is an abnormal decrease in platelet count that causes purpural hemorrhages.
D69.4	Other primary thrombocytopenia is reported with this subcategory as follows:
D69.41	Evans syndrome
D69.42	Congenital and hereditary thrombocytopenia purpura. A notation appears in the code book that instructs the coder to "Code first congenital or hereditary disorder, such as: thrombocytopenia with absent radius (TAR syndrome) (Q87.2)".
D69.49	This code reports other primary thrombocytopenia, including megakaryocytic hypoplasia and primary thrombocytopenia.
D69.51 and D69.59	Secondary thrombocytopenia is reported using these codes. D69.51 reports posttransfusion purpure, while D69.59 reports other secondary thrombocytopenia.
D69.6	Thrombocytopenia, unspecified, is reported with this code. If the documentation does not specify the type of thrombocytopenia, this code is used for thrombocytopenia, unspecified.
D69.8	Other specified hemorrhagic conditions that include capillary fragility and vascular pseudohemophilia are reported with this code.
D69.9	An unspecified hemorrhagic condition is reported with this code.

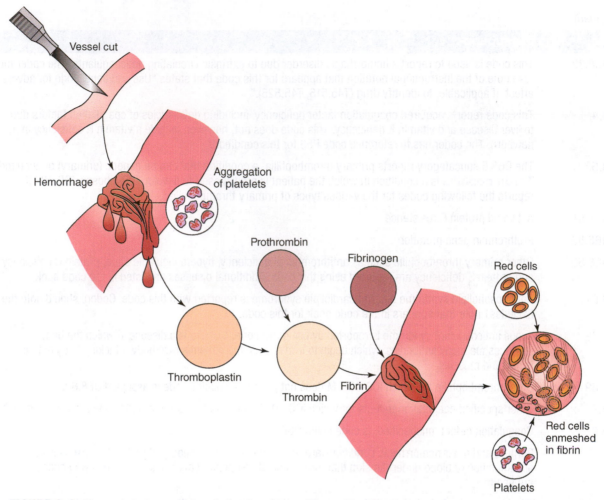

FIGURE 8-3 Normal stages of blood clotting (From Rizzo, *Fundamentals of Anatomy and Physiology*, 2nd ed. (Clifton Park, NY: Delmar, 2003, Cengage Learning), p. 306.).

Disease Highlight—Von Willebrand's Disease

Von Willebrand's disease, also known as **angiohemophilia**, is the most common of the inherited bleeding disorders. This disease is caused by a deficiency in the clotting factor and platelet function and is categorized as a hereditary autosomal dominant disorder.

Signs and Symptoms:

Patients with von Willebrand's disease have an increase in mucosal bleeding that includes:

- Epistaxis
- Gingival bleeding
- Monorrhagia
- Gastrointestinal bleeding

Other symptoms include an increase in the amount of bleeding following surgery, injury, and dental procedures.

Clinical Testing:

Laboratory tests show prolonged bleeding time and a decrease in the vW factor level in plasma.

Treatment:

- Patients diagnosed with von Willebrand's disease are to avoid using aspirin because it exacerbates bleeding.
- Patients who have lost a significant amount of blood will have a transfusion of plasma cryoprecipitate.
- Antifibrinolytic agents are administered to patients during surgery and dental procedures to decrease bleeding.
- Desmopressin acetate is also given to patients to control the disease.

Exercise 8.6—Coding Exercise: Anemia and Coagulation Coding

Use an ICD-10-CM coding book to code the following diagnoses.

Diagnosis	Code
1. idiopathic aplastic anemia	
2. leukoerythroblastic anemia	
3. sideroblastic anemia	
4. angiohemophilia	
5. primary thrombophilia	
6. transient acquired pure red cell aplasia	
7. panmyelophthisis	
8. familial hypoplastic anemia	
9. dyshematopoietic anemia	
10. Factor IX deficiency	

Other Disorders of the Blood and Blood-Forming Organs (Category Codes D70–D77)

This category of codes encompasses more blood disorders, mainly genetic blood disorders and disorders of the white blood cells.

Neutropenia is an abnormal decrease of granular leukocytes in the blood and is coded to this category of codes. Additional codes are required for any associated fever and mucositis. Transient neonatal neutropenia is not included in this series of codes.

The following lists the codes associated with these disorders and explains some of the conditions:

Code	Description
D70	Category D70 reports neutropenia, which is further defined in ICD-10-CM as follows:
D70.0	Congenital agranulocytosis, congenital neutropenia, infantile genetic agranulocytosis, and Kostmann's disease are reported with this code.
D70.1	When assigning a code for agranulocytosis secondary to cancer chemotherapy, code D70.1, the coder is instructed to code any underlying neoplasms and to "Use an additional code for adverse affect, if applicable, to identify drug (T45.1X5)."
D70.2	Other drug-induced agranulocytosis is reported using this code along with the appropriate T code (T36–T50 with fifth or sixth character 5) to identify the drug used.
D70.3	Code D70.3 reports neutropenia due to infection.
D70.4	Cyclic neutropenia, cyclic hematopoiesis, and periodic neutropenia are reported with this code.
D70.8	Other neutropenia
D70.9	Neutropenia, unspecified

(continues)

(continued)

Code	Description
D71	Functional disorders of **polymorphonuclear neutrophils** are reported using this code. Polymorphonuclear neutrophils are white blood cells found in the peripheral blood and are the most numerous of the white blood cells.
D72	Other disorders of white blood cells are reported with this category, which is differentiated as follows:
D72.0	Genetic anomalies of leukocytes and other conditions listed in the extensive notation found in the code are reported with this code.
D72.1	Code D72.1 reports **eosinophilia**, a condition in which the eosinophil white blood cell is found in excess in the blood or body tissues. This code is further divided. Reference the code manual for the complete listing of the codes such as code D72.110 which reports idiopathic hypereosinophilic syndrome and note the use of the fifth and sixth characters.
D72.8	In this category, other specified disorders of white blood cells are differentiated more specifically in ICD-10-CM by use of the following codes:
D72.81	This subcategory, Decreased white blood cell count, is further divided at the sixth character level to include:
D72.810	Lymphocytopenia
D72.818	Other decreased white blood cell count. The coder should read the listing of diseases that appear in the code book to become familiar with diseases that are reported via this code.
D72.819	Decreased white blood cell count, unspecified
D72.82	This category reports elevated white blood cell count, and it further specifies to the sixth character level as follows:
D72.820	Lymphocytosis (symptomatic) and elevated lymphocytes
D72.821	Monocytosis (symptomatic)
D72.822	Plasmacytosis
D72.823	Leukemoid reaction
D72.824	Basophilia
D72.825	Bandemia
D72.828	Other elevated white blood cell count
D72.829	Elevated white blood cell count, unspecified
D72.89 and D72.9	D72.89 reports other specified disorders of white blood cells, while D72.9 reports a disorder of white blood cells, unspecified, as well as abnormal leukocyte differential.
D73	Diseases of the spleen are coded to this category. The **spleen** is located in the upper left quadrant of the abdomen. The spleen forms lymphocytes and monocytes and also stores erythrocytes. This category is further divided using the following codes:
D73.0	Hyposplenism
D73.1	Hypersplenism
D73.2	Chronic congestive splenomegaly
D73.3	Abscess of spleen
D73.4	Cyst of spleen
D73.5	This code is used to report infarction of the spleen, nontraumatic splenic rupture, and torsion of the spleen.
D73.8	Other diseases of the spleen are further differentiated as follows:
D73.81	Neutropenic splenomegaly
D73.89	Other diseases of spleen

(continues)

(continued)

Code	Description
D73.9	Disease of the spleen, unspecified, is reported with this code.
D74	**Methemoglobinemia** is a disorder of the hemoglobin in which oxygen is not transported by the cells. The codes are further divided:
D74.0	Congenital methemoglobinemia
D74.8	Other methemoglobinemias include the acquired methemoglobinemia conditions.
D74.9	Methemoglobinemia, unspecified
D75	Other and unspecified diseases of blood and blood-forming organs are reported with codes from the D75 category and are differentiated as follows:
D75.0	This code for familial erythrocytosis includes benign and familial polycythemia.
D75.1	Secondary polycythemia and other conditions that are listed in the extensive note for this code are reported with code D75.1.
D75.8	Subcategory D75.8 reports other specified diseases of blood and blood-forming organs. This is further divided as follows:
D75.81	Myelofibrosis. Numerous instructional notations appear in the code book for this code and must be followed for accurate code assignment.
D75.82	Heparin-induced thrombocytopenia (HIT)
D75.89	Other specified diseases of blood and blood-forming organs
D75.9	Disease of blood and blood-forming organs, unspecified, is reported with this code.
D75.A	Glucose-6-phosphate dehydrogenase (G6PD) deficiency without anemia. There is an EXCLUDES1 note for this code description that states that glucose-6-phosphate dehydrogenase (G6PD) deficiency with anemia is to be coded using code D55.0.
D76	Certain diseases involving lymphoreticular and reticulohistocytic tissue are reported with the specific codes that follow. (The extensive Excludes1 note guides the coder in code selection.)
D76.1	Hemophagocytic lymphohistiocytosis
D76.2	This code is reported for hemophagocytic syndrome, infection-associated. The coder is instructed that an additional code is needed to identify the infectious agent or disease.
D76.3	D76.3 reports other histiocytosis syndromes, including xanthogranuloma, reticulohistiocytoma, and sinus histiocytosis with massive lymphadenopathy.
D77	Other disorders of the blood and blood-forming organs in diseases classified elsewhere are reported with this code.

Courtesy of the Centers for Medicare & Medicaid Services, www.cms.gov

Exercise 8.7—Other Disorders of the Blood and Blood-Forming Organs

Using an ICD-10-CM coding book, code the diagnoses.

Diagnosis	Code
1. congenital neutropenia	_____
2. cyclic neutropenia	_____
3. hyposplenism	_____
4. nontraumatic splenic rupture	_____
5. leukopenia	_____

Intraoperative and Postprocedural Complications of the Spleen (Category Code D78)

This code category includes accidental punctures and lacerations of the spleen during a procedure, as well as postprocedural hemorrhaging. The specific codes for these conditions are as follows:

Code	Description
D78	This category reports intraoperative and postprocedural complications of the spleen, and the codes are differentiated as follows:
D78.0	Intraoperative hemorrhage and hematoma of the spleen complicating a procedure are further divided and reported using the following codes:
D78.01	Intraoperative hemorrhage and hematoma of the spleen complicating a procedure on the spleen
D78.02	Intraoperative hemorrhage and hematoma of the spleen complicating other procedure
D78.1	Accidental puncture and laceration of the spleen during a procedure is reported using:
D78.11	Accidental puncture and laceration of the spleen during a procedure on the spleen
D78.12	Accidental puncture and laceration of the spleen during other procedure
D78.2	Postprocedural hemorrhage of the spleen following a procedure is reported with one of the following codes:
D78.21	Postprocedural hemorrhage of the spleen following a procedure on the spleen
D78.22	Postprocedural hemorrhage of the spleen following other procedure
D78.31–D78.34	This range of codes reports postprocedural hematoma and seroma of the spleen following a procedure.
D78.8	Other intraoperative and postprocedural complications of spleen are reported by using codes D78.81 or D78.89. It should be noted that these codes are governed by the instructional notation that states "Use additional code, if applicable, to further specify disorder."
D78.81	Other intraoperative complications of the spleen
D78.89	Other postprocedural complications of the spleen

Courtesy of the Centers for Medicare & Medicaid Services, www.cms.gov

Certain Disorders Involving the Immune Mechanism (Category Codes D80–D89)

The **immune system** is the body's defense mechanism against disease and other foreign agents. This category of codes includes defects in the complement system and immunodeficiency disorders, except for HIV. Also excluded from this block of codes are some systemic autoimmune diseases and functional disorders of polymorphonuclear neutrophils (discussed earlier in the chapter). The following list contains the codes found in these categories:

Code	Description
D80	Immunodeficiency with predominantly antibody defects are reported using codes that are differentiated as follows:
D80.0	Hereditary hypogammaglobulinemia, such as autosomal recessive agammaglobulinemia. **Agammaglobulinemia** is a hereditary disorder in which the immunoglobulin or immune proteins are extremely low, leaving the person open to frequent infections.
D80.1	Nonfamilial hypogammaglobulinemia
D80.2	Selective deficiency of immunoglobulin A [IgA]
D80.3	Selective deficiency of immunoglobulin G [IgG] subclasses
D80.4	Selective deficiency of immunoglobulin M [IgM]
D80.5	Immunodeficiency with increased immunoglobulin M [IgM]
D80.6	Antibody deficiency with near-normal immunoglobulins or with hyperimmunoglobulinemia

(continues)

(continued)

Code	Description
D80.7	Transient hypogammaglobulinemia of infancy
D80.8	Other immunodeficiencies with predominantly antibody defects
D80.9	Immunodeficiency with predominantly antibody defects, unspecified
D81	Combined immunodeficiencies are reported with the specific codes that follow. Coders should note the Excludes1 note at this level.
D81.0	Severe combined immunodeficiency [SCID] with reticular dysgenesis
D81.1	Severe combined immunodeficiency [SCID] with low T- and B-cell numbers
D81.2	Severe combined immunodeficiency [SCID] with low or normal B-cell numbers
D81.3	Adenosine deaminase [ADA] deficiency
D81.30	Adenosine deaminase deficiency, unspecified
D81.31	Severe combined immunodeficiency due to adenosine deaminase deficiency
D81.32	Adenosine deaminase 2 deficiency. It should be noted that a "Code also" note appears for this code that instructs the coder to code associated manifestations. Review the code in the ICD-10-CM coding manual for more specific information.
D81.39	Other adenosine deaminase deficiency. Review the ICD-10-CM coding manual for a listing of the various deficiencies types that are reported to this code.
D81.4	Nezelof's syndrome
D81.5	Purine nucleoside phosphorylase [PNP] deficiency
D81.6	Major histocompatibility complex class I deficiency
D81.7	Major histocompatibility complex class II deficiency
D81.8	Other combined immunodeficiencies are coded with increased granularity as follows:
D81.81	Biotin-dependent carboxylase deficiency disorders are specified as follows in ICD-10-CM. Providers may have to be queried to differentiate the deficiency so that a specific code can be assigned.
D81.810	Biotinidase deficiency
D81.818	Other biotin-dependent carboxylase deficiency
D81.819	Biotin-dependent carboxylase deficiency, unspecified
D81.89	Other combined immunodeficiencies not given a specific code in ICD-10-CM are reported with this code.
D81.9	Combined immunodeficiency, unspecified, including severe combined immunodeficiency disorder, is reported with this code.
D82	Immunodeficiency associated with other major defects is reported with codes from this category as follows:
D82.0	Wiskott-Aldrich syndrome
D82.1	Di George's syndrome
D82.2	Immunodeficiency with short-limbed stature
D82.3	Immunodeficiency following hereditary defective response to Epstein-Barr virus
D82.4	Hyperimmunoglobulin E [IgE] syndrome
D82.8	Immunodeficiency associated with other specified major defects
D82.9	Immunodeficiency associated with major defect, unspecified
D83	This category is used to report common variable immunodeficiencies. Documentation is essential when selecting codes because the codes are very specific as to the cell abnormalities. The diseases are reported as follows:
D83.0	Common variable immunodeficiency with predominant abnormalities of B-cell numbers and function

(continues)

(continued)

Code	Description
D83.1	Common variable immunodeficiency with predominant immunoregulatory T-cell disorders
D83.2	Common variable immunodeficiency with autoantibodies to B- or T-cells
D83.8	Other common variable immunodeficiencies
D83.9	Common variable immunodeficiency, unspecified
D84	Other immunodeficiencies are coded using this category, which is differentiated as follows:
D84.0	Lymphocyte function antigen-1 [LFA-1] defect
D84.1	Defects in the complement system
D84.8	Other specified immunodeficiencies are reported with codes at this level that are at times denoted to the the fifth and sixth character level. Review the coding manual for the specific characters.
D84.9	Immunodeficiency, unspecified
D86	Category D86 is used to report various forms of sarcoidosis. The following codes identify the sites of the sarcoidosis:
D86.0	Sarcoidosis of lung
D86.1	Sarcoidosis of lymph nodes
D86.2	Sarcoidosis of lung with sarcoidosis of lymph nodes
D86.3	Sarcoidosis of skin
D86.8	Sarcoidosis of other sites are further differentiated within ICD-10-CM as follows:
D86.81	Sarcoid meningitis
D86.82	Multiple cranial nerve palsies in sarcoidosis
D86.83	Sarcoid iridocyclitis
D86.84	Sarcoid pyelonephritis
D86.85	Sarcoid myocarditis
D86.86	Sarcoid arthropathy
D86.87	Sarcoid myositis
D86.89	Sarcoidosis of other sites
D86.9	Sarcoidosis, unspecified, is reported with this code. Prior to the assignment of this code, the provider should be queried to determine whether more specific information is available.
D89	Other disorders involving the immune mechanism, not elsewhere classified, is reported and governed by the Excludes1 and Excludes2 notations that appear after the category heading in the code book. The codes are divided as follows:
D89.0	Polyclonal hypergammaglobulinemia
D89.1	Cryoglobulinemia is reported with this code, as well as the other diseases listed in the extensive notation that follows this code.
D89.2	This code reports Hypergammaglobulinemia, unspecified.
D89.3	This code reports Immune Reconstitution Syndrome.
D89.4	This subcategory reports mast cell activation syndrome and related disorders using various fifth character levels for specificity.
D89.8	Other specified disorders involving the immune mechanism, not elsewhere classified, are specified at the fifth and sixth character level in ICD-10-CM. The "Code first" and "Use additional" notations also govern code assignment.
D89.9	Disorders involving the immune mechanism, unspecified code D89.9, reports unspecified disorders involving the immune mechanism and immune disease.

Summary

- Erythrocytes are red blood cells; leukocytes are white blood cells.
- Leukocytes are divided into two groups: granulocytes and agranulocytes.
- Thrombocytes function in the initiation of blood clotting.
- Anemia occurs when there is a decrease in red blood cells, hemoglobin, and/or hematocrit.
- Sickle-cell trait and sickle-cell anemia are separately identifiable conditions that are classified with different codes.
- Aplastic anemia can be congenital or acquired.
- Coagulation defects cause prolonged clotting time and can result in serious bleeding, which can lead to death.

Internet Links

To learn about various types of anemia, visit **www.mayoclinic.org** and type the key term *anemia*.

For a comprehensive review of research and information on blood disorders, visit *https://synapseresearchinstitute.com/*.

Chapter Review

True/False

Indicate whether each statement is true (T) or false (F).

1. _____ Different fluids and electrolyte balance are maintained by the flow of the blood through the body.

2. _____ Monocytes, basophils, and eosinophils are all types of granulocytes.

3. _____ A platelet plug slows or stops bleeding.

4. _____ Transcobalamin II deficiency is a common recessive disease.

5. _____ Thalassemia is a condition in which the white blood cells are not formed or functioning properly and the globulin gene arrangement is affected.

Multiple Choice

Select the answer that best completes the statement or answers the question.

6. Of the following, which is not a function of blood? _____
   a. transportation of nutrients
   b. transportation of bone marrow
   c. transportation of waste

7. The bone marrow is where _____ is/are formed.
   a. red blood cells   b. hemoglobin   c. plasma

8. Which of the following statements is *not* true of white blood cells? _____
   a. WBCs are less numerous than RBCs.
   b. WBCs contain hemoglobin and have an irregular ball-like shape.
   c. WBCs are classified into two major groups: granulocytes and agranulocytes.

9. A marked decrease in red blood cells, hemoglobin, and/or hematocrit could result in a diagnosis of _____.

    a.   anemia   b.   anaphylactic shock   c.   phagocytosis

10. A type of iron-deficiency anemia that becomes so severe the patient has difficulty swallowing, in addition to other symptoms of anemia, is known as _____.

    a.   aplastic anemia   b.   vitamin B_{12} anemia   c.   sideropenic dysphagia

Coding Assignments

Instructions: Using an ICD-10-CM code book, assign the proper diagnosis code to the following diagnostic statements.

1. sarcoidosis of the skin   _____

2. hypergammaglobulinemia   _____

3. DiGeorge's syndrome   _____

4. biotin-dependent carboxylase deficiency   _____

5. selective deficiency of IgA   _____

6. cryoglobulinemia   _____

7. sarcoid myositis   _____

8. LFA-1 defect   _____

9. common variable immunodeficiency with predominant
    immunoregulatory T cell disorder   _____

10. postprocedural complication of the spleen   _____

11. microangiopathic hemolytic anemia   _____

12. IgE syndrome   _____

13. Wiskott-Aldrich syndrome   _____

14. Nezelof's syndrome   _____

15. iridocyclitis in sarcoidosis   _____

16. polycythemia acquired   _____

17. cyst of the spleen   _____

18. intraoperative hemorrhage of the spleen, complicating a procedure   _____

19. myelofibrosis   _____

20. plasmacytosis   _____

21. prothrombin gene mutation   _____

22. congenital thrombocytopenia   _____

23. protein C deficiency   _____

24. fibrinolytic purpura   _____

25. congenital Heinz body anemia   _____

26. transcobalamin II deficiency   _____

27. hereditary persistence of fetal hemoglobin   _____

28. sickle-cell/Hb-C disease with acute chest syndrome   _____

29. abnormal hemoglobin   _____

30. cytokine release syndrome, grade 4   _____

Case Studies

Instructions: Review each case study and select the correct ICD-10-CM diagnostic code.

Case 1

Discharge Summary

PATIENT NAME: Polly Patch

AGE: 72 years old

Polly was admitted from home because she passed out from dizziness. Her daughter called my office, and I admitted her to the medical unit because this is the third time in 2 weeks that she passed out.

On initial examination she was conscious and alert and appeared pale. Physical findings can be found on the history and physical dated 02/13/XX.

CBC, chest x-ray, and EKG were ordered.

CBC revealed a low platelet count of 53,000, supporting a diagnosis of idiopathic thrombocytopenia. Chest x-ray and EKG were normal.

The rest of her 2-day admission was uneventful, and she was discharged home. She was instructed
to follow up in my office in 2 weeks or to call my office if her symptoms increase.

ICD-10-CM Code Assignment: _____

Case 2

Hospital Note: 3/4/xx

Bob was admitted on Monday with a diagnosis of anemia associated with a primary malignancy of the prostate. Today I ordered a blood transfusion due to his low blood count. CBC is to be repeated after the transfusion. I instructed the charge nurse to call me with the results.

ICD-10-CM Code Assignment: _____

Case 3

Postsurgical Note

Mary is now 1-day postop for a right breast mass excision. During the surgery she lost a significant amount of blood due to uncontrolled bleeding. A CBC was ordered that showed an abnormally low hematocrit and hemoglobin confirming anemia due to blood loss. She was given a transfusion and has tolerated the transfusion well.

ICD-10-CM Code Assignment: _____

Case 4

Office Note

This 6-year-old female was suffering from abdominal pain and was complaining of being tired when she presented to my office 2 days ago. She returns with her mother today because testing confirmed a diagnosis of pernicious anemia. Today she will be started on Vitamin B_{12} injections and will follow up with me in 2 weeks or if symptoms increase.

ICD-10-CM Code Assignment: _____

Case 5

Office Note

This female patient was feeling very weak and lethargic over the last month. She was also suffering from pain in her major joints. Testing confirmed sickle-cell anemia. She is here today to discuss this disease.

ICD-10-CM Code Assignment: _____

Case 6

Skilled Nursing Facility Note

This 73-year-old male patient was seen today at the request of the nursing staff. He is experiencing a purple spotted skin rash, abdominal pain, and joint inflammation. He recently had a respiratory bacterial infection, which has cleared. He is also complaining of a headache and loss of appetite.

Assessment: All symptoms support a diagnosis of allergic purpura.

Plan: The patient is to be given Tylenol for pain and Prednisone to relieve GI symptoms.

ICD-10-CM Code Assignment: _____

Case 7

Discharge Note

This 39-year-old male patient is being discharged today following a splenectomy. The splenectomy was completed because the patient had hypersplenism, which could not be treated by other more conservative measures. The patient tolerated the procedure and has been instructed to follow the postoperative orders that I have given him. He is to see me in my office in 1 week.

ICD-10-CM Code Assignment: _____

Case 8

Office Note

This 72-year-old female patient is being seen in the office today for a follow-up after a series of diagnostic testing. She has been complaining of fatigue, weight loss, fever, shortness of breath, and bone pain in her legs. Diagnostic testing confirmed myelofibrosis. I am going to refer her to Dr. Smith, who specializes in the treatment of this disease. All diagnostic testing results with be forwarded to Dr. Smith.

ICD-10-CM Code Assignment: _____

Case 9

Office Note

This 45-year-old male patient was seen 4 days ago for his annual physical. Blood and urine samples were taken. The patient will return today to discuss the findings. The blood test showed elevated leukocytes, the cause of which is undetermined at this time. I am referring him to Dr. Yan in hematology to follow up on this finding.

ICD-10-CM Code Assignment: _____

Case 10

Hospital Discharge Note

This female 49-year-old patient is being discharged today after a 2-day stay for a transfusion of plasma cryoprecipitate to manage her von Willebrand's disease. Her course of treatment was uneventful, and she is instructed to follow up with me in the office in 2 weeks or sooner if symptoms occur.

ICD-10-CM Code Assignment: _____

Endocrine, Nutritional, and Metabolic Diseases

Chapter Outline

Chapter Objectives

At the conclusion of this chapter, you should be able to:

1. Explain how hormones impact functions within the body.
2. Distinguish between the different types of diabetes and select ICD-10-CM codes for the various types of diabetes.
3. Interpret the ICD-10-CM coding guidelines that apply to endocrine, nutritional, and metabolic diseases.
4. Accurately code endocrine, nutritional, and metabolic diseases.
5. Select and code diagnoses from case studies.

Key Terms

Adult onset diabetes

Cushing's syndrome

Diabetes mellitus

Endocrine system

Glucose

Goiter

Hormones

Hyperparathyroidism

Hyperthyroidism

Hypoparathyroidism

Hypothyroidism

Insulin

Insulin-dependent
diabetes mellitus
(IDDM)

Juvenile diabetes, IDDM

Metabolism

Noninsulin-dependent
diabetes mellitus
(NIDDM)

Pancreas

Thyroid gland

Thyrotoxic crisis

Thyrotoxic storm

Type 1 diabetes mellitus

Type 2 diabetes mellitus

REMINDER: As you work through this chapter, you will need to have a copy of the ICD-10-CM coding book to reference. For this chapter, you will also need to reference the ICD-10-CM Official Guidelines for Coding and Reporting. These guidelines can be found in Appendix A which are now available on the Student Companion site and MINDTAP From Cengage.

Introduction

Chapter 4 of ICD-10-CM, "Endocrine, Nutritional, and Metabolic Diseases," classifies conditions that affect the endocrine system, as well as nutritional and metabolic diseases. A common disease coded to this chapter is **diabetes mellitus**, which is a chronic disorder resulting from a problem with the pancreas. The **pancreas** is located under the stomach in the upper abdomen and performs various physiological functions. One of these functions is secreting digestive hormones into the gastrointestinal tract to aid in digestion. The other function is to regulate insulin in the body. **Insulin** is used in the body to process glucose. If the pancreas does not regulate the insulin properly or does not produce insulin at all, glucose levels are thrown out of control. **Glucose** is needed for the cells to properly supply energy for the body's metabolic functions. Nutritional and metabolic disorders, with the exception of anemias caused by nutritional deficiencies, are

 NOTE:

> Some endocrine and metabolic disturbances—such as conditions that affect pregnancy and neonates and certain types of anemia resulting from nutritional deficiencies—are coded to other chapters in ICD-10-CM. Coders should read the Excludes notes throughout Chapter 4 to become familiar with the conditions excluded from this chapter.

also classified to this chapter. Anemias caused by nutritional deficiencies are classified to Chapter 3 of ICD-10-CM, "Diseases of the Blood and Blood-Forming Organs and Certain Disorders Involving the Immune Mechanism." The nutritional and metabolic disorders classified to Chapter 4 of ICD-10-CM are caused by deficiencies of vitamins, minerals, and proteins, as well as other conditions such as obesity, malnutrition, and carbohydrate and lipid imbalances.

Introduction to the Body System

The **endocrine system** (*endo-* means "within," and *-crin* means "secrete") consists of several different internal groups of glands and structures that produce or secrete hormones. Figure 9-1 illustrates the structures of the endocrine system. **Hormones** are chemical substances produced by the body to keep organs and tissues functioning properly. Each hormone has a specific function, as summarized in Figure 9-2.

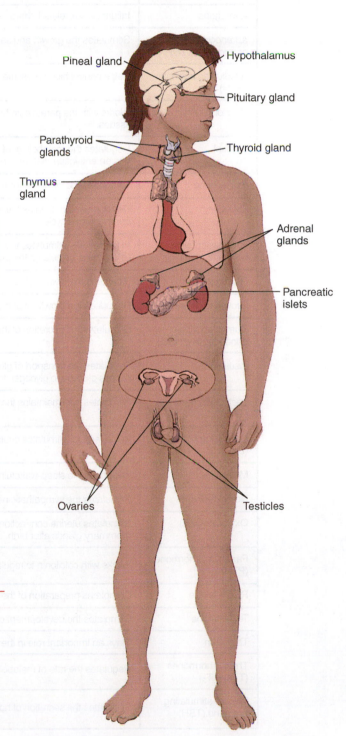

FIGURE 9-1 Structures of the endocrine system

When chemical changes occur in the body, hormone release may be either increased or decreased, provided that the organ producing the hormone is functioning properly. When endocrine body structures do not function properly, hormones are not released.

Hormone	Functions
Aldosterone	Aids in regulating the levels of salt and water in the body.
Androgens	Influence sex-related characteristics.
Adrenocorticotropic hormone (ACTH)	Stimulates the growth and secretions of the adrenal cortex.
Antidiuretic hormone (ADH)	Helps control blood pressure by reducing the amount of water that is excreted.
Calcitonin	Works with the parathyroid hormone to regulate calcium levels in the blood and tissues.
Cortisol	Regulates the metabolism of carbohydrates, fats, and proteins in the body. Also has an anti-inflammatory action.
Epinephrine	Stimulates the sympathetic nervous system.
Estrogen	Develops and maintains the female secondary sex characteristics and regulates the menstrual cycle.
Follicle-stimulating hormone (FSH)	In the female, stimulates the secretion of estrogen and the growth of ova (eggs). In the male, stimulates the production of sperm.
Glucagon	Increases the level of glucose in the bloodstream.
Growth hormone (GH)	Regulates the growth of bone, muscle, and other body tissues.
Human chorionic gonadotropin (HCG)	Stimulates the secretion of the hormones required to maintain the pregnancy.
Insulin (In)	Regulates the transport of glucose to body cells and stimulates the conversion of excess glucose to glycogen for storage.
Lactogenic hormone (LTH)	Stimulates and maintains the secretion of breast milk.
Luteinizing hormone (LH)	In the female, stimulates ovulation. In the male, stimulates testosterone secretion.
Melatonin	Influences the sleep-wakefulness cycles.
Norepinephrine	Stimulates the sympathetic nervous system.
Oxytocin (OXT)	Stimulates uterine contractions during childbirth. Causes milk to flow from the mammary glands after birth.
Parathyroid hormone (PTH)	Works with calcitonin to regulate calcium levels in the blood and tissues.
Progesterone	Completes preparation of the uterus for possible pregnancy.
Testosterone	Stimulates the development of male secondary sex characteristics.
Thymosin	Plays an important role in the immune system.
Thyroid hormones (T_4 and T_3)	Regulates the rate of metabolism.
Thyroid-stimulating hormone (TSH)	Stimulates the secretion of hormones by the thyroid gland.

FIGURE 9-2 Hormones and their functions

EXAMPLE: The thyroid gland secretes hormones that regulate growth and metabolism. A condition known as hypothyroidism occurs when the thyroid is not as active as it should be, creating a deficiency of thyroid hormone secretion. An underactive thyroid, left undiagnosed, can cause conditions such as depression, sensitivity to cold, and fatigue. Medications can be prescribed to stimulate or replace the needed hormones to get the thyroid hormones back in balance.

Coding of Endocrine, Nutritional, and Metabolic Diseases

Chapter 4 of ICD-10-CM is organized into the following blocks:

- E00–E07,   Disorders of thyroid gland
- E08–E13,   Diabetes mellitus
- E15–E16,   Other disorders of glucose regulation and pancreatic internal secretion
- E20–E35,   Disorders of other endocrine glands
- E36,   Intraoperative complications of endocrine system
- E40–E46,   Malnutrition
- E50–E64,   Other nutritional deficiencies
- E65–E68,   Overweight, obesity, and other hyperalimentation
- E70–E88,   Metabolic disorders
- E89,   Postprocedural endocrine and metabolic complications and disorders, not elsewhere classified

At the start of Chapter 4 of ICD-10-CM, a notation appears that governs the entire chapter, as shown in Figure 9-3. Coders need to understand this notation and be guided by these instructions.

Disorders of the Thyroid Gland (Category Codes E00–E07)

ICD-10-CM classifies disorders of the thyroid gland to category codes E00–E07. The primary function of the thyroid gland is to regulate the body's metabolism, which is the rate at which the body uses energy and at which body functions occur.

Common conditions that are classified to this code range are different types of goiters. When hormone secretions fall within normal limits but the thyroid itself becomes enlarged, this condition is known as a goiter. A lack of iodine can cause goiters. Categories E01 and E04 contain codes for various types of goiters. Category E01 reports iodine-deficiency related thyroid disorders and allied conditions, including iodine-deficiency related

---

Chapter 4—Endocrine, nutritional, and metabolic diseases (E00-E89)

All neoplasms, whether functionally active or not, are classified in Chapter 2. Appropriate codes in this chapter (i.e., E05.8, E07.0, E16-E31, E34.-) may be used as additional codes to indicate either functional activity by neoplasms and ectopic endocrine tissue or hyperfunction and hypofunction of endocrine glands associated with neoplasms and other conditions classified elsewhere.

EXCLUDES1: transitory endocrine and metabolic disorders specific to newborn (P70-P74)

Courtesy of the Centers for Medicare & Medicaid Services, www.cms.gov

FIGURE 9-3 Start of Chapter 4 of ICD-10-CM

diffuse (endemic) goiter E01.0, iodine-deficiency related multinodular (endemic) goiter E01.1, and other iodine-deficiency related thyroid disorders and allied conditions E01.8. Category E04 reports nontoxic goiters and is differentiated at the fourth character level as follows:

E04.0—Nontoxic diffuse goiter

E04.1—Nontoxic single thyroid nodule

E04.2—Nontoxic multinodular goiter

E04.8—Other specified nontoxic goiter

E04.9—Nontoxic goiter, unspecified

Other conditions affecting the thyroid are hypothyroidism, which is an underactive thyroid, and **hyperthyroidism**, which occurs when the thyroid oversecretes hormones, causing excessive amounts of thyroid hormones in the blood. Hyperthyroidism can cause weight loss, nervousness, tachycardia, and goiters. In some extreme cases of hyperthyroidism, known as **thyrotoxic crisis** or **thyrotoxic storm**, the symptoms of hyperthyroidism are so severe that they put the patient in a life-threatening situation or crisis.

ICD-10-CM category E02 classifies subclinical iodine-deficiency hypothyroidism, and category E03 is used for other types of hypothyroidism. Hyperthyroidism, or thyrotoxicosis, is classified to category E05. Fourth digits identify whether a goiter, toxic nodule or nodules, factitia, or ectopic thyroid tissue are present. Fifth digits indicate whether thyrotoxic crisis or storm is present.

Disease Highlight—Hypothyroidism

Hypothyroidism occurs when there is a decrease in the production of the thyroid hormone secondary to the dysfunction of the thyroid gland. The causes of the decreased function may relate to:

- Surgery
- Inflammatory conditions
- Irradiation therapy
- Chronic autoimmune thyroid diseases

Signs and Symptoms:

In the early stages of hypothyroidism, the patient presents with:

- Fatigue
- Weakness
- Muscle cramps
- Constipation
- Arthralgias
- Headache
- Thinning of nails and hair

In the later stages the patient may have:

- Slow speech
- Thickening of the tongue
- Puffiness of the face and eyelids
- Decreased sense of smell and taste
- Dyspnea
- Pitting edema
- Hypoventilation
- Hypoxia
- Hypothermia
- Hyponatremia
- Hypotension

Clinical Testing:

The following results of lab testing indicate hypothyroidism:

- An increase in serum cholesterol and prolactin
- Elevated liver enzymes and creatine
- An increase in TSH
- Low-to-normal serum T4 levels

Treatment:

Patients are treated with medication, the most common of which is Levothyroxine.

Disease Highlight—Hyperthyroidism

Hyperthyroidism, also known as hyperactivity of the thyroid, occurs when the thyroid gland secretes excessive amounts of thyroxine.

Signs and Symptoms:

- Enlarged thyroid gland
- Accelerated metabolic processes of the body
- Tachycardia
- Nervousness
- Excessive excitability
- Increased appetite with weight loss
- Tremors
- Fatigue
- Heat intolerance
- Diarrhea
- Moist skin
- Extreme thirst

Clinical Testing:

- Serum T3, T4, thyroid resin uptake, and free thyroxine index are elevated.

- TSI levels are usually high.
- Serum ANA and anti-double-stranded DNA antibodies are usually elevated.
- Thyroid radioactive iodine uptake and scan are often performed.
- MRI, CT scanning, and ultrasound are performed to visualize ophthalmopathy.

Treatment:

Depending on the intensity of the hyperthyroidism, the following treatment options are considered:

- Medications, such as propylthiouracil or methimazole
- Radioactive iodine to destroy the overfunctioning of the thyroid tissue
- Thyroid surgery to remove part or all of the thyroid gland (When removal of the entire thyroid gland occurs, hormonal supplements are needed for the rest of the patient's life.)
- Radiation of the thyroid

Other common conditions classified to this code block are different types of thyroiditis, an inflammation of the thyroid gland. This is classified to category E06, which is summarized as follows:

Code	Description
E06.0	Acute thyroiditis, abscess of the thyroid, pyogenic thyroiditis, and suppurative thyroiditis are assigned this code. An additional code is needed to identify the infectious agent that is present.
E06.1	Subacute thyroiditis, which includes granulomatous thyroiditis, giant-cell thyroiditis, and viral thyroiditis, are coded with this code.
E06.2	Code E06.2 reports chronic thyroiditis with transient thyrotoxicosis. An Excludes1 note appears in the code book that excludes autoimmune thyroiditis from this code.
E06.3	Autoimmune thyroiditis, Hashimoto's thyroiditis, hashitoxicosis (transient), lymphadenoid goiter, lymphocytic thyroiditis, and struma lymphomatosa are classified in this code.
E06.4	Drug-induced thyroiditis is classified with this code. The code book instructs coders to "Use additional code for adverse effect, if applicable, to identify drug (T36-T50 with fifth or sixth character 5)."
E06.5	Other chronic forms of thyroiditis are coded here, including chronic fibrous thyroiditis, chronic thyroiditis NOS, ligneous thyroiditis, and Riedel thyroiditis.
E06.9	The last code in this subcategory is used to code unspecified thyroiditis.

Courtesy of the Centers for Medicare & Medicaid Services, www.cms.gov

Exercise 9.1—Coding Disorders of the Thyroid Gland

Select the appropriate ICD-10-CM code for each diagnostic statement.

Diagnosis	Code
1. multinodular goiter	_____
2. congenital hypothyroidism	_____
3. acquired atrophy of thyroid	_____
4. congenital atrophy of thyroid	_____
5. cyst of thyroid	_____
6. pyogenic thyroiditis	_____
7. Hashimoto's disease	_____
8. chronic lymphocytic thyroiditis	_____
9. Iatrogenic hypothyroidism	_____
10. thyrotoxicosis with thyrotoxic crisis	_____
11. mixed type endemic cretinism	_____
12. Riedel thyroiditis	_____
13. cystic goiter	_____
14. chronic thyroiditis	_____
15. myxedema	_____

Diabetes Mellitus E08–E13

Codes for diabetes mellitus, a complex metabolic disease characterized by hyperglycemia, caused by defects in insulin secretion, insulin action, or both, are classified to code range E08–E13 except for gestational diabetes. Various types of diabetes are identified by the severity of the disorder in the pancreas and the onset of the disease. In ICD-10-CM, the diabetes codes are organized as follows:

- Category E08, Diabetes mellitus due to underlying condition
- Category E09, Drug or chemical induced diabetes mellitus
- Category E10, Type 1 diabetes mellitus
- Category E11, Type 2 diabetes mellitus
- Category E13, Other specified diabetes mellitus

Coders need to be familiar with the notations that appear under the headings for the various categories. For example, the instructional note shown in Figure 9-4 appears for category E08. This notation instructs the coder to code first the underlying condition and then the diabetes code from this category. An additional code is also needed to identify any insulin use. Read the start of all of the diabetes mellitus category codes to become familiar with the notations that appear.

Fourth-digit characters for these categories are used to define specified complications. Fifth digits are used to classify the specific manifestation of the disease, such as neuropathy, retinopathy, skin ulcerations, peripheral angiopathy, and the like. To provide additional information on manifestations, sixth characters are used. The coder has to read the medical record to determine the manifestations of diabetes. If the information is not documented, the coder has to query the providers so that the code selected will most accurately reflect the patient's diagnostic condition. Providers should be educated on the terminology used for the diabetes codes in relation to their documentation and proper code assignment.

E08 Diabetes mellitus due to underlying condition

Code first the underlying condition, such as:

      Congenital rubella (P35.0)

      Cushing's syndrome (E24.-)

      Cystic fibrosis (E84.-)

      Malignant neoplasm (C00-C96)

      Malnutrition (E40-E46)

      Pancreatitis and other diseases of the pancreas (K85-K86.-)

Use additional code to identify control using:

  insulin (Z79.4)

  oral antidiabetic drugs (Z79.84)

  oral hypoglycemic drugs (Z79.84)

Excludes1:   drug or chemical induced diabetes mellitus (E09.-)

            gestational diabetes (O24.4-)

            neonatal diabetes mellitus (P70.2)

            postpancreatectomy diabetes mellitus (E13.-)

            postprocedural diabetes mellitus (E13.-)

            secondary diabetes mellitus (E13.-)

            type 1 diabetes mellitus (E10.-)

            type 2 diabetes mellitus (E11.-)

FIGURE 9-4 Start of Category E08

Courtesy of the Centers for Medicare & Medicaid Services, www.cms.gov

Types of Diabetes Mellitus

When the pancreas does not secrete insulin at all or secretes an insufficient amount, the patient might be diagnosed as having **type 1 diabetes mellitus**. The onset for type 1 diabetes is generally between puberty and adulthood, but it can also occur at birth. Thus, the term **juvenile diabetes, IDDM** (as well as juvenile type, juvenile onset, or ketosis-prone diabetes) is used to describe this type of diabetes. Symptoms of the disease are increased hunger, frequent urination, and thirst. A person with type 1 diabetes takes injections of insulin to replace the insulin not being produced by the pancreas. These insulin injections are necessary to keep the person alive. Blood sugars need to be monitored very carefully to prevent serious or even life-threatening conditions.

The other type of diabetes is **type 2 diabetes mellitus**, or **adult onset diabetes**. Type 2 diabetes results from the body's inability either to produce sufficient amounts of insulin or to process the insulin it does produce. This type of diabetes usually develops later on in life and is far more common than type 1 diabetes. The symptoms of type 2 diabetes are the same as those of type 1. While patients with type 1 diabetes require injections of insulin to maintain control of their diabetes, type 2 diabetes is controlled by diet, exercise, and oral medications. If the oral medications are not successful in bringing insulin levels under control, then insulin injections may be necessary.

Providers rarely write out the insulin dependency of a patient; the abbreviations *IDDM* or *NIDDM* are used instead. These two abbreviations stand for **insulin-dependent diabetes mellitus** and **noninsulin-dependent diabetes mellitus**. The coder may see "type 2 NIDDM" or "type 2 IDDM" on a note to distinguish the use of insulin or not. Type 2 diabetics can be either insulin-dependent or noninsulin-dependent, and clarification is needed before the encounter is coded. Type 1 diabetes is always insulin dependent.

When selecting codes for diabetes, ICD-10-CM Coding Guidelines need to be followed:

ICD-10-CM Official Guidelines

a. Diabetes mellitus

The diabetes mellitus codes are combination codes that include the type of diabetes mellitus, the body system affected, and the complications affecting that body system. As many codes within a particular category as are necessary to describe all of the complications of the disease may be used. They should be sequenced based on the reason for a particular encounter. Assign as many codes from categories E08–E13 as needed to identify all of the associated conditions that the patient has.

1) Type of diabetes

The age of a patient is not the sole determining factor, though most type 1 diabetics develop the condition before reaching puberty. For this reason type 1 diabetes mellitus is also referred to as juvenile diabetes.

2) Type of diabetes mellitus not documented

If the type of diabetes mellitus is not documented in the medical record the default is E11.-, Type 2 diabetes mellitus.

3) Diabetes mellitus and the use of insulin, oral hypoglycemics, and injectable non-insulin drugs

If the documentation in a medical record does not indicate the type of diabetes but does indicate that the patient uses insulin, code E11-, Type 2 diabetes mellitus, should be assigned. An additional code should be assigned from category Z79 to identify the long-term (current) use of insulin or oral hypoglycemic drugs. If the patient is treated with both oral medications and insulin, only the code for long-term (current) use of insulin should be assigned. If the patient is treated with both insulin and an injectable non-insulin antidiabetic drug, assign codes Z79.4, Long-term (current) use of insulin, and Z79.899, Other long term (current) drug therapy. If the patient is treated with both oral hypoglycemic drugs and an injectable non-insulin antidiabetic drug, assign codes Z79.84, Long-term (current) use of oral hypoglycemic drugs, and Z79.899, Other long-term (current) drug therapy. Code Z79.4 should not be assigned if insulin is given temporarily to bring a type 2 patient's blood sugar under control during an encounter.

4) Diabetes mellitus in pregnancy and gestational diabetes

See Section I.C.15. Diabetes mellitus in pregnancy.

See Section I.C.15. Gestational (pregnancy induced) diabetes.

5) Complications due to insulin pump malfunction

(a) Underdose of insulin due to insulin pump failure

An underdose of insulin due to an insulin pump failure should be assigned to a code from subcategory T85.6, Mechanical complication of other specified internal and external prosthetic devices, implants and grafts, that specifies the type of pump malfunction, as the principal or first listed code, followed by code T38.3x6–, Underdosing of insulin and oral hypoglycemic [antidiabetic] drugs. Additional codes for the type of diabetes mellitus and any associated complications due to the underdosing should also be assigned.

(b) Overdose of insulin due to insulin pump failure

The principal or first listed code for an encounter due to an insulin pump malfunction resulting in an overdose of insulin, should also be T85.6–, Mechanical complication of other specified internal and external prosthetic devices, implants and grafts, followed by code T38.3x1–, Poisoning by insulin and oral hypoglycemic [antidiabetic] drugs, accidental (unintentional).

6) Secondary diabetes mellitus

Codes under categories E08, Diabetes mellitus due to underlying condition, E09, Drug or chemical induced diabetes mellitus, and E13, other specified diabetes mellitus, identify complications/manifestations associated with secondary diabetes mellitus. Secondary diabetes is always caused by another condition or event (e.g., cystic fibrosis, malignant neoplasm of pancreas, pancreatectomy, adverse effect of drug, or poisoning).

(a) Secondary diabetes mellitus and the use of insulin or oral hypoglycemic drugs

For patients with secondary diabetes mellitus who routinely use insulin or oral hypoglycemic drugs, an additional code from category Z79 should be assigned to identify the long-term (current) use of insulin or oral hypoglycemic drugs. If the patient is treated with both oral medications and insulin, only the code for long-term (current) use of insulin should be assigned. If the patient is treated with both insulin and an injectable non-insulin antidiabetic drug, assign codes Z79.4, Long-term (current) use of insulin, and Z79.899, Other long term (current) drug therapy. If the patient is treated with both oral hypoglycemic drugs and an injectable non-insulin antidiabetic drug, assign codes Z79.84, Long-term (current) use of oral hypoglycemic drugs, and Z79.899, Other long-term (current) drug therapy.

Code Z79.4 should not be assigned if insulin is given temporarily to bring a secondary diabetic patient's blood sugar under control during an encounter.

(b) Assigning and sequencing secondary diabetes codes and its causes

The sequencing of the secondary diabetes codes in relationship to codes for the cause of the diabetes is based on the Tabular List instructions for categories E08, E09, and E13.

(i) Secondary diabetes mellitus due to pancreatectomy

For postpancreatectomy diabetes mellitus (lack of insulin due to the surgical removal of all or part of the pancreas), assign code E89.1, Postprocedural hypoinsulinemia. Assign a code from category E13 and a code from subcategory Z90.41, Acquired absence of pancreas, as additional codes.

(ii) Secondary diabetes due to drugs

Secondary diabetes may be caused by an adverse effect of correctly administered medications, poisoning or sequela of poisoning.

See section I.C.19.e for coding of adverse effects and poisoning, and section I.C.20 for external cause code reporting. (See Appendix A, Section, C4, a, 1-6.)

Exercise 9.2—Coding of Diabetes

Enter the appropriate term(s) to complete each statement.

1. A condition that occurs when the thyroid is not as active as it should be is referred to as _____.

2. A chronic disorder that results from a problem with the pancreas not secreting insulin properly is called _____.

3. The thyroid gland secretes hormones that regulate _____.

4. Diabetes mellitus falls into the _____ block of codes.

5. The type of diabetes that is always insulin dependent is type _____.

6. Code _____ is used to code type 2 diabetes with periodontal disease.

7. To code type 1 diabetes with ketoacidosis with coma, the coder should select code _____.

8. Type 2 DM with moderate nonproliferative diabetic retinopathy with macular edema is coded with code _____.

9. Type 1 DM with diabetic peripheral angiopathy with gangrene is coded with code _____.

10. Type 2 DM with diabetic neuropathy is coded with _____.

Other Disorders of Glucose Regulation and Pancreatic Internal Secretion (Category Codes E15–E16)

This block of codes includes codes for the following conditions:

- *Nondiabetic hypoglycemic coma (E15)*—This includes drug induced insulin coma in nondiabetics, hyperinsulinism with hypoglycemic coma, and hypoglycemic coma NOS.

- *Other disorders of pancreatic internal secretion (E16)*—Fourth digits differentiate the codes as follows:

E16.0—Drug-induced hypoglycemia without coma. Coders are directed by the following instructional notation: "Use additional code for adverse effect, if applicable, to identify drug (T36-T50 with fifth or sixth character 5)." Coders should also be directed by the following: Excludes1: diabetes with hypoglycemia without coma (E09.649), that appears after the code description.

E16.1—Other hypoglycemia. An Excludes1 note appears for this code that excludes diabetes with hypoglycemia (E08.649, E10.649, E11.649, E13.649), hypoglycemia in an infant of a diabetic mother, and neonatal hypoglycemia from being reported with this code.

E16.2—Hypoglycemia, unspecified. Note the Excludes1 notation that appears in the coding manual.

E16.3—Increased secretion of glucagon

E16.4—Increased secretion of gastrin

E16.8—Other specified disorders of pancreatic internal secretion

E16.9—Disorder of pancreatic internal secretion, unspecified

Disorders of Other Endocrine Glands (Category Codes E20–E35)

Category codes that are found in this section of ICD-10-CM include (It should be noted that there is an EXCLUDES1 notation after the E20 to E35 block heading in the Tabular List of ICD-10-CM.):

- E20, Hypoparathyroidism—This includes idiopathic, pseudo hypothyroidism, and other forms. **Hypoparathyroidism** is defined as an abnormal insufficient secretion of parathyroid hormone by the parathyroid glands caused by primary parathyroid dysfunction or by an elevated serum calcium level.

- E21, Hyperparathyroidism and other disorders of parathyroid gland—This category is divided into primary, secondary, and other types of hyperparathyroidism as well as disorders of the parathyroid. **Hyperparathyroidism** is defined as an abnormal condition of the parathyroid glands in which there is an excessive secretion of parathyroid hormone.

- E22, Hyperfunction of pituitary gland—This category includes acromegaly and pituitary gigantism as well as hyperprolactinemia.

- E23, Hypofunction and other disorders of the pituitary gland—Hypopituitarism, diabetes insipidus, and other hypothalamic dysfunction are classified to this code. Coders should be guided by the Includes note that appears following the category heading that states: "Includes: the listed conditions whether the disorder is in the pituitary or the hypothalamus."

- E24, Cushing's syndrome—Various forms of Cushing's syndrome are coded using category E24. **Cushing's syndrome** results from the excessive and chronic production of cortisol by the adrenal cortex or by the administration of glucocorticoids in large doses for a period of several weeks or longer.

- E25, Adrenogenital disorders—This category includes both female and male adrenogenital disorders. Coders should be familiar with the extensive Includes note listed by the start of this category.

- E26, Hyperaldosteronism—The fourth digits differentiate primary, secondary, and other forms of hyperaldosteronism.

- E27, Other disorders of the adrenal gland—Some of the diseases classified here include adrenocortical overactivity, Addisonian crisis, drug-induced and other adrenocortical insufficiencies, as well as adrenomedullary hyperfunction.

- E28, Ovarian dysfunction—Included in this category are codes for primary ovarian failure, polycystic ovarian syndrome, and other ovarian dysfunctions.

- E29, Testicular dysfunction—Hyperfunction and hypofunction testicular diseases are classified to this category.

- E30, Disorders of puberty, not elsewhere classified—Delayed, precocious, and other disorders of puberty are coded here.

- E31, Polyglandular dysfunction—This category codes diseases that involve dysfunction of multiple glands such as Schmidt's syndrome and multiple endocrine neoplasia syndromes.

- E32, Disease of the thymus—This category is differentiated by the fourth-digit level to indicate persistent hyperplasia of the thymus, abscess of thymus, and other diseases of the thymus.

- E34, Other endocrine disorders—This category classifies other endocrine disorders and syndromes.

- E35, Disorders of endocrine glands in diseases classified elsewhere—Notations appear after the heading of this category to instruct the coder to "Code first underlying disease" and "Use additional code." Review the ICD-10-CM code book and note the specific information related to these notations.

- E36, Intraoperative complications of endocrine system—This category codes complications of the endocrine system, such as an intraoperative hematoma, that occurs during a procedure. The fourth and fifth digits identify the type of complication.

Malnutrition (Category Codes E40–E46)

This block of codes is used to code malnutrition and includes the following categories (It should be noted that there are EXCLUDES1 and EXCLUDES2 notes at the start of the E40 to E46 block heading in the Tabular List that govern this block of codes.):

- E40, Kwashiorkor
- E41, Nutritional marasmus
- E42, Marasmic kwashiorkor
- E43, Unspecified severe protein-calorie malnutrition
- E44, Protein-calorie malnutrition of moderate and mild degree
- E45, Retarded development following protein-calorie malnutrition
- E46, Unspecified protein-calorie malnutrition

Other Nutritional Deficiencies (Category Codes E50–E64) and Overweight, Obesity, and Other Hyperalimentation (Category Codes E65–E68)

Nutritional deficiencies are commonly seen as a result of poverty, substance abuse, and the so-called diet craze. Malnourished patients commonly have vitamin deficiencies, but these deficiencies can also be found in patients who exhibit problems such as malabsorption of nutrients. Although malabsorption typically is found in infants, children, and the elderly, the condition can be found in anyone.

ICD-10-CM classifies nutritional deficiencies to codes E50–E64, differentiating by type.

Codes E65–E68 are used to classify overweight, obesity, and other hyperalimentation. Category E66 differentiates the type of obesity as obesity due to excess calories, drug-induced obesity, morbid obesity, and other and unspecified obesity. Following the category heading for E66, the following instructional notations appear: "Code first obesity complicating pregnancy, childbirth and the puerperium, if applicable (O99.21-)" and "Use additional code to identify body mass index (BMI), if known (Z68.-)." Coders should also be guided by the Excludes1 note that appears for this category.

Metabolic Disorders and Postprocedural Complications (Category Codes E70–E89)

Conditions classified in the E70–E89 blocks of codes include disorders of metabolism and postprocedural endocrine and metabolic complications and disorders. The coder should review the numerous notations that are found throughout this section including the EXCLUDES1 notation that appears after the E70 to E88 block heading in the Tabular List of ICD-10-CM. It should also be noted that many of the codes in the E70 to E88 range contain much detail in the code descriptions.

> **EXAMPLE:** For example in category E73 lactose intolerance codes are described as to the type of intolerance. If a patient has congenital lactase deficiency code E73.0 is assigned. If a patient has secondary lactase deficienciey code E73.1 is assigned.

Summary

- The endocrine system is comprised of structures that produce or secrete hormones.
- Hormones keep organs and tissues functioning properly.
- The thyroid gland secretes hormones that regulate growth and metabolism.
- Diabetes is a chronic condition that can affect the proper functioning of organs and systems in the body.
- ICD-10-CM uses categories E08–E13 to classify the various types of diabetes.
- Documentation is key to coding diabetes and reflecting the manifestations of the disease.
- Nutritional deficiencies and other metabolic and immunity disorders are coded from Chapter 4 of ICD-10-CM.

Internet Links

Visit **www.diabetes.org** to learn about diabetes.

Additional information about the endocrine system can be found at **www.endocrineweb.com**.

The National Institute of Diabetes and Digestive and Kidney Disease has a website that contains a wealth of information at **www.endocrine.niddk.nih.gov**.

Chapter Review

True/False

Indicate whether each statement is true (T) or false (F).

1. _____ When the pancreas does not secrete insulin, the patient typically has type 2 diabetes.
2. _____ Hypothyroidism is a thyroid that is not as active as it should be.
3. _____ Type 2 diabetes is also known as adult onset diabetes.

4. _____ Ketoacidosis is most commonly found in type 2 diabetics.

5. _____ Gestational diabetes develops during childhood.

Fill-in-the-Blank

Enter the appropriate term(s) to complete the phrase.

6. Hyperthyroidism, also known as hyperactivity of the thyroid, occurs when the thyroid gland secretes excessive amounts of _____.

7. Hyperthyroidism with extreme crisis is also known as _____, or _____.

8. When hormone secretions fall within normal limits but the thyroid itself becomes enlarged, this is known as a(n) _____.

9. Type 1 diabetes is also referred to as juvenile type, juvenile onset, or _____ diabetes.

10. Patients with hypothyroidism are often treated with the medication _____.

Multiple Choice

Select the answer that best completes the statement or answers the question.

11. Which code is assigned for thyroiditis? _____
    a. E06
    b. E06.0
    c. E06.9
    d. E07

12. To code a disorder of the hypersecretion of intestinal hormones, the coder should reference the term _____ in the alphabetic index.
    a. disorder
    b. hormones
    c. hypersecretion
    d. intestinal

13. Severe malnutrition with nutritional edema with dyspigmentation of skin and hair is coded using code(s) _____.
    a. E40
    b. E40 and E41
    c. E41
    d. E46

14. Sam Somo is diagnosed with a deficiency of vitamins E and K. This is coded as _____.
    a. E56.0
    b. E56.1
    c. E56.0, E56.1
    d. E56.8

15. Which of the following diagnoses is *not* coded to E72.3? _____.
    a. hydroxylysinemia
    b. ornithinemia type1
    c. glutaric aciduria
    d. hyperlysinemia

Coding Guidelines True/False

Review the ICD-10-CM Official Guidelines for Coding and Reporting and indicate if the statement(s) is true or false.

16. _____ The diabetes mellitus codes are combination codes that include the type of diabetes mellitus, the body system affected, and the complications affecting that body system.

17. _____ The age of a patient is not the sole determining factor, though most type 1 diabetics develop the condition before reaching puberty.

18. _____ If the type of diabetes mellitus is not documented in the medical record, the default is type 1 diabetes mellitus.

19. _____ If the documentation in a medical record does not indicate the type of diabetes but does indicate that the patient uses insulin, code E11-, type 2 diabetes mellitus, should be assigned.

20. _____ For patients with secondary diabetes mellitus who routinely use insulin or oral hypoglycemic drugs, an additional code from category Z79 should be assigned to identify the long-term (current) use of insulin or oral hypoglycemic drugs. If the patient is treated with both oral medications and insulin, only the code for long-term (current) use of insulin should be assigned.

Coding Assignments

Instructions: Using an ICD-10-CM code book, assign the proper diagnosis code to the following diagnostic statements.

1. hyperthyroidism _____

2. fructose intolerance _____

3. hyperlipidemia NOS _____

4. morbid obesity _____

5. Wilson's disease with Kayser-Fleischer ring, right eye _____

6. hypoglycemia _____

7. vitamin D–resistant rickets _____

8. type 1 diabetes _____

9. type 2 diabetes with hyperosmolarity _____

10. type 2 diabetes with retinopathy _____

11. simple nontoxic goiter _____

12. cystathioninemia _____

13. mild-degree of malnutrition _____

14. type 1 diabetic, under good control, with gangrene of the right great toe _____

15. type 2 diabetic, with hyperosmolarity with coma _____

16. nondiabetic insulin coma _____

17. vitamin B_{12} deficiency _____

18. galactosemia _____

19. vitamin A deficiencies with night blindness _____

20. hypophosphatasia _____

21. multinodular nontoxic goiter _____

22. ovarian hyperfunction _____

23. acquired iodine deficient hypothyroidism _____

24. nutritional dwarfism   _____

25. hypopotassemia   _____

26. fluid overload   _____

27. combined hyperlipidemia   _____

28. metabolic alkalosis   _____

29. MELAS syndrome   _____

30. ocular albinism   _____

31. increased secretion of glucagon   _____

32. asymptomatic postprocedural ovarian failure   _____

33. hypochloremia   _____

34. struma lymphomatosa   _____

35. myxedema coma   _____

Case Studies

Instructions: Review each case study and select the correct ICD-10-CM diagnostic code.

Case 1

Physician Office Visit

This 39-year-old female recently underwent GYN surgery and now is experiencing sleeplessness, headache, and lack of concentration. Her physical exam is negative. Diagnostic workup concludes ovarian failure. I am referring her to a specialist. Diagnosis: symptomatic postprocedural ovarian failure.

ICD-10-CM Code Assignment: _____

Case 2

Clinic Visit

The patient presents today with symptoms of excessive thirst and frequent urination, which has been going on for approximately 1 month. The patient states that these symptoms are affecting her sleep, and she is concerned that there might be something wrong. Patient denies any shortness of breath, nausea, or stomach cramping. The patient does state that her mother had type 2 diabetes, and she is fearful since the symptoms are similar. The patient states that she was borderline diabetic during her pregnancy.

(continues)

(*continued*)

WEIGHT: 198 lb Temp: 98.7 BP: 110/70

HEART: No murmurs, RRR

LUNGS: Normal

SKIN: Warm and dry

EXTREMITIES: No edema

We did a finger stick, which indicated an elevated blood sugar level of 201. An HgA1C was ordered, which came back at a level 9. With these results and the symptoms involved, type 2 diabetes is the diagnosis. We will try to control her diabetes with diet, exercise, and Glucophage. She will be set up for diabetic education as soon as possible.

ICD-10-CM Code Assignment: _____

Case 3

S: This patient is a 68-year-old female presenting with severe muscle cramps most evenings. Sometimes the cramping wakes her out of a sound sleep. This has been going on for several months and doesn't seem to be getting better.

O: Pleasant older female, well nourished, and in no acute distress. Weight is 175 lb; blood pressure is 176/72; temperature, 98.4; pulse, 72; and respiration, 18. Skin: Normal and dry to touch; no rashes. Heart: No murmurs. Lungs: Clear. Extremities: No edema, clubbing, or cyanosis.

LAB RESULTS: Hemoglobin, 11.6; hematocrit, 35.3; potassium is 5.6, which is slightly elevated.

A & P: Hyperkalemia. I gave the patient a form that lists foods high in potassium content. I asked her to limit her intake of these foods as much as possible. If this approach works and the cramping lessens, we can avoid medication. She is willing to try this for 2 weeks. If she has not improved over that time, we will explore other options.

ICD-10-CM Code Assignment: _____

Case 4

This patient presents today with a history of thyroid problems 6 years prior to today's visit. Today she is complaining of some tingling in the hands and feet, some lethargy, and some anxiety. We ran some lab tests, which showed low serum and urinary calcium, as well as low urinary phosphate with increase in the serum phosphate. Parathyroid hormone levels were almost absent. It was determined that the patient has hypoparathyroidism.

ICD-10-CM Code Assignment: _____

Case 5

A 2-month-old male presents with chronic, severe diarrhea and fatigue. His growth is stunted. His family is concerned because he has been treated for several different disorders, none of which have been the problem. After extensive lab testing over the last week, we found very low-density lipoprotein levels. We now have a definite diagnosis of Andersen's disease and will begin vitamin E therapy.

ICD-10-CM Code Assignment: _____

Case 6

The patient presents today as a follow-up for her type 2 DM with Charcot's joints. There is no change in her medical, family, or social history. On exam, there are no abnormal findings in the cardiac, abdominal, or respiratory systems. Her knees are swollen with instability. Pain is moderate at this time. She is instructed to continue on her current medications with no changes. She is to follow up with me in 4 months.

ICD-10-CM Code Assignment: _____

Case 7

Physician's Office Visit

John, a 56-year-old male, presents to the office today to discuss the results of recent laboratory tests.

Chief compliant: Over the last 2 months, John has felt lethargic and drowsy after eating large meals. He complains of extreme thirst and frequent urination.

Physical Exam:

HEENT: All exam areas are within normal limits. His breath has a fruity odor.

Heart: Normal rate and rhythm

Abdomen: Soft, nontender

Extremities: No edema, skin dry and clear

Physical exam is unremarkable

Laboratory Findings: For the last 3 weeks, John has had a fasting plasma glucose level that has been over 140 mg/dL on three of three occasions.

(continues)

(*continued*)

Discussion with Patient: I discussed with John that he has diabetes mellitus. Patient educational information was given and he was referred to the Diabetic Clinic to attend educational classes. He was given information about the need to maintain a well-balanced, nutritious diet. His diabetes will be managed by diet therapy. He is to schedule an appointment and to return to my office in 4 weeks.

Assessment: type 2 diabetes

ICD-10-CM Code Assignment: _____

Case 8

Skilled Nursing Facility Visit

This 86-year-old female patient has resided in the facility for 18 months.

Skin: There is a chronic ulceration of the skin of the left heel and midfoot. There is not breakdown into the fatty layer, muscle, or bone.

Assessment: DM, type 2 diabetes, with skin ulceration on heel and midfoot

ICD-10-CM Code Assignment: _____

Case 9

Inpatient Progress Note

This 10-year-old male patient is a type 1 diabetic. He was admitted from the emergency room because he is in a coma. He is being seen today for discharge. His insulin levels were adjusted and he can be discharged.

Discharge Diagnosis:

Type 1 diabetes with ketoacidosis with coma

ICD-10-CM Code Assignment: _____

Case 10

Physician's Office Visit

This 69-year-old patient is seen today for type 2 diabetes with diabetic neuropathy, controlled with insulin. The patient was instructed to follow up in 2 months or sooner if glucose levels change.

ICD-10-CM Code Assignment: _____

Mental, Behavioral, and Neurodevelopmental Disorders

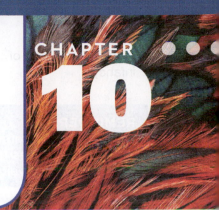

CHAPTER
10

Chapter Outline

Chapter Objectives
Key Terms
Introduction
Introduction to the Body System
Coding of Mental, Behavioral, and
    Neurodevelopmental Disorders

Summary
Internet Links
Chapter Review
Coding Assignments
Case Studies

Chapter Objectives

At the conclusion of this chapter, you should be able to:

1. Define mental health disorders and conditions.
2. Summarize how the coding for this specialty is different from the other specialties and why the coding is challenging.
3. Determine the assignment and sequencing of codes for drug and alcohol abuse and dependence.
4. Apply ICD-10-CM coding guidelines to accurately code mental, behavioral, and neurodevelopmental disorders.
5. Select and code diagnoses from case studies.

Key Terms

Alcohol abuse
Alcohol dependence
Alcoholism
Anxiolytics
Bed wetting
Conversion disorders
Delusional disorders
Dementia
Developmental dyspraxia

Diagnostic and Statistical Manual of Mental Disorders, Fifth Revision (DSM-5)
Dissociative disorders
Drug abuse
Drug dependence
Encopresis
Enuresis
Factitious disorder

Hallucinogens
Hypnotics
Impulse disorders
Inhalants
Intellectual disabilities
Kleptomania
Mild intellectual disabilities
Moderate intellectual disabilities

Nicotine
Nocturnal enuresis
Obsessive-compulsive disorder
Paraphilias
Pica
Polysubstance drug use
Profound intellectual disabilities

Pyromania	Schizophrenia	Severe intellectual	Tic disorder
Rumination disorder of infancy	Sedatives	disabilities	Trichotillomania
		Somatoform disorders	

> **REMINDER:** As you work through this chapter, you will need to have a copy of the ICD-10-CM coding book to reference. For this chapter, you will also need to reference the ICD-10-CM Official Guidelines for Coding and Reporting. These guidelines can be found in Appendix A which are now available on the Student Companion site and MINDTAP From Cengage.

Introduction

Chapter 5 of ICD-10-CM, "Mental, Behavioral, and Neurodevelopmental Disorders," classifies disorders of psychological development. It includes mental disorders that are due to known physiological conditions and substance use, along with other psychotic and nonpsychotic mental disorders.

Introduction to the Body System

Mental disorders are disorders that affect the ability of a person to function in a healthy, socially acceptable way and are classified to Chapter 5 of ICD-10-CM. Persons with the same mental disorder are not always affected the same way. The severity may be different, or a person's reaction to treatment may differ from those of other patients. Because psychiatric terminology changes frequently, coders need to have reference materials. For the most current definitions of psychiatric conditions, coders should reference **http://allpsych.com**.

Psychiatric disorders diagnosed by psychiatrists most commonly are recorded according to a nomenclature established by the American Psychiatric Association, the **Diagnostic and Statistical Manual of Mental Disorders, Fifth Revision (DSM-5)**. Although most psychiatrists use the terminology from DSM-V, the ICD-10-CM codes are used to report mental disorders to third-party payers. To learn more about the *Diagnostic and Statistical Manual of Mental Disorders*, visit **www.dsm5.org/Pages/Default.aspx**. The latest edition of the DSM-5 was released in May 2013.

Exercise 10.1—Defining Psychiatric Terms

Define the following psychiatric terms by using the preceding website or a medical dictionary:

1. anxiety _____
2. depression _____
3. panic attack _____
4. hallucination _____
5. personality disorder _____
6. paranoid reaction _____
7. schizophrenia _____
8. dementia _____
9. attention deficit disorder _____
10. dissociative amnesia _____

Coding of Mental, Behavioral, and Neurodevelopmental Disorders

Chapter 5, "Mental, Behavioral, and Neurodevelopmental Disorders," in the ICD-10-CM coding book is divided into the following blocks of codes:

- F01–F09, Mental disorders due to known physiological conditions
- F10–F19, Mental and behavioral disorders due to psychoactive substance use
- F20–F29, Schizophrenia, schizotypal and delusional, and other non-mood psychotic disorders
- F30–F39, Mood [affective] disorders
- F40–F48, Anxiety, dissociative, stress-related, somatoform, and other nonpsychotic mental disorders
- F50–F59, Behavioral syndromes associated with physiological disturbances and physical factors
- F60–F69, Disorders of adult personality and behavior
- F70–F79, Intellectual disabilities
- F80–F89, Pervasive and specific developmental disorders
- F90–F98, Behavioral and emotional disorders with onset usually occurring in childhood and adolescence
- F99, Unspecified mental disorder

Mental Disorders Due to Known Physiological Conditions (Category Codes F01–F09)

The F01–F09 block of codes includes mental disorders that have an etiology in cerebral disease, brain injury, or other cause that has led to cerebral dysfunction. This etiology can lead to forms of dementia. **Dementia** is a loss of brain function that impacts memory, language, judgment, and the ability to think logically. This block of codes can best be summarized by reading the following notation that appears under the code block heading.

Mental Disorders Due To Known Physiological Conditions (F01–F09)
This block comprises a range of mental disorders grouped together on the basis of their having in common a demonstrable etiology in cerebral disease, brain injury, or other insult leading to cerebral dysfunction. The dysfunction may be primary, as in diseases, injuries, and insults that affect the brain directly and selectively; or secondary, as in systemic diseases and disorders that attack the brain only as one of the multiple organs or systems of the body that are involved.

Codes that are included in this block are the following:

Category Code	Description
F01	This category is used to classify vascular dementia and includes arteriosclerotic dementia. A notation also appears in the Tabular Listing that instructs the coder to "Code first the underlying physiological condition or sequelae of cerebrovascular disease."
F02	Dementia in other diseases classified elsewhere is classified to category F02. A notation appears at the category level that instructs the coder to "Code first the underlying physiological condition, such as:" Alzheimer's, cerebral lipidosis, epilepsy, and recurrent seizures, to name a few that are listed. This indicates to the coder that if a patient's dementia is caused by an underlying physiological condition, the physiological condition must be listed first. For example, if a patient has Alzheimer's dementia, the proper code sequence is G30.9, Alzheimer's disease, unspecified, and then F02.80, Dementia in other diseases classified elsewhere, without behavioral disturbance.

(continues)

(continued)

Category Code	Description
F03	F03 is used to classify unspecified dementia. Examples of diagnoses that are classified to F03 include: • Presenile dementia. • Presenile psychosis. • Primary degenerative dementia. • Senile dementia. • Senile dementia, depressed or paranoid type. • Senile psychosis. This category is differentiated at the fifth character level to identify dementia without or with behavioral disturbances.
F04	Amnestic disorders due to known physiological conditions are classified to category F04. This includes nonalcoholic Korsakov's psychosis or syndrome. The underlying physiological condition that caused the amnestic disorder should also be coded and listed first, as instructed by the coding notation.
F05	Delirium due to a known physiological condition is classified to F05. This code is used for: • Acute or subacute brain syndrome. • Acute or subacute confusional state (nonalcoholic). • Acute or subacute infective psychosis. • Acute or subacute organic reaction. • Acute or subacute psycho-organic syndrome. • Delirium of mixed etiology. • Delirium superimposed on dementia. • Sundowning. It should be noted that coders are to be guided by the instructional notation for this category that states "Code first the underlying physiological condition" as well as the Excludes1 and Excludes2 notes that appear in the code book.
F06	Other mental disorders due to known physiological condition is classified to category F06. This category is differentiated at the fourth and fifth character levels to indicate catatonic, psychotic, mood, anxiety, and other specified mental disorders due to known physiological conditions. The coder should be guided by the numerous Excludes1 and Excludes2 notes that appear at the code levels within this category.
F07	F07 codes personality and behavioral disorders due to known physiological conditions. The fourth and fifth characters are used to define the specific disorders. Coders are instructed to "Code first the underlying physiological condition" for codes assigned.
F09	Code F09, Unspecified mental disorder due to known physiological condition, is used to code: • Mental disorder NOS due to known physiological condition. • Organic brain syndrome NOS. • Organic mental disorder NOS. • Organic psychosis NOS. • Symptomatic psychosis NOS. Coders should heed the notation to "Code first the underlying physiological condition."

Courtesy of the Centers for Medicare & Medicaid Services, www.cms.gov

Mental and Behavioral Disorders Due to Psychoactive Substance Use (Category Codes F10–F19)

Mental disorders related to the excessive use of substances are classified to the F10–F19 codes. The codes in this block identify the drug of choice and the level of abuse or dependence. Common addictive drugs are listed in Figure 10-1.

Alcohol abuse is defined as drinking alcohol to excess but not having a physical dependence on the alcohol. **Alcohol dependence**, also known as **alcoholism**, occurs when a person has become dependent on alcohol and is unable to stop drinking even though the alcoholism has negative effects on the person's health, social relationships, and normal daily activities, such as work. **Drug abuse** is defined as taking drugs to excess but not having a dependence on them. **Drug dependence** occurs when a chronic use of drugs creates a compulsion to take the drug in order to experience the effects from the drug.

Opiates
- Buprenex (buprenorphine)
- Darvon, Darvocet (propoxyphene)
- Demerol (meperidine)
- Dilaudid (hydromorphone)
- Fentanyl
- Heroin
- Immodium (loperamide)
- Lomotil (diphenoxylate)
- Lorcet (hydrocodone)
- MS Contin/morphine
- Methadone (Dolophine, Dolobid), LAAM (levomethadyl)
- Nubain (nalbuphine)
- Nyquil, cough syrups (dextromethorphan)
- OxyContin (oxycodone)
- Percocet, Percodan
- Stadol (butorphanol)
- Talwin (pentazocine)
- Ultram (trammodol)
- Vicodin (hydrocodone)

Benzodiazipines
- Ambien (zoldipem)
- Ativan (lorazepam)
- Dalmane (flurazepam)
- Halcion (triazolam)
- Klonopin (clonazepam)
- Librium (chlordiazepoxide)
- Restoril (temazepam)
- Serax (oxazepam)
- Tranzene (chlorazepate)
- Valium (diazepam)
- Versed (midlazolam)
- Xanax (alprazolam)

Barbituates
- Amytal (amobarbital)
- Fiorinal (butalbital)
- Nembutal (pentobarbital)
- Phenobarbital
- Seconal (secobarbital)

Hallucinogens
- Ecstasy (methylenedioxymethamphetamine or MDMA)
- Ketamine
- LSD (lysergic acid diethylamide)
- Marijuana
- Mescaline
- MDA (methylenedioxyamphetamine)
- Mushrooms
- PCP (phtencyclidine)
- Peyote
- XTC

Stimulants
- Amphetamine diet pills
- Cocaine
- Dexadrine
- Ephedrine
- Methamphetamine
- Pseudoephedrine
- Ritalin (methylphenidate)

Inhalants
- Anesthetic gases
- Diprivan (propofol)
- Gasoline/paint thinner
- Poppers, snappers (nitrous oxide)
- Propellant

Others
- Benadryl (diphenhydramine)
- Chloral hydrate
- Flexeril (cyclobenzaprine)
- Miltown (meprobamate)
- Placidyl (ethchlorvynol)
- Skelaxin (methaxalone)
- Soma (carisoprodol)

FIGURE 10-1 Common addictive drugs

When selecting codes from the F10–F19 code block, the coder must first carefully read the medical documentation in the patient's record to select the fifth and sixth characters used in this code range. The F10–F19 categories are organized as follows:

Category Code	Description
F10	Alcohol-related disorders are classified to category F10. The category is further divided into F10.1, Alcohol abuse; F10.2, Alcohol dependence; and F10.9, Alcohol use, unspecified. Each of these subcategories is then divided into fifth and at times sixth characters, which further specify disorders and conditions accompanying the abuse or dependence. To select the most detailed codes, the coder must read the medical records to determine whether the patient is exhibiting other disorders such as delirium, psychotic disorders with delusions or hallucinations, anxiety disorders, withdrawal and the like. One of the common code sets utilized is the F10.230–F10.239 block, Alcohol dependence with withdrawal. These codes are used when a patient has been diagnosed as having a dependence on alcohol and is experiencing withdrawal.

(continues)

(continued)

Category Code	Description
F11	Opioid-related disorders are coded using the F11 category. The category is divided to indicate abuse, dependence, or unspecified use. The fifth and sixth characters are used to identify intoxication, mood disorders, and other disturbances that the patient may be experiencing due to the use of opioids.
F12	Cannabis-related disorders are coded using the F12 category. This category includes disorders related to the use of marijuana. The fifth and six characters are organized in the same manner as in the F10 and F11 categories. ICD-10-CM follows the same pattern for the fifth and sixth characters for all of the F10–F19 codes.
F13	Sedative-, hypnotic-, or anxiolytic-related disorders are coded using the F13 category. **Sedatives** are drugs that induce a relaxed state and calm or tranquilize a patient. **Hypnotics** are sleep-inducing agents. **Anxiolytics** relieve anxiety.
F14	Cocaine-related disorders are coded using the F14 category. ICD-10-CM provides a separate category for cocaine-related disorders, even though cocaine is actually a stimulant.
F15	Stimulant-related disorders, other than cocaine, are coded using the F15 category. This category includes amphetamine-related disorders and caffeine-related disorders.
F16	Hallucinogen-related disorders are coded using the F16 category. **Hallucinogens** are substances that induce a perception of something being present that has no external cause. The patient may have a perception of a visual image or a sound that is not present.
F17	Nicotine dependence is coded using the F17 category. **Nicotine** is a poisonous alkaloid found in tobacco. Codes from F17 should only be assigned when the provider has documented that the patient has a nicotine dependence. If the documentation states that the patient uses tobacco, then code Z72.0 should be assigned. If the patient had a history of tobacco dependence, assign code Z87.891.
F18	Inhalant-related disorders are coded using the F18 category. **Inhalants** are substances that are inhaled for their euphoric effect. Common inhalants are glue, paint, and paint thinner.
F19	Other psychoactive-substance-related disorders are coded using the F19 category. This category includes **polysubstance drug use**, which is the indiscriminate use of multiple substances.

Courtesy of the Centers for Medicare & Medicaid Services, www.cms.gov

The following guidelines need to be referenced when selecting codes for mental and behavioral disorders due to psychoactive substance use.

ICD-10-CM Official Coding Guideline

Mental and behavioral disorders due to psychoactive substance use

1) In Remission

Selection of codes for "in remission" for categories F10-F19, Mental and behavioral disorders due to psychoactive substance use (categories F10-F19 with -.11, -.21) requires the provider's clinical judgment. The appropriate codes for "in remission" are assigned only on the basis of provider documentation (as defined in the Official Guidelines for Coding and Reporting), unless otherwise instructed by the classification.

Mild substance use disorders in early or sustained remission are classified to the appropriate codes for substance abuse in remission, and moderate or severe substance use disorders in early or sustained remission are classified to the appropriate codes for substance dependence in remission.

2) Psychoactive Substance Use, Abuse And Dependence

When the provider documentation refers to use, abuse and dependence of the same substance (e.g., alcohol, opioid, cannabis,), only one code should be assigned to identify the pattern of use based on the following hierarchy:

- If both use and abuse are documented, assign only the code for abuse
- If both abuse and dependence are documented, assign only the code for dependence

- If use, abuse and dependence are all documented, assign only the code for dependence
- If both use and dependence are documented, assign only the code for dependence

3) Psychoactive Substance Use, *Unspecified*

As with all other unspecified diagnoses, the codes for unspecified psychoactive substance use disorders (F10.9-, F11.9-, F12.9-, F13.9-, F14.9-, F15.9-, F16.9-, F18.9-, F19.9-) should only be assigned based on provider documentation and when they meet the definition of a reportable diagnosis (see Section III, Reporting Additional Diagnoses). These codes are to be used only when the psychoactive substance use is associated with a physical, disorder included in chapter 5 (such as sexual dysfunction and sleep disorder), or a mental or behavioral disorder, and such a relationship is documented by the provider. (See Appendix A, Section I, C5, b 1-3.)

Courtesy of the Centers for Medicare & Medicaid Services. www.cms.gov

Schizophrenia, Schizotypal, Delusional, and Other Non-Mood Psychotic Disorders (Category Codes F20–F29)

The F20–F29 block of codes is used for the following disorders:

Category Code	Description
F20	Schizophrenia is classified to F20. Schizophrenia is a psychotic disorder characterized by disruptive behavior, hallucinations, delusions, and disorganized speech. ICD-10-CM differentiates the types of schizophrenia at the fourth-character level to include paranoid schizophrenia, disorganized schizophrenia, catatonic schizophrenia, undifferentiated schizophrenia, residual schizophrenia, and other forms. Coders need to become familiar with the various terms used to describe the types of schizophrenia that are listed in the code book under each fourth-character level.
F21	Schizotypal disorder is classified to F21 and includes: • Borderline schizophrenia. • Latent schizophrenia. • Latent schizophrenic reaction. • Prepsychotic schizophrenia. • Prodromal schizophrenia. • Pseudoneurotic schizophrenia. • Pseudopsychopathic schizophrenia. • Schizotypal personality disorder.
F22	Category F22 is used to classify delusional disorders. **Delusional disorders** include the feeling of paranoia in which the patient has a constant distrust and suspicion of others.
F23	Brief psychotic disorder is the title of category F23, and it includes paranoid reactions and psychogenic paranoid psychosis.
F24	F24 classifies shared psychotic disorder and includes folie à deux, induced paranoid disorder, and induced psychotic disorders.
F25	Schizoaffective disorders are classified to F25. This category is defined at the fourth-character level to identify the various types of schizoaffective disorders that include bipolar type, depressive type, and other forms.
F28	Other psychotic disorders not due to a substance or known physiological condition are classified to this category. A diagnosis of chronic hallucinatory psychosis is coded here.
F29	The last category in this block of codes is unspecified psychosis not due to a substance or known physiological condition. The diagnosis of psychosis is coded here.

Mood [Affective] Disorders (Category Codes F30–F39)

Mood disorders, also known as affective disorders, are characterized by abnormal emotional states. This range of codes is differentiated as follows:

- F30, Manic episode—The fourth and fifth characters are used to identify the presence or absence of psychotic symptoms and the severity of the symptoms if they are present.

- F31, Bipolar disorder—Numerous fourth and fifth characters are used to classify the various forms of bipolar disorder. The coder needs to identify whether the patient is having a current episode of bipolar disorder or is in partial remission, and the level of severity.

- F32, Major depressive disorder, single episode—The coder should note the numerous diagnoses listed as an Includes note for this category. The coder also needs to read the patient's record to determine whether the disorder is a single or recurrent episode and the severity of the episode. Providers may have to be queried to determine the level of detail needed for code selection.

- F33, Major depressive disorder, recurrent—The coder should consult the Includes note that appears under the F33 category heading. The severity of the depressive disorder also needs to be determined for code selection: mild, moderate, severe, and associated psychotic symptoms.

- F34, Persistent mood [affective] disorders—This category includes cyclothymic disorders such as affective personality disorder, cycloid personality, cyclothymia, and cyclothymic personality, which are classified to F34.0. Dysthymic disorders are classified to F34.1 and include depressive neurosis, depressive personality disorder dysthymia, neurotic depression, and persistent anxiety depression. F34.8 classifies other persistent mood [affective] disorders, and F34.9 classifies persistent mood [affective] disorder, unspecified.

- F39, Unspecified mood [affective] disorder—This code includes affective psychosis.

Anxiety, Dissociative, Stress-Related, Somatoform, and Other Nonpsychotic Mental Disorders (Category Codes F40–F48)

The F40–F48 block of codes classifies anxiety, dissociate, stress-related, somatoform, and other nonpsychotic mental disorders. The categories include:

- F40, Phobic anxiety disorder—Common phobias classified here include agoraphobia, social phobias, and isolated phobias such as claustrophobia, acrophobia, fear of flying, and the like. Fourth, fifth, and sixth characters provide additional information.

- F41, Other anxiety disorder—Panic disorder, generalized and other mixed anxiety disorders are classified at the fourth-character levels in this category. F41.9, Anxiety, is a commonly used code in this category.

- F42, Obsessive-compulsive disorder—**Obsessive-compulsive disorder** is a psychoneurotic disorder. The patient has obsessions or compulsions and suffers extreme anxiety or depression that can interfere with the patient's ability to function occupationally, interpersonally, or socially.

- F43, Reaction to severe stress, and adjustment disorders—This category includes codes for combat fatigue, grief reaction, post-traumatic stress disorder, and other reactions to stress. Fourth characters are used to provide specificity to the codes.

- F44, Dissociative and conversion disorders—**Dissociative disorders** are characterized by emotional conflicts; the patient represses his or her emotions in such a manner that a separation in the personality occurs. The result can be a confusion in identity or an altered state of consciousness. **Conversion disorders** occur when a patient represses emotional conflicts, and sensory, motor, or visceral symptoms occur. The symptoms can include involuntary muscle movements, blindness, paralysis, aphonia, hallucinations, and choking sensations, to name a few. ICD-10-CM uses the fourth- and fifth-character levels to identify the disorder and the symptoms that occur.

- F45, Somatoform disorders—**Somatoform disorders** are characterized by symptoms that suggest a physical illness or disease but for which there is no organic cause or physiologic dysfunction. Fourth and fifth characters identify the specific somatoform disorder.

- F48, Other nonpsychotic mental disorders—The last category in this block of codes includes codes for neurosis, Dhat syndrome, neurasthenia, occupational neurosis, psychasthenia, and other nonpsychotic mental disorders. Fourth characters and instructional notations need to be referenced for this category.

It should be noted that the following ICD-10-CM Official Coding Guideline governs code selection for codes F45.41 and F45.42.

ICD-10-CM Official Coding Guideline

Pain disorders related to psychological factors

Assign code F45.41, for pain that is exclusively related to psychological disorders. As indicated by the Excludes1 note under category G89, a code from category G89 should not be assigned with code F45.41.

Code F45.42, Pain disorders with related psychological factors, should be used with a code from category G89, Pain, not elsewhere classified, if there is documentation of a psychological component for a patient with acute or chronic pain.

See Section I.C.6. Pain

(See Appendix A, Section I, C5, a.)

Courtesy of the Centers for Medicare & Medicaid Services, www.cms.gov

Behavioral Syndromes Associated with Physiological Disturbances and Physical Factors (Category Codes F50–F59)

Categories F50–F59 classify behavioral syndromes associated with physiological disturbances and physical factors, including the following categories:

- F50, Eating disorders—Anorexia nervosa and bulimia nervosa are classified here. Fourth and fifth characters provide additional detail for this category.

- F51, Sleep disorders not due to substance or known physiological condition. Coders need to reference the notations that appear at the various character levels within this category.

- F52, Sexual dysfunction not due to a substance or known physiological condition. Fourth and fifth characters provide additional code detail.

- F53, Mental and behavioral disorders associated with the puerperium, not elsewhere classified- This category is further divided to F53.0, Postpartum depression, and F53.1 Puerperal psychosis. Reference the ICD-10-CM coding manual and note the EXCLUDES1 note that governs this category.

- F54, Psychological and behavioral factors associated with disorders or diseases classified elsewhere—An instructional notation instructs the coder to "Code first the associated physical disorder, such as . . ."; therefore, two codes are needed. Please see the code book for the specific notation.

- F55, Abuse of nonpsychoactive substances—This category classifies, at the fourth character level, the abuse of substances such as antacids, herbal or folk remedies, laxatives, steroids, hormones, vitamins, and other substances.

- F59, Unspecified behavioral syndromes associated with physiological disturbances and physical factors— This includes psychogenic physiological dysfunction.

Exercise 10.2—Coding Disorders from Categories F01–F59

Select the appropriate ICD-10-CM code for each diagnostic statement.

Diagnosis	Code
1. alcohol abuse with intoxication delirium, blood alcohol level 26 mg/100 ml	_____
2. hebephrenic schizophrenia	_____
3. bipolar disorder, current episode depressed, moderate	_____
4. chronic post-traumatic stress disorder	_____
5. multiple psychosomatic disorder	_____
6. atypical bulimia nervosa	_____

Disorders of Adult Personality and Behavior (Category Codes F60–F69)

Disorders of adult personality and behavior are classified to F60–F69. This block includes the following categories:

- F60, Specific personality disorders—Paranoid personality disorder, schizoid personality disorder, antisocial personality disorder, borderline personality disorder, histrionic personality disorder, obsessive-compulsive personality disorder, avoidant personality disorder, dependent personality disorder, and other personality disorders are differentiated at the fourth or fifth character levels within this category.

- F63, Impulse disorder—**Impulse disorders** are characterized by a sudden desire or urge to act without consideration of consequences that may result. Fourth and/or fifth characters identify pathological gambling, **pyromania** (fire setting), **kleptomania** (pathological stealing), **trichotillomania** (hair plucking), and other impulse disorders.

- F64, Gender identity disorders—This includes dual role transvestism and transsexualism. Coders need to read the instructional notations for this category for proper code assignment.

- F65, Paraphilias—**Paraphilias** are sexual perversions or deviations. Fourth characters are used to differentiate the types of paraphilias.

- F66, Other sexual disorders—These are classified to category F66 and include sexual maturation disorder and sexual relationship disorder.

- F68, Other disorders of adult personality and behavior—Codes F68.10 to F68.13 classify **factitious disorders**, which are characterized by disease symptoms that have been caused by the patient's deliberate actions to gain attention.

   The following guideline applies to factitious disorder.

ICD-10-CM Official Coding Guideline

c. Factitious Disorder

Factitious disorder imposed on self or Munchausen's syndrome is a disorder in which a person falsely reports or causes his or her own physical or psychological signs or symptoms. For patients with documented factitious disorder on self or Munchausen's syndrome, assign the appropriate code from subcategory F68.1-, Factitious disorder imposed on self.

Munchausen's syndrome by proxy (MSBP) is a disorder in which a caregiver (perpetrator) falsely reports or causes an illness or injury in another person (victim) under his or her care, such as a child, an elderly adult, or a person who has a disability. The condition is also referred to as "factitious disorder imposed on another" or "factitious disorder by proxy." The perpetrator, not the victim, receives this diagnosis. Assign code F68.A, factitious disorder imposed on another, to the perpetrator's record. For the victim of a patient suffering from MSBP, assign the appropriate code from categories T74, adult and child abuse, neglect and other maltreatment, confirmed, or T76, adult and child abuse, neglect and other maltreatment, suspected.

See Section I.C.19.f. Adult and child abuse, neglect and other maltreatment

(See Appendix A, Section I, C5, c.)

- F69, Unspecified disorder of adult personality and behavior—This category is used for disorders that are not specified by the provider as to the specific disorder.

Intellectual Disabilities (Category Codes F70–F79)

The coding in this block of codes is based on the person's current level of functioning. Intellectual disabilities are classified and defined in ICD-10-CM as follows:

- **Mild intellectual disabilities**—Code F70, an IQ of 50–55 to approximately 70, also referred to as mild mental subnormality or mild mental retardation

- **Moderate intellectual disabilities**—Code F71, an IQ of 35–40 to 50–55, also referred to as moderate mental subnormality or moderate mental retardation
- **Severe intellectual disabilities**—Code F72, an IQ of 20–25 to 35–40, also referred to as severe mental subnormality or severe mental retardation
- **Profound intellectual disabilities**—Code F73, an IQ below 20–25, also referred to as profound mental subnormality or profound mental retardation
- Other intellectual disabilities—Code F78
- Unspecified **intellectual disabilities**—Code F79, used when the medical documentation states that the patient has intellectual disabilities but the level of functioning is not recorded; includes mental deficiency and mental subnormality

Disease Highlight—Intellectual Disabilities

Intellectual disabilities are genetic or acquired conditions in which there is decreased intelligence. The genetic causes of intellectual disabilities are:

- Down's syndrome
- Hypothyroidism
- Phenylketonuria

Acquired causes include:

- Birth injuries
- Anoxia
- Head trauma
- Poor nutrition
- Premature birth
- Prenatal maternal rubella or syphilis
- Blood type incompatibility

Signs and Symptoms:

Children with intellectual disabilities show signs of decreased mental functioning compared to other children of the same age.

Clinical Testing:

IQ testing and observation of a child's functional levels confirm the diagnosis.

Treatment:

Treatment of patients with intellectual disabilities varies depending on their functioning level. Persons with severe intellectual disabilities are institutionalized because they are unable to care for themselves without assistance. Persons with mild intellectual disabilities are able to live fairly normal lives and to find employment with little psychological and social assistance.

Pervasive and Specific Developmental Disorders (Category Codes F80–F89)

This code block is used to classify developmental disorders according to the following categories:

Category Code	Description
F80	Specific developmental disorders of speech and language are classified to the F80 category. The category is further divided to identify the types of disorder: • Phonological disorders (F80.0) • Expressive language disorder (F80.1) • Mixed receptive–expressive language disorder (F80.2) • Speech and language development delay due to hearing loss (F80.4) • Other developmental disorders of speech or language (F80.8), which is differentiated at the fifth-character level to indicate childhood-onset fluency disorder, F80.81, social pragmatic communication disorder, F80.82, and other developmental disorders of speech and language, F80.89. • Developmental disorder of speech or language, unspecified (F80.9) Code F80.4 contains an instructional notation for the coder to "Code also type of hearing loss (H90.–, H91.–)."

(continues)

(continued)

Category Code	Description
F81	Specific developmental disorders of scholastic skills are coded to the F81 category and are divided at the fourth or fifth character level to identify the specific delay. This category lists various terms used to describe the scholastic skills delay, such as developmental dyslexia, specific reading disability, developmental arithmetical disorder, and specific spelling disorder.
F82	F82 identifies specific developmental disorder of motor function and includes clumsy child syndrome, developmental coordination disorder, and developmental dyspraxia. **Developmental dyspraxia** is defined as an impaired ability to perform coordinated movements in the absence of any defect in sensory or motor functions.
F84	At the start of this category, Pervasive developmental disorders, an instructional notation tells the coder to "Use additional code to identify any associated medical condition and intellectual disabilities." This category is used to code: • F84.0, Autistic disorder. • F84.2, Rett's syndrome. • F84.3, Other childhood disintegrative disorder. (The code book lists various diagnoses that are coded here. An instructional notation also appears to "Use additional code to identify any associated neurological condition.") • F84.5, Asperger's syndrome. • F84.8, Other pervasive developmental disorders. • F84.9, Pervasive developmental disorder, unspecified.
F88	Other disorders of psychological development are classified to category F88.
F89	F89 is used to classify an unspecified disorder of psychological development and developmental disorder.

Behavioral and Emotional Disorders with Onset Usually Occurring in Childhood and Adolescence (Category Codes F90–F98)

Although the title for the F90–F98 block of codes leads the reader to believe that these codes are assigned only for disorders that occur in childhood and adolescence, coders should follow the notation that appears under the heading for this range of codes:

> **Behavioral and emotional disorders with onset usually occurring in childhood and adolescence (F90–F98)**
>
> Note: Codes within categories F90–F98 may be used regardless of the age of a patient. These disorders generally have onset within the childhood or adolescent years, but may continue throughout life or not be diagnosed until adulthood.

This range of codes is differentiated as follows:

- F90, Attention-deficit hyperactivity disorders—This category includes attention-deficit disorder with hyperactivity and attention-deficit syndrome with hyperactivity. Fourth characters are used to differentiate inattentive type, hyperactive, combined, other, or unspecified types of this disorder.

- F91, Conduct disorders—When selecting codes from this category, coders need to carefully read the Excludes notes at the category level. Coders should also become familiar with the diagnoses listed at the F91.1, F91.2, and F91.9 codes; the listed diagnoses are included to provide further definition to the code descriptions.

- F93, Emotional disorders with onset specific to childhood—Separation anxiety disorders of childhood and other childhood emotional disorders are classified to this category with detail at the fourth character level.

- F94, Disorders of social functioning with onset specific to childhood and adolescence—This category is divided into the following fourth-character codes:
  - F94.0, Selective mutism
  - F94.1, Reactive attachment disorder of childhood

- F94.2, Disinhibited attachment disorder of childhood
- F94.8, Other childhood disorders of social functioning
- F94.9, Childhood disorder of social functioning, unspecified
- F95, Tic disorder—A **tic disorder** is defined as a repetitive involuntary muscle spasm that is usually psychogenic and can increase due to stress or anxiety. Fourth characters are used to identify the types of tic disorders, such as transient tic disorder, chronic motor or vocal tic disorder, and Tourette's disorder.
- F98, Other behavioral and emotional disorders with onset usually occurring in childhood and adolescence—This category is used to code the following:
  - F98.0, Enuresis not due to a substance or known physiological condition—**Enuresis** is incontinence of urine. **Nocturnal enuresis**, also known as **bed wetting**, is incontinence of urine that occurs at night. Note that this category is for enuresis with no known physiological cause or not due to a substance.
  - F98.1, Encopresis not due to a substance or known psychological condition—**Encopresis** is the involuntary passage of feces. An instructional notation for this code tells the coder to "Use additional code to identify the cause of any coexisting constipation."
  - F98.2, Other feeding disorders of infancy and childhood—This category includes **rumination disorder of infancy**, which is when a person regurgitates and chews previously swallowed food, and other feeding disorders. Fifth characters provide additional detail to the codes.
  - F98.3, Pica of infancy and childhood—**Pica** occurs when a person has an abnormal craving and eating of substances that are not normally eaten by humans. Common ingested substances are chalk, paper, and ashes.
  - F98.4, Stereotyped movement disorders—This category also includes stereotype and habit disorders.
  - F98.5, Adult onset fluency disorder. An Excludes1 note appears that states that the following conditions are excluded from this code:

    Childhood onset fluency disorder (F80.81)

    Dysphasia (R47.02)

    Fluency disorder in conditions classified elsewhere (R47.82)

    Fluency disorder (stuttering) following cerebrovascular disease (I69. with final characters -23)

    Tic disorders (F95.-)
  - F98.8, Other specified behavioral and emotional disorders with onset usually occurring in childhood and adolescence—This category includes excessive masturbation, nail biting, nose picking, and thumb sucking.
  - F99.9, Unspecified behavioral and emotional disorders with onset usually occurring in childhood and adolescence.

Unspecified Mental Disorder (Category Code F99)

The last category in this chapter, F99, is for mental disorders that are not specified elsewhere or that are listed in the patient's record as mental illness not otherwise specified.

Summary

- Chapter 5 of ICD-10-CM classifies mental disorders.
- Provider documentation must be reviewed, and it must be used to justify the codes selected for mental disorders.
- ICD-10-CM and DSM-5 are both used to classify mental disorders.
- Dementia is a form of psychosis.

- Fourth, fifth, and sixth characters are frequently used with Chapter 5 of ICD-10-CM. Therefore, coders need to thoroughly review provider documentation before selecting codes.
- Alcohol use, abuse and alcohol dependence are classified separately in ICD-10-CM.
- Drug use, abuse and drug dependence are classified separately in ICD-10-CM.
- Abuse occurs when there is excess use of a substance; dependence occurs when person has become dependent on a substance and is unable to stop using the substance.
- Any diagnoses that fall in Chapter 5 must be clearly supported by provider documentation for code selection.
- Mental disabilities are classified in ICD-10-CM by a person's functional level and are described as mild, moderate, severe, profound, or unspecified.

Internet Links

To learn about addictions, Alzheimer's, depression, stress, personality disorders, and other psychiatric conditions, go to **www.apa.org**, the home page of the American Psychological Association.

To learn more about the diagnosis and treatment of mental and emotional illness and substance use disorders, go to **www.psych.org**, the home page of the American Psychiatric Association.

For information on current treatment, research, and prevention of drug abuse, go to **www.drugabuse.gov**, the home page of the National Institute on Drug Abuse.

The American Academy of Addiction Psychiatry provides information about the treatment of addiction and research on the etiology, prevention, and identification of addictions at **www.aaap.org**.

The Alcohol Medical Scholars Program provides information on the identification and care of individuals with alcohol use disorders and other substance-related problems at **www.alcoholmedicalscholars.org**.

To learn more about the treatment of mental disorders, visit **www.mentalhealth.org** and **http://psychcentral.com/disorders**.

Chapter Review

True/False

Indicate whether each statement is true (T) or false (F).

1. _____ DSM-5 is the preferred nomenclature of mental disorders for third-party reimbursement.

2. _____ Alcohol abuse and dependence are classified to different codes in ICD-10-CM.

3. _____ Mild intellectual disabilites are diagnosed when a person has an IQ of 30.

4. _____ Mental disorders are always congenital.

5. _____ Ginger Gin is admitted to New Days Drug and Alcohol Treatment Facility with the following diagnoses: gastritis due to alcoholism, continuous alcohol dependence. The code for the alcohol dependence should be sequenced first when payment for services is billed.

Fill-in-the-Blank

Enter the appropriate term(s) to complete each statement.

6. A slowly progressive decrease in mental abilities that includes lack of judgment, decreased memory, and a decrease in the ability to pay attention is known as _____.

7. A chronic use of drugs that creates a compulsion to take the drug in order to experience the effects from the drug is known as _____.

8. Psychiatric disorders diagnosed most commonly by psychiatrists are recorded by using _____, thus making coding challenging.

9. Mood disorders, also known as _____ disorders, are characterized by abnormal emotional states.

10. A person with an IQ of 30 would be diagnosed as having _____ intellectual disabilities.

Multiple Choice

Select the best answer that completes the statement or answers the question.

11. Which code is used for the diagnosis of infantile autism?
    a. F84
    b. F84.0
    c. F84.5
    d. F84.9

12. Which of the following diagnoses would *not* be coded to F60.0?
    a. expansive paranoid personality disorder
    b. fanatic personality disorder
    c. inadequate personality disorder
    d. sensitive paranoid personality disorder

13. Category F53 is used to code:
    a. aversion sexual disorder.
    b. hypoactive sexual disorder.
    c. nymphomania.
    d. puerperal psychosis.

14. Which of the following diagnoses are coded with F51.01?
    a. adjustment insomnia
    b. paradoxical insomnia
    c. primary insomnia
    d. unspecified insomnia

15. Category F03 includes all of the following diagnoses *except*:
    a. presenile dementia.
    b. presenile psychosis.
    c. senile dementia.
    d. senility.

Coding Guidelines True/False

Review the ICD-10-CM Official Guidelines for Coding and Reporting and indicate if the statement(s) is true or false.

16. _____ When the provider documentation refers to use and abuse of the same substance, assign only one code. If both use and abuse are documented, assign only the code for use.

17. _____ When the provider documentation refers to abuse and dependence of the same substance assign only one code for the dependence.

18. _____ When the provider documentation refers to use, abuse, and dependence of the same substance, assign only one code for the abuse.

19. _____ Assign code F45.41 for pain that is exclusively related to psychological disorders. As indicated by the Excludes1 note under category G89, a code from category G89 should be assigned with code F45.41.

20. _____ Code F45.42, Pain disorders with related psychological factors, should be used with a code from category G89, Pain, not elsewhere classified, if there is documentation of a psychological component for a patient with acute or chronic pain.

Coding Assignments

Instructions: Using an ICD-10-CM code book, assign the proper diagnosis code to the following diagnostic statements.

1.   presenile dementia with violent behavior   _____

2.   obsessive-compulsive disorder   _____

3.   anxiety   _____

4.   borderline personality disorder   _____

5.   social phobia   _____

6.   narcissistic personality disorder   _____

7.   intellectual disabilities, IQ of 29   _____

8.   premature ejaculation   _____

9.   heroin dependence   _____

10. passive personality disorder   _____

11. acute stress reaction   _____

12. anorexia nervosa   _____

13. psychogenic dysuria   _____

14. neurotic depression   _____

15. marijuana abuse, current   _____

16. alcoholic paranoia   _____

17. alcohol withdrawal syndrome   _____

18. hyperorexia nervosa   _____

19. alcoholic dementia   _____

20. chronic paranoid schizophrenia   _____

21. delusional dysmorphophobia   _____

22. vascular dementia   _____

23. organic psychosis   _____

24. psychogenic confusion   _____

25. hypomanic-type psychosis   _____

26. organic psychosyndrome   _____

27. mild alcohol use disorder   _____

28. dissocial personality disorder   _____

29. compulsive gambling   _____

30. developmental Wernicke's aphasia   _____

Case Studies

Instructions: Review each case study and select the correct ICD-10-CM diagnostic code.

Case 1

PATIENT: Tom Smith DATE OF SERVICE: 9/10/XX

BLOOD PRESSURE: 140/90 WEIGHT: 164 PULSE: Rapid TEMPERATURE: 100

Tom was seen today at the request of his wife for what she suspects is a recurrence of his cocaine dependence.

On physical examination, the following was noted:

EARS, EYES, NOSE, AND THROAT: Pupils are dilated.

HEART: Heart rate is increased; blood pressure is 140/90.

ABDOMEN: Soft, nontender, no abnormal masses

PSYCHIATRIC: Oriented to time and place. Patient is very talkative and admits to not eating for the last 36 hours with no sleep for the last 48 hours. The lack of sleep is cocaine induced. Patient admits to using cocaine over the last month and recent days.

Referral made for inpatient treatment.

ICD-10-CM Code Assignment: _____

Case 2

Nursing Facility Note of 2/7/XX

Sally Andover was admitted on 2/5/XX because of her medical conditions and her inability to care for herself at home. She was mildly cooperative throughout the exam. However, her dementia makes her obviously confused, and she has a diagnosis of senile dementia. Her medications were reviewed. Her full medical history and physical was completed 2/5/XX by Dr. Jones.

HEENT: Normal

LUNGS: Clear

ABDOMEN: Soft, nontender; active bowel sound; no masses noted

HEART: Regular rhythm without murmurs, pulses normal

TEMPERATURE: 98.8 BLOOD PRESSURE: 125/85 PULSE: Regular

Medication orders written.

ICD-10-CM Code Assignment: _____

Case 3

Psychiatric Office Note

Terry was seen today experiencing symptoms of mania, speech disturbances, and lack of sleep for 3 days due to his bipolar disorder. Patient states that he has not been taking his medications. I discussed with the patient the importance of taking his medications and instructed him to regularly take them. Current issues that create stress for the patient were discussed, including marital distress and financial issues. Patient was instructed to follow up at 1 month due to this current manic bipolar episode.

ICD-10-CM Code Assignment: _____

Case 4

Emergency Department Note

PATIENT: Samantha Hill DATE OF SERVICE: 12/31/XX

AGE: 23

Samantha was brought in by ambulance. She was at a New Year's Eve's party, and she had been drinking alcohol for 4 hours and passed out. According to her friend who accompanied her to the ER, Mary does not have an alcohol addiction and has no known medical conditions.

Physical Exam:

Pupils are dilated.

HEART: Heart rate is decreased.

ABDOMEN: No abnormal findings

Patient has limited response to questions. While she was in the emergency room, she started to vomit. She was observed for 7 hours and then sent home. She was advised to seek counseling for possible alcohol addiction.

DIAGNOSIS: Alcohol use with intoxication

ICD-10-CM Code Assignment: _____

Case 5

Physician's Office Note

NAME: John Nown DATE OF SERVICE: 3/1/XX

BLOOD PRESSURE: 130/83 WEIGHT: 168 TEMPERATURE: 98.6

(continues)

(continued)

John is being seen today at his request because he has felt tired and has lost his appetite for the last 3 weeks since his wife died. He has no other complaints at this time.

He said he wants to make sure that he has no physical problems. Reviewing his record, I noted that all of his immunizations are current and that he is not due for any additional preventative medicine testing at this time.

Physical Exam:

HEENT: Within normal limits

HEART: Normal R&R, no murmurs

ABDOMEN: Soft and nontender, no masses; active bowel sounds

EXTREMITIES: Within normal limits

Patient is oriented to time, person, and surroundings with no confusion. Patient expressed that he is sad because of the loss of his wife. I told the patient that his tiredness is most likely due to the loss of his wife and that there are no abnormal physical findings at this time.

DIAGNOSIS: Adjustment disorder with depressed mood.

PLAN: Patient refused antidepressive medications and said he would seek counseling if he felt he needed it. He was instructed to call the office if he experienced any other symptoms and said he wanted to follow up with me in 3 weeks.

ICD-10-CM Code Assignment: _____

Case 6

Office Visit

This 39-year-old male patient is being seen today to follow up on his treatment for bouts of decreased need for sleep, optimism, and marked hyperactivity and talkativeness. He states that these have decreased over the last month since he has been regularly taking his medications. I instructed him to continue on meds as prescribed and to follow up with me in 2 months, or sooner if symptoms increase. Assessment: Ongoing hypomania

ICD-10-CM Code Assignment: _____

Case 7

Emergency Department Note

The 48-year-old woman is brought to the ED today by her mother. This patient is profoundly retarded, which is complicating the examination. Mother states that the patient has had bouts of hypoglycemia and she is not eating well today. The patient has been very "low on energy" per mother.

Vital signs: B/P: 120/85, Temperature: 100.1, Weight: 160 pounds

HEENT: Normal

Abdomen: Soft, nontender. No masses noted.

Lungs: Clear

Blood sugar was taken and found to be 45.

Patient was started on IV. Blood sugar was then again taken and rose to 90. Patient's mother was given information about hypoglycemia and instructed to follow up with the patient's primary care provider as soon as possible.

ICD-10-CM Code Assignment: _____

Case 8

Outpatient Addiction Clinic Note

This 48-year-old male presents today at the clinic and appears to be intoxicated. He states that he has been treated numerous times for his addiction to alcohol and needs to be seen today. Review of his records indicates alcohol dependence. His blood alcohol level is currently 125 mg/100 ml. He was seen by the crisis team and they determined that he needs to have further treatment. This was discussed with the patient and he agreed to be transferred to an inpatient facility for detox and admission.

ICD-10-CM Code Assignment: _____

Case 9

Discharge Note

This 59-year-old male patient is being discharged today following a 34-day length of stay due to his latent schizophrenia. The details of his treatment can be found in the treatment plan. He has been making steady progress throughout his stay. He will continue to be monitored by outpatient services.

ICD-10-CM Code Assignment: _____

Case 10

Admission Note

This 63-year-old female is being admitted to rehab for opioid use. Laboratory testing confirmed opioid use. At this time she is exhibiting perceptual disturbances due to the opioid intoxication. She is to be admitted for further evaluation.

ICD-10-CM Code Assignment: _____

CHAPTER

11 Diseases of the Nervous System

Chapter Outline

Chapter Objectives

Key Terms

Introduction

Introduction to the Body System

Coding of Diseases of the Nervous System

Summary

Internet Links

Chapter Review

Coding Assignments

Case Studies

Chapter Objectives

At the conclusion of this chapter, you should be able to:

1. Identify the major structures of the nervous system.
2. Explain conditions that involve the nervous system.
3. Apply the ICD-10-CM coding guidelines to accurately code diseases of the nervous system.
4. Select and code diagnoses from case studies.

Key Terms

Alzheimer's disease

Autonomic nervous system

Central nervous system (CNS)

Cerebral palsy

Encephalitis

Encephalomyelitis

Epilepsy

Grand mal

Hemiparesis

Hemiplegia

Meningitis

Multiple sclerosis

Myelitis

Nervous system

Parkinson's disease

Peripheral nervous system (PNS)

Petit mal

REMINDER: As you work through this chapter, you will need to have a copy of the ICD-10-CM coding book to reference. For this chapter, you will also need to reference the ICD-10-CM Official Guidelines for Coding and Reporting. These guidelines can be found in Appendix A which are now available on the Student Companion site and MINDTAP From Cengage.

Introduction

Chapter 6 of ICD-10-CM, entitled Diseases of the Nervous System, classifies conditions that impact the nervous system. Categories G00 through G99 are used within this chapter of ICD-10-CM.

Introduction to the Body System

The **nervous system** controls all bodily activities and is divided into two main parts. The **central nervous system (CNS)** is the part of the nervous system made up of the brain and spinal cord. The **peripheral nervous system (PNS)** is the part of the nervous system that directly branches off the central nervous system. The 12 pairs of cranial nerves and 31 pairs of spinal nerves make up this system. Included in the peripheral nervous system is what is known as the **autonomic nervous system**. The autonomic nervous system regulates the activities of the cardiac muscle, smooth muscle, and glands. Ultimately, the brain controls all bodily activities. If the brain dies, the body dies. Figure 11-1 illustrates the organization of the central nervous system and the peripheral nervous system.

Coding of Diseases of the Nervous System

Chapter 6 of ICD-10-CM is organized into the following blocks:

- G00–G09, Inflammatory diseases of the central nervous system
- G10–G14, Systemic atrophies primarily affecting the central nervous system
- G20–G26, Extrapyramidal and movement disorders
- G30–G32, Other degenerative diseases of the nervous system
- G35–G37, Demyelinating diseases of the central nervous system
- G40–G47, Episodic and paroxysmal disorders
- G50–G59, Nerve, nerve root, and plexus disorders
- G60–G65, Polyneuropathies and other disorders of the peripheral nervous system
- G70–G73, Diseases of myoneural junction and muscle
- G80–G83, Cerebral palsy and other paralytic syndromes
- G89–G99, Other disorders of the nervous system

Inflammatory Diseases of the Central Nervous System (Category Codes G00–G09)

The first block in this chapter classifies inflammatory diseases of the central nervous system. A diagnosis that is commonly coded to this block is meningitis. **Meningitis** is an inflammation of the membranes, or the meninges,

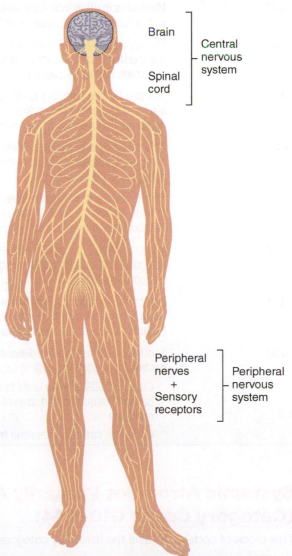

FIGURE 11-1 Central and peripheral nervous systems (From Ehrlich A, Schroeder CI. *Medical Terminology for Health Professions*, 4th ed. Clifton Park, NY: Delmar Cengage Learning, 2001.).

of the spinal cord or brain. Meningitis can be bacterial, nonbacterial, viral, or aseptic. ICD-10-CM classifies meningitis according to the type of organism or cause.

Other conditions that code to these categories of the nervous system include **encephalitis**, an inflammation of the brain; **myelitis**, an inflammation of the spinal cord; and **encephalomyelitis**, an inflammation of both the brain and the spinal cord. The G00–G09 block is summarized as follows:

Category Code	Description
G00	This category is used to code bacterial meningitis, not elsewhere classified, and is differentiated at the fourth-character level to identify the type of meningitis, such as hemophilus, pneumococcal, streptococcal, staphylococcal, and other forms. To identify the type of bacterial meningitis present, reference the laboratory reports.
G01	G01 is used to code meningitis in bacterial diseases classified elsewhere. This category contains an instructional notation stating "Code first underlying disease."
G02	Meningitis in other infectious and parasitic diseases classified elsewhere is coded here. As in G01, an instructional notation appears to "Code first underlying disease."
G03	Meningitis due to other and unspecified causes is classified with this category and is differentiated at the fourth-character level according to the following types of meningitis: nonpyogenic, chronic, benign recurrent, and other causes. Meningitis, unspecified is coded to G03.9.
G04	The title for this category is "encephalitis, myelitis, and encephalomyelitis." Fourth and fifth characters are used to identify the various forms of the conditions. There are several Includes and Excludes notations that need to be referred to prior to code selection.
G05	This category reports encephalitis, myelitis, and encephalomyelitis in diseases classified elsewhere. This category contains an instructional notation to "Code first underlying disease." The lengthy Excludes1 note should be reviewed.
G06	"Intracranial and intraspinal abscess and granuloma" is the title of this category. Fourth characters provide additional detail. Additional codes should be added to identify infectious agents present, as instructed by the notation that appears after the G06 category heading in the code book.
G07	Intracranial and intraspinal abscess and granuloma in diseases classified elsewhere are included in this category. A "Code first underlying disease" note appears in the code book for this category as well as an Excludes1 note.
G08	Intracranial and intraspinal phlebitis and thrombophlebitis are assigned this code. This code is used for various forms of septic conditions of the venous sinuses and veins. Coders need to read the notation and Excludes1 note that appears after this category heading for guidance when selecting this code.
G09	Sequelae of inflammatory diseases of central nervous system are assigned this code. This category contains the following note to explain the purpose of this code: Category G09 is to be used to indicate conditions whose primary classification is to G00-G08 as the cause of sequelae, themselves classifiable elsewhere. The "sequelae" include conditions specified as residuals. Code first condition resulting from (sequela) of inflammatory diseases of central nervous system.

Courtesy of the Centers for Medicare & Medicaid Services, www.cms.gov

Systemic Atrophies Primarily Affecting the Central Nervous System (Category Codes G10–G14)

This block of codes contains the following categories:

- G10, Huntington's disease

- G11, Hereditary ataxia. Fourth and fifth characters identify the type of ataxia.

- G12, Spinal muscular atrophy and related syndromes. Fourth and fifth characters provide further detail to this category.

- G13, Systematic atrophies primarily affecting central nervous system in diseases classified elsewhere. Coders need to assign fourth characters and reference the notations that are present in the code book at the fourth character level.
- G14, Postpolio syndrome. Coders should be guided by the Excludes1 note present.

This block of codes includes some congenital disorders such as code G11.0, Congenital nonprogressive ataxia. Coders must carefully read the diagnostic statement and match it with one of the many diagnostic descriptions in this block. For example, code G12.1, other inherited spinal muscular atrophy, has many diagnostic descriptions following the heading.

EXAMPLE: Dr. Jamel records a diagnosis of distal spinal muscular atrophy for Rased Zong. Later in the day Dr. Jamel records a diagnosis of progressive bulbar palsy of childhood for patient Suz Yeng. Both of these conditions are inherited spinal muscular atrophy disorders and are reported with code G12.1.

Extrapyramidal and Movement Disorders (Category Codes G20–G26)

This block of codes includes codes for Parkinson's disease and other degenerative diseases of basal ganglia, dystonia, and other movement disorders.

Parkinson's disease, a progressive disease characterized by a mask-like facial expression, weakened muscles, tremors, and involuntary movement, is classified by this section of ICD-10-CM to category codes G20–G21. With Parkinson's disease, the coder must identify any other associated conditions that may exist because these can affect code assignment. When assigning codes from category G21, it should be noted that the instructional notations of "Use additional code for adverse effect..." and "Code first..." appears at various fourth- and fifth-character levels.

Exercise 11.1—Coding from Category Codes G00-G26

For each diagnostic statement, select the correct ICD-10-CM code.

1. congenital nonprogressive ataxia _____
2. genetic torsion dystonia _____
3. tropical spastic paraplegia _____
4. late-onset cerebellar ataxia _____
5. tics of organic origin _____
6. spasmodic torticollis _____
7. progressive bulbar palsy _____
8. chronic meningitis _____
9. myelitis _____
10. motor neuron disease _____

Other Degenerative Diseases of the Nervous System (Category Codes G30–G32)

Alzheimer's disease, a disease in which brain structure changes lead to memory loss, personality changes, and ultimately impaired ability to function, is coded to category G30. When reporting Alzheimer's disease, additional codes should be assigned to identify delirium, dementia with behavioral disturbance, and dementia without behavioral disturbance. Reference the instructional notation that appears in the code book at the start of category

G30. Coders should be guided by the instructional notation at the start of category G30 that states "Use additional code to identify: dementia, if applicable (F05), dementia with behavioral disturbance (F02.81) and dementia without behavioral disturbance (F02.80)." Category G31 is used to report other degenerative diseases of the nervous system such as frontotemporal dementia, senile degeneration of the brain, and mild cognitive impairment. For this category coders should be guided by the following notations that are found after the category description:

For codes G31.0–G31.83, G31.85–G31.9, use additional code to identify: dementia with behavioral disturbance (F02.81), dementia without behavioral disturbance (F02.80) and the Excludes2 note that reads: Excludes2: Reye's syndrome (G93.7).

Category G32 reports other degenerative disorders of the nervous system in diseases classified elsewhere. Within the subcategories, various instructional notations appear that direct the assignment of the first listed code. Reference code G32.0 and G32.8 to make note of these instructional notations. The use of fifth characters should also be noted in the G31 and G32 categories.

Demyelinating Diseases of the Central Nervous System (Category Codes G35–G37)

This block of codes has only three categories:

- G35, Multiple sclerosis
- G36, Other acute disseminated demyelination. Fourth characters are assigned for this category.
- G37, Other demyelinating diseases of central nervous system. Fourth characters are also assigned for this category.

Multiple sclerosis is a demyelinating disorder in which patches of hardened tissue form in the brain or spinal cord and cause partial or complete paralysis and muscle tremors.

Disease Highlight—Multiple Sclerosis

Multiple sclerosis (MS) is a chronic disease that attacks the central nervous system. The patient's own body attacks the myelin fibers, causing scarring or sclerosis. This sclerosis interrupts the nerve impulses traveling to and from the brain and spinal cord. There is no clear conclusive clinical evidence of any type of pathogenesis that would cause MS.

Signs and Symptoms:

The symptoms of MS vary from person to person and include:

- Numbness in the limbs
- Visual disturbances
- Muscle weakness
- Emotional problems, such as mood swings and depression

- Urinary problems, such as incontinence, urgency, or frequency

Clinical Testing:

MS is difficult to diagnose. Testing may include:

- Electrophoresis
- Computed tomography (CT) and magnetic resonance imaging (MRI) scans
- Lumbar puncture
- Electroencephalography (EEG)

Treatment:

Patients with MS receive symptomatic treatment, such as physical therapy and steroid treatment, to relieve the symptoms.

Episodic and Paroxysmal Disorders (Category Codes G40–G47)

One of the most common disorders assigned in this code block is epilepsy and recurrent seizures. Category G40 is used to report these disorders with fourth, fifth, and sixth characters that provide further detail. This category is very detailed in the description of the codes, and coders may have to query providers to assign codes when diagnostic statements are not detailed.

Epilepsy is a transient disturbance of cerebral function that is recurrent and characterized by episodes of seizures. The most severe seizure is the **grand mal**. Less severe seizures are identified as **petit mal**. The seizure may involve convulsions, abnormal behavior, and loss of consciousness. Because seizures can occur in other diseases or conditions, the coder should not assume that epilepsy is present unless the provider specifically documents the cause of the patient's seizures as epilepsy. A diagnosis of epilepsy carries serious legal consequences, such as loss of a driver's license or the inability to obtain insurance, so extreme care needs to be taken when assigning this diagnosis.

Category G43 is used to report migraine and is differentiated by use of additional characters, to indicate the various types of migraine, such as migraine with aura, status migrainosus, hemiplegic migraine, menstrual migraine, persistent migraine, and chronic migraine.

Other headache syndromes are coded to category code G44 with additional characters to provide detail as to the type of headache syndrome. Cluster, vascular, post-traumatic, and drug induced are some of the differentiations.

G45 reports transient cerebral ischemic attacks and related syndromes, and G46 reports vascular syndromes of the brain in cerebrovascular diseases. Category G47 is used to report sleep disorders such as insomnia, hypersomnia, sleep apnea, narcolepsy, and parasomnia. Categories G45, G46, and G47 require four or five or six characters to complete code selection.

Nerve, Nerve Root, and Plexus Disorders (Category Codes G50–G59)

This block of codes is used to report various nerve disorders. The categories are differentiated according to the nerve involved. Coders must identify the nerve involvement for proper code assignment. For example, G52.0 reports disorders of the olfactory nerve and code G52.1 reports disorders of glossopharyngeal nerve.

Polyneuropathies and Other Disorders of the Peripheral Nervous System (Category Codes G60–G65)

An Excludes1 note appears in the code book after the block heading that excludes the following conditions from G60 to G65:

Neuralgia NOS (M79.2)

Neuritis NOS (M79.2)

Peripheral neuritis in pregnancy (O26.82-)

Radiculitis NOS (M54.10)

Hereditary and idiopathic neuropathies are classified with category code G60. Fourth characters provide detail for category G60.

An extensive list of diagnoses is classified to code G60.0, as evidenced by the diagnoses listed after the code heading. Codes G61–G65 report other types of polyneuropathies. Code G62.0 reports drug-induced polyneuropathy. When reporting this code, the coder must "Use additional code for adverse effect, if applicable, to identify drug (T36-T50 with fifth or sixth character 5)." Coders should be guided by the numerous instructional notations that are present for this block of codes.

Diseases of Myoneural Junction and Muscle (Category Code G70–G73)

This block of codes contains category G70- myasthenia gravis and other myoneural disorders, category E71- primary disorders of muscles, category E72- other and unspecified myopathies and category E73- disorders of myoneural junction and muscle in diseases classified elsewhere.

Category E71 provides extensive detail in code assignment. Locate these codes in the ICD-10-CM coding manual. G71.0, muscular dystrophy is further divided to the fifth character level. The G71.1 codes, myotonic disorders, are further differentiated by the type of myotonic condition, such as congenital, drug induced, and other forms. G71.2 codes report congenital myopathies and contain five and/or six characters. Coders must identify the specific types of disorder to accurately assign codes.

> **EXAMPLE:** Sally is diagnosed with Becker muscular dystrophy while James is diagnosed with facioscapulohumeral muscular dystrophy. Although both patients have muscular dystrophy there are unique codes for each type. Becker muscular dystrophy is coded with code G71.01 while facioscapulohumeral muscular dystrophy is coded with code G71.02.

Category G72 reports other and unspecified myopathies with code specificity to identify the types of myopathy. For example G72.0 reports drug induced myopathy while code G72.1 reports alcoholic myopathy. Review the G72 category in the ICD-10-CM coding manual and note the instructional notations that are found within the category and at the code level.

Disorders of the myoneural junction and muscles in diseases classified elsewhere are reported with codes from category G73. Review the ICD-10-CM coding manual. To accurately assign codes, coders must identify the specific type of disorder and note the instructional notations that instruct coders to "Code first …" the underlying neoplasm or diseases. For example, when assigning code G73.1- Lambert-Eaton syndrome in neoplastic disease the coder is instructed to "Code first underlying neoplasm (C00–D49)."

Cerebral Palsy and Other Paralytic Syndromes (Category Codes G80–G83)

This block of codes is divided as follows:

- G80, Cerebral palsy. Fourth characters provide additional detail of the category.
- G81, Hemiplegia and hemiparesis. Fourth and fifth characters provide detail.
- G82, Paraplegia (paraparesis) and quadriplegia (quadriparesis). Fourth and fifth characters are necessary for this category.
- G83, Other paralytic syndromes. Fourth characters and for some codes fifth characters are required for this category.

Cerebral palsy, a disorder in which the motor function of the brain is impaired, is present at birth, and is chronic and nonprogressive. The disorder is coded in this section. **Hemiplegia** is a condition in which one side of the body is paralyzed due to brain hemorrhage, cerebral thrombosis, embolism, or a tumor of the cerebrum. **Hemiparesis** is a synonym for hemiplegia.

This block of codes is governed by the following coding guideline:

ICD-10-CM Official Coding Guidelines

a. Dominant/nondominant side

Codes from category G81, Hemiplegia and hemiparesis, and subcategories G83.1, Monoplegia of lower limb, G83.2, Monoplegia of upper limb, and G83.3, Monoplegia, unspecified, identify whether the dominant or nondominant side is affected. Should the affected side be documented, but not specified as dominant or nondominant, and the classification system does not indicate a default, code selection is as follows:

- For ambidextrous patients, the default should be dominant.
- If the left side is affected, the default is non-dominant.
- If the right side is affected, the default is dominant. (See Appendix A, Section I C6, a.)

Courtesy of the Centers for Medicare & Medicaid Services, www.cms.gov

Other Disorders of the Nervous System (Category Codes G89–G99)

This block of codes includes codes for pain. The following coding guidelines should be followed when selecting codes from this block.

ICD-10-CM Official Coding Guidelines

b. Pain—Category G89

1) General coding information

Codes in category G89, Pain, not elsewhere classified, may be used in conjunction with codes from other categories and chapters to provide more detail about acute or chronic pain and neoplasm-related pain, unless otherwise indicated below.

If the pain is not specified as acute or chronic, post-thoracotomy, postprocedural, or neoplasm-related, do not assign codes from category G89.

A code from category G89 should not be assigned if the underlying (definitive) diagnosis is known, unless the reason for the encounter is pain control/management and not management of the underlying condition.

When an admission or encounter is for a procedure aimed at treating the underlying condition (e.g., spinal fusion, kyphoplasty), a code for the underlying condition (e.g., vertebral fracture, spinal stenosis) should be assigned as the principal diagnosis. No code from category G89 should be assigned.

(a) Category G89 Codes as Principal or First-Listed Diagnosis

Category G89 codes are acceptable as principal diagnosis or the first-listed code:

- When pain control or pain management is the reason for the admission/encounter (e.g., a patient with displaced intervertebral disc, nerve impingement and severe back pain presents for injection of steroid into the spinal canal). The underlying cause of the pain should be reported as an additional diagnosis, if known.

- When a patient is admitted for the insertion of a neurostimulator for pain control, assign the appropriate pain code as the principal or first listed diagnosis. When an admission or encounter is for a procedure aimed at treating the underlying condition and a neurostimulator is inserted for pain control during the same admission/encounter, a code for the underlying condition should be assigned as the principal diagnosis and the appropriate pain code should be assigned as a secondary diagnosis.

(b) Use of Category G89 Codes in Conjunction with Site-Specific Pain Codes

(i) Assigning Category G89 and Site-Specific Pain Codes

Codes from category G89 may be used in conjunction with codes that identify the site of pain (including codes from Chapter 18) if the category G89 code provides additional information. For example, if the code describes the site of the pain, but does not fully describe whether the pain is acute or chronic, then both codes should be assigned.

(ii) Sequencing of Category G89 Codes with Site-Specific Pain Codes

The sequencing of category G89 codes with site-specific pain codes (including Chapter 18 codes) is dependent on the circumstances of the encounter/admission as follows:

- If the encounter is for pain control or pain management, assign the code from category G89 followed by the code identifying the specific site of pain (e.g., encounter for pain management for acute neck pain from trauma is assigned code G89.11, Acute pain due to trauma, followed by code M54.2, Cervicalgia, to identify the site of pain).

- If the encounter is for any other reason except pain control or pain management, and a related definitive diagnosis has not been established (confirmed) by the provider, assign the code for the specific site of pain first, followed by the appropriate code from category G89.

2) Pain due to devices, implants, and grafts

See Section I.C.19. Pain due to medical devices

3) Postoperative Pain

The provider's documentation should be used to guide the coding of postoperative pain, as well as Section III. Reporting Additional Diagnoses and Section IV. Diagnostic Coding and Reporting in the Outpatient Setting.

The default for post-thoracotomy and other postoperative pain not specified as acute or chronic is the code for the acute form.

Routine or expected postoperative pain immediately after surgery should not be coded.

(a) Postoperative pain not associated with specific postoperative complication

Postoperative pain not associated with a specific postoperative complication is assigned to the appropriate postoperative pain code in category G89.

(b) Postoperative pain associated with specific postoperative complication

Postoperative pain associated with a specific postoperative complication (such as painful wire sutures) is assigned to the appropriate code(s) found in Chapter 19, Injury, poisoning, and certain other consequences of external causes. If appropriate, use additional code(s) from category G89 to identify acute or chronic pain (G89.18 or G89.28).

4) Chronic pain

Chronic pain is classified to subcategory G89.2. There is no time frame defining when pain becomes chronic pain. The provider's documentation should be used to guide use of these codes.

5) Neoplasm Related Pain

Code G89.3 is assigned to pain documented as being related, associated or due to cancer, primary or secondary malignancy, or tumor. This code is assigned regardless of whether the pain is acute or chronic.

This code may be assigned as the principal or first-listed code when the stated reason for the admission/encounter is documented as pain control/pain management. The underlying neoplasm should be reported as an additional diagnosis.

When the reason for the admission/encounter is management of the neoplasm and the pain associated with the neoplasm is also documented, code G89.3 may be assigned as an additional diagnosis. It is not necessary to assign an additional code for the site of the pain.

See Section I.C.2 for instructions on the sequencing of neoplasms for all other stated reasons for the admission/encounter (except for pain control/pain management).

6) Chronic pain syndrome

Central pain syndrome (G89.0) and chronic pain syndrome (G89.4) are different than the term "chronic pain," and therefore codes should only be used when the provider has specifically documented this condition.

See Section I.C.5. Pain disorders related to psychological factors (See Appendix A, Section I, C6, b 1-6.)

Summary

- The nervous system is comprised of the central nervous system and the peripheral nervous system.
- Nervous system codes are found in categories G00–G99.
- Meningitis is an inflammation of the meninges.
- Some congenital nervous system disorders are coded in this chapter.

Internet Links

To learn more about Parkinson's disease, visit **www.pdf.org**.

Visit **www.biausa.org** and **www.neuroexam.com** to learn about neurological disorders and **www.epilepsy.com** to learn about epilepsy.

Chapter Review

True/False

Indicate whether each statement is true (T) or false (F).

1. _____ Parkinson's disease is a congenital disease.

2. _____ The autonomic nervous system is part of the central nervous system.

3. _____ Myelitis is an inflammation of the spinal cord.

4. _____ Encephalomyelitis is an inflammation of the spinal cord and meninges.

5. _____ Multiple sclerosis is a disease in which brain structure changes lead to memory loss, personality changes, and impaired ability to function.

Fill-in-the-Blank

Enter the appropriate term(s) to complete each statement.

6. Numbness in the limbs, visual disturbances, muscle weakness, and urinary problems can all be symptoms of _____.

7. PNS stands for _____.

8. The most severe seizure is a _____ seizure.

9. A chronic and nonprogressive disorder that is present at birth and that impacts the motor function of the brain is _____.

10. Hemiparesis is a synonym for _____.

Coding Guidelines True/False

Review the ICD-10-CM Official Guidelines for Coding and Reporting and indicate if the statement(s) is true or false.

11. _____ If pain is not specified as acute or chronic, post-thoracotomy, postprocedural, or neoplasm-related, do not assign codes from category G89.

12. _____ A code from category G89 should be assigned if the underlying (definitive) diagnosis is known, unless the reason for the encounter is pain control/ management and not management of the underlying condition.

13. _____ Chronic pain is classified to subcategory G89.2. There is no time frame defining when pain becomes chronic pain. The provider's documentation should be used to guide use of these codes.

14. _____ Central pain syndrome (G89.0) and chronic pain syndrome (G89.4) are the same as the term "chronic pain."

15. _____ Codes from category G89 may be used in conjunction with codes that identify the site of pain (including codes from Chapter 18) if the category G89 code provides additional information.

Coding Assignments

Instructions: Using an ICD-10-CM code book, assign the proper diagnosis code to the following diagnostic statements.

1. communicating hydrocephalus   _____

2. Alpers' disease   _____

3. multiple sclerosis _____

4. intractable epilepsy _____

5. transient global amnesia _____

6. intractable menstrual migraine _____

7. anterior cerebral artery syndrome _____

8. REM sleep behavior disorder _____

9. lesion of sciatic nerve, left side _____

10. carpal tunnel syndrome _____

11. facial palsy _____

12. atypical facial pain _____

13. spastic diplegic cerebral palsy _____

14. hydrocephalus _____

15. central pain syndrome _____

16. cerebral edema _____

17. postviral fatigue syndrome _____

18. paralysis of both lower limbs _____

19. cerebral palsy _____

20. Horner's syndrome _____

21. pneumococcal meningitis _____

22. intractable cyclical vomiting _____

23. episodic cluster headache _____

24. spasm of cerebral artery _____

25. hypersomnia related to menses _____

26. benign recurrent meningitis _____

27. cerebral ventriculitis _____

28. hereditary cerebellar degeneration _____

29. progressive isolated aphasia _____

30. myasthenia gravis in crisis _____

31. familial tremor _____

32. stiff-man syndrome _____

33. Lewy body disease _____

34. migraine with prolonged aura _____

35. idiopathic hypersomnia without long sleep time _____

Case Studies

Instructions: Review each case study and select the correct ICD-10-CM diagnostic code.

Case 1

Clinic Note

This 57-year-old female patient comes to the clinic today for her annual physical.

HEENT: Normal

LUNGS: Clear

ABDOMEN: Soft, nontender

RECTAL EXAM: Refused

NEUROLOGICAL: Congenital spastic paralysis, left leg

There are no physical findings that need to be addressed at this time. I have reviewed her care plan, and she should continue per her care plan at the residential home where she resides.

ICD-10-CM Code Assignment: _____

Case 2

Sleep Clinic Note

This patient returns today following sleep testing completed last week. The testing revealed abnormal sleep patterns. I discussed with the patient if she is experiencing any stress or anxiety. She denies both. She also stated that she does not want to take any sleep-aid medications at this time. I referred her to the educator at this clinic to discuss treatment options other than medications. She should return in 1 month.

DIAGNOSIS: Delayed sleep phase syndrome

ICD-10-CM Code Assignment: _____

Case 3

Office Note

This 49-year-old secretary is being seen today for pain that is present in her right hand. She has had a series of imaging that showed no fractures or other abnormalities.

Upon exam she has weakness and pain, and she complains of disturbances of sensations in her right hand.

DIAGNOSIS: carpal tunnel syndrome

ICD-10-CM Code Assignment: _____

Case 4

This 39-year-old male presents today because of pain in his right leg that occurs at night. He describes this as a cramping feeling. He states that he has not injured his leg in the past or in the recurrent days.

EXAM:

HEENT: Normal

LUNGS: Clear

EXTREMITIES: Normal to touch and neurological testing

I instructed him to heat his leg prior to going to bed and offered to give him a referral to PT at this time. He stated he wanted to try the at-home treatment first. Since this is only occurring at night when sleeping, I feel that this is sleep-related leg cramps.

ICD-10-CM Code Assignment: _____

Case 5

Inpatient Drug and Alcohol Facility Progress Note

I was called by the nurse to see this newly admitted patient. He is having drug-induced tremor. At this time we have not determined his drug of choice. He will be placed in the detox unit to be monitored for 48 hours.

ICD-10-CM Code Assignment: _____

Case 6

Sleep Clinic Assessment

This 59-year-old male completed a 14-hour sleep analysis. He was able to sleep during the analysis. He was found to have abnormal breathing during the testing period. After analysis of all data, a diagnosis of primary central sleep apnea is supported. The patient was instructed to make an appointment to follow up on these findings in my office.

ICD-10-CM Code Assignment: _____

Case 7

Clinic Note

This 13-year-old male presents to the clinic today because there has been an increase in the frequency of his seizures. Vital Signs: BP 115/ 75, weight 126 pounds, temperature 98.6.

(continues)

(*continued*)

HEENT: Normal

Lungs: Clear

Heart: Normal rate and rhythm

Abdomen: Non-distended, no splenomegaly or masses.

Extremities: Reflexes within normal limits.

I discussed with the patient's mother the need to adjust his medications. She was instructed to increase the dose as per order. I would like to see the patient in 4 weeks to follow up to see if the epileptic simple partial seizures are continuing to increase.

ICD-10-CM Code Assignment: _____

Case 8

Discharge Note

Mary Smith, a 43-year-old, is being discharged home today following her admission 3 days ago. At the time of admission she was experiencing a severe headache. After diagnostic testing, it was confirmed that she had a persistent migraine, with aura with cerebral infarction with refractory migraine and status migrainosus. She is to follow up with me in my office in 2 weeks.

ICD-10-CM Code Assignment: _____

Case 9

Office Note

This 84-year-old male patient is seen today to follow up on the results of various tests to determine the cause of the pain he experiences on the left side of his face. Diagnostic findings from testing have been nonconclusive. At this time there is no underlying reason for the atypical facial pain. He was given Vicodin and instructed to take when pain level is over 5. If other symptoms occur, he was instructed to call the office or go to the emergency room.

ICD-10-CM Code Assignment: _____

Case 10

Inpatient Admission Note

This 73-year-old female is being admitted today because she has ovarian cancer and she continues to experience pain. She has refused all treatment for the cancer. The pain is very acute at the present time and she is admitted for IV pain management. Nurses were advised to follow pain management protocols.

ICD-10-CM Code Assignment: _____

CHAPTER 12

Disorders of the Eye and Adnexa

Chapter Outline

Chapter Objectives
Key Terms
Introduction
Abbreviations
Introduction to the Body System
Coding Disorders of the Eye and Adnexa

Summary
Internet Links
Chapter Review
Coding Assignments
Case Studies

Chapter Objectives

At the conclusion of this chapter, you should be able to:

1. Identify the major structures of the eye and adnexa.
2. Explain disorders that impact the eye and adnexa.
3. Interpret abbreviations that apply to disorders of the eye and adnexa.
4. Apply ICD-10-CM coding guidelines to accurately code disorders of the eye and adnexa.
5. Select and code diagnoses from case studies.

Key Terms

Adnexa	Ciliary body	Glaucoma	Posterior chamber
Anterior chamber	Conjunctiva	Hordeolum	Pterygium
Aqueous humor	Cornea	Iris	Pupil
Blepharitis	Dacryoadenitis	Lacrimal duct	Retina
Blepharochalasis	Entropion	Lacrimal gland	Sclera
Canthus	Epiphora	Lagophthalmos	Suspensory
Cataracts	Eyelashes	Lens	ligaments
Chalazion	Eyelids, upper	Optic disc	Trichiasis
Choroids	and lower	Optic nerve	Vitreous humor

REMINDER: As you work through this chapter, you will need to have a copy of the ICD-10-CM coding book to reference. For this chapter, you will also need to reference the ICD-10-CM Official Guidelines for Coding and Reporting. These guidelines can be found in Appendix A which are now available on the Student Companion site and MINDTAP From Cengage.

Introduction

Chapter 7 of ICD-10-CM classifies diseases of the eye and adnexa. It excludes certain conditions that originate in the perinatal period, certain infectious and parasitic diseases, congenital malformations, diabetes-related eye conditions, injuries, and neoplasms that impact the eye and adnexa. Coders should reference the Excludes note that appears at the start of the chapter. Chapter 7 of ICD-10-CM contains the following blocks of codes:

- H00–H05, Disorders of eyelid, lacrimal system, and orbit
- H10–H11, Disorders of conjunctiva
- H15–H22, Disorders of sclera, cornea, iris, and ciliary body
- H25–H28, Disorders of lens
- H30–H36, Disorders of choroid and retina
- H40–H42, Glaucoma
- H43–H44, Disorders of vitreous body and globe
- H46–H47, Disorders of optic nerve and visual pathways
- H49–H52, Disorders of ocular muscles, binocular movement, accommodation, and refraction
- H53–H54, Visual disturbances and blindness
- H55–H57, Other disorders of eye and adnexa
- H59, Intraoperative and postprocedural complications and disorders of eye and adnexa, not elsewhere classified

Abbreviations

The following abbreviations are commonly used for the eye and adnexa:

ARMD	age-related macular degeneration
EOM	extraocular movement
IOL	intraocular lens
IOP	intraocular pressure
OD	right eye
Ophth	ophthalmology
OS	left eye
OU	both eyes
PERRLA	pupils equal, round, reactive to light and accommodation

Introduction to the Body System

When coding disorders of the eye, the coder must understand the anatomy of the eye or have detailed diagrams and well-documented provider notes to assist with the coding. Figures 12-1 and 12-2 illustrate the complexity of the eye anatomy. **Adnexa** is a term for the accessory or appendage of an organ. Figure 12-3 diagrams the adnexa of the eyes.

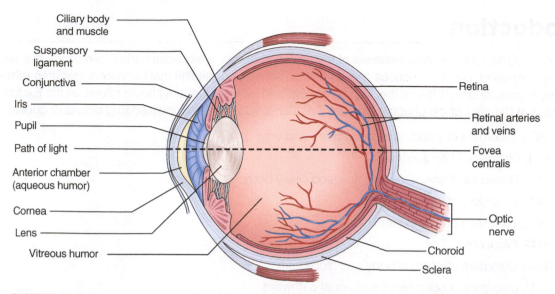

FIGURE 12-1 Cross section of the structures of the eyeball (From Ehrlich A, Schroeder Cl. *Medical Terminology for Health Professions*, 4th ed. Clifton Park, NY: Delmar, Cengage Learning, 2001.).

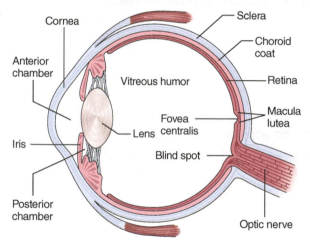

FIGURE 12-2 Structures of the eye (From Ehrlich A, Schroeder Cl. *Medical Terminology for Health Professions*, 4th ed. Clifton Park, NY: Delmar, Cengage Learning, 2001.).

The parts of the eye are as follows:

- **Sclera**—The white portion of the eye that is a fibrous membrane, that serves as a protective covering for the eye, and that maintains the shape of the eyeball
- **Iris**—The colored portion of the eye
- **Pupil**—The center of the iris that controls the amount of light entering the eye
- **Conjunctiva**—The colorless mucous membrane that lines the anterior part of the eye
- **Lacrimal gland**—The gland that produces tears
- **Lacrimal duct**—The duct that drains the tears from the eye and that is located at the inner edge of the eye, which is known as the **canthus**
- **Upper and lower eyelids**—The lids that protect the eyes and help to keep the surface of the eyeball lubricated

- **Eyelashes**—Hairs that are located along the edge of the eyelids to protect the eye from foreign materials
- **Cornea**—A transparent nonvascular structure located on the anterior portion of the sclera
- **Choroids**—The layer just beneath the sclera containing capillaries that provide the blood supply and nutrients to the eye
- **Lens**—Posterior to the iris, a colorless structure that allows the eye to focus on images
- **Ciliary body**—The muscles responsible for adjusting the lens
- **Suspensory ligaments**—Attached to the ciliary body, the ligaments that attach to the lens and hold it in place
- **Retina**—The nerve cell layer of the eye that changes light rays into nerve impulses
- **Optic nerve**—The nerve that transmits impulses to the brain from the eye

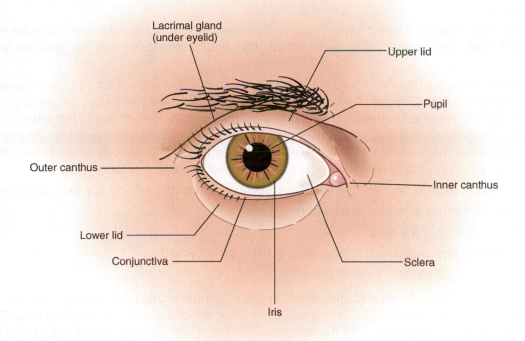

FIGURE 12-3 Major structures and adnexa of the right eye (From Ehrlich A, Schroeder Cl. *Medical Terminology for Health Professions*, 4th ed. Clifton Park, NY: Delmar, Cengage Learning, 2001.).

- **Optic disc**—The blind spot on the optic nerve that is the point of entry for the artery supplying blood to the retina
- **Aqueous humor**—The fluid that fills the two cavities of the interior of the eye
- **Anterior chamber**—A chamber located in front of the lens
- **Posterior chamber**—A chamber located behind the lens
- **Vitreous humor**—The clear, jelly-like fluid that fills the posterior chamber of the eye and helps shape the eye

Coding Disorders of the Eye and Adnexa

Chapter 7 of ICD-10-CM is organized according to the anatomical structures of the eye and adnexa. When selecting codes, the coder should read the medical documentation to determine whether the condition or disorder is impacting one or both eyes because many codes delineate the eye or eyes affected.

Disorders of Eyelid, Lacrimal System, and Orbit (Category Codes H00–H05)

This block of codes classifies disorders of the eyelid, lacrimal system, and orbit. It includes the following categories:

- H00, Hordeolum and chalazion—**Hordeolum**, commonly known as a sty, and **chalazion**, a small tumor of the eyelid caused by the retention of secretions of the meibomian gland, are classified to this category. This category, as with many of the categories found in this chapter of ICD-10-CM, details the specific anatomic site of the condition in code assignment. For example Code H00.011 reports hordeolum externum, right upper eyelid, while code H00.012 reports hordeolum externum, right lower eyelid.

- H01, Other inflammation of eyelid—This category classifies **blepharitis**, an inflammation of the eyelids, and noninfectious dermatoses of the eyelid. Fourth, fifth, and/or sixth characters are assigned for this category.

- H02, Other disorders of eyelid—This category is used to report the various forms of **entropion**, the turning inward of the border of the eyelid against the eyeball, and **trichiasis**, the turning inward of the eyelashes that often causes the eyeball to become irritated. Also coded to this category is **lagophthalmos**, the inability to close the eyelids completely, and **blepharochalasis**, atrophy of the intercellular tissue that causes a relaxation of the skin of the eyelid. To provide greater detail in this category, fourth, fifth, and/or sixth characters are assigned for code selection.

- H04, Disorders of lacrimal system—Coded to this category, with fourth, fifth, and/or sixth characters, are:
  - **Dacryoadenitis**—Inflammation of the lacrimal gland
  - **Epiphora**—Tearing of the eyes
  - Acute, chronic, and unspecified inflammation of the lacrimal system
  - Stenosis and insufficiency of lacrimal passages

- H05, Disorders of orbit—Acute and chronic inflammation of the orbit, exophthalmic conditions, deformities of the orbit, and enophthalmos and other disorders of the orbit are classified here. Coders need to review the coding manual for the assignment of fourth, fifth, and/or sixth characters for this category of codes.

Disorders of Conjunctiva (Category Codes H10–H11)

Many common conditions are classified to this range of codes:

- H10, Conjunctivitis—The various forms of conjunctivitis are coded to this category. The coder needs to determine whether the condition is acute or chronic. Blepharoconjunctivitis and other forms of conjunctivitis are also classified here. Coders should note the Excludes1 note that appears after the category heading that states "Excludes1: keratoconjunctivitis (H16.2-)." Also coders should note the assignment of fourth, fifth, or sixth characters for this category.

> **EXAMPLE:** Dr. Raz reports that his patient has bilateral acute follicular conjunctivitis. This is reported to the sixth character by assigning code H10.013.

- H11, Other disorders of conjunctiva—This category includes **pterygium**, which is a thick patch of hypertrophied tissue that extends from the nasal border of the cornea to the inner canthus of the eye. Also classified in this category are conjunctival degenerations and deposits, scars, hemorrhage, and other conjunctival vascular disorders. Fourth, fifth, and/or sixth characters are needed for code assignment within this category.

Disorders of Sclera, Cornea, Iris, and Ciliary Body (Category Code H15–H22)

This block of codes is divided into the following categories, with the use of fourth, fifth, and/or sixth characters for valid code assignment:

- H15, Disorders of sclera
- H16, Keratitis
- H17, Corneal scars and opacities

- H18, Other disorders of cornea
- H20, Iridocyclitis
- H21, Other disorders of iris and ciliary body
- H22, Disorders of iris and ciliary body in diseases classified elsewhere

Disorders of Lens (Category Codes H25–H28)

Cataracts, the abnormal loss of transparency of the lens of the eye, are classified to this block of codes with the use of fourth, fifth, and/or sixth characters. The types of cataracts and other disorders of the lens are classified as follows:

- H25, Age-related cataract. This category also reports senile cataract.
- H26, Other cataract
- H27, Other disorders of lens
- H28, Cataract in diseases classified elsewhere

It is important for coders to note the numerous instructional notations that appear throughout the categories for the cataract codes.

Disease Highlight—Cataracts

Cataracts occur in the lens of the eye when there is a clouding of the lens. Cataracts commonly develop in persons 70 years of age and older, and affect about 60% of this population. The clouding of the lens occurs because of a change in metabolism and nutrition. Trauma, birth defects, and other diseases, such as diabetes mellitus, can also cause cataracts.

Sign and Symptoms:

- Decrease in visual acuity
- Patient complains of not being able to see
- Blurred vision
- Glare

- Decrease in color perception
- White or cloudy appearance of the pupil

Clinical Testing:

Slit lamp examination of the eye will confirm the diagnosis.

Treatment:

Removal of the cloudy lens, known as cataract extraction, with the insertion of an artificial lens, known as an intraocular lens, is the common treatment for cataracts. See Figure 12-4. If a person has bilateral cataracts, the surgery will be completed on one eye and then weeks later be completed on the second eye so the person will always have use of one eye.

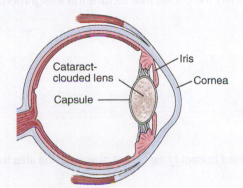 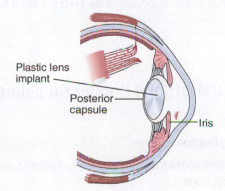

FIGURE 12-4 Cataract extraction with placement of intraocular lens.

Disorders of Choroid and Retina (Category Codes H30–H36)

This block of codes includes chorioretinal inflammation, chorioretinal scars, choroidal degeneration, choroidal hemorrhage and rupture, and choroidal detachment. Also classified to this block are retinal detachments and breaks, coded with category H33. Category H34 classifies the various types of retinal vascular occlusions. Category H35 classifies other retinal disorders, such as background retinopathy and retinal vascular changes, retinopathy of prematurity, degeneration of macular and posterior pole, peripheral retinal degeneration, and hereditary retinal dystrophy. Coders need to review the coding manual for the selection of fourth, fifth, and/or sixth characters for valid code assignment. H36 reports retinal disorders in diseases classified elsewhere.

Exercise 12.1—Coding Diseases of the Eye

For each diagnostic statement, assign an ICD-10-CM code:

1. detachment of retina, left eye _____
2. bilateral cyst of ora serrata _____
3. subluxation of lens of right eye _____
4. cataract with neovascularization, left eye _____
5. aphakia _____
6. posterior dislocation of lens of the left eye _____
7. left eye total traumatic cataract _____
8. bilateral ectopic pupil _____
9. right eye, miotic pupillary cyst _____
10. recurrent acute iridocyclitis of both eyes _____

Glaucoma (Category Codes H40–H42)

Glaucoma, an eye disease marked by increased pressure in the eyeball that may result in damage to the optic disk and the gradual loss of vision, is reported using category codes H40–H42. The codes are differentiated according to the types of glaucoma and whether the disease is impacting one or both eyes. Some of the subcategories, such as H40.3 and H40.4, contain instructional notations directing the coder to "Code also underlying condition." It should also be noted for these subcategories, a seventh character is needed to identify the stage of the glaucoma. H40.5 instructs the coder to "Code also underlying eye disorder," and H40.6 instructs the coder to "Use additional code for adverse effect, if applicable, to identify drug (T36–T50 with fifth or sixth character 5). Coders need to carefully read the headings that follow subcategories H40.1–H40.6 to identify the codes that require the assignment of a seventh character."

ICD-10-CM Official Coding Guidelines

a. Glaucoma

1) Assigning Glaucoma Codes

Assign as many codes from category H40, Glaucoma, as needed to identify the type of glaucoma, the affected eye, and the glaucoma stage.

2) Bilateral glaucoma with same type and stage

When a patient has bilateral glaucoma and both eyes are documented as being the same type and stage, and there is a code for bilateral glaucoma, report only the code for the type of glaucoma, bilateral, with the seventh character for the stage.

When a patient has bilateral glaucoma and both eyes are documented as being the same type and stage, and the classification does not provide a code for bilateral glaucoma (i.e., subcategories H40.10 and H40.20) report only one code for the type of glaucoma with the appropriate seventh character for the stage.

3) Bilateral glaucoma stage with different types or stages

When a patient has bilateral glaucoma and each eye is documented as having a different type or stage, and the classification distinguishes laterality, assign the appropriate code for each eye rather than the code for bilateral glaucoma.

When a patient has bilateral glaucoma and each eye is documented as having a different type, and the classification does not distinguish laterality (i.e., subcategories H40.10 and H40.20), assign one code for each type of glaucoma with the appropriate seventh character for the stage.

When a patient has bilateral glaucoma and each eye is documented as having the same type, but different stage, and the classification does not distinguish laterality (i.e., subcategories H40.10 and H40.20), assign a code for the type of glaucoma for each eye with the seventh character for the specific glaucoma stage documented for each eye.

4) Patient admitted with glaucoma and stage evolves during the admission

If a patient is admitted with glaucoma and the stage progresses during the admission, assign the code for highest stage documented.

5) Indeterminate stage glaucoma

Assignment of the seventh character "4" for "indeterminate stage" should be based on the clinical documentation. The seventh character "4" is used for glaucomas whose stage cannot be clinically determined. This seventh character should not be confused with the seventh character "0", unspecified, which should be assigned when there is no documentation regarding the stage of the glaucoma.

(See Appendix A, Section I, c7, a 1-5.)

Disorders of Vitreous Body and Globe (Category Codes H43–H44)

The H43–H44 categories are used to report disorders of the vitreous body and globe. The H43 category codes vitreous prolapse, hemorrhage, deposits, opacities, and other disorders of the vitreous body. Fourth, fifth, and/or six characters are used within this category. Code H44 reports disorders of the globe that include purulent endophthalmitis, degenerative myopia, hypotony of the eye, degenerative conditions of the globe, and other disorders. Retained foreign body particles are also coded to H44 category codes. Coders need to reference the coding manual to identify fourth, fifth, and/or sixth characters.

EXAMPLE: The patient presents with a diagnosis of chronic vitreous abscess of right eye. To correctly code this diagnosis the coder must report code H44.021 that includes all six characters.

Disorders of Optic Nerve and Visual Pathways (Category Codes H46–H47)

Optic neuritis is reported using category code H46. Code H47 reports other disorders of optic nerve and visual pathways. The H47.4, H47.5, and H47.6 subcategories of codes has an instructional notation stating "Code also underlying condition." Both categories H46 and H47 require the assignment of fourth, fifth, and/or sixth characters.

Disorders of Ocular Muscles, Binocular Movement, Accommodation, and Refraction (Category Codes H49–H52)

This block of codes is divided into the following categories, and coders need to reference the coding manual for additional fourth, fifth, and/or sixth characters:

- H49, Paralytic strabismus—This category is differentiated according to the nerve involved in the palsy. The H49.0 codes involve the third nerve, H49.1 codes involve the fourth nerve, and H49.2 codes involve the sixth nerve.
- H50, Other strabismus—This category reports esotropia, exotropia, vertical strabismus, intermittent heterotropia, other and unspecified heterotropia.
- H51, Other disorders of binocular movement—Disorders reported here include convergence insufficiency and excess and internuclear ophthalmoplegia.
- H52, Disorders of refraction and accommodation—Myopia, hypermetropia, astigmatism, anisometropia, presbyopia, and other disorders of accommodation are classified to this category.

Visual Disturbances and Blindness (Category Codes H53–H54)

This category, with the use of fourth, fifth, sixth, and/or seventh characters, reports visual disturbance and blindness. Legal blindness, as defined in the United States, is classified by severity. In the ICD-10-CM code book under the code H54.8, a table lists the classification of the severity of visual impairment. The notation directly above the table assists the coder in selecting codes for the terms *low vision* and *blindness*.

The following guidelines provide guidance for the coding of low vision and blindness.

ICD-10-CM Official Coding Guideline

b. Blindness

If "blindness" or "low vision" of both eyes is documented but the visual impairment category is not documented, assign code H54.3, Unqualified visual loss, both eyes. If "blindness" or "low vision" in one eye is documented but the visual impairment category is not documented, assign a code from H54.6-, unqualified visual loss, one eye. If "blindness" or "visual loss" is documented without any information about whether one or both eyes are affected, assign code H54.7, Unspecified visual loss. (See Appendix A, Section 1, c7, b.)

Other Disorders of Eye and Adnexa (Category Codes H55–H59)

The last block of codes found in Chapter 7 of ICD-10-CM reports other disorders of the eye and adnexa, using fourth, fifth, and/or sixth characters, and includes the following categories:

- H55, Nystagmus and other irregular eye movements
- H57, Other disorders of eye and adnexa, such as anomalies of papillary function and ocular pain
- H59, Intraoperative and postprocedural complications and disorders of eye and adnexa, not elsewhere classified, including complications following cataract surgery and other procedures. Coders should make note of the Excludes1 note that appears in the code book for this code.

Summary

- Chapter 7 of ICD-10-CM classifies diseases of the eye and adnexa.
- A cataract is the abnormal loss of transparency of the eye's lens.
- Glaucoma is an eye disease marked by increased pressure in the eyeball that may result in damage to the optic disk and the gradual loss of vision.
- Legal blindness, as defined in the United States, is classified by severity.

Internet Links

To learn about glaucoma, visit **www.glaucoma.org**.

To learn about cataracts, visit **https://nei.nih.gov/health/cataract/**.

To learn about the eye, visit **www.medicinenet.com** and search on the specific eye disorder.

Chapter Review

True/False

Indicate whether each statement is true (T) or false (F).

1. _____ The transparent nonvascular structure located on the anterior portion of the sclera is the cornea.

2. _____ The structure that is posterior to the iris and is a colorless structure that allows the eye to focus on images is the lens.

3. _____ Epiphora is an inflammation of the lacrimal gland.

4. _____ Category code H04 classifies disorders of the eyelid.

5. _____ Amyloid pterygium of the right eye is reported with code H11.011.

Fill-in-the-Blank

Enter the appropriate term(s) to complete each statement.

6. The layer just beneath the sclera that contains capillaries that provide the blood supply and nutrients to the eye is the _____.

7. The muscles that are responsible for adjusting the lens are the _____.

8. Tearing of the eyes is _____.

9. To report conjunctival granuloma of both eyes, use code _____.

10. Posterior cyclitis would be classified to code _____.

Coding Guidelines True/False

Review the ICD-10-CM Official Guidelines for Coding and Reporting and indicate if the statement(s) is true or false.

11. _____ Assign only one code from category H40, Glaucoma, to identify the type of glaucoma, the affected eye, and the glaucoma stage.

12. _____ When a patient has bilateral glaucoma and both eyes are documented as being the same type and stage, and the classification does not provide a code for bilateral glaucoma (i.e., subcategories H40.10 and H40.20) report only one code for the type of glaucoma with the appropriate seventh character for the stage.

13. _____ When a patient has bilateral glaucoma and each eye is documented as having a different type, and the classification does not distinguish laterality (i.e., subcategories H40.10 and H40.20), assign one code for each type of glaucoma with the appropriate seventh character for the stage.

14. _____ If a patient is admitted with glaucoma and the stage progresses during the admission, assign the code for stage of the glaucoma documented at the time of the admission.

15. _____ Assignment of the seventh character "4" for "indeterminate stage" should be based on the clinical documentation. The seventh character "4" is used for glaucomas whose stage cannot be clinically determined. This seventh character should not be confused with the seventh character "0", unspecified, which should be assigned when there is no documentation regarding the stage of the glaucoma.

Coding Assignments

Instructions: Using an ICD-10-CM code book, assign the proper diagnosis code to the following diagnostic statements.

1. acute atopic conjunctivitis _____

2. angular blepharoconjunctivitis _____

3. macular keratitis _____

4. left eye photokeratitis _____

5. perforated corneal ulceration of the right eye _____

6. scleral ectasia, bilateral _____

7. conjunctival hyperemia, both eyes _____

8. Mooren's corneal ulcer, left eye _____

9. left eye ghost vessels _____

10. diffuse interstitial keratitis _____

11. descemetocele, OD _____

12. band keratopathy _____

13. bilateral degeneration of ciliary body _____

14. pupillary occlusion _____

15. iris atrophy, right eye _____

16. bilateral choroidal rupture _____

17. diffuse secondary atrophy of choroid _____

18. serous choroidal detachment, OS _____

19. partial retinal artery occlusion _____

20. parasitic cyst of retina, OD _____

21. bilateral tonic pupil _____

22. irregular astigmatism, OS _____

23. alternating exotropia with A pattern _____

24. bilateral trochlear nerve palsy _____

25. left eye, degeneration of chamber angle _____

26. mild low-tension glaucoma, right eye _____

27. bilateral preglaucoma _____

28. left eye retinal hemorrhage _____

29. bilateral lattice degeneration of retina _____

30. bilateral flat anterior chamber hypotony of eye _____

31. conjunctivochalasis, right eye _____

32. anterior scleritis, bilateral _____

33. Equatorial staphyloma, OS   _____

34. central corneal ulcer, OD   _____

35. bilateral exposure keratoconjunctivitis   _____

Case Studies

Instructions: Review each case study and select the correct ICD-10-CM diagnostic code.

Case 1

Office Note

This 7-year-old male presents today with redness OU. Upon examination, the conjunctiva are swollen. He is experiencing no other symptoms.

Dx: acute conjunctivitis

Eye ointment given. Instructed to return in 10 days.

ICD-10-CM Code Assignment: _____

Case 2

ER Visit Note

This 37-year-old male presents to the ER with pain in his eye. Exam shows an object in the right lower eyelid. Because the object is deeply embedded in the skin, I am asking for a consultation from Dr. Ferrar. The object is retained in the lower right eyelid. The patient was sent to Dr. Ferrar's office.

ICD-10-CM Code Assignment: _____

Case 3

Office Visit Note

This 54-year-old man works on a dairy farm and 2 weeks ago he "got something in my eye." Exam of the eyes reveals that there are no foreign objects in the eyes at this time. The left eye is red and there is an abscess of the right upper eyelid. The patient was given antibiotics, drops, and patient education material. He was instructed to follow up with me if the eye becomes worse or in 10 days.

ICD-10-CM Code Assignment: _____

Case 4

Ambulatory Surgery Discharge Note

This 74-year-old female patient underwent cataract extraction with intraocular lens replacement in her left eye due to anterior subcapsular polar senile cataracts. The surgery was uneventful and she was instructed to follow up in my office in 6 days.

ICD-10-CM Code Assignment: _____

Case 5

Office Note

This 1-year-old male child presents to the office today from a referral from Dr. Smith in pediatrics. Dr. Smith has noted altered eye movements upon examination.

Examination: The child's left eye has a monocular convergent concomitant strabismus. Right eye is normal.

Treatment: At this time I am going to conservatively treat the child and cover the right eye to force the left eye to function normally. If the eye does not respond, I will then discuss with the parents the need for corrective lenses or surgical intervention if more conservative treatment fails.

ICD-10-CM Code Assignment: _____

Case 6

Office Note

This 53-year-old female patient returns to the office today to follow up after having fluorescien angiography. She still reports loss of central vision. At this time she is still able to read. She is also a smoker. I have reviewed the angiography report, which confirms macular degeneration in both eyes. I informed the patient that cigarette smoking is a risk factor that contributes to the disease and advised her to stop smoking. I also informed her that she should wear sunglasses that block ultraviolet light and gave her information about the disease process. She is to read the information that contains information about laser surgery and the risks and benefits of this surgery for this disease. I would like to see her in 4 months to assess the disease process.

ICD-10-CM Code Assignment: _____

Case 7

Office Note

This 4-year-old male patient is brought to my office today by his mother. She states that he is consistently confusing the colors red and green. I had the child view various Ishirara Color test plates and testing revealed color blindness.

ICD-10-CM Code Assignment: _____

Case 8

This 69-year-old male patient presents to the office today complaining of an irregular floating spot in his left eye and blurred vision.

Ophthalmoscope Examination: Examination revealed no findings in the right eye.

In the left eye there is a separation of the inner layers of the retina with fluid in the subretinal space. There is also a retinal break.

Assessment: retinal detachment with retinal break

Plan: Patient will be scheduled for surgery

ICD-10-CM Code Assignment: _____

Case 9

Observation Note

This patient is being placed in observation due to an increase in the symptoms of her acute angle-closure glaucoma in her right eye, severe stage. She is being placed on IV meds to see if symptoms decrease. She will be monitored and then admission for peripheral iridectomy will be made if needed.

ICD-10-CM Code Assignment: _____

Case 10

Office Note

Upon examination there is a small mass on the patient's right upper eyelid. On eversion of the lid there is elevated reddish yellow area on the conjunctival surface. The patient was instructed to apply warm compresses to open the mass and to place Sulfomamide eye drops in the eye as prescribed.

Assessment: chalazion

ICD-10-CM Code Assignment: _____

13 Diseases of the Ear and Mastoid Process

Chapter Outline

Chapter Objectives

Key Terms

Introduction

Introduction to the Body System

Coding Diseases of the Ear
   and Mastoid Process

Summary

Internet Links

Chapter Review

Coding Assignments

Case Studies

Chapter Objectives

At the conclusion of this chapter, you should be able to:

1. Identify diseases of the ear and mastoid process.
2. Indentify the anatomy of the ear.
3. Explain diseases of the ear and mastoid process.
4. Accurately code diseases of the ear and mastoid process.
5. Select and code diagnoses from case studies.

Key Terms

Auditory ossicles

Auditory tube

Auricle

Bony labyrinth

Cerumen

Ceruminous glands

Cilia

Cochlea

Cochlear duct

Ear lobe

Endolymph

Eustachian tube

External auditory
   canal

External auditory
   meatus

External ear

Incus

Labyrinth

Malleus

Membranous labyrinth

Middle ear

Organ of Corti

Otalgia

Otitis externa

Otorrhagia

Otorrhea

Otosclerosis

Oval window

Perilymph

Pharyngotympanic tube

Pinna

Saccule

Semicircular canals

Semicircular ducts

Stapes

Tympanic cavity

Tympanic membrane

Utricle

Vestibule

REMINDER: As you work through this chapter, you will need to have a copy of the ICD-10-CM coding book to reference. Please note that for Chapter 8 of ICD-10-CM, entitled Diseases of the Ear and Mastoid Process, there are no ICD-10-CM Official Guidelines for Coding and Reporting.

Introduction

Chapter 8 of ICD-10-CM, "Diseases of the Ear and Mastoid Process," contains the following blocks of codes:

- H60–H62, Diseases of external ear
- H65–H75, Diseases of middle ear and mastoid
- H80–H83, Diseases of inner ear
- H90–H94, Other disorders of ear
- H95,   Intraoperative and postprocedural complications and disorders of ear and mastoid process, not elsewhere classified

Introduction to the Body System

The ear is considered part of the nervous system and has the following functions:

- It allows hearing to occur by picking up sound waves and sending them to the brain.
- It helps maintain a person's balance.

The ear is divided into three regions: the external ear, the middle ear, and the inner ear. Figure 13-1 illustrates the regions of the ear.

The outermost part of the ear, known as the **external ear**, is the visible part of the ear and is not within the structure of the skull. The external ear consists of the auricle and the external auditory meatus. The **auricle**, also known as the **pinna**, is a flexible cartilaginous flap that has a bottom portion known as the **ear lobe**. The auricle allows sound waves to enter the ear canal, which is known as the **external auditory canal** or the **external auditory meatus**. Along the external auditory canal, tiny hairs called **cilia** aid in transmitting the sound waves inward to other auditory structures. Also within the external auditory canal are sweat glands, called **ceruminous glands**, that secrete a honey-colored, thick, waxy substance known as earwax, or **cerumen**.

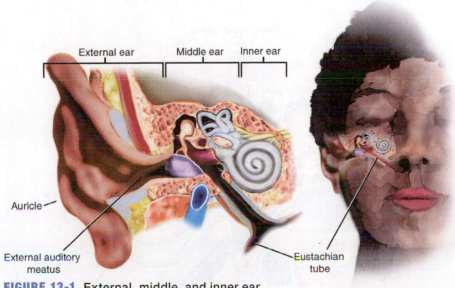

External ear   Middle ear   Inner ear

Auricle

External auditory
meatus

Eustachian
tube

FIGURE 13-1 External, middle, and inner ear.

Cerumen helps protect and lubricate the ear. In combination with the cilia, the cerumen helps to protect the eardrum from foreign objects.

The **tympanic membrane**, commonly called the eardrum, separates the external ear from the middle ear. The tympanic membrane is a thin, semitransparent membrane, silvery gray in color. The membrane transmits sound vibrations to the inner ear through the **auditory ossicles**.

The **middle ear**, also known as the **tympanic cavity**, is found within the temporal bone and houses the auditory ossicles and the eustachian tube. The auditory ossicles consist of three small bones that transmit and amplify sound waves. The bones are named according to their shapes:

- **Malleus**—Shaped like a hammer
- **Incus**—Shaped like an anvil
- **Stapes**—Shaped like a stirrup

The **eustachian tube**, also known as the **auditory tube** or **pharyngotympanic tube**, connects the bony structures of the middle ear to the pharynx. The purpose of the eustachian tube is to equalize air pressure in the middle ear.

The middle ear is separated from the inner ear by the **oval window**. In the inner ear, also known as the **labyrinth**, are bony structures and membranous structures. The bony structures, called the **bony labyrinth**, consist of the following:

- **Vestibule**—The central portion of the inner ear, this structure contains the **utricle** and the **saccule**, which are membranous sacs that aid in maintaining balance.
- **Semicircular canals**—Located behind the vestibule are three bony structures, filled with fluid, that also help to maintain balance. The **semicircular ducts** are also found in this area and aid in balance.
- **Cochlea**—This snail-shaped, bony structure contains **endolymph** and **perilymph**, which are auditory fluids that transmit sound. The **organ of Corti**, also found in the cochlea, is the true organ of hearing. The **cochlear duct**, a membranous structure, is found in this area of the ear and aids in the hearing process.

Membranous labyrinth is a term used to describe the utricle, saccule, semicircular ducts, and cochlear ducts because these structures are all membranous structures.

Figure 13-2 illustrates the numerous structures found in the ear, whereas Figure 13-3 illustrates the inner ear structures in greater detail.

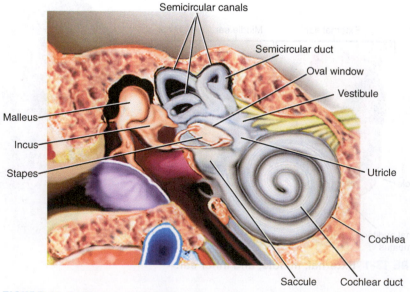

FIGURE 13-2 Structures of the ear.

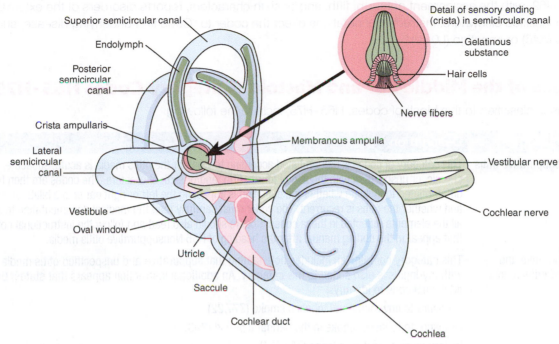

FIGURE 13-3 Inner ear structures.

Coding Diseases of the Ear and Mastoid Process

Codes for diseases of the ear and mastoid process are organized according to the anatomy of the ear. Coders should note the "Note" and Excludes2 note that appear after the chapter title in the coding manual.

Diseases of the External Ear (Category Codes H60–H62)

Category H60 applies to **otitis externa**, an inflammation of the external auditory canal. This category is differentiated according to the various types of otitis, with fourth, fifth, and sixth characters providing additional detail about the condition:

- Abscess of external ear
- Cellulitis of external ear
- Malignant otitis externa
- Infective otitis externa
- Cholesteatoma of external ear
- Acute noninfective otitis externa

EXAMPLE: A patient presents with an abscess of right external ear. This diagnosis is reported to the fifth character level using code H60.01. A second patient represents with a bilateral external abscess of the ears. This is reported to the fifth character level using code H60.03. Note how the fifth characters provide additional information about the diagnoses reported.

Category H61, with the assignment of fourth, fifth, and/or sixth characters, is used to report other disorders of the external ear, including:

- Chondritis and perichondritis of the external ear
- Noninfective disorders of the pinna
- Impacted cerumen
- Acquired stenosis of the external ear canal
- Exostosis of the external ear

Category H62, with the assignment of fourth, fifth, and/or sixth characters, reports disorders of the external ear in diseases classified elsewhere. Instructional notations direct the coder to "Code first underlying disease, such as erysipelas (A46) or impetigo (L01.0)."

Diseases of the Middle Ear and Mastoid (Category Codes H65–H75)

The diseases classified to this block of codes, H65–H75, include the following:

Category Code	Description
H65, Nonsuppurative otitis media	This category of codes is differentiated according to whether the otitis media is acute, subacute, chronic, or unspecified with the use of fourth, fifth, and/or sixth characters. The codes are then further differentiated to indicate whether the condition is impacting the left or right ear or is a bilateral condition and whether the otitis is recurrent. The coder must carefully read the medical documentation to capture all the elements reflected in these codes. Coders should also read and follow the instructional notations that appear in the coding manual after the heading of H65 Nonsuppurative otitis media.
H66, Suppurative and unspecified otitis media	This category contains an Includes note stating that suppurative and unspecified otitis media with myringitis is also coded to this category. An additional instruction appears that states: Use additional code to identify:
	exposure to environmental tobacco smoke (Z77.22)
	exposure to tobacco smoke in the perinatal period (P96.81)
	history of tobacco dependence (Z87.891)
	occupational exposure to environmental tobacco smoke (Z57.31)
	tobacco dependence (F17.-)
	tobacco use (Z72.0)
	It should also be noted that fourth, fifth, and/or sixth characters are used within this category.
H67, Otitis media in diseases classified elsewhere	Instructional notation guides the coder to "Code first the underlying disease," such as plasminogen deficiency (E88.02) viral disease NEC (B00–B34), and to "Use additional code for any associated perforated tympanic membrane (H72.-)." The coder should also note the extensive Excludes1 note that appears for this category. Category H67 also requires fourth characters for valid code assignment.
H68, Eustachian salpingitis and obstruction	Conditions that are classified here include eustachian salpingitis and obstructions of the eustachian tube. Coders need to reference the coding manual for fourth, fifth, and/or sixth characters within this category.
H69, Other and unspecified disorders of eustachian tube	Patulous eustachian tube and other specified disorders of the eustachian tube that are not listed elsewhere are coded to this category with the assignment of fourth and fifth characters.
H70, Mastoiditis and related conditions	The codes in this category are differentiated by acute or chronic mastoiditis, petrositis, and other mastoiditis, and related conditions with the use of fourth, fifth, and/or sixth characters.
H71, Cholesteatoma of middle ear	These codes are differentiated, with the use of fourth and fifth characters, according to the anatomical structure impacted by the cholesteatoma and whether the condition is impacting the left or right ear or is bilateral or the laterality is unspecified.
H72, Perforation of tympanic membrane	This category includes persistent post-traumatic perforation of the eardrum and postinflammatory perforation of the eardrum. An instructional notation appears that instructs the coder to "Code first any associated otitis media (H65.–, H66.1–, H66.2–, H66.3–, H66.4–, H66.9–, H67.–)." Fourth, fifth and/or sixth characters provide greater detail in code assignment.
H73, Other disorders of tympanic membrane	Included in this category are acute, chronic, and unspecified myringitis; other specified disorders of the tympanic membrane; and unspecified disorders of the tympanic membrane. Coders should note the Excludes1 note that follows H73.0 and H73.1 and the assignment of the fourth, fifth, and/or sixth characters for this category.
H74, Other disorders of middle ear mastoid	Diseases classified in this category include tympanosclerosis, adhesive middle ear disease, discontinuity and dislocation of ear ossicles, polyp of middle ear, and other and unspecified disorders of the middle ear and mastoid. Coders should note the Excludes2 note that appears at the start of this category and the use of fourth, fifth, and/or sixth characters.

(continues)

(continued)

Category Code	Description
H75, Other disorders of middle ear and mastoid in diseases classified elsewhere	This category includes mastoiditis in infectious and parasitic diseases and other specified disorders of the middle ear and mastoid in diseases classified elsewhere. An instructional notation directs the coder to "Code first underlying disease." Fourth and fifth characters provide greater detail within this category.

Exercise 13.1—Coding Diseases from Code Range H60–H75

Using an ICD-10-CM code book, select the diagnostic code for each diagnosis.

1. chronic perichondritis of right external ear   _____
2. bilateral abscess of external ear   _____
3. acute contact otitis externa, right ear   _____
4. bilateral impacted cerumen   _____
5. chondritis of left external ear   _____
6. chronic allergic otitis media   _____
7. recurrent, right ear acute serous otitis media   _____
8. bilateral chronic eustachian tube salpingitis   _____
9. right ear diffuse cholesteatosis   _____
10. left ear attic perforation of tympanic membrane   _____

Diseases of Inner Ear (Category Codes H80–H83)

This block of codes, with the use of fourth, fifth, and/or sixth characters, is used to report diseases of the inner ear. The categories that are present include:

- H80, Otosclerosis—**Otosclerosis** is the growth of spongy bone in the inner ear. The growth can progress, causing the obstruction of the oval or round window and progressive deafness. This category is differentiated according to the site of the otosclerosis and the ear involved.

- H81, Disorders of vestibular function—Included in this category of codes is Ménière's disease, benign paroxysmal vertigo, vestibular neuronitis, other peripheral vertigo, and other vestibular disorders.

- H82, Vertiginous syndromes in diseases classified elsewhere—An instructional notation directs the coder to "Code first underlying disease."

- H83, Other diseases of inner ear—This category is used to code labyrinthitis, labyrinthine fistula, labyrinthine dysfunction, noise effects on the inner ear, and other diseases.

Other Disorders of Ear (Category Codes H90–H94) and Intraoperative and Postprocedural Complications and Disorders of Ear and Mastoid Process, Not Elsewhere Classified (H95)

The last block of codes in this chapter of ICD-10-CM consists of the following categories, with the use of fourth, fifth, and/or sixth characters:

- H90, Conductive and sensorineural hearing loss—This category is differentiated to identify the type of hearing loss and whether the hearing loss is unilateral or bilateral. The types of hearing loss include conductive, sensorineural, and mixed.

- H91, Other and unspecified hearing loss—This category is used to report other and unspecified hearing loss, including ototoxic, presbycusis, sudden idiopathic, and other specified and unspecified forms of hearing loss.

- H92, Otalgia and effusion of ear—A number of common disorders are coded to this category:
  - **Otalgia**—Earache
  - **Otorrhea**—Discharge from the external ear
  - **Otorrhagia**—Hemorrhage from the ear
- H93, Other disorders of ear, not elsewhere classified—Degenerative and vascular disorders of the ear, tinnitus, other abnormal auditory perceptions, disorders of the acoustic nerve, and other specified disorders of the ear are categorized here.
- H94, Other disorders of ear in diseases classified elsewhere—Coders are instructed to "Code first underlying disease, such as parasitic disease (B65-B89)" for this category. Reference the headings of H94.0 and H94.8 to review the instructional notations.
- H95, Intraoperative and postprocedural complications and disorders of ear and mastoid process, not elsewhere classified—This category is used to report complications in the ear and mastoid process that occurred during a procedure or postprocedure.

Summary

- Chapter 8 of ICD-10-CM is "Diseases of the Ear and Mastoid Process."
- The ear is considered part of the nervous system.
- The ear is divided into three regions: external ear, middle ear, and inner ear.
- Codes for diseases of the ear and mastoid process are organized according to ear anatomy.
- Coders must be able to identify the ear or ears impacted by the disorder to correctly assign codes for Chapter 8 of ICD-10-CM.

Internet Links

To learn more about the diseases of the ear and mastoid process, visit the following sites for information:

www.mayoclinic.org and search on terms such as "ear infections", "hearing loss," and "impacted cerumen" for a wealth of information on various diseases and current treatments.

www.everydayhealth.com and search on the name of the disease of the ear and mastoid process.

https://medlineplus.gov/eardisorders.html and review information about diseases of the ear and mastoid process.

Chapter Review

True/False

Indicate whether each statement is true (T) or false (F).

1. _____ The auricle is also known as the external auditory canal.
2. _____ The cochlea is a snail-shaped, bony structure that contains endolymph and perilymph.
3. _____ Category H83 classifies labyrinthitis.
4. _____ Aural vertigo is classified to category H80.
5. _____ Code H66.0 is used to classify acute suppurative otitis externa.

Fill-in-the-Blank

Enter the appropriate term(s) to complete each statement.

6. The canals located behind the vestibule that are three bony structures and that are filled with fluid are known as the _____.

7. Category H65 is used to classify _____.

8. Bilateral sensorineural hearing loss is coded to _____.

9. Right ear ototoxic hearing loss is coded to _____.

10. Bilateral acute eczematoid otitis externa is coded to _____.

Coding Assignments

Instructions: Using an ICD-10-CM code book, assign the proper diagnosis code to the following diagnostic statements.

1. congenital auditory imperception _____

2. right ear otalgia _____

3. bilateral labyrinthitis _____

4. left ear aural vertigo _____

5. bilateral multiple perforations of tympanic membrane _____

6. exostosis of right external ear canal _____

7. acquired stenosis of external ear canal, both ears _____

8. hematoma of pinna, left ear, nontraumatic _____

9. acute chemical otitis externa, both ears _____

10. chronic serous otitis media, left ear _____

11. bilateral Ménière's disease _____

12. bilateral acoustic nerve disorder _____

13. otorrhagia, bilateral _____

14. presbycusis _____

15. right ear auditory recruitment _____

16. chronic inflammation of postmastoidectomy cavity, left side _____

17. right ear osseous obstruction of eustachian tube _____

18. chronic mucoid otitis media, bilateral _____

19. left ear chronic allergic otitis media _____

20. bilateral chondritis of pinna _____

21. cellulitis of left external ear _____

22. acute perichondritis of right external ear _____

23. suppurative otitis media, right ear _____

24. bilateral petrositis _____

25. bilateral adhesive middle ear disease   _____

26. bilateral cellulitis of external ear   _____

27. acute eczematoid otitis externa, left ear   _____

28. chondritis of right external ear   _____

29. bilateral hematoma of pinna   _____

30. cholesteatoma of mastoid, right ear   _____

31. abscess of left external ear   _____

32. hemorrhagic otitis externa, bilateral   _____

33. Swimmer's ear   _____

34. diffuse otitis externa of the left ear   _____

35. acute actinic otitis externa of both ears   _____

Case Studies

Instructions: Review each case study and select the correct ICD-10-CM diagnostic code.

Case 1

Emergency Department Note

This 9-year-old male patient was brought to the ER by his mother. His left external ear is warm to touch, and it appears red and swollen. He has had a fever of 100 for the past 2 days. Upon otoscopic exam, the middle and inner ear are reviewed with no findings. There is definitely cellulitis of the external auditory canal. Antibiotics were given, and the patient was instructed to return to his doctor in 7 days or to call if the symptoms worsen.

ICD-10-CM Code Assignment: _____

Case 2

Office Note

This 19-year-old female has been complaining of ear pain for 3 days and feeling tired.

EXAM

EYES: Appear normal

NOSE: No findings

CERVICAL LYMPH NODES: Unremarkable

EARS: The right ear shows otitis media is present.

Antibiotics and drops given. Instructed to return in 10 days.

ICD-10-CM Code Assignment: _____

Case 3

Audiology Note

This 54-year-old male patient is being seen by me today to review the results of previous hearing tests and to determine a course of action for the hearing loss. Diagnostic testing reveals bilateral conductive hearing loss. The outcome of the testing was discussed with the patient and the patient will follow up with the audiology department to further discuss treatment options.

ICD-10-CM Code Assignment: _____

Case 4

Office Note

This is the third time in a 4-month period this year that this patient has been seen for myringitis. The patient was also seen last year three times for the same condition. Treatment options have not controlled the myringitis. I have referred the patient to Dr. Payal in the audiology department for further treatment for the chronic myringitis of the left ear.

ICD-10-CM Code Assignment: _____

Case 5

Hospital Discharge Note

This 31-year-old male is being discharged today following correction of deformity of the right pinna that he acquired during a automobile accident. His stay was uneventful, the surgery corrected the deformity, and there were no complications. He is instructed to follow the discharge orders that were given to him and follow up in my office in one week.

ICD-10-CM Code Assignment: _____

Case 6

Office Note

This 84-year-old patient presents today with a complaint of loss of hearing, tinnitus, and pain in her left ear.

Vital Signs: BP: 130/80, Weight: 194 pounds

Ear: Inspection of right ear—no findings

Inspection of left ear—there is impacted cerumen in the ear.

Mineral oil was placed in her ear and then the ear was irrigated and the wax removed.

ICD-10-CM Code Assignment: _____

Case 7

Office Note

This patient is returning to the office today to discuss having a stapedectomy or obtaining a hearing aid to treat bilateral otosclerosis. The patient has discussed this with his family and he would rather not have surgery at this time. I have referred him to the hearing clinic to be fitted for a hearing aid in both ears.

ICD-10-CM Code Assignment: _____

Case 8

Emergency Department Note

This 10-year-old patient is complaining of ringing in his left ear and a headache for the last 3 days. He has had a fever of 101 for the last 2 days. Otoscopic examination is suggestive of acute mastoiditis. CT scan revealed inflammation of the mastoid bone in the left ear. Antibiotics were prescribed and he was instructed to follow up with his primary care provider in 5 days.

ICD-10-CM Code Assignment: _____

Case 9

Office Note

This 10-month-old patient is brought to the office by his father. The father states that the child is pulling on his right ear, has been running a fever, and has been crying for no reason. Temperature is 100.4.

Otoscopic examination reveals a bulging tympanic membrane in the right ear, which is red and swollen. Left ear is normal.

Assessment: acute suppurative otitis media

Plan: Tylenol for pain and amoxicillin as written

ICD-10-CM Code Assignment: _____

Case 10

Skilled Nursing Facility Note

This 86-year-old female has been tested for hearing loss. I am seeing her today to discuss the need for a hearing aid. She is not able to hear well in both ears, as confirmed by testing, due to sensorineural hearing loss. Today I am writing a script for her so she can be fitted for hearing aids.

ICD-10-CM Code Assignment: _____

Diseases of the Circulatory System

Chapter Outline

Chapter Objectives

At the conclusion of this chapter, you should be able to:

1. Identify the structures and function of the circulatory system.
2. Explain diseases of the circulatory system.
3. Apply the ICD-10-CM coding guidelines to accurately code diseases of the circulatory system.
4. List the types of hypertension and select codes for the various types of hypertension.
5. Select and code diagnoses from case studies.

Key Terms

Angina pectoris
Arteries
Cardiomyopathy
Cerebral hemorrhage
Cerebrovascular accident (CVA)
Cerebrovascular disease
Diastolic blood pressure
Endocarditis

Healed myocardial infarction
Heart
Heart attack
Heart failure
Hypertension
Hypotension
Ischemic heart disease
Lymphadenitis
Myocardial infarction (MI)

Myocarditis
Occlusion
Occlusion of cerebral and precerebral arteries
Old myocardial infarction
Pericarditis
Pericardium
Phlebitis
Portal vein thrombosis

Secondary hypertension
Stenosis
Stroke
Systolic blood pressure
Thrombolytic therapy
Thrombophlebitis
Transient hypertension
Unstable angina
Varicose veins
Veins

> **REMINDER:** As you work through this chapter, you will need to have a copy of the ICD-10-CM coding book to reference. For this chapter, you will also need to reference the ICD-10-CM Official Guidelines for Coding and Reporting. These guidelines can be found in Appendix A which are now available on the Student Companion site and MINDTAP From Cengage.

Introduction

Chapter 9 of ICD-10-CM, "Diseases of the Circulatory System," contains codes for diseases of the circulatory system, except circulatory conditions that occur during pregnancy, childbirth, and the puerperium or conditions that are determined to be a congenital anomaly. Circulatory disorders that occur during the obstetrical period are coded to Chapter 15 of ICD-10-CM, "Pregnancy, Childbirth, and the Puerperium." Circulatory congenital anomalies are coded to Chapter 17 of ICD-10-CM, "Congenital Malformations, Deformations, and Chromosomal Abnormalities."

> **EXAMPLE:** Hypertensive diseases code to I10–I16, excluding hypertensive diseases that complicate pregnancy, childbirth, or the puerperium, which code to O10–O11, O13–O16, or neonatal hypertension that codes to P29.2. The diagnosis of essential hypertension codes to I10, whereas a diagnosis of preexisting essential hypertension complicating childbirth codes to O10.02, as found in Chapter 15 of ICD-10-CM, "Pregnancy, Childbirth, and the Puerperium."

Chapter 9 of ICD-10-CM contains the following blocks:

- I00–I02, Acute rheumatic fever
- I05–I09, Chronic rheumatic heart diseases
- I10–I16, Hypertensive diseases
- I20–I25, Ischemic heart diseases
- I26–I28, Pulmonary heart disease and diseases of pulmonary circulation
- I30–I52, Other forms of heart disease
- I60–I69, Cerebrovascular diseases
- I70–I79, Diseases of arteries, arterioles, and capillaries
- I80–I89, Diseases of veins, lymphatic vessels, and lymph nodes, not elsewhere classified
- I95–I99, Other and unspecified disorders of the circulatory system

Introduction to the Body System

The body structures found in this chapter of ICD-10-CM are also referred to as the *cardiovascular system* or *circulatory system*. This system consists of the following organs and body structures:

- **Arteries**—Carry oxygen-rich blood from the heart to the body (with the exception of the pulmonary artery, which carries deoxygenated blood from the heart to the lungs)
- **Veins**—Carry deoxygenated blood from the body back to the heart (with the exception of the pulmonary vein, which carries oxygenated blood back to the heart)
- **Heart**—A muscular organ, located between the lungs and to the left of the midline of the body, that pumps blood throughout the body

The blood vessels of the body are considered the longest system of the body. The heart is considered one of the strongest organs of the body, pumping an average of 4,000 gallons of blood a day for an adult. Coders must be able to identify the various arteries, veins, and specific parts and structures of the heart.

Occlusion, occluded

- anus K62.4

- - congenital Q42.3

- - - with fistula Q42.2

- aortoiliac (chronic) I74.09

-aqueduct of Sylvius G91.1

- congenital Q03.0

- - - with spina bifida —*see* Spina bifida, by site, with hydrocephalus

- artery (*see also* Atherosclerosis, artery) I70.9

- - auditory, internal I65.8

- - basilar I65.1

- - - with

- - - - infarction I63.22

- - - - - due to

- - - - - - embolism I63.12

- - - - - - thrombosis I63.02

- - hypophyseal —*see* Occlusion, artery, precerebral, specified NEC

- - iliac I74.5

- - lower extremities due to stenosis or stricture I77.1

- - mesenteric (embolic) (thrombotic) (see also Infarct, intestine) K55.069

- - perforating —*see* Occlusion, artery, cerebral, specified NEC

Courtesy of the Centers for Medicare & Medicaid Services, www.cms.gov

FIGURE 14-1 Alphabetic entry for occlusion.

EXAMPLE: A patient has been diagnosed with left posterior tibial artery occlusion due to stenosis. To accurately code this diagnosis, the coder must be able to identify that this artery is found in the lower extremities. To select a code, the term *occlusion* is located in the Alphabetic Index, which is further divided into anatomical structures. Figure 14-1 illustrates the index entry. To locate the correct code, the coder references the entry of occlusion, then artery, then lower extremities due to stenosis or stricture. Here code I77.1 appears in the Alphabetic Index.

Because not all arteries and veins have separate entries in the Alphabetical Index, the coder has to understand arterial circulation (Figure 14-2), venous circulation (Figure 14-3), and heart pulmonary circulation (Figure 14-4) to make a correct code selection.

Exercise 14.1—Identifying Arteries and Veins

For each of the arteries and veins listed, state where the structure is located using the following legend: abdominal cavity (A), lower extremities (L), thoracic (T), and upper extremities (U). (Reference Figures 14-2 to 14-4.)

(continues)

Exercise 14.1—*continued*

1. right femoral artery
2. left renal vein
3. left great saphenous vein
4. right ulnar artery
5. arch of aorta
6. left ovarian vein
7. pulmonary artery
8. superior palmar arch
9. peroneal artery
10. hepatic artery

_____

_____

_____

_____

_____

_____

_____

_____

_____

_____

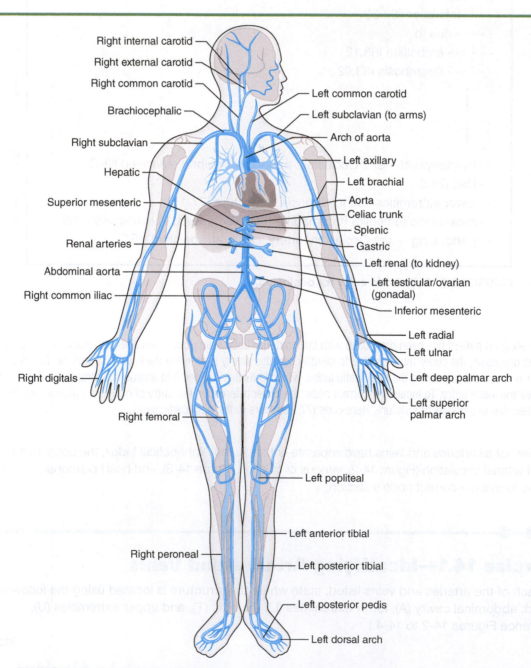

Right internal carotid

Right external carotid

Right common carotid

Brachiocephalic

Right subclavian

Hepatic

Superior mesenteric

Renal arteries

Abdominal aorta

Right common iliac

Left common carotid

Left subclavian (to arms)

Arch of aorta

Left axillary

Left brachial

Aorta

Celiac trunk

Splenic

Gastric

Left renal (to kidney)

Left testicular/ovarian (gonadal)

Inferior mesenteric

Left radial

Left ulnar

Left deep palmar arch

Left superior palmar arch

Right digitals

Right femoral

Left popliteal

Left anterior tibial

Right peroneal

Left posterior tibial

Left posterior pedis

Left dorsal arch

FIGURE 14-2 Arterial circulation.

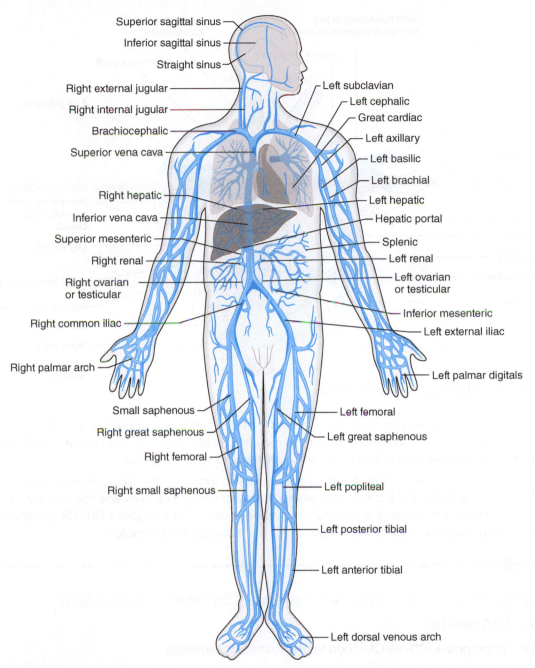

FIGURE 14-3 Venous circulation.

Coding of Diseases of the Circulatory System

Many circulatory system disorders are interrelated. A cardiovascular disease can affect many vessels throughout the entire cardiovascular system and damage organs. Circulatory system disorders can be caused by infections as well as by physiological factors.

Acute and Chronic Rheumatic Fever (Category Codes I00–I09)

Acute rheumatic fever develops, usually in children ages 5 to 15 years, following a group A hemolytic *Streptococci* infection of the pharynx. ICD-10-CM classifies acute cases of the disease to categories I00–I02 and chronic rheumatic heart disease to categories I05–I09. Symptoms of acute rheumatic fever include abdominal pain, fever,

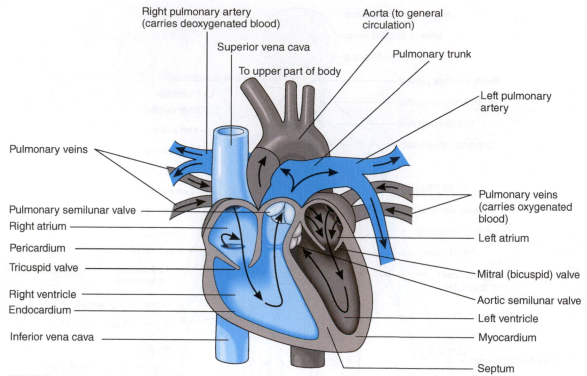

FIGURE 14-4 Heart pulmonary circulation.

joint pain, skin changes, chorea (involuntary movements of the face, tongue, and upper extremities), and lesions of the heart, blood vessels, and connective tissue. Chronic rheumatic heart disease results from an attack or attacks of rheumatic fever that cause damage to the heart, particularly the aortic and mitral valves.

Chronic rheumatic heart disease can impact the mitral, aortic, tricuspid, or multiple valves. Category codes I05–I08 differentiate the valves that are impacted when chronic rheumatic heart disease has occurred. For accurate coding, the coder must be able to identify the valves involved. For categories I00–I09, coders need to reference the coding manual to identify the assignment of fourth and/or fifth characters.

Exercise 14.2—Coding Acute and Chronic Rheumatic Heart Diseases

Select the appropriate ICD-10-CM code for the following diagnoses.

1. rheumatic aortic stenosis with insufficiency   _____
2. acute rheumatic endocarditis   _____
3. rheumatic aortic and mitral valve insufficiency   _____
4. rheumatic chorea with heart involvement   _____
5. rheumatic tricuspid stenosis   _____
6. mitral valve insufficiency and stenosis, rheumatic   _____
7. rheumatic mitral valve insufficiency   _____
8. rheumatic aortic valve insufficiency   _____
9. aortic valve insufficiency and stenosis, rheumatic   _____
10. chronic rheumatic myopericarditis   _____

Hypertensive Diseases (Category Codes I10–I16)

Hypertension, hypertensive heart disease, and hypertensive chronic kidney disease are coded to category codes I10–I16. Because of the interrelationship of hypertension and other hypertensive conditions, coders must pay close attention to the instructional notations found in both the Alphabetic Index and the Tabular List. Coders need to reference the coding manual to identify appropriate fourth and/or fifth character assignment.

Hypertension

Hypertension is an increase in **systolic blood pressure** (the pressure on the arterial walls during the heart muscle contraction), in **diastolic blood pressure** (the pressure on the arterial walls during relaxation of the heart muscle), or in both.

At times physicians may describe hypertension as "controlled" or "uncontrolled." There is no way to differentiate between controlled and uncontrolled states of hypertension within the ICD-10-CM coding system; so follow these guidelines:

ICD-10-CM Official Coding Guidelines

8) Hypertension, Controlled—

This diagnostic statement usually refers to an existing state of hypertension under control by therapy. Assign the appropriate code from categories I10–I15, Hypertensive diseases.

9) Hypertension, Uncontrolled—

Uncontrolled hypertension may refer to untreated hypertension or hypertension not responding to current therapeutic regimen. In either case, assign the appropriate code from categories I10–I15, Hypertensive diseases.

10) Hypertensive Crisis

Assign a code from category I16, Hypertensive crisis, for documented hypertensive urgency, hypertensive emergency or unspecified hypertensive crisis. Code also any identified hypertensive disease (I10–I15). The sequencing is based on the reason for the encounter.

(See Appendix A, Section I, C9, a, 8–10.)

Courtesy of the Centers for Medicare & Medicaid Services, www.cms.gov

EXAMPLE: Tim Long was seen by Dr. Hardy for uncontrolled hypertension, and his medications were adjusted. The appropriate code to assign is I10.

Before assigning a code for hypertension, medical documentation must be available clearly stating that the patient has hypertension rather than an elevated blood pressure reading. ICD-10-CM code R03.0 is used when a patient has elevated blood pressure but the physician has not made a diagnosis of hypertension. Some physicians refer to elevated blood pressure as **transient hypertension**.

Secondary Hypertension

Secondary hypertension is defined as high arterial blood pressure due to another disease such as central nervous system disorders, renal disorders, and endocrine and vascular diseases. Secondary hypertension is coded to category code I15, which is divided as follows:

- I15.0, Renovascular hypertension
- I15.1, Hypertension secondary to other renal disorders
- I15.2, Hypertension secondary to endocrine disorders
- I15.8, Other secondary hypertension
- I15.9, Secondary hypertension, unspecified

NOTE:

At the start of this category, an instructional notation directs the coder to "Code also underlying condition." Thus, the following coding guideline needs to be followed:

ICD-10-CM Official Coding Guidelines

Hypertension, Secondary

Secondary hypertension is due to an underlying condition. Two codes are required: one to identify the underlying etiology and one from category I15 to identify the hypertension. Sequencing of codes is determined by the reason for admission/encounter. (See Appendix Section I, C9, a, 6.)

Courtesy of the Centers for Medicare & Medicaid Services, www.cms.gov

EXAMPLE: Gale Carerro is admitted to Sunny Valley Hospital to address her secondary malignant hypertension that is caused by adult polycystic kidney disease. Because she was admitted to treat the secondary malignant hypertension, this is sequenced first. The appropriate codes to assign are I15.1 and Q61.2.

Coding Guidelines for Hypertension

Coders need to be familiar with the following coding guidelines that impact the coding of hypertension and other conditions associated with hypertension.

ICD-10-CM Official Coding Guidelines

Hypertension

The classification presumes a causal relationship between hypertension and heart involvement and between hypertension and kidney involvement, as the two conditions are linked by the term "with" in the Alphabetic Index. These conditions should be coded as related even in the absence of provider documentation explicitly linking them, unless the documentation clearly states the conditions are unrelated.

For hypertension and conditions not specifically linked by relational terms such as "with," "associated with" or "due to" in the classification, provider documentation must link the conditions in order to code them as related.

1) Hypertension with Heart Disease

Hypertension with heart conditions classified to I50.– or I51.4–I51.7, I51.89, I51.9, are assigned to, a code from category I11, Hypertensive heart disease. Use an additional code(s) from category I50, Heart failure, to identify the type(s) of heart failure in those patients with heart failure.

The same heart conditions (I50.–, I51.4–I51.7, I51.89, I51.9) with hypertension are coded separately if the provider has documented they are unrelated to the hypertension. Sequence according to the circumstances of the admission/encounter.

2) Hypertensive Chronic Kidney Disease

Assign codes from category I12, Hypertensive chronic kidney disease, when both hypertension and a condition classifiable to category N18, Chronic kidney disease (CKD), are present. CKD should not be coded as hypertensive if the provider indicates the CKD is not related to the hypertension.

The appropriate code from category N18 should be used as a secondary code with a code from category I12 to identify the stage of chronic kidney disease.

See Section I.C.14, Chronic kidney disease.

If a patient has hypertensive chronic kidney disease and acute renal failure, the acute renal failure should also be coded. Sequence according to the circumstances of the admission/encounter.

3) Hypertensive Heart and Chronic Kidney Disease

Assign codes from combination category I13, Hypertensive heart and chronic kidney disease, when there is hypertension with both heart and kidney involvement. If heart failure is present, assign an additional code from category I50 to identify the type of heart failure.

The appropriate code from category N18, Chronic kidney disease, should be used as a secondary code with a code from category I13 to identify the stage of chronic kidney disease.

See Section I.C.14. Chronic kidney disease.

The codes in category I13, Hypertensive heart and chronic kidney disease, are combination codes that include hypertension, heart disease and chronic kidney disease. The Includes note at I13 specifies that the conditions included at I11 and I12 are included together in I13. If a patient has hypertension, heart disease and chronic kidney disease then a code from I13 should be used, not individual codes for hypertension, heart disease, and chronic kidney disease, or codes from I11 or I12.

For patients with both acute renal failure and chronic kidney disease, the acute renal failure should also be coded. Sequence according to the circumstances of the admission/encounter.

4) Hypertensive Cerebrovascular Disease

For hypertensive cerebrovascular disease, first assign the appropriate code from categories I60–I69, followed by the appropriate hypertension code.

5) Hypertensive Retinopathy

Subcategory H35.0, Background retinopathy and retinal vascular changes, should be used with a code from category I10–I15, Hypertensive disease to include the systemic hypertension. The sequencing is based on the reason for the encounter.

(See Appendix A, Section I, C9, a, 1–5.)

Courtesy of the Centers for Medicare & Medicaid Services. www.cms.gov

Exercise 14.3—Coding of Hypertension

Select the appropriate ICD-10-CM diagnostic codes for each diagnosis.

1. essential hypertension   _____
2. hypertension due to primary malignant neoplasm of brain   _____
3. uncontrolled malignant hypertension   _____
4. hypertension, benign   _____
5. hypertensive chronic kidney disease, stage 3   _____
6. hypertensive renal disease, stage 2   _____
7. elevated blood pressure   _____
8. hypertensive heart disease without heart failure   _____
9. systemic hypertension   _____
10. arterial hypertension   _____

Ischemic Heart Diseases (Category Codes I20–I25)

Ischemic heart disease occurs when there is an inadequate supply of blood to the heart, which is caused by a blockage, also called an **occlusion**, or constriction of an arterial blood vessel. The vessels commonly become blocked or constricted because of the presence of fatty deposits on the walls of the arteries. Ischemic heart disease is also referred to as:

- Arteriosclerotic coronary artery disease (ACAD)
- Arteriosclerotic heart disease (ASHD)

- Atherosclerosis
- Coronary artery disease (CAD)
- Coronary arteriosclerosis
- Coronary heart disease
- Coronary ischemia

NOTE:

An instructional notation in the Tabular List of ICD-10-CM, after the heading of Ischemic Heart Disease, tells the coder to "Use additional code to identify presence of hypertension (I10–I16)."

Angina Pectoris (Category Code I20)

Angina pectoris, which is assigned to ICD-10-CM category code I20 with an appropriate fourth character, is defined as severe chest pain caused by an insufficient amount of blood reaching the heart. It is relieved rapidly by rest or nitrates. Factors that usually bring on an angina attack include exertion, heavy eating, and stress.

Unstable angina, which is assigned to ICD-10-CM code I20.0, is an accelerating, or crescendo, pattern of chest pain that occurs at rest or during mild exertion, typically lasting longer than does angina pectoris, and that is not responsive to medications. Unstable angina can progress to infarction or may heal and return to a stable condition. This code is assigned only when there is no documentation of infarction. Diseases that code to I20.0 are accelerated angina, crescendo angina, de novo effort angina, intermediate coronary syndrome, preinfarction syndrome, and worsening effort angina. Figure 14-5 illustrates the most common patterns of angina. Patients typically complain of tightness in the chest that radiates to the left arm, neck, and jaw.

The following note appears after the category heading I20, Angina pectoris. It directs coders to use additional codes with category I20.

Use additional code to identify:
exposure to environmental tobacco smoke (Z77.22)
history of tobacco dependence (Z87.891)
occupational exposure to environmental tobacco smoke (Z57.31)
tobacco dependence (F17.–)
tobacco use (Z72.0)

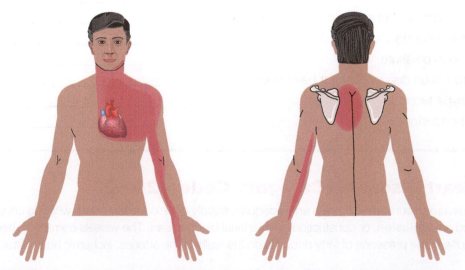

FIGURE 14-5 Most common patterns of angina (From Neighbors M & Tannehill-Jones R. *Human Diseases*, 2nd ed. Clifton Park, NY: Delmar, Cengage Learning, p. 141.).

Coding guidelines that apply to this range of codes include the following:

ICD-10-CM Official Coding Guidelines

Atherosclerotic coronary artery disease and angina

ICD-10-CM has combination codes for atherosclerotic heart disease with angina pectoris. The subcategories for these codes are I25.11, Atherosclerotic heart disease of native coronary artery with angina pectoris and I25.7, Atherosclerosis of coronary artery bypass graft(s) and coronary artery of transplanted heart with angina pectoris.

When using one of these combination codes it is not necessary to use an additional code for angina pectoris. A causal relationship can be assumed in a patient with both atherosclerosis and angina pectoris, unless the documentation indicates the angina is due to something other than the atherosclerosis.

If a patient with coronary artery disease is admitted due to an acute myocardial infarction (AMI), the AMI should be sequenced before the coronary artery disease.

See Section I.C.9. Acute myocardial infarction (AMI)

(See Appendix A, Section I, C 9,b.)

Courtesy of the Centers for Medicare & Medicaid Services, www.cms.gov

Myocardial Infarction

An acute **myocardial infarction (MI)**, commonly called a **heart attack**, occurs when there is inadequate blood supply to a section or sections of the heart.

Disease Highlight—Myocardial Infarction

A myocardial infarction (MI) occurs when there is a decrease in the blood flow through one of the coronary arteries, causing a decrease in the amount of oxygen supplied to the heart tissue. The decreased blood flow causes myocardial ischemia and necrosis.

Sign and Symptoms:

- Severe chest pain that typically radiates down the left arm and up to the neck and jaw
- Sweating
- Nausea
- Vomiting
- Shortness of breath
- Weakness
- Dysrhythmias

Clinical Testing:

- Electrocardiography—An ST segment elevation or depression, symmetric inversion of T waves, and evolving Q waves
- Blood tests—Elevation of cardiac enzymes in the blood
- Cardiac imaging studies—Appearance of segmental wall motion abnormality

- Chest x-ray—Possible signs of congestive heart failure, which may develop behind other clinical findings

Treatment:

If the patient is currently having an MI:

- Place the patient in a lying position. If cardiac arrest occurs, cardiopulmonary resuscitation should be administered.
- Medical treatment is directed at pain management and the administration of oxygen.
- If the patient is experiencing arrhythmias, medications are administered.
- **Thrombolytic therapy**, the intravenous administration of thrombolytic agents, is often completed to open the coronary artery occlusion and to restore blood flow to the cardiac tissue.

Following the management of the acute MI:

- Patients may undergo cardiac catheterization to evaluate the heart.
- Angioplasty and/or coronary artery bypass surgery may be indicated depending on the clinical findings.
- Cardiac rehabilitation and patient education are also part of the treatment regimen.

In ICD-10-CM, myocardial infarctions are coded to categories I21–I22. Category I21 is used to code a myocardial infarction specified as acute or with a stated duration of 4 weeks (28 days) or less from onset. This category also includes:

- Cardiac infarction
- Coronary (artery) embolism
- Coronary (artery) occlusion
- Coronary (artery) rupture
- Coronary (artery) thrombosis
- Infarction of heart, myocardium, or ventricle

Coders are instructed, via an instructional notation that appears after the heading for category I21, to use an additional code to identify:

- Exposure to environmental tobacco smoke (Z77.22)
- History of tobacco dependence (Z87.891)
- Occupational exposure to environmental tobacco smoke (Z57.31)
- Status post administration of tPA (rtPA) in a different facility within the last 24 hours prior to admission to current facility (Z92.82)
- Tobacco dependence (F17.–)
- Tobacco use (Z72.0)

Category I22 is used to report an acute myocardial infarction occurring within 4 weeks (28 days) of a previous acute myocardial infarction, regardless of site. This category also includes:

- Cardiac infarction
- Coronary (artery) embolism
- Coronary (artery) occlusion
- Coronary (artery) rupture
- Coronary (artery) thrombosis
- Infarction of heart, myocardium, or ventricle
- Recurrent myocardial infarction
- Reinfarction of myocardium
- Rupture of heart, myocardium, or ventricle
- Subsequent type1 myocardial infarction

As with category I21, the following instructional notation appears after the heading of category I22:

Use an additional code to identify:
• exposure to environmental tobacco smoke (Z77.22)
• history of tobacco dependence (Z87.891)
• occupational exposure to environmental tobacco smoke (Z57.31)
• status post administration of tPA (rtPA) in a different facility within the last 24 hours prior to admission to current facility (Z92.82)
• tobacco dependence (F17.–)
• tobacco use (Z72.0)

 **NOTE:**

As per coding guidelines a code from category I22 must be used in conjunction with a code from category I21. The sequencing of the I22 and I21 codes depends on the circumstances of the encounter.

The following coding guidelines are to be followed when assigning codes for myocardial infarctions:

ICD-10-CM Official Coding Guidelines

Acute myocardial infarction (AMI)

1) Type 1 ST elevation myocardial infarction (STEMI) and non ST elevation myocardial infarction (NSTEMI)

The ICD-10-CM codes for type 1 acute myocardial infarction (AMI) identify the site, such as anterolateral wall or true posterior wall. Subcategories I21.0–I21.2 and code I21.3 are used for type 1 ST elevation myocardial infarction (STEMI). Code I21.4, Non-ST elevation (NSTEMI) myocardial infarction, is used for type 1 non ST elevation myocardial infarction (NSTEMI) and nontransmural MIs. If a type 1 NSTEMI evolves to STEMI, assign the STEMI code. If a type 1 STEMI converts to NSTEMI due to thrombolytic therapy, it is still coded as STEMI.

For encounters occurring while the myocardial infarction is equal to, or less than, four weeks old, including transfers to another acute setting or a postacute setting, and the myocardial infarction meets the definition for "other diagnoses" (see Section III, Reporting Additional Diagnoses), codes from category I21 may continue to be reported. For encounters after the 4 week time frame and the patient is still receiving care related to the myocardial infarction, the appropriate aftercare code should be assigned, rather than a code from category I21. For old or healed myocardial infarctions not requiring further care, code I25.2, Old myocardial infarction, may be assigned.

2) Acute myocardial infarction, unspecified

Code I21.9, Acute myocardial infarction, unspecified, is the default for the unspecified acute myocardial infarction or unspecified type. If only type 1 STEMI or transmural MI without the site is documented, assign code I21.3, ST elevation (STEMI) myocardial infarction of unspecified site.

3) AMI documented as nontransmural or subendocardial but site provided

If an AMI is documented as nontransmural or subendocardial, but the site is provided, it is still coded as a subendocardial AMI.

See Section I.C.21.3 for information on coding status post administration of tPA in a different facility within the last 24 hours.

4) Subsequent acute myocardial infarction

A code from category I22, Subsequent ST elevation (STEMI) and non ST elevation (NSTEMI) myocardial infarction, is to be used when a patient who has suffered a type 1 or unspecified AMI has a new AMI within the 4 week time frame of the initial AMI. A code from category I22 must be used in conjunction with a code from category I21. The sequencing of the I22 and I21 codes depends on the circumstances of the encounter.

Do not assign code I22 for subsequent myocardial infarctions other than type 1 or unspecified. For subsequent type 2 AMI assign only code I21.A1. For subsequent type 4 or type 5 AMI, assign only code I21.A9.

If a subsequent myocardial infarction of one type occurs within 4 weeks of a myocardial infarction of a different type, assign the appropriate codes from category I21 to identify each type. Do not assign a code from I22. Codes from category I22 should only be assigned if both the initial and subsequent myocardial infarctions are type 1 or unspecified.

5) Other Types of Myocardial Infarction

The ICD-10-CM provides codes for different types of myocardial infarction. Type 1 myocardial infarctions are assigned to codes I21.0–I21.4.

Type 2 myocardial infarction (myocardial infarction due to demand ischemia or secondary to ischemic imbalance) is assigned to code I21.A1, Myocardial infarction type 2 with a code for the underlying cause coded first. Do not assign code I24.8, Other forms of acute ischemic heart disease for the demand ischemia. If a type 2 AMI code is described as NSTEMI or STEMI, only assign code I21.A1. Codes I21.01–I21.4 should only be assigned for type 1 AMIs.

Acute myocardial infarctions type 3, 4a, 4b, 4c and 5 are assigned to code I21.A9, Other myocardial infarction type.

The "Code also" and "Code first" notes should be followed related to complications, and for coding of postprocedural myocardial infarctions during or following cardiac surgery.

(See Appendix A, Section I, C9, e, 1–5.)

Old Myocardial Infarction

Code I25.2 is assigned for an **old myocardial infarction**, sometimes referred to as a **healed myocardial infarction**. This code is used when a past MI is diagnosed by electrocardiogram (EKG) or other investigation and the patient is not presenting with any symptoms. The code is not assigned when current symptoms or ischemic heart disease is present. It actually records a history of an MI and is most commonly used when a past MI has been diagnosed after a diagnostic study or EKG has been completed. The coder must determine from the medical documentation that no symptoms are present before this code is assigned.

EXAMPLE: Don Duckster presented to the physician's office for a follow-up visit 6 months after an EKG showed a slight MI. The patient complained of no symptoms. Code I25.2 is appropriately assigned for this visit.

Pulmonary Heart Disease and Diseases of Pulmonary Circulation (Category Codes I26–I28)

Category I26, with the appropriate fourth and fifth characters, reports pulmonary embolisms and includes pulmonary (artery or vein):

- Infarction
- Thromboembolism
- Thrombosis

Category code I27, with the appropriate fourth and/or fifth characters, reports other pulmonary heart diseases such as primary pulmonary hypertension, kyphoscoliotic heart disease, and other specified pulmonary diseases.

Category code I28, with the appropriate fourth character, reports other diseases of pulmonary vessels such as arteriovenous fistula of pulmonary vessels, aneurysm of pulmonary artery, and other diseases of pulmonary vessels.

The following coding guideline is to be used when assigning codes from I27:

ICD-10-CM Official Coding Guideline

Pulmonary Hypertension

Pulmonary hypertension is classified to category I27, Other pulmonary heart diseases. For secondary pulmonary hypertension (I27.1, I27.2-), code also any associated conditions or adverse effects of drugs or toxins. The sequencing is based on the reason for the encounter, except for adverse effects of drugs (See Section I.C.19.e.) (See Appendix A, Section I, C9, a, 11.)

Other Forms of Heart Disease (Category Codes I30–I52)

This block of codes, using fourth, fifth, and/or sixth characters, classifies other forms of heart disease:

- Acute **pericarditis**—code I30. Inflammation of the outer layers of the heart, known as the **pericardium**.

- Other diseases of pericardium—category code I31. This includes other types of pericarditis, hemopericardium, and other diseases.
- Pericarditis in diseases classified elsewhere—category code I32. It should be noted that the code book contains an instructional notation that states "Code first underlying disease."
- Acute and subacute **endocarditis**—category code I33. Inflammation of the inner layer of the heart. Code I33.0 reports acute and subacute infective endocarditis. Coders must "Use additional code (B95–B97) to identify infectious agent" when code I33.0 is assigned.
- Nonrheumatic mitral valve disorders—category code I34. Coders should note the extensive Excludes1 note that appears for this subcategory.
- Nonrheumatic aortic valve disorders—category code I35. An extensive Excludes1 note also appears for this category.
- Nonrheumatic tricuspid valve disorders—category code I36. Review the Excludes1 note that appears for this category.
- Nonrheumatic pulmonary valve disorders—category code I37.
- Endocarditis, valve unspecified—category code I38. This category includes:

  endocarditis (chronic) NOS

  valvular incompetence NOS

  valvular insufficiency NOS

  valvular regurgitation NOS

  valvular stenosis NOS

  valvulitis (chronic) NOS

  The Excludes1 note for this category needs to be referenced prior to code assignment.

- Endocarditis and heart valve disorders in diseases classified elsewhere—category code I39. Coders should be guided by the extensive Excludes1 and "Code first underlying disease" notations that appear for this category.
- Acute myocarditis—category code I40. The I40 category also reports subacute myocarditis; however, acute rheumatic myocarditis is excluded from this category.

  When reporting code I40.0, "Use additional code (B95–B97) to identify infectious agent."

- **Myocarditis** in diseases classified elsewhere—category code I41. Inflammation of the heart muscle. When reporting code I41, coders must "Code first underlying disease, such as: typhus (A75.0–A75.9),"
- **Cardiomyopathy**—category codes I42–I43. Diseases of the heart muscle. Category I42 reports cardiomyopathy and includes myocardiopathy. Coders should reference the Excludes2 note and the note that states "Code first preexisting cardiomyopathy complicating pregnancy and puerperium (O99.4)." Category I43 contains an Excludes1 note and an instructional notation that states "Code first underlying disease:..." and directs the coder in code assignment.
- Atrioventricular and left bundle-branch block—category code I44. This category is differentiated at the fourth-character level to indicate:
  - the degree of the block (first degree, second degree, complete, and other) for atrioventricular blocks
  - the site of the block (left anterior or left posterior) for fascicular blocks
  - other and unspecified fascicular block I44.6, which is further differentiated to the fifth-character level
  - a left bundle-branch block, code I44.7
- Other conduction disorders—category code I45. This category identifies various types of blocks and pre-excitation syndromes.
- Cardiac arrest—category code I46. This category is differentiated at the fourth-character level to indicate the cause of the cardiac arrest: due to underlying cardiac condition (I46.2), due to other underlying condition

(I46.8), and cause unspecified (I46.9). For codes I46.2 and I46.8, the coder is instructed to "Code first underlying condition."

- Paroxysmal tachycardia—category code I47. This category contains an instructional notation that instructs the coder to "Code first tachycardia..." and an extensive Excludes1 note.

- Atrial fibrillation and flutter—category code I48. This category is differentiated at the fourth or fifth level to identify specific types of atrial fibrillation and flutter.

- Other cardiac arrhythmias—category code I49. Coders should become familiar with the extensive Excludes1 notation present for this category. A "Code first" notation also gives coders direction in code sequencing.

- **Heart failure**—category code I50—A decreased ability of the heart to pump a sufficient amount of blood to the body's tissue. Code I50.9 is used to report congestive heart failure NOS. Figure 14-6 illustrates signs of congestive heart failure. It should be noted that "Code first" and Excludes1 and Excludes2 notations are present for category I50.

- Complications and ill-defined descriptions of heart disease—category code I51. Prior to assigning codes from category I51, coders should reference the Excludes1 note that appears following the I51 heading. This will direct coders to more specific codes for various complications and ill-defined descriptions of heart disease.

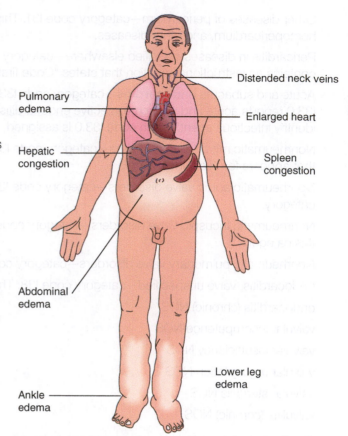

FIGURE 14-6 Signs of congestive heart failure (From Marianne Neighbors & Ruth Tannehill-Jones. *Human Diseases*, 2nd ed. Clifton Park, NY: Delmar, Cengage Learning, p. 143.).

- Other heart disorders in diseases classified elsewhere—code I52. Prior to assigning code I52, coders should be guided by the extensive Excludes1 note as well as the "Code first" notation for this code.

When selecting codes in this section of the code book, the coder must be able to identify modifying terms associated with the main diagnostic term. For example, myocarditis has numerous causes. The coder needs to reference the main term *myocarditis* and then search for any modifying terms such as *bacterial*. This leads the coder to the correct form of myocarditis.

Cerebrovascular Diseases (Category Codes I60–I69)

ICD-10-CM category codes I60–I69, with appropriate fourth, fifth, and/or sixth characters, are used to code various forms of cerebrovascular diseases. **Cerebrovascular disease** includes abnormal nontraumatic conditions that affect the cerebral arteries:

- **Cerebral hemorrhage**—Bleeding within the brain or layers of brain lining

- **Cerebrovascular accident (CVA)**—The disruption in the normal blood supply to the brain, commonly called a **stroke**

- **Occlusion of cerebral and precerebral arteries**—The blocking of the artery

- **Stenosis** of the cerebral arteries—The narrowing of the cerebral arteries that supply blood to the brain

The categories are as follows:

- I60, Nontraumatic subarachnoid hemorrhage
- I61, Nontraumatic intracerebral hemorrhage
- I62, Other and unspecified nontraumatic intracranial hemorrhage
- I63, Cerebral infarction
- I65, Occlusion and stenosis of precerebral arteries, not resulting in cerebral infarction
- I66, Occlusion and stenosis of cerebral arteries, not resulting in cerebral infarction
- I67, Other cerebrovascular diseases
- I68, Cerebrovascular disorders in diseases classified elsewhere
- I69, Sequelae of cerebrovascular disease

Category codes I60–I69 are governed by the following coding guidelines.

> **NOTE:**
>
> Many of the codes are differentiated by the side of the body that the disease occurs on. For example, subcategory I63.0 differentiates between right versus left vertebral artery. The coder must glean the details for code assignment from the medical documentation of the case.

ICD-10-CM Official Coding Guideline

Sequelae of Cerebrovascular Disease

1) Category I69, Sequelae of cerebrovascular disease

Category I69 is used to indicate conditions classifiable to categories I60–I67 as the causes of sequela (neurologic deficits), themselves classified elsewhere. These "late effects" include neurologic deficits that persist after initial onset of conditions classifiable to categories I60–I67. The neurologic deficits caused by cerebrovascular disease may be present from the onset or may arise at any time after the onset of the condition classifiable to categories I60–I67.

Codes from category I69, Sequelae of cerebrovascular disease, that specify hemiplegia, hemiparesis and monoplegia identify whether the dominant or nondominant side is affected. Should the affected side be documented, but not specified as dominant or nondominant and the classification system does not indicate a default code selection is as follows:

- For ambidextrous patients, the default should be dominant.
- If the left side is affected, the default is non-dominant.
- If the right side is affected, the default is dominant.

2) Codes from category I69 with codes from I60–I67

Codes from category I69 may be assigned on a health care record with codes from I60–I67, if the patient has a current cerebrovascular disease and deficits from an old cerebrovascular disease.

3) Codes from category I69 and Personal history of transient ischemic attack (TIA) and cerebral infarction (Z86.73)

Codes from category I69 should not be assigned if the patient does not have neurologic deficits.

See Section I.C.21.4. History (of) for use of personal history codes (See Appendix A, Section I, C9,d, 1–3.)

Courtesy of the Centers for Medicare & Medicaid Services, www.cms.gov

Disease of Arteries, Arterioles, and Capillaries (Category Codes I70–I79)

Coders should reference a diagram of the body's arteries when coding in this section. Many of the codes require identification of the specific diseased artery. Coders must also identify whether the disease is affecting the patient's own arteries or grafted or transplanted arteries.

EXAMPLE: Atherosclerosis, category code I70, is divided to identify atherosclerosis of the native arteries of the extremities and bypass grafts of the extremities. Subcategory I70.2 identifies atherosclerosis of native arteries of the extremities, and subcategory I70.3 identifies atherosclerosis of unspecified type of bypass grafts of the extremities.

The detail in the I70–I79 code range is great. For accurate coding, coders need to thoroughly read the diagnosis being coded and match it with the descriptions in the code book.

Diseases of Veins, Lymphatic Vessels, and Lymph Nodes, Not Elsewhere Classified (Category Codes I80–I89)

Code block I80–I89 includes numerous commonly treated conditions. The category codes found in this section of the code book are:

- I80, **Phlebitis**, inflammation of a vein, and **thrombophlebitis**, inflammation of a vein with the formation of a thrombus
- I81, **Portal vein thrombosis**, the formation of a blood clot in the main vein of the liver
- I82, Other venous embolism and thrombosis. An instructional notation appears in the code book in regard to reporting embolisms and thrombosis that are complicating abortion, ectopic or molar pregnancy, pregnancy, childbirth, and the puerperium.

  Codes I82.40–I82.499 describe embolism and thrombosis of the deep veins of the lower extremities with codes to identify left versus right and the specific vein involved.

- I83, **Varicose veins** of the lower extremities—Dilated superficial veins of the legs. When assigning codes from this category, coders need to identify the specific extremity and site of the varicose veins. It should also be noted that at some subcategory levels, such as I83.0 and I83.2, coders are instructed via an instructional notation to "Use additional code to identify severity of ulcer (L97.–)."
- I85, Esophageal varices. For this category an instructional notation requires using an additional code to identify alcohol abuse and dependence.
- I86, Varicose veins of other sites—Varicose veins of the sublingual, scrotal, pelvic, gastric, vulval, and other specified areas are classified to this code category.
- I87, Other disorders of veins—This category includes the following disorders: postphlebitic syndrome, compression of vein, venous insufficiency, and chronic venous hypertension.
- I88, Nonspecific lymphadenitis—**Lymphadenitis** is the inflammation of the lymph nodes.
- I89, Other noninfective disorders of lymphatic vessels and lymph nodes. This category reports lymphedema, lymphangitis, and other noninfective disorders of the lymphatic vessels and lymph nodes.

Other and Unspecified Disorders of the Circulatory System (Category Codes I95–I99)

The last code block of this chapter is I95–I99:

- I95, **Hypotension**—Low blood pressure. This category is differentiated at the fourth or fifth character level to identify the type of hypotension, such as idiopathic, orthostatic, hypotension due to drugs, hypotension of hemodialysis, and other forms.
- I96, Gangrene, not elsewhere classified—Includes gangrenous cellulitis
- I97, Intraoperative and postprocedural complications and disorders of circulatory system, not elsewhere classified. Fourth, fifth, and/or sixth characters are required within this category.
- I99, Other and unspecified disorders of circulatory system—Codes from this category are not specific. The coder should query the provider to determine whether more specific information is available before assigning codes.

The following coding guideline applies to the coding of intraoperative and postprocedural cerebrovascular accidents.

ICD-10-CM Official Coding Guideline

c. Intraoperative and Postprocedural Cerebrovascular Accident

Medical record documentation should clearly specify the cause-and-effect relationship between the medical intervention and the cerebrovascular accident in order to assign a code for intraoperative or postprocedural cerebrovascular accident.

Proper code assignment depends on whether it was an infarction or hemorrhage and whether it occurred intraoperatively or postoperatively. If it was a cerebral hemorrhage, code assignment depends on the type of procedure performed. (See Appendix A, Section I, c9, c.)

Courtesy of the Centers for Medicare & Medicaid Services, www.cms.gov

Summary

- ICD-10-CM Chapter 9 covers diseases of the circulatory system.
- The primary structures of the circulatory system are arteries, veins, and the heart.
- Cardiovascular disease can affect many vessels throughout the body.
- Secondary hypertension is high arterial blood pressure due to another disease.
- Hypertensive heart disease includes heart disease caused by hypertension.
- Hypertensive renal disease includes renal disease caused by hypertension.
- Cerebrovascular disease includes abnormal nontraumatic conditions that affect the cerebral arteries.
- Chronic ischemic heart disease is also referred to as arteriosclerotic heart disease.
- Cerebrovascular disease includes abnormal nontraumatic conditions that affect the cerebral arteries.

Internet Links

To learn more about peripheral vascular disease, visit **www.footcare4u.com**.

To better understand the various forms of heart disease, visit **www.medicinenet.com** and search the term *heart disease*.

Chapter Review

True/False

Indicate whether each statement is true (T) or false (F).

1. _____ Angina pectoris and unstable angina are classified to the same code.

2. _____ Veins carry deoxygenated blood from the body back to the heart with one exception, the pulmonary vein.

3. _____ Rheumatic tricuspid stenosis is assigned code I07.9.

4. _____ Diastolic blood pressure is the pressure on the arterial walls during heart muscle contraction.

5. _____ Hypertension is an increase in systolic blood pressure, diastolic blood pressure, or both.

Fill-in-the-Blank

Enter the appropriate term(s) to complete each statement.

6. Uncontrolled hypertension may refer to _____ hypertension or hypertension not responding to current _____.

7. Hypertensive cardiomegaly and hypertensive heart failure are types of _____ disease.

8. Stenosis of the cerebral arteries is caused by a _____ of the cerebral arteries that supply blood to the brain.

9. Circulatory system disorders can be caused by infections as well as _____ factors.

10. An acute _____ is commonly called a heart attack.

Coding Guidelines True/False

Review the ICD-10-CM Official Guidelines for Coding and Reporting and indicate if the statement(s) is true or false.

11. _____ Assign a code from category I16, Hypertensive crisis, for documented hypertensive urgency, hypertensive emergency, or unspecified hypertensive crisis. Code also any identified hypertensive disease (I10–I15). Sequence the I16 category code first.

12. _____ For hypertension and conditions not specifically linked by relational terms such as "with," "associated with," or "due to" in the classification, provider documentation must link the conditions in order to code them as related.

13. _____ For hypertensive cerebrovascular disease, first assign the appropriate code from categories I60–I69, followed by the appropriate hypertension code.

14. _____ Uncontrolled hypertension may refer to untreated hypertension or hypertension not responding to current therapeutic regimen. In either case, assign the appropriate code from categories I10–I15, Hypertensive diseases.

15. _____ Controlled hypertension usually refers to an existing state of hypertension under control by therapy, therefore do not assign a code.

Coding Assignments

Instructions: Using an ICD-10-CM code book, assign the proper diagnosis code to the following diagnostic statements.

1. benign essential hypertension _____

2. moderate arterial hypertension _____

3. Raynaud's syndrome with gangrene _____

4. dissection of carotid artery _____

5. rheumatic aortic regurgitation _____

6. unstable angina _____

7. angina pectoris with essential hypertension _____

8. spasm-induced angina _____

9. congestive heart failure _____

10. peripheral venous insufficiency _____

11. alcoholic cardiomyopathy _____

12. cardiac arrest _____

13. Dressler's syndrome _____

14. circulation defect _____

15. acute pericarditis _____

16. atrial flutter _____

17. cardiomegaly _____

18. aortic aneurysm _____

19. chronic ischemic heart disease _____

20. acute myocardial infarction _____

21. obstructive hypertrophic cardiomyopathy _____

22. extrasystolic arrhythmia _____

23. aneurysm of renal artery _____

24. arterial stricture _____

25. esophageal varices _____

26. phlebosclerosis _____

27. subacute lymphangitis _____

28. atheroembolism of left lower extremity _____

29. endomyocardial fibrosis _____

30. idiopathic pulmonary arteriosclerosis _____

31. nonrheumatic mitral valve regurgitation _____

32. longstanding persistent atrial fibrillation _____

33. mitral valve stenosis _____

34. left ventricular failure _____

35. intraoperative cardiac arrest during cardiac surgery _____

Case Studies

Instructions: Review each case study and select the correct ICD-10-CM diagnostic code.

Case 1

Physician Office Note

VITAL SIGNS: Temperature: 100.2, Blood pressure: 130/80, Weight: 175 pounds

Bridgit presents today with a chief complaint of pain in her left leg that has been present on and off for the last week. She has previously experienced phlebitis in her left leg.

(continues)

(*continued*)

EXAM:

HEENT: Normal

CHEST: Clear

EXTREMITIES: There is edema in her left leg. An area on her calf is tender to palpation. She states that the pain is also unbearable when I touch it.

Because of her previous phlebitis, I sent her to the x-ray department for a STAT venogram that revealed thrombophlebitis of the left tibial vein.

Patient was given heparin, and a prescription was written for antibiotics. The left leg was immobilized, and she was instructed to return to me in 3 days.

ICD-10-CM Code Assignment: _____

Case 2

DISCHARGE SUMMARY:

Admitted 2/03/XX

Discharged 2/07/XX

Admitting Diagnosis:

Unstable angina

Atrial fibrillation

HISTORY: This 69-year-old man was admitted through the ER with chest pain that began while he was eating his lunch. After lunch he went to do his grocery shopping, and he began to develop discomfort in his chest as well as in his jaw. He drove himself to the ER. The ER physician admitted the patient due to unstable angina.

Vital signs at time of admission: BP: 140/60, Heart rate: 110 to 120

HEART: Patient complains of chest pain.

All other physical findings were within normal limits.

HOSPITAL COURSE:

Cardiac enzymes—CPK of 105, Troponin—4.7 with a relative index of 5.4

Digoxin level was 1.8.

All other lab values were normal.

EKG was positive for a new anterior wall infarction.

The patient was maintained on Imdur 30 mg daily and metoprolol 50 mg in the morning and evening.

The patient stabilized and was instructed to see me in 7 days.

Discharge Diagnosis:

(continues)

(continued)

Acute anterolateral transmural Q wave infarction

Hypertension

ICD-10-CM Code Assignment: _____

Case 3

Skilled Nursing Facility Physician Monthly Progress Note

4/22/XX

This patient was admitted in January of last year with a primary diagnosis of ischemic heart disease, history of bladder cancer, and uncontrolled malignant hypertension. Patient continues to be stable. On exam, he appears comfortable and still has some coughing spells during my physical examination.

Vital signs include a weight of 223.8 lb. Compared to last 3 months, it varies from 222 to 225. No weight gain or weight loss.

BLOOD PRESSURE: 160/90, which is not under control; pulse—70 per minute, regular; respirations—24.

LUNGS: Still occasional rhonchi but no wheeze

HEART: Regular rhythm with no change in systolic murmur

Abdomen is soft. Bowel sounds are active.

EXTREMITIES: No pedal edema; no clubbing or cyanosis

Medications, including Advil, Cytotec, Ascriptin, Tylenol, Tenormin, Pulmoaid therapy, Senna laxative, Artificial Tears, Analgesic Balm, Casadex, Mycolog, to be continued, along with the standing orders.

I will see the patient in 30 days or at the request of the charge nurse.

ICD-10-CM Code Assignment: _____

Case 4

Physician's Office Note

Mr. Cafferty presents today with some ascites and complaint of exertional dyspnea. When queried about any other symptoms, he stated that at night he sometimes wakes up coughing, which in his words is described as "real dry." He has a history of congestive heart failure and microvascular spasms.

(continues)

(continued)

On physical examination, mild ascites, tachycardia, and peripheral edema are noted. Previous diagnostic testing was reviewed, which confirmed cardiomyopathy.

ICD-10-CM Code Assignment: _____

Case 5

Physician's Office Note

VITAL SIGNS: Temperature: 98.8, Blood pressure: 120/70, Weight 185 pounds

This 42-year-old male presents today with shortness of breath, fatigue, ankle edema, and anxiety. He states that these symptoms have begun to increase in severity, and he is concerned.

Chest x-ray and EKG confirmed congestive heart failure.

ICD-10-CM Code Assignment: _____

Case 6

Discharge Note

This 85-year-old male patient is being discharged to Sunny Side Nursing facility. He has had a 4-day length of stay due to a number of issues. Today he is stable and he is to be discharged. His final diagnosis is:

Stage 4 chronic renal disease accompanied by congestive heart failure due to hypertension.

I will follow up with him at the nursing facility in 10 days or sooner if needed.

ICD-10-CM Code Assignment: _____

Case 7

Emergency Department Note

This 54-year-old male patient presents to the ED with angina. Review of his records indicates that he has atherosclerotic heart disease. After he was given nitro, the angina stabilized. He has not had any previous cardiac surgery. I am calling the cardiac team to review this case.

ICD-10-CM Coding Assignment: _____

Case 8

Consultation Inpatient Note

This patient was referred to me by Dr. Smith. The patient was admitted from the ER.

She is 65 years old and has a history of a previous MI 4 years old and has not had any previous bypass surgery. She has coronary artery disease and today she is experiencing unstable angina. I discussed with her the need to have a cardiac catheterization. She says she would like to have her husband and daughter come in to speak with me prior to scheduling the cath.

ICD-10-CM Code Assignment: _____

Case 9

Office Visit

This 83-year-old patient is being seen in the office today to monitor his essential hypertension that he has experienced for the last 2 years. The blood workup that he had last week showed a vitamin D deficiency. There were no other abnormalities.

HEENT: Normal

Heart: Regular rate and rhythm

Abdomen: Soft, no masses

Extremities: No edema

Plan: He is to continue on his prescribed diet and continue to take his cardiac medications. I also instructed him to take 2000 units of vitamin D per day. He is to follow up with me in 3 months.

ICD-10-CM Code Assignment: _____

Case 10

Emergency Department Note

This 46-year-old female patient presents to the ED with palpitations, an atrial rate of 420 bpm, nausea, weakness, and fatigue. She was given Quinidine to convert rhythm. ECG showed absence of P waves, and uniform-shaped QRS complexes with irregular intervals. She is being admitted to the cardiac unit with a diagnosis of atrial fibrillation.

ICD-10-CM Code Assignment: _____

CHAPTER 15

Diseases of the Respiratory System

Chapter Outline

Chapter Objectives

Key Terms

Introduction

Introduction to the Body System

Coding Diseases of the Respiratory System

Summary

Internet Links

Chapter Review

Coding Assignments

Case Studies

Chapter Objectives

At the conclusion of this chapter, you should be able to:

1. Identify the major functions and structures of the respiratory system.
2. Explain the diseases and conditions that impact the respiratory system.
3. Summarize coding guidelines for diseases of the respiratory system.
4. Apply ICD-10-CM coding guidelines to accurately code conditions and diseases of the respiratory system.
5. Select and code diagnoses from case studies.

Key Terms

Acute bronchitis

Aspiration pneumonia

Bronchi

Bronchitis

Chronic bronchitis

Chronic sinusitis

Emphysema

Influenza

Larynx

Lungs

Pharyngitis

Pharynx

Pneumonia

Respiratory system

Tonsils

Trachea

Vocal cords

REMINDER: As you work through this chapter, you will need to have a copy of the ICD-10-CM coding book to reference. For this chapter, you will also need to reference the ICD-10-CM Official Guidelines for Coding and Reporting. These guidelines can be found in Appendix A which are now available on the Student Companion site and MINDTAP From Cengage.

Introduction

Chapter 10 of ICD-10-CM, "Diseases of the Respiratory System" (category codes J00–J99), classifies conditions such as acute respiratory infections, diseases of the upper respiratory tract, acute respiratory failure, asthma, pneumonia, influenza, and chronic obstructive pulmonary disease.

The following blocks of codes are present in this chapter:

- J00–J06, Acute upper respiratory infections
- J09–J18, Influenza and pneumonia
- J20–J22, Other acute lower respiratory infections
- J30–J39, Other diseases of upper respiratory tract
- J40–J47, Chronic lower respiratory diseases
- J60–J70, Lung diseases due to external agents
- J80–J84, Other respiratory diseases principally affecting the interstitium
- J85–J86, Suppurative and necrotic conditions of the lower respiratory tract
- J90–J94, Other diseases of the pleura
- J95, Intraoperative and postprocedural complications and disorders of respiratory system, not elsewhere classified
- J96–J99, Other diseases of the respiratory system

Introduction to the Body System

The respiratory system begins its function when air enters the body through the nose or mouth. The **respiratory system** is comprised of structures that exchange oxygen and carbon dioxide in the body.

The main organs of the respiratory system are the **lungs**, where this gas exchange occurs. The lungs also work as a purification or filtering system for the air the body takes in. Two lobes, one on the right and one on the left, hold the bronchi. The **bronchi** are formed when the **trachea**, or windpipe, branches off in the chest. Figure 15-1 illustrates the structures of the respiratory system.

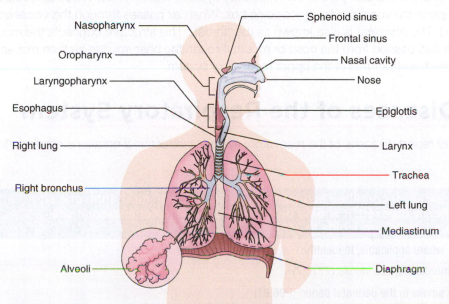

FIGURE 15-1 Structures of the respiratory system (From Ehrlich A, Schroeder CL. Medical Terminology for Health Professionals, 4th ed. Clifton Park, NY: Delmar, Cengage Learning, 2001.).

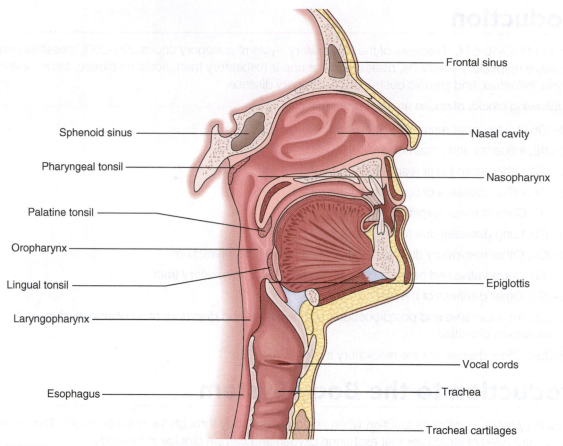

FIGURE 15-2 Structures of the upper respiratory system (From Ehrlich A, Schroeder CL. Medical Terminology for Health Professionals, 4th ed. Clifton Park, NY: Delmar, Cengage Learning, 2001.).

The larynx and pharynx are also part of the respiratory system. The **larynx** is made up of cartilage and ligaments that compose the vocal cords, or the voice box. When air passes through the **vocal cords**, sound or speech is produced. The **pharynx** is also known as the "throat." This structure connects the mouth and nose to the larynx. Once air has passed from the nose or mouth through the pharynx, the air then moves into the trachea. Figure 15-2 illustrates the structures of the upper respiratory system.

Coding Diseases of the Respiratory System

Categories J00–J99 report diseases of the respiratory system. Instructional notations appear after the chapter heading that state:

Note: When a respiratory condition is described as occurring in more than one site and is not specifically indexed, it should be classified to the lower anatomic site (e.g., tracheobronchitis to bronchitis in J40).
Use additional code, where applicable, to identify:
exposure to environmental tobacco smoke (Z77.22)
exposure to tobacco smoke in the perinatal period (P96.81)
history of tobacco dependence (Z87.891)
occupational exposure to environmental tobacco smoke (Z57.31)
tobacco dependence (F17.–)
tobacco use (Z72.0)

These instructions must be followed for proper code selection. Coders should also keep in mind that provider documentation is key in the diagnostic coding for respiratory disease. Laboratory results, on their own, are not enough to assign a diagnosis code in this chapter. The coder must also reference provider diagnostic statements for code selection. It should also be noted that an extensive Excludes2 note appears after the chapter heading that governs the entire chapter.

Acute Upper Respiratory Infections (Category Codes J00–J06)

This block of codes, with use of fourth and fifth characters, contains some of the more common diagnostic codes used by a primary care office:

- J00, Acute nasopharyngitis [common cold]
- J01, Acute sinusitis
- J02, Acute pharyngitis
- J03, Acute tonsillitis
- J04, Acute laryngitis and tracheitis
- J05, Acute obstructive laryngitis [croup] and epiglottitis
- J06, Acute upper respiratory infections of multiple and unspecified sites

Acute **pharyngitis**, or what is commonly called a "sore throat," is coded to category code J02. There are many causes of pharyngitis, such as a virus, bacteria, and tobacco abuse. The category J02 is for acute pharyngitis and should not be used if the condition is chronic, which codes to J31.2. If the pharyngitis is due to an infection, codes from the "Certain Infectious and Parasitic Diseases" chapter should be reported to identify the cause of the infection. A notation appears after code J02.8 that directs the coder to "Use additional code (B95–B97) to identify infectious agents."

EXAMPLE:

Patient 1

An 8-year-old girl presents today with a runny nose, cough, and sore throat. A rapid strep test is done, which comes back negative.

DX: Cold and sore throat

Code assignment: J00 and J02.9

Patient 2

A 10-year-old boy presents today with a runny nose, cough, and sore throat. A rapid strep test is done, which comes back positive.

DX: Strep throat

Code assignment: J02.0

When coding in this section, be sure your documentation supports an acute condition. If there is any question, consult the provider for clarification.

Influenza and Pneumonia (Category Codes J09–J18)

This category of codes includes influenza and pneumonia. Some forms of influenza and pneumonia are not coded to these categories. The types of influenza and pneumonia that are excluded from these categories appear in Excludes1 notes. For example, the following are Excludes1 notes for category J09:

Excludes1:
influenza A/H1N1 (J10.–)
influenza due to other identified influenza virus (J10.–)
influenza due to unidentified influenza virus (J11.–)
seasonal influenza due to other identified influenza virus (J10.–)
seasonal influenza due to unidentified influenza virus (J11.–)

This block of codes has many instructional notations that instruct coders to code first any associated conditions and to use additional codes to identify the presence of a virus.

The following category codes are present in this block of codes:

- J09, Influenza due to certain identified influenza viruses
- J10, Influenza due to other identified influenza virus
- J11, Influenza due to unidentified influenza virus
- J12, Viral pneumonia, not elsewhere classified
- J13, Pneumonia due to *Streptococcus pneumoniae*
- J14, Pneumonia due to *Hemophilus influenzae*
- J15, Bacterial pneumonia, not elsewhere classified
- J16, Pneumonia due to other infectious organisms, not elsewhere classified
- J17, Pneumonia in diseases classified elsewhere
- J18, Pneumonia, unspecified organism

Influenza, a highly contagious respiratory disease that is caused by various viruses, is coded in ICD-10-CM to category codes J09–J11. The following coding guideline needs to be referenced when coding from categories J09–J11.

ICD-10-CM Official Coding Guidelines

c. Influenza due to certain identified influenza viruses

Code only confirmed cases of influenza due to certain identified influenza viruses (category J09) and due to other identified influenza virus (category J10). This is an exception to the hospital inpatient guideline Section II, H. (Uncertain Diagnosis).

In this context, "confirmation" does not require documentation of positive laboratory testing specific for avian or other novel influenza A or identified influenza virus. However, coding should be based on the provider's diagnostic statement that the patient has avian influenza, or other novel influenza A, for category J09, or has another particular identified strain of influenza, such as H1N1 or H3N2, but not identified as novel or variant, for category J10.

If the provider records "suspected" or "possible" or "probable" avian influenza or novel influenza, or other identified influenza, then the appropriate influenza code from category J11, Influenza due to unidentified influenza virus, should be assigned. A code from category J09, Influenza due to certain identified influenza viruses, should not be assigned nor should a code from category J10, Influenza due to other identified influenza virus. (See Appendix A, Section I, C10, c.)

Pneumonia is a condition in which liquid, known as "exudate," and pus infiltrate the lung and cause an inflammation. Bacteria, viruses, inhaled irritants, or fungi can cause pneumonia. There are many types of pneumonia, so it is very important to verify the type of pneumonia documented in the medical record. ICD-10-CM classifies pneumonia by the organism or irritant causing the pneumonia.

At times a provider documents the term *lobar pneumonia*. When there is mention of pneumonia in a lobe of the lung, it is lobar pneumonia only if documented by the provider as such. If you reference the term *lobar pneumonia* in the Alphabetic Index of ICD-10-CM, you will note numerous entries under the term *lobar*. Therefore, coders may have to clarify with the provider as to the type of lobar pneumonia that is present. Lobar pneumonia is usually caused by *Streptococcus pneumoniae,* and it is coded to J13.

Other Acute Lower Respiratory Infections (Category Codes J20–J22)

This block of codes, with use of fourth digits for categories J20 and J21, is divided into the following categories:

- J20, Acute bronchitis
- J21, Acute bronchiolitis
- J22, Unspecified acute lower respiratory infection

Bronchitis, an inflammation of the bronchus, can be diagnosed as both acute and chronic. ICD-10-CM provides separate codes for the acute and chronic manifestations of bronchitis. The J20 category is used for acute bronchitis. **Acute bronchitis** is an inflammation of the bronchus that lasts for a short period of time and is typically caused by a spreading of an inflammation from the nasopharynx. Symptoms of acute bronchitis include fever, cough, and substernal pain.

Chronic bronchitis is a prolonged inflammation of the bronchus, lasting for more than 3 months and occurring for two consecutive years. Chronic bronchitis can occur because of exposure to bronchial irritants such as cigarette smoking. Symptoms of chronic bronchitis include a severe, persistent cough and large amounts of discolored sputum. Chronic bronchitis is classified to category codes J40–J42.

Other Diseases of Upper Respiratory Tract (Category Codes J30–J39)

This block of codes reports other diseases of the upper respiratory tract, with use of fourth and/or fifth characters within the categories.

This section of the chapter contains many of the codes needed to code the chronic inflammatory diseases of the upper respiratory tract (see Figure 15-2). This section also classifies conditions that affect the accessory structures of the respiratory system such as the sinus cavities, tonsils and adenoids, larynx, and vocal cords.

One of the more common conditions coded to this section is **chronic sinusitis**, category code J32, which is a prolonged inflammation of one or more of the sinus cavities. Chronic sinusitis can be a result of exposure to something the patient may be allergic to or an infective agent. Acute sinusitis is coded to category J01.

Chronic diseases of the tonsils are coded to this section. The **tonsils** protect the entrance to the respiratory system from invading organisms. Abscess of the tonsils is coded to J36, Peritonsillar abscess. Acute tonsillitis is coded to J03.90. Other chronic conditions found here are chronic laryngitis, J37.0, and chronic rhinitis, J31.0.

 NOTE:

Coders must reference the many instructional notations throughout this entire block when selecting codes.

Exercise 15.1—Coding Category Codes J00–J39

Select the appropriate ICD-10-CM code for the diagnosis listed.

1. bacterial pneumonia _____
2. pneumonia due to *Mycoplasma pneumoniae* _____
3. *E. coli* pneumonia _____
4. common cold _____
5. acute tonsillitis _____
6. acute laryngopharyngitis _____
7. pneumonia due to *Hemophilus influenzae* _____
8. chronic maxillary sinusitis _____
9. hypertrophy of tonsils _____
10. allergic rhinitis _____

Chronic Lower Respiratory Diseases (Category Codes J40–J47)

This block of codes is divided as follows, with the use of fourth, fifth, and/or sixth characters within certain categories:

- J40, Bronchitis, not specified as acute or chronic
- J41, Simple and mucopurulent chronic bronchitis
- J42, Unspecified chronic bronchitis
- J43, Emphysema
- J44, Other chronic obstructive pulmonary disease
- J45, Asthma
- J47, Bronchiectasis

Emphysema, a loss of lung function due to progressive decrease in the number of alveoli in the bronchus of the lung, is coded to category code J43. Asthma is a stricture of the airway that causes difficulty breathing. Asthma is usually an allergic disorder in which wheezing and coughing are common indicators. The J45 category, Asthma, is further divided to indicate the type of asthma: mild intermittent, mild persistent, moderate persistent, etc.

The following coding guideline should also be noted when coding from categories J44 to J45.

ICD-10-CM Official Coding Guidelines

a. Chronic Obstructive Pulmonary Disease [COPD] and Asthma

1) Acute exacerbation of chronic obstructive bronchitis and asthma

The codes in categories J44 and J45 distinguish between uncomplicated cases and those in acute exacerbation. An acute exacerbation is a worsening or a decompensation of a chronic condition. An acute exacerbation is not equivalent to an infection superimposed on a chronic condition, though an exacerbation may be triggered by an infection. (See Appendix A, Section I, c10, a.)

Courtesy of the Centers for Medicare & Medicaid Services, www.cms.gov

Lung Diseases Due to External Agents (Category Codes J60–J70)

This block of codes is used to code lung diseases that are due to external agents such as solids, liquids, chemicals, gases, fumes, and vapors. This block includes such diseases as black lung disease, asbestosis, pneumoconiosis, any airway disease due to organic dust, and pneumonitis due to solids and liquids.

A common condition that is coded to J69.0 is aspiration pneumonia. **Aspiration pneumonia** occurs when a solid or liquid is inhaled into the lung. Aspiration pneumonia can be caused by the inhalation of food, gastric secretions, milk, and vomit, among other things.

Other Respiratory Diseases Principally Affecting the Interstitium (Category Codes J80–J84)

This block of codes contains the following categories, with the assignment of fourth, fifth, and/or sixth characters within specific categories:

- J80, Acute respiratory distress syndrome
- J81, Pulmonary edema
- J82, Pulmonary eosinophilia, not elsewhere classified
- J84, Other interstitial pulmonary diseases

Pulmonary edema, category J81, contains an instructional notation that instructs the coder to:

Use additional code to identify:
exposure to environmental tobacco smoke (Z77.22)
history of tobacco dependence (Z87.891)
occupational exposure to environmental tobacco smoke (Z57.31)
tobacco dependence (F17.–)
tobacco use (Z72.0)

An Excludes1 note reads:

Excludes1:
chemical (acute) pulmonary edema (J68.1)
hypostatic pneumonia (J18.2)
passive pneumonia (J18.2)
pulmonary edema due to external agents (J60–J70)
pulmonary edema with heart disease NOS (I50.1)
pulmonary edema with heart failure (I50.1)

Coders need to be guided by these notations when selecting codes for acute and chronic pulmonary edema.

Suppurative and Necrotic Conditions of the Lower Respiratory Tract (Category Codes J85–J86)

This block of codes reports abscess of the lung and mediastinum with category J85 and pyothorax with category J86. For category J85 the following appears: "Use additional code (B95–B97) to identify infectious agent."

The J85 category is differentiated as follows:

- J85.0, Gangrene and necrosis of lung

- J85.1, Abscess of lung with pneumonia
  Code also the type of pneumonia

- J85.2, Abscess of lung without pneumonia
  Abscess of lung NOS

- J85.3, Abscess of   mediastinum

  If the provider does not document the infectious agent the coder should query the provider to determine the infectious agent.

  Category J86 is differentiated to identify the presence of fistula and also contains the following: "Use additional code (B95–B97) to identify infectious agent."

EXAMPLE:

Patient 1

Dr. Wong documents abscess of lung with pneumonia. The abscess of the lung with pneumonia is coded with J85.1 however the provider did not document the infectious agent the provider needs to be queried to determine the type of pneumonia.

Patient 2

Dr. Yeng documents staphylococcal abscess of pleura without fistula. Since the provider recorded the

type of infectious agent the coder would code J86.9 and code B95.8.

Other Diseases of the Pleura (Category Codes J90–J94) and Intraoperative and Postprocedural Complications and Disorders of Respiratory System, Not Elsewhere Classified (Category Code J95)

This block of codes is divided as follows:

- J90, Pleural effusion, not elsewhere classified
- J91, Pleural effusion in condition classified elsewhere
- J92, Pleural plaque
- J93, Pneumothorax and air leak
- J94, Other pleural conditions

Prior to code selection for categories J90–J94, coders need to become familiar with the Excludes1 and Excludes2 and "Code first" notations that appear at various code levels.

- J95, Intraoperative and postprocedural complications and disorders of respiratory system, not elsewhere classified

The following gives the coder direction when coding ventilator-associated pneumonia.

ICD-10-CM Official Coding Guidelines

d. Ventilator associated Pneumonia

1) Documentation of Ventilator associated Pneumonia

As with all procedural or postprocedural complications, code assignment is based on the provider's documentation of the relationship between the condition and the procedure.

Code J95.851, Ventilator associated pneumonia, should be assigned only when the provider has documented ventilator associated pneumonia (VAP). An additional code to identify the organism (e.g., Pseudomonas aeruginosa, code B96.5) should also be assigned. Do not assign an additional code from categories J12–J18 to identify the type of pneumonia.

Code J95.851 should not be assigned for cases where the patient has pneumonia and is on a mechanical ventilator and the provider has not specifically stated that the pneumonia is ventilator-associated pneumonia. If the documentation is unclear as to whether the patient has a pneumonia that is a complication attributable to the mechanical ventilator, query the provider.

2) Ventilator associated Pneumonia Develops after Admission

A patient may be admitted with one type of pneumonia (e.g., code J13, Pneumonia due to Streptococcus pneumonia) and subsequently develop VAP. In this instance, the principal diagnosis would be the appropriate code from categories J12–J18 for the pneumonia diagnosed at the time of admission. Code J95.851, Ventilator associated pneumonia, would be assigned as an additional diagnosis when the provider has also documented the presence of ventilator associated pneumonia. (See Appendix A, Section I, c10, d.)

Other Diseases of the Respiratory System (Category Codes J96–J99)

This block of codes has three categories:

- J96, Respiratory failure, not elsewhere classified
- J98, Other respiratory disorders
- J99, Respiratory disorders in diseases classified elsewhere

The following coding guideline governs these codes:

ICD-10-CM Official Coding Guidelines

b. Acute Respiratory Failure

1) Acute respiratory failure as principal diagnosis

A code from subcategory J96.0, Acute respiratory failure, or subcategory J96.2, Acute and chronic respiratory failure, may be assigned as a principal diagnosis when it is the condition established after study to be chiefly responsible for occasioning the admission to the hospital, and the selection is supported by the Alphabetic Index and Tabular List. However, chapter-specific coding guidelines (such as obstetrics, poisoning, HIV, newborn) that provide sequencing direction take precedence.

2) Acute respiratory failure as secondary diagnosis

Respiratory failure may be listed as a secondary diagnosis if it occurs after admission, or if it is present on admission, but does not meet the definition of principal diagnosis.

3) Sequencing of acute respiratory failure and another acute condition

When a patient is admitted with respiratory failure and another acute condition, (e.g., myocardial infarction, cerebrovascular accident, aspiration pneumonia), the principal diagnosis will not be the same in every situation. This applies whether the other acute condition is a respiratory or nonrespiratory condition. Selection of the principal diagnosis will be dependent on the circumstances of admission. If both the respiratory failure and the other acute condition are equally responsible for occasioning the admission to the hospital, and there are no chapter-specific sequencing rules, the guideline regarding two or more diagnoses that equally meet the definition for principal diagnosis (Section II, C.) may be applied in these situations.

If the documentation is not clear as to whether acute respiratory failure and another condition are equally responsible for occasioning the admission, query the provider for clarification. (See Appendix A, Section I, c10, b.)

Courtesy of the Centers for Medicare & Medicaid Services, www.cms.gov

Vaping-related Disorders

The final guideline found in the chapter specific guidelines for the Respiratory System provides the coder guidance for the coding of vaping-related disorders. Vaping-related disorders are coded in Chapter 22 of ICD-10-CM. The vaping-related codes and guidelines will be addressed in Chapter 26 of this textbook.

Summary

- The respiratory system works as a purifying system, filtering air and carrying oxygen to the blood cells and carrying carbon dioxide out of the body.
- The lungs are the main organ of the respiratory system.
- The larynx is where the vocal cords are located.
- The trachea branches off into each lung; the branches are called bronchi.
- Respiratory conditions are commonly identified as acute, chronic, or both acute and chronic.
- ICD-10-CM classifies pneumonia by the organism or irritant causing the pneumonia.
- ICD-10-CM provides separate codes for the acute and chronic manifestations of bronchitis.
- Acute and chronic sinusitis are classified to different category codes in ICD-10-CM.
- The ICD-10-CM Official Guidelines for Coding and Reporting give instructions for coding acute exacerbation of chronic obstructive bronchitis and asthma, acute respiratory failure, and influenza due to avian influenza virus.

Internet Links

To learn more about diseases of the respiratory system, visit **www.lungusa.org** and **www.emphysema.net**. The Pulmonary Education and Research Foundation also provides current information at **www.perf2ndwind.org**.

For information about diseases of the respiratory system, visit
https://www.niehs.nih.gov/health/topics/conditions/lung-disease/index.cfm.

Chapter Review

True/False

Indicate whether each statement is true (T) or false (F).

1. _____ The bronchi are located in the lungs.

2. _____ The respiratory system begins its function when air enters the body.

3. _____ When air passes through the pharynx, sound is produced.

4. _____ Code J02.9 reports acute pharyngitis.

5. _____ The code for maxillary sinusitis is J32.0.

Fill-in-the-Blank

Enter the appropriate term(s) to complete each statement.

6. Acute respiratory failure is coded to _____.

7. An inflammation of the bronchus that lasts for a short time and suddenly occurs is called _____.

8. The vocal cords are located in the _____.

9. Chronic bronchitis is a bronchial infection that lasts longer than _____.

10. Acute _____ is commonly called a sore throat.

Coding Guidelines True/False

Review the ICD-10-CM Official Guidelines for Coding and Reporting and indicate if the statement(s) is true or false.

11. _____ Code only confirmed cases of influenza due to certain identified influenza viruses (category J09) and due to other identified influenza virus (category J10). This is an exception to the hospital inpatient guideline Section II, H. (Uncertain Diagnosis).

12. _____ If the provider records "suspected" or "possible" or "probable" avian influenza or novel influenza, or other identified influenza, then the appropriate influenza code from category J11, Influenza due to unidentified influenza virus, should not be assigned.

13. _____ The codes in categories J44 and J45 distinguish between uncomplicated cases and those in acute exacerbation. An acute exacerbation is a worsening or a decompensation of a chronic condition. An acute exacerbation is equivalent to an infection superimposed on a chronic condition, though an exacerbation may be triggered by an infection.

14. _____ Code J95.851, Ventilator associated pneumonia, should be assigned only when the provider has documented ventilator associated pneumonia (VAP). An additional code to identify the organism (e.g., Pseudomonas aeruginosa, code B96.5) should also be assigned. Do not assign an additional code from categories J12–J18 to identify the type of pneumonia.

15. _____ If the documentation is not clear as to whether acute respiratory failure and another condition are equally responsible for occasioning the admission, query the provider for clarification.

Coding Assignments

Instructions: Using an ICD-10-CM code book, assign the proper diagnosis code to the following diagnostic statements.

1. acute tonsillitis _____
2. edema of pharynx _____
3. chronic ethmoidal sinusitis _____
4. acute tracheitis without obstruction _____
5. farmer's lung _____
6. acute and chronic respiratory failure _____
7. chronic pulmonary insufficiency following surgery _____
8. chronic laryngitis _____
9. allergic rhinitis due to dog hair _____
10. chronic tonsillitis and adenoiditis _____
11. COPD _____
12. parapharyngeal abscess _____
13. acute tracheitis with acute laryngitis _____
14. hypertrophy of nasal turbinates _____
15. acute epiglottitis with obstruction _____
16. black lung disease _____
17. hay fever with asthma _____
18. necrotic pneumonia _____
19. spontaneous tension pneumothorax _____
20. interstitial pneumonia _____
21. Löffler's syndrome _____
22. hypostatic bronchopneumonia _____
23. postprocedural respiratory failure _____
24. Maltworker's lung _____
25. smokers' cough _____
26. cyst of pharynx _____
27. pneumonia due to streptococcus, group B _____
28. acute bronchitis due to rhinovirus _____
29. chronic sphenoidal sinusitis _____
30. panlobular emphysema _____
31. acute recurrent streptococcal tonsillitis _____
32. acute upper respiratory disease _____

33. Chlamydial pneumonia   _____

34. paralysis of vocal cords and larynx, unilateral   _____

35. moderate persistent asthma with status asthmaticus   _____

Case Studies

Instructions: Review each case study and select the correct ICD-10-CM diagnostic code.

Case 1

CHIEF COMPLAINT: This 71-old-year male, whom I have treated for a number of years, returns today with a persistent cough.

HISTORY OF THE PRESENT ILLNESS: The patient has a 4-month history of a cough. He also experienced this last year.

PAST MEDICAL HISTORY: Acute bronchitis and pneumonia

SOCIAL HISTORY: Patient is a 2-pack-a-day smoker. Denies alcohol use. Is tobacco dependent.

ALLERGIES: NKA

EXAM: BP 125/80, Pulse 72, Respirations 22

HEENT: No findings

LUNGS: Bilateral wheezing and scattered rales. Sputum is discolored.

Abdomen: No findings

Chest x-ray ordered. Sputum C&S.

I feel that the patient has progressed to a chronic state of bronchitis due to his cigarette smoking. Patient to follow up in 2 weeks. Medications ordered as per med sheet.

ICD-10-CM Code Assignment: _____

Case 2

CHIEF COMPLAINT: A 36-year-old male patient presents with headache and pressure in his head.

VITAL SIGNS: Temperature 100.3, BP 130/70

HEENT: Pain over the eyes in the frontal area of the forehead. Palpation increases pain. Throat appears red. There is a discolored discharge from his nose.

LUNGS: Clear

ABDOMEN: Normal findings

Patient has responded to Z-pac in the past for acute recurrent frontal sinusitis. Therefore, this was ordered.

ICD-10-CM Code Assignment: _____

Case 3

Katy presented to the ED at 5:00 a.m. very flushed with difficulty breathing, chest tightness, and tachycardia. She was examined by the ED physician, who ordered a pulmonary function test, arterial blood gases, chest x-ray, and ECG. Katy was diagnosed with an acute exacerbation of asthma. She was given two nebulizer treatments, which helped. After 12 hours of observation, she was sent home.

ICD-10-CM Code Assignment: _____

Case 4

This 72-year-old male presents today with productive cough, fever, chills, dyspnea, and chest pain. He was given a complete examination, which included a chest x-ray, EKG, and blood and sputum cultures.

The cultures came back with a positive for pneumonia infection due to *Streptococcus*, group A. We have begun antibiotic therapy and will have him set up with 1 liter of O_2 at night if he needs it.

ICD-10-CM Code Assignment: _____

Case 5

Mary, age 14, presented to our office today with complaints of tearing, sneezing, headache, and problems "catching her breath." When asked whether she noted any changes in her routine, body lotions, or laundry soap, she said no. She did say that she is spending more time outside. Her mother said she noticed this same thing happening last spring as well. We did a blood chemistry as well as some allergy sensitivity testing. Mary was diagnosed with allergic rhinitis. She was started on antihistamine therapy.

ICD-10-CM Code Assignment: _____

Case 6

Office Visit Note

This 3-year-old female patient presents to the office today running a low-grade fever and with congestion in the nasopharyngeal area. Examination of the ears is negative. Nasal area and pharynx are inflamed.

Assessment: Nasopharyngitis

Plan: Patient should be given Tylenol every 4 hours and should follow up with me if symptoms are not gone in 5 to 7 days.

ICD-10-CM Code Assignment: _____

Case 7

Skilled Nursing Facility Note

This 74-year-old female presents with a temperature of 100.1, and cough. She states that she is experiencing body aches and a headache. Examination of her lungs suggests pneumonia. A bedside x-ray was completed that confirmed double pneumonia.

ICD-10-CM Code Assignment: _____

Case 8

Emergency Department Note

This 14-year-old female presents to the ER due to an acute exacerbation of moderate persistent asthma. She was given a respiratory treatment and the asthma subsided. She is to follow up with her primary care provider if symptoms increase.

ICD-10-CM Code Assignment: _____

Case 9

Skilled Nursing Facility Note

I was called to the unit by the nursing staff because this resident shows signs of dyspnea and hypotension. Chest rales and cyanosis are observed. The nurses report that the patient did aspirate some food last week. He is currently being treated for gastroesophageal reflux which contributed to the aspiration of the food. Pneumonia is present due to food aspiration. Antibiotics were prescribed and an order for respiratory therapy was written. Oxygen was started. If the patient does not improve the nurses are to contact me.

ICD-10-CM Code Assignment: _____

Case 10

Discharge Note

This 5-year-old child has been hospitalized for the last 3 days. She presented to my office on the day of admission with a fever of 102, chest pain, and a severe cough. I suspected pneumonia and admitted her. Testing confirmed streptococcal group B pneumonia. IV antibiotics were given and the fever resided. She is to follow up in my office in 5 days or if symptoms increase.

ICD-10-CM Code Assignment: _____

CHAPTER 16

Diseases of the Digestive System

Chapter Outline

Chapter Objectives

At the conclusion of this chapter, you should be able to:

1. Identify anatomical structures and functions of the digestive system.
2. Explain conditions that are related to the digestive system.
3. Accurately code diagnoses of the digestive system.
4. Select and code diagnoses from case studies.

Key Terms

Accessory organs	Diverticula	Gastrointestinal (GI) tract	Pancreas
Alimentary canal	Diverticulitis	Gastrojejunal ulcer	Peptic ulcer
Appendicitis	Diverticulosis	Geographic tongue	Periapical abscess
Appendix	Duodenal ulcer	Hepatic	Peritonitis
Bile	Duodenum	Hernia	Pulp
Cecum	Enteritis	Hiatal hernia	Pulpitis
Cholecystitis	Esophagitis	Ileum	Regional enteritis
Cholelithiasis	Esophagus	Indirect inguinal hernia	Stomach
Colitis	Gallbladder	Inguinal hernia	Ulcerative colitis
Crohn's disease	Gastric ulcer	Jejunum	
Direct inguinal hernia	Gastroesophageal reflux disease (GERD)	Liver	

REMINDER: As you work through this chapter, you will need to have a copy of the ICD-10-CM coding book to reference. Please note that for Chapter 11 of ICD-10-CM, entitled Diseases of the Digestive System, there are no ICD-10-CM Official Guidelines for Coding and Reporting.

Introduction

Chapter 11 of ICD-10-CM, "Diseases of the Digestive System," classifies conditions of the digestive system, which is also known as the **gastrointestinal (GI) tract**. The category codes found in this chapter include:

- K00–K14, Diseases of oral cavity and salivary glands
- K20–K31, Diseases of esophagus, stomach, and duodenum
- K35–K38, Diseases of appendix
- K40–K46, Hernia
- K50–K52, Noninfective enteritis and colitis
- K55–K64, Other diseases of intestines
- K65–K68, Diseases of peritoneum and retroperitoneum
- K70–K77, Diseases of liver
- K80–K87, Disorders of gallbladder, biliary tract, and pancreas
- K90–K95, Other diseases of the digestive system

Introduction to the Body System

The digestive system is also referred to as the **alimentary canal** (*aliment-* means "nourishment" and *-ary* means "pertaining to"; thus *alimentary* means "pertaining to nourishment"). The oral cavity (mouth), pharynx (throat), esophagus, stomach, small intestine, large intestine, rectum, and anus are the major organs and structures of the digestive system. Figure 16-1 illustrates the major organs and anatomical structures of this system.

The digestive process begins when food is taken into the mouth for nourishment and is broken down for digestion and absorption of nutrients. The process ends with the elimination of waste. The breakdown of food begins with chewing and continues as chemicals in the body further break food down and assist in the absorption and elimination process.

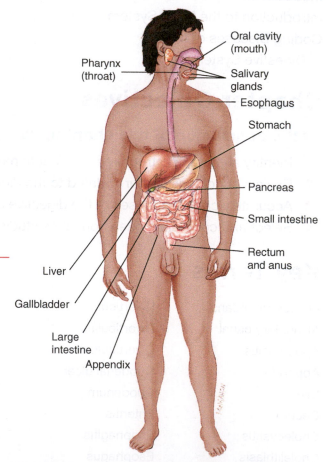

FIGURE 16-1 **Major and accessory structures of the digestive system** (From Ehrlich A, Schroeder CL. *Medical Terminology for Health Professionals*, 4th ed. Clifton Park, NY: Delmar, Cengage Learning, 2001, p. 166.).

Coding Diseases of the Digestive System

This chapter of ICD-10-CM is organized according to the anatomical order of the digestive tract, starting with the mouth through the intestines to the rectum and anus. This helps the coder determine the correct areas of the chapter for code selection. Disorders of the liver, gallbladder, and pancreas also code to this section because they are considered **accessory organs**, or secondary organs, of the digestive system.

Diseases of the Oral Cavity and Salivary Glands (Category Codes K00–K14)

These categories of codes classify disorders of the oral cavity, such as tooth development anomalies, disturbances of tooth formation, dental caries, and other periodontal diseases.

When coding disorders of the oral cavity, the coder should refer to a diagram of the mouth and teeth. Figures 16-2 and 16-3 illustrate the structures of the tooth and oral cavity.

Diseases of the enamel, hard tissue of the teeth, and center of the teeth, known as **pulp**, are classified to this section of the book. **Pulpitis**, reported with code K04.01 for reversible pulpitis or code K04.02 for irreversible pulpitis, is an abscess of the pulp, usually of bacterial origin. Another condition that is encountered in this category of codes is **periapical abscess**, which is an infection of the pulp and surrounding tissue.

Other conditions coded to this section of the chapter are gingivitis, diseases of the jaw and salivary glands, and diseases and conditions of the tongue, such as geographic tongue. **Geographic tongue**, K14.1, is a condition in which irregularly shaped patches are present on the tongue and resemble landforms on a map. The cause is unknown, but the condition usually goes away on its own or, in some cases, with a topical steroid.

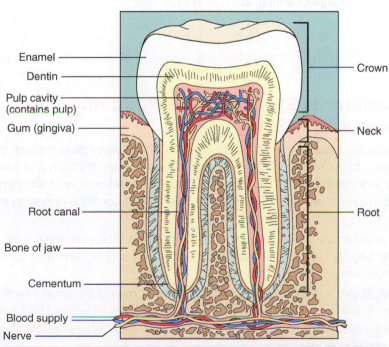

FIGURE 16-2 Structures and tissues of the tooth (From Ehrlich A, Schroeder CL. *Medical Terminology for Health Professionals*, 4th ed. Clifton Park, NY: Delmar, Cengage Learning, 2001, p. 168.).

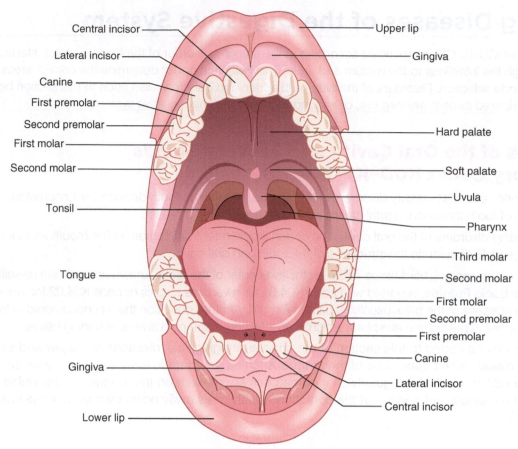

FIGURE 16-3 Structures of the oral cavity (From Ehrlich A, Schroeder CL. *Medical Terminology for Health Professionals*, 4th ed. Clifton Park, NY: Delmar, Cengage Learning, 2001, p. 167.).

Disease of Esophagus, Stomach, and Duodenum (Category Codes K20–K31)

The **esophagus** connects the throat to the stomach. When food and water pass through the oral cavity, they travel down the esophagus to the stomach. When a person has an upset stomach and vomits, the reverse occurs. **Esophagitis** is an inflammation of the esophagus due to the reflux of acid and pepsin from the stomach into the esophagus. **Gastroesophageal reflux disease (GERD)** is a common condition that primary care providers treat.

The esophagus connects to the **stomach**, a pouch-like structure. The stomach connects to the **duodenum**, where the small intestine begins. Figure 16-4 illustrates the stomach and its structures as well as its relation to the esophagus and the duodenum.

The duodenum extends to the **jejunum**, which is the middle portion of the small intestine. The jejunum connects the duodenum to the **ileum**, which is the last part of the small intestine. The ileum connects to the **cecum**, which is the beginning of the large intestine. Coders must know where certain structures stop and start so that they assign the correct codes.

Coding of Gastrointestinal Ulcers

Ulcerations of the gastrointestinal (GI) tract occur when there is erosion of the mucous membrane.

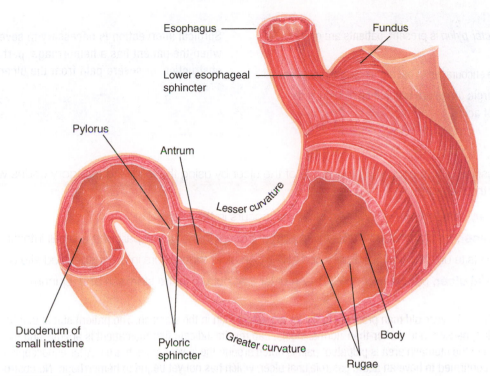

FIGURE 16-4 Structures of the stomach (From Ehrlich A, Schroeder CL. *Medical Terminology for Health Professionals*, 4th ed. Clifton Park, NY: Delmar, Cengage Learning, 2001, p. 169.).

Disease Highlight—Gastrointestinal Ulcers

Gastrointestinal ulcers occur throughout the gastrointestinal tract and include gastric, duodenal, peptic, and gastrojejunal ulcers. All ulcers involve the destruction of tissue occurring in areas that are exposed to acid and/or pepsin. The mucous membrane penetrates through the muscularis mucosa and becomes inflamed. The etiology of ulcers is unclear, but contributing factors include the reflux of bile or hyperacidity in the stomach, the extended use of anti-inflammatory drugs such as aspirin, the heavy intake of steroids and alcohol, smoking, and the presence of *Helicobacter pylori* bacteria.

Signs and Symptoms:

Patients with gastrointestinal ulcers complain of burning pain in the stomach or epigastric region, which may or may not subside with food intake or use of antacids. Patients also experience:

- Weight loss
- Nausea
- Vomiting
- Anemia

Clinical Testing:

Ulcers are diagnosed by means of:

- Upper GI and barium studies (endoscopy), which shows the ulceration
- Lab tests that review the patient's hemoglobin, hematocrit, and serum gastric and amylase levels. Hemoglobin and hematocrit are decreased in patients with bleeding from the ulcer. Serum gastrin and serum amylase levels are increased.
- Stool sample, which can be positive for occult blood

Treatment:

Treatment for patients with ulcers is directed at decreasing the acidity of the ulcer site, thereby promoting the healing of the mucosa.

- Elimination of contributing factors is essential.
- Antacids and dietary restrictions neutralize the gastric acids.

- If *Helicobacter pylori* is present, patients are given antibiotics.
- Patients are encouraged to eat nutritious and regular meals.
- Anticholinergic drugs are prescribed to reduce the secretion of acid.
- Surgical intervention is necessary in severe cases when the patient has a hemorrhage, perforation, obstruction, or severe pain from the ulcer site.

ICD-10-CM classifies ulcers according to the site of the ulcer by using the following category codes with the appropriate fourth character:

- **Gastric ulcer**, category code K25—An ulcer that occurs in the stomach
- **Duodenal ulcer**, category code K26—An ulcer that occurs in the upper part of the small intestine
- **Peptic ulcer** (site unspecified), category code K27—An ulcer that occurs in an unspecified site of the GI tract
- **Gastrojejunal ulcer**, category code K28—An ulcer that occurs in the stomach and jejunum

EXAMPLE: An 82-year-old man presents today for persistent pain in the stomach. The patient states that he suffers from indigestion, nausea, and darker-than-normal stools. Lab results indicate that the patient is anemic and that the guaiac is positive. When the stomach area is palpated, pain is noted around the lower stomach area. After endoscopic examination, the patient is confirmed to have an acute gastrojejunal ulcer, which has not yet begun to hemorrhage. No obstructions are noted, and, because we have not encountered hemorrhaging, medication is prescribed at this time for treatment.

Because the confirmed diagnosis of acute gastrojejunal ulcer is given, the code assigned is K28.3, Acute gastrojejunal ulcer without mention of hemorrhage or perforation. The K25–K28 category codes are differentiated by whether the ulcer is acute, chronic, or unspecified and whether hemorrhage and/or perforation are present.

Diseases of Appendix (Category Codes K35–K38)

The **appendix** is a wormlike structure that is found, in most people, at the blind end of the cecum. When the appendix becomes inflamed or infected, a condition known as **appendicitis**, the patient may experience pain and the white blood cell count becomes elevated. The appendix does not serve any known purpose in the digestive system, but it is the most common nonobstetrical problem encountered during pregnancy. Figure 16-5 illustrates the location of the appendix.

In the case of appendicitis, the coder must determine whether any other complications are associated with the appendicitis, such as generalized peritonitis or peritoneal abscess. The coder should also note whether the term is modified by the terms *acute, chronic,* or *recurrent*. These complications and terms all affect code assignment.

EXAMPLE: The diagnostic statement of appendicitis codes to K37, Unspecified appendicitis. Chronic appendicitis and recurrent appendicitis code to K36. Acute appendicitis codes to category K35 with differentiation to indicate the following:

- K35.20, Acute appendicitis with generalized peritonitis without abscess, and K35.21, acute appendicitis with generalized peritonitis, with abscess.
- K35.30, Acute appendicitis with localized peritonitis without perforation or gangrene, K35.31, acute appendicitis with localized peritonitis and gangrene, without perforation, K35.32, acute appendicitis with perforation and localized peritonitis without abscess and K35.33, acute appendicitis with perforation and localized peritonitis with abscess.
- K35.80, Acute appendicitis, unspecified
- K35.890, Other acute appendicitis without perforation or gangrene and K35.891, Other acute appendicitis without perforation with gangrene

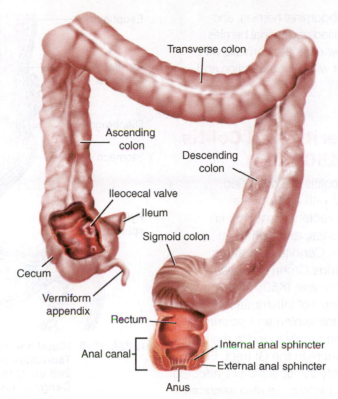

FIGURE 16-5 Large intestine and location of appendix.

Hernia (Category Codes K40–K46)

At the start of this block of codes, a notation appears that states "Note: Hernia with both gangrene and obstruction is classified to hernia with gangrene." A **hernia** is simply a protrusion or bulge through the tissue that normally contains the structure. There are several different types of hernias.

An **inguinal hernia** occurs when a part of the intestine passes through a weak point or tear in the wall that holds the abdominal organs. Sometimes the doctor's note refers to a "**direct inguinal hernia**," which is a protrusion in the groin area. An **indirect inguinal hernia** is a protrusion that has moved to the scrotum. These types of hernias code to the K40 category and require additional characters to indicate whether the hernia is unilateral or bilateral, whether it is recurrent, and whether gangrene or an obstruction is present.

> **EXAMPLE:** A 23-year-old man presents with a bulging in the scrotal area on the right side. The patient experiences sharp pain on the right when urinating. Over the last week, patient has noticed pain in the area at the end of his workday. The patient has not experienced this before and is quite concerned. Upon examination, it was determined that the patient is suffering from an indirect inguinal hernia. We will refer him to a surgeon for further evaluation.

Code assignment in our example is K40.90. The K40.90, unilateral inguinal hernia, without obstruction or gangrene, not specified as recurrent, is chosen based on the information given in the note. There is no mention of obstruction or gangrene, which may change with the surgeon's evaluation. With the information given, the hernia appears to be on only the right side and is not recurrent.

Other types of hernias are a femoral hernia (category K41), umbilical hernia (category K42), ventral hernia (category K43), diaphragmatic hernia (category K44), and hiatal hernia. Hiatal hernias are common and are coded to category K44. A **hiatal hernia** is the sliding of part of the stomach into the chest cavity (see Figure 16-6).

Category K45 reports other abdominal hernias, and category K46 reports unspecified abdominal hernias. The coder needs to indicate whether the hernia is with obstruction, with gangrene, or without obstruction and gangrene.

Noninfective Enteritis and Colitis (Category Code K50–K52)

Noninfectious enteritis and colitis are classified to category codes K50–K52 with appropriate fourth, fifth, and/or sixth characters. **Enteritis** is an inflammation of the intestines, and **colitis** is an inflammation of the colon. Conditions that are classified to this section include Crohn's disease and ulcerative colitis. **Crohn's disease** (K50), also known as **regional enteritis**, is a form of inflammatory bowel disease that can cause the thickening and scarring of the abdominal wall; most commonly found in the large intestine, it can attack anywhere in the GI tract. Fourth characters are used to identify the specific site affected. Additional fifth and sixth characters are also assigned.

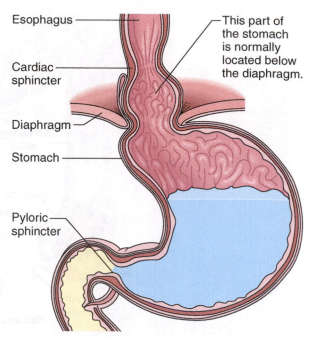

FIGURE 16-6 Hiatal hernia (From Neighbors M, Tannehill-Jones R. *Human Diseases*, 2nd ed. Clifton Park, NY: Delmar, Cengage Learning, 2001, p. 191.).

EXAMPLE: Mark presented with diarrhea, which has occurred for the last week, along with abdominal pain, fever, and noticeable weight loss. The physician ordered a barium enema and small bowel x-ray. The results of these tests confirmed a diagnosis of Crohn's disease of the small intestine.

Crohn's disease of the small intestine is classified to subcategory K50.0, Crohn's disease of the large intestine is classified to subcategory K50.1, Crohn's disease of both the small and large intestine is classified to subcategory K50.8, and Crohn's disease, unspecified, is classified to subcategory K50.9. Additional characters are used with all of these subcategories to indicate whether rectal bleeding, intestinal obstruction, fistula, abscess, or some other complication is present. **Ulcerative colitis** affects the colon by causing frequent diarrhea. The colon becomes inflamed, and ulcers develop in the lining of the intestine. Ulcerative colitis is classified to category code K51 with additional characters to identify the site affected.

To accurately code Crohn's disease and ulcerative colitis, the coder needs to identify the site by reviewing the patient's medical record. If the site cannot be determined from review of the medical documentation, query the provider.

Other Diseases of the Intestines (Category Codes K55–K64)

Common conditions that are classified to this section of the code book are diverticulosis and diverticulitis. **Diverticula** are abnormal pouches or sacs in the lining of the intestine that cause a condition known as **diverticulosis**. If these sacs become inflamed, the patient is diagnosed with **diverticulitis**. A note at the beginning of the K57.0, K57.2, K57.4, and K57.8 subcategories indicates that diverticulitis with peritonitis is included in these subcategories. **Peritonitis** is an inflammation of the lining of the abdominal cavity.

When coding diverticulosis or diverticulitis, coders must determine the site of the condition: either the small intestine or large intestine. Coders must also determine whether the condition occurs with or without bleeding and whether perforation and an abscess are present.

Category K58 is used to report irritable bowel syndrome, irritable colon, and spastic colon. Category K59 is used to report other functional intestinal disorders such as constipation, functional diarrhea, neurogenic bowel, anal spasm, and other functional intestinal disorders.

Fissure and fistula of the anal and rectal regions are reported with category K60. This category is differentiated at the fourth-character levels to indicate anal versus rectal and to identify acute and chronic states of the disease.

Category K61 reports an abscess of anal and rectal regions, and K62 reports other diseases of the anus and rectum. K63 reports other diseases of the intestine. Hemorrhoids and perianal venous thrombosis are reported with category K64. The degree of the hemorrhoids is differentiated at the fourth digit with codes K64.0 to K64.3.

Diseases of Peritoneum and Retroperitoneum (Category Codes K65–K68)

This block of codes is used to report the following:

- K65, Peritonitis
- K66, Other disorders of the peritoneum
- K67, Disorders of peritoneum in infectious diseases classified elsewhere
- K68, Disorders of retroperitoneum

NOTE:

Coders need to become familiar with the numerous instructional notations and Excludes1 notes in this section, as well as the assignment of appropriate fourth and/or fifth characters.

Disease of Liver (Category Codes K70–K77)

This block of codes includes codes for diseases of the liver. The liver is considered one of the accessory organs of the digestive system (see Figure 16-7). The **liver** filters red blood cells, produces glycogen, and secretes **bile**, which breaks down fat. A coder may encounter the term **hepatic**, which means pertaining to the liver.

The category codes, with the appropriate fourth and/or fifth characters, for this block are:

- K70, Alcoholic liver disease. An additional code is used to identify alcohol abuse and dependence.
- K71, Toxic liver disease. "Code first" and "Use additional code" notations appear after the K71 category heading.
- K72, Hepatic failure, not elsewhere classified. The extensive Includes, Excludes1 and Excludes2 notations that follow the category heading need to be reviewed prior to code assignment.
- K73, Chronic hepatitis, not elsewhere classified. Various forms of chronic hepatitis are excluded from this category, as identified by the Excludes1 note.
- K74, Fibrosis and cirrhosis of liver. If viral hepatitis is present with diseases coded by this category, the coder should be guided by the "Code also" notation.
- K75, Other inflammatory liver diseases. This category includes abscess of liver, phlebitis of the portal vein, various types of hepatitis, and other inflammatory liver diseases.
- K76, Other diseases of liver. Coders should be guided by the extensive Excludes2 notation that appears for this category.
- K77, Liver disorders in diseases classified elsewhere. Coders need to make note of the "Code first" notation and the extensive Excludes1 notations.

Disorders of Gall Bladder, Biliary Tract, and Pancreas (Category Codes K80–K87)

The **gallbladder** is found under the liver and is connected to the liver via the cystic duct. The purpose of the gallbladder is to store bile secreted by the liver until the bile is needed in digestion. The **pancreas** is located behind the stomach and is connected to the gallbladder and the liver by the common bile duct. This organ has a function in both the digestive system and the endocrine system. The pancreas secretes juices necessary for digestion but also regulates blood sugar levels through the release of the hormone insulin.

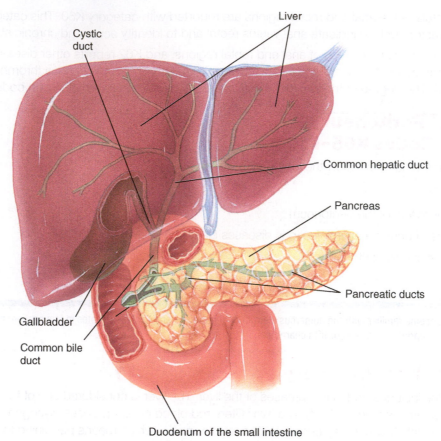

FIGURE 16-7 Accessory digestive organs (From Ehrlich A, Schroeder CL. *Medical Terminology for Health Professionals*, 4th ed. Clifton Park, NY: Delmar, Cengage Learning, 2001, p. 170.).

Cholecystitis and Cholelithiasis

Cholecystitis, a sudden and severe onset of inflammation of the gallbladder, and **cholelithiasis**, the formation or presence of gallstones, are classified to this section of the code book. Cholecystitis and cholelithiasis can occur with or without the other condition. The coder must therefore review the medical documentation carefully to identify the clinical picture of the patient.

Cholelithiasis is classified to category K80, with additional characters used to identify the location of the gallstones and whether cholecystitis is present or not. Additional characters are also used to identify an obstruction.

EXAMPLE:

Patient 1

Diagnosis: Calculus of gallbladder with chronic cholecystitis with obstruction

Code reported: K80.11

Patient 2

Diagnosis: Calculus of gallbladder with chronic cholecystitis without obstruction

Code reported: K80.10

Note that the fifth character identifies the presence or absence of an obstruction. The fifth digit of 1 identifies with obstruction and the fifth digit of 0 identifies without obstruction.

Cholecystitis is classified to category K81. This category contains the following codes:

- K81.0, Acute cholecystitis
- K81.1, Chronic cholecystitis
- K81.2, Acute cholecystitis with chronic cholecystitis
- K81.9, Cholecystitis, unspecified

Category K82 reports other diseases of gallbladder, and category K83 reports other diseases of the biliary tract. Acute pancreatitis is reported with category code K85, other diseases of the pancreas are reported with K86, and K87 reports disorders of the gallbladder, biliary tract, and pancreas in diseases classified elsewhere. Coders need to reference the coding manual for the assignment of fourth and/or fifth characters for categories K80–K87 and carefully compare the diagnosis recorded by the provider with the specific descriptions that are found in these codes.

Other Diseases of the Digestive System (Category Codes K90–K95)

The last block of codes reports other diseases of the digestive system. This includes the following category codes, with the appropriate fourth, fifth, and/or sixth characters:

- K90, Intestinal malabsorption
- K91, Intraoperative and postprocedural complications and disorders of digestive system, not elsewhere classified
- K92, Other diseases of digestive system
- K94, Complications of artificial openings of the digestive system. The K94 category codes differentiate colostomy, enterostomy, gastrostomy, and esophagostomy complications.
- K95, Complications of bariatric procedures

Summary

- The digestive process begins when food is taken into the mouth for nourishment and finishes its work with the elimination of waste.
- The *alimentary canal* and the *gastrointestinal tract* are terms used to describe the digestive system.
- Diseases of the oral cavity, including the teeth, are included in Chapter 11 of ICD-10-CM.
- Accessory organs, such as the appendix, liver, gallbladder, and pancreas, are also classified to Chapter 11 off ICD-10-CM.
- Appendicitis can be accompanied by peritonitis or peritoneal abscess.
- Hernias are classified in ICD-10-CM according to the site of the hernia.
- Noninfectious enteritis and colitis are classified to Chapter 11 of ICD-10-CM.
- Diverticula are abnormal sacs in the lining of the intestine.
- Diverticulitis occurs when there is an inflammation of the diverticula.

Internet Links

To learn more about diseases and conditions of the digestive system, visit **www.gastro.org** and **www.saem.org**.

The Cleveland Clinic has a website that can be found at **http://my.clevelandclinic.org**. Search the names of diseases of the gastrointestinal system. This site has abundant information on gastrointestinal disorders.

Additional information can also be found at **www.iffgd.org**. This site is maintained by the International Foundation for Functional Gastrointestinal Disorders.

Chapter Review

True/False

Indicate whether the statement is true (T) or false (F).

1. _____ Food is broken down for nourishment by the digestive tract.

2. _____ Cholelithiasis means kidney stones.

3. _____ The pancreas is not an accessory organ.

4. _____ Irregularly shaped patches that appear on the tongue are known as mapped tongue.

5. _____ The stomach is a pouch-like structure that connects to the esophagus on one end and to the ileum on the other.

Fill-in-the-Blank

Enter the appropriate term(s) to complete each statement.

6. An infection of the pulp and the surrounding tissue in the mouth is called _____.

7. An inflammation of the esophagus due to acid reflux is known as _____.

8. The _____ secretes bile, which breaks down fat.

9. The _____ has functions in both the digestive and endocrine systems.

10. Abnormal pouches or sacs in the lining of the intestines cause a condition known as _____.

Coding Assignments

Instructions: Using an ICD-10-CM code book, assign the proper diagnosis code to the following diagnostic statements.

1. chronic pulpitis, reversible

2. reflux esophagitis

3. odontogenesis imperfecta

4. recurrent bilateral femoral hernia

5. hematemesis

6. denture hyperplasia

7. phlebitis of portal vein

8. stenosis of cystic duct

9. sliding hiatal hernia

10. GERD

11. gastric diverticulum

12. umbilical hernia

13. dental pulp degeneration

14. granulomatous colitis

15. dentinal dysplasia

16. pyloric stenosis

17. fecalith of appendix

18. Barrett's esophagus

19. hypertrophic gastritis with hemorrhage

20. biliary cirrhosis

21. IBS with diarrhea

22. calculus of gallbladder and bile duct with acute cholecystitis with obstruction   _____

23. hepatic infarction   _____

24. fistula of bile duct   _____

25. pancreatic steatorrhea   _____

26. stenosis of esophagus   _____

27. gastrocolic fistula   _____

28. Crohn's diseases of small intestine with intestinal obstruction   _____

29. left-sided colitis with fistula   _____

30. prolapse of anal canal   _____

31. chronic cholecystitis   _____

32. adhesions of cystic duct   _____

33. focal nodular hyperplasia of liver   _____

34. hepatic fibrosis with hepatic sclerosis   _____

35. chronic hepatic failure without coma   _____

Case Studies

Instructions: Review each case study and select the correct ICD-10-CM diagnostic code.

Case 1

CHIEF COMPLAINT: Abdominal pain

HISTORY: This is a 70-year-old man who had a diagnostic sigmoidoscopy done 3 days ago for rectal bleeding. He is having some abdominal pain. He has noted some nausea and pain when he eats solid food. He says he feels better if he has only liquids, and once he has a bowel movement he feels better. When asked if he knew the results of his sigmoidoscopy, he replied that the doctor had told him he had some diverticula. He denies any diarrhea but said there is some constipation. He also denies chest pain or shortness of breath. He has had some coughing, but no other symptoms are noted. All other reviews of systems are noted as normal.

PAST MEDICAL HISTORY: Positive for diverticulosis. No known allergies, no diabetes. Patient had thyroidectomy 25 years ago.

EXAM:

HEENT: Normal

MOUTH: Partially edentulous; gums look healthy.

HEART: Regular sinus rate and rhythm; heart sounds are good.

LUNGS: Clear to auscultation and percussion.

ABDOMEN: Soft; slight tenderness on palpation in lower left quadrant; no organomegaly; no

(continues)

(continued)

GENITALIA: Normal male

RECTAL: Good sphincter tone; guaiac testing shows occult blood; blood is noted upon visual exam.

EXTREMITIES: No edema, ulceration, or discoloration; pedal pulses are normal.

NEUROLOGICAL: Normal

IMPRESSION: Diverticulitis with hemorrhage

PLAN: We will begin antibiotic therapy with Flagyl.

ICD-10-CM Code Assignment: _____

Case 2

This is a 25-year-old female with a history of ulcerative colitis who presents today with diarrhea and bleeding. She was hospitalized last June with a similar problem and had been on IV steroids and then oral steroids prior to discharge. She has been off the steroids now for approximately 2 months and had been doing fairly well. She now is having abdominal cramping and loose stools, which have become bloody. She noted that over the last 48 hours, her bowel movements have increased dramatically, which is why she has presented to the ER. She has been drinking and eating very bland foods, as well as avoiding dairy products. Nothing seems to help.

PHYSICAL EXAM: This is a 25-year-old female who appears slightly dehydrated and in mild distress.

VITAL SIGNS: Temp: 98.1, Respiratory rate: 20, Pulse: 110 and regular, BP: 100/70

HEENT: Normal; oral cavity is moist without lesions.

NECK: Supple, no thyromegaly or lymphadenopathy

CHEST: Clear to auscultation and percussion

HEART: No murmurs, rubs, or gallops

ABDOMEN: Nondistended. Normal bowel sounds. Some epigastric tenderness with deep palpation, without radiation. Has some right lower quadrant discomfort without rebound or guarding associated.

RECTAL: Some internal hemorrhoids noted. Stool is light brown and not bloody at this time.

IMPRESSION and PLAN: Exacerbation of ulcerative colitis with rectal bleeding. Admit patient at this time. Would like to start IV rehydration and also intravenous steroids. Will observe stool count, consistency, and whether there is blood in the stool. Amylase, creatinine, BUN, WBC, Hgb, and MCV ordered.

ICD-10-CM Code Assignment: _____

Case 3

Skilled Nursing Facility Monthly Progress Note

This resident was admitted in May of this year with the primary diagnoses of diabetes mellitus and chronic gastritis. The patient has been complaining of heartburn and is occasionally irritated by bananas and some cereals. She denies any nausea or vomiting, but she thinks that every time she eats there is fullness in the stomach.

PHYSICAL EXAMINATION:

She is alert, conscious, not in any acute pain or distress. Fasting blood sugar is 86; BP, 120/74; P, 80 per minute and regular; R, 20; and temp, 95.7. Her weight is 110.

Abdomen is soft. Bowel sounds are positive; it is not distended, and there is tenderness.

HEART: Regular rhythm with no change in the systolic murmur.

LUNGS: Clear to auscultation

MEDICATIONS INCLUDE: See medication list for her current medications. Start Maalox 15cc three times a day for chronic gastritis. I will reevaluate her if she needs additional medication for her gastritis.

ICD-10-CM Code Assignment: _____

Case 4

ED Summary Note

Sylvia presented to the ED with abdominal distention and pain, along with nausea, and reported an earlier bout of vomiting. Upon examination, no bowel sounds were noted, but an increase in white cell count was noted. Barium studies showed a twisting of the intestine. A surgical consult was requested for Sylvia.

ICD-10-CM Code Assignment: _____

Case 5

ED Summary Note

Kyle presented to the ED with abdominal distention and tenderness, a fever of 102, and a complaint of nausea. Kyle has a history of perforated peptic ulcer. Physical exam was

(continues)

(*continued*)

performed, along with arterial blood gases (which showed lowered potassium and carbon dioxide), urinalysis, and lab tests, all of which confirm the diagnosis of generalized acute peritonitis.

ICD-10-CM Code Assignment: _____

Case 6

Ambulatory Surgery Discharge Note

This 49-year-old female patient is stabilized after having surgery for choledocholithiasis with acute cholangitis and obstruction. She has been able to drink fluids and has voided. She is to follow up in my office in 7 days.

ICD-10-CM Code Assignment: _____

Case 7

Consultation Note

This patient was admitted yesterday and was referred to me by Dr. Jones. Dr. Jones ordered an abdominal scan that confirmed an acute gastric ulcer with hemorrhage. I explained to the patient that I will be ordering additional diagnostic tests and she will be given antacids. I will see her later when the results of the lab work are available.

ICD-10-CM Code Assignment: _____

Case 8

Office Note

This 39-year-old patient was referred to me because she has strangulated 4th-degree hemorrhoids. Conservative treatment has not been successful. She wants to discuss surgery. I explained the benefits and the risk and she gave consent for surgery. Surgery will be scheduled within 1 week.

ICD-10-CM Code Assignment: _____

Case 9

Office Note

This 26-year-old male patient is being seen today to follow up on his Crohn's disease. At this time he is being managed with medications. He states that over the last 2 months he has not had any acute exacerbations. At this time we will continue the current course of treatment. I will see him if symptoms develop or in 3 months.

ICD-10-CM Code Assignment: _____

Case 10

Office Note

This 37-year-old male patient presents today complaining of groin pain. He reports that this pain increases when he lifts and the pain subsides when he lies down. CT scan confirms a diagnosis of inguinal hernia.

ICD-10-CM Code Assignment: _____

Diseases of the Skin and Subcutaneous Tissue

Chapter Outline

Chapter Objectives

At the conclusion of this chapter, you should be able to:

1. Identify and name the layers of the skin.
2. Explain the diseases and conditions that impact the skin and subcutaneous tissue.
3. Interpret the ICD-10-CM coding guidelines that apply to diseases of the skin and subcutaneous tissue.
4. Apply the ICD-10-CM coding guidelines to accurately code diseases of the skin and subcutaneous tissue.
5. Select and code diagnoses and procedures from case studies.

Key Terms

Abscess	Decubitus ulcers	Hives	Pressure ulcers
Alopecia	Dermatitis	Integumentary	Sebaceous glands
Bedsores	Dermis	Melanocytes	Subcutaneous
Carbuncles	Epidermis	Melanoma	Ulcers
Cellulitis	Hair	Nails	Urticaria
Cutane	Hirsutism	Pressure sores	

REMINDER: As you work through this chapter, you will need to have a copy of the ICD-10-CM coding book to reference. For this chapter, you will also need to reference the ICD-10-CM Official Guidelines for Coding and Reporting. These guidelines can be found in Appendix A which are now available on the Student Companion site and MINDTAP From Cengage.

Introduction

Diseases of the skin and subcutaneous tissue, category code range L00–L99, are classified in Chapter 12 of ICD-10-CM, "Diseases of the Skin and Subcutaneous Tissue." The following blocks of codes are in this chapter:

- L00–L08, Infections of the skin and subcutaneous tissue
- L10–L14, Bullous disorders
- L20–L30, Dermatitis and eczema
- L40–L45, Papulosquamous disorders
- L49–L54, Urticaria and erythema
- L55–L59, Radiation-related disorders of the skin and subcutaneous tissue
- L60–L75, Disorders of skin appendages
- L76, Intraoperative and postprocedural complications of skin and subcutaneous tissue
- L80–L99, Other disorders of the skin and subcutaneous tissue

Introduction to the Body System

The coding in this chapter classifies disorders and diseases of the integumentary system, or the skin. **Integumentary** means "covering" or "outer layer." The integumentary system acts as a shield for the body and is considered the largest body system. The functions of the integumentary system include the protection of deeper tissue by retaining fluid in the body and the regulation of body temperature by controlling heat loss. This natural shield also works as a factor in the immune system by blocking bacteria and other foreign materials from entering the body. Receptors for touch are located on the skin. Because the skin is porous, it protects the body from ultraviolet radiation from the sun while letting the ultraviolet light in so that the body can produce vitamin D. The skin also temporarily stores the fat, glucose, water, and salts that are absorbed by the blood and used by various organs of the body.

The skin is specialized tissue made up of three layers. The **epidermis** is the outermost layer of the skin. Epithelial tissues make up the epidermis. There are no blood vessels or connective tissue within the epidermis, so this layer of skin depends on the lower layers for nourishment.

The color of the skin is determined by the amount of melanin pigment contained in **melanocytes**, or cells that produce dark pigment. When these cells exhibit abnormal behavior, a person might be diagnosed with melanoma. **Melanoma** is a fast-growing cancer of the skin, usually identified as a mole that has changed in some way.

The **dermis** is the thick layer of tissue located directly below the epidermis. This is the layer of skin that enables a person to recognize touch, pain, pressure, and temperature changes. This layer of skin contains blood and lymph vessels, so it is more sensitive and self-sufficient than the epidermis.

The layer of skin that connects to the muscle surface is called the **subcutaneous** layer. **Cutane** means "skin," so *subcutaneous* means "below the skin." Fat cells are found in this layer of skin. Figure 17-1 illustrates the three layers of skin and some of the structures they contain.

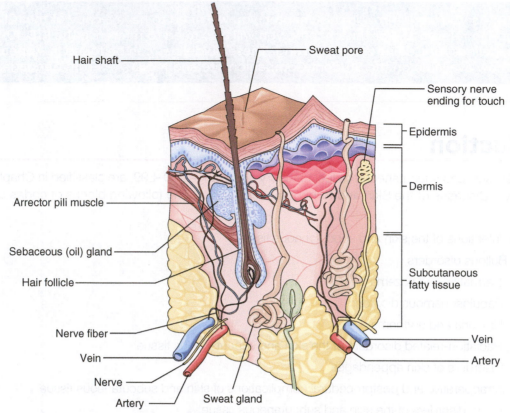

FIGURE 17-1 Cross section of the skin (From Scott AS, Fong E. *Body Structures and Functions*, 9th ed. Clifton Park, NY: Delmar, Cengage Learning, 1998, p. 58.).

Coding of Diseases of the Skin and Subcutaneous Tissue

Coding for this chapter includes diseases and disorders not only of the skin but also of the nails, sweat glands, hair, and hair follicles. Figure 17-2 illustrates various diseases of the skin.

Infections of Skin and Subcutaneous Tissue (Category Codes L00–L08)

The first section of this chapter classifies disorders such as cellulitis, carbuncles, and furuncles, which may be caused by bacterial organisms. The following notation appears right after the heading for this block of codes:

Use additional code (B95–B97) to identify infectious agent.

Therefore, two codes may be needed to code diagnostic statements.

Category code L00 reports staphylococcal scalded skin syndrome, and category code L01 reports impetigo. Category L01 uses fourth and fifth characters to identify the type of impetigo. Cutaneous abscess, furuncle, and carbuncle are reported using category code L02.

NONPALPABLE

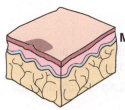

Macule:
Localized changes in skin
color of less than 1 cm
in diameter
Example: Freckle

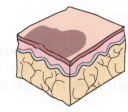

Patch:
Localized changes in skin
color of greater than 1 cm
in diameter
Examples: Vitiligo, stage 1
of pressure ulcer

PALPABLE

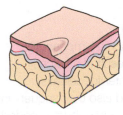

Papule:
Solid, elevated lesion less
than 0.5 cm in diameter
Examples: Warts,
elevated nevus

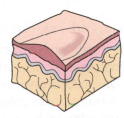

Plaque:
Solid, elevated lesion
greater than 0.5 cm
in diameter
Example: Psoriasis

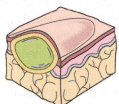

Nodules:
Solid and elevated,
but extending deeper than
papules into the dermis or
subcutaneous tissues,
0.5–2.0 cm
Examples: Lipoma, erythema
nodosum, cyst

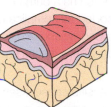

Wheal:
Localized edema in the
epidermis causing irregular
elevation that may be red
or pale
Examples: Insect bite,
hives

FLUID-FILLED CAVITIES WITHIN THE SKIN

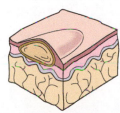

Vesicle:
Accumulation of fluid between
the upper layers of the skin;
elevated mass containing
serous fluid; less than 0.5 cm
Examples: Herpes simplex,
herpes zoster, chickenpox

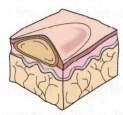

Bulla:
Same as a vesicle only
greater than 0.5 cm
Examples: Contact
dermatitis, large second-
degree burns, bulbous
impetigo, pemphigus

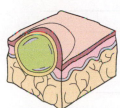

Pustule:
Vesicles or bullae that
become filled with pus,
usually described as less
than 0.5 cm in diameter
Examples: Acne, impetigo,
furuncles, carbuncles,
folliculitis

FIGURE 17-2 Disorders of the skin (From Sormunen C. *Terminology for Allied Health Professions,*
5th ed. Clifton Park, NY: Delmar, Cengage Learning, 2003, p. 103.).

Carbuncles occur when furuncles cluster and form a pus-filled sac. Additional characters are used in the L02 category to identify the anatomic site of the abscess, furuncle, or carbuncle.

> **EXAMPLE:**
>
> S: Patient presents with a "bump on my neck" that is beginning to hurt. Patient cannot recall any injury to the area. Patient has started with a low-grade fever of 99.3 and has noticed an increase in the pain over the last day or two.
>
> O: Upon examination, a large red lump is located at the base of the posterior side of the neck. The lump is fluctuating and causes pain upon touch.
>
> A & P: Carbuncle of the neck. At this time we will start antibiotics and warm compresses. If this does not relieve some of the pain and some improvement is not noticed in the next 5 days, he will return and we will look at other options.

The code for this example is L02.13, Carbuncle of neck.

Categories L03, with the use of fourth, fifth, and/or sixth characters, classify cellulitis and acute lymphangitis. **Cellulitis** is another type of infection that develops within the layers of the skin that can be a result of an ulcer, laceration, or wound. In some cases, two codes are necessary when coding a patient encounter for cellulitis. Reference to provider documentation is necessary for determining the need for two codes and also their sequencing. If cellulitis is noticed when a patient is being treated for an open wound or a burn, the open wound or burn is coded first with an additional code for the cellulitis. If the cellulitis is what brought the patient in after treatment has already been rendered for another condition, such as a burn or open wound, the cellulitis is coded first with the burn or open wound second. The open wound is coded as complicated in either case because complication indicates infection. Also, if cellulitis is associated with an open wound that has been repaired, the documentation should reflect whether the cellulitis is a postoperative infection. These issues are discussed further in Chapter 24 of this textbook when injuries are discussed.

This section of the chapter also classifies abscesses. An **abscess** is a localized collection of pus and indicates tissue destruction. As with cellulitis, if an organism is identified as the cause of the abscess, this finding should be coded in addition to the code for the abscess. For example, code L02.411 is the code for cutaneous abscess of right axilla. If the organism staphylococcus was identified, an additional code of B95.8 would be assigned to identify the organism.

Documentation is critical for these categories of the chapter. The coder needs to reference the provider note to accurately code the condition, the sequencing, and the site of the cellulitis or abscess.

Exercise 17.1—Coding Category Codes L00–L08

For each diagnostic statement, select the appropriate ICD-10-CM code(s).

1. carbuncle of face _____
2. pyoderma _____
3. acute lymphangitis of trunk _____
4. cutaneous abscess of right lower limb _____
5. acute lymphangitis of right axilla _____
6. acute lymphadenitis of face _____
7. cellulitis of toes _____
8. furuncle of right hand _____
9. cellulitis of neck _____
10. furuncle of the right axilla _____

Bullous Disorders (Category Codes L10–L14)

This block of codes is divided into the following categories:

- L10, Pemphigus
- L11, Other acantholytic disorders
- L12, Pemphigoid
- L13, Other bullous disorders
- L14, Bullous disorders in diseases classified elsewhere

Each category is further divided into various types of the disorders with the use of fourth and/or fifth characters.

Dermatitis and Eczema (Category Codes L20–L30)

This section of the chapter contains codes for common conditions such as cradle cap, dermatitis, eczema, and erythematosquamous dermatosis. **Dermatitis** is an inflammation of the upper layer of the skin and is classified to this section of the chapter. Various types of dermatitis exist; therefore, if a provider documents a specific type of dermatitis, a coder must select a code to identify the type, such as category code L20, Atopic dermatitis, or category code L21, Seborrheic dermatitis. Categories L20 and L21 also use fourth and fifth characters to further specify the conditions.

Another type of dermatitis coded to this section of the chapter is dermatitis due to medication. A distinction is made here between drugs ingested and drugs or plants that come into contact with the skin topically. Category L27, Dermatitis due to substances taken internally, is used if the coder sees the diagnosis of drug eruption, dermatitis medicamentosa, or medication properly administered with an allergic reaction or adverse side effect. A reaction to medication ingested is when a patient ingests the proper medication prescribed by a medical professional at the proper dosage. A notation appears for code L27.0 and L27.1 that instructs the coder to "Use additional code for adverse effect, if applicable, to identify drug (T36–T50 with fifth or sixth character 5)."

> **EXAMPLE:**
>
> S: A 21-month-old male presents today with low-grade fever, hives, and slight swelling in the joints of the lower extremities. Mother notes that child was started on Amoxicillin, 500 mg, for an ear infection. Child started medication 1 day ago. Review was made with mom on the dosage. Child was given proper dosage but now appears to have had an allergic reaction.
>
> O: Upon examination, child is alert and in no acute distress. He is a bit lethargic but is not crying or fussy. He allows examination of ears: TMs red, some fluid. Rest of HEENT is unremarkable. Skin is warm to touch, and it should be noted that child has low-grade temp of 99.8. He is showing a localized skin eruption on the trunk, and it is now moving to the extremities. Joints of the upper extremities are fine, but the lower extremities are showing signs of slight swelling. As for rest of exam, heart and lungs are normal. No other problems noted in either of these areas.
>
> A: Allergic reaction to Amoxicillin
>
> P: Will start child on Benadryl and change the antibiotic to Ceclor for the ear infection. If he is not exhibiting signs of reduced hives and disappearance of joint swelling in 24 hours or if temperature spikes and reaction starts to become worse, mom will bring child back here, if during regular office hours, or to the Emergency Room, if after hours.

This example clearly describes an allergic reaction to Amoxicillin. The documentation supports that the medication was given properly. The coding for this example is L27.1 and T36.0x5A.

Papulosquamous Disorders (Category Codes L40–L45) and Urticaria and Erythema (Category Codes L49–L54)

These two blocks of codes are used to report the following disorders:

- L40, Psoriasis
- L41, Parapsoriasis
- L42, Pityriasis rosea
- L43, Lichen planus
- L44, Other papulosquamous disorders
- L45, Papulosquamous disorders in diseases classified elsewhere
- L49, Exfoliation due to erythematous conditions according to extent of body surface involved
- L50, Urticaria
- L51, Erythema multiforme
- L52, Erythema nodosum
- L53, Other erythematous conditions
- L54, Erythema in diseases classified elsewhere

The L50 category, Urticaria, is used to report **urticaria**, commonly known as **hives**. Fourth digits are needed to specify the type of urticaria: allergic, idiopathic, urticaria due to cold and heat, dermatographic, vibratory, cholinergic, contact, and other forms.

Disease Highlight—Urticaria

Urticaria is a skin disorder in which there are raised edematous areas of skin accompanied by intense itching. Urticaria may be an indication of an allergic reaction to foods, inhaled allergens, drugs, or an insect bite. Nonallergic reactions can be caused by an infection or some type of external physical stimuli.

Signs and Symptoms:

The patient presents with lesions that have very distinct dermal wheals accompanied by erythematous areas surrounding the lesions. In the areas of the wheals there is severe itching.

Clinical Testing:

The following tests may be performed to confirm or rule out an inflammatory process:

- Allergy testing
- Urinalysis
- Sedimentation rate
- CBC

Treatment:

Patients are given antihistamines and instructed to avoid the allergen if the urticaria is caused by an allergic reaction. Topical ointments may also be given.

Radiation-Related Disorders of the Skin and Subcutaneous Tissue (Category Codes L55–L59)

This block of codes is divided as follows:

- L55, Sunburn
- L56, Other acute skin changes due to ultraviolet radiation
- L57, Skin changes due to chronic exposure to nonionizing radiation
- L58, Radiodermatitis
- L59, Other disorders of skin and subcutaneous tissue related to radiation

Sunburn, category L55 with the use of fourth characters, is divided according to the degree of the burn. L56 includes drug phototoxic response and photoallergic response. An instructional notation appears to "Use additional code to identify the source of the ultraviolet radiation (W89, X32)." Under codes L56.0 and L56.1 are instructional notations to "Use additional code for adverse effect, if applicable, to identify drug (T36–T50 with fifth or sixth character 5)."

Disorders of Skin Appendages (Category Codes L60–L75)

This block of codes includes disorders that impact the nails, hair, and skin. Disorders of nails are coded to this section because **nails** are hardened cells of the epidermis. Some of the conditions a coder sees are ingrown nail, code L60.0, and onycholysis, code L60.1.

Conditions involving the hair are coded to this section because hair follicles extend out of the dermis. **Hair** is a form of protection used by the body to keep foreign material from entering through the skin. Some of the conditions a coder might have to code from this section are **hirsutism**, excessive hair growth, codes to L68.0, and **alopecia**, the loss of hair, codes to codes within category L63.

The **sebaceous glands** are located in the skin and produce an oily secretion that conditions the skin. Oversecretion of the sebaceous glands can cause acne. Acne is coded to the L70 category of codes, with fourth digits used to identify the type of acne.

Intraoperative and Postprocedural Complications of Skin and Subcutaneous Tissue (Category Code L76)

This next block contains only one category, L76. This category is further differentiated according to the type of skin complication. Complications include hemorrhage, seroma, hematoma, puncture, and lacerations.

Other Diseases of the Skin and Subcutaneous Tissue (Category Codes L80–L99)

This block of codes contain the following categories:

- L80, Vitiligo
- L81, Other disorders of pigmentation
- L82, Seborrheic keratosis
- L83, Acanthosis nigricans
- L84, Corns and callosities
- L85, Other epidermal thickening
- L86, Keratoderma in diseases classified elsewhere
- L87, Transepidermal elimination disorders
- L88, Pyoderma gangrenosum
- L89, Pressure ulcer
- L90, Atrophic disorders of skin
- L91, Hypertrophic disorders of skin
- L92, Granulomatous disorders of skin and subcutaneous tissue
- L93, Lupus erythematosus
- L94, Other localized connective tissue disorders
- L95, Vasculitis limited to skin, not elsewhere classified
- L97, Nonpressure chronic ulcer of lower limb, not elsewhere classified
- L98, Other disorders of skin and subcutaneous tissue, not elsewhere classified
- L99, Other disorders of skin and subcutaneous tissue in diseases classified elsewhere

The L89 category of the chapter contains codes for pressure ulcers. **Ulcers** are erosions of the skin in which the tissue becomes inflamed and then is lost. Ulcers not only appear on the skin but can be found within the body. A **decubitus ulcer** is a result of continuous pressure in an area that eventually limits or stops circulation and oxygen flow to an area. Decubitus ulcers are also called **pressure ulcers**, **bedsores**, or **pressure sores**.

Ulcers are staged as one through four depending on their severity. The staging affects the coding assignment. ICD-10-CM defines the stages of ulceration as follows:

- Stage I, limited to persistent focal edema
- Stage II, abrasion, blister, partial-thickness skin loss involving epidermis and/or dermis
- Stage III, full-thickness skin loss involving damage or necrosis of subcutaneous tissue
- Stage IV, necrosis of soft tissues through to underlying muscle, bone, and supporting structures (i.e., the tendon or joint capsule)

The ICD-10-CM Official Guidelines for Coding give the following direction for coding pressure ulcers:

ICD-10-CM Official Coding Guidelines

a. Pressure ulcer stage codes

1) Pressure ulcer stages

Codes in category L89, Pressure ulcer, identify the site and stage of the pressure ulcer.

The ICD-10-CM classifies pressure ulcer stages based on severity, which is designated by stages 1–4, deep tissue pressure injury, unspecified stage and unstageable.

Assign as many codes from category L89 as needed to identify all the pressure ulcers the patient has, if applicable.

See Section I.B.14 for pressure ulcer stage documentation by clinicians other than patient's provider.

2) Unstageable pressure ulcers

Assignment of the code for unstageable pressure ulcer (L89.--0) should be based on the clinical documentation. These codes are used for pressure ulcers whose stage cannot be clinically determined (e.g., the ulcer is covered by eschar or has been treated with a skin or muscle graft). This code should not be confused with the codes for unspecified stage (L89.--9). When there is no documentation regarding the stage of the pressure ulcer, assign the appropriate code for unspecified stage (L89.--9).

3) Documented pressure ulcer stage

Assignment of the pressure ulcer stage code should be guided by clinical documentation of the stage or documentation of the terms found in the Alphabetic Index. For clinical terms describing the stage that are not found in the Alphabetic Index, and there is no documentation of the stage, the provider should be queried.

4) Patients admitted with pressure ulcers documented as healed

No code is assigned if the documentation states that the pressure ulcer is completely healed at the time of admission.

5) Pressure ulcers documented as healing

Pressure ulcers described as healing should be assigned the appropriate pressure ulcer stage code based on the documentation in the medical record. If the documentation does not provide information about the stage of the healing pressure ulcer, assign the appropriate code for unspecified stage.

If the documentation is unclear as to whether the patient has a current (new) pressure ulcer or if the patient is being treated for a healing pressure ulcer, query the provider. For ulcers that were present on admission but healed at the time of discharge, assign the code for the site and stage of the pressure ulcer at the time of admission.

6) Patient admitted with pressure ulcer evolving into another stage during the admission

If a patient is admitted to an inpatient hospital with a pressure ulcer at one stage and it progresses to a higher stage, two separate codes should be assigned: one code for the site and stage of the ulcer on admission and a second code for the same ulcer site and the highest stage reported during the stay.

7) Pressure-induced deep tissue damage

For pressure-induced deep tissue damage or deep tissue pressure injury, assign only the appropriate code for pressure-induced deep tissue damage (L89. – 6). (See Appendix A, Section I, c12, a.)

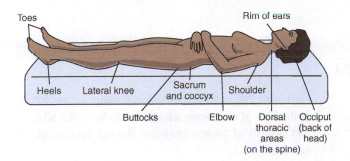

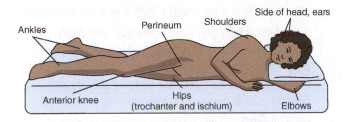

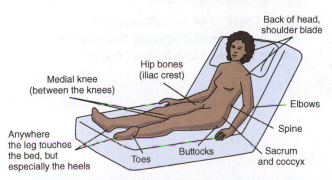

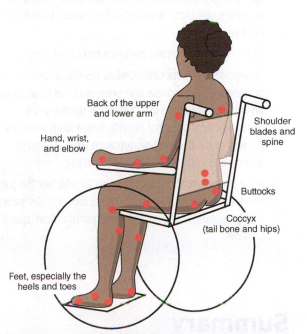

FIGURE 17-3 Decubitus ulcer sites of bed-bound patient (From Hegner BR, Acello B, Caldwell E. *Nursing Assistant: A Nursing Process Approach*, 9th ed. Clifton Park, NY: Delmar, Cengage Learning, 2004, p. 591.).

FIGURE 17-4 Decubitus ulcer sites of wheelchair-bound patient (From Hegner BR, Acello B, Caldwell E. *Nursing Assistant: A Nursing Process Approach*, 9th ed. Clifton Park, NY: Delmar, Cengage Learning, 2004, p. 591.).

When selecting codes for pressure ulcers, the coder must be able to identify the site of the ulceration and the stage. If the stage is not recorded, the coder should query the provider or assign the code to indicate that the stage is unspecified.

Patients who are confined to bed or in a wheelchair are at risk for developing decubitus ulcers. Figures 17-3 and 17-4 illustrate common sites of decubitus ulcers for patients confined to bed or a wheelchair.

A notation appears after the category L89 heading that reads, "Code first any associated gangrene (I96)."

EXAMPLE: Debbie Diabetic presents with a heel pressure ulcer. The ulcer has developed gangrene on the wound. I have referred her to the Wound Care Center for treatment today. She will return in approximately 1 week.

The codes for our example are L89.609 for the ulcer and I96 for the gangrene. As with all coding, the medical documentation must be used as a guide in the selection and the sequencing of the codes. The ICD-10-CM Official Guidelines for Coding give the following direction for coding non-pressure ulcers:

ICD-10-CM Official Coding Guidelines

b. Non-Pressure Chronic Ulcers

1) Patients admitted with non-pressure ulcers documented as healed

No code is assigned if the documentation states that the non-pressure ulcer is completely healed at the time of admission.

2) Non-pressure ulcers documented as healing

Non-pressure ulcers described as healing should be assigned the appropriate non-pressure ulcer code based on the documentation in the medical record. If the documentation does not provide information about the severity of the healing non-pressure ulcer, assign the appropriate code for unspecified severity.

If the documentation is unclear as to whether the patient has a current (new) non-pressure ulcer or if the patient is being treated for a healing non-pressure ulcer, query the provider.

For ulcers that were present on admission but healed at the time of discharge, assign the code for the site and severity of the non-pressure ulcer at the time of admission.

3) Patient admitted with non-pressure ulcer that progresses to another severity level during the admission

If a patient is admitted to an inpatient hospital with a non-pressure ulcer at one severity level and it progresses to a higher severity level, two separate codes should be assigned: one code for the site and severity level of the ulcer on admission and a second code for the same ulcer site and the highest severity level reported during the stay.

See Section I.B.14 for pressure ulcer stage documentation by clinicians other than patient's provider. (See Appendix A, Section I, c12, b.)

Courtesy of the Centers for Medicare & Medicaid Services, www.cms.gov

Summary

- This chapter codes diseases of the skin, hair, nails, and sebaceous glands.
- The skin is also known as the integumentary system and is made up of three layers: the epidermis, the dermis, and the subcutaneous layers.
- Conditions of the integumentary system include melanoma, furuncles, carbuncles, cellulitis, abscesses, and dermatitis.
- Conditions of the nails are coded to this chapter.
- Codes for skin ulcers are found in this chapter.

Internet Links

To learn more about disorders of the skin and subcutaneous system, visit **www.medicinenet.com/atopic_dermatitis/article.htm** and **www.emedicine.com**, search on conditions of the skin.

To learn more about decubitus ulcers, visit **http://en.wikipedia.org/wiki/Decubitus_ulcer**.

Chapter Review

True/False

Indicate whether each statement is true (T) or false (F).

1. _____ Pressure ulcers are also known as bedsores.

2. _____ Patient presents with an open wound of the leg area. During the examination, it is noted that the patient has cellulitis. The wound is coded first, then the cellulitis.

3. _____ The dermis layer is located below the subcutaneous layer of skin.

4. _____ Sclerodactyly is coded with code L94.3.

5. _____ An inflammation of the upper layer of the skin is called alopecia.

Fill-in-the-Blank

Enter the appropriate term(s) to complete each statement.

6. Another name for bedsore or pressure ulcer is _____.

7. The outermost layer of the skin is called the _____.

8. Corns are coded to _____.

9. The subcutaneous layer connects the bottom layer of the skin to the top surface of _____.

10. Another name for skin is _____.

Coding Guidelines True/False

Review the ICD-10-CM Official Guidelines for Coding and Reporting and indicate if the statement(s) is true or false.

11. _____ No code is assigned if the documentation states that the non-pressure ulcer is completely healed at the time of admission.

12. _____ If a patient is admitted to an inpatient hospital with a non-pressure ulcer at one severity level and it progresses to a higher severity level, assign a code for the highest severity level of the site.

13. _____ Codes from category L89, Pressure ulcer, identify the site of the pressure ulcer as well as the stage of the ulcer.

14. _____ Non-pressure ulcers described as healing should be assigned the appropriate non-pressure ulcer code based on the documentation in the medical record. If the documentation does not provide information about the severity of the healing non-pressure ulcer, assign the appropriate code for unspecified severity.

15. _____ The ICD-10-CM classifies pressure ulcer stages based on severity, which is designated by stages 1–6, unspecified stage and unstageable.

Coding Assignments

Instructions: Using an ICD-10-CM code book, assign the proper diagnosis code to the following diagnostic statements.

1. seborrheic infantile dermatitis   _____

2. cellulitis of cheek   _____

3. stage 2 decubitus ulcer, buttock

4. hidradenitis

5. paronychia of right toe

6. pyogenic granuloma

7. impetigo

8. vitiligo

9. acne varioliformis

10. vegetans dermatitis

11. ingrown toenail

12. carbuncle of left lower leg

13. ulcer of ankle

14. pilonidal cyst with abscess

15. cheloid

16. sunburn

17. acne vulgaris

18. subcutaneous calcification

19. urticaria due to cold and heat

20. stage 3 bedsore of left hip

21. xerosis cutis

22. cicatrix

23. lichen nitidus

24. septic dermatitis

25. benign mucous membrane pemphigoid

26. cutaneous abscess buttock

27. acute lymphangitis of perineum

28. chronic bullous disease of childhood

29. pruritus vulvae

30. lichen striatus

31. acute lymphangitis of left finger

32. bullous lichen planus

33. plaque psoriasis

34. infectious eczematoid dermatitis

35. circumscribed neurodermatitis

Case Studies

Instructions: Review each case study and select the correct ICD-10-CM diagnostic code.

Case 1

S: A 15-year-old male presents with acne. Patient says that he has had continual breakouts over the last 6 months, which appear, to the patient, to be getting worse. He tries not to touch his face and washes it three or four times a day.

O: Examination reveals a well-nourished, well-developed 15-year-old male with acne lesions on the face. There are also a few lesions on the chest and back. The rest of the skin exam is unremarkable.

A: Acne

P: I explained to patient that washing the face too much is just as harmful as not washing enough.

Patient will wash once in the morning and then again before bed with a mild soap, followed by Differin q.h.s., and will start doxycycline once a day, 100 mg p.o. q.d. He will return in 1 month for follow-up.

ICD-10-CM Code Assignment: _____

Case 2

Skilled Nursing Facility Note

VITAL SIGNS: See nurse's vital signs sheet.

This patient was admitted in March and she is wheelchair bound.

EXAM:

HEENT: Within normal limits

ABDOMEN: Soft, no masses

HEART: Normal

SKIN: There is skin breakdown in the sacrum area, which shows some necrotic tissue in the ulcerative area. It shows some granulation, and there is drainage at this time. Stage 4 decubitus present.

PLAN: I have instructed the nurses to treat with Sorbsan, packing twice a day and using a dry sterile dressing.

ICD-10-CM Code Assignment: _____

Case 3

Physician Office Note

Patient presents with a complaint of pain in left hand and has been running a low-grade fever.

EXAM:

EXTREMITIES: Right arm and hand within normal limits. Left hand and thumb are sore to touch. The nail around the thumb is swollen, and the cuticle is edematous and red. The cuticle lifts away from the base, and there is pus present. Paronychia of thumb present. Antibiotics ordered as per med sheet. Patient encouraged to wash hands frequently. Patient instructed to follow up in 10 days or if symptoms worsen.

ICD-10-CM Code Assignment: _____

Case 4

Physician Office Note

Tim is a 5-year-old male who presents today with a red area on his right finger. Mom noticed this spot about 3 weeks ago and said that it has gotten darker than when it first appeared.

The child is having no problems eating or drinking. Upon examination, it is noted that there is a considerable amount of inflammation on the right second finger. This spot is tender. No other spots, lesions, or abnormalities are noted. The diagnosis for this child is cellulitis of right finger.

ICD-10-CM Code Assignment: _____

Case 5

Physician Office Note

Tess presented today with a complaint of burning and itching around her abdominal scar. The scar is a result of an automobile accident she was in approximately 3 years ago. Upon examination, the scar is approximately 15 cm in length and appears to be elevated and slightly irregular in shape. I believe this to be a keloid and will administer a steroid injection at the site to relieve the symptoms. Tess will return to the office in 2 weeks for follow-up or sooner if necessary.

ICD-10-CM Code Assignment: _____

Case 6

Observation Unit Note

This elderly patient was placed on the observation unit due to cellulitis present on her left foot that has been present for the last week. She was started on oral antibiotics 6 days ago but the cellulitis is not improving. The foot is red and swollen and is tender to touch. Her temperature is 99.7. An ultrasound was completed to rule out deep vein thrombosis. The ultrasound was normal. She is being treated with IV antibiotics and I will observe her for the next 10 hours and then decide if admission is necessary.

ICD-10-CM Code Assignment: _____

Case 7

Emergency Department Note

This 45-year-old male patient, who is a logger, presents to the ED complaining of pain and swelling of his left index finger. I asked him if he has recently injured the finger and he said that he has not. Examination of hands is normal except for the left index finger, which is swollen, red, and appears gangrenous. I suggested to the patient that he should be started on IV antibiotics, which he refused. I ordered oral antibiotics and told him to take Tylenol for the pain. The area was cleaned and dressed. The patient stated that he will follow up with his primary care provider tomorrow and he refused any additional treatment today.

ASSESSMENT: Abscess of skin with dry gangrene

ICD-10-CM Code Assignment: _____

Case 8

Office Note

This 6-month-old male infant has a reddened area on his scalp with greasy-looking yellow scales. His mother states that this has been present for 4 days and the mother is very concerned about the condition. I informed the mother that this is seborrheic dermatitis, commonly referred to as cradle cap. I instructed her to go to the drug store on the way home and purchase an over-the-counter (OTC) medicated shampoo. If the condition does not improve in 1 week she is to bring the infant back to be reexamined.

ICD-10-CM Code Assignment: _____

Case 9

Office Note

This 18-year-old male patient presents to the office today complaining of a painful area on his right arm. Examination of the arm shows a red area of skin that is tender when I touch it. The skin also feels warm. There is a small sebaceous cyst present. I instructed the patient to place a warm, moist compress on the cyst to reduce the pain and to promote drainage. If the cyst does not drain within 3 days I instructed the patient to return to the office.

ICD-10-CM Code Assignment: _____

Case 10

This 16-year-old female patient returns to the office today for follow-up. She is currently experiencing an acute flare-up of her chronic eczema. I wrote a script of topical cortisone cream and told her to take an antihistamine. If symptoms do not subside in 5 days she is to call the office.

ICD-10-CM Code Assignment: _____

Diseases of the Musculoskeletal System and Connective Tissue

Chapter Outline

Chapter Objectives
Key Terms
Introduction
Introduction to the Body System
Coding of Diseases of the Musculoskeletal
   System and Connective Tissue

Summary
Internet Links
Chapter Review
Coding Assignments
Case Studies

Chapter Objectives

At the conclusion of this chapter, you should be able to:

1. Identify the anatomical structures of the musculoskeletal system.
2. Explain the conditions and disorders that affect the musculoskeletal system.
3. Intrepret the ICD-10-CM coding guidelines related to the conditions of the musculoskeletal system.
4. Apply the ICD-10-CM coding guidelines to accurately code diseases of the musculoskeletal system and connective tissue.
5. Select and code diagnoses from case studies.

Key Terms

Ankylosing spondylitis
Ankylosis
Aporosity
Arthritis
Bones
Bursa
Bursitis
Cartilage
Colles' fracture

Compression fractures
  of the spine
Degenerative joint
  disease
Dorsopathies
Dowager's hump
Fascia
Herniated disc
Infectious arthropathies

Joints
Ligaments
Malunion fracture
Muscles
Myelopathy
Myositis
Nonunion fracture
Osteoarthritis (OA)
Osteoporosis

Pathologic fracture
Rheumatism
Rheumatoid arthritis
  (RA)
Spondylitis
Stress fracture
Synovia
Tendons

REMINDER: As you work through this chapter, you will need to have a copy of the ICD-10-CM coding book to reference. For this chapter, you will also need to reference the ICD-10-CM Official Guidelines for Coding and Reporting. These guidelines can be found in Appendix A which are now available on the Student Companion site and MINDTAP From Cengage.

Introduction

Chapter 13 of ICD-10-CM classifies musculoskeletal disorders and conditions that occur as a disease process. Injuries that affect the musculoskeletal system, such as a fracture, are classified to Chapter 19 of ICD-10-CM, "Injury, Poisoning and Certain Other Consequences of External Causes," with the exception of stress fractures and pathologic fractures; these are classified to Chapter 13 of ICD-10-CM. This chapter contains the following blocks of codes:

- M00–M02, Infectious arthropathies
- M04, Autoinflammatory Syndromes
- M05–M14, Inflammatory polyarthropathies
- M15–M19, Osteoarthritis
- M20–M25, Other joint disorders
- M26–M27, Dentofacial anomalies (including malocclusion) and other disorders of jaw
- M30–M36, Systemic connective tissue disorders
- M40–M43, Deforming dorsopathies
- M45–M49, Spondylopathies
- M50–M54, Other dorsopathies
- M60–M63, Disorders of muscles
- M65–M67, Disorders of synovium and tendon
- M70–M79, Other soft tissue disorders
- M80–M85, Disorders of bone density and structure
- M86–M90, Other osteopathies
- M91–M94, Chondropathies
- M95, Other disorders of the musculoskeletal system and connective tissue
- M96, Intraoperative and postprocedural complications and disorders of musculoskeletal system, not elsewhere classified
- M97, Periprosthetic fracture around internal prosthetic joint
- M99, Biomechanical lesions, not elsewhere classified

Introduction to the Body System

When coding diseases of the musculoskeletal system and connective tissue, the coder must have good reference materials, a sound understanding of anatomy and physiology, and specific documentation from the provider to guide the coder in making the correct code assignment.

This chapter of the coding book classifies diseases of the musculoskeletal system. *Musculoskeletal* refers to

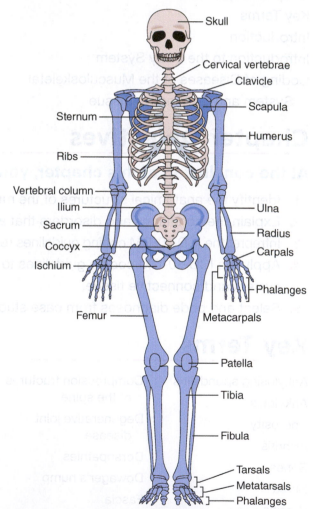

FIGURE 18-1 Anterior view of the human skeleton (From Ehrlich A, Schroeder CL. *Medical Terminology for Health Professionals*, 4th ed. Clifton Park, NY: Delmar, Cengage Learning, 2001, p. 49.).

the **muscles**, which hold the body erect and allow movement, and the **bones**, which are connective tissue that protect the internal organs and form the framework of the body. For correct code assignments to be made from this chapter, coders must understand the terms associated with the musculoskeletal system.

- **Cartilage** is smooth, nonvascular connective tissue that comprises the more flexible parts of the skeleton, such as the outer ear.
- **Joints** allow for bending and rotating movements.
- **Ligaments** are bands of connective tissue that connect the joints.
- **Tendons** connect muscle to bone.
- **Synovia** is the fluid that acts as a lubricant for the joints, tendon sheath, or bursa.
- The **bursa** is the synovial-filled sac that works as a cushion to assist in movement.
- **Fascia** is the connective tissue that not only covers but also supports and separates muscles.

Figures 18-1, 18-2, and 18-3 illustrate the anatomical features of the musculoskeletal system.

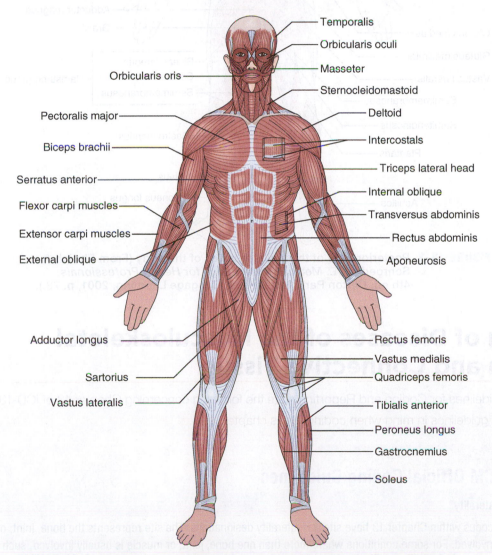

FIGURE 18-2 Anterior view of the major muscles of the body (From Ehrlich A, Schroeder CL. *Medical Terminology for Health Professionals*, 4th ed. Clifton Park, NY: Delmar, Cengage Learning, 2001, p. 78.).

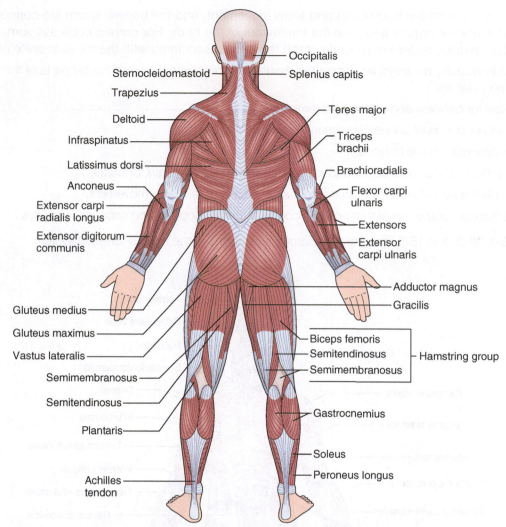

FIGURE 18-3 Posterior view of the major muscles of the body (From Ehrlich A, Schroeder CL. *Medical Terminology for Health Professionals*, 4th ed. Clifton Park, NY: Delmar, Cengage Learning, 2001, p. 78.).

Coding of Diseases of the Musculoskeletal System and Connective Tissue

The Official Guidelines for Coding and Reporting state the following concerning Chapter 13 of ICD-10-CM:

Keep these guidelines in mind when coding in this chapter.

ICD-10-CM Official Coding Guidelines

a) Site and laterality

Most of the codes within Chapter 13 have site and laterality designations. The site represents the bone, joint, or the muscle involved. For some conditions where more than one bone, joint, or muscle is usually involved, such as osteoarthritis, there is a "multiple sites" code available. For categories where no multiple site code is provided and more than one bone, joint, or muscle is involved, multiple codes should be used to indicate the different sites involved.

Courtesy of the Centers for Medicare & Medicaid Services, www.cms.gov

1) Bone versus joint

For certain conditions, the bone may be affected at the upper or lower end (e.g., avascular necrosis of bone, M87, Osteoporosis, M80, M81). Though the portion of the bone affected may be at the joint, the site designation will be the bone, not the joint.

b) Acute traumatic versus chronic or recurrent musculoskeletal conditions

Many musculoskeletal conditions are a result of previous injury or trauma to a site, or are recurrent conditions. Bone, joint, or muscle conditions that are the result of a healed injury are usually found in Chapter 13. Recurrent bone, joint, or muscle conditions are also usually found in Chapter 13. Any current, acute injury should be coded to the appropriate injury code from Chapter 19. Chronic or recurrent conditions should generally be coded with a code from Chapter 13. If it is difficult to determine from the documentation in the record which code is best to describe a condition, query the provider. (See Appendix A, Section I, C.13.a-b.)

Infectious Arthropathies (Category Codes M00–M02)

Infectious arthropathies are disorders of the joints that are caused by an infectious agent. The Tabular List of ICD-10-CM explains this block of codes as follows:

This block comprises arthropathies due to microbiological agents. Distinction is made between the following types of etiological relationship:

a) direct infection of joint, where organisms invade synovial tissue and microbial antigen is present in the joint;

b) indirect infection, which may be of two types: a reactive arthropathy, where microbial infection of the body is established but neither organisms nor antigens can be identified in the joint, and a postinfective arthropathy, where microbial antigen is present but recovery of an organism is inconstant and evidence of local multiplication is lacking.

Coders have to identify the type of arthropathy present because ICD-10-CM differentiates the categories as follows: M00, Pyogenic arthritis; M01, Direct infections of joint in infectious and parasitic diseases classified elsewhere; and M02, Postinfective and reactive arthropathies. Within category M00 the specific codes differentiate the type of organism causing the infectious condition. Categories M01 and M02 contain instructional notations that state: "Code first underlying disease …." The site of the disease, for example right wrist, left wrist, or unspecified wrist, is also identified in the codes. Coders need to reference the code book to note the fourth, fifth, and/or sixth characters that are valid for these categories.

Autoinflammatory Syndromes (M04) and Inflammatory Polyarthropathies (Category Codes M05–M14)

These blocks of codes include the following categories, with fourth, fifth, and/or sixth characters:

- M04, Autoinflammatory syndromes
- M05, Rheumatoid arthritis with rheumatoid factor
- M06, Other rheumatoid arthritis
- M07, Enteropathic arthropathies
- M08, Juvenile arthritis
- M1a, Chronic gout. This category requires a seventh character.
- M10, Gout

- M11, Other crystal arthropathies
- M12, Other and unspecified arthropathy
- M13, Other arthritis
- M14, Arthropathies in other diseases classified elsewhere

Arthritis, an inflammation of a joint, is a common condition coded to this block of the musculoskeletal chapter. Another common condition coded to this block is **rheumatism**, which is a general term for the deterioration and inflammation of connective tissues, including muscles, tendons, synovium, and bursa.

One of the most painful types of arthritis is **rheumatoid arthritis (RA)**, which is a disease of the autoimmune system in which the synovial membranes are inflamed and thickened. Rheumatoid arthritis can affect children or adults, and it can affect one site or many sites throughout the body. Rheumatoid arthritis may also be referenced as "progressive arthritis" and "proliferative arthritis." Medical documentation needs to specify the site or sites affected so that the appropriate code can be assigned. Because joint swelling and pain are considered an integral part of the condition, they should not be coded separately when a definitive diagnosis of rheumatoid arthritis is given.

EXAMPLE: A patient presents with pain and swelling of the right shoulder and the right elbow. The patient is known to have rheumatoid arthritis of the right shoulder and right elbow. This encounter would be coded with codes M06.011 and M06.021. The pain and swelling of the joints are not coded as they are considered a component of the rheumatoid arthritis.

Osteoarthritis (Category Codes M15–M19)

This block of codes reports the following categories:

- M15, Polyosteoarthritis—This category reports osteoarthritis of multiple sites.
- M16, Osteoarthritis of hip—Category M16 is used to report unilateral and bilateral osteoarthritis of the hip. Laterality is identified within the category.
- M17, Osteoarthritis of knee—Codes are differentiated within this category to reflect laterality.
- M18, Osteoarthritis of first carpometacarpal joint—This category is used to report only osteoarthritis of the first carpometacarpal joint.
- M19, Other and unspecified osteoarthritis—This category reports osteoarthritis of other joints that are not classified to categories M15 to M18.

The most common form of arthritis is known as **osteoarthritis (OA)**. Osteoarthritis is also referred to as "degenerative arthritis" because it causes the degeneration of the articular cartilage. Osteoarthritis also causes enlargement of the bone. It occurs almost always in older patients. The term **degenerative joint disease** is frequently used to describe this type of osteoarthritis.

Other Joint Disorders (Category Codes M20–M25)

The block of codes includes the following:

- M20, Acquired deformities of fingers and toes
- M21, Other acquired deformities of limbs
- M22, Disorder of patella
- M23, Internal derangement of knee
- M24, Other specific joint derangements
- M25, Other joint disorders, not elsewhere classified

This block of codes is very detailed as to the type of deformity or disorder present. Coders must reference the medical documentation to ensure proper code assignment. For example when coding ankylosis, fifth characters identify the site and sixth characters further identify laterality. To code ankylosis of the right shoulder, the coder would select code M24.611, ankylosis, right shoulder.

Dentofacial Anomalies [Including Malocclusion] and Other Disorders of Jaw (Category Codes M26–M27)

The anomalies classified to categories M26–M27 include those of the jaw, jaw-cranial base, dental arch, tooth position, malocclusion, dentofacial function, and temporomandibular joint disorders. Other diseases of the jaw, such as developmental disorders and inflammatory jaw conditions, are also classified here.

Systemic Connective Tissue Disorders (Category Codes M30–M36)

This block of codes reports systemic connective tissue disorders that include:

- M30, Polyarteritis nodosa and related conditions—Codes are differentiated at the fourth-character level to identify the specific condition.
- M31, Other necrotizing vasculopathies—This category reports such conditions as thrombotic microangiopathy (M31.1), and giant cell arteritis with polymyalgia rheumatica (M31.5).
- M32, Systemic lupus erythematosus (SLE)—This category is differentiated to identify the type of lupus and organ or system involvement.
- M33, Dermatopolymyositis—This category identifies various forms of dermatopolymyositis and the site of organ involvement.
- M34, Systemic sclerosis [scleroderma]—Fourth characters within this category identify the type of sclerosis. Coders need to make note of the instructional notations that appear following code M34.2 that identify sequencing and additional code assignment.
- M35, Other systemic involvement of connective tissue—Fourth characters identify various syndromes and systemic diseases. Coders should note the various Excludes1 notations that appear throughout this category. Fifth characters are needed for the subcategory of M35.0.
- M36, Systematic disorders of connective tissue in diseases classified elsewhere—There are numerous instructional notations within category M36 that instruct coders to "Code first …".

Coders need to reference the coding manual to review the fourth and fifth characters required for categories M30 to M36 and review the instructional notations that are present for these codes.

For example, reporting code M36.2, Hemophilic arthropathy, the coder should be aware of the following instructional notation:

Code first underlying disease, such as:
factor VIII deficiency (D66)
with vascular defect (D68.0)
factor IX deficiency (D67)
hemophilia (classical) (D66)
hemophilia B (D67)
hemophilia C (D68.1)

This signals to the coder that two codes are needed to fully code the disease.

Exercise 18.1—Coding for Categories M00–M36

For each diagnostic statement, select the appropriate ICD-10-CM diagnostic code.

Diagnosis	Code
1. enteropathic arthropathy left ankle and foot	_____
2. right shoulder juvenile arthritis	_____
3. gout due to renal impairment, right wrist	_____
4. polyosteoarthritis	_____
5. mallet finger of left finger	_____
6. chronic postrheumatic arthropathy, left elbow	_____
7. recurrent subluxation of patella, left knee	_____
8. loose body in right knee	_____
9. contracture of left hip	_____
10. hemarthrosis knee	_____

Dorsopathies (Category Codes M40–M54)

Dorsopathies, which are disorders of the back, are reported using the following ranges of codes, with the assignment of fourth, fifth, and at times sixth and seventh characters:

- M40–M43, Deforming dorsopathies
- M45–M49, Spondylopathies
- M50–M54, Other dorsopathies

One of the conditions encountered in this section is **ankylosing spondylitis**, a form of rheumatoid arthritis. It is a chronic inflammation of the spine and sacroiliac joints, which leads to stiffening of the spine. **Ankylosis** is the complete fusion of the vertebrae. **Spondylitis** is an inflammation of the vertebrae. Ankylosing spondylitis is also referred to as Marie-Strümpell or Bekhterev's disease. The cause is unknown, but it is progressive and affects mainly the small joints of the spine. This condition is classified to category code M45.

Category code M46 reports other inflammatory spondylopathies, and category code M47 reports spondylosis.

The term **myelopathy** refers to any disorder of the spinal cord. Back disorders that involve herniation of the intervertebral disc or spondylitis need the distinction of "with myelopathy" or "without myelopathy."

A **herniated disc** is a result of the rupture of the nucleus pulposus, or the material in the center of the disc. The rupture causes the nucleus pulposus to move outward, placing pressure on the spinal cord. Because back pain is an integral part of a herniated disc, it is not coded separately. Sciatica is another symptom and is not coded separately. Herniated discs are classified to intervertebral disc displacement codes and are classified by the site of the displacement, such as M51.2 codes, Other thoracic, thoracolumbar and lumbosacral intervertebral disc displacement, and M50.2 codes, Other cervical disc displacement.

Soft Tissue Disorders (Category Codes M60–M79)

Soft tissue disorders are grouped into the following blocks of codes, with fourth, fifth, and at times sixth characters:

- M60–M63, Disorders of muscles
- M65–M67, Disorders of synovium and tendon
- M70–M79, Other soft tissue disorders

Myositis, an inflammation of the muscle, is coded using category code M60. The various types of myositis are differentiated. Muscle wasting and atrophy, commonly seen in the elderly, is reported using the M62.5 codes with the appropriate fifth and sixth characters.

Synovitis and tenosynovitis are reported using category M65. Codes M65.30- to M65.35-, Trigger finger, are commonly reported.

Bursitis, an inflammation of the bursa, is reported with codes from category M71. The type of bursitis needs to be determined for proper code selection. Fibromyalgia is reported with code M79.7.

Osteopathies and Chondropathies (Category Codes M80–M94)

Osteopathies and chondropathies are divided into the following blocks of codes, with fourth, fifth, and at times sixth and seventh characters:

- M80–M85, Disorders of bone density and structure
- M86–M90, Other osteopathies
- M91–M94, Chondropathies

One of the most common diseases reported to this section of the code book is osteoporosis, M80–M81. **Osteoporosis** is a reduction in bone mass that is responsible for different conditions that can affect a person's health. The more severe condition that affects patients with osteoporosis is fractures.

Disease Highlight—Osteoporosis

Osteoporosis is a bone disorder, related to metabolism, in which bone mass is lost due to decreased bone formation and increased bone resorption. The disease causes **aporosity**, or a Swiss cheese appearance, of the bones, creating a decrease in bone mass. The numerous causes of osteoporosis include:

- Malnutrition
- Decreased calcium absorption
- Inadequate calcium intake
- Estrogen deficiency
- As a side effect of some chronic diseases

Signs and Symptoms:

Osteoporosis is a slowly developing disease that may take decades before symptoms present. Compression fractures of the spine and pathologic wrist fractures commonly present as an early sign of osteoporosis.

As the disease progresses, the patient may have:

- Kyphosis (see Figure 18-4)
- Pain in the back and trunk area
- A decrease in the size of the chest and abdominal cavity
- A loss of height
- The appearance of **Dowager's hump**, an abnormal curvature in the upper thoracic spine (Figure 18-5

illustrates the loss in height and the appearance of Dowager's hump in a patient with osteoporosis.)

As the disease advances, the patient's risk of fracturing a bone increases. Common fracture sites include the distal radius and proximal femur. Figure 18-4 illustrates these fracture sites.

Clinical Testing:

Osteoporosis is diagnosed by:

- Taking bone mass measurements, bone biopsy, and x-rays
- Completing blood testing to determine the serum calcium, phosphorus, and alkaline phosphatase levels

Treatment:

Because osteoporosis is irreversible, there is no treatment to reverse the bone mass loss.

- Patients are encouraged to take calcium and vitamin D and to complete a daily exercise routine.
- Reducing risk factors, such as decreasing caffeine and alcohol consumption and not smoking, is also encouraged.
- Physical therapy, estrogen therapy, and the surgical correction of pathological fractures are also treatment options for some patients.
- The drug alendronate (Fosamax) is often prescribed in an effort to increase bone mass.

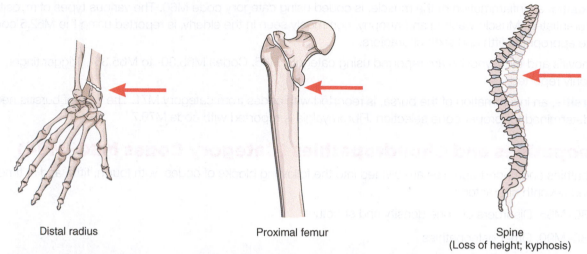

Distal radius   Proximal femur   Spine
(Loss of height; kyphosis)

FIGURE 18-4 Fracture and related osteoporosis (From Neighbors M, Tannehill-Jones, R. *Human Disease*, 2nd ed. Clifton Park, NY: Delmar, Cengage Learning, 2001, p. 91.).

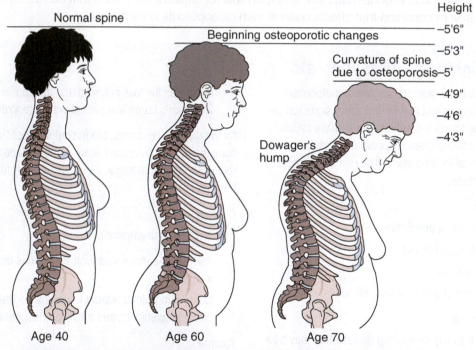

FIGURE 18-5 Dowager's hump (From Neighbors M, Tannehill-Jones, R. *Human Disease*, 2nd ed. Clifton Park, NY: Delmar, Cengage Learning, 2001, p. 91.).

The ICD-10-CM Official Guidelines for Coding and Reporting state the following in relation to coding osteoporosis:

ICD-10-CM Official Coding Guidelines

d) Osteoporosis

Osteoporosis is a systemic condition, meaning that all bones of the musculoskeletal system are affected. Therefore, site is not a component of the codes under category M81, Osteoporosis without current pathological fracture. The site codes under category M80, Osteoporosis with current pathological fracture, identify the site of the fracture, not the osteoporosis.

Courtesy of the Centers for Medicare & Medicaid Services, www.cms.gov

1) Osteoporosis without pathological fracture

Category M81, Osteoporosis without current pathological fracture, is for use for patients with osteoporosis who do not currently have a pathologic fracture due to the osteoporosis, even if they have had a fracture in the past. For patients with a history of osteoporosis fractures, status code Z87.310, Personal history of (healed) osteoporosis fracture, should follow the code from M81.

2) Osteoporosis with current pathological fracture

Category M80, Osteoporosis with current pathological fracture, is for patients who have a current pathologic fracture at the time of an encounter. The codes under M80 identify the site of the fracture. A code from category M80, not a traumatic fracture code, should be used for any patient with known osteoporosis who suffers a fracture, even if the patient had a minor fall or trauma, if that fall or trauma would not usually break a normal, healthy bone. (See Appendix A, Section I, C13.d.)

Three types of fractures are commonly associated with osteoporosis. (1) Pathologic or **compression fractures of the spine** occur when the vertebrae in the spine become weak and collapse under low stress. (2) **Colles' fracture** is a wrist fracture that typically occurs when a person tries to break a fall by extending the arm. (3) The last type, and the most dangerous, is a hip fracture. The hip fracture can be caused by a fall or, in some cases, can occur spontaneously. Loss of mobility or even death can be the result of this type of fracture. Coders must determine whether the fracture occurred because of a weakened diseased bone or as a result of an injury. Fractures that occur because of a traumatic injury, such as a child who falls and breaks an arm while playing, are classified to Chapter 19 of ICD-10-CM, "Injury, Poisoning and Certain Other Consequences of External Causes." For correct code assignment, coders must read the medical record to identify whether the fracture is pathologic or due to a traumatic injury.

The following types of fractures are coded to this section of Chapter 13 of the ICD-10-CM code book:

- M84.4–M84.6, **Pathologic fractures**—A pathologic fracture is a break of a diseased bone that occurs from a minor stress or injury that would not normally occur in healthy bone. Pathologic fractures can also occur spontaneously. Note that a seventh character is added to this group. The following instructional notation appears at the start of M84.4, M84.5, and M84.6:

The appropriate 7th character is to be added to each code from subcategory M84.4, M84.5, M84.6:
A initial encounter for fracture
D subsequent encounter for fracture with routine healing
G subsequent encounter for fracture with delayed healing
K subsequent encounter for fracture with nonunion
P subsequent encounter for fracture with malunion
S sequela

- M84.3, **Stress fractures**—Stress fractures occur when repetitive force is applied to a bone over a period of time. Other terms used for stress fractures are "fatigue fracture," "march fracture," and "stress reaction." Individuals who run or exercise frequently may develop stress fractures. Stress fractures are not always visualized by x-ray initially when they are suspected.

Two terms that are also associated with fractures are **malunion fracture** and **nonunion fracture**. A malunion occurs when the fracture site is misaligned. A nonunion occurs when the fracture fragments fail to unite.

The ICD-10-CM Official Guidelines for Coding and Reporting give coders directions for the coding of pathologic fractures:

Courtesy of the Centers for Medicare & Medicaid Services, www.cms.gov

ICD-10-CM Official Coding Guidelines

c) Coding of Pathologic Fractures

7th character A is for use as long as the patient is receiving active treatment for the fracture. While the patient may be seen by a new or different provider over the course of treatment for a pathological fracture, assignment of the 7th character is based on whether the patient is undergoing active treatment and not whether the provider is seeing the patient for the first time.

7th character, D is to be used for encounters after the patient has completed active treatment for the fracture and is receiving routine care for the fracture during the healing or recovery phase. The other 7th characters, listed under each subcategory in the Tabular List, are to be used for subsequent encounters for treatment of problems associated with the healing, such as malunions, nonunions, and sequelae.

Care for complications of surgical treatment for fracture repairs during the healing or recovery phase should be coded with the appropriate complication codes.

See Section I.C.19. Coding of traumatic fractures. (See Appendix A, C.13.c.)

Other Disorders of the Musculoskeletal System and Connective Tissue (Category Code M95)

This code category includes other acquired deformities of musculoskeletal system and connective tissue. The codes are differentiated according to the site. Coders should note the extensive Excludes2 notation that appears at the start of category M95.

Intraoperative and Postprocedural Complications and Disorders of Musculoskeletal System, Not Elsewhere Classified (Category Code M96) Periprosthetic Fracture Around Internal Prosthetic Joint (Category Code M97) and Biomechanical Lesions, Not Elsewhere Classified (Category Code M99)

These categories report complications and biomechanical lesions that are not classified elsewhere in Chapter 13. Category M96 reports such conditions as postsurgical lordosis (M96.4) and postradiation scoliosis (M96.5). Category M97 reports periprosthetic fracture around an internal prosthetic joint and is differentiated by site and laterality. Seventh characters are required for category M97. Category M99 reports biomechanical lesions, not elsewhere classified in ICD-10-CM. Category M99 should not be used if the condition can be classified elsewhere.

Summary

- Chapter 13 of ICD-10-CM classifies musculoskeletal disorders and conditions that occur as a disease process.
- Stress fractures and pathologic fractures are coded with Chapter 13 of ICD-10-CM.
- Most of the codes in Chapter 13 of ICD-10-CM have site and laterality designations.
- Bone, joint, or muscle conditions that are the result of a healed injury are found in Chapter 13 of ICD-10-CM.
- Osteoporosis with or without a current pathological fracture is reported with category codes M80 and M81.

Internet Links

The learn more about the musculoskeletal system, visit **www.aaos.org**.

To learn about rheumatoid arthritis, visit **www.rheumatoidarthritis.com**.

Chapter Review

True/False

Indicate whether each statement is true (T) or false (F).

1. _____ All fractures are coded to Chapter 13 of ICD-10-CM, "Diseases of the Musculoskeletal System and Connective Tissue."

2. _____ A compression fracture can occur when a person tries to break a fall by extending an arm.

3. _____ All congenital disorders of the back are classified to Chapter 13 of ICD-10-CM.

4. _____ Coxa plana, right hip, is coded to code M91.21.

5. _____ Aneurysmal bone cyst is coded to code M85.51.

Fill-in-the-Blank

Enter the appropriate term(s) to complete each statement.

6. Tendons connect muscle to _____.

7. _____ is an inflammation of a joint.

8. _____ separates and covers the muscles.

9. Disorders of bone density and structure are classified to block _____.

10. _____ acts as a lubricant for joints.

Coding Guidelines True/False

Review the ICD-10-CM Official Guidelines for Coding and Reporting and indicate if the statement(s) is true or false.

11. _____ Most of the codes within Chapter 13 have site and laterality designations. The site represents the bone, joint, or the muscle involved. For some conditions where more than one bone, joint, or muscle is usually involved, such as osteoarthritis, there is a "multiple sites" code available.

12. _____ Osteoporosis is a systemic condition, meaning that all bones of the musculoskeletal system are affected. Therefore, site is not a component of the codes under category M81, Osteoporosis without current pathological fracture. The site codes under category M80, Osteoporosis with current pathological fracture, identify the site of the fracture, not the osteoporosis.

13. _____ For certain conditions, the bone may be affected at the upper or lower end (e.g., avascular necrosis of bone, M87, Osteoporosis, M80, M81). Though the portion of the bone affected may be at the joint, the site designation will be the bone, not the joint.

14. _____ Many musculoskeletal conditions are a result of previous injury or trauma to a site, or are recurrent conditions. Bone, joint, or muscle conditions that are the result of a healed injury are

usually found in Chapter 13. Recurrent bone, joint, or muscle conditions are also usually found in Chapter 13. Any current, acute injury should be coded to the appropriate injury code from Chapter 13.

15. _____ Care for complications of surgical treatment for fracture repairs during the healing or recovery phase should be coded with the appropriate complication codes.

Coding Assignments

Instructions: Using an ICD-10-CM code book, assign the proper diagnosis code to the following diagnostic statements.

1. cauliflower ear, left ear _____

2. coccygodynia _____

3. kyphosis due to radiation _____

4. hypertrophy of right humerus _____

5. senile osteoporosis _____

6. pathological fracture of left humerus, subsequent encounter with nonunion _____

7. pain in limb _____

8. polymyositis _____

9. spinal stenosis, thoracolumbar region _____

10. joint mice, right knee _____

11. Felty's syndrome left shoulder _____

12. rheumatoid arthritis _____

13. acute osteomyelitis of shoulder _____

14. low back pain _____

15. Baker's cyst, left knee _____

16. mandibular hyperplasia _____

17. effusion of right elbow _____

18. cervical spondylolysis _____

19. osteoporosis _____

20. contracture of left hand _____

21. pneumococcal arthritis, left hip _____

22. cavus deformity of foot, acquired _____

23. flexion deformity, left shoulder _____

24. displacement of cervical intervertebral disc without myelopathy _____

25. bunion _____

26. acute hematogenous osteomyelitis left shoulder _____

27. Reiter's disease, left elbow _____

28. idiopathic chronic gout _____

29. traumatic arthropathy, left shoulder _____

30. acquired clawhand, right hand _____

31. rheumatoid arthritis of right wrist _____

32. rheumatoid nodule of left ankle and foot _____

33. enteropathic arthropathies of left knee _____

34. idiopathic chronic gout of left knee _____

35. familial chondrocalcinosis of the right shoulder _____

Case Studies

Instructions: Review each case study and select the correct ICD-10-CM diagnostic code.

Case 1

Physician Office Visit

VITAL SIGNS: BP: 125/80, Temperature: 98.9, Weight: 164 pounds

HEENT: Normal

ABDOMEN: Soft, tender. No masses, spleen normal.

CHEST/HEART: Within normal limits

EXTREMITIES: Extremities were examined and revealed joint inflammation due to arthritis. Patient was instructed to avoid wearing tight footwear. Patient was advised to schedule an appointment with Dr. Town, a podiatrist, for an evaluation.

Follow up in 1 month.

ICD-10-CM Code Assignment: _____

Case 2

Emergency Room Visit

This 16-year-old female was running at track practice today and started to experience foot pain. This has occurred in the past when she runs, but today the pain is at an increased level.

VITAL SIGNS: Temperature: 98.6, BP: 120/75, Weight: 124 pounds

EXAM:

HEENT: Within normal limits

HEART: Normal

ABDOMEN: Normal, with no complaints

(continues)

(continued)

EXTREMITIES: Left foot pain present, and pain increases to touch in the metatarsal area.

x-ray ordered.

Clinical diagnosis of stress fracture of second toe on left foot, confirmed by x-ray.

Referred to orthopedics.

ICD-10-CM Code Assignment: _____

Case 3

Skilled Nursing Facility Note

Mary was admitted in June with a diagnosis of dementia and osteoporosis. She is seen today at the request of the charge nurse because she is complaining of pain in her right midthigh area. She has not fallen or injured herself.

EXAM:

EXTREMITIES: When the patient's right leg is moved, she complains of pain in her thigh. She does not complain of pain in her left leg.

Onsite x-ray was ordered, which showed a fracture of the shaft of the femur.

Patient was sent to hospital for treatment.

CLINICAL IMPRESSION: Fracture due to postmenopausal osteoporosis.

ICD-10-CM Code Assignment: _____

Case 4

Physician Office Visit

Mark presents today for follow-up of a torn meniscus. The injury occurred while skiing 2 years ago. He was going downhill, fell, and twisted his right knee during this fall. He was in a wheelchair for 2 weeks and then moved to crutches and physical therapy. He is now walking and performing activities of daily living without assistance. The diagnosis given for today's visit is old bucket handle tear of medial meniscus of the right knee.

ICD-10-CM Code Assignment: _____

Case 5

Physician Office Visit

Mrs. Kennedy presents today with "terrible pain in my knees." It has been 6 months since I have seen her. We discussed the medications she is taking, which are limited to Advil or Tylenol.

(continues)

(*continued*)

Examination reveals decreased range of motion and a slight change in gait. It was decided to run a few lab tests and also take some x-rays, which confirmed the diagnosis of osteoarthritis of the knee, bilaterally. We decided that glucosamine plus chondroitin sulfate, which are OTC medications, could be tried at this time prior to anything stronger. If she experiences no relief in the next 3 to 4 weeks, we will explore other options.

ICD-10-CM Code Assignment: _____

Case 6

Physician Office Note

This 54-year-old patient returns to my office today to follow up on her degenerative arthritis present in her left elbow. She is experiencing tenderness and joint pain. She states that when she awakens in the morning she has stiffness in the elbow. The pain has increased in the last 3 months from an average of 4 on the pain scale to an average of 8. I am ordering an x-ray to determine if there is a narrowing of the joint space. I offered a corticosteroid injection but she refused the treatment. I instructed her to apply heat to the joint when she awakens and to take NSAIDs as prescribed. She is to follow up with me in 3 months.

ICD-10-CM Code Assignment: _____

Case 7

Physician Office Note

This 10-year-old female was referred to me following a school physical which identified a lateral curvature of the spine. The child has stated to her mother that she has had a backache for the last 2 months or so.

EXAM:

EXTREMITIES: Normal range of motion and no abnormalities noted.

SPINE: I estimate that there is a 25-degree curvature of the thoracic area.

I am going to have her spine imaged via an x-ray to determine the degree of the curvature. I have given her some exercises to do at this time. She is to follow up with me after the results of the x-ray are obtained.

ASSESSMENT: Scoliosis, thoracogenic

ICD-10-CM Code Assignment: _____

Case 8

Physician Office Note

This 34-year-old female presents to the office today with back pain on her right side. She said she woke up feeling this way this morning. The pain is radiating down her side buttocks and legs. Upon exam there is a limitation of straight-leg raising and loss of reflexes on her right side. I instructed her to rest in bed for 2 or 3 days and apply heat. I wrote a prescription for a muscle relaxant and told her to take Advil. If the symptoms have not resided in 4 days she is to call the office.

ASSESSMENT: Sciatica with lumbago

ICD-10-CM Code Assignment: _____

Case 9

Physician Office Note

This 12-year-old female is a gymnast who trains 6 days a week. She states that her left lower extremity is painful. There has been no injury that would cause this pain. x-ray was completed and there is no fracture. There is restricted movement.

ASSESSMENT: Achilles tendinitis

PLAN: Apply alternating heat and ice and take Advil for five days. If symptoms persist return to the office.

ICD-10-CM Code Assignment: _____

Case 10

Office Note

This 46-year-old male carpenter presents to the office today complaining of pain in his right thigh area, which has increased throughout the day. Exam showed no limitations in ROM or reflexes. Skin is intact. Neurological exam is within normal limits. I instructed him to heat the area and to take Tylenol for the pain. He is to return to the office if symptoms do not resolve in 1 week.

ICD-10-CM Code Assignment: _____

Diseases of the Genitourinary System

Chapter Outline

Chapter Objectives

At the conclusion of this chapter, you should be able to:

1. Identify the anatomical structures and functions of the urinary system.
2. Identify the anatomical structures of the male and female genital tracts.
3. Explain the conditions related to the genitourinary system.
4. Apply the ICD-10-CM coding guidelines to accurately code diseases of the genitourinary system.
5. Select and code diagnoses from case studies.

Key Terms

Acute kidney failure

Benign prostatic hypertrophy (BPH)

Calculus

Chronic kidney disease (CKD)

Chronic renal failure

Complete prolapse

Cystitis

Dysplasia

Endometriosis

End-stage renal disease (ESRD)

Female genital prolapse

Female genitalia

Glomerulonephritis

Incomplete prolapse

Kidneys

Male genitalia

Menopause

Micturate

Nephritis

Nephrons

Nephropathy

Nephrosis

Ovarian cysts

Penis

Perimenopausal

Postmenopausal

Premenopausal

Prostate gland

Renal colic

Ureters

Urethra

Urethral stricture

Urethritis

Urinary bladder

Urinary system

Urinary tract infection (UTI)

Urine

Voiding

Introduction

Chapter 14 of ICD-10-CM, "Diseases of the Genitourinary System," classifies conditions of the urinary system and of the male and female genital tracts except for certain genitourinary transmissible infections, neoplasms, and conditions associated with pregnancy, childbirth, and the puerperium. This chapter contains the following blocks:

- N00–N08, Glomerular diseases
- N10–N16, Renal tubulo-interstitial diseases
- N17–N19, Acute kidney failure and chronic kidney disease
- N20–N23, Urolithiasis
- N25–N29, Other disorders of kidney and ureter
- N30–N39, Other diseases of the urinary system
- N40–N53, Diseases of male genital organs
- N60–N65, Disorders of breast
- N70–N77, Inflammatory diseases of female pelvic organs
- N80–N98, Noninflammatory disorders of female genital tract
- N99,   Intraoperative and postprocedural complications and disorders of genitourinary system, not elsewhere classified

Introduction to the Body System

The urinary system is comprised of the kidneys, ureter, bladder, and urethra. The main function of the **urinary system** is to maintain a balance of the contents of the fluids within the body. Urea is removed from the bloodstream and then, along with other excess fluids and waste products, is converted to **urine**, which is expelled from the body by way of the bladder. Figure 19-1 illustrates the structures of the urinary system.

The kidneys are the primary organs of the urinary system. A person usually has two kidneys, which are located against the dorsal wall of the abdominal cavity and lie on either side of the vertebral column. The **kidneys** filter blood constantly to remove waste and secrete urine. The **nephrons**, microscopic units of the kidneys, are the structures that actually form urine.

Urine is moved from the kidney to the bladder by way of the **ureters**. The ureters are very narrow tubes, which can easily be damaged in certain types of surgery. They must function properly for the urinary system to function properly.

The ureters connect to the **urinary bladder**, which holds urine until it moves to the urethra. The **urethra** is a small tube extending from the bladder to outside the body. When the bladder fills, pressure is

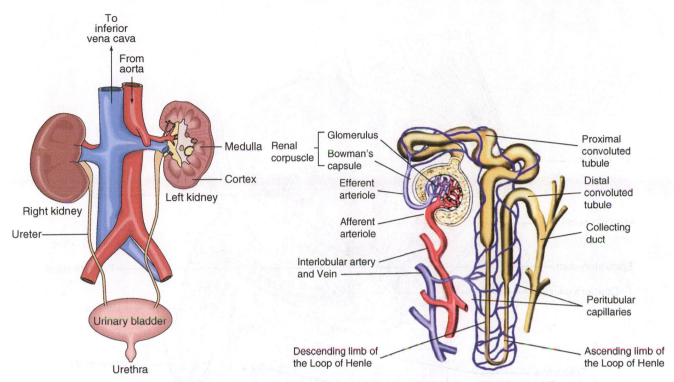

FIGURE 19-1 Structures and blood flow of the kidneys (From Ehrlich A, Schroeder CL. *Medical Terminology for Health Professionals*, 4th ed. Clifton Park, NY: Delmar, Cengage Learning, 2001, p. 189.).

exerted on the urethra, causing the urge to urinate. The coder may note the terms **micturate** or **voiding**, which are synonymous terms for urination. Coders must be very careful to identify the proper body part and the spelling of *urethra* and *ureter*. The spellings of these structures are very close, so paying attention to the specific terminology used in the medical record when locating a code is critical.

The **male genitalia** are made up of the scrotum, testicles, and the penis. The function of these organs is primarily for reproduction, but they also function as part of the urinary system; hence they are included in this chapter.

In the male, the urethra passes through the penis to outside the body. The **penis** functions in both the urinary and reproductive systems. The ureters move urine from the kidneys to the bladder. The urethra moves the urine from the urinary bladder to outside the body. In the reproductive function, semen moves through the vas deferens to the urethra from the ejaculatory duct.

The prostate gland, also part of the male genitalia, is located under the bladder and on the upper end of the urethra. The **prostate gland** secretes a fluid that is part of the semen and also aids in the motility of the sperm. Figure 19-2 illustrates a cross section of the male genitalia and its relation to the urethra and the urinary bladder.

The primary function of the **female genitalia** is the same as that of the male genitalia—reproduction—but because of its proximity to the urinary system, it is included in this chapter.

The female genitalia are made up of the uterus, vagina, ovaries, fallopian tubes, cervix, perineum, clitoris, labia, and mammary glands, or breasts. Figure 19-3 illustrates a cross section of the female genitalia and its relation to the urinary system.

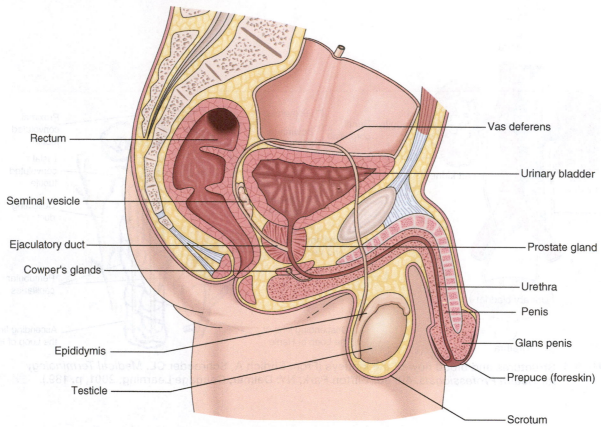

FIGURE 19-2   Cross section of the male reproductive organs (From Ehrlich A, Schroeder CL. *Medical Terminology for Health Professionals*, 4th ed. Clifton Park, NY: Delmar, Cengage Learning, 2001, p. 296.).

Coding Diseases of the Genitourinary System

This chapter of ICD-10-CM includes genitourinary diseases for both males and females.

Glomerular Diseases (Category Codes N00–N08)

This block of codes includes the following categories:

- N00, Acute nephritic syndrome
- N01, Rapidly progressive nephritic syndrome
- N02, Recurrent and persistent hematuria
- N03, Chronic nephritic syndrome
- N04, Nephrotic syndrome
- N05, Unspecified nephritic syndrome
- N06, Isolated proteinuria with specified morphological lesion
- N07, Hereditary nephropathy, not elsewhere classified
- N08, Glomerular disorders in diseases classified elsewhere

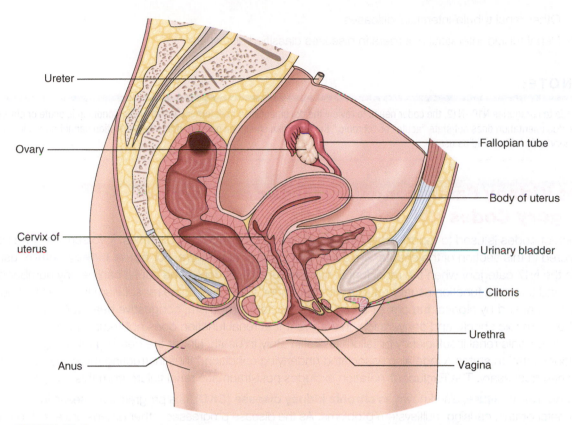

FIGURE 19-3 Cross section of the female reproductive organs (From Ehrlich A, Schroeder CL. *Medical Terminology for Health Professionals*, 4th ed. Clifton Park, NY: Delmar, Cengage Learning, 2001, p. 301.).

This block of codes reports **nephritis**, an inflammation of the kidneys. **Nephrosis** refers to a disease or disorder of the kidney. The coder may also encounter the term **nephropathy**, which is a synonymous term for nephrosis.

Some conditions that are classified to this section of the code book have separate codes for the acute and chronic manifestations of the disease. One such condition is **glomerulonephritis**, an inflammation of the glomeruli of the kidney. Acute glomerulonephritis is classified to category N00, Acute nephritic syndrome, whereas chronic glomerulonephritis is classified to category N03.

EXAMPLE: Polly Patient came in for a follow-up of her chronic glomerulonephritis. She has been feeling a little tired and she thought she should communicate this to me.

For this example, the correct code to use is N03.9.

Renal Tubulo-Interstitial Diseases (Category Codes N10–N16)

This block of codes also codes various forms of nephritis. The blocks are arranged as follows:

- N10, Acute pyelonephritis
- N11, Chronic tubulo-interstitial nephritis
- N12, Tubulo-interstitial nephritis, not specified as acute or chronic
- N13, Obstructive and reflux uropathy
- N14, Drug- and heavy-metal-induced tubulo-interstitial and tubular conditions

- N15, Other renal tubulo-interstitial diseases
- N16, Renal tubulo-interstitial disorders in diseases classified elsewhere

 NOTE:

To code to categories N10–N12, the coder needs to review the documentation to determine whether the condition is acute or chronic. If the documentation does not state "acute" or "chronic," the physician should be queried. If the determination cannot be made, then category code N12 should be used.

Acute Kidney Failure and Chronic Kidney Disease (Category Codes N17–N19)

This block of codes is used to report acute kidney failure and chronic kidney diseases. Two serious conditions encountered in this section of the chapter are acute and chronic renal failure. For **acute kidney failure**, use codes in the N17 category when the renal function is interrupted suddenly. The cause can be any number of reasons, and the renal function usually returns with treatment. Causes of acute renal failure include blockage of urine flow caused by stones, tumors, or an enlarged prostate; embolism; congestive heart failure; surgical shock; hemorrhagic shock; and dehydration. In the event that renal function does not return, the condition may progress to chronic renal insufficiency or failure and ultimately to death. Under the heading for category N17, an instructional notation states "Code also associated underlying condition," thus instructing the coder to use two codes when necessary. The Excludes1 notation excludes post-traumatic renal failure from this category.

Chronic renal failure, also known as **chronic kidney disease (CKD)**, is a progressive disease in which renal function deteriorates, causing multisystem problems. As the disease progresses, other organs are affected until the patient advances to the late stages of chronic renal failure, which is then considered **end-stage renal disease (ESRD)**. Patients with chronic renal failure may be on dialysis or awaiting a kidney transplant. Chronic kidney disease code determination is based on the stage of the disease. The diagnosis code category for chronic kidney disease is N18, and fourth or fifth characters are used to indicate the stage.

- Stage 1 involves some kidney damage with a glomerular filtration rate (GFR) slightly greater than 90, which is considered a normal GFR.
- Stage 2 has a GFR of 60–89 with mild or minor kidney damage.
- Stage 3 involves more damage to the kidney with a GFR of 30–59.
- Stage 4 has a GFR of 15–29 with severe kidney damage.
- Stage 5 involves severe kidney damage with a GFR less than 15.
- At stage 5, the patient is on dialysis or awaiting a transplant.

Category N18 contains instructional notations that appear in the Tabular List as follows:

N18 Chronic kidney disease (CKD)
Code first any associated:
diabetic chronic kidney disease (E08.22, E09.22, E10.22, E11.22, E13.22)
hypertensive chronic kidney disease (I12.–, I13.–)
Use additional code to identify kidney transplant status, if applicable (Z94.0)

Review of medical documentation is essential when coding for chronic renal failure/chronic kidney disease. The coder may encounter such phrases as "chronic renal insufficiency," "chronic renal failure," "chronic renal disease," and "chronic uremia," all of which are coded to N18.9 because the terms do not indicate the stage of the disease.

Laboratory tests are generally an indication of chronic renal failure. Elevated serum creatinine or blood urea nitrogen (BUN) values may indicate this condition. Clinical manifestations such as anemia, hypocalcemia, and renal osteodystrophy may be documented. Unless the provider has documented specifically that the patient has ESRD, renal failure, chronic renal failure, or renal insufficiency, clarification must be made before a code is assigned. Coders may assign only a diagnosis that can be supported by medical documentation, so they must be in communication with the provider for clarification of the diagnosis before assigning a code.

The ICD-10-CM Official Guidelines for Coding and Reporting on the coding of chronic kidney disease are as follows:

ICD-10-CM Official Coding Guidelines

Chronic kidney disease

1) Stages of chronic kidney disease (CKD)

The ICD-10-CM classifies CKD based on severity. The severity of CKD is designated by stages 1–5. Stage 2, code N18.2, equates to mild CKD; stage 3, codes N18.30–N18.32, equates to moderate CKD; and stage 4, code N18.4, equates to severe CKD. Code N18.6, End stage renal disease (ESRD), is assigned when the provider has documented end-stage renal disease (ESRD).

If both a stage of CKD and ESRD are documented, assign code N18.6 only.

2) Chronic kidney disease and kidney transplant status

Patients who have undergone kidney transplant may still have some form of chronic kidney disease (CKD), because the kidney transplant may not fully restore kidney function. Therefore, the presence of CKD alone does not constitute a transplant complication. Assign the appropriate N18 code for the patient's stage of CKD and code Z94.0, Kidney transplant status. If a transplant complication such as failure or rejection or other transplant complication is documented, see section I.C.19.g for information on coding complications of a kidney transplant. If the documentation is unclear as to whether the patient has a complication of the transplant, query the provider.

3) Chronic kidney disease with other conditions

Patients with CKD may also suffer from other serious conditions, most commonly diabetes mellitus and hypertension. The sequencing of the CKD code in relationship to codes for other contributing conditions is based on the conventions in the Tabular List.

See I.C.9. Hypertensive chronic kidney disease.

See I.C.19. Chronic kidney disease and kidney transplant complications. (See Appendix A, Section I, C14, 1–3.)

Urolithiasis (Category Codes N20–N23)

This block of codes is used to report some very common situations:

- N20, Calculus of kidney and ureter—A **calculus** is a stone. In this case, a kidney stone is in the kidney and/or ureter.

- N21, Calculus of lower urinary tract. This category includes calculus of the lower urinary tract with cystitis and urethritis.

- N22, Calculus of urinary tract in diseases classified elsewhere. It should be noted for category N22 that an instructional notation appears that states "Code first underlying disease, such as: gout (M1A.–, M10.–), schistosomiasis (B65.0–B65.9)."

- N23, Unspecified renal colic—**Renal colic** is an acute pain caused by the passage of a kidney stone from the kidney through the ureter.

Other Disorders of Kidney and Ureter (Category Codes N25–N29)

This block includes the following categories:

- N25, Disorders resulting from impaired renal tubular function
- N26, Unspecified contracted kidney
- N27, Small kidney of unknown cause
- N28, Other disorders of kidney and ureter, not elsewhere classified
- N29, Other disorders of kidney and ureter in diseases classified elsewhere

The N28.0 code classifies some common disorders that include renal artery embolism, renal artery obstruction, renal artery occlusion, renal artery thrombosis, and renal infarct. Other common disorders of the kidney and ureter are also coded to category N28. The fourth and fifth characters differentiate the disorders.

> **EXAMPLE:**
> Patient 1 presents with an acquired cyst of the kidney. This is reported with code N28.1.
>
> Patient 2 presents with hypertrophy of kidney. This is reported with code N28.81.
>
> Patient 3 presents with a diagnosis of megaloureter. This is reported with code N28.82.
>
> In the ICD-10-CM manual, reference category N28 for the complete code descriptions for category N28.

Other Diseases of the Urinary System (Category Codes N30–N39)

This block of codes includes:

- N30, Cystitis—**Cystitis** is an inflammation of the bladder.
- N31, Neuromuscular dysfunction of bladder, not elsewhere classified—This category includes neuropathic conditions that affect bladder function.
- N32, Other disorders of the bladder—This includes various obstructions, fistula, diverticulum of the bladder, and other specified bladder disorders.
- N33, Bladder disorders in diseases classified elsewhere
- N34, Urethritis and urethral syndrome—**Urethritis** is an inflammation of the urethra.
- N35, **Urethral stricture**—the narrowing of the urethra
- N36, Other disorders of the urethra
- N37, Urethral disorders in diseases classified elsewhere
- N39, Other disorders of urinary system

A commonly seen condition that is classified to this block of ICD-10-CM is the **urinary tract infection (UTI)**, which is an abnormal presence of microorganisms in the urine. UTIs, unspecified, are classified to code N39.0, Urinary tract infection, site not specified. The following notation appears in the Tabular List for subcategory code N39.0, which coders must use when coding UTIs:

> Use additional code (B95–B97) to identify infectious agent.

The Excludes1 notation should also be referenced because it lists UTIs that are excluded from this code.

Urinary tract infections can occur in various sites throughout the urinary tract. Figure 19-4 identifies various UTI sites. When a specific infection site is identified, ICD-10-CM assigns codes from the following categories:

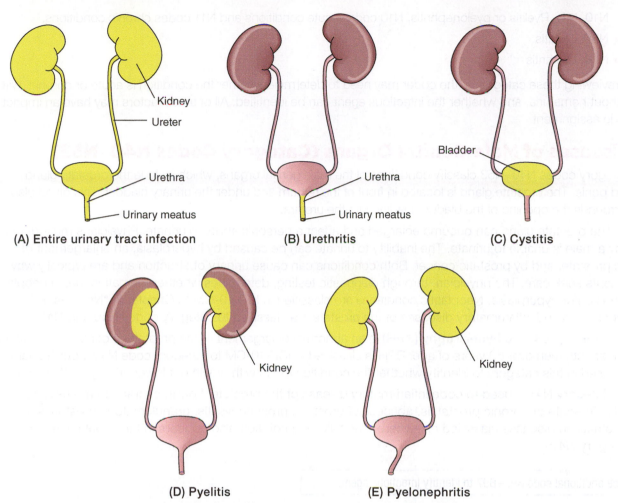

(A) Entire urinary tract infection

(B) Urethritis

(C) Cystitis

(D) Pyelitis

(E) Pyelonephritis

FIGURE 19-4 Sites of urinary tract infections.

Exercise 19.1—Code Selection for Category Codes N00–N39

For each diagnostic statement, select the appropriate ICD-10-CM diagnostic code.

Diagnosis   **Code**

1. urethral fistula   _____
2. renal failure   _____
3. ureteric stone   _____
4. pyonephrosis   _____
5. acute cortical necrosis   _____
6. vesicorectal fistula   _____
7. uremia   _____
8. abscess of urethral gland _____
9. renal osteodystrophy   _____
10. nonvenereal urethritis   _____

- N10–N11, Pyelitis or pyelonephritis, N10 codes acute conditions and N11 codes chronic conditions.
- N30, Cystitis
- N34, Urethritis

In reviewing these categories, the coder may need to determine whether the condition is acute or chronic, with or without hematuria, and whether the infectious agent can be identified. All of these factors may have an impact on code assignment.

Diseases of Male Genital Organs (Category Codes N40–N53)

Category codes N40–N53 classify conditions of the male genital organs, which include the prostate gland and penis. The prostate gland is located in front of the rectum and under the urinary bladder. This gland also surrounds the opening of the bladder leading into the urethra.

The prostate gland can become enlarged and affect a person's ability to urinate. Physicians must determine why a male is unable to urinate. The inability to urinate can be caused by hyperplasia, an enlargement of the prostate, and by prostatic cancer. Both conditions can cause urinary obstruction and are typically why patients seek care. The physician, through diagnostic testing, determines whether the patient has a neoplastic condition or hyperplasia. Neoplastic conditions are classified in ICD-10-CM to Chapter 2, "Neoplasms." Hyperplasia and inflammatory diseases of the prostate are classified to category codes N40 and N41.

Benign prostatic hypertrophy (BPH) is an abnormal enlargement of the prostate, a common condition that affects men over 60 years of age. BPH is classified in ICD-10-CM to category code N40. Fourth characters are used in this category to identify whether the condition exists with or without lower urinary tract symptoms.

Category N41 is used to code inflammatory disease of the prostate. Fourth characters are used to indicate acute or chronic prostatitis, abscess of prostate, prostatocystitis, granulomatous prostatitis, or prostatitis in diseases classified elsewhere. The following notation also appears in the Tabular List for category N41:

Use additional code B95–B97 to identify infectious agent.

Therefore, coders have to distinguish whether a specific organism has been identified as the cause of the prostatitis. Be aware of this instructional notation.

The remaining codes found in this block classify disorders of the testes, penis, and seminal vesicles. Male erectile dysfunction, N52, uses fourth and fifth characters to identify the cause of the dysfunction.

EXAMPLE:
Patient 1
DX: Erectile dysfunction due to arterial insufficiency
ICD-10-CM code: N52.01

Patient 2
DX: Erectile dysfunction following radical prostatectomy
ICD-10-CM code: N52.31

Patient 3
DX: Erectile dysfunction following simple prostatectomy
ICD-10-CM code: N52.34

Note that the fourth and fifth characters differentiate the types of erectile dysfunction. In the ICD-10-CM coding manual, reference category N52 for a completed listing of the codes for male erectile dysfunction.

Disorders of Breast (Category Codes N60–N65)

This block of codes classifies disorders of the breast. The codes are used for both males and females. Disorders of the breast are coded to different chapters within ICD-10-CM. Neoplastic conditions are classified to Chapter 2,

"Neoplasms," and other disorders of the breast that occur during pregnancy or during the postpartum period are classified to Chapter 15, "Pregnancy, Childbirth, and the Puerperium." The remaining disorders of the breast are classified to category code N60, Benign mammary dysplasia; category code N61, Inflammatory disorders of breast; category code N62, Hypertrophy of breast; N63, Unspecified lump in breast; N64, Other disorders of breast; and N65, Deformity and disproportion of reconstructed breast. It should be noted that categories N60 and N63 delineate laterality.

Review of the medical record is essential when you are coding disorders of the breast. If you have any questions about the cause of the disorders, query the provider. When a provider documents terms such as "breast lump," "cyst," or "growth," clarification is needed to determine whether the condition is of neoplastic origin. Biopsies of breast tissue are completed to determine whether the growth is neoplastic, and coders need to reference pathology reports before assigning codes for neoplastic conditions. When a provider records "mass in breast," "lump," "cyst," or "growth," use code N63, Unspecified lump in breast, until further diagnostic testing reveals the cause of the mass.

Other common non-neoplastic disorders of the breast that are classified to these codes are:

- N60.01–N60.09, Cyst of breast—A single encapsulated fluid-filled sac of the breast
- N60.11–N60.19, Diffuse cystic mastopathy, including cystic breast and fibrocystic disease of the breast—The presence of a single cyst or multiple cysts of the breast

Inflammatory Diseases of Female Pelvic Organs (Category Codes N70–N77)

This block of codes is used to report the following categories:

- N70, Salpingitis and oophoritis
- N71, Inflammatory disease of uterus, except cervix
- N72, Inflammatory disease of cervix uteri
- N73, Other female pelvic inflammatory diseases
- N74, Female pelvic inflammatory disorders in diseases classified elsewhere
- N75, Diseases of Bartholin's gland
- N76, Other inflammation of the vagina and vulva
- N77, Vulvovaginal ulceration and inflammation in diseases classified elsewhere

At the start of categories N70, N71, N72, N73, and N76, instructional notations instruct the coder to "Use additional code (B95–B97), to identify infectious agent," signaling that two codes may be needed for some diagnostic phrases. Category N74 includes a notation to "Code first underlying disease." Coders need to become familiar with the numerous notations and listings of Includes notes in this block.

Noninflammatory Disorders of the Female Genital Tract (Category Codes N80–N98)

The following disorders of the female genital tract are classified in this ICD-10-CM chapter according to the following blocks:

- N80, **Endometriosis**—This is an abnormal growth of the endometrium outside the uterus.
- N81, **Female genital prolapse**—This is the downward displacement of the genital organs. Coders must also identify whether the prolapse is diagnosed as a **complete prolapse**, when the entire uterus descends and protrudes beyond the introitus and the vagina becomes inverted, or as an **incomplete prolapse**, when the uterus descends into the introitus.
- N82, Fistulae involving female genital tract—This includes vesicovaginal fistula, uterovesical fistula, cervicovesical fistula, and other specified types of fistula.

- N83, Noninflammatory disorders of the ovary, fallopian tube, and broad ligament—This category includes **ovarian cysts**, encapsulated sacs of the ovary that are filled with a semisolid or liquid material.
- N84, Polyp of female genital tract—This category includes polyps of the corpus uteri, cervix uteri, vagina, vulva, and other parts of the female genital tract.
- N85, Other noninflammatory disorders of uterus, except cervix—This includes hypertrophy of the uterus, subinvolution of the uterus, and other malpositions of the uterus.
- N86, Erosion and ectropion of cervix uteri
- N87, Dysplasia of cervix uteri
- N88, Other non-inflammatory disorders of cervix uteri
- N89, Other noninflammatory disorders of vagina—This category includes **dysplasia**, the abnormal development or growth of cells.
- N90, Other noninflammatory disorders of the vulva and perineum
- N91, Absent, scanty, and rare menstruation
- N92, Excessive, frequent, and irregular menstruation
- N93, Other abnormal uterine and vaginal bleeding
- N94, Pain and other conditions associated with female genital organs and menstrual cycle
- N95, Menopausal and other perimenopausal disorders—This category includes menopausal and perimenopausal disorders. **Menopause** refers to the time of a woman's life when her menstrual cycle ceases. A woman may experience problems that are **premenopausal** (the time period right before menopause), **perimenopausal** (when symptoms of menopause begin, such as hot flashes), menopausal (which is marked by a woman's not having a period for one year), and **postmenopausal** (when a woman has not had a period for at least one year until the time she celebrates her 100th birthday).
- N96, Recurrent pregnancy loss
- N97, Female infertility
- N98, Complications associated with artificial fertilization

Intraoperative and Postprocedural Complications and Disorders of Genitourinary System, Not Elsewhere Classified (Category Code N99)

This category classifies intraoperative and postprocedural complications and disorders of the genitourinary system. The category is further differentiated to include the specific complication.

Summary

- The urinary system and the genital system are so closely connected that in some cases the function of one depends on the ability of the other to work properly.
- Not classified in Chapter 14 of ICD-10-CM, "Diseases of the Genitourinary System," are certain genitourinary transmissible infections, neoplasms, and conditions associated with pregnancy, childbirth, and the puerperium.
- The late stage of chronic renal failure is considered end-stage renal disease.
- The coder needs to be cautious in this chapter because of the many notes for coding underlying disease and for additional codes to identify organisms.
- Noninflammatory disorders of the female genital tract are classified to Chapter 14 of ICD-10-CM.

Internet Links

To learn more about the genitourinary system, visit **www.auanet.org/** and search on diseases of the genitourinary system.

To take an online quiz about the anatomy of the genitourinary system, visit **https://www.getbodysmart.com/urinary-system**.

To learn more about the male and female reproductive systems, visit **www.malehealthcenter.com** and **www.healthywomen.org**.

Chapter Review

True/False

Indicate whether the statement is true (T) or false (F).

1. _____ The urethra is a narrow tube connecting the kidney to the bladder.

2. _____ The mammary glands are located in the breasts.

3. _____ The prostate gland is part of the male urinary system.

4. _____ Nephrosis refers to a disease or disorder of the kidney.

5. _____ If renal failure is confirmed as being acute, codes from the N20 category are used.

Fill-in-the-Blank

Enter the appropriate term(s) to complete each statement.

6. The _____ holds urine until it is expelled from the body.

7. _____ is a progressive disease in which renal function deteriorates.

8. _____ is synonymous with nephropathy.

9. _____ marks the end of a woman's menstrual cycle.

10. The _____ filters blood to remove waste, and the _____ actually form urine.

Coding Guidelines True/False

Review the ICD-10-CM Official Guidelines for Coding and Reporting and indicate if the statement(s) is true or false.

11. _____ The ICD-10-CM classifies chronic kidney disease based on severity.

12. _____ The severity of chronic kidney disease is designated by stages 1–7.

13. _____ Code N18.7, End stage renal disease (ESRD), is assigned when the provider has documented end-stage-renal disease (ESRD).

14. _____ If both a stage of chronic kidney disease and ESRD are documented, assign code N18.6 only.

15. _____ Patients with CKD may also suffer from other serious conditions, most commonly diabetes mellitus and hypertension. The sequencing of the CKD code in relationship to codes for other contributing conditions is based on the conventions in the ICD-10-CM Index to Diseases and Injuries.

Coding Assignments

Instructions: Using an ICD-10-CM code book, assign the proper diagnosis code to the following diagnostic statements.

1. atrophy of kidney _____
2. galactorrhea not associated with childbirth _____
3. bilateral small kidneys _____
4. paralysis of the bladder _____
5. chronic renal failure _____
6. postmenopausal bleeding _____
7. dysplasia of the cervix, uteri _____
8. acute renal failure with acute cortical necrosis _____
9. hyperplasia of prostate with urinary obstruction _____
10. prolapsed urethral mucosa _____
11. renal tubular necrosis _____
12. benign prostatic hypertrophy _____
13. UTI _____
14. weakening of pubocervical tissue _____
15. ureterolithiasis _____
16. renal cortical necrosis NOS _____
17. chronic interstitial cystitis _____
18. Peyronie's disease _____
19. acute salpingo-oophoritis _____
20. overactive bladder _____
21. fibrosclerosis of breast _____
22. atrophy of the spermatic cord _____
23. azoospermia _____
24. abscess of the epididymis _____
25. glomerulitis _____
26. acute pyelitis _____
27. pyelonephritis _____
28. acquired bladder-neck stenosis _____
29. benign cyst of prepuce _____
30. atrophy of breast _____
31. diffuse cystic mastopathy of right breast _____
32. right testicular pain _____
33. acquired buried penis _____

34. leukoplakia of penis   _____

35. benign cyst of testis   _____

Case Studies

Instructions: Review each case study and select the correct ICD-10-CM diagnostic code.

Case 1

Physician Office Note

This 50-year-old patient was seen today in follow-up for renal insufficiency.

HISTORY OF THE PRESENT ILLNESS: The patient had a renal biopsy that showed focal and segmental glomerular sclerosis. He was placed on Vasotec but developed hyperkalemia, and then the Vasotec was stopped.

ALLERGIES: NKA

PHYSICAL EXAM:

BP: 170/90, Pulse: 88, Respirations: 19

HEENT: Fundi are unremarkable. PERRLA

NECK: No JVD, adenopathy, or goiter

LUNGS: Clear

CARDIAC: Regular rate and rhythm without murmurs, rubs, or gallops

ABDOMEN: Soft, nontender, no masses

LABORATORY DATA: His most recent data completed on August 1, 20XX, showed his sedimentation rate at 50, potassium at 5.3, BUN 75, creatinine 3.8, potassium down to 5.1, and calcium 9.6 with an albumin of 3.2. WBC is 16.4, hemoglobin 9.1, and platelets 530.

DIAGNOSTIC IMPRESSION: Chronic nephritic syndrome with focal and segmental sclerosis

MEDICATIONS ORDERED: Diovan 80 mg daily

Instructed him to follow a low-potassium diet and follow up with me in 1 month.

ICD-10-CM Code Assignment: _____

Case 2

Discharge Summary

PERTINENT HISTORY: The patient is a 31-year-old white female admitted from my office because of increasing abdominal pain. The patient is gravida II, para II. The pain has been

(continues)

(continued)

present for the last 6 months, occurring more severely the day before the onset of menses. The pain radiated down her back, vagina, and her lower abdomen.

HOSPITAL COURSE:

Pelvis exam revealed generalized tenderness. A laparoscopy revealed endometriosis of pelvic peritoneum. The patient was counseled as to available treatment options, which include hormonal therapy, surgical resection, or electrocautery. After pain management, she was discharged in 1 day. She wishes to discuss the treatment options with her husband.

DISCHARGE INSTRUCTIONS TO PATIENT: Patient was instructed to see me in my office in 3 days.

ICD-10-CM Code Assignment: _____

Case 3

Skilled Nursing Facility Progress Note

VITAL SIGNS: BP: 120/80, Weight: 165 pounds, Temperature: 100.1

This 84-year-old man was seen today at the request of the charge nurse. The patient is experiencing urinary retention. No other complaints were noted by patient.

EXAM:

HEENT: Normal

CHEST: Lungs are clear.

HEART: Normal sinus rhythm. No murmurs noted.

ABDOMEN: Soft, nontender. No masses noted.

RECTAL: Smooth enlarged prostate, no other findings noted.

Because of the enlarged prostate I ordered a PSA to rule out prostate cancer because the patient has not had a previous PSA completed. The following tests were also ordered: urinalysis and urine culture.

Patient will be seen again when results are received.

ICD-10-CM Code Assignment: _____

Case 4

ED Summary Note

Eric presented to the ED with severe flank pain, hematuria, and a palpable flank mass. He said the pain was 10 on the pain scale. He had a dull pain for most of the day, but pain escalated

(continues)

(*continued*)

over the last hour. Dr. Smith ordered a renal scan and ultrasound. Eric was diagnosed with hydronephrosis. He was sent home on pain medications and antibiotic therapy.

ICD-10-CM Code Assignment: _____

Case 5

Physician Office Visit

Mrs. Vinton presents with complaint of painful urination. She states she has pain and burning when urinating. She also notes that she feels urgency and has recently started with low back pain over the last 24 hours. A urinalysis was positive for pyuria, the culture showing 150,000 organisms/mL. She was diagnosed with cystitis. She was started on antibiotics.

ICD-10-CM Code Assignment: _____

Case 6

Physician Office Note

This 25-year-old female patient presents today with dysuria, flank pain, and low back pain. Symptoms have been present for 3 days. Urinalysis was completed and showed 110,000 bacteria per milliliter and C&S showed *E. coli* present. Prescription was written for antibiotics to treat the urinary tract infection. Patient was to return to my office in 10 days for follow-up urinalysis.

ICD-10-CM Code Assignment: _____

Case 7

Emergency Department Note

This 51-year-old male patient presents to the ED with extreme pain stating that "This is the worst pain I have ever had in my life." The pain is in his lower back area. Urinalysis shows hematuria. Ultrasound shows renal calculi of the kidney and ureter. I have called in Dr. Smith for a urinary consultation.

ICD-10-CM Code Assignment: _____

Case 8

Discharge Summary

This 73-year-old male patient is being discharged today following a 4-day length of stay for his stage 4 renal disease. During this admission he received dialysis and we discussed that the disease is progressing. His medications were adjusted and he will continue dialysis as an outpatient.

ICD-10-CM Code Assignment: _____

Case 9

Hospital Admission Note

This 46-year-old female is being admitted today for IV antibiotic therapy because she has been treated for acute pyelonephritis for the last 10 days with no improvement in her symptoms. She is experiencing chills, fever, and flank pain and nausea. I have scheduled an ultrasound to determine if the kidney is enlarged. I will return to see her later today following the results of the ultrasound.

ICD-10-CM Code Assignment: _____

Case 10

Ambulatory Surgery Discharge Note

This male patient underwent a hydrocelectomy following trauma to his scrotum that resulted in a hydrocele on his left testis. The surgery was uneventful and he is instructed to return to my office in 1 week.

ICD-10-CM Code Assignment: _____

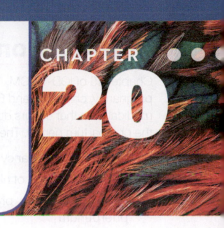

Pregnancy, Childbirth, and the Puerperium

Chapter Outline

Chapter Objectives

At the conclusion of this chapter, you should be able to:

1. Identify the terminology related to pregnancy.
2. Explain the complications encountered during pregnancy and how they affect code assignment.
3. Apply the ICD-10-CM coding guidelines to accurately code conditions during pregnancy, childbirth, and the puerperium.
4. Select the final character indicating the trimester of pregnancy.
5. Select and code diagnoses from case studies.

Key Terms

Abruptio placentae	Embryo	Missed abortion	Postpartum
Antepartum	Fetus	Molar pregnancy	Puerperium
Childbirth	Labor and delivery	Obstetrical care	Uterus
Complete placenta previa	Legally induced	Partial placenta previa	
Ectopic pregnancy	abortion	Placenta previa	

REMINDER: As you work through this chapter, you will need to have a copy of the ICD-10-CM coding book to reference. For this chapter, you will also need to reference the ICD-10-CM Official Guidelines for Coding and Reporting. These guidelines can be found in Appendix A which are now available on the Student Companion site and MINDTAP From Cengage.

Introduction

Chapter 15 of ICD-10-CM, "Pregnancy, Childbirth, and the Puerperium," classifies conditions that occur during pregnancy, childbirth, and 6 weeks after delivery. This chapter also codes normal deliveries. **Obstetrical care**, medical care that occurs during pregnancy and delivery, is divided into the antepartum period, labor and delivery, and the postpartum period. The blocks of codes found in this chapter are as follows:

- O00–O08, Pregnancy with abortive outcome
- O09, Supervision of high-risk pregnancy
- O10–O16, Edema, proteinuria, and hypertensive disorders in pregnancy, childbirth, and the puerperium
- O20–O29, Other maternal disorders predominantly related to pregnancy
- O30–O48, Maternal care related to the fetus and amniotic cavity and possible delivery problems
- O60–O77, Complications of labor and delivery
- O80–O82, Encounter for delivery
- O85–O92, Complications predominantly related to the puerperium
- O94–O9A, Other obstetric conditions, not elsewhere classified

Introduction to the Body System

To code from this section correctly, coders need to understand the terminology associated with the different stages of maternity and delivery care. Through the eighth week of pregnancy, the developing child is known as an **embryo**. From the ninth week until birth, the developing child is referred to as a **fetus**. When a fetus has reached the point at which it is capable of living outside the uterus, childbirth occurs. Figure 20-1 illustrates the position of a fetus at term. The **uterus** sits above the cervix and is the part of the female anatomy that houses the fetus until birth. Pregnancy, in most cases, takes 40 weeks. In some instances, conditions or problems alter the length of time a woman is pregnant.

Antepartum encompasses the time before childbirth. **Childbirth** refers to the delivery of one or more infants and is referred to as **labor and delivery**. The term **puerperium** relates to the postpartum period, which begins immediately after delivery and lasts for 6 weeks. **Postpartum** means after childbirth.

The ICD-10-CM Official Guidelines for Coding and Reporting define the postpartum and peripartum periods in the guidelines as follows:

ICD-10-CM Official Coding Guidelines

1) Peripartum and postpartum periods

The postpartum period begins immediately after delivery and continues for six weeks following delivery. The peripartum period is defined as the last month of pregnancy to five months postpartum.

2) Peripartum and Postpartum complication

A postpartum complication is any complication occurring within the six-week period. (See Appendix A, Section I, C15, o 1-2.)

Courtesy of the Centers for Medicare & Medicaid Services, www.cms.gov

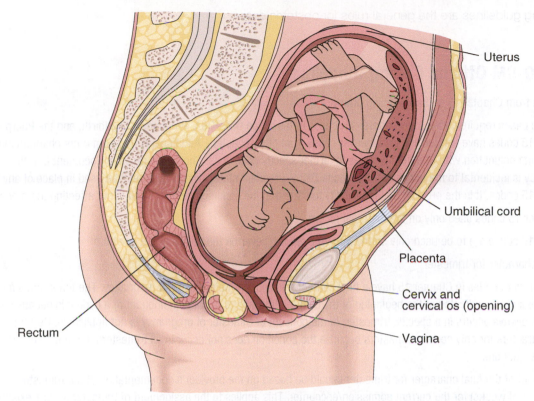

FIGURE 20-1 Position of a fetus at term (From Lindh WQ. *Delmar's Comprehensive Medical Assisting: Administrative and Clinical Competencies,* 2nd ed. Clifton Park, NY: Delmar, Cengage Learning, 2002, p. 461.).

Coding for Pregnancy, Childbirth, and the Puerperium

Chapter 15 of ICD-10-CM, "Pregnancy, Childbirth and the Puerperium," is governed by numerous notations that appear at the start of the chapter. For proper code selection, you must understand and follow three notations that appear in the coding manual after the heading for Chapter 15. The notations state the following:

 N O T E :

Codes from this chapter are for use only on maternal records, never on newborn records.

Codes from this chapter are for use for conditions related to or aggravated by pregnancy, childbirth, or by the puerperium (maternal causes or obstetric cause).

 N O T E :

Trimesters are counted from the first day of the last menstrual period. They are defined as follows:

1st trimester—less than 14 weeks 0 days

2nd trimester—14 weeks 0 days to less than 28 weeks 0 days

3rd trimester—28 weeks 0 days until delivery

Use additional code from category Z3A, weeks of gestation, to identify the specific week of the pregnancy if known.

The following guidelines are the general rules for obstetric cases:

ICD-10-CM Official Coding Guidelines

1) Codes from Chapter 15 and sequencing priority

Obstetric cases require codes from Chapter 15, codes in the range O00–O9A, Pregnancy, Childbirth, and the Puerperium. Chapter 15 codes have sequencing priority over codes from other chapters. Additional codes from other chapters may be used in conjunction with Chapter 15 codes to further specify conditions. Should the provider document that the pregnancy is incidental to the encounter, then code Z33.1, Pregnant state, incidental, should be used in place of any Chapter 15 codes. It is the provider's responsibility to state that the condition being treated is not affecting the pregnancy.

2) Chapter 15 codes used only on the maternal record

Chapter 15 codes are to be used only on the maternal record, never on the record of the newborn.

3) Final character for trimester

The majority of codes in Chapter 15 have a final character indicating the trimester of pregnancy. The timeframes for the trimesters are indicated at the beginning of the chapter. If trimester is not a component of a code it is because the condition always occurs in a specific trimester, or the concept of trimester of pregnancy is not applicable. Certain codes have characters for only certain trimesters because the condition does not occur in all trimesters, but it may occur in more than just one.

Assignment of the final character for trimester should be based on the provider's documentation of the trimester (or number of weeks) for the current admission/encounter. This applies to the assignment of trimester for pre-existing conditions as well as those that develop during or are due to the pregnancy. The provider's documentation of the number of weeks may be used to assign the appropriate code identifying the trimester.

Whenever delivery occurs during the current admission, and there is an "in childbirth" option for the obstetric complication being coded, the "in childbirth" code should be assigned.

4) Selection of trimester for inpatient admissions that encompass more than one trimester

In instances when a patient is admitted to a hospital for complications of pregnancy during one trimester and remains in the hospital into a subsequent trimester, the trimester character for the antepartum complication code should be assigned on the basis of the trimester when the complication developed, not the trimester of discharge. If the condition developed prior to the current admission/encounter or represents a pre-existing condition, the trimester character for the trimester at the time of the admission/encounter should be assigned.

5) Unspecified trimester

Each category that includes codes for trimester has a code for "unspecified trimester." The "unspecified trimester" code should rarely be used, such as when the documentation in the record is insufficient to determine the trimester and it is not possible to obtain clarification.

6) 7th character for fetus identification

Where applicable, a 7th character is to be assigned for certain categories (O31, O32, O33.3–O33.6, O35, O36, O40, O41, O60.1, O60.2, O64 and O69) to identify the fetus for which the complication code applies.

Assign 7th character "0":

- For single gestations
- When the documentation in the record is insufficient to determine the fetus affected and it is not possible to obtain clarification.
- When it is not possible to clinically determine which fetus is affected.

(See Appendix A, Section I, C15, a 1-6.)

Courtesy of the Centers for Medicare & Medicaid Services, www.cms.gov

Any conditions encountered during a pregnancy or postpartum period are coded to this chapter as a complication unless the provider documents that such a condition is incidental to the pregnancy. The documentation must clearly state that the visit was not directly related to the pregnancy. In this case, a Z33.1, Pregnant state, incidental, should be used instead of codes from this chapter.

> **EXAMPLE:** A female presents with sinus pressure and pain for the past 3 days; no over-the-counter (OTC) medications were tried because she is pregnant for approximately 24 weeks. The diagnosis is acute sinusitis. Although the decision for medication is affected by the pregnancy, the visit is for a condition not directly related to it. The code assignment is J01.90 as the primary diagnosis for the acute sinusitis, along with the Z33.1 as the second code.

Pregnancy with Abortive Outcome (Category Codes O00–O08) and Supervision of High-Risk Pregnancy (Category Code O09)

This block of codes is divided into the following categories, with the use of fourth, fifth, and at times sixth characters:

- O00, Ectopic pregnancy
- O01, Hydatidiform mole
- O02, Other abnormal products of conception
- O03, Spontaneous abortion
- O04, Complications following (induced) termination of pregnancy
- O07, Failed attempted termination of pregnancy
- O08, Complications following ectopic and molar pregnancy
- O09, Supervision of high-risk pregnancy

Category O00, Ectopic pregnancy, and code O02.0, Blighted ovum and nonhydatidiform mole, classify ectopic and molar pregnancy. An **ectopic pregnancy** is one that occurs outside the uterus. Abdominal, tubal, and ovarian pregnancies are all included in this section. If a blighted ovum in the uterus develops into a mole or benign tumor, this is considered a **molar pregnancy**. The products of conception have not yet developed into a fetus in these cases. When the current episode of care is for an ectopic or molar pregnancy, a code is assigned to represent the ectopic or molar pregnancy as the principal or first-listed diagnosis. A code from the O08 category can be used secondarily to describe the complication. Figure 20-2 illustrates an ectopic pregnancy.

Code O02.1 is used for a missed abortion. A **missed abortion** is one in which a fetus has died before the completion of 20 weeks' gestation with the retention of the dead fetus. Abnormal products of conception, which include carneous mole, hydatidiform mole, and blighted ovum, are reported by using category O01, Hydatidiform mole, or category O02, Other abnormal products of conception. It should be noted that following categories O01 and O02 an instructional notation appears that states: "Use additional code from category O08 to identify an associated complication." Categories O01 and O02 contain additional characters for which the coding manual needs to be referenced.

Category O03 reports spontaneous abortions. A spontaneous abortion is the complete or incomplete expulsion of products of conception before a pregnancy goes beyond 22 weeks' gestation. The O03 category is differentiated according to the types of complications.

Category O04 reports complications following (induced) termination of pregnancy. The coding manual needs to be referenced for the assignment of fourth, and at times fifth characters for category O04. An abortion that is induced by medical personnel working within the law is considered a **legally induced abortion**. The legally induced abortion can be elective or for therapeutic reasons such as when the mother's health is in danger.

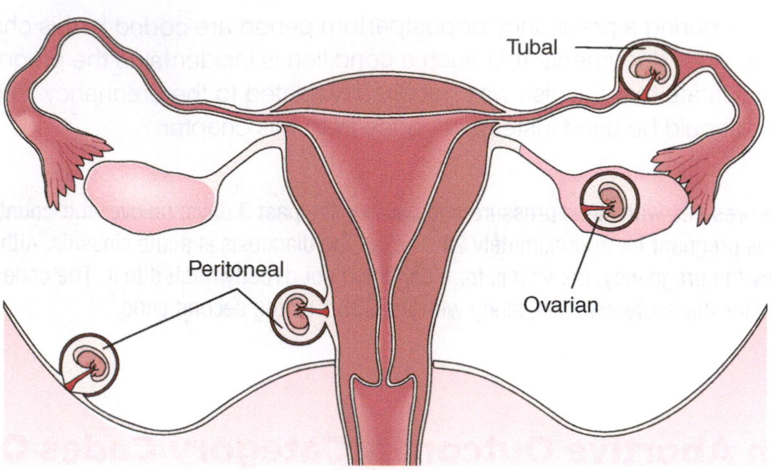

FIGURE 20-2 An ectopic pregnancy (From Lindh WQ. *Delmar's Comprehensive Medical Assisting: Administrative and Clinical Competencies,* 2nd ed. Clifton Park, NY: Delmar, Cengage Learning, 2002, p. 463.).

The following coding guidelines are used for coding abortions:

ICD-10-CM Official Coding Guidelines

q. Termination of Pregnancy and Spontaneous Abortions

1) Abortion with Liveborn Fetus

When an attempted termination of pregnancy results in a liveborn fetus assign code Z33.2, Encounter for elective termination of pregnancy and a code from category Z37, Outcome of Delivery.

2) Retained Products of Conception following an abortion

Subsequent encounters for retained products of conception following a spontaneous abortion or elective termination of pregnancy, without complications are assigned O03.4, Incomplete spontaneous, abortion without complication or codes O07.4, Failed attempted termination of pregnancy without complication. This advice is appropriate even when the patient was discharged previously with a discharge diagnosis of complete abortion. If the patient has a specific complication associated with the spontaneous abortion or elective termination of pregnancy in addition to retained products of conception, assign the appropriate complication code (e.g., O03.-, O04.-, O07.-) instead of code O03.4 or O07.4.

3) Complications leading to abortion

Codes from Chapter 15 may be used as additional codes to identify any documented complications of the pregnancy in conjunction with codes in categories in O04, O07 and O08.

(See Appendix A, Section I. C15.q 1-3.)

Courtesy of the Centers for Medicare & Medicaid Services, www.cms.gov

Category O07 reports failed attempted termination of pregnancy. This includes failure of attempted induction of termination of pregnancy and incomplete elective abortion. Fourth characters identify complications following the failed attempted termination of pregnancy. Fifth characters are also needed for some conditions.

Category O08 reports complications following an ectopic or molar pregnancy. Sepsis following ectopic or molar pregnancy is reported with code O08.82. The following guideline applies to this code and to other Chapter 15 codes for sepsis that complicates abortion, pregnancy, childbirth, and the puerperium:

ICD-10-CM Official Coding Guidelines

j. Sepsis and septic shock complicating abortion, pregnancy, childbirth, and the puerperium

When assigning a Chapter 15 code for sepsis complicating abortion, pregnancy, childbirth, and the puerperium, a code for the specific type of infection should be assigned as an additional diagnosis.
If severe sepsis is present, a code from subcategory R65.2, Severe sepsis, and code(s) for associated organ dysfunction(s) should also be assigned as additional diagnoses.

k. Puerperal sepsis

Code O85, Puerperal sepsis, should be assigned with a secondary code to identify the causal organism (e.g., for a bacterial infection, assign a code from category B95-B96, Bacterial infections in conditions classified elsewhere). A code from category A40, Streptococcal sepsis, or A41, Other sepsis, should not be used for puerperal sepsis. If applicable, use additional codes to identify severe sepsis (R65.2-) and any associated acute organ dysfunction. Code O85 should not be assigned for sepsis following an obstetrical procedure (See Section I.C.1.d.5.b., Sepsis due to a postprocedural infection). (See Appendix A, Section I. C15. j-k.)

Courtesy of the Centers for Medicare & Medicaid Services, www.cms.gov

Category O09, Supervision of high-risk pregnancy, is used when a provider is managing the care for a woman who is a high-risk pregnancy. The pregnancy can be high risk due to:

- A history of infertility
- A history of ectopic or molar pregnancy
- Other poor reproductive or obstetric history
- Insufficient antenatal care
- Grand multiparity
- Elderly primigravida and multigravida—elderly is defined as a pregnancy for a 35-year-old female and older at expected date of delivery.
- Young primigravida and multigravida—young is defined as a pregnancy for a female less than 16 years old at expected date of delivery.
- Social problems
- Use of assisted reproductive technology

The following coding guideline applies:

ICD-10-CM Official Coding Guidelines

Supervision of high-risk pregnancy

Codes from category O09, Supervision of high-risk pregnancy, are intended for use only during the prenatal period. For complications during the labor or delivery episode as a result of a high-risk pregnancy, assign the applicable complication code from Chapter 15. If there are no complications during the labor or delivery episode, assign code O80, Encounter for full-term uncomplicated delivery.

For routine prenatal outpatient visits for patients with high-risk pregnancies, a code from category O09, Supervision of high-risk pregnancy, should be used as the first-listed diagnosis. Secondary Chapter 15 codes may be used in conjunction with these codes if appropriate. (See Appendix A, Section I. C15. b.2.)

Courtesy of the Centers for Medicare & Medicaid Services, www.cms.gov

Routine Outpatient Prenatal Visits

When routine outpatient prenatal visits occur, the following coding guideline applies to code assignment:

ICD-10-CM Official Coding Guidelines

1. Routine outpatient prenatal visits

For routine outpatient prenatal visits when no complications are present, a code from category Z34, Encounter for supervision of normal pregnancy, should be used as the first-listed diagnosis. These codes should not be used in conjunction with Chapter 15 codes. (See Appendix A, Section I, C15,b 1.)

Edema, Proteinuria, and Hypertensive Disorders in Pregnancy, Childbirth, and the Puerperium (Category Codes O10–O16)

This block of codes reports edema, proteinuria, and hypertensive disorders complicating pregnancy, childbirth, and the puerperium:

- O10, Preexisting hypertension complicating pregnancy, childbirth, and the puerperium
- O11, Preexisting hypertension with pre-eclampsia
- O12, Gestational [pregnancy-induced] edema and proteinuria without hypertension
- O13, Gestational [pregnancy-induced] hypertension without significant proteinuria
- O14, Pre-eclampsia
- O15, Eclampsia
- O16, Unspecified maternal hypertension

The following guidelines apply to this section:

ICD-10-CM Official Coding Guidelines

c. Pre-existing conditions versus conditions due to the pregnancy

Certain categories in Chapter 15 distinguish between conditions of the mother that existed prior to pregnancy (pre-existing) and those that are a direct result of pregnancy. When assigning codes from Chapter 15, it is important to assess if a condition was pre-existing prior to pregnancy or developed during or due to the pregnancy in order to assign the correct code.

Categories that do not distinguish between pre-existing and pregnancy-related conditions may be used for either. It is acceptable to use codes specifically for the puerperium with codes complicating pregnancy and childbirth if a condition arises postpartum during the delivery encounter.

d. Pre-existing hypertension in pregnancy

Category O10, Pre-existing hypertension complicating pregnancy, childbirth, and the puerperium, includes codes for hypertensive heart and hypertensive chronic kidney disease. When assigning one of the O10 codes that includes hypertensive heart disease or hypertensive chronic kidney disease, it is necessary to add a secondary code from the appropriate hypertension category to specify the type of heart failure or chronic kidney disease.

See Section I.C.9. Hypertension. (See Appendix A, Section I. C15.c-d.)

Other Maternal Disorders Predominantly Related to Pregnancy (Category Codes O20–O29)

This block of codes reports the following:

- O20, Hemorrhage in early pregnancy
- O21, Excessive vomiting in pregnancy
- O22, Venous complications and hemorrhoids in pregnancy
- O23, Infections of genitourinary tract in pregnancy
- O24, Diabetes mellitus in pregnancy, childbirth, and the puerperium
- O25, Malnutrition in pregnancy, childbirth, and the puerperium
- O26, Maternal care for other conditions predominantly related to pregnancy
- O28, Abnormal findings on antenatal screening of mother
- O29, Complications of anesthesia during pregnancy

This block of codes reports many types of disorders, including:

- O20.0, Threatened abortion
- O21.0–O21.1, Hyperemesis
- O26.20–O26.23, Pregnancy care of habitual aborter

A complication that should be noted is gestational diabetes (category code O24). The following guidelines apply to diabetes mellitus in pregnancy and gestational diabetes:

ICD-10-CM Official Coding Guidelines

g. Diabetes mellitus in pregnancy

Diabetes mellitus is a significant complicating factor in pregnancy. Pregnant women who are diabetic should be assigned a code from category O24, Diabetes mellitus in pregnancy, childbirth, and the puerperium, first, followed by the appropriate diabetes code(s) (E08–E13) from Chapter 4.

h. Long-term use of insulin

See section I.C.4.a.3 for information on the long term use of insulin and oral hypoglycemic.

i. Gestational (pregnancy induced) diabetes

Gestational (pregnancy induced) diabetes can occur during the second and third trimester of pregnancy in women who were not diabetic prior to pregnancy. Gestational diabetes can cause complications in the pregnancy similar to those of pre-existing diabetes mellitus. It also puts the woman at greater risk of developing diabetes after the pregnancy. Codes for gestational diabetes are in subcategory O24.4, Gestational diabetes mellitus. No other code from category O24, Diabetes mellitus in pregnancy, childbirth, and the puerperium, should be used with a code from O24.4.

The codes under subcategory O24.4 include diet controlled, insulin controlled, and controlled by oral hypoglycemic drugs. If a patient with gestational diabetes is treated with both diet and insulin, only the code for insulin-controlled is required. If a patient with gestational diabetes is treated with both diet and oral hypoglycemic medications, only the code for "controlled by oral hypoglycemic drugs" is required.

Code Z79.4, Long-term (current) use of insulin or code Z79.84, Long-term (current) use of oral hypoglycemic drugs, should not be assigned with codes from subcategory O24.4.

An abnormal glucose tolerance in pregnancy is assigned a code from subcategory O99.81, Abnormal glucose complicating pregnancy, childbirth, and the puerperium. (See Appendix A, Section I. C15. g-i.)

Courtesy of the Centers for Medicare & Medicaid Services, www.cms.gov

Maternal Care Related to the Fetus and Amniotic Cavity and Possible Delivery Problems (Category Codes O30-O48)

This block contains the following categories:

- O30, Multiple gestation
- O31, Complications specific to multiple gestation
- O32, Maternal care for malpresentation of fetus
- O33, Maternal care for disproportion
- O34, Maternal care for abnormality of pelvic organs
- O35, Maternal care for known or suspected fetal abnormality and damage
- O36, Maternal care for other fetal problems
- O40, Polyhydramnios
- O41, Other disorders of amniotic fluid and membranes
- O42, Premature rupture of membranes
- O43, Placental disorders
- O44, Placenta previa
- O45, Premature separation of placenta (abruptio placentae)
- O46, Antepartum hemorrhage, not elsewhere classified
- O47, False labor
- O48, Late pregnancy

Category O35, Maternal care for known or suspected fetal abnormality and damage, and category O36, Maternal care for other fetal problems, are governed by the following coding guideline:

ICD-10-CM Official Coding Guidelines

Fetal Condition Affecting the Management of the Mother

1) Codes from categories O35 and O36

Codes from categories O35, Maternal care for known or suspected fetal abnormality and damage, and O36, Maternal care for other fetal problems, are assigned only when the fetal condition is actually responsible for modifying the management of the mother, i.e., by requiring diagnostic studies, additional observation, special care, or termination of pregnancy. The fact that the fetal condition exists does not justify assigning a code from this series to the mother's record.

2) In utero surgery

In cases when surgery is performed on the fetus, a diagnosis code from category O35, Maternal care for known or suspected fetal abnormality and damage, should be assigned identifying the fetal condition. Assign the appropriate procedure code for the procedure performed.

No code from Chapter 16, the perinatal codes, should be used on the mother's record to identify fetal conditions. Surgery performed in utero on a fetus is still to be coded as an obstetric encounter. (See Appendix A, Section I. C15. e 1-2.)

Courtesy of the Centers for Medicare & Medicaid Services, www.cms.gov

Two conditions that can complicate pregnancies are Abruptio placentae, category O45, and Placenta previa, category O44.

Disease Highlight—Abruptio Placentae

When there is a premature sudden separation of the placenta from the uterus prior to or during labor, the patient is said to have **abruptio placentae**. The abrupt separation can be caused by trauma, chronic hypertension, convulsions, and multiple births (see Figure 20-3).

Signs and Symptoms:

The presenting signs and symptoms are determined by the amount of separation of the placenta. When a partial separation occurs, the patient may be asymptomatic. When a complete separation occurs:

- The patient needs to seek medical care quickly because a complete separation can lead to maternal and fetal death.
- The mother may experience severe abdominal pain with vaginal bleeding.
- Shock can also occur.
- Fetal heart tones and fetal activity decrease due to the lack of oxygen and nutrition being supplied to the fetus.

Clinical Testing:

Because of the urgency of the condition, diagnosis is made based on clinical history and observation. At times a uterine ultrasound is completed.

Treatment:

If the placenta separation is partial, the patient is placed on bed rest and may be hospitalized to monitor the mother and fetus.

If the placenta separation is complete:

- The patient is prepared for delivery.
- Continuous fetal monitoring is started to determine fetal distress.
- Often a cesarean section is performed.
- If the mother has lost a significant amount of blood, she is given units of blood.

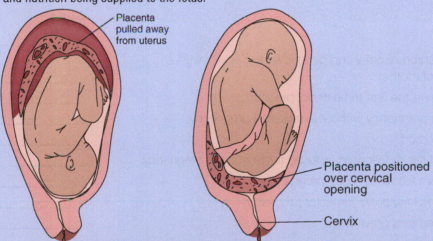

Placenta pulled away from uterus

Placenta positioned over cervical opening

Cervix

FIGURE 20-3 Abruptio placentae and placenta previa (From Neighbors M., Tannehill-Jones R. *Human Diseases,* 2nd ed. Clifton Park, NY: Delmar, Cengage Learning, 2002, p. 323.).

Placenta previa is another complication that occurs during pregnancy.

Disease Highlight—Placenta Previa

Placenta previa is the abnormal positioning of the placenta in the lower uterus so that the cervical os is partially or completely covered.

- A **complete placenta previa** occurs when the placenta entirely covers the cervical os.

- A **partial placenta previa** occurs when the placenta covers part of the cervical os.

Risk factors include:

- Maternal age greater than 35
- Large or abnormal placenta formation

- Multiparity
- Previous uterine surgery
- Smoking

Signs and Symptoms:

The patient has spotting during the first and second trimester. During the third trimester, the patient may have bright red vaginal bleeding and uterine cramping. If the bleeding is severe, the patient may experience shock, which can be life threatening.

Clinical Testing:

Pelvic ultrasound is completed to visualize the placenta.

Treatment:

The treatment is determined by the extent of the placenta previa.

- Medications may be administered to prevent premature labor and to stop contractions.
- If there is minimal bleeding, the patient is placed on bed rest and observed.
- If the bleeding is severe or if the fetus is in distress, an emergency cesarean section is performed.

Blood transfusions may also be necessary.

Exercise 20.1—Coding for Categories O00–O48

For each diagnostic statement, select the appropriate ICD-10-CM diagnostic code. Do not assign Z codes for this exercise.

Diagnosis	Code
1. false labor	_____
2. abnormal chromosomal and genetic finding on antenatal screening of mother	_____
3. malnutrition in the first trimester of pregnancy	_____
4. left ovarian pregnancy without intrauterine pregnancy	_____
5. missed abortion	_____
6. acute renal failure following induced termination of pregnancy	_____
7. fat embolism following molar pregnancy	_____
8. hemorrhoids in second-trimester pregnancy	_____
9. mild hyperemesis gravidarum	_____
10. polyhydramnios	_____

Complications of Labor and Delivery (Category Codes O60–O77)

Complications that occur during labor and delivery are classified to category codes O60–O77. These include preterm labor, failed induction of labor, abnormalities of forces of labor, long labor, obstructed labor, complication of intrapartum hemorrhage, abnormality of fetal acid-base balance, umbilical cord complications, perineal laceration during labor, obstetric trauma, postpartum hemorrhage, retained placenta, and other complications during labor and delivery.

Coders should carefully read the medical documentation to determine the type of complication that occurred during labor and delivery. To locate these codes, coders should reference the main term "Delivery" in the Alphabetic Index and then the subterm "complicated" and then further reference the complications listed.

Use category O64, Obstructed labor due to malposition and malpresentation of fetus, to report labor obstructed by abnormal positions and presentation of the newborn. Figure 20-4 illustrates various delivery positions.

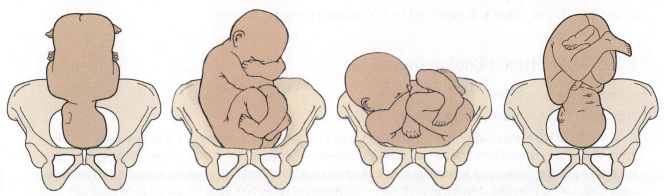

FIGURE 20-4 Delivery positions: (A) occiput anterior (normal); (B) breech; (C) transverse; (D) occiput posterior (From Sormunen C. *Terminology for Allied Health Professions,* 5th ed. Clifton Park, NY: Delmar, Cengage Learning, 2002, p. 420.).

Encounter for Delivery (Category Codes O80 and O82)

Two category codes are used to code deliveries: O80, Encounter for full-term uncomplicated delivery, and O82, Encounter for cesarean delivery without indication. These categories are defined in the tabular listing as follows:

O80 Encounter for full-term uncomplicated delivery
Delivery requiring minimal or no assistance, with or without episiotomy, without fetal manipulation [e.g., rotation version] or instrumentation [forceps] of a spontaneous, cephalic, vaginal, full-term, single, live-born infant. This code is for use as a single diagnosis code and is not to be used with any other code from Chapter 15. Use additional code to indicate outcome of delivery (Z37.0)
O82 Encounter for cesarean delivery without indication
This code must be accompanied by a delivery code from the appropriate procedure classification. Use additional code to indicate outcome of delivery (Z37.0)

Figure 20-5 illustrates the presentation of a fetus during normal delivery.

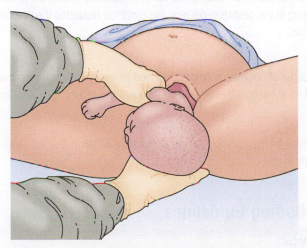

FIGURE 20-5 Presentation of a fetus during normal delivery (From Ehrlich A, Schroeder CL. *Medical Terminology for Health Professionals,* 4th ed. Clifton Park, NY: Delmar, Cengage Learning, 2001, p. 311.).

Code O80, Normal delivery, is governed by the following coding guidelines:

ICD-10-CM Official Coding Guidelines

n. Normal Delivery, Code O80

1) Encounter for full term uncomplicated delivery

Code O80 should be assigned when a woman is admitted for a full-term normal delivery and delivers a single, healthy infant without any complications antepartum, during the delivery, or postpartum during the delivery episode. Code O80 is always a principal diagnosis. It is not to be used if any other code from Chapter 15 is needed to describe a current complication of the antenatal, delivery, or postnatal period. Additional codes from other chapters may be used with code O80 if they are not related to or are in any way complicating the pregnancy.

2) Uncomplicated delivery with resolved antepartum complication

Code O80 may be used if the patient had a complication at some point during the pregnancy, but the complication is not present at the time of the admission for delivery.

3) Outcome of delivery for O80

Z37.0, Single live birth, is the only outcome of delivery code appropriate for use with O80. (See Appendix A, Section I. C15.n 1-3.)

Delivery cases are also governed by these additional guidelines:

ICD-10-CM Official Coding Guidelines

4) When a delivery occurs

When an obstetric patient is admitted and delivers during that admission, the condition that prompted the admission should be sequenced as the principal diagnosis. If multiple conditions prompted the admission, sequence the one most related to the delivery as the principal diagnosis. A code for any complication of the delivery should be assigned as an additional diagnosis. In cases of cesarean delivery, if the patient was admitted with a condition that resulted in the performance of a cesarean procedure, that condition should be selected as the principal diagnosis. If the reason for the admission was unrelated to the condition resulting in the cesarean delivery, the condition related to the reason for the admission should be selected as the principal diagnosis.

5) Outcome of delivery

A code from category Z37, Outcome of delivery, should be included on every maternal record when a delivery has occurred. These codes are not to be used on subsequent records or on the newborn record. (See Appendix A, Section I. C15. b 4-5.)

At times a pregnant patient presents for care because of a complication but no delivery occurs. In such cases, the following coding guideline applies:

ICD-10-CM Official Coding Guidelines

3) Episodes when no delivery occurs

In episodes when no delivery occurs, the principal diagnosis should correspond to the principal complication of the pregnancy which necessitated the encounter. Should more than one complication exist, all of which are treated or monitored, any of the complications codes may be sequenced first. (See Appendix A, Section I. C15. b3.)

Complications Predominately Related to the Puerperium (Category Codes O85–O92)

Category codes O85–O92 report complications predominately relating to the puerperium: puerperal sepsis, other puerperal infections, obstetric embolism, complications of anesthesia during the puerperium, infections of breast associated with pregnancy, and other disorders of lactation. When selecting codes from these categories, coders need to identify the instructional notations that instruct coders to assign additional codes. For example, following the heading for category O85 an instructional notation appears that states: "Use additional code (B95–B97), to identify infectious agent" and "Use additional code (R65.2-) to identify severe sepsis, if applicable." These categories also contain numerous Excludes1 and Excludes2 notes.

Code O90.3 is governed by the following coding guideline:

ICD-10-CM Official Coding Guidelines

5) Pregnancy associated cardiomyopathy

Pregnancy associated cardiomyopathy, code O90.3, is unique in that it may be diagnosed in the third trimester of pregnancy but may continue to progress months after delivery. For this reason, it is referred to as peripartum cardiomyopathy. Code O90.3 is only for use when the cardiomyopathy develops as a result of pregnancy in a woman who did not have pre-existing heart disease.

(See Appendix A, Section I. C15.o 5.)

Courtesy of the Centers for Medicare & Medicaid Services, www.cms.gov

Other Obstetric Conditions, Not Elsewhere Classified (Category Codes O94–O9A)

Category codes O94–O9A report other obstetric conditions that are not classified elsewhere in this chapter.

Category O94, Sequelae of complications of pregnancy, childbirth, and the puerperium, is governed by the following guidelines:

ICD-10-CM Official Coding Guidelines

p. Code O94, Sequelae of complication of pregnancy, childbirth, and the puerperium

1) Code O94

Code O94, Sequelae of complication of pregnancy, childbirth, and the puerperium, is for use in those cases when an initial complication of a pregnancy develops a sequelae requiring care or treatment at a future date.

2) After the initial postpartum period

This code may be used at any time after the initial postpartum period.

3) Sequencing of Code O94

This code, like all sequela codes, is to be sequenced following the code describing the sequelae of the complication. (See Appendix A, Section I. C 15.p 1-3.)

Courtesy of the Centers for Medicare & Medicaid Services, www.cms.gov

Code assignment for patients admitted because of an HIV-related illness should follow the following coding guideline:

ICD-10-CM Official Coding Guidelines

f. HIV Infection in Pregnancy, Childbirth, and the Puerperium

During pregnancy, childbirth, or the puerperium, a patient admitted because of an HIV-related illness should receive a principal diagnosis from subcategory O98.7–, Human immunodeficiency [HIV] disease complicating pregnancy, childbirth, and the puerperium, followed by the code(s) for the HIV-related illness(es).

Patients with asymptomatic HIV infection status admitted during pregnancy, childbirth, or the puerperium should receive codes of O98.7– and Z21, Asymptomatic human immunodeficiency virus [HIV] infection status. (See Appendix A, Section I. C15. f.)

The following coding guidelines govern alcohol and tobacco use complicating pregnancy, childbirth, and the puerperium:

ICD-10-CM Official Coding Guidelines

l. Alcohol, tobacco and drug use during pregnancy, childbirth, and the puerperium

1) Alcohol use during pregnancy, childbirth, and the puerperium

Codes under subcategory O99.31, Alcohol use complicating pregnancy, childbirth, and the puerperium, should be assigned for any pregnancy case when a mother uses alcohol during the pregnancy or postpartum. A secondary code from category F10, Alcohol related disorders, should also be assigned to identify manifestations of the alcohol use.

2) Tobacco use during pregnancy, childbirth, and the puerperium

Codes under subcategory O99.33, Smoking (tobacco) complicating pregnancy, childbirth, and the puerperium, should be assigned for any pregnancy case when a mother uses any type of tobacco product during the pregnancy or postpartum. A secondary code from category F17, Nicotine dependence should also be assigned to identify the type of nicotine dependence.

3) Drug use during pregnancy, childbirth and the puerperium

Codes under subcategory O99.32, Drug use complicating pregnancy, childbirth, and the puerperium, should be assigned for any pregnancy case when a mother uses drugs during the pregnancy or postpartum. This can involve illegal drugs, or inappropriate use or abuse of prescription drugs. Secondary code(s) from categories F11-F16 and F18-F19 should also be assigned to identify manifestations of the drug use. (See Appendix A, Section I. C15.l. 1-3.)

Another coding guideline applies to injuries, poisonings, and certain other consequences of external causes during pregnancy, childbirth, and the puerperium.

ICD-10-CM Official Coding Guidelines

m. Poisoning, toxic effects, adverse effects, and underdosing in a pregnant patient

A code from subcategory O9A.2, Injury, poisoning, and certain other consequences of external causes complicating pregnancy, childbirth, and the puerperium, should be sequenced first, followed by the appropriate injury, poisoning, toxic effect, adverse effect, or underdosing code, and then the additional code(s) that specifies the condition caused by the poisoning, toxic effect, adverse effect, or underdosing.

See Section I.C.19. Adverse effects, poisoning, underdosing, and toxic effects. (See Appendix A, Section I. C15. m.)

Coders need to be familiar with these guidelines for proper code selection.

Additional Coding Guidelines

The following additional coding guidelines apply to this chapter of ICD-10-CM:

ICD-10-CM Official Coding Guidelines

3) Pregnancy-related complications after 6 week period

Chapter 15 codes may also be used to describe pregnancy-related complications after the peripartum or postpartum period if the provider documents that a condition is pregnancy related.

4) Admission for routine postpartum care following delivery outside hospital

When the mother delivers outside the hospital prior to admission and is admitted for routine postpartum care and no complications are noted, code Z39.0, Encounter for care and examination of mother immediately after delivery, should be assigned as the principal diagnosis. (See Appendix A, Section I, C15, o 3-4.)

Abuse in a pregnant patient

For suspected or confirmed cases of abuse of a pregnant patient, a code(s) from subcategories O9A.3, Physical abuse complicating pregnancy, childbirth, and the puerperium, O9A.4, Sexual abuse complicating pregnancy, childbirth, and the puerperium, and O9A.5, Psychological abuse complicating pregnancy, childbirth and the puerperium, should be sequenced first, followed by the appropriate codes (if applicable) to identify any associated current injury due to physical abuse, sexual abuse, and the perpetrator of abuse.

See Section I.C.19, Adult and child abuse, neglect and other maltreatment. (See Appendix A, Section I,C15,r.)

Courtesy of the Centers for Medicare & Medicaid Services, www.cms.gov

COVID-19 Infection in Pregnancy, Childbirth, and the Puerperium

The ICD-10-CM Official Coding Guidelines provide specific information for the reporting of COVID-19 during pregnancy, childbirth and the puerperium. The specific guidelines and codes will be discussed in Chapter 26 of this textbook.

Summary

- Understanding terminology is extremely important in assigning the correct codes.
- The codes in Chapter 15 of ICD-10-CM apply to the medical record or encounter of the mother.
- Any conditions encountered during a pregnancy or postpartum period are coded to this chapter as a complication unless the provider documents that such a condition is incidental to the pregnancy.

Internet Links

To learn more about pregnancy, childbirth, and the puerperium, visit Dr. Donnica's Women's Health site at **www.drdonnica.com** and the National Women's Health Resource Center at **www.healthywomen.org**. For information on labor and delivery, visit **www.babies.sutterhealth.org**.

Chapter Review

True/False

Indicate whether each statement is true (T) or false (F).

1. _____ Through the tenth week of pregnancy, the developing child is known as an embryo.

2. _____ The second trimester is from 14 to 20 weeks.

3. _____ The phrase "unspecified episode of care" is used only if there is absolutely no other information available.

4. _____ A spontaneous abortion is classified to category O03. Additional characters are needed for correct code assignment.

5. _____ Codes from this chapter should appear only on the mother's encounter.

Fill-in-the-Blank

Enter the appropriate term(s) to complete each statement.

6. A blighted ovum that has developed into a benign tumor is called a(n) _____.

7. A pregnancy that occurs outside the uterus is called a(n) _____.

8. A developing child from 9 weeks until birth is known as a(n) _____.

9. An encounter for cesarean delivery without indication is reported with code _____.

10. The time before childbirth is called _____.

11. Through 8 weeks of pregnancy, the developing child is known as a(n) _____.

12. The puerperium, or postpartum period, lasts up to _____ weeks after delivery.

13. A premature sudden separation of the placenta from the uterus prior to or during labor is called _____.

14. The only outcome of delivery code assigned with code O80 is _____.

15. During pregnancy, childbirth, or the puerperium, a patient admitted because of an HIV-related illness should be coded with a principal diagnosis from subcategory _____.

Coding Assignments

Instructions: Using an ICD-10-CM code book, assign the proper diagnosis code(s) to the following diagnostic statements.

1. postpartum fibrinolysis   _____

2. severe pre-eclampsia, 16 weeks   _____

3. antepartum hemorrhage, 10 weeks   _____

4. vomiting complicating pregnancy, 8 weeks   _____

5. low-lying placenta (during pregnancy, no hemorrhage)   _____

6. tubal pregnancy, 5 weeks   _____

7. spontaneous termination of pregnancy complicated by renal failure, 13 weeks   _____

8. miscarriage at 10 weeks' gestation   _____

9. cervical pregnancy, 14 weeks   _____

10. uterine fibroid found, 29 weeks   _____

11. twin pregnancy, 20 weeks   _____

12. cervical incompetence, Shirodkar suture needed to hold pregnancy   _____

13. premature rupture of membranes   _____

14. threatened abortion at 15 weeks' gestation, no delivery   _____

15. obstruction of delivery during labor caused by prolapsed arm of fetus, 41 weeks

_____

16. pelvic peritonitis following incomplete spontaneous abortion, 12 weeks

_____

17. delivery with retained placenta with manual removal of retained placenta, 42 weeks

_____

18. contraction ring dystocia, 42 weeks

_____

19. postpartum hemorrhage

_____

20. false labor at 38 weeks

_____

21. hydatidiform mole, 5 weeks

_____

22. pelvic peritonitis with an ectopic pregnancy, 6 weeks

_____

23. syphilis during pregnancy

_____

24. liver disorders in childbirth

_____

25. antepartum anemia complicating pregnancy

_____

26. pregnancy with essential long-standing hypertension at 15 weeks

_____

27. hypertension, gestational at 25 weeks

_____

28. early spontaneous incomplete abortion

_____

29. mural pregnancy

_____

30. left ovarian pregnancy without intrauterine pregnancy

_____

Case Studies

Instructions: Review each case study and select the correct ICD-10-CM diagnostic code.

Case 1

Physician Office Note of 2/04/XX

WEIGHT: 150 pounds. This is a weight gain of 7 pounds since her last visit 3 weeks ago. Blood pressure: 140/80. Lab: Urinalysis reveals protein present.

Patient is complaining of increased headaches and dizziness.

VAGINAL EXAM: Normal

HEENT: Face appears swollen.

EXTREMITIES: Edema of hands and feet

Patient symptoms indicate mild pre-eclampsia during her 39th week. Patient advised to decrease salt intake and to follow up in 2 weeks.

ICD-10-CM Code Assignment: _____

Case 2

Discharge Summary

ADMISSION DATE: 5/6/XX, Discharge date: 5/8/XX

HISTORY:

This patient is gravida 2, para 1 and was seen in my office for all of her prenatal visits. Her prenatal course was uneventful. She was admitted with a history of contractions every 3 to 5 minutes. Cervix was 100% effaced and 9 cm dilated.

HOSPITAL COURSE:

At the time of admission, patient received IV and was placed on a fetal monitor. Her water broke at 2 a.m. After 3 hours the patient delivered a baby boy with apgar scores of 8 at 1 minute and 10 at 5 minutes. Postpartum care was uneventful. The patient was discharged 2 days later.

INSTRUCTIONS TO PATIENT: Diet as tolerated. Tylenol every 4 hours for pain. She is to follow up in my office in 2 weeks.

ICD-10-CM Code Assignment: _____

Case 3

Physician Office Note

This patient presents today in the 38th week of her pregnancy. She complains of increased fatigue over the last month, edema of both legs, shortness of breath, and difficulty breathing when lying down.

I have monitored her closely for the last 2 months. Last week I sent her for an EKG, chest x-ray, and coronary angiography. Today I am reviewing the results with her.

EXAM: Reveals an obese, gravida 1, para 0, 29-year-old woman.

HEENT: Normocephalic, palpebrale conjunctiva, pinkish, PERRLA

NECK: Supple. No mass noted.

HEART: Tachycardia present. Slight murmur.

LUNGS: There is congestion in both lungs.

ABDOMEN: Protuberant, soft, and nontender. Liver and spleen not palpable. Uterus enlarged to gestational size. Fetal heart tones are noted to be normal.

PELVIC: External genitalia, normal. Vagina, clear. Membranes, intact.

EXTREMITIES: There is edema in both legs.

Review of diagnostic testing: EKG, chest x-ray, and coronary angiography results support a diagnosis of peripartum cardiomyopathy.

(continues)

(continued)

I discussed with the patient the need for medications to improve her heart function, decrease edema, and prevent the formation of blood clots that can occur with the diagnosis of peripartum cardiomyopathy.

Medications were ordered as per medication record.

INSTRUCTIONS TO PATIENT: I explained to the patient the need to take her medications as prescribed.

She is to follow up with me in 5 days.

ICD-10-CM Code Assignment: _____

Case 4

Discharge Note

Linda presented to the hospital in active labor. She was admitted, and a fetal monitor was used, which showed a very unstable fetal heart rate of 100–125. After physical examination, it was determined that she was fully dilated but the baby was in breech position. Linda was instructed to begin pushing, at which time the fetal heart rate dropped. It was decided that an attempt would be made to turn the baby, but this attempt was unsuccessful. At this point, an emergency cesarean delivery was successfully performed.

ICD-10-CM Code Assignment: _____

Case 5

Physician Office Visit

This 27-year-old female, who is 12 weeks pregnant, is experiencing increased thirst, increased urination, increased fatigue, and bouts of nausea. An in-office blood sugar reading was 245, so a glucose tolerance test was ordered. The results confirmed gestational diabetes. Insulin is not necessary at this time.

ICD-10-CM Code Assignment: _____

Case 6

Physician Office Visit

This 25-year-old patient is being seen today for follow-up care. She has gestational diabetes that is controlled by diet. The pregnancy is progressing well. Vital signs are within normal limits. The fetal heartbeat was normal. She is to follow up with me in 3 weeks. This is the 30th week of pregnancy.

ICD-10-CM Code Assignment: _____

Case 7

Physician Office Visit

This 25-year-old, 29-weeks-pregnant patient presents to the office today stating that she is experiencing urinary urgency, dysuria, and low back pain. Urinalysis and C/S confirmed UTI due to *E. coli*. A prescription for antibiotics was written.

ICD-10-CM Code Assignment: _____

Case 8

Discharge Summary

This 13-weeks-pregnant patient is being discharged today following a 7-day length of stay for severe hyperemesis with electrolyte imbalance. She was given IV prenatal vitamin supplement and was NPO. After 4 days the vomiting subsided. She is now able to tolerate small amounts of food. She is discharged home at this time with instructions to call me if the vomiting persists throughout an entire day.

ICD-10-CM Code Assignment: _____

Case 9

Office Visit Note

This 42-year-old pregnant patient is being seen today for a 24-week prenatal visit. This is her first pregnancy. Vital signs are normal. Blood glucose is within normal limits. Fetal heartbeat is normal. The pregnancy is progressing well. I will see her again in 2 weeks.

ICD-10-CM Code Assignment: _____

Case 10

Office Visit Note

This patient returns to my office today following delivery of a female infant 2 weeks ago. She states that she is having bilateral breast pain that is increasing in intensity for the last 4 days. Upon exam both breasts appear red and warm to the touch, confirming puerperal mastitis. The patient is very anxious about this and I informed the patient that this is nothing to be alarmed about. The patient was instructed to apply a heated compress to both breasts and to take Tylenol for the discomfort and to wear a firm supporting bra to increase her comfort.

She was instructed to return to me if the symptoms increase.

ICD-10-CM Code Assignment: _____

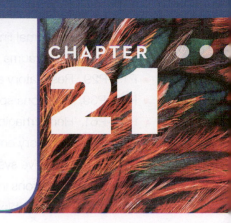

Certain Conditions Originating in the Perinatal Period

Chapter Outline

Chapter Objectives

At the conclusion of this chapter, you should be able to:

1. Describe how perinatal conditions of the mother affect the fetus or newborn and code assignment.
2. Define perinatal conditions and terms used that relate to the perinatal period.
3. Apply the ICD-10-CM coding guidelines to accurately code conditions originating in the perinatal period.
4. Select and code diagnoses from case studies.

Key Terms

Omphalitis

Perinatal period

> **REMINDER:** As you work through this chapter, you will need to have a copy of the ICD-10-CM coding book to reference. For this chapter, you will also need to reference the ICD-10-CM Official Guidelines for Coding and Reporting. These guidelines can be found in Appendix A which are now available on the Student Companion site and MINDTAP From Cengage.

Introduction

The time before the birth of the child through the 28th day following birth is considered the **perinatal period**. The codes in Chapter 16 of ICD-10-CM are organized into the following blocks of codes:

- P00–P04, Newborn affected by maternal factors and by complications of pregnancy, labor, and delivery
- P05–P08, Disorders of newborn related to length of gestation and fetal growth

- P09,   Abnormal findings on neonatal screening
- P10–P15, Birth trauma
- P19–P29, Respiratory and cardiovascular disorders specific to the perinatal period
- P35–P39, Infections specific to the perinatal period
- P50–P61, Hemorrhagic and hematological disorders of newborn
- P70–P74, Transitory endocrine and metabolic disorders specific to newborn
- P76–P78, Digestive system disorders of newborn
- P80–P83, Conditions involving the integument and temperature regulation of newborn
- P84,   Other problems with newborn
- P90–P96, Other disorders originating in the perinatal period

Coding Guidelines for Certain Conditions Originating in the Perinatal Period

The ICD-10-CM Official Coding Guidelines state the following:

ICD-10-CM Official Coding Guidelines

For coding and reporting purposes the perinatal period is defined as before birth through the 28th day following birth. The following guidelines are provided for reporting purposes.

a. General Perinatal Rules

1) Use of Chapter 16 Codes

Codes in this chapter are never for use on the maternal record. Codes from Chapter 15, the obstetric chapter, are never permitted on the newborn record. Chapter 16 codes may be used throughout the life of the patient if the condition is still present.

2) Principal Diagnosis for Birth Record

When coding the birth episode in a newborn record, assign a code from category Z38, Liveborn infants according to place of birth and type of delivery, as the principal diagnosis. A code from category Z38 is assigned only once, to a newborn at the time of birth. If a newborn is transferred to another institution, a code from category Z38 should not be used at the receiving hospital.

A code from category Z38 is used only on the newborn record, not on the mother's record.

3) Use of Codes from other Chapters with Codes from Chapter 16

Codes from other chapters may be used with codes from Chapter 16 if the codes from the other chapters provide more specific detail. Codes for signs and symptoms may be assigned when a definitive diagnosis has not been established. If the reason for the encounter is a perinatal condition, the code from Chapter 16 should be sequenced first.

4) Use of Chapter 16 Codes after the Perinatal Period

Should a condition originate in the perinatal period, and continue throughout the life of the patient, the perinatal code should continue to be used regardless of the patient's age.

5) Birth Process or Community Acquired Conditions

If a newborn has a condition that may be either due to the birth process or community acquired and the documentation does not indicate which it is, the default is due to the birth process and the code from Chapter 16 should be used. If the condition is community-acquired, a code from Chapter 16 should not be assigned.

For COVID-19 infection in a newborn, see guideline I.C.16.h.

6) Code All Clinically Significant Conditions

All clinically significant conditions noted on routine newborn examination should be coded. A condition is clinically significant if it requires:

- clinical evaluation; or
- therapeutic treatment; or
- diagnostic procedures; or
- extended length of hospital stay; or
- increased nursing care and/or monitoring; or
- has implications for future health care needs

Note: The perinatal guidelines listed above are the same as the general coding guidelines for "additional diagnoses", except for the final point regarding implications for future health care needs. Codes should be assigned for conditions that have been specified by the provider as having implications for future health care needs.

b. Observation and Evaluation of Newborns for Suspected Conditions not found.

1) Use of Z05 codes

Assign a code from category Z05, Observation and evaluation of newborns and infants for suspected conditions ruled out, to identify those instances when a healthy newborn is evaluated for a suspected condition that is determined after study not to be present. Do not use a code from category Z05 when the patient has identified signs or symptoms of a suspected problem; in such cases code the sign or symptom.

2) Z05 on Other than the Birth Record

A code from category Z05 may also be assigned as a principal or first-listed code for readmissions or encounters when the code from category Z38 code no longer applies. Codes from category Z05 are for use only for healthy newborns and infants for which no condition after study is found to be present.

3) Z05 on a birth record

A code from category Z05 is to be used as a secondary code after the code from category Z38, Liveborn infants according to place of birth and type of delivery.

(See Appendix A, Section I, C16 a to b.)

Courtesy of the Centers for Medicare & Medicaid Services, www.cms.gov

Newborn Affected by Maternal Factors and by Complications of Pregnancy, Labor, and Delivery (Category Codes P00–P04)

This block of codes is explained by the note that appears at the start of the block.

 NOTE:

These codes are for use when the listed maternal conditions are specified as the cause of confirmed morbidity or potential morbidity which have their origin in the perinatal period (before birth through the first 28 days after birth).

When assigning codes from this section, the coder must carefully read the recorded medical information to determine the proper code assignment. The descriptions for these codes are very detailed. Many instructional notations appear in these categories. For example, following categories P00, P01, P02, and P03, a notation appears that states: "Code first any current condition in the newborn." This notation provides sequencing guidance when assigning codes. Coders also need to reference the code book for the assignment of fourth and at times fifth characters.

Disorders of Newborn Related to Length of Gestation and Fetal Growth (Category Codes P05–P08)

This block of codes includes the following categories:

- P05, Disorders of newborn related to slow fetal growth and fetal malnutrition
- P07, Disorders of newborn related to short gestation and low birth weight, not elsewhere classified. Be aware of the note and the Includes notations that appear in the Tabular list at the start of category P07.
- P08, Disorders of newborn related to long gestation and high birth weight. Be aware of the note and the Includes notations that appear in the code book at the start of category P08.

A situation that can affect newborns is prematurity and/or fetal growth retardation. The Official Coding Guidelines give the following direction to coders in this situation:

ICD-10-CM Official Coding Guidelines

d. Prematurity and Fetal Growth Retardation

Providers utilize different criteria in determining prematurity. A code for prematurity should not be assigned unless it is documented. Assignment of codes in categories P05, Disorders of newborn related to slow fetal growth and fetal malnutrition, and P07, Disorders of newborn related to short gestation and low birth weight, not elsewhere classified, should be based on the recorded birth weight and estimated gestational age.

When both birth weight and gestational age are available, two codes from category P07 should be assigned, with the code for birth weight sequenced before the code for gestational age.

e. Low Birth Weight and Immaturity Status

Codes from category P07, Disorders of newborn related to short gestation and low birth weight, not elsewhere classified, are for use for a child or adult who was premature or had a low birth weight as a newborn and this is affecting the patient's current health status. See Section I.C.21. Factors influencing health status and contact with health services, Status.

(See Appendix A, Section I, c16, d-e.)

Abnormal Findings on Neonatal Screening (Category Code P09)

The title of this category makes it self-explanatory in that it records abnormal findings on neonatal screenings. A notation appears after the category heading instructing the coder to "Use additional code to identify signs, symptoms, and conditions associated with the screening."

Birth Trauma (Category Codes P10–P15)

This block of codes, with the assignment of fourth characters, reports injuries that occurred during birth:

- P10, Intracranial laceration and hemorrhage due to birth injury
- P11, Other birth injuries to central nervous system
- P12, Birth injury to scalp
- P13, Birth injury to skeleton
- P14, Birth injury to peripheral nervous system
- P15, Other birth injuries

To assign these codes, you must have supporting documentation that the injury is a birth trauma.

The following two coding guidelines apply to coding multiple birth traumas and the entire chapter:

ICD-10-CM Official Coding Guidelines

c. Coding Additional Perinatal Diagnoses

1) Assigning codes for conditions that require treatment

Assign codes for conditions that require treatment or further investigation, prolong the length of stay, or require resource utilization.

2) Codes for conditions specified as having implications for future health care needs

Assign codes for conditions that have been specified by the provider as having implications for future health care needs.

Note: This guideline should not be used for adult patients. (See Appendix A, Section I.C16, c 1-2.)

Courtesy of the Centers for Medicare & Medicaid Services, www.cms.gov

Respiratory and Cardiovascular Disorders Specific to the Perinatal Period (Category Codes P19–P29)

This block of codes is used to report metabolic acidemia in the newborn (P19), respiratory distress of the newborn (P22), congenital pneumonia (P23), neonatal aspiration (P24), interstitial emphysema and related conditions originating in the perinatal period (P25), pulmonary hemorrhage (P26), chronic respiratory disease (P27), and other respiratory conditions (P28), and cardiovascular disorders that originated in the perinatal period (P29).

Infections Specific to the Perinatal Period (Category Codes P35–P39)

Category codes P35–P39 include infections acquired in utero, during birth via the umbilicus, or during the first 28 days after birth:

- P35, Congenital viral diseases
- P36, Bacterial sepsis of newborn
- P37, Other congenital infectious and parasitic diseases
- P38, **Omphalitis** of newborn (an inflammation of the navel)
- P39, Other infections specific to the perinatal period

Category P36, Bacterial sepsis of newborn, is governed by the following guideline:

ICD-10-CM Official Coding Guidelines

f. Bacterial Sepsis of Newborn

Category P36, Bacterial sepsis of newborn, includes congenital sepsis. If a perinate is documented as having sepsis without documentation of congenital or community acquired, the default is congenital and a code from category P36 should be assigned. If the P36 code includes the causal organism, an additional code from category B95, Streptococcus, Staphylococcus, and Enterococcus as the cause of diseases classified elsewhere, or B96, Other bacterial agents as the cause of diseases classified elsewhere, should not be assigned. If the P36 code does not include the causal organism, assign an additional code from category B96. If applicable, use additional codes to identify severe sepsis (R65.2–) and any associated acute organ dysfunction. (See Appendix A, Section I. C16. f.)

Courtesy of the Centers for Medicare & Medicaid Services, www.cms.gov

Exercise 21.1—Coding for Categories P00–P39

For each diagnostic statement listed, select the appropriate ICD-10-CM diagnostic code.

Diagnosis	Code
1. newborn suspected to be affected by prolapsed cord ruled out	_____
2. fracture of skull due to birth injury	_____
3. meconium aspiration	_____
4. neonatal candidiasis	_____
5. exceptionally large newborn, 4600 grams	_____
6. subconjunctival hemorrhage due to birth injury	_____
7. congenital malaria	_____
8. neonatal aspiration of blood	_____
9. congenital rubella pneumonitis	_____
10. idiopathic tachypnea of newborn	_____

Hemorrhagic and Hematologic Disorders of Newborn (Category Codes P50–P61)

The block of codes in this section of the code book includes the following categories:

- P50, Newborn affected by intrauterine (fetal) blood loss
- P51, Umbilical hemorrhage of newborn
- P52, Intracranial nontraumatic hemorrhage of newborn
- P53, Hemorrhagic disease of newborn
- P54, Other neonatal hemorrhages
- P55, Hemolytic disease of newborn
- P56, Hydrops fetalis due to hemolytic disease
- P57, Kernicterus
- P58, Neonatal jaundice due to other excessive hemolysis
- P59, Neonatal jaundice from other and unspecified causes
- P60, Disseminated intravascular coagulation of newborn
- P61, Other perinatal hematological disorders

Coders need to pay attention to the numerous notations and code descriptions in this block of codes. For example, code P54.5 lists a number of diagnoses that are coded here as well as an important Excludes2 notation.

Transitory Endocrine and Metabolic Disorders Specific to Newborn (Category Codes P70–P74)

This block of codes includes transitory endocrine and metabolic disturbances caused by the infant's response to maternal endocrine and metabolic factors or its adjustment to extrauterine environment. Some of the commonly reported codes from this block of codes include:

- Neonatal diabetes mellitus (P70.2)
- Neonatal goiter (P72.0)
- Dehydration of newborn (P74.1)

Digestive System Disorders of Newborn (Category Codes P76–P78)

Three categories in this block of codes are used to report an intestinal obstruction of the newborn (P76), necrotizing enterocolitis of the newborn (P77), and other perinatal digestive system disorders (P78). Some common diagnoses that are reported from these categories include:

Meconium plug syndrome P76.0

Meconium peritonitis P78.0

Neonatal peritonitis P78.1

Neonatal diarrhea P78.3

Conditions Involving the Integument and Temperature Regulation of Newborn (Category Codes P80–P83) and Other Problems with Newborns (Category Code P84)

Hypothermia of the newborn, disturbances of temperature regulation, and conditions of integument specific to the newborn are reported using category codes P80–P83.

Category P84 reports the following problems with a newborn:

- Acidosis
- Anoxia NOS
- Asphyxia NOS
- Hypercapnia
- Hypoxemia
- Hypoxia
- Mixed metabolic and respiratory acidosis

Other Disorders Originating in the Perinatal Period (Category Codes P90–P96)

The last block of codes in this chapter reports other disorders originating in the perinatal period:

- P90, Convulsions of newborn
- P91, Other disturbances of cerebral status of newborn. It should be noted that codes P91.821 to P91.829, neonatal cerebral infarction, delineate the side of the brain that the cerebral infarction has impacted. As stated in the coding guidelines if the coder knows the side that a condition impacts the coder needs to identify this in code selection. If the side is not specified the coder should query the provider. If the side impacted is not known then the coder should select code P81.829 neonatal cerebral infarction, unspecified side.

- P92, Feeding problems of newborn
- P93, Reactions and intoxications due to drugs administered to newborn
- P94, Disorders of muscle tone of newborn
- P95, Stillbirth
- P96, Other conditions originating in the perinatal period

Category P95 is governed by the following coding guideline:

ICD-10-CM Official Coding Guidelines

g. Stillbirth

Code P95, Stillbirth, is only for use in institutions that maintain separate records for stillbirths. No other code should be used with P95. Code P95 should not be used on the mother's record. (See Appendix A, Section I.C16. g.)

Courtesy of the Centers for Medicare & Medicaid Services, www.cms.gov

---

COVID-19 Infection in Newborn

The ICD-10-CM Official Coding Guidelines provide instructions for coding COVID-19 that impacts a newborn. The specific guidelines will be discussed in Chapter 26 of this textbook.

Summary

- The codes from Chapter 16 of ICD-10-CM classify conditions that affect the fetus or newborn.
- These codes are used on the chart of the newborn *only*; they *never* appear in the mother's medical record.
- Congenital conditions that are not detected until later in life should be coded from this section.
- Numerous coding guidelines apply to this chapter of ICD-10-CM.
- When coding from Chapter 16 of ICD-10-CM, the coder must determine that the condition being coded originated in the perinatal period.

Internet Links

To learn more about conditions that arise in the perinatal period, go to the following websites:

U.S. Department of Health and Human Services at **www.hhs.gov**

Neonatal Resuscitation Program at **www.aap.org**

Chapter Review

True/False

Indicate whether each statement is true (T) or false (F).

1. _____ Code P95 reports stillbirth.
2. _____ Codes from this chapter can be found in the record of either the mother or the newborn.
3. _____ Low birth weight may be referred to as "fetal immaturity."
4. _____ Code P83.9 would be used to report congenital hydrocele.
5. _____ Acidosis of the newborn would be reported with code P70.

Fill-in-the-Blank

Enter the appropriate term(s) to complete each statement.

6. The perinatal period extends from birth up to _____.

7. Code _____ reports massive umbilical hemorrhage of the newborn.

8. Code P29.0 reports _____.

9. Respiratory failure of the newborn is reported with code _____.

10. Congenital tuberculosis is coded with code _____.

Coding Guidelines True/False

Review the ICD-10-CM Official Guidelines for Coding and Reporting and indicate if the statement(s) is true or false.

11. _____ ICD-10-CM Chapter 16 codes may be used throughout the life of the patient if the condition is still present.

12. _____ If a newborn is transferred to another institution, a code from category Z38 should be assigned at the receiving hospital.

13. _____ A code from category Z05 should not be used as a secondary code after the code from category Z38, Liveborn infants according to place of birth and type of delivery.

14. _____ A code for prematurity should not be assigned unless it is documented.

15. _____ Code P95 should be used on the mother's record.

Coding Assignments

Instructions: Using an ICD-10-CM code book, assign the proper diagnosis code to the following diagnostic statements.

1. maternal hypertension affecting the fetus _____

2. neonatal bradycardia _____

3. dehydration of newborn _____

4. post-term infant, 41 weeks _____

5. neonatal peritonitis _____

6. premature baby, birth weight of 1900 grams _____

7. fetal malnutrition, 6 days old, 1300 grams _____

8. meconium peritonitis _____

9. congenital hypertonia _____

10. cold injury syndrome of the newborn _____

11. transitory neonatal hypoglycemia _____

12. neonatal thyrotoxicosis _____

13. CNS dysfunction in newborn due to birth injury _____

14. polycythemia neonatorum _____

15. neonatal tachycardia _____

16. stillbirth _____

17. mild birth asphyxia _____

18. pulmonary hemorrhage originating in the perinatal period _____

19. bronchopulmonary dysplasia originating in the perinatal period _____

20. neonatal moniliasis _____

21. neonatal bruising _____

22. placenta previa affecting the fetus _____

23. neonatal hypertension _____

24. acidosis of newborn _____

25. birth injury to brachial plexus _____

26. perinatal intestine perforation _____

27. underfeeding of newborn _____

28. Grey baby syndrome _____

29. neonatal hypomagnesemia _____

30. iatrogenic neonatal hypoglycemia _____

31. neonatal cerebral infarction left side of brain _____

32. fracture of clavicle of newborn due to birth injury _____

33. hyaline membrane disease of newborn _____

34. anemia of prematurity of newborn _____

35. late metabolic acidosis of newborn _____

Case Studies

Instructions: Review each case study and select the correct ICD-10-CM diagnostic code.

Case 1

Inpatient Physician's Progress Note

12/20/XX Two-day-old infant examined today to follow up after the results of diagnostic tests.

BLOOD GAS: Study indicates reduced oxygen tension and ineffective gas exchange.

CHEST X-RAY: Presence of infiltrate

Infant continues to exhibit signs of infant respiratory distress syndrome, type 2.

ORDERS: Continue titrated oxygen and aerosol infusion of Survanta.

ICD-10-CM Code Assignment: _____

Case 2

Inpatient Physician's Progress Note

2/3/XX Five-hour-old neonate is jaundiced, and delivering physician has just determined that the child is Rh-positive and mother is Rh-negative. The mother just moved to the area, and it cannot be determined from history whether the mother had screening for Rh incompatibility prior to delivery.

EXAM:

ABDOMEN: Liver and spleen are enlarged.

CHEST: Lungs are clear.

PLAN: Phototherapy and albumin infusion standard protocol as per written orders.

IMPRESSION: Hemolytic disease of the newborn due to Rh isoimmunization.

ICD-10-CM Code Assignment: _____

Case 3

Discharge Summary

The patient was discharged in stable condition on 1/20/XX. She is to continue on breast milk and can be supplemented with Similac with iron.

This patient is the product of a full-term gestation. The Apgars were 9 and 10. Birth weight was 6 pounds 10 ounces. Physical examination shortly after birth was negative. The infant's temperature was elevated, and urinalysis revealed a urinary tract infection. The plan was to observe the patient. Antibiotic therapy was started.

She had no difficulty nursing and ate well while she was in the hospital. She had no problems with her bowel movements. On the day of discharge, the patient's weight was down 3 ounces from birth. She will be seen in my office in 7 days.

ICD-10-CM Code Assignment: _____

Case 4

Hospital Visit Note

The patient is a female, born 36 hours ago and now experiencing convulsions. The product of a normal delivery with birth weight of 7 pounds 2 ounces. Her vital signs are normal at this time. The nursing staff contacted this physician immediately upon noting the convulsions, which they said lasted several seconds. An EEG and ECG have been ordered, along with a complete blood workup. The baby will be monitored closely until all test results are back.

ICD-10-CM Code Assignment: _____

Case 5

Hospital Visit Note

The patient is a newborn infant male, born 2 hours ago to a mother who was experiencing severe hypertension prior to her pregnancy. The mother was being monitored closely for this condition during her current pregnancy because she had difficulty during her last one. It appears now that this baby boy is experiencing some respiratory distress due to the maternal hypertension. Pulse ox reading was 70, and his respirations were elevated. His vital signs at this time are all within normal limits since we started the oxygen. His pulse ox reading is now at 98. He will be monitored until such time as there is no need for the oxygen and his vital signs remain normal.

ICD-10-CM Code Assignment: _____

Case 6

Discharge Note

This 15-day-old infant was born in the hospital and discharged. Ten days after discharge she developed a high fever and she was seen in my office. Diagnostic testing indicated sepsis due to group B streptococcus. She is stable at this time and she is being discharged home.

ICD-10-CM Code Assignment: _____

Case 7

Discharge Note

This 7-pound, 2-ounce female infant was born 4 days ago and there were no complications during the delivery. The following day the child appeared jaundice and a diagnosis of hyperbilirubinemia was made. She was given phototherapy. She is now stabilized and she is being discharged with no other complications.

ICD-10-CM Code Assignment: _____

Case 8

Physician Office Note

This 12-day-old infant presents to the office today with numerous pustules that have a yellow crust over the lesions. The lesions are on the infant's face and hands consistent with neonatal pyoderma. I instructed the mother to bath the child twice a day and to apply an antibiotic ointment. If the skin does not clear within 1 week they should return to the office.

ICD-10-CM Code Assignment: _____

Case 9

Discharge Note

This 4-day-old infant is being discharged today following a normal delivery. The child did experience noninfectious diarrhea for the last 2 days that has now stabilized. I instructed the mother to supplement her breast feeding with Pedialyte and to call me if the diarrhea increases.

ICD-10-CM Code Assignment: _____

Case 10

Physician Office Note

This 20-day-old infant is being seen in my office today because at the time of birth he experienced a cardiac dysrhythmia suggestive of tachycardia. But the rhythm was normal at the time of discharge. His cardiac rhythm still is tachycardic at this time. I am having the infant and his mother go from my office directly to the ED, where they will be met by the pediatric cardiologist.

ICD-10-CM Code Assignment: _____

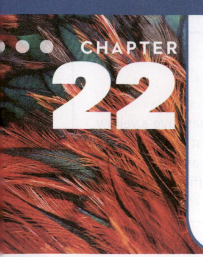

CHAPTER 22

Congenital Malformations, Deformations, and Chromosomal Abnormalities

Chapter Outline

Chapter Objectives

Key Terms

Introduction

Introduction to the Body System

Coding Congenital Malformations, Deformations, and Chromosomal Abnormalities

Summary

Internet Links

Chapter Review

Coding Assignments

Case Studies

Chapter Objectives

At the conclusion of this chapter, you should be able to:

1. Define the terms *congenital anomaly*, *deformity*, and teratogens.
2. Discuss the organization of Chapter 17 of ICD-10-CM.
3. Differentiate between congenital and acquired conditions.
4. Apply the ICD-10-CM coding guidelines to accurately code congenital malformations, deformations, and chromosomal abnormalities.
5. Select and code diagnoses from case studies.

Key Terms

Acquired conditions

Anomaly

Birth defect

Cleft lip

Cleft palate

Congenital anomaly

Deformity

Harelip

Hydrocephalus

Polycystic kidney disease

Spina bifida

Teratogens

Valgus deformities of feet

Varus deformities of feet

Volkmann's deformity

REMINDER: As you work through this chapter, you will need to have a copy of the ICD-10-CM coding book to reference. For this chapter, you will also need to reference the ICD-10-CM Official Guidelines for Coding and Reporting. These guidelines can be found in Appendix A which are now available on the Student Companion site and MINDTAP From Cengage.

Introduction

Congenital anomalies, category codes Q00–Q99, are classified in Chapter 17 of ICD-10-CM. This chapter is organized according to anatomical site. The blocks found in this chapter are:

- Q00–Q07, Congenital malformations of the nervous system
- Q10–Q18, Congenital malformations of eye, ear, face, and neck
- Q20–Q28, Congenital malformations of the circulatory system
- Q30–Q34, Congenital malformations of the respiratory system
- Q35–Q37, Cleft lip and cleft palate
- Q38–Q45, Other congenital malformations of the digestive system
- Q50–Q56, Congenital malformations of genital organs
- Q60–Q64, Congenital malformations of the urinary system
- Q65–Q79, Congenital malformations and deformations of the musculoskeletal system
- Q80–Q89, Other congenital malformations
- Q90–Q99, Chromosomal abnormalities, not elsewhere classified

Introduction to the Body System

To understand the conditions that are classified to this chapter of ICD-10-CM, coders need to understand its terminology. A **congenital anomaly** is a disorder that exists at the time of birth and may be a result of genetic factors, agents causing defects in the embryo, or both. Agents that cause defects in an embryo are called **teratogens**. ICD-10-CM makes a clear distinction between an anomaly and a deformity. A **deformity** is a problem in the structure or form, which may or may not be disfiguring. An example of this is **Volkmann's deformity**, which is a congenital deformity of the foot due to tibiotarsal dislocation. An **anomaly**, or **birth defect**, is a deviation from what is normal in the development of a structure or organ. An example of an anomaly is spina bifida cystica. **Spina bifida** is a congenital condition in which the spinal canal fails to close around the spinal cord.

Coding Congenital Malformations, Deformations, and Chromosomal Abnormalities

When selecting codes for congenital anomalies and defects, coders must closely review the Alphabetic Index. Many conditions are identified in ICD-10-CM as both congenital and acquired. **Acquired conditions** occur during a person's life. ICD-10-CM makes a distinction in the Alphabetic Index between congenital and acquired conditions, with the terms *acquired* or *congenital* in parentheses for some conditions. The terms in parentheses act as modifiers for the condition being coded because they further describe it.

EXAMPLE: Holly presented to the emergency room with extreme pain in the right wrist joint. Holly is 10 years old. Upon examination, it was noted that the joint was somewhat deformed in that it was indented in the middle of the joint. Patient cannot flex the wrist. Mom noted that the wrist has been like this since birth. Until she has finished growing, surgery is not an option. The condition will be treated with ibuprofen and ice until the patient can be seen by primary care.

Clinical Impression: congenital deformity of the right wrist

When coding the diagnostic statement "deformity of the joint," the coder finds the following in the Alphabetic Index:

Deformity
wrist (joint) (acquired)—see also Deformity, limb, forearm
congenital Q68.8
contraction—see Contraction, Joint, wrist

In the Alphabetic Index, both acquired and congenital categories are listed, with the term *acquired* appearing in parentheses and the term *congenital* appearing as an indentation. The coder has to be able to read the documentation when confronted with this type of situation to assign the correct code. If this is not possible based on the available information, then the coder needs to get clarification from the provider. For this example, code Q68.8 is the correct code assignment.

When selecting codes for this chapter of ICD-10-CM, coders need to be familiar with the following coding guidelines:

ICD-10-CM Official Coding Guidelines

Chapter 17: Congenital malformations, deformations, and chromosomal abnormalities (Q00–Q99)

Assign an appropriate code(s) from categories Q00–Q99, Congenital malformations, deformations, and chromosomal abnormalities when a malformation/deformation/or chromosomal abnormality is documented. A malformation/deformation/or chromosomal abnormality may be the principal/first listed diagnosis on a record or a secondary diagnosis.

When a malformation/deformation/or chromosomal abnormality does not have a unique code assignment, assign additional code(s) for any manifestations that may be present.

When the code assignment specifically identifies the malformation/deformation/or chromosomal abnormality, manifestations that are an inherent component of the anomaly should not be coded separately. Additional codes should be assigned for manifestations that are not an inherent component.

Codes from Chapter 17 may be used throughout the life of the patient. If a congenital malformation or deformity has been corrected, a personal history code should be used to identify the history of the malformation or deformity. Although present at birth, a malformation/deformation/or chromosomal abnormality may not be identified until later in life. Whenever the condition is diagnosed by the provider, it is appropriate to assign a code from codes Q00–Q99.

For the birth admission, the appropriate code from category Z38, Liveborn infants, according to place of birth and type of delivery, should be sequenced as the principal diagnosis, followed by any congenital anomaly codes, Q00–Q99. (See Section I, 17.)

Courtesy of the Centers for Medicare & Medicaid Services, www.cms.gov

 NOTE:

The codes in this chapter are not assigned by age. Some congenital conditions do not manifest themselves until later in life even though they may have been present at birth. Also, a condition that occurs during the birthing process is considered a perinatal condition; a condition that is due to birth injury is coded to Chapter 16, "Conditions in the Perinatal Period."

Congenital Malformations of the Nervous System (Category Codes Q00–Q07)

Block Q00–Q07 is divided into the following categories:

- Q00, Anencephaly and similar malformations
- Q01, Encephalocele

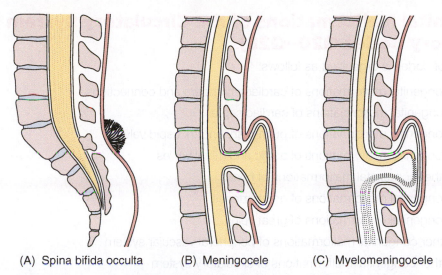

(A) Spina bifida occulta   (B) Meningocele   (C) Myelomeningocele

FIGURE 22-1   **Types of spina bifida (From Neighbors M., Tannehill-Jones R. *Human Diseases*, 2nd ed. Clifton Park, NY: Delmar, Cengage Learning, 2002, p. 374.).**

- Q02, Microcephaly
- Q03, Congenital hydrocephalus
- Q04, Other congenital malformations of brain
- Q05, Spina bifida
- Q06, Other congenital malformations of spinal cord
- Q07, Other congenital malformations of nervous system

Spina bifida is classified to category code Q05, except for spina bifida occulta, which is classified to code Q76.0. Figure 22-1 illustrates the different types of spina bifida. **Hydrocephalus**, an accumulation of fluid in the cranial meninges, is also found in the Q05 category when associated with spina bifida.

Congenital Malformations of Eye, Ear, Face, and Neck (Category Codes Q10–Q18)

This block of codes includes congenital malformations of the eye, ear, face, and neck and is classified to the following categories:

- Q10, Congenital malformations of eyelid, lacrimal apparatus, and orbit
- Q11, Anophthalmos, microphthalmos, and macrophthalmos
- Q12, Congenital lens malformations
- Q13, Congenital malformations of anterior segment of eye
- Q14, Congenital malformations of posterior segment of eye
- Q15, Other congenital malformations of eye
- Q16, Congenital malformations of ear causing impairment of hearing
- Q17, Other congenital malformations of ear
- Q18, Other congenital malformations of face and neck

As evidenced by their titles, the categories in this section are organized according to the specific sites and types of malformation. For many of the codes, numerous diagnostic descriptions and instructional notations are given. Careful attention to documentation is necessary for proper code assignment.

Congenital Malformations of the Circulatory System (Category Codes Q20–Q28)

This block of codes is organized as follows:

- Q20, Congenital malformations of cardiac chambers and connections
- Q21, Congenital malformations of cardiac septa
- Q22, Congenital malformations of pulmonary and tricuspid valves
- Q23, Congenital malformations of aortic and mitral valves
- Q24, Other congenital malformations of heart
- Q25, Congenital malformations of great arteries
- Q26, Congenital malformations of great veins
- Q27, Other congenital malformations of peripheral vascular system
- Q28, Other congenital malformations of circulatory system

Congenital anomalies of the cardiovascular system involve the heart and other structures of the circulatory system. The category codes are organized according to the anatomical structures affected by the anomaly. The terminology is the most challenging aspect of coding in this part of the code book. Because of the complexity of some of the conditions encountered in this part of the chapter, coders must research any questions regarding terminology, site, or abbreviations. Once a coder is familiar with the provider's documentation on these types of anomalies, code assignments become easier. Coders also need to identify that the cardiac condition being coded is congenital.

> **EXAMPLE:** Stenosis of the mitral valve can be congenital or acquired. Congenital stenosis of the mitral valve is coded to Q23.2, and mitral valve stenosis is coded to I05.0. Reading the documentation in the medical record and querying the provider are key in determining the proper code assignment.

Congenital Malformations of the Respiratory System (Category Codes Q30–Q34)

Congenital malformations of the respiratory system affect the nose, larynx, trachea, bronchus, lung, and pleura and are reported with the following categories:

- Q30, Congenital malformations of nose
- Q31, Congenital malformations of larynx
- Q32, Congenital malformations of trachea and bronchus
- Q33, Congenital malformations of lung
- Q34, Other congenital malformations of the respiratory system

Many congenital malformations, such as congenital stenosis of nares (Q30.0), congenital absence of lung (Q33.3), and congenital anomaly of pleura (Q34.0), are located in this section. Keep in mind, though, that some of these anomalies or deformities may not be diagnosed until months or years after the person is born, but the conditions are still reported with these codes. If they are determined to be congenital, they are still coded from this section.

Cleft Lip and Cleft Palate (Category Codes Q35–Q37)

This block of codes reports Q35, Cleft palate; Q36, Cleft lip; and Q37, Cleft palate with cleft lip. An instructional notation after the block heading reads, "Use additional code to identify associated malformations of the nose (Q30.2)."

A **cleft palate** is a congenital groove or opening of the palate that involves the hard palate, soft palate, or both, as well as the upper lip. A **cleft lip**, also referred to as **harelip**, is a congenital defect that results in a deep groove or opening of the lip running upward to the nose.

Other Congenital Malformations of the Digestive System (Category Codes Q38–Q45)

Congenital malformations of the tongue, mouth, pharynx, esophagus, upper alimentary tract, small and large intestines, gallbladder, bile ducts, and liver are reported with category codes Q38–Q45.

The categories are differentiated by anatomical site and then by the specific malformation. The categories are organized as follows:

- Q38, Other congenital malformations of tongue, mouth, and pharynx
- Q39, Congenital malformations of esophagus
- Q40, Other congenital malformations of upper alimentary tract
- Q41, Congenital absence, atresia, and stenosis of small intestine
- Q42, Congenital absence, atresia, and stenosis of large intestine
- Q43, Other congenital malformations of intestine
- Q44, Congenital malformations of gallbladder, bile ducts, and liver
- Q45, Other congenital malformations of digestive system

Exercise 22.1—Congenital Malformations

Match the code in column 1 with the description in column 2.

Column 1

_____ **1.** Q01.8
_____ **2.** Q04.6
_____ **3.** Q06.4
_____ **4.** Q13.5
_____ **5.** Q13.1
_____ **6.** Q18.4
_____ **7.** Q24.2
_____ **8.** Q22.4

Column 2

a. schizencephaly
b. macrostomia
c. congenital tricuspid stenosis
d. encephalocele of other sites
e. blue sclera
f. hydroachis
g. cor triatriatum
h. aniridia

Congenital Malformations of Genital Organs (Category Codes Q50–Q56)

Categories Q50–Q56 include malformations of both male and female genital organs. These codes are organized by anatomical site and then by the specific malformation. The categories are organized as follows:

- Q50, Congenital malformations of ovaries, fallopian tubes, and broad ligaments
- Q51, Congenital malformations of uterus and cervix

- Q52, Other congenital malformations of female genitalia
- Q53, Undescended and ectopic testicle
- Q54, Hypospadias
- Q55, Other congenital malformations of male genital organs
- Q56, Indeterminate sex and pseudohermaphroditism

Congenital Malformations of the Urinary System (Category Codes Q60–Q64)

The following five categories are used to report congenital malformations of the urinary system:

- Q60, Renal agenesis and other reduction defects of kidney
- Q61, Cystic kidney disease
- Q62, Congenital obstructive defects of renal pelvis and congenital malformations of ureter
- Q63, Other congenital malformations of kidney
- Q64, Other congenital malformations of the urinary system

Category code Q61 reports the various forms of cystic kidney disease. **Polycystic kidney disease**, a slowly progressive disorder in which the normal tissue of the kidneys is replaced with multiple grape-like cysts, is reported from this range of codes.

Disease Highlight—Polycystic Kidney Disease

Polycystic kidney disease is an inherited disorder in which the kidneys gradually lose the ability to function due to the grape-like clusters of cysts that form. The fluid-filled cysts cause a gradual inability of the kidneys to function because the renal tissue becomes compressed and eventually stops working. Figure 22-2 illustrates a polycystic kidney.

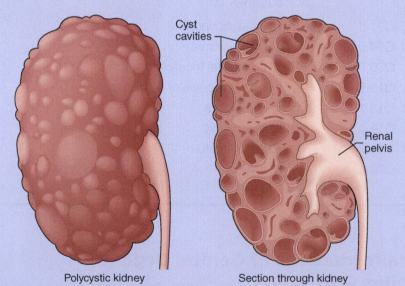

Polycystic kidney   Section through kidney

FIGURE 22-2 **Polycystic kidney (From Neighbors M., Tannehill-Jones R.** *Human Diseases,* **2nd ed. Clifton Park, NY: Delmar, Cengage Learning, 2002, p. 230.).**

Signs and Symptoms:

As the disease progresses, renal tissue is destroyed and hypertension typically develops. Lumbar pain, blood in the urine, and frequent urinary tract infections occur. In some cases, renal failure occurs.

Clinical Testing:

- A family history of polycystic kidney disease determines whether a patient is at risk.
- An intravenous pyelogram confirms the diagnosis.
- Urine tests, ultrasound, CT scans, and lab tests would be used to check creatinine levels and also confirm the diagnosis.

Treatment:

- There is no cure for the disease, but treatment of symptoms and surgical intervention may be necessary.
- If the kidney fails, dialysis is necessary.
- A kidney transplant is needed for end-stage management of the disease.
- Treatment is also directed by managing the hypertension and urinary tract infections.

Congenital Malformations and Deformations of the Musculoskeletal System (Category Codes Q65–Q79)

Category codes Q65–Q79 report musculoskeletal deformities of the hip, feet, head, face, fingers, knee, skull, limbs, ribs, spine, and chest. The categories are organized as follows:

- Q65, Congenital deformities of hip
- Q66, Congenital deformities of feet
- Q67, Congenital musculoskeletal deformities of head, face, spine, and chest
- Q68, Other congenital musculoskeletal deformities
- Q69, Polydactyly
- Q70, Syndactyly
- Q71, Reduction defects of upper limb
- Q72, Reduction defects of lower limb
- Q73, Reduction defects of unspecified limb
- Q74, Other congenital malformations of limb(s)
- Q75, Other congenital malformations of skull and face bones
- Q76, Congenital malformations of spine and bony thorax
- Q77, Osteochondrodysplasia with defects of growth of tubular bones and spine
- Q78, Other osteochondrodysplasias
- Q79, Congenital malformations of musculoskeletal system, not elsewhere classified

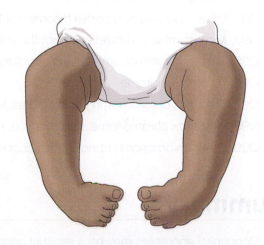

FIGURE 22-3 Varus deformity (From Neighbors M., Tannehill-Jones R. *Human Diseases*, 2nd ed. Clifton Park, NY: Delmar, Cengage Learning, 2002, p. 58.).

Category Q66 is used to report congenital deformities of the feet, including clubfoot, or talipes varus. **Varus deformities of feet** refer to the congenital turning inward of the feet, and **valgus deformities of feet** refer to the congenital outward turning of the feet. Figure 22-3 illustrates a talipes varus deformity of the feet. It should also be noted that within a number of categories laterality is identified for code assignment. For example, when reporting webbed fingers the codes are differentiated by the fifth characters as follows: Q70.10, Webbed fingers, unspecified hand; Q70.11, Webbed fingers, right hand; Q70.12, Webbed fingers, left hand; Q70.13, Webbed fingers, bilateral.

Other Congenital Malformations (Category Codes Q80–Q89) and Chromosomal Abnormalities, Not Elsewhere Classified (Category Codes Q90–Q99)

Category codes Q80–Q89 include:

- Q80, Congenital ichthyosis
- Q81, Epidermolysis bullosa
- Q82, Other congenital malformations of skin
- Q83, Congenital malformations of breast
- Q84, Other congenital malformations of integument
- Q85, Phakomatoses, not elsewhere classified
- Q86, Congenital malformation syndromes due to known exogenous causes, not elsewhere classified
- Q87, Other specified congenital malformation syndromes affecting multiple systems
- Q89, Other congenital malformations, not elsewhere classified

Chromosomal abnormalities reported with categories Q90–Q99 include:

- Q90, Down syndrome
- Q91, Trisomy 18 and trisomy 13
- Q92, Other trisomies and partial trisomies of the autosomes, not elsewhere classified
- Q93, Monosomies and deletions from the autosomes, not elsewhere classified
- Q95, Balanced rearrangements and structural markers, not elsewhere classified
- Q96, Turner's syndrome
- Q97, Other sex chromosome abnormalities, female phenotype, not elsewhere classified
- Q98, Other sex chromosome abnormalities, male phenotype, not elsewhere classified
- Q99, Other chromosome abnormalities, not elsewhere classified

Summary

- Congenital anomalies may be a result of genetic factors, teratogens, or both.
- The anomalies can be present at birth and obvious, or they may not be identified until later in life.
- Documentation is critical, and the coder must be clear on the diagnoses to be certain of the code assignment.
- ICD-10-CM classifies anomalies to congenital and acquired states. Therefore, for accurate coding to occur, medical documentation must clearly identify whether the anomaly is congenital.

Internet Links

To learn more about congenital anomalies, visit the National Institutes of Health at *www.health.nih.gov* and the National Library of Medicine at *www.nlm.nih.gov*.

Chapter Review

True/False

Indicate whether each statement is true (T) or false (F).

1. _____ The agents causing defects in an embryo are called teratogens.

2. _____ The codes in this chapter are assigned by age.

3. _____ The first block of codes in the chapter deals with anomalies of the nervous system.

4. _____ Anomalies of the eye are coded to the specific site of the defect.

5. _____ Spina bifida is a congenital condition in which the spinal canal fails to close around the spinal cord.

Fill-in-the-Blank

Enter the appropriate term(s) to complete each statement.

6. A _____ is a disorder that exists at the time of birth.

7. Code Q01.0 reports _____.

8. A birth defect is also known as a(n) _____.

9. _____ is a condition in which there is an accumulation of fluid in the cranial meninges.

10. A _____ is a problem in the structure or form that may or may not be disfiguring.

Coding Guidelines True/False

Review the ICD-10-CM Official Guidelines for Coding and Reporting and indicate if the statement(s) is true or false.

11. _____ A malformation/deformation/or chromosomal abnormality may be only listed as a principal diagnosis on a record.

12. _____ Codes from Chapter 17 of ICD-10-CM may only be used at the time of birth.

13. _____ When a malformation/deformation or chromosomal abnormality does not have a unique code assignment, assign additional code(s) for any manifestations that may be present.

14. _____ When a code assignment specifically identifies the malformation/deformation/or chromosomal abnormality, manifestations that are an inherent component of the anomaly should not be coded separately.

15. _____ If a congenital malformation or deformity has been corrected, a personal history code should be used to identify the history of the malformation or deformity.

Coding Assignments

Instructions: Using an ICD-10-CM code book, assign the proper diagnosis code to the following diagnostic statements.

1. congenital hydrocephalus _____

2. macrocheilia _____

3. unspecified anomaly of the ear with impairment of hearing _____

4. congenital deformity of the auricle of the heart _____

5. Arnold–Chiari syndrome _____

6. congenital branchial cleft malformation _____

7. Klippel–Feil syndrome _____

8. complete transposition of great vessels, congenital _____

9. congenital upper-limb vessel anomaly _____

10. hydromyelia _____

11. congenital renal dysplasia _____

12. exstrophy of urinary bladder _____

13. microcephalus _____

14. trisomies due to extra rings, normal individual _____

15. congenital deformity of lip _____

16. congenital clubnail _____

17. tuberous sclerosis _____

18. macrotia _____

19. Meckel's diverticulum _____

20. congenital coronary artery anomaly _____

21. fragile X syndrome _____

22. velo-cardio-facial syndrome _____

23. scrotal transposition, congenital _____

24. embryonal nuclear cataract _____

25. hemicephaly _____

26. congenital malformation of retina _____

27. congenital ptosis _____

28. absence of eustachian tube _____

29. absence of iris _____

30. congenital subglottic stenosis _____

31. congenital fibrocystic kidney _____

32. congenital vasocutaneous fistula _____

33. atresia of bile ducts present at birth _____

34. Apple peel syndrome _____

35. congenital torsion of ovary _____

Case Studies

Instructions: Review each case study and select the correct ICD-10-CM diagnostic code.

Case 1

Inpatient Orthopedic Consultation

Mary is a 3-year-old female child I am seeing at the request of Dr. Sharp. She is presently admitted to remove a cystic hygroma on her neck. She was born 4 weeks premature and

(continues)

(*continued*)

spent 5 weeks in the NICU and was diagnosed with congenital contracture of the left hip. Her development has been extremely delayed due to cerebral palsy.

EXAM:

Increased tone on her left side than on her right. There is a significant contracture of her left hip.

IMPRESSION:

Congenital coxa valga contracture of left hip.

RECOMMENDATIONS: The status of her hip adductors may cause her hip to dislocate, and an x-ray was ordered. She was scheduled for an adductor tenotomy to prevent her hip from dislocating.

ICD-10-CM Code Assignment: _____

Case 2

Office Visit

Samantha returns today for follow-up of her elbow and knee flexion contractures.

EXAM:

UPPER EXTREMITIES: Rigid bilateral 37-degree elbow flexion contractures.

PELVIC JOINTS: She has no contractures of her hips.

LOWER EXTREMITIES: Rigid bilateral 40-degree knee flexion contractures

ANKLES: There are no contractures of her ankles.

X-RAYS REVIEWED: AP pelvis, AP and lateral knee, and AP and lateral elbow x-rays show no significant findings. The findings are consistent with multiplex, congenital arthrogryposis involving the elbows and knees.

RECOMMENDATIONS: Measurements have been taken to have elbow and knee night splints made. She was scheduled for fitting and a 1-month follow-up visit.

ICD-10-CM Code Assignment: _____

Case 3

Ambulatory Surgery Discharge Note

This is a 7-year-old female who presented with a problem swallowing. The mother states that she took the child to her pediatrician for evaluation when she started having problems eating and holding food down. The pediatric office sent over results of CT scans of the neck, chest, and trunk as well as lab test results. Upon review of the CT scans, it is noted that a slight mass is present on the esophagus that has probably been present since birth. Today a surgical

(*continues*)

(*continued*)

removal of the mass and path examination was completed. The postoperative diagnosis of esophageal cyst (congenital) was made.

ICD-10-CM Code Assignment: _____

Case 4

Physician Office Note

This is a 5-year-old male who presents today with a complaint of abdominal pain. His mother has noted a history of complaints of abdominal pain in the past. He is now experiencing vomiting since last night around 1 a.m. and is quite lethargic and in mild distress. Examination reveals the abdomen is distended and tender. An abdominopelvic CT scan reveals a stricture in the small bowel. This appears to have been present since birth, but due to the child's growth it has now become a problem. He will be admitted to the hospital for surgical correction.

ICD-10-CM Code Assignment: _____

Case 5

Pediatric Office Note

Theresa Louise presents today for a 2-week checkup after a normal vaginal delivery. Mom says baby is eating well and is alert, responds appropriately when she hears noise, and is overall healthy. Upon examination there is a slight murmur when listening to the heart. We performed an EKG and chest x-ray.

There appears to be a small ventricular septal defect, which would have been present at birth. We will not do anything further at this time but will monitor this condition to see if it corrects itself over this coming year.

ICD-10-CM Code Assignment: _____

Case 6

Physician Office Note

This 84-year-old male patient, recently diagnosed with polycystic kidney disease, presents today to discuss his treatment options. At this point he is not experiencing any end-stage disease symptoms or any acute symptoms. I discussed with him and his wife that this is a progressive disease and it is more than likely he will need dialysis as the disease progresses. He was instructed to follow up with me in 8 weeks.

ICD-10-CM Code Assignment: _____

Case 7

Discharge Note

This 4-month-old female is being discharged following an admission for a surgical closure of a cervical spine meningocele. The surgery was successful and the meningocele was repaired without any complications. Prescription for liquid Tylenol with codeine was written for pain management. The patient should return to my office in 10 days.

ICD-10-CM Code Assignment: _____

Case 8

NICU Consultation

I was called in on consultation for this 16-hour-old newborn due to a loud systolic heart murmur. A chest x-ray shows a decreased pulmonary vascular marking and boot-shaped cardiac silhouette. EKG demonstrated a right ventricular hypertrophy and right axis deviation and right atrial hypertrophy. Additional diagnostic imaging and echocardiography confirms tetralogy of Fallot.

ICD-10-CM Code Assignment: _____

Case 9

Inpatient Consultation

This 25-hour-old male infant has Down syndrome. Upon exam there is a cardiac murmur that varies in frequency. EKG demonstrates a left and right ventricular hypertrophy. Echocardiography confirms a large ventricular septal defect. These findings will be discussed with the patient's parents.

ICD-10-CM Code Assignment: _____

Case 10

Office Visit

This 3-year-old female child and her parents are returning to the office today to follow up after a series of tests that included a muscle biopsy and electromyography. Upon examination the child is walking with a *waddling* gait, and toe walking. The findings from the diagnostic testing confirm muscular dystrophy. I am referring the child to physical therapy and to be evaluated for leg braces.

ICD-10-CM Code Assignment: _____

CHAPTER 23

Symptoms, Signs, and Abnormal Clinical Laboratory Findings

Chapter Outline

Chapter Objectives

At the conclusion of this chapter, you should be able to:

1. Identify terms used in locating codes for symptoms, signs, and ill-defined conditions found in Chapter 18 of ICD-10-CM.
2. Explain terms found in documentation that would lead a coder to Chapter 18 of ICD-10-CM.
3. Describe the conditions classified to Chapter 18 of ICD-10-CM.
4. Apply the ICD-10-CM coding guidelines to accurately code symptoms, signs, and abnormal clinical laboratory findings.
5. Select and code signs, symptoms, and ill-defined conditions from case studies.

Key Terms

Altered states of
   consciousness

Coma

Sign

Symptom

Syncope

REMINDER: As you work through this chapter, you will need to have a copy of the ICD-10-CM coding book to reference. For this chapter, you will also need to reference the ICD-10-CM Official Guidelines for Coding and Reporting. These guidelines can be found in Appendix A which are now available on the Student Companion site and MINDTAP From Cengage.

Introduction

Chapter 18 of ICD-10-CM, "Symptoms, Signs, and Abnormal Clinical and Laboratory Findings, Not Elsewhere Classified," allows the coder to locate codes for the abnormal results of laboratory or other investigative procedures, as well as for signs and symptoms for conditions that do not have a specific diagnosis code found elsewhere in ICD-10-CM. The codes for symptoms that affect only one body system are classified to the relevant chapters of ICD-10-CM, whereas symptoms that affect multiple systems or more than one disease are found in Chapter 18.

The code blocks found in this code range are:

- R00–R09, Symptoms and signs involving the circulatory and respiratory systems
- R10–R19, Symptoms and signs involving the digestive system and abdomen
- R20–R23, Symptoms and signs involving the skin and subcutaneous tissue
- R25–R29, Symptoms and signs involving the nervous and musculoskeletal systems
- R30–R39, Symptoms and signs involving the genitourinary system
- R40–R46, Symptoms and signs involving cognition, perception, emotional state, and behavior
- R47–R49, Symptoms and signs involving speech and voice
- R50–R69, General symptoms and signs
- R70–R79, Abnormal findings on examination of blood, without diagnosis
- R80–R82, Abnormal findings on examination of urine, without diagnosis
- R83–R89, Abnormal findings on examination of other body fluids, substances, and tissues, without diagnosis
- R90–R94, Abnormal findings on diagnostic imaging and in function studies, without diagnosis
- R97, Abnormal tumor markers
- R99, Ill-defined and unknown cause of mortality

Coding of Symptoms, Signs, and Abnormal Clinical and Laboratory Findings, Not Elsewhere Classified

Chapter 18 of ICD-10-CM contains codes for signs, symptoms, and ill-defined conditions such as abnormal clinical or laboratory findings that impact the medical care and management of the patient. A **symptom** is reported by the patient and typically is what brings the patient to seek medical attention. A symptom is considered subjective information because it can be evaluated or measured only by the patient. A **sign** is observed by the physician and is objective evidence of a disease. It can be measured or evaluated.

> **EXAMPLE:** Marie Merry presents with itching and burning of the right forearm. Upon examination, a patch of small blisters is noticed. The itching and burning are considered symptoms because they can be described and evaluated only by the patient. The blisters are a sign because they can be observed and evaluated by the physician.

Ill-defined conditions also code to this chapter but should never be used if a more definitive diagnosis has been made. These codes are used when no other diagnosis is found in the available medical information or a code cannot be found in another chapter of ICD-10-CM. Until a specific diagnosis is assigned, the signs and symptoms are coded.

EXAMPLE: Mrs. Marble presents today with her 3-month-old daughter, who is not eating well and is quite fussy. She cries after she has had her bottle and has projectile vomiting. She has been like this over the last several days, and now Mrs. Marble would like her to be examined. The report is as follows:

Examination reveals nothing out of the ordinary. This is a normal, 3-month-old baby girl. Heart and lungs are clear; bowel sounds are active and normal. Abdomen is soft with no splenomegaly.

Diagnosis: Projectile vomiting

Plan: Will contact the pediatric GI office and set up a consult with possible workup.

The diagnosis in this example is R11.12, Projectile vomiting, because a definitive diagnosis was not made. If the pediatric gastroenterologist (GI) makes a definitive diagnosis, then the diagnosis is *not* R11.12 but whatever diagnosis the gastroenterologist gives.

Before selecting codes from this chapter, the coder should be familiar with the notations in the Tabular List after the chapter heading. The notations explain the purpose and use of the codes found in Chapter 18 of ICD-10-CM. The following is the note that appears for Chapter 18 of ICD-10-CM at the start of the chapter.

NOTE:

This chapter includes symptoms, signs, abnormal results of clinical or other investigative procedures, and ill-defined conditions regarding which no diagnosis classifiable elsewhere is recorded.

Signs and symptoms that point rather definitely to a given diagnosis have been assigned to a category in other chapters of the classification. In general, categories in this chapter include the less well-defined conditions and symptoms that, without the necessary study of the case to establish a final diagnosis, point perhaps equally to two or more diseases or to two or more systems of the body.

Practically all categories in the chapter could be designated "not otherwise specified", "unknown etiology," or "transient". The Alphabetical Index should be consulted to determine which symptoms and signs are to be allocated here and which to other chapters. The residual subcategories, numbered .8, are generally provided for other relevant symptoms that cannot be allocated elsewhere in the classification.

The conditions and signs or symptoms included in categories R00—R94 consist of:

(a)   cases for which no more specific diagnosis can be made even after all the facts bearing on the case have been investigated;

(b)   signs or symptoms existing at the time of initial encounter that proved to be transient and whose causes could not be determined;

(c)   provisional diagnosis in a patient who failed to return for further investigation or care;

(d)   cases referred elsewhere for investigation or treatment before the diagnosis was made;

(e)   cases in which a more precise diagnosis was not available for any other reason;

(f)   certain symptoms, for which supplementary information is provided, that represent important problems in medical care in their own right.

It is common to select codes from Chapter 18 for coding outpatient encounters. Outpatients seek care for relief of symptoms, and the results of diagnostic workups are not always available at the time of the encounter. The codes from Chapter 18 are used to describe the reason for the encounter when a more definitive diagnosis is not yet available.

Coding Guidelines for Symptoms, Signs, and Abnormal Clinical and Laboratory Findings, Not Elsewhere Classified

The ICD-10-CM Official Guidelines for Coding and Reporting provide the coder with guidance as to when to use codes from Chapter 18. These guidelines, at times, are different for inpatient and outpatient encounters; however, some of the guidelines apply to both the inpatient and the outpatient settings.

The first guideline that applies to coding symptoms and signs appears in Section I, B, 4 of the ICD-10-CM Official Coding Guidelines for Coding and Reporting. It reads as follows:

ICD-10-CM Official Coding Guidelines

Signs and Symptoms

Codes that describe symptoms and signs, as opposed to diagnoses, are acceptable for reporting purposes when a related definitive diagnosis has not been established (confirmed) by the provider. Chapter 18 of ICD-10-CM, Symptoms, Signs, and Abnormal Clinical and Laboratory Findings, Not Elsewhere Classified (codes R00.0–R99) contain many, but not all codes for symptoms. (See Appendix A, Section I, B, 4.)

Courtesy of the Centers for Medicare & Medicaid Services, www.cms.gov

Guideline for Principal Diagnosis

An additional guideline in Section II, A of the ICD-10-CM Official Guidelines for Coding and Reporting applies to the selection of one or more principal diagnoses for inpatient, short-term, acute care, long-term care, home health agencies, rehabilitative facilities, and psychiatric hospital records:

ICD-10-CM Official Coding Guidelines

A. Codes for symptoms, signs, and ill-defined conditions

Codes for symptoms, signs, and ill-defined conditions from Chapter 18 are not to be used as a principal diagnosis when a related definitive diagnosis has been established. (See Appendix A, section II, A.)

Courtesy of the Centers for Medicare & Medicaid Services, www.cms.gov

This guideline instructs the coder to report a definitive diagnosis when it is established and not use a code from Chapter 18. If a definitive diagnosis is not established, then a code from Chapter 18 can be used. In an inpatient setting, symptom codes are not sequenced as a principal diagnosis when a related condition has been confirmed unless the patient was admitted for the purpose of treating the symptom and no care, treatment, or evaluation of the underlying disease occurred. For example, if a patient is admitted with intractable renal colic known to be caused by kidney stones and only pain management occurs, the code for renal colic, N23, is used. Therefore, the symptom can be coded as a principal diagnosis if the patient is being treated for only the symptom and not for the underlying condition. If there is any question about sequencing, the coder should always go back to the reason for the encounter.

Symptoms and Signs as Secondary Codes

The ICD-10-CM Official Guidelines for Coding and Reporting state the following in relation to reporting signs and symptoms as additional diagnoses. This guideline applies to both inpatient and outpatient settings:

ICD-10-CM Official Coding Guidelines

5. Conditions that are an integral part of a disease process

Signs and symptoms that are associated routinely with a disease process should not be assigned as additional codes unless otherwise instructed by the classification. (See Appendix A, Section I, B, 5.)

Courtesy of the Centers for Medicare & Medicaid Services, www.cms.gov

The coder must have clinical documentation, as well as reference materials available, to properly code patient admissions and encounters in which signs and symptoms are documented in addition to a disease process. The coder must be able to identify the signs and symptoms that are implicit in a diagnostic statement because, according to the Official Coding Guidelines, these signs and symptoms are not coded separately. For example, if a patient presents with abdominal pain, and it is determined that the patient has gastroenteritis, the abdominal pain is not coded because the abdominal pain is an integral part of the gastroenteritis.

However, when a patient presents with signs and symptoms that are not routinely associated with a disease, the following coding guideline applies:

ICD-10-CM Official Coding Guidelines

6. Conditions that are not an integral part of a disease process

Additional signs and symptoms that may not be associated routinely with a disease process should be coded when present. (See Appendix A, Section I, B, 6.)

Courtesy of the Centers for Medicare & Medicaid Services, www.cms.gov

Difference Between Inpatient and Outpatient Coding Guidelines

For inpatient hospital visits, suspected, rule-out, and possible diagnoses can be coded. For outpatient or office visits, suspected, rule-out, and possible diagnoses cannot be coded. Therefore, often in the outpatient setting, codes from Chapter 18 of ICD-10-CM are used until a physician can establish a definitive diagnosis. The following guideline applies to outpatient settings and is found in Section IV of the ICD-10-CM Official Guidelines for Coding and Reporting:

ICD-10-CM Official Coding Guidelines

H. Uncertain diagnoses

Do not code diagnoses documented as "probable," "suspected," "questionable," "rule out," "compatible with," "consistent with," or "working diagnosis" or other similar terms indicating uncertainty. Rather, code the conditions(s) to the highest degree of certainty for that encounter/visit, such as symptoms, signs, abnormal test results, or other reason for the visit.

Please note: This differs from the coding practices used by short-term, acute care, long-term care, and psychiatric hospitals. (See Appendix A, Section IV, H.)

Courtesy of the Centers for Medicare & Medicaid Services, www.cms.gov

EXAMPLE: Patty Patient presents to the ER with acute rebound tenderness in the lower right quadrant and a fever of 99. The ER doctor orders a lab workup to be done to rule out appendicitis. The diagnosis on lab order is rebound tenderness, fever, possible appendicitis.

The coding is going to hinge on the fact that this patient is being seen in the emergency room and is therefore still considered an outpatient. The diagnosis of "possible appendicitis" cannot be coded when the provider does not state it as a definitive diagnosis. In the outpatient setting, the symptoms of rebound tenderness, R10.823, and fever, R50.9, are coded because these are the reasons the patient presented to the emergency room.

The coder should reference other coding guidelines before assigning codes from this chapter. As we move through the chapter-specific categories, we will reference the applicable guidelines further.

Chapter 18 Specific Coding Guidelines

Chapter 18 of ICD-10-CM is governed by the following guidelines:

ICD-10-CM Official Coding Guidelines

Chapter 18: Symptoms, signs, and abnormal clinical and laboratory findings, not elsewhere classified (R00–R99)

Chapter 18 includes symptoms, signs, abnormal results of clinical or other investigative procedures, and ill-defined conditions regarding which no diagnosis classifiable elsewhere is recorded. Signs and symptoms that point to a specific diagnosis have been assigned to a category in other chapters of the classification.

a. Use of symptom codes

Codes that describe symptoms and signs are acceptable for reporting purposes when a related definitive diagnosis has not been established (confirmed) by the provider.

b. Use of a symptom code with a definitive diagnosis code

Codes for signs and symptoms may be reported in addition to a related definitive diagnosis when the sign or symptom is not routinely associated with that diagnosis, such as the various signs and symptoms associated with complex syndromes. The definitive diagnosis code should be sequenced before the symptom code.

Signs or symptoms that are associated routinely with a disease process should not be assigned as additional codes, unless otherwise instructed by the classification.

c. Combination codes that include symptoms

ICD-10-CM contains a number of combination codes that identify both the definitive diagnosis and common symptoms of that diagnosis. When using one of these combination codes, an additional code should not be assigned for the symptom. (See Appendix A, Section I. C18. a–c.)

Courtesy of the Centers for Medicare & Medicaid Services, www.cms.gov

Symptoms and Signs Involving the Circulatory and Respiratory Systems (Category Codes R00–R09)

The codes in this block include those for shortness of breath, hemoptysis, cardiac murmur, and snoring. This code block also includes elevated blood pressure without a diagnosis of hypertension (R03.0). The code block is organized as follows:

- R00, Abnormalities of heart beat
- R01, Cardiac murmurs and other cardiac sounds

- R03, Abnormal blood-pressure reading without diagnosis
- R04, Hemorrhage from respiratory passages
- R05, Cough
- R06, Abnormalities of breathing
- R07, Pain in throat and chest
- R09, Other symptoms and signs involving the circulatory and respiratory system

Symptoms and Signs Involving the Digestive System and Abdomen (Category Codes R10–R19)

For any abdominal pain, whether it is abdominal tenderness, localized or generalized pain, or rebound pain, the codes are found in these categories. The extensive Excludes2 note at the beginning of the block of codes should be referenced before the code is assigned. The block organization is as follows:

- R10, Abdominal and pelvic pain—It should be noted that the abdominal quadrant in which the pain is present is differentiated in the code.
- R11, Nausea and vomiting
- R12, Heartburn
- R13, Aphagia and dysphagia
- R14, Flatulence and related conditions
- R15, Fecal incontinence
- R16, Hepatomegaly and splenomegaly, not elsewhere classified
- R17, Unspecified jaundice
- R18, Ascites
- R19, Other symptoms and signs involving the digestive system and abdomen

Symptoms and Signs Involving the Skin and Subcutaneous Tissue (Category Codes R20–R23)

This block of codes reports disturbances of skin sensation, rashes and other nonspecific skin eruptions, and other skin changes. Also included is hypoesthesia of the skin, pallor, and scaling of the skin. The block is organized as follows:

- R20, Disturbances of skin sensation
- R21, Rash and other nonspecific skin eruption
- R22, Localized swelling, mass and lump of skin and subcutaneous tissue
- R23, Other skin changes

Symptoms and Signs Involving the Nervous and Musculoskeletal Systems (Category Codes R25–R29)

Tremors, abnormal reflexes, and paralytic gait are included in this range of codes, as well as loss of heat and facial weakness. The Excludes1 notes specifies various disorders that are not coded from these codes. The block is organized as follows:

- R25, Abnormal involuntary movements
- R26, Abnormalities of gait and mobility

- R27, Other lack of coordination
- R29, Other symptoms and signs involving the nervous and musculoskeletal systems

When assigning code R29.6, the following guideline needs to be taken into consideration:

ICD-10-CM Official Coding Guidelines

d. Repeated falls

Code R29.6, Repeated falls, is for use for encounters when a patient has recently fallen and the reason for the fall is being investigated.

Code Z91.81, History of falling, is for use when a patient has fallen in the past and is at risk for future falls. When appropriate, both codes R29.6 and Z91.81 may be assigned together. (See Appendix A, Section I.C18.d.)

Symptoms and Signs Involving the Genitourinary System (Category Codes R30–R39)

Hematuria, urinary retention, oliguria, polyuria, and urgency are all coded to this code range. The instructional notation for category R39.1 instructs the coder to "Code first, if applicable, any causal condition, such as: enlarged prostate (N40.1)." The block is organized as follows:

- R30, Pain associated with micturition
- R31, Hematuria
- R32, Unspecified urinary incontinence
- R33, Retention of urine
- R34, Anuria and oliguria
- R35, Polyuria
- R36, Urethral discharge
- R37, Sexual dysfunction, unspecified
- R39, Other and unspecified symptoms and signs involving the genitourinary system

Symptoms and Signs Involving Cognition, Perception, Emotional State, and Behavior (Category Codes R40–R46)

This block of codes is organized as follows:

- R40, Somnolence, stupor, and coma
- R41, Other symptoms and signs involving cognitive functions and awareness
- R42, Dizziness and giddiness
- R43, Disturbances of smell and taste
- R44, Other symptoms and signs involving general sensations and perceptions
- R45, Symptoms and signs involving emotional state
- R46, Symptoms and signs involving appearance and behavior

A **coma** is a condition in which the person is in a deep state of unconsciousness. There is usually no spontaneous eye movement or response to painful stimuli. In **altered states of consciousness**, such as transient alteration of awareness, the patient does not lose consciousness completely but may stare or have a loss of awareness.

Subcategory R40.2 is used to assign codes for coma. At the start of the R40.2 subcategory, the following notation appears: "Code first any associated:

coma in fracture of skull (S02.-)

coma in intracranial injury (S06.-)"

The coder is also instructed that seventh characters are to be added to each code from subcategory R40.21-, R40.22-, R40.23-, and R40.24-.

When assigning codes from subcategory R40.2-, the following guideline needs to be taken into consideration:

ICD-10-CM Official Coding Guidelines

e. Coma scale

The coma scale codes (R40.2-) can be used in conjunction with traumatic brain injury codes. These codes are primarily for use by trauma registries, but they may be used in any setting where this information is collected. The coma scale codes should be sequenced after the diagnosis code(s).

These codes, one from each subcategory, are needed to complete the scale. The 7th character indicates when the scale was recorded. The 7th character should match for all three codes.

At a minimum, report the initial score documented on presentation at your facility. This may be a score from the emergency medicine technician (EMT) or in the emergency department. If desired, a facility may choose to capture multiple coma scale scores.

Assign code R40.24, Glasgow coma scale, total score, when only the total score is documented in the medical record and not the individual score(s).

Do not report codes for individual or total Glasgow coma scale scores for a patient with a medically induced coma or a sedated patient.

See Section I.B.14 for coma scale documentation by clinicians other than patient's provider. (See Appendix A, Section I.C18.e.)

Symptoms and Signs Involving Speech and Voice (Category Codes R47–R49)

Category codes R47 to R49 report symptoms and signs involving speech and voice. Many of the codes contained in these categories are used by speech therapists when they are reporting diagnoses for their initial and subsequent therapies that they provide to patients. The categories are summarized as follows:

- R47, Speech disturbances, not elsewhere classified—This category contains codes for dysphasia (R47.02), aphasia (R47.01), dysarthria and anarthria (R47.1), slurred speech (R47.81), and fluency disorder in conditions classified elsewhere (R47.82), other speech disturbances (R47.89), and unspecified speech disturbances (R47.9).

- R48, Dyslexia and other symbolic dysfunctions, not elsewhere classified—This category contains codes for dyslexia and alexia (R48.0), agnosia (R48.1), apraxia (R48.2), visual agnosia (R48.3), other symbolic dysfunctions (R48.8), and unspecified symbolic dysfunctions (R48.9).

- R49, Voice and resonance disorders—This category contains codes for dysphonia (R49.0), aphonia (R49.1), hypernasality (R49.21), hyponasality (R49.22), other voice and resonance disorders (R49.8), and unspecified voice and resonance disorder (R49.9).

 NOTE:

If you are unfamiliar with any of the medical terms that are used as category titles or as a diagnosis, you should reference a medical dictionary.

General Symptoms and Signs (Category Codes R50–R69)

This block of codes is organized as follows:

- R50, Fever of other and unknown origin
- R51, Headache
- R52, Pain, unspecified
- R53, Malaise and fatigue
- R54, Age-related physical debility
- R55, Syncope and collapse
- R56, Convulsions, not elsewhere classified
- R57, Shock, not elsewhere classified
- R58, Hemorrhage, not elsewhere classified
- R59, Enlarged lymph nodes
- R60, Edema, not elsewhere classified
- R61, Generalized hyperhidrosis
- R62, Lack of expected normal physiological development in childhood and adults
- R63, Symptoms and signs concerning food and fluid intake
- R64, Cachexia
- R65, Symptoms and signs specifically associated with systemic inflammation and infection
- R68, Other general symptoms and signs
- R69, Illness, unspecified

Syncope, also known as fainting, is a condition in which there is a brief loss of consciousness due to a lack of oxygen to the brain. When no specific disease process is identified as causing the condition, syncope is reported with code R55. Other common symptoms and signs that are reported to this block of codes include:

- Fever, R50.9
- Headache, R51.9
- Chronic fatigue syndrome, R53.82
- Old age, R54
- Hemorrhage, R58
- Fluid retention, R60.9
- Loss of appetite, R63.0
- Excessive sweating, R61

Coders should also note the coding guideline that is associated with codes R65.10 and R65.11.

When assigning codes from category R65, the following guideline needs to be followed:

ICD-10-CM Official Coding Guidelines

g. SIRS due to Non-Infectious Process

The systemic inflammatory response syndrome (SIRS) can develop as a result of certain non-infectious disease processes, such as trauma, malignant neoplasm, or pancreatitis. When SIRS is documented with a non-infectious condition, and no subsequent infection is documented, the code for the underlying condition, such as an injury, should be assigned, followed by code R65.10, Systemic inflammatory response syndrome (SIRS) of non-infectious origin without acute organ dysfunction, or code R65.11, Systemic inflammatory response syndrome (SIRS) of non-infectious origin with acute organ dysfunction. If an associated acute organ dysfunction is documented, the appropriate code(s) for the specific type of organ dysfunction(s) should be assigned in addition to code R65.11. If acute organ dysfunction is documented, but it cannot be determined if the acute organ dysfunction is associated with SIRS or due to another condition (e.g., directly due to the trauma), the provider should be queried. (See Appendix A, Section I.C18.g.)

Abnormal Findings on Examination of Blood Without Diagnosis (Category Codes R70–R79) and Abnormal Findings on Examination of Urine Without Diagnosis (Category Codes R80–R82)

Conditions that are classified as abnormal findings without a definitive diagnosis are coded from this range of codes. Such conditions can be located in the Alphabetic Index under entries such as "Findings, abnormal, without diagnosis," "Elevation," and "Abnormal, abnormality, abnormalities." If the documentation implies but does not specifically state a diagnosis, clarification from the provider is needed; if the physician clarifies the documentation, an addendum is added to it.

A problem that is frequently encountered in a primary care office is a patient who presents with elevated blood glucose but no history of diabetes mellitus. Nothing in the history or examination indicates that this is a chronic condition. Category R73 is used to report the elevated blood glucose. If this same patient presents to the office with elevated blood glucose, is a diagnosed diabetic, and is on medication to control the diabetes, the code for diabetes is used and not the R73 category.

This block of codes is organized as follows:

- R70, Elevated erythrocyte sedimentation rate and abnormality of plasma viscosity
- R71, Abnormality of red blood cells
- R73, Elevated blood glucose level
- R74, Abnormal serum enzyme levels
- R75, Inconclusive laboratory evidence of human immunodeficiency virus [HIV]
- R76, Other abnormal immunological findings in serum
- R77, Other abnormalities of plasma proteins
- R78, Findings of drugs and other substances, not normally found in blood
- R79, Other abnormal findings of blood chemistry
- R80, Proteinuria
- R81, Glycosuria
- R82, Other and unspecified abnormal findings in urine

Abnormal Findings on Examination of Other Body Fluids, Substances, and Tissues, Without Diagnosis (Category Codes R83–R89)

Abnormal microbiological findings, abnormal levels of hormones, abnormal levels of enzymes, and abnormal histological findings are coded to these category codes. These codes are used if no definitive diagnosis is found.

Coders have to refer to the documentation to be sure that there is not information supporting a diagnosis found in another chapter of ICD-10-CM.

This code block is arranged as follows:

- R83, Abnormal findings in cerebrospinal fluid
- R84, Abnormal findings in specimens from respiratory organs and thorax
- R85, Abnormal findings in specimens from digestive organs and abdominal cavity
- R86, Abnormal findings in specimens from male genital organs
- R87, Abnormal findings in specimens from female genital organs
- R88, Abnormal findings in other body fluids and substances
- R89, Abnormal findings in specimens from other organs, systems, and tissues

Abnormal Findings on Diagnostic Imaging and in Function Studies, Without Diagnosis (Category Codes R90–R94), Abnormal Tumor Markers (Category Code R97), and Ill-defined and Unknown Cause of Mortality (Category Code R99)

This block of codes is organized as follows:

- R90, Abnormal findings on diagnostic imaging of central nervous system
- R91, Abnormal findings on diagnostic imaging of lung
- R92, Abnormal and inconclusive findings on diagnostic imaging of breast
- R93, Abnormal findings on diagnostic imaging other body structures
- R94, Abnormal results of function studies
- R97, Abnormal tumor markers
- R99, Ill-defined and unknown cause of mortality

Remember that before assigning these codes, the coder needs to review all the available medical documentation to ensure that a more definitive diagnosis has not been determined.

When assigning code R99, ill-defined and unknown cause of mortality, the following guideline needs to be taken into consideration:

ICD-10-CM Official Coding Guidelines

h. Death NOS

Code R99, Ill-defined and unknown cause of mortality, is only for use in the very limited circumstance when a patient who has already died is brought into an emergency department or other healthcare facility and is pronounced dead upon arrival. It does not represent the discharge disposition of death. (See Appendix A, Section I.C18.h.)

i. NIHSS

The NIH stroke scale (NIHSS) codes (R29.7--) can be used in conjunction with acute stroke codes (I63) to identify the patient's neurological status and the severity of the stroke. The stroke scale codes should be sequenced after the acute stroke diagnosis code(s).

At a minimum, report the initial score documented. If desired, a facility may choose to capture multiple stroke scale scores.

See Section I.B.14. for NIHSS stroke scale documentation by clinicians other than patient's provider.

(See Appendix A, Section I.C.18.h-i.)

Courtesy of the Centers for Medicare & Medicaid Services, www.cms.gov

Summary

- Chapter 18 of ICD-10-CM, "Symptoms, Signs and Abnormal Clinical and Laboratory Findings, Not Elsewhere Classified," contains codes for symptoms and signs that affect the medical care and management of the patient.
- Abnormal findings and ill-defined conditions are also coded to Chapter 18 of ICD-10-CM.
- Codes from this chapter should not be used if a more definitive diagnosis is available.
- Until a specific diagnosis is assigned, the signs and symptoms are coded.
- Symptoms are not usually sequenced as a principal diagnosis when a related condition has been confirmed.
- Suspected, rule-out, and possible diagnoses cannot be coded in an outpatient setting.

Chapter Review

True/False

Indicate whether each statement is true (T) or false (F).

1. _____ A symptom is objective and a sign is subjective.
2. _____ Diagnosis codes from Chapter 18 of ICD-10-CM are not used if a definitive diagnosis is given.
3. _____ In an outpatient setting, rule-out diagnoses can be coded.
4. _____ Symptoms involving the respiratory and digestive systems are coded to the same categories of codes.
5. _____ Ascites is reported with code R18.8.

Fill-in-the-Blank

Enter the appropriate term(s) to complete each statement.

6. Until a specific diagnosis is assigned, the _____ and _____ are coded instead.
7. Another term for fainting is _____.
8. A _____ is a condition in which the person is in a deep state of unconsciousness.
9. Sinus bradycardia is reported with code _____.
10. Precordial pain is reported with code _____.

Coding Guidelines True/False

Review the ICD-10-CM Official Guidelines for Coding and Reporting and indicate if the statement(s) is true or false.

11. _____ Code R99 represents the discharge disposition of death.
12. _____ The NIH stroke scale (NIHSS) codes (R29.7–) can be used in conjunction with acute stroke codes (I63) to identify the patient's neurological status and the severity of the stroke. The stroke scale codes should be sequenced before the acute stroke diagnosis code(s).
13. _____ Code R29.6, Repeated falls, is for use for encounters when a patient has recently fallen and the reason for the fall is being investigated.

14. _____ Assign code R40.24, Glasgow coma scale, total score, when only the total score is documented in the medical record and not the individual score(s).

15. _____ Codes for signs and symptoms may be reported in addition to a related definitive diagnosis when the sign or symptom is not routinely associated with that diagnosis, such as the various signs and symptoms associated with complex syndromes. The definitive diagnosis code should be sequenced after the symptom code.

Coding Assignments

Instructions: Using an ICD-10-CM code book, assign the proper diagnosis code to the following diagnostic statements.

1. palpitations   _____

2. left lower quadrant abdominal tenderness   _____

3. hypoesthesia of skin   _____

4. nausea and vomiting   _____

5. painful respirations   _____

6. periumbilical rebound tenderness   _____

7. meningismus   _____

8. cardiac bruit   _____

9. ataxia   _____

10. loss of height   _____

11. orthopnea   _____

12. elevated blood pressure reading without diagnosis of hypertension   _____

13. epigastric pain   _____

14. tendency to fall   _____

15. eructation   _____

16. cyanosis   _____

17. auditory hallucinations   _____

18. restlessness   _____

19. painful urination   _____

20. malaise   _____

21. failure to thrive, child   _____

22. cardiogenic shock   _____

23. poor urinary stream   _____

24. retrograde amnesia   _____

25. abnormal glucose in a nondiabetic   _____

26. hemorrhage from throat   _____

27. hyperventilation   _____

28. mouth breathing   _____

29. dysphagia, oral phase   _____

30. hyperperistalsis   _____

31. slow heartbeat   _____
32. left upper quadrant abdominal tenderness   _____
33. inability to swallow   _____
34. induration of skin   _____
35. extravasation of urine   _____

Case Studies

Instructions: Review each case study and select the correct ICD-10-CM diagnostic code.

Case 1

Physician Office Visit

CHIEF COMPLAINT: Patient fell walking up her steps last night. She states that she is also having a severe headache since the fall.

PHYSICAL EXAMINATION:

HEENT: Normal

CHEST: Normal

On examination, there is no swelling of the ankles and no other areas of pain reported. The patient was instructed to go to the hospital radiology department for a CT of the skull. Tylenol 3 was ordered for her headache. Patient will be contacted following results of CT.

ICD-10-CM Code Assignment: _____

Case 2

Emergency Room Visit—Physician's Note

S: This 75-year-old patient was shoveling snow when he became short of breath. His wife insisted that he come to the emergency room to be evaluated. He states that he has had no other symptoms.

O: HEENT: Normal

CHEST: Normal heart rate, no significant findings; EKG normal

LUNGS: Clear, no congestion

ABDOMEN: Soft, nontender; no organ enlargement

LABS: All returned normal.

A: Shortness of breath, ruled out MI.

P: Instructed patient to see his primary care provider for full physical examination.

ICD-10-CM Code Assignment: _____

Case 3

Physician Office Note

The patient is a 72-year-old male who presents today with complaints of abdominal discomfort, some shortness of breath, and pain "in my gut." The patient denied any recent injury or trauma to the abdomen. He says he feels fine otherwise. Social history is positive for alcohol × 6 per day, and cigarette smoking 3 × 1 pack per day.

Examination reveals an obese Caucasian male who has a distended abdomen. No palpable masses in the abdomen.

SKIN: Skin color is normal; no bruises or discoloration

HEENT: No significant findings

HEART: Normal rate and rhythm

Lab results reveal WBC count to be at 400 cells/milliliter.

The diagnosis at this time is generalized ascites. The patient has been counseled on limiting sodium intake and is now taking Aldactone.

ICD-10-CM Code Assignment: _____

Case 4

Physician Office Visit

Marcus is an 8-year-old male who presented yesterday to the nurse's office at school with a nosebleed that occurred on the playground after Marcus and another student collided on the swing set. Other than the nosebleed, he was fine and able to go back to class. Today Marcus presents to this office with another nosebleed after he fell out of his bed while wrestling with his brother. His mother is concerned because of the two incidents happening so close together and because she had a bit of difficulty getting this nosebleed to stop.

On examination, Marcus is a normal, healthy, 8-year-old male in NAD with evidence of a recent nosebleed. At this time, there is a slight trickle of blood coming from the right nare. Internal exam reveals no serious problems. Marcus does not complain of a headache, blurred vision, or any other pain in the head and neck. We packed the nostril and told the mother to return if any further bleeding occurs.

Diagnosis for today's visit is nosebleed. We will continue to follow him to rule out possible chronic blood disorders.

ICD-10-CM Code Assignment: _____

Case 5

Physician Clinic Note

Mrs. Black presents today with complaints of "feeling tired" all the time. Upon questioning, she notes that for the most part her routine has not changed very much. She is a 56-year-old female who has two grown children who do not live with her. Her husband is 57 years old and semiretired. She said that her husband helps her around the house and also that she helps him around the yard. When asked if she is sleeping all right, she said she is getting up once or twice a night but falls right back to sleep. At this time, I advised Mrs. Black that maybe she should try to get a good walk in during the day and also watch her diet. If the malaise and fatigue don't subside or do not improve over the next 2 months with these changes, we will do further testing. Labs were drawn today to look at levels.

EXAM:

HEENT: Normal

ABDOMEN: Nondistended, no masses

HEART: RRR

EXTREMITIES: Normal

Oriented to time, person, and place

No significant physical findings noted.

ICD-10-CM Code Assignment: _____

Case 6

Emergency Department

This 37-year-old female patient presents to the ED with abdominal pain. The pain is present in the right lower quadrant. The patient says she is having nausea and has vomited four times in the last 3 hours. The vomiting has been occurring since last night. Laboratory tests were performed and all where within normal limits. The ED physician wrote "nausea and vomiting, possible appendicitis."

ICD-10-CM Code Assignment: _____

Case 7

Physician Office Visit

This 76-year-old male patient is returning to the office today to discuss a finding from a routine x-ray of his lungs. The radiology report states that there is a mass on his right lung. The left lung

(continues)

(*continued*)

appears within normal limits. I explained to the patient that this mass should be biopsied to rule out cancer of the lung. He agreed to the biopsy. The biopsy will be scheduled for Friday.

ICD-10-CM Code Assignment: _____

Case 8

Inpatient Gastroenterology Consultation Note

This 53-year-old male patient has had weight loss over the last 3 months. He is experiencing consistent diarrhea. He has not had a baseline colonoscopy so his primary care physician has asked me to complete one. I will complete the colonoscopy later today to rule out cancer of colon and polyps.

ICD-10-CM Code Assignment: _____

Case 9

Employment Drug Testing Results

A blood sample was obtained from this 39-year-old male. The sample showed that there is cocaine in the blood sample. The employer's supervisor will be notified and the employee will be sent for further evaluation.

ICD-10-CM Code Assignment: _____

Case 10

Physician Office Visit

This 74-year-old female patient presents to the office today. She says that over the last month she is experiencing chest pain when she is taking deep breaths. Today she says that the chest pain is more frequent than it has been. EKG is normal. BP is 120/85.

Physical Exam:

Lungs: Clear to auscultation. No rales, rhonci, or wheezing

Heart: Regular rate, no murmurs.

Neck: No masses present.

Abdomen: Good bowel sounds, soft. No pain or masses or tenderness. No hepatosplenomegaly.

Impression: Painful respiration

Plan: I am sending the patient to the hospital for a chest x-ray and a complete blood workup.

ICD-10-CM Code Assignment: _____

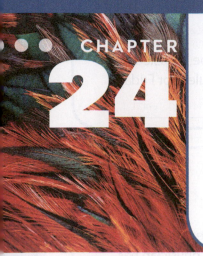

Injury, Poisoning, and Certain Other Consequences of External Causes

Chapter Outline

Chapter Objectives

At the conclusion of this chapter, you should be able to:

1. Identify the organizational structure of Chapter 19 of ICD-10-CM and related tables.
2. Explain the various types of fractures.
3. Define medical terms that relate to Chapter 19 of ICD-10-CM.
4. Apply the ICD-10-CM coding guidelines to accurately code injuries, poisonings, and other consequences of external causes.
5. Select and code diagnoses from case studies.

Key Terms

Adverse effect	Concussion	Luxation	Spiral fracture
Anterior	Corrosions	Medial	Sprain
Avulsion	Depressed fracture	Medicaments	Strain
Burn	Dislocation	Open fracture	Stress fracture
Closed fracture	First-degree burn	Paralysis	Subluxation
Comminuted fracture	Fissured fracture	Poisoning	Third-degree burn
Complete fracture	Fracture (Fx)	Posterior	Underdosing
Complicated fracture	Greenstick fracture	Reduction	Vault of the skull
Compound fracture	Impacted fracture	Second-degree burn	Vertebral column
Compression fracture	Lateral	Simple fracture	

> **REMINDER:** As you work through this chapter, you will need to have a copy of the ICD-10-CM coding book to reference. For this chapter, you will also need to reference the ICD-10-CM Official Guidelines for Coding and Reporting. These guidelines can be found in Appendix A which are now available on the Student Companion site and MINDTAP From Cengage.

Introduction

This chapter is quite different from the chapters encountered to this point. This chapter is not confined to one part of the body or to one body system. It is an eclectic collection of injuries that can occur in almost any area of the body. The injuries range from fractures and crush injuries to burns, spinal cord injuries, and late effects of injuries.

Injuries are coded according to the type of injury first and then to its location. Coders must use the Tabular List in conjunction with the Alphabetic Index because Includes and Excludes notes are used extensively. Correct code assignments cannot be made if the notes are not followed and if the documentation is not clear.

The block of codes in this chapter are as follows:

- S00–S09, Injuries to head
- S10–S19, Injuries to neck
- S20–S29, Injuries to the thorax
- S30–S39, Injuries to the abdomen, lower back, lumbar spine, pelvis, and external genitals
- S40–S49, Injuries to shoulder and upper arm
- S50–S59, Injuries to the elbow and forearm
- S60–S69, Injuries to wrist, hand, and fingers
- S70–S79, Injuries to hip and thigh
- S80–S89, Injuries to knee and lower leg
- S90–S99, Injuries to the ankle and foot
- T07,　　 Injuries involving multiple body regions
- T14,　　 Injury of unspecified body region
- T15–T19, Effects of foreign body entering through natural orifice
- T20–T25, Burns and corrosions of external body surface, specified by site
- T26–T28, Burns and corrosions confined to the eye and internal organs
- T30–T32, Burns and corrosions of multiple and unspecified body regions
- T33–T34, Frostbite
- T36–T50, Poisoning by, adverse effect of, and underdosing of drugs, medicaments, and biological substances
- T51–T65, Toxic effects of substances chiefly nonmedicinal as to source
- T66–T78, Other and unspecified effects of external causes
- T79,　　 Certain early complications of trauma
- T80–T88, Complications of surgical and medical care, not elsewhere classified

 NOTE:

The injury code blocks begin at the head and work their way down the body. This sequence can help you determine that you are coding from the correct section in a chapter.

In this chapter, the S codes are used for coding different types of injuries related to single body regions. T codes reflect injuries to unspecified body regions, as well as poisoning and certain other consequences of external causes.

Coding Guidelines

The ICD-10-CM Official Guidelines for Coding and Reporting provide many guidelines and much guidance for the coding of injuries and poisoning. Because more than one injury can occur at the same time, the official guidelines state the following:

ICD-10-CM Official Coding Guidelines

Chapter 19: Injury, poisoning, and certain other consequences of external causes (S00-T88)

a. Application of 7th Characters in Chapter 19

Most categories in Chapter 19 have a 7th character requirement for each applicable code. Most categories in this chapter have three 7th character values (with the exception of fractures): A, initial encounter, D, subsequent encounter and S, sequela. Categories for traumatic fractures have additional 7th character values. While the patient may be seen by a new or different provider over the course of treatment for an injury, assignment of the 7th character is based on whether the patient is undergoing active treatment and not whether the provider is seeing the patient for the first time.

For complication codes, active treatment refers to treatment for the condition described by the code, even though it may be related to an earlier precipitating problem. For example, code T84.50XA, Infection and inflammatory reaction due to unspecified internal joint prosthesis, initial encounter, is used when active treatment is provided for the infection, even though the condition relates to the prosthetic device, implant or graft that was placed at a previous encounter.

7th character "A", initial encounter is used for each encounter where the patient is receiving active treatment for the condition.

7th character "D" subsequent encounter is used for encounters after the patient has completed active treatment of the condition and is receiving routine care for the condition during the healing or recovery phase.

The aftercare Z codes should not be used for aftercare for conditions such as injuries or poisonings, where 7th characters are provided to identify subsequent care. For example, for aftercare of an injury, assign the acute injury code with the 7th character "D" (subsequent encounter).

7th character "S", sequela, is for use for complications or conditions that arise as a direct result of a condition, such as scar formation after a burn. The scars are sequelae of the burn. When using 7th character "S", it is necessary to use both the injury code that precipitated the sequela and the code for the sequela itself. The "S" is added only to the injury code, not the sequela code. The 7th character "S" identifies the injury responsible for the sequela. The specific type of sequela (e.g., scar) is sequenced first, followed by the injury code. (See Section I.B.10 Sequelae, (Late Effects))

b. Coding of Injuries

When coding injuries, assign separate codes for each injury unless a combination code is provided, in which case the combination code is assigned. Codes from category T07, Unspecified multiple injuries should not be assigned in the inpatient setting unless information for a more specific code is not available. Traumatic injury codes (S00–T14.9) are not to be used for normal, healing surgical wounds or to identify complications of surgical wounds.

The code for the most serious injury, as determined by the provider and focus of treatment, is sequenced first.

1. Superficial injuries

Superficial injuries such as abrasions or contusions are not coded when associated with more severe injuries of the same site.

2. Primary injury with damage to nerves/blood vessels

When a primary injury results in minor damage to peripheral nerves or blood vessels, the primary injury is sequenced first with additional code(s) for injuries to nerves and spinal cord (such as category S04), and/or injury to blood vessels (such as category S15). When the primary injury is to the blood vessels or nerves, that injury should be sequenced first.

3. Iatrogenic injuries

Injury codes from Chapter 19 should not be assigned for injuries that occur during, or as a result of, a medical intervention. Assign the appropriate complication code(s). (See Appendix A, Section I, C19, a-b.)

Courtesy of the Centers for Medicare & Medicaid Services, www.cms.gov

Terminology

Terminology is very important when coding from this chapter. Knowledge of the terminology allows the coder to make a more accurate code selection.

Fractures

Fractures, sometimes seen in a provider note as **Fx**, are broken bones resulting from undue force or pathological changes. Malunions or nonunions are not found in this chapter. These types of fractures were described in the chapter "Diseases of the Musculoskeletal System and Connective Tissue."

Knowing whether the fracture is open or closed is the starting point for coding fractures. An **open fracture**, also known as a **compound fracture**, is a fracture that has broken through the skin at the fracture site. The bone may or may not be protruding through the skin, but an open wound is always associated with this type of fracture. Because the tissues are exposed, these fractures present a high risk for infection. Surgery is almost always required. Foreign bodies, or "missiles," may need to be surgically removed from the tissues.

A **closed fracture** is a type of fracture in which the bone is broken but not the skin. This type of fracture is also known as a **complete** or **simple fracture**.

The following quick reference for terminology related to closed fractures is not comprehensive. If you encounter a term that is not listed here, seek clarification from the provider. If the fracture is not specified as open or closed and you cannot get any further information from the provider, code it as closed.

Type of Closed Fracture	Definition
Comminuted	Bone is crushed, may be splintered.
Compression	Bone is pressed on itself.
Depressed	Relating to skull, bone is broken but pushed inward.
Fissured	Bone has a narrow split that does not go through to the other side.
Greenstick	As with a greenstick of a tree, the bone bends as well as breaks.
Impacted	One end of the broken bone is wedged into the other end.
Spiral	Severe twisting motion caused bone to twist apart.
Stress	Excessive impact on bone causes small hairline crack in the bone.

Figure 24-1 illustrates types and patterns of fractures. If an internal organ has been injured as a direct result of the fracture, it is called a **complicated fracture**. Either the bone itself or just a fragment of the bone may cause the injury.

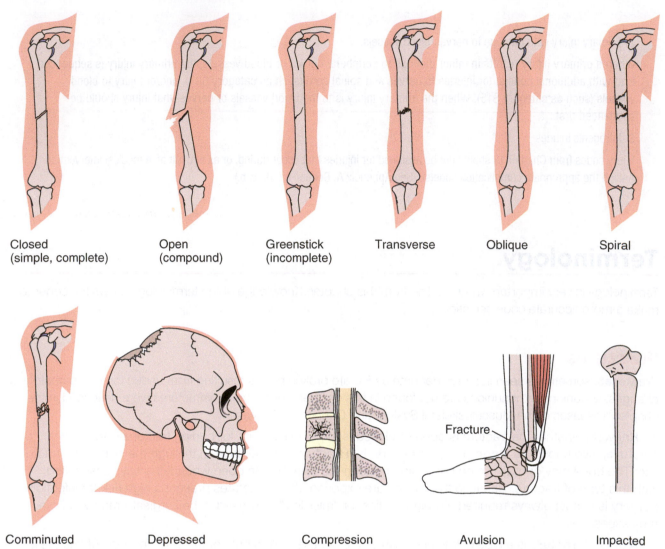

FIGURE 24-1 Types and patterns of fractures (From Hegner BR, Acello B, Caldwell E. *Nursing Assistant: A Nursing Process Approach*, 9th ed. Clifton Park, NY: Delmar, Cengage Learning, 2001, p. 644.).

Coders should also be aware of the following guidelines:

ICD-10-CM Official Coding Guidelines

c. Coding of Traumatic Fractures

The principles of multiple coding of injuries should be followed in coding fractures. Fractures of specified sites are coded individually by site in accordance with both the provisions within categories S02, S12, S22, S32, S42, S49, S52, S59, S62, S72, S79, S82, S89, and S92, and the level of detail furnished by medical record content.

A fracture not indicated as open or closed should be coded to closed. A fracture not indicated whether displaced or not displaced should be coded to displaced.

More specific guidelines are as follows:

1) Initial vs. Subsequent Encounter for Fractures

Traumatic fractures are coded using the appropriate 7th character for initial encounter (A, B, C) for each encounter where the patient is receiving active treatment for the fracture. The appropriate 7th character for initial encounter should also be assigned for a patient who delayed seeking treatment for the fracture or nonunion.

Fractures are coded using the appropriate 7th character for subsequent care for encounters after the patient has completed active treatment of the fracture and is receiving routine care for the fracture during the healing or recovery phase.

Care for complications of surgical treatment for fracture repairs during the healing or recovery phase should be coded with the appropriate complication codes.

Care of complications of fractures, such as malunion and nonunion, should be reported with the appropriate 7th character for subsequent care with nonunion (K, M, N) or subsequent care with malunion (P, Q, R).

Malunion/nonunion: The appropriate 7th character for initial encounter should also be assigned for a patient who delayed seeking treatment for the fracture or nonunion. The open fracture designations in the assignment of the 7th character for fractures of the forearm, femur, and lower leg, including ankle are based on the Gustilo open fracture classification. When the Gustilo classification type is not specified for open fracture, the 7th character for open fracture type I or II should be assigned (B,E,H,M,Q).

A code from category M80, not a traumatic fracture code, should be used for any patient with known osteoporosis who suffers a fracture, even if that patient had a minor fall or trauma, if that fall or trauma would not usually break a normal, healthy bone. See Section I.C.13. Osteoporosis.

The aftercare Z codes should not be used for aftercare for traumatic fractures. For aftercare of a traumatic fracture assign the acute fracture code with the appropriate 7th character.

2) Multiple Fractures Sequencing

Multiple fractures are sequenced in accordance with the severity of the fracture.

3) Physeal fractures

For physeal fractures, assign only the code identifying the type of physeal fracture. Do not assign a separate code to identify the specific bone that is fractured. (See Appendix A, Section I, C19, c.)

Should the coder identify a situation that indicates both open and closed fractures in the same site, the open fracture is coded because it takes priority over the closed fracture. A patient who might present with multiple fractures after an accident may have both open and closed fractures. In this case, as stated in the guidelines, the fractures are sequenced according to severity.

Gustilo Classification of Fractures

As stated in the coding guidelines, traumatic fractures are coded using the appropriate seventh character. Many of the seventh-character extensions designate the specific type of open fracture based on the Gustilo Classification of Fractures. The Gustilo classification classifies open fractures into three major categories based on the mechanism of injury, degree of soft tissue damage, and degree of skeletal involvement or bone injury. The types are defined as follows:

Type I

- Wound is less than 1 centimeter.
- Soft tissue injury is minimal.
- Wound bed is clean.
- Commonly a low-energy type of injury.
- Fractures are typically a simple transverse fracture, short oblique fracture, or minimally comminuted.

Type II

- Wound is greater than 1 centimeter.
- Soft tissue injury is moderate.

- Wound bed has no contamination or is minimally contaminated.
- Commonly a low-energy type of injury.
- Fractures are typically a simple transverse fracture, short oblique fracture, or minimally comminuted.

Type III

- Wound is greater than 1 centimeter.
- Extensive damage to soft tissue, including muscle, skin, and neurovascular structures.
- Commonly a high-energy type of injury with a severe crushing component.
- Types of injury patterns that are classified as type III include:
  - Open segmental fracture, regardless of size of the wound
  - Gunshot wounds
  - Open fracture with neurovascular injury
  - Farm injuries with contamination from soil
  - Traumatic amputations
  - Open fractures with treatment delay of over 8 hours
  - Mass casualties, such as from war or tornados

Type III subtypes

Subtype IIIA

- Adequate soft tissue coverage despite soft tissue laceration, or flaps, or high-energy trauma
- Includes segmental fractures or severely comminuted fractures

Subtype IIIB

- Extensive tissue damage with periosteal stripping, bone exposure, or a vascular injury requiring repair
- Usually accompanied by mass contamination

Subtype IIIC

- Major arterial (vascular) damage and injury
- Repair of injury necessary to salvage limb

S Codes

After the Chapter 19 heading in the ICD-10-CM code book the following appears:

 NOTE:

Use secondary code(s) from Chapter 20, External cause of morbidity, to indicate cause of injury. Codes within the T section that include the external cause do not require an additional external cause code.

Use additional code to identify any retained foreign body, if applicable (Z18.-).

EXCLUDES1   birth trauma (P10–P15)
                        obstetric trauma (O70–O71)

The chapter uses the S-section for coding different types of injuries related to single body regions and the T-section to cover injuries to unspecified body regions as well as poisoning and certain other consequences of external causes.

Coders need to follow these instructions while assigning codes from Chapter 19.

Injuries to the Head (Category Codes S00–S09)

The injuries that are coded to this block include the following:

- S00, Superficial injury of head
- S01, Open wound of head
- S02, Fracture of skull and facial bones
- S03, Dislocation and sprain of joints and ligaments of head
- S04, Injury of cranial nerve
- S05, Injury of eye and orbit
- S06, Intracranial injury
- S07, Crushing injury of head
- S08, Avulsion and traumatic amputation of part of head
- S09, Other and unspecified injuries of head

This code block includes codes for injuries that occur from the scalp down to just past the jaw. Some knowledge of anatomy is necessary to navigate through these sections when coding for injuries of the teeth, tongue, gums, and oral cavity.

The **vault of the skull** is made up of three bones: the two parietal bones and the frontal bone. The chapter identifies different types of fractures of the head and face.

These categories classify intracranial injury, such as concussions. A **concussion** is a violent shaking or jarring of the brain. The main axis for coding concussions hinges on whether the patient lost consciousness and, if so, to what degree. When selecting codes in this block, as well as in other blocks of Chapter 19 of ICD-10-CM, coders need to pay close attention to the assignment of the appropriate seventh character. For example, category S00 requires an appropriate seventh character to identify: A- initial encounter, for example, B- subsequent encounter, S- sequela. When coding the statement "contusion of scalp, initial encounter," the proper code assignment would be S00.03xA. Coders are required to use a placeholder of x in the character position that does not have a value in the code book, thus "filling in" the sixth-character position in this example. The placeholder of x is to be used in all character positions that do not have a value when a seventh character is required for the category. Therefore, more than one x may have to be inserted by the coder.

Injuries to the Neck (Category Codes S10–S19)

The next section reports injuries to the neck, supraclavicular region, and throat. The injuries found in this code block include superficial injuries, contusions, open wounds, and fractures. This code block includes fractures of the cervical vertebra and other parts of neck (S12). When selecting codes for a cervical vertebra fracture, the specific vertebra should be known for specific code assignment to occur. The **vertebral column**, which shields the spinal cord, is made up of cervical, thoracic, and lumbar vertebra. To properly code an injury to the spinal cord or a vertebra, you need to know the location of the injury. An injury to this area of the body can cause **paralysis**, which is the loss of sensation or voluntary motion. This loss may be permanent or temporary, depending on the type and site of the injury.

Dislocation and sprain of joints and ligaments at the neck level are reported with codes from category S13. The term **dislocation** means that a body part has moved out of place, in this case a bone. The bone has moved or displaced completely from where it should be. A synonymous term for dislocation is **luxation**. In cases of a partial dislocation, or **subluxation**, only part of the joint surface has moved away from where it should be.

Like fractures, dislocations can be open or closed. An open dislocation is prone to infection. A **reduction** is the usual procedure needed to put the joint back into place, whether the dislocation is open or closed.

The coding of dislocations requires knowing whether the dislocation is open or closed, as well as the location of the displaced bone in relation to where its proper placement should be in the joint. The terms to look for in provider documentation are "anterior," "posterior," "lateral," and/or "medial."

- **Anterior** means "in front of" or "forward of."
- **Posterior** is the opposite of anterior and means "in back of" or "behind."
- **Medial** is closest or nearest to the midline of a structure.
- **Lateral** means "away from midline" toward the side.

Dislocations can be very serious when major joints are involved, specifically the shoulders, knees, and hips. Vascular complications can occur with these types of dislocations, which can have long-lasting or even permanent adverse affects.

When a dislocation occurs with a fracture, the dislocation is included in the code for the fracture and is not coded separately. This category of codes is used when no fracture is present. As with fractures, dislocations are coded as closed unless the provider has specifically stated that the dislocation is open.

Sometimes the terms *sprain* and *strain* are used interchangeably. They are not the same, and coders should seek clarification if there is any question about the condition. A **sprain** is an injury to a joint, specifically the ligament of the joint, which becomes stretched. A **strain** is not an injury at the joint site but to the muscle or to the tendon attachment. In provider documentation, the coder may note that the severity of sprain or strain has been graded or typed, with type I as the least severe through type III as the most severe. When there are multiple sprains or strains, the typing of these sprains and strains is helpful in determining which site to code first.

 NOTE:

In the Alphabetic Index, not many sites are listed under the main term *strain*, but the term *sprain* has a large range of anatomical sites.

Commonly a patient is prescribed RICE therapy (rest, ice, compression, and elevation) to treat strains and sprains.

Injuries to the Thorax (Category Codes S20–29)

Injuries in this block of codes include injuries of the breast, chest wall, and the interscapular area. The type of injuries included in this code range are superficial injuries, abrasions, open wounds, fractures, subluxation and dislocations, and crush injuries.

Injuries to the Abdomen, Lower Back, Lumbar Spine, Pelvis, and External Genitals (Category Codes S30–S39)

The anatomy included in this section includes the abdominal wall, anus, buttock, external genitalia, flank, and groin. As in other categories, superficial injuries, contusions, open wounds, and lacerations are coded to this code range, as well as fractures and dislocations of the lumbar spine and pelvis.

This code range also includes injuries to the intra-abdominal organs, including the kidneys, the ureters, the bladder, the fallopian tubes, and the uterus. Attention to the specific anatomical sites injured helps with code selection. Documentation must support the codes selected.

Injuries to the Shoulder and Arm, Elbow, Wrist, and Hand (Category Codes S40–S69)

Injuries to all areas from the shoulder to the tip of the fingers are included in this code range, which distinguishes between right and left sides. Refer to the documentation for the correct site of the injury. Superficial wounds, lacerations, open wounds, and fractures are reported from this code range, as well as injuries to the muscle, fascia, and tendons of the shoulder area.

The note at the start of this section includes open wounds caused by animal bites, cuts, lacerations, puncture wounds, and traumatic amputations. Also included here are avulsions. An **avulsion** is a ripping or tearing away.

Avulsions are usually documented in reference to fingernails or toenails or a portion of an organ, but they can also occur on arms or legs. Sometimes the coder encounters the term *complicated*, referring to an open wound, such as "complicated open wound of the back."

Injuries to the Hip and Thigh, Knee and Lower Leg, Ankle and Foot, and Toes (Category Codes S70–S99)

The injuries in this code range include dislocations, fractures, and muscle injuries. Refer to the documentation for the necessary details to assign a code. This range of codes contains many Includes and Excludes notations, which must be referenced before code assignment is made.

Exercise 24.1—Fractures, Dislocation, Sprains, and Strains

True/False: Indicate whether each statement is true (T) or false (F).

1. _____ Injuries are coded according to location first, then type of injury.

2. _____ Sprains and strains are not the same type of injury.

3. _____ When coding fractures, attention to the type of fracture and the location is necessary for proper code assignment.

4. _____ To properly code fractures, the coder needs to know whether the fracture is dislocated or not.

5. _____ The vertebral column shields the spinal cord.

Fill-in-the-Blank: Enter the appropriate term(s) to complete each statement.

6. "Fx" in a provider note refers to a _____.

7. A _____ is an injury to a ligament of the joint, whereas a _____ is an injury to a muscle.

8. Comminuted is a type of _____ fracture.

9. A synonymous term for luxation is _____.

10. A _____ fracture occurs when a bone is pressed on itself.

Instructions: Using an ICD-10-CM coding book, select the code for each diagnostic statement.

Diagnosis	Code
11. comminuted right ankle fracture, initial encounter	_____
12. nondisplaced fracture of the lower epiphysis of the right femur, initial encounter	_____
13. initial encounter for sprain of the sternoclavicular joint	_____
14. initial encounter for fracture of the proximal end of the left tibia	_____
15. closed dislocation of the C6/C7 vertebrae, initial visit	_____
16. open fracture, sternum, initial care	_____
17. nondisplaced closed avulsion fracture of the ilium, initial visit	_____
18. initial care for closed displaced fracture of lateral malleolus of right fibula	_____
19. initial visit for open dislocation of the right carpometacarpal joint	_____
20. initial care for nondisplaced condyle fracture of lower end of right femur	_____

T Codes

As stated earlier, T codes reflect injuries to unspecified body regions, as well as poisoning and certain other consequences of external causes. T codes contain many instructional notations, so any codes found in the Alphabetic Index need to be referenced in the Tabular List to pick up the instructional notations before making a code selection.

Injuries Involving Unspecified Multiple Body Regions (Category Code T07)

This category is used to identify unspecified multiple injuries. The coder should note that this code is used only when no documentation is available to identify the specific injury or site of injury. This code is not acceptable in the inpatient setting.

Injury of Unspecified Body Region (Category Code T14)

Category T14 requires seventh character assignment. T14 is not appropriate for use in the inpatient setting.

Effects of Foreign Body Entering Through Natural Orifice (Category Codes T15–T19)

The T codes in this range reflect foreign bodies in the ear and multiple parts of the eye. It also includes codes for foreign bodies in the respiratory and alimentary tracts.

Pay careful attention to the details of the documentation because the codes in this range do not need an additional external cause code if the external cause is included in the code description.

> **EXAMPLE:** Mary suffered a sore throat due to a chicken bone getting caught in the trachea. The code is T17.428, Food in trachea causing other injury. The Includes note under the T17.42 code identifies bones and seeds in the trachea. For this reason, no additional code is needed.

Burns and Corrosions (Category Codes T20–T32)

Coding for burns can be very difficult and confusing if the coding guidelines are not followed. A **burn** is an injury to body tissue as a result of heat, flame, sun, chemicals, radiation, or electricity. Coding a burn is determined by its severity, or degree, and its location. Codes from the T31 or T32 category are used to identify the extent of body surfaced involved. The code descriptions are very detailed, and the documentation supporting code selection needs to be detailed as well.

Burns are classified as first, second, and third degree.

- **First-degree burns** do not present a danger to the patient and are limited to the outer layer of the epidermis. An example is a mild sunburn.

- **Second-degree burns** are partial-thickness burns, which form blisters. A second-degree burn, not properly treated, can result in an infection at the burn site.

- **Third-degree burns** are full-thickness burns and affect the epidermis, dermis, and subcutaneous layers. This type of burn can lead to necrosis and even the loss of the body part.

Because a burn is the destruction of the skin, which protects the body from infection, the patient must receive proper treatment. Infection is a very serious problem in burn victims, as is the loss of blood supply to the areas of third-degree burns. Without blood supply to the area, necrosis can occur. Figure 24-2 illustrates the types of burns.

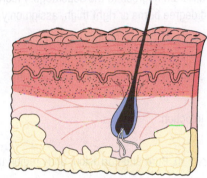

Skin red, dry

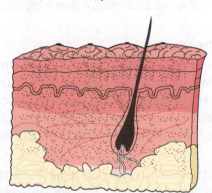

Blistered, skin moist, pink or red

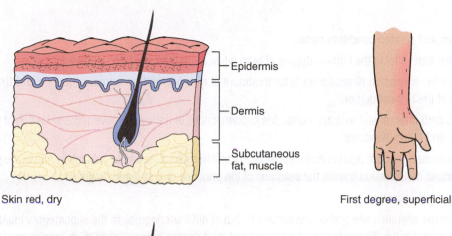

Epidermis

Dermis

Subcutaneous fat, muscle

First degree, superficial

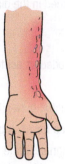

Second degree, partial thickness

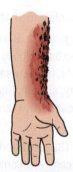

Charring, skin black, brown, red

Third degree, full thickness

FIGURE 24-2 First-, second-, and third-degree burns (From Ehrlich A, Schroeder CL. *Medical Terminology for Health Professionals*, 4th ed. Clifton Park, NY: Delmar, Cengage Learning, 2001, p. 264.).

ICD-10-CM Official Coding Guidelines

Coding of Burns and Corrosions

The ICD-10-CM makes a distinction between burns and corrosions. The burn codes are for thermal burns, except sunburns, that come from a heat source, such as a fire or hot appliance. The burn codes are also for burns resulting from electricity and radiation. **Corrosions** are burns due to chemicals. The guidelines are the same for burns and corrosions.

Current burns (T20–T25) are classified by depth, extent and by agent (X code). Burns are classified by depth as first degree (erythema), second degree (blistering), and third degree (full-thickness involvement). Burns of the eye and internal organs (T26–T28) are classified by site, but not by degree.

1) Sequencing of burn and related condition codes

Sequence first the code that reflects the highest degree of burn when more than one burn is present.

a. When the reason for the admission or encounter is for treatment of external multiple burns, sequence first the code that reflects the burn of the highest degree.

b. When a patient has both internal and external burns, the circumstances of admission govern the selection of the principal diagnosis or first-listed diagnosis.

c. When a patient is admitted for burn injuries and other related conditions such as smoke inhalation and/or respiratory failure, the circumstances of admission govern the selection of the principal or first-listed diagnosis.

2) Burns of the same anatomic site

Classify burns of the same anatomic site and on the same side but of different degrees to the subcategory identifying the highest degree recorded in the diagnosis (e.g., for second and third degree burns or right thigh, assign only code T24.311-)

3) Non-healing burns

Non-healing burns are coded as acute burns. Necrosis of burned skin should be coded as a non-healed burn.

4) Infected burn

For any documented infected burn site, use an additional code for the infection.

5) Assign separate codes for each burn site

When coding burns, assign separate codes for each burn site. Category T30, Burn and corrosion, body region unspecified is extremely vague and should rarely be used.

Codes for burns of "multiple sites" should only be assigned when the medical record documentation does not specify the individual sites.

6) Burns and corrosions classified according to extent of body surface involved

Assign codes from category T31, Burns classified according to extent of body surface involved, or T32, Corrosions classified according to extent of body surface involved, when the site of the burn is not specified or when there is a need for additional data. It is advisable to use category T31 as additional coding when needed to provide data for evaluating burn mortality, such as that needed by burn units. It is also advisable to use category T31 as an additional code for reporting purposes when there is mention of a third-degree burn involving 20 percent or more of the body surface.

Categories T31 and T32 are based on the classic "rule of nines" in estimating body surface involved: head and neck are assigned 9 percent, each arm 9 percent, each leg 18 percent, the anterior trunk 18 percent, posterior trunk 18 percent, and genitalia 1 percent. Providers may change these percentage assignments where necessary to accommodate infants and children who have proportionately larger heads than adults, and patients who have large buttocks, thighs, or abdomen that involve burns.

7) Encounters for treatment of sequela of burns

Encounters for the treatment of the late effects of burns or corrosions (i.e., scars or joint contractures) should be coded with a burn or corrosion code with the 7th character "S" for sequela.

8) Sequelae with a late effect code and current burn

When appropriate, both a code for a current burn or corrosion with 7th character "A" or "D" and a burn or corrosion code with 7th character "S" may be assigned on the same record (when both a current burn and sequelae of an old burn exist). Burns and corrosions do not heal at the same rate and a current healing wound may still exist with sequela of a healed burn or corrosion. See Section I.B.10 Sequela (Late Effects)

9) Use of an external cause code with burns and corrosions

An external cause code should be used with burns and corrosions to identify the source and intent of the burn, as well as the place where it occurred. (See Appendix A, Section I, C19, d.)

With these few guidelines in mind, this example helps to illustrate how they are applied.

> **EXAMPLE:** A 56-year-old male presents to the ER with first- and multiple second-degree burns on the right arm. The right leg contains third-degree burns to the thigh, knee, and calf area.
>
> To properly code this example, the first listed code is the code for the burn area of the right thigh because the third-degree burns are the most severe of the burns. Category T24, Burn and corrosion of lower limb, except ankle and foot, would be used to code this burn. To report the most severe burns, use code T24.391A, Burn of third degree of multiple sites of right lower limb, except ankle and foot, initial encounter. To report the next severe burn, use code T22.291A, Burn of second degree of multiple sites of right shoulder and upper limb, except wrist and hand, initial encounter.

The extent of the body surface burned is coded according to the rule of nines. This rule is based on the premise that the adult body can be divided into anatomic regions with surface area percentages that are multiples of nine. The rule of nines breaks down as follows:

- Head and neck, 9%
- Arms, 9% each
- Legs, 18% each
- Anterior trunk, 18%
- Posterior trunk, 18%
- Genitalia, 1%

Section I, C19,d, 6 of the ICD-10-CM Official Guidelines for Coding and Reporting presents the complete details.

Following the category and subcategory headings for many of the codes, there is an instructional notation that an additional code is needed to identify the source, place, and intent of the burn. The coder needs to review the Tabular Listing to make note of and follow these instructional notations.

Frostbite (Category Codes T33–T34)

Category T33 reports superficial frostbite and is differentiated according to site. Category T34 reports frostbite with tissue necrosis and also differentiates the site. Both of these categories require the use of a seventh character and are governed by the Excludes2 notation that appears after the block heading. The Excludes2 note states: "hypothermia and other effects of reduced temperature (T68, T69-)," which tells the coder to add these conditions if the conditions are present for the case being coded.

Poisoning by Adverse Effects of and Underdosing of Drugs, Medicaments, and Biological Substances (Category Codes T36–T50)

ICD-10-CM defines **poisoning** as an overdose of substances or a wrong substance given or taken in error. When the substance is not used as prescribed or not used properly, this is poisoning. If the documentation does not state specifically that the situation is a poisoning, then it is coded as an adverse effect. **Medicaments** is a term for medicine.

An **adverse effect** is defined as *hypersensitivity, reaction*, etc. to a correct substance properly administered. The coder may encounter certain terms that indicate an adverse effect, for example, *allergic reaction, paradoxical, synergistic*, or *idiosyncratic reaction*. Also seen in the documentation are phrases like *hypersensitivity to drugs, toxicity, toxic effect*, or *intoxication due to prescription drugs*, and the like.

Underdosing is defined as taking less of a medication than what is prescribed or instructed by the physician or the manufacturer, whether deliberately or inadvertently.

Refer to the Official Coding Guidelines when there is any question as to how to code these conditions. (Please note that the Table of Drugs and Chemicals appears in the ICD-10-CM Index to Diseases and Injuries after the Neoplasm Table and before the External Causes Index.)

ICD-10-CM Official Coding Guidelines

e. Adverse Effects, Poisoning, Underdosing and Toxic Effects

Codes in categories T36–T65 are combination codes that include the substance that was taken as well as the intent. No additional external cause code is required for poisonings, toxic effects, adverse effects, and underdosing codes.

1) Do not code directly from the Table of Drugs

Do not code directly from the Table of Drugs and Chemicals. Always refer back to the Tabular List.

2) Use as many codes as necessary to describe

Use as many codes as necessary to describe completely all drugs, medicinal, or biological substances.

3) If the same code would describe the causative agent

If the same code would describe the causative agent for more than one adverse reaction, poisoning, toxic effect, or underdosing, assign the code only once.

4) If two or more drugs, medicinal, or biological substances

If two or more drugs, medicinal, or biological substances are taken, code each individually unless a combination code is listed in the Table of Drugs and Chemicals.

If multiple unspecified drugs, medicinal or biological substances were taken, assign the appropriate code from subcategory T50.91, Poisoning by, adverse effect of and underdosing of multiple unspecified drugs, medicaments and biological substances.

5) The occurrence of drug toxicity is classified in ICD-10-CM as follows:

(a) Adverse Effect

When coding an adverse effect of a drug that has been correctly prescribed and properly administered, assign the appropriate code for the nature of the adverse effect followed by the appropriate code for the adverse effect of the drug (T36-T50). The code for the drug should have a 5th or 6th character "5" (for example T36.0X5-). Examples of the nature of an adverse effect are tachycardia, delirium, gastrointestinal hemorrhaging, vomiting, hypokalemia, hepatitis, renal failure, or respiratory failure.

(b) Poisoning

When coding a poisoning or reaction to the improper use of a medication (e.g., overdose, wrong substance given or taken in error, wrong route of administration), first assign the appropriate code from categories T36–T50. The poisoning codes have an associated intent as their 5th or 6th character: accidental, intentional self-harm, assault, and undetermined. If the intent of the poisoning is unknown or unspecified, code the intent as accidental intent. The undetermined intent is only for use if the documentation in the record specifies that the intent cannot be determined. Use additional code(s) for all manifestations of poisonings.

If there is also a diagnosis of abuse or dependence of the substance, the abuse or dependence is assigned as an additional code.

Examples of poisoning include:

(i) Error was made in drug prescription

Errors made in drug prescription or in the administration of the drug by provider, nurse, patient, or other person.

(ii) Overdose of a drug intentionally taken

If an overdose of a drug was intentionally taken or administered and resulted in drug toxicity, it would be coded as a poisoning.

(iii) Nonprescribed drug taken with correctly prescribed and properly administered drug

If a nonprescribed drug or medicinal agent was taken in combination with a correctly prescribed and properly administered drug, any drug toxicity or other reaction resulting from the interaction of the two drugs would be classified as a poisoning.

Courtesy of the Centers for Medicare & Medicaid Services, www.cms.gov

(iv) Interaction of drug(s) and alcohol

When a reaction results from the interaction of a drug(s) and alcohol, this would be classified as poisoning.

See Section I.C.4. if poisoning is the result of insulin pump malfunctions.

(c) Underdosing

Underdosing refers to taking less of a medication than is prescribed by a provider or a manufacturer's instruction. Discontinuing the use of a prescribed medication on the patient's own initiative (not directed by the patient's provider) is also classified as an underdosing. For underdosing, assign the code from categories T36–T50 (5th or 6th character "6").

Codes for underdosing should never be assigned as principal or first-listed codes. If a patient has a relapse or exacerbation of the medical condition for which the drug is prescribed because of the reduction in dose, then the medical condition itself should be coded.

Noncompliance (Z91.12–, Z91.13– and Z91.14–) or complication of care (Y63.6–Y63.9) codes are to be used with an underdosing code to indicate intent, if known.

(See Appendix A, Section I, C19, e.)

Toxic Effects of Substances Chiefly Nonmedicinal as to Source (Category Codes T51–T65)

As with other blocks of codes, ICD-10-CM has official guidelines related to toxic effects:

ICD-10-CM Official Coding Guidelines

(d) Toxic Effects

When a harmful substance is ingested or comes in contact with a person, this is classified as a toxic effect. The toxic effect codes are in categories T51–T65.

Toxic effect codes have an associated intent: accidental, intentional self-harm, assault, and undetermined.

(See Appendix A, Section 1, C19, e,5,d.)

Courtesy of the Centers for Medicare & Medicaid Services, www.cms.gov

This code block includes toxic effects of ethanol, methanol, benzene, and tetrachloroethylene. Most of the categories in this range require a seventh character. The Tabular List needs to be referenced before a code is assigned to determine the appropriate seventh character needed for code assignment.

Other and Unspecified Effects of External Causes (Category Codes T66–T78)

Radiation sickness, the effects of heat and light, heatstroke and sunstroke, heat exhaustion, and heat edema are conditions coded to this block of codes. These codes are also used to report hypothermia and asphyxiation due to plastic bags and pillows.

Category T74 reports adult and child abuse, neglect, and other maltreatment, confirmed. Category T76 reports adult and child abuse, neglect, and other maltreatment, suspected. The diagnosis must be confirmed by the physician or provider documentation to support assignment of a T74 code. Additional codes should be applied to identify any associated current injury or to identify the perpetrator, if known. If the abuse is suspected but not yet confirmed, reference the T76 code range. These codes should never be used without a confirmation from the physician/provider.

Official Coding Guidelines address the rules for code assignment in cases of abuse:

ICD-10-CM Official Coding Guidelines

f. Adult and child abuse, neglect, and other maltreatment

Sequence first the appropriate code from categories T74.- (Adult and child abuse, neglect and other maltreatment, confirmed) or T76.- (Adult and child abuse, neglect and other maltreatment, suspected) for abuse, neglect and other maltreatment, followed by any accompanying mental health or injury code(s).

If the documentation in the medical record states abuse or neglect it is coded as confirmed (T74.-). It is coded as suspected if it is documented as suspected (T76.-).

For cases of confirmed abuse or neglect an external cause code from the assault section (X92–Y09) should be added to identify the cause of any physical injuries. A perpetrator code (Y07) should be added when the perpetrator of the abuse is known. For suspected cases of abuse or neglect, do not report external cause or perpetrator code.

If a suspected case of abuse, neglect, or mistreatment is ruled out during an encounter code Z04.71, Encounter for examination and observation following alleged physical adult abuse, ruled out, or code Z04.72, Encounter for examination and observation following alleged child physical abuse, ruled out, should be used, not a code from T76.

If a suspected case of alleged rape or sexual abuse is ruled out during an encounter code Z04.41, Encounter for examination and observation following alleged adult rape or code Z04.42, Encounter for examination and observation following alleged child rape should be used, not a code from T76.

If a suspected case of forced sexual exploitation or forced labor exploitation is ruled out during an encounter, code Z04.81, Encounter for examination and observation of victim following forced sexual exploitation, or code Z04.82, Encounter for examination and observation of victim following forced labor exploitation, should be used, not a code from T76.

See Section I.C.15. Abuse in a pregnant patient.

(See Appendix A, Section 1, C19, f.)

Courtesy of the Centers for Medicare & Medicaid Services, www.cms.gov

Throughout the code block T66–T78, numerous instructional notations appear. A seventh-character assignment might also be necessary; therefore, coders must reference the Tabular Listing and note the instructional notations and seventh characters required.

Complications of Surgical and Medical Care, Not Elsewhere Classified (Category Codes T80–T88)

This code block contains a wide range of codes and complications. It is not referenced if more specific codes can be found elsewhere. An additional code from the Y62–Y82 range may be needed to identify devices involved and details of circumstances. Included in this code range are codes for Rh incompatibility reaction, disruption of an operation wound, or an obstruction due to a foreign body accidentally left in the body following a procedure. The code block also reports complications of organ transplants, grafts, and infections. The following guidelines need to be followed when coding complications of care:

ICD-10-CM Official Coding Guidelines

g. Complications of care

1) General guidelines for complications of care

(a) Documentation of complications of care

See Section I.B.16. for information on documentation of complications of care.

2) Pain due to medical devices

Pain associated with devices, implants or grafts left in a surgical site (for example painful hip prosthesis) is assigned to the appropriate code(s) found in Chapter 19, Injury, poisoning, and certain other consequences of external causes. Specific codes for pain due to medical devices are found in the T code section of the ICD-10-CM. Use additional code(s) from category G89 to identify acute or chronic pain due to presence of the device, implant or graft (G89.18 or G89.28).

3) Transplant complications

(a) Transplant complications other than kidney

Codes under category T86, Complications of transplanted organs and tissues, are for use for both complications and rejection of transplanted organs. A transplant complication code is only assigned if the complication affects the function of the transplanted organ. Two codes are required to fully describe a transplant complication: the appropriate code from category T86 and a secondary code that identifies the complication.

Pre-existing conditions or conditions that develop after the transplant are not coded as complications unless they affect the function of the transplanted organs.

See I.C.21. for transplant organ removal status

See I.C.2. for malignant neoplasm associated with transplanted organ.

(b) Kidney transplant complications

Patients who have undergone kidney transplant may still have some form of chronic kidney disease (CKD) because the kidney transplant may not fully restore kidney function. Code T86.1- should be assigned for documented complications of a kidney transplant, such as transplant failure or rejection or other transplant complication. Code T86.1- should not be assigned for post kidney transplant patients who have chronic kidney disease (CKD) unless a transplant complication such as transplant failure or rejection is documented. If the documentation is unclear as to whether the patient has a complication of the transplant, query the provider.

Conditions that affect the function of the transplanted kidney, other than CKD, should be assigned a code from subcategory T86.1, Complications of transplanted organ, Kidney, and a secondary code that identifies the complication.

For patients with CKD following a kidney transplant, but who do not have a complication such as failure or rejection, see section I.C.14, Chronic kidney disease and kidney transplant status.

4) Complication codes that include the external cause

As with certain other T codes, some of the complications of care codes have the external cause included in the code. The code includes the nature of the complication as well as the type of procedure that caused the complication. No external cause code indicating the type of procedure is necessary for these codes.

5) Complications of care codes within the body system chapters

Intraoperative and postprocedural complication codes are found within the body system chapters with codes specific to the organs and structures of that body system. These codes should be sequenced first, followed by a code(s) for the specific complication, if applicable.

Complication codes from the body system chapters should be assigned for intraoperative and postprocedural complications (e.g., the appropriate complication code from Chapter 9 would be assigned for a vascular intraoperative or postprocedural complication) unless the complication is specifically indexed to a T code in Chapter 19. (See Appendix A, Section C.19. g.)

Courtesy of the Centers for Medicare & Medicaid Services, www.cms.gov

The ICD-10-CM Official Coding Guidelines instructs the coder to review provider documentation prior to assigning codes for complications of care. The coding guidelines reads as follows:

ICD-10-CM Official Coding Guidelines

16. Documentation of Complications of Care

Code assignment is based on the provider's documentation of the relationship between the condition and the care or procedure, unless otherwise instructed by the classification. The guideline extends to any complications of care, regardless of the chapter the code is located in. It is important to note that not all conditions that occur during or following medical care or surgery are classified as complications. There must be a cause-and-effect relationship between the care provided and the condition, and an indication in the documentation that it is a complication. Query the provider for clarification, if the complication is not clearly documented.

(See Appendix A, Section B.16.)

Summary

- When coding injuries, assign a separate code for each injury unless a combination code is provided.
- When coding from Chapter 19, follow the ICD-10-CM Official Guidelines for injuries, poisoning, and other consequences of external causes.
- When a dislocation occurs with a fracture, include the dislocation in the code for the fracture.
- A sprain is an injury to a joint, and a strain is an injury to the muscle or the tendon attachment.
- Intracranial injuries that are diagnosed with cerebral lacerations are coded with a combination code.
- Seventh digits are commonly used when coding injuries of the thorax, abdomen, and pelvis.
- A burn is an injury to body tissue as a result of heat, flame, sun, chemicals, radiation, or electricity.
- Burns are classified by the severity: first, second, or third degree.
- The extent of the body surface burned is coded according to the rule of nines.
- An adverse effect occurs when a drug or other substance is used as prescribed or correctly according to directions.
- A seventh-digit character may or may not be needed; refer to the instructional notations before assigning codes.

Internet Links

For more information on fractures and the different types of fractures, visit **www.orthoinfo.aaos.org**.

For more information on types of sprains and strains that involve the feet, go to **www.apma.org** and search on sprains and strains.

Chapter Review

True/False

Indicate whether the statement is true (T) or false (F).

1. _____ The codes S00–T14.9 are used for normal, healing surgical wounds or to identify complications of puncture wounds.

2. _____ A fracture that is not specified as displaced or not displaced should be coded to displaced.

3. _____ Category codes S10–S19 report injuries to the head.

4. _____ The rule of nines is used to figure the total percentage of body surface burned.

5. _____ When a harmful substance is ingested or comes in contact with a person, this is classified as a toxic effect.

Fill-in-the-Blank

Enter the appropriate term(s) to complete each statement.

6. The term _____ means that a body part has moved out of place.

7. The first column listed in the Table of Drugs and Chemicals is _____.

8. A violent shaking or jarring of the brain is known as _____.

9. If a substance that is given causes an allergic reaction even though it is used correctly it is called a(n) _____.

10. According to the rule of nines, each arm is valued at _____ percent.

Coding Guidelines True/False

Review the ICD-10-CM Official Guidelines for Coding and Reporting and indicate if the statement(s) is true or false.

11. _____ Superficial injuries such as abrasions or contusions are not coded when associated with more severe injuries of the same site.

12. _____ For any documented infected burn site, do not use an additional code for the infection.

13. _____ When coding an adverse effect of a drug that has been correctly prescribed and properly administered, assign the appropriate code for the nature of the adverse effect followed by the appropriate code for the adverse effect of the drug (T36–T50).

14. _____ Codes for underdosing should never be assigned as principal or first-listed codes.

15. _____ As with certain other T codes, some of the complications of care codes have the external cause included in the code. The code includes the nature of the complication as well as the type of procedure that caused the complication. An external cause code indicating the type of procedure is necessary for these codes.

Coding Assignments

Instructions: Using an ICD-10-CM code book, assign the proper diagnosis code to the following diagnostic statements. (Do not code procedures at this time.)

1. initial visit of laceration with foreign body, abdominal wall   _____

2. surfer's knot, initial encounter   _____

3. infection of the right lower leg amputation stump, first visit _____

4. initial care for corneal transplant rejection _____

5. exhaustion due to exposure, initial care _____

6. Alpine sickness, subsequent care _____

7. first-degree corrosion of the neck, first visit (no Y code at this time) _____

8. anaphylactic shock due to properly administered substance, aspirin _____

9. initial care for open wound of left middle finger with
    splinter that had to be removed _____

10. external constriction of the right upper arm, initial visit _____

11. subsequent encounter for crush injury of the skull _____

12. second-degree burn of the chest wall (no Y code at this time) _____

13. traumatic subdural hemorrhage with loss of consciousness for 2 hours _____

14. first visit for seasickness _____

15. late effect of 0.5 cm laceration of left eyelid and periocular area _____

16. spiral displaced fracture of the shaft of the right femur, initial care _____

17. toxic effect of natural gas (subsequent visit) _____

18. underdosing of tetracycline, initial care _____

19. initial care for superficial frostbite of right hand _____

20. toxic effect of ingested mushrooms, accidental, initial care _____

21. mechanical breakdown of infusion catheter _____

22. bone graft failure _____

23. complex tear of right medial meniscus, current _____

24. heart-lung transplant failure _____

25. epidural hemorrhage with loss of consciousness, <30 minutes _____

26. initial encounter for open fracture of nasal bones _____

27. initial encounter for avulsion of right eye _____

28. initial encounter for closed fracture of coccyx _____

29. subsequent encounter for sprain of metacarpophalangeal
    joint of right index finger _____

30. initial encounter for laceration of blood vessels of left ring finger _____

Case Studies

Instructions: Review each case study and select the correct ICD-10-CM diagnostic code.

Case 1

Physician Office Note

S: The patient's wife brought the patient to my office after the patient tried to separate a raccoon and their dog, which were fighting. While trying to separate the animals, the patient was bitten. He is not sure whether the raccoon or the dog bit him.

EXAM:

The patient's left forearm has bite marks on it. The wound is bleeding and is deep, and there is tendon involvement.

The nurse cleaned the wound, and a tetanus shot was given. Because the wound is deep and there is tendon involvement, I called Dr. Black for a surgical consult. The wound was dressed to control the bleeding.

ICD-10-CM Code Assignment: _____

Case 2

ER Note

CHIEF COMPLAINT: This 2-year-old patient presents with a cut on his face.

History of the present illness: Patient fell off a kitchen chair and struck his face on the seat of the chair.

VITAL SIGNS: Pulse: 117, Respirations: 28, BP: 103/43

RESPIRATORY: Airway clear

BREATH SOUNDS: Clear

SKIN: 1.5-cm laceration to the forehead.

LACERATION REPAIR NOTE: The patient was papoosed with his mother's knowledge and presence. The wound was injected with 2 percent plain Lidocaine, and the wound edges were approximated with three #6-0 nylon sutures.

The patient was sent for an x-ray to rule out any facial bone fractures.

PLAN: Follow up with family physician in 1 week.

ICD-10-CM Code Assignment: _____

Case 3

Physician Office Note

CHIEF COMPLIANT: Pain in right arm.

HISTORY OF PRESENT ILLNESS: This 39-year-old female was carrying groceries into her house when she slipped on ice and fell. She landed on her right side and on her arm.

EXAM: EXTREMITIES: Her right arm is swollen, and it appears to be broken due to its abnormal appearance.

An in-office x-ray was completed that showed a complete fracture of the shaft of the humerus. Patient was referred to Dr. Break, the orthopedic surgeon on call. Patient was sent to Dr. Break's office.

ICD-10-CM Code Assignment: _____

Case 4

Clinic Visit Note

This is a 63-year-old type II diabetic male who presents 4 weeks after left foot amputation due to his diabetes. The patient presented to this office at the time of the injury due to concerns he had regarding possible complications stemming from his amputation, as his stump is quite red.

Upon examination, there was no streaking at this time, but some clear drainage is noted. The patient is afebrile, and other vital signs are within normal limits.

The diagnosis at this time is infection of amputation stump, left lower leg. We are starting the patient on antibiotics and have also treated and dressed the wound.

ICD-10-CM Code Assignment: _____

Case 5

Emergency Department Note

This patient is a 27-year-old male who was brought to the emergency department by ambulance after being bitten by a rattlesnake while hiking in the desert. The bite is located just above the ankle. The patient was wearing sneakers instead of hiking boots. The area of the bite is now red and a bit swollen.

(continues)

(continued)

The patient says the pain is about 9 out of 10 on the pain scale.

Examination reveals two small puncture marks on the medial side of the lower leg above the ankle.

Vital signs are within normal limits. The skin is swollen, red, and warm to touch. Patient was given a shot of antivenom and admitted for 24-hour observation.

ICD-10-CM Code Assignment: _____

Case 6

Office Visit

This 16-year-old male patient returns to the office today due to increased pain in his left upper leg. He had a previous traumatic fracture of the neck of the left femur. An x-ray was taken that showed a nonunion of the fracture.

ICD-10-CM Code Assignment: _____

Case 7

Discharge Note

This 34-year-old patient was admitted via the ED 3 days ago due to a traumatic rupture of the collateral ligament of the left wrist. Repair of the ligament was completed and the patient had no complications. She is instructed to see me in 2 weeks.

ICD-10-CM Code Assignment: _____

Case 8

Emergency Department Note

This female patient presents to the ER today with severe pain in her right index finger. She does not recall injuring the finger but there is a dislocation of the finger. I was able to manipulate the joint and realign it. I instructed her to follow up with orthopedics if more pain and discomfort occurs.

ICD-10-CM Code Assignment: _____

Case 9

This 59-year-old male previously had knee surgery in his left knee with a prosthesis inserted. He comes to the office today complaining of pain. Imaging of the knee and blood work confirm an infection surrounding the prosthesis. He is being referred to orthopedics to discuss treatment and I have prescribed an antibiotic.

ICD-10-CM Code Assignment: _____

Case 10

Office Visit Note

This patient presents today complaining of discomfort in her lower back. X-ray shows no signs of fracture. She is able to move without difficultly. She does not recall any injury to her back.

Vital Signs: BP: 120/80, Pulse: regular

Skin: On exam there is a contusion on her left lower back.

Heart: Normal

Lung: Clear

Extremities: ROM within normal limits, no contusions or wounds noted.

There are no other injuries noted at this time.

ICD-10-CM Code Assignment: _____

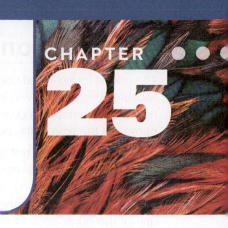

External Causes of Morbidity

Chapter Outline

Chapter Objectives

At the conclusion of this chapter, you should be able to:

1. Define "external cause" code categories and terms and when a code is appropriately assigned.
2. Sequence V, W, X, and Y codes.
3. Apply relevant ICD-10-CM coding guidelines to accurately code external causes of morbidity.
4. Select and code V, W, X, or Y codes for case studies.

Key Terms

Animate object	Inanimate object	Pedal cycle	Terrorism
Assault	Morbidity	Pedestrian	

REMINDER: As you work through this chapter, you will need to have a copy of the ICD-10-CM coding book to reference. For this chapter, you will also need to reference the ICD-10-CM Official Guidelines for Coding and Reporting. These guidelines can be found in Appendix A which are now available on the Student Companion site and MINDTAP From Cengage.

Introduction

The codes found in the code range V00 through Y99 are used to describe external causes of morbidity. **Morbidity** is another way of saying "diseased state." The codes are used as secondary codes to describe further how an injury happened or what caused a particular health condition, the place of occurrence, the activity of the person at the time of the event, and the person's status.

Some payers do not recognize or require the use of these codes. The data provided by the use of these codes assists in the evaluation and research of the cause and prevention strategies of injuries or certain health conditions. Also conveyed with this code block is whether the condition is intentionally inflicted and the place where the injury or the event occurred. The external causes of morbidity codes can be used with any of the other codes from the A00.0–T88.9 range, as well as with the other supplemental code category Z00–Z99.

The following blocks are found in this chapter:

- V00–V09, Pedestrian injured in transport accident
- V10–V19, Pedal cycle rider injured in transport accident
- V20–V29, Motorcycle rider injured in transport accident
- V30–V39, Occupant of three-wheeled motor vehicle injured in transport accident
- V40–V49, Car occupant injured in transport accident
- V50–V59, Occupant of pickup truck or van injured in transport accident
- V60–V69, Occupant of heavy transport vehicle injured in transport accident
- V70–V79, Bus occupant injured in transport accident
- V80–V89, Other land transport accidents
- V90–V94, Water transport accidents
- V95–V97, Air and space transport accidents
- V98–V99, Other and unspecified transport accidents
- W00–X58, Other external causes of accidental injury
- W00–W19, Slipping, tripping, stumbling, and falls
- W20–W49, Exposure to inanimate mechanical forces
- W50–W64, Exposure to animate mechanical forces
- W65–W74, Accidental non-transport drowning and submersion
- W85–W99, Exposure to electric current, radiation, and extreme ambient air temperature and pressure
- X00–X08, Exposure to smoke, fire, and flames
- X10–X19, Contact with heat and hot substances
- X30–X39, Exposure to forces of nature
- X50, Overexertion and strenuous or repetitive movements
- X52, X58, Accidental exposure to other specified factors
- X71–X83, Intentional self-harm
- X92–Y09, Assault
- Y21–Y33, Event of undetermined intent
- Y35–Y38, Legal intervention, operations of war, military operations, and terrorism
- Y62–Y84, Complications of medical and surgical care
- Y62–Y69, Misadventures to patients during surgical and medical care

- Y70–Y82, Medical devices associated with adverse incidents in diagnostic and therapeutic use
- Y83–Y84, Surgical and other medical procedures as the cause of abnormal reaction of the patient, or of later complication, without mention of misadventure at the time of the procedure
- Y90–Y99, Supplementary factors related to causes of morbidity classified elsewhere

Coding External Causes of Morbidity

As previously stated, the codes found in the V00–Y99 range are never used as a principal or first-listed diagnosis. They are applicable in any health care setting and are used in research and statistical gathering of data.

The Index to External Causes is located immediately after the Table of Drugs and Chemicals and immediately before the Tabular List of Disease and Injuries.

Some of the main terms used in the Index to External Causes include *accident, activity, contact, exposure, incident,* and *place of occurrence.*

No code from this code range should ever be used unless the provider documentation clearly states the specifics of an injury or accident, which support the V00–Y99 code choice.

The codes found in this code block can contain up to seven characters. The seventh character indicates the type of encounter, whether it is initial or subsequent, for which the patient is being seen. This character adds another level of detail to the information being reported. Keep in mind that more than one code from this code range may be necessary to accurately paint the picture of the person's accident or illness. The coder should pay close attention to the course of events, as documented in the medical record, before making the decision to use two codes or one combination code.

> **EXAMPLE:** Nina was on a college campus walking to her next class with a friend when they came upon a fight already in progress. As they were trying to get around the fight, one of the campus security persons accidentally kicked Nina in the course of trying to break up the fight. The blow landed on the left thigh and caused her to fall down two concrete steps, hitting her head. She was brought to the emergency department with multiple abrasions and contusions.
>
> If we break this down by the course of events, we would reference the Index to External Causes as follows:
>
> - Place of occurrence—college campus, Y92.214
> - Kicked by—person, in fight injuring bystander, Y35.892A (In this case, Nina was not one of the people involved in the fight; so the fact that security was trying to break up the fight and that she was an injured bystander is conveyed with this one code.)
> - Fall—fell down two concrete steps, W10.9xxA

Coders must check the codes found in the Index to External Causes against the Tabular List to be sure they have selected the correct code. Reference all necessary instructional notations and be sure all characters necessary to accurately report the incident have been identified.

To locate a code from the V00–Y99 range, refer to the Index to External Causes, located after the Alphabetic Index. The codes are then referenced in sequence in the Tabular List.

> **EXAMPLE:** In the case of Nina's injury:
>
> - Code Y92.214—College as the place of occurrence of the external cause
> - Code Y35.892A—Legal intervention involving other specified means, bystander injured (requires the seventh character)
> - Code W10.9—Fall (on)(from) other stairs and steps (In this case the appropriate seventh character needs to be selected. This code is four characters, so the placeholders need to be used to complete the valid code W10.9xxA. This is only determined by referencing the Tabular List.)
>
> *(continues)*

Our final external cause code assignment is:

- W10.9xxA—assigned first because this code best identifies how the actual injury occurred
- Y92.214
- Y35.892A

The Official Coding Guidelines governing the assignment of these codes are as follows:

ICD-10-CM Official Coding Guidelines

Chapter 20: External Causes of Morbidity (V00–Y99)

The external causes of morbidity codes should never be sequenced as the first-listed or principal diagnosis.

External cause codes are intended to provide data for injury research and evaluation of injury prevention strategies. These codes capture how the injury or health condition happened (cause), the intent (unintentional or accidental; or intentional, such as suicide or assault), the place where the event occurred, the activity of the patient at the time of the event, and the person's status (e.g., civilian, military).

There is no national requirement for mandatory ICD-10-CM external cause code reporting. Unless a provider is subject to a state-based external cause code reporting mandate or these codes are required by a particular payer, reporting of ICD-10-CM codes in Chapter 20, External Causes of Morbidity, is not required. In the absence of a mandatory reporting requirement, providers are encouraged to voluntarily report external cause codes, as they provide valuable data for injury research and evaluation of injury prevention strategies.

a. General External Cause Coding Guidelines

1) Used with any code in the range of A00.0–T88.9, Z00–Z99

An external cause code may be used with any code in the range of A00.0–T88.9, Z00–Z99, classification that represents a health condition due to an external cause. Though they are most applicable to injuries, they are also valid for use with such things as infections or diseases due to an external source, and other health conditions, such as a heart attack that occurs during strenuous physical activity.

2) External cause code used for length of treatment

Assign the external cause code, with the appropriate 7th character (initial encounter, subsequent encounter or sequela) for each encounter for which the injury or condition is being treated.

Most categories in Chapter 20 have a 7th character requirement for each applicable code. Most categories in this chapter have three 7th character values: A, initial encounter, D, subsequent encounter and S, sequela. While the patient may be seen by a new or different provider over the course of treatment for an injury or condition, assignment of the 7th character for external cause should match the 7th character of the code assigned for the associated injury or condition for the encounter.

3) Use the full range of external cause codes

Use the full range of external cause codes to completely describe the cause, the intent, the place of occurrence, and if applicable, the activity of the patient at the time of the event, and the patient's status, for all injuries, and other health conditions due to an external cause.

4) Assign as many external cause codes as necessary

Assign as many external cause codes as necessary to fully explain each cause. If only one external code can be recorded, assign the code most related to the principal diagnosis.

Courtesy of the Centers for Medicare & Medicaid Services, www.cms.gov

5) The selection of the appropriate external cause code

The selection of the appropriate external cause code is guided by the Alphabetic Index of External Causes and by Inclusion and Exclusion notes in the Tabular List.

6) External cause code can never be a principal diagnosis

An external cause code can never be a principal (first-listed) diagnosis.

7) Combination external cause codes

Certain of the external cause codes are combination codes that identify sequential events that result in an injury, such as a fall which results in striking against an object. The injury may be due to either event or both. The combination external cause code used should correspond to the sequence of events regardless of which caused the most serious injury.

8) No external cause code needed in certain circumstances

No external cause code from Chapter 20 is needed if the external cause and intent are included in a code from another chapter (e.g., T36.0X1- Poisoning by penicillins, accidental (unintentional)).

(See Appendix A, Section I, C20, 1-8.)

Exercise 25.1—Introduction Summary

Complete the following statements.

1. The codes found in Chapter 20 are used as _____ codes in addition to codes from other chapters in ICD-10-CM.
2. Category codes _____ report complications of medial and surgical care.
3. Water transport accidents are coded to the _____ code block.
4. Misadventures to patients during surgical and medical care are coded to the _____ block.
5. There is the potential for up to _____ characters in the V00–Y99 code range.

Transport Accidents (Category Codes V00–V99)

This block of codes is broken down into 12 groups. Each group identifies whether the accident was on land or in the water and then further identifies the mode of transportation. The most important issue to identify is the type of vehicle involved and whether the injured person is a passenger, driver, or bystander. Definitions of the different transport vehicles are found at the beginning of Chapter 20, in the Tabular List that allows for a more accurate code assignment. Coders need to read the definitions that appear after the heading.

For example, a **pedestrian** is defined as any person involved in an accident who was not at the time of the accident riding in or on a motor vehicle, railway train, streetcar or animal-drawn or other vehicle, or on a pedal cycle or animal. This includes a person changing a tire or working on a parked car. It also includes the use of a pedestrain conveyance such as a baby carriage, ice skates, roller skates, a skateboard, a nonmotorized wheelchair, a motorized mobility scooter, and a nonmotorized scooter.

The block of codes is defined as follows:

- V00–V09, Pedestrian injured in transport accident
- V10–V19, Pedal cycle rider injured in transport accident
- V20–V29, Motorcycle rider injured in transport accident
- V30–V39, Occupant of three-wheeled motor vehicle injured in transport accident

- V40–V49, Car occupant injured in transport accident
- V50–V59, Occupant of pickup truck or van injured in transport accident
- V60–V69, Occupant of heavy transport vehicle injured in transport accident
- V70–V79, Bus occupant injured in transport accident
- V80–V89, Other land transport accidents
- V90–V94, Water transport accidents
- V95–V97, Air and space transport accidents
- V98–V99, Other and unspecified transport accidents

Each of these blocks will be further discussed.

Pedestrian Injured in Transport Accident (Category Codes V00–V09)

To be coded as a transport accident, the vehicle involved must be used for transport purposes, and must be moving or running at the time of the accident. Coders need to see the Includes and Excludes notes before codes are assigned. Numerous instructional notations appear at the category level that identify the appropriate seventh characters.

- A, Initial encounter
- D, Subsequent encounter
- S, Sequela

This code range is quite extensive. Pedestrian conveyance accidents, rolling-type pedestrian conveyance accidents, and gliding-type pedestrian conveyance accidents are found at the beginning of the code range. The codes become very detailed regarding the pedestrian colliding with skateboards and scooters and other types of transports.

Pedal Cycle Rider Injured in Transport Accident (Category Codes V10–V19)

A **pedal cycle** is operated by a person who is operating the vehicle without the help of a motor. An accident involving a person who might be riding in a sidecar or a trailer that is attached to a pedal cycle is categorized to this code block unless the sidecar or trailer is animal drawn.

Codes found in this code block include a person injured in a collision with a two-or three-wheeled motor vehicle; a pedal cycle rider injured in a collision with a car, pickup truck, or van; and a pedal cycle rider injured in a collision with railway train or railway vehicle. Pedal cycle riders injured in a noncollision transport accident, which would include a fall from a pedal cycle, whether the person was thrown or the pedal cycle overturned, are coded to the V18 category.

Motorcycle Rider Injured in Transport Accident (Category Codes V20–V29)

Included in this code block are motorcycle riders and passengers on a motorcycle, including those seated in a sidecar. Other included vehicles are mopeds, motorized bicycles, and motor scooters. A three-wheeled motor vehicle is excluded. The motor vehicles in this code range are exclusively two-wheeled motor vehicles with a riding saddle. If the sidecar is attached to the motorcycle, it is considered part of the motorcycle.

Occupant of Three-Wheeled Motor Vehicle Injured in Transport Accident (Category Codes V30–V39)

This block of codes includes motorized tricycles, rickshaws, and three-wheeled motor cars. Fourth characters are assigned to identify the driver, passenger, or unspecified occupant. Appropriate seventh-character assignment is also needed.

Exercise 25.2—Category Codes V00–V39

Using an ICD-10-CM code book, assign a code from the V00–V39 code range.

Diagnosis **Code**

1. a passenger on a motorcycle who was injured in an accident in which a bear ran into the road and hit the motorcycle (subsequent encounter) _____

2. person on roller skates injured in a collision with a bike in a nontraffic accident (initial encounter) _____

3. an ice-skater who collided with a railroad tie that was set along side the pond (initial encounter) _____

4. passenger on a bicycle injured after being sideswiped by a bus on a busy street (subsequent encounter) _____

5. person walking on the sidewalk hit by a car backing out of a driveway (initial encounter) _____

Car Occupant Injured in Transport Accident (Category Codes V40–V49)

This code block is primarily used to report accidents occurring in a four-wheeled motor vehicle designed to carry up to seven passengers. A trailer or camper that is being pulled by an automobile is also included in this range. These categories do not include a minivan or van. The following box further explains the V40–V49 code block.

Category	Description
V40, Car occupant injured in collision with pedestrian or animal	This category is used to report a driver or passenger injured in a collision. The distinction is made as to the type of accident and who was injured, the driver or passenger.
V41, Car occupant injured in collision with pedal cycle	A car collision with a bicycle either in or out of traffic is reported with this category. The person injured may be a passenger or the driver injured in the vehicle or entering or leaving the vehicle.
V42, Car occupant injured in collision with two- or three-wheeled motor vehicle	As with previous code categories, the driver or passenger of the car needs to be identified. The place of the accident has to be identified, as well as whether the accident was in or out of traffic.
V43, Car occupant injured in collision with car, pickup truck, or van	The driver or passenger needs to be identified before code selection can occur. The identification of the other vehicle needs to be made because the code selection depends on whether the accident occurred with a car, pickup truck, van, or sport utility vehicle and on whether the accident was a traffic or nontraffic accident.

Courtesy of the Centers for Medicare & Medicaid Services, www.cms.gov

The remainder of the code categories, V44–V49, involve car accidents involving buses, trains, railway vehicles, or cars in an accident with a stationary object. Careful attention to the details of the documentation indicating who was injured, what the vehicle might have hit, and whether the accident happened in traffic are necessary to assign the proper code.

Occupant of Pickup Truck or Van Injured in Transport Accident (Category Codes V50–V59)

This block of codes includes four- or six-wheel motor vehicles that primarily carry passengers and property but weighing less than the local limit for classification as a heavy goods vehicle. This would include minibus, minivan, sport utility vehicle, truck, or van. The information needed to code from this range is the same as with the previous categories. Knowing whether the driver or passenger was injured in a traffic accident is necessary to choose a correct code.

Occupant of Heavy Transport Vehicle Injured in Transport Accident (Category Codes V60–V69)

Heavy transport vehicles are designed for carrying property, meeting local criteria for classification as a heavy goods vehicle in terms of weight and requiring a special driver's license, such as a commercial driver's license (CDL). This definition includes armored cars, panel trucks, and 18-wheelers. Injury of a driver or passenger in or out of traffic is the information necessary to properly assign a code.

Bus Occupant Injured in Transport Accident (Category Codes V70–V79)

A bus transport is a vehicle that is designed to carry more than 10 passengers and that requires a special license to operate. A motorcoach falls into this category as well. The coder must know whether the patient is the driver or a passenger who was injured in the bus accident. The type of accident and the knowledge of whether the accident happened as part of a traffic or nontraffic accident are also necessary information in determining a code.

Other Land Transport Accidents (Category Codes V80–V89)

The land transport vehicles that fall into this category include animals, animal-drawn vehicles, and all-terrain vehicles. The specific codes are chosen from this category just as they are selected from other codes in the transport accident blocks of codes. Passengers, drivers, and the type of accident are all considerations that need to be determined prior to code selection.

Exercise 25.3—Category Codes V40–V89

Using an ICD-10-CM code book, assign the proper code for the accident described.

Diagnosis	Code
1. driver of a car injured when a deer jumped out of the woods into the road in front of the moving vehicle (initial encounter)	_____
2. person on the outside of a car who is injured in a collision with an SUV as part of a traffic accident (subsequent encounter)	_____
3. passenger in a pickup truck injured in a collision with a bus in a traffic accident (initial encounter)	_____
4. passenger in a dune buggy injured in an accident on the dunes (initial encounter)	_____
5. person injured in a farm accident involving the driver of a tractor who was injured when he lost his footing while getting off the tractor out in the field (initial encounter)	_____

Water Transport Accidents (Category Codes V90–V94)

Within ICD-10-CM, watercraft accidents include boats, ships, hovercrafts, and any other transportation that works on the water. The included incidents are drowning due to an accident on the water, crush injuries involving watercraft, burns and falls encountered on the water or involving watercrafts, and injuries or accidents involving machinery on board a watercraft. Inflatable watercraft such as rafts and inner tubes are included in the code choices under V94, Other and unspecified water transport accidents.

There are many Excludes notes throughout this category. The coder needs to pay close attention to these notes in order to properly assign the correct code. The documentation needs to contain as many specifics of the accident as possible to support the code selection.

Air and Space Transport Accidents (Category Codes V95–V97)

The definition of aircraft includes any vehicle used to transport persons or goods in the air. This includes any aircraft except for military aircraft, which are covered in the Y codes. The following further explains the V95–V97 code block:

Category	Description
V95, Accident to powered aircraft causing injury to occupant	This code category includes helicopter accidents; ultralight, microlight, or powered glider; and fixed-wing aircraft. Also included are codes for spacecraft accidents.
V96, Accident to nonpowered aircraft causing injury to occupant	This category includes accidents that involve balloons, hang gliders, and other nonpowered aircraft accidents.
V97, Other specified air transport accidents	This category includes occupants of aircrafts who have fallen in or from an aircraft. Parachute accidents are also coded to this section.

Courtesy of the Centers for Medicare & Medicaid Services, www.cms.gov

Other and Unspecified Transport Accidents (Category Codes V98–V99)

This block contains codes used to report accidents involving a cable car not on rails, land yacht, ice yacht, and ski lift. The codes in this section are referenced after all other code choices have been exhausted.

Other External Causes of Accidental Injury (Category Codes W00–X58)

Slipping, Tripping, Stumbling, and Falls (Category Codes W00–W19)

The external cause codes found in this code range begin with falls due to ice and snow; falls from a curb; and falls from a wheelchair, bed, chair, playground equipment, tree, ladder, and scaffolding. The majority of the codes found in the W00–W16.4 range are falls *from, into,* or *off* of something. The coder must be able to make that distinction because the next range of codes, beginning with W16.5, describes *jumping* into something.

The W00–W16.4 code range includes falling into a swimming pool, into a natural body of water, or into a bathtub. Once the category of code is chosen, the coder needs to make the determination from the documentation provided as to whether the patient was injured due to striking the water or another structure in the water.

> **EXAMPLE:** Roger was playing in the pool with his cousin when he fell from its side into the water, landing flat on his stomach. He hit the water so hard it knocked the wind out of him, and he had to have help getting to the ladder. Once on the ladder, he caught his breath but felt dizzy, so his mother took him to the doctor to be examined. He did have some bruising on the anterior trunk. We would assign external cause code W16.012A, Fall into swimming pool striking water surface causing other injury. At the beginning of the category, there is an instructional notation that a character is needed to indicate the status of the encounter. The seventh character of A is chosen because it is the initial encounter for this problem.

Category W16.5 begins the code range for jumping or diving into a swimming pool, lake, or other body of water. The coder needs to determine whether the patient was submerged, drowned, or injured. Refer to the documentation for this information.

Category W17 is referenced for falls from one level to another, such as down an embankment or into a hole or well.

Categories W18 and W19 complete the code block with codes used to indicate slipping, tripping, and/or stumbling. If the type of fall is not found in the previous code categories, these categories are referenced.

Also found in this block of external cause codes are falls due to bumping against an object, such as glass or sports equipment, and falls in the shower or bathtub.

These categories specify slipping, tripping, and stumbling without falling. Refer to the documentation for verification of a fall. Never assume that, because patients are injured due to slipping, tripping, or stumbling, they actually fell. This is not always the case. If the documentation is not clear on this point, query the originator of the documentation.

> **EXAMPLE:** Lisa got up from the couch to get a drink of water. On her way from the living room to the kitchen, her heel caught on the carpet and she stumbled forward, twisting her ankle. She caught herself on the side of the door before she actually fell. Even though Lisa stumbled, she did not fall; so the code assignment is W18.49XA, Other slipping, tripping, and stumbling without falling, initial encounter.

Exposure to Inanimate Mechanical Forces (Category Codes W20–W49)

An **inanimate object** is one that is not alive or able to move (animate) on its own power. The beginning of this category of codes contains an Excludes1 note that this category does not include assault, contact, or collision with animals or persons; exposure to inanimate mechanical forces involving the military or war operations; or intentional self-harm.

This code block does, however, include being struck by thrown or projected objects, such as cave-ins, or by sports equipment (e.g., footballs, baseballs, volleyballs). A patient might present with an injury caused by a cleat or skate blade. These incidents are found in the W21 category.

Category W22 reports striking against or struck by other objects which includes such objects as walls, furniture, and airbags. This category contains some Exclude notations that should be addressed before codes are assigned.

Crush and contact injuries are found in the code block for exposure to inanimate mechanical forces. The documentation must clearly state what caused the injury so that the coder can determine the correct code.

The W23–W31 categories are referenced for these types of injuries. Contact codes are quite detailed and include contact with glass, knives, garden tools, kitchen utensils, and paper cutters. These categories contain further detail that needs to be referenced after the documentation is reviewed.

The W32–W34 categories contain codes that reflect the external cause codes for the accidental discharge of a weapon. The weapons include firearms such as handguns, pistols, revolvers, pellet guns, rifles, and air guns. The codes become more specific, identifying guns specifically as hunting rifles and machine guns.

Categories W35–W40 report the following:

Catergory	Description
W35, Explosion and rupture of boiler	This code includes the explosion and/or rupture of a boiler in a structure. A rupture of a boiler on a watercraft is coded to V93.4- instead of this code.
W36, Explosion and rupture of gas cylinder	This code range includes aerosol cans, air tanks, pressurized gas tanks, and gas cylinders.
W37, Explosion and rupture of pressurized tire, pipe, or hose	Included in this code range are car or bicycle tires.
W38, Explosion and rupture of other specified pressurized devices	An injury related to an explosion and rupture of other specified pressurized devices, that are not defined in ICD-10-CM, is reported with this category code.
W39, Discharge of firework	An injury related to the discharge of fireworks is reported with the code for the injury and this W code as an additional descriptor.
W40, Explosion of other materials	This range of codes includes blasting material such as blasting caps, detonators, and dynamite. This range also includes explosive gases and other explosive material.

The remaining codes in this block are a somewhat eclectic mix of "contact" issues. There are external cause codes reflecting foreign bodies or objects entering through the skin, such as a nail, paper, or lid of a can. Other codes report contact with a hypodermic needle and exposure to abnormal gravitational forces (G force).

Exposure to Animate Mechanical Forces (Category Codes W50–W64)

An **animate object** is a living being capable of movement on its own. The code range includes:

- Accidental injuries by another person, distinguished according to how the injury took place (e.g., hitting, kicking, biting, or scratching)
- Being crushed by a crowd
- Injury caused by contact with rodents, dogs, cats, horses, or other mammals
- Contact with reptiles, venomous or nonvenomous

Accidental Non-Transport Drowning and Submersion (Category Codes W65–W74)

This is not a very extensive code block. Found here are codes for accidental drowning and submersion while in the bathtub or other water but *not* due to a fall.

Exposure to Electric Current, Radiation, and Extreme Ambient Air Temperature and Pressure (Category Codes W85–W99)

This code block contains Includes and Excludes notes that need to be reviewed prior to code selection. This code block reports exposure to broken power lines, to industrial or residential wiring, and to the wiring of appliances that might have caused injury.

The detail extends to injury caused by exposure to the ultraviolet light of a welding light or tanning bed. Also found is contact with heating appliances; with hot engines, machinery, and tools; and with hot metal.

One of the unique features of this chapter is the category for exposure to changes in high and low air pressure, which include injuries occurring in the air, in deep water, or due to other rapid changes in air pressure. Like other codes in the external cause chapter, a seventh-character assignment is necessary for most of the codes in this block.

Exercise 25.4—Coding from the W Code Section

Using an ICD-10-CM code book, assign a W code.

Diagnosis	Code
1. exposure to infrared radiation (late effect)	_____
2. bitten by a parrot (initial encounter)	_____
3. explosion of propane (initial encounter)	_____
4. contact with a lathe (subsequent encounter)	_____
5. fall from the toilet, striking head on the vanity (initial encounter)	_____

Exposure to Smoke, Fire, and Flames (Category Codes X00–X08)

The X codes are actually a continuation of the exposure codes, so they are not broken out into their own section within the external cause chapter of ICD-10-CM. Even though there are more than 68,000 codes in ICD-10-CM, many sections leave room for expansion. The W and X codes are two such blocks.

The X codes begin with X00, Exposure to uncontrolled fire in building or structure. The codes found in the X00–X08 range are also referenced when reporting exposure to flames in a controlled or uncontrolled building or structure fire, as well as the ignition of highly flammable material such as gasoline, kerosene, or even melting clothing. Exposure to ignition of plastic jewelry, bed fires, and other furniture fires is also reported from this code range.

Contact with Heat and Hot Substances (Category Codes X10–X19)

Unfortunately, many people are burned each year. The causes vary from hot water, to flames, to hot air, to appliances. This code block has very specific forms of contact injuries for reporting these exposures.

> **EXAMPLE:** Marcy got home late from work and was very tired. She decided to have a toasted bagel with a little peanut butter and a cup of tea, and call it a night. She was heating water on her hot-plate for some tea while the bagel was toasting. When the bagel popped up from the toaster, she went to prepare it. As she was reaching for the knife to apply peanut butter to her bagel, her hand went down on the hotplate by accident. Even though she tried to take care of it, she ended up at the emergency room and had silver nitrate applied to her hand for the second-degree burn she received due to contact with the hot-plate.
>
> The burn is the primary diagnosis. How Marcy obtained the burn is reported with X15.2XXA, Contact with hotplate, initial encounter.

Exposure to Forces of Nature (Category Codes X30–X39)

Exposure to forces of nature include exposure to sunlight, earthquake, volcanic eruption, hurricane, tornado, blizzard, and dust storm, to name a few. These codes are used to report any type of incident that is considered caused by nature but excludes human-made heat or radiation.

Overexertion and Strenuous or Repetitive Movement (Category Code X50) and Accidental Exposure to Other Specified Factors (Category Codes X52, X58)

Category X50 reports overexertion, strenuous and repetitive movements. Code X52 is for prolonged stay in a weightless environment. This is reported by astronauts after prolonged exposure in a training environment or after an extended stay in space. Code X58 reports Exposure to other specified factors.

Intentional Self-Harm (Category Codes X71–X83)

This block includes codes for identifying suicide attempts and self-inflicted intentional injuries. In some instances, a person causes self-harm just for the attention, without trying to commit suicide. The coder should *never* assign a code for suicide or a suicide attempt unless the physician or provider has been queried and confirms the diagnosis.

Reported from this block of codes is intentional self-harm by drowning, by shotgun or other firearm, or by smoke, fire, flames, or sharp object. Like the other blocks in this chapter, the appropriate seventh character needs to be added when indicated to make the code as specific as possible.

Assault (Category Codes X92–Y09)

Assault is a violent crime committed against another. This block of codes is used to identify various types of assault, including homicide or injuries inflicted by another with the intent to injure or kill. The Excludes1 notation identifies injuries due to legal intervention, operations of war, or terrorism.

Assaults by smoke, fire, or flames, steam, hot vapors, hot objects, and firearms or sharp objects are found in the X94–X99 code range. The Y codes begin with Y00, Assault by blunt object.

 NOTE:

The codes for assault include both X and Y codes.

The codes for Y07, Perpetrator of assault, maltreatment, and neglect, are very specific and should be used cautiously. The *only* time a coder includes one of these codes on a claim form is if there is a confirmed case of abuse and the person has been positively identified with supporting documentation. Use of this code without such documentation can leave the door open to a defamation of character suit and cause a legal nightmare for the coder, the provider, and the employing organization.

Event of Undetermined Intent (Category Codes Y21–Y33)

This code block is referenced when no determination is documented as to the intent of the injury. The coder needs to reference accidental or unintentional events if the intent is documented.

Found in this code block are drowning; the discharge of firearms; contact with explosive materials or sharp objects; and exposure to smoke, fire, and flames. Again, the documentation must state that the intent of the injury could not be determined.

Legal Intervention, Operations of War, Military Operations, and Terrorism (Category Codes Y35–Y38)

This code block includes codes for injuries received as a result of an encounter with law enforcement officials serving on or off duty in any capacity at the time of an encounter. The following box further explains these codes and when to use them:

Y35, Legal intervention	This block of codes is extensive in the types of legal intervention injuries. The category begins with firearm discharge codes and goes through pellet rifles and handguns. Injuries also obtained by exposure to tear gas or blunt objects can be found here. The codes identify law enforcement personnel, suspects, and bystanders. Refer to the documentation for the support of the proper code selection and determination of who was injured.
Y36, Operation of war	This code block identifies injuries received by military personnel, as well as civilians, that are caused by war and/or civil insurrection. Such occurrences include explosions of marine weapons and military watercraft or aircraft, as well as fragments from a bomb, artillery shell, grenade, land mine, or shrapnel. Codes for the secondary effects of nuclear weapons during war operations are also found in this category. The distinctions among codes in this category are made by the documentation stating whether the injury was due to friendly fire or enemy fire and whether the person injured was a civilian or a member of the military.
Y37, Military operation	Sometimes injuries occur on military property, such as base of operations, during routine military operations. This block of codes identifies such injuries involving military personnel or civilians. In this case, military property does *not* extend to military vehicles, including aircraft or watercraft, involved in transport accidents or other accidents with civilian vehicles; these are reported with codes from the V code section.
Y38, Terrorism	ICD-10-CM guides the coder with the following note at the beginning of this code block, which is the FBI definition of terrorism: "These codes are for use to identify injuries resulting from the unlawful use of force or violence against persons or property to intimidate or coerce a government, the civilian population, or any segment, thereof, in furtherance of political or social objective." An additional code from the Y92 category is needed to indicate the place of occurrence. The codes distinguish among a public safety official, a civilian, or a terrorist being injured. When the cause of the injury is clearly identified by the federal government (FBI) as terrorism, the Y38 code should always be sequenced first. If, however, the cause is suspected terrorism, the injury is identified with a code from the assault code set. Code Y38.9-, Terrorism, secondary effects, is used for conditions occurring after the terrorist event and may be used with other Y38 codes.

Complications of Medical and Surgical Care (Category Codes Y62–Y84)

The blocks of codes that are found in this section of Chapter 20 include:

- Misadventures to Patients During Surgical and Medical Care (Category Codes Y62–Y69)
- Medical Devices Associated with Adverse Incidents in Diagnostic and Therapeutic Use (Category Codes Y70–Y82)
- Surgical and Other Medical Procedures as the Cause of Abnormal Reaction of the Patient, or of Later Complication, Without Mention of Misadventure at the Time of the Procedure (Category Codes Y83–Y84)

Included in this block of codes are complications of medical devices, surgical and medical procedures as the cause of an abnormal reaction of the patient, or of later complication, without mention of misadventure at the time of the procedure.

The code selections found in the Y62–Y69 range include failure of sterile precautions for organ transplant, bypass or graft surgery, amputation of a limb, or reconstruction, to name a few.

 NOTE:

Beginning with the Y62-Y69 block of codes, a seventh-character assignment may or may not be appropriate. Coders need to refer to the Tabular List to be sure that they are assigning an accurate code containing all the characters necessary to process a claim.

Supplementary Factors Related to Causes of Morbidity Classified Elsewhere (Category Codes Y90–Y99)

This block of codes is not used except in conjunction with other codes. Details surrounding the codes are outlined in the following box:

Code	Description
Y90, Evidence of alcohol involvement determined by blood alcohol level	The Y90.0–Y90.9 codes indicate blood alcohol levels that have been determined by an actual blood test. The levels range from less than 20 mg/100 ml to 240 mg/100 ml. There is a "Code first" note indicating that a code from the F10 codes for alcohol-related disorders should be coded before a code from the Y90 series.
Y92, Place of occurrence of the external cause	These codes are used with an activity code to identify the place of occurrence of the external cause. Place of occurrence codes are used only for the initial encounter and are not repeated at subsequent visits. Place of occurrence codes include, but are not limited to, private driveways, private garages, gardens, mobile homes, apartments, institutional residence, nursing homes, and military bases.
Y93, Activity code	The activity code block contains codes that indicate the activity of the injured person at the time of the injury. These codes are used when a person suffers a health condition, such as a stroke or heart attack, and the activity being performed at the time of the heart attack or stroke needs to be reported. A couple of things to note for this category: <ul><li>The codes can be used for both acute injuries and conditions due to long-term cumulative activities.</li><li>The codes are appropriate for use with external cause codes for cause and intent, if identifying the activity provides additional information on the event.</li></ul>

The following guidelines also govern the assignment of codes from Chapter 20 of ICD-10-CM:

ICD-10-CM Official Coding Guidelines

b. Place of Occurrence Guideline

Codes from category Y92, Place of occurrence of the external cause, are secondary codes for use after other external cause codes to identify the location of the patient at the time of injury or other condition.

Generally, place of occurrence code is assigned only once, at the initial encounter for treatment. However, in the rare instance that a new injury occurs during hospitalization, an additional place of occurrence code may be assigned. No 7th characters are used for Y92.

Do not use place of occurrence code Y92.9 if the place is not stated or is not applicable.

c. Activity Code

Assign a code from category Y93, Activity code, to describe the activity of the patient at the time the injury or other health condition occurred.

An activity code is used only once, at the initial encounter for treatment. Only one code from Y93 should be recorded on a medical record.

The activity codes are not applicable to poisonings, adverse effects, misadventures or sequela.

Do not assign Y93.9, Unspecified activity, if the activity is not stated.

A code from category Y93 is appropriate for use with external cause and intent codes if identifying the activity provides additional information about the event.

d. Place of Occurrence, Activity, and Status Codes Used with other External Cause Code

When applicable, place of occurrence, activity, and external cause status codes are sequenced after the main external cause code(s). Regardless of the number of external cause codes assigned, there should be only one place of occurrence code, one activity code, and one external cause status code assigned to an encounter. However in the rare instance that a new injury occurs during hospitalization, an additional place of occurrence code may be assigned.

e. If the Reporting Format Limits the Number of External Cause Codes

If the reporting format limits the number of external cause codes that can be used in reporting clinical data, report the code for the cause/intent most related to the principal diagnosis. If the format permits capture of additional external cause codes, the cause/intent, including medical misadventures, of the additional events should be reported rather than the codes for place, activity, or external status.

f. Multiple External Cause Coding Guidelines

More than one external cause code is required to fully describe the external cause of an illness or injury. The assignment of external cause codes should be sequenced in the following priority:

If two or more events cause separate injuries, an external cause code should be assigned for each cause. The first-listed external cause code will be selected in the following order:

External codes for child and adult abuse take priority over all other external cause codes.

See Section I.C.19., Child and Adult abuse guidelines.

External cause codes for terrorism events take priority over all other external cause codes except child and adult abuse.

External cause codes for cataclysmic events take priority over all other external cause codes except child and adult abuse and terrorism.

External cause codes for transport accidents take priority over all other external cause codes except cataclysmic events, child and adult abuse and terrorism.

Activity and external cause status codes are assigned following all causal (intent) external cause codes.

The first-listed external cause code should correspond to the cause of the most serious diagnosis due to an assault, accident, or self-harm, following the order of hierarchy listed above.

g. Child and Adult Abuse Guideline

Adult and child abuse, neglect and maltreatment are classified as assault. Any of the assault codes may be used to indicate the external cause of any injury resulting from the confirmed abuse.

For confirmed cases of abuse, neglect and maltreatment, when the perpetrator is known, a code from Y07, Perpetrator of maltreatment and neglect, should accompany any other assault codes.

See Section I.C.19. Adult and child abuse, neglect and other maltreatment.

h. Unknown or Undetermined Intent Guideline

If the intent (accident, self-harm, assault) of the cause of an injury or other condition is unknown or unspecified, code the intent as accidental intent. All transport accident categories assume accidental intent.

1) Use of undetermined intent

External cause codes for events of undetermined intent are only for use if the documentation in the record specifies that the intent cannot be determined.

i. Sequelae (Late Effects) of External Cause Guidelines

1) Sequelae external cause codes

Sequela are reported using the external cause code with the 7th character "S" for sequela. These codes should be used with any report of a late effect or sequela resulting from a previous injury. See Section I.B.10 Sequela (Late Effects)

2) Sequela external cause code with a related current injury

A sequela external cause code should never be used with a related current nature of injury code.

3) Use of sequela external cause codes for subsequent visits

Use a late effect external cause code for subsequent visits when a late effect of the initial injury is being treated. Do not use a late effect external cause code for subsequent visits for follow-up care (e.g., to assess healing, to receive rehabilitative therapy) of the injury when no late effect of the injury has been documented.

j. Terrorism Guidelines

1) Cause of injury identified by the Federal Government (FBI) as terrorism

When the cause of an injury is identified by the Federal Government (FBI) as terrorism, the first-listed external cause code should be a code from category Y38, Terrorism. The definition of terrorism employed by the FBI is found at the inclusion note at the beginning of category Y38. Use additional code for place of occurrence (Y92.-). More than one Y38 code may be assigned if the injury is the result of more than one mechanism of terrorism.

2) Cause of an injury is suspected to be the result of terrorism

When the cause of an injury is suspected to be the result of terrorism, a code from category Y38 should not be assigned. Suspected cases should be classified as assault.

3) Code Y38.9, Terrorism, secondary effects

Assign code Y38.9, Terrorism, secondary effects, for conditions occurring subsequent to the terrorist event. This code should not be assigned for conditions that are due to the initial terrorist act.

It is acceptable to assign code Y38.9 with another code from Y38 if there is an injury due to the initial terrorist event and an injury that is a subsequent result of the terrorist event.

k. External cause status

A code from category Y99, External cause status, should be assigned whenever any other external cause code is assigned for an encounter, including an Activity code, except for the events noted below. Assign a code from category Y99, External cause status, to indicate the work status of the person at the time the event occurred. The status code indicates whether the event occurred during military activity, whether a nonmilitary person was at work, whether an individual including a student or volunteer was involved in a non-work activity at the time of the causal event.

A code from Y99, External cause status, should be assigned, when applicable, with other external cause codes, such as transport accidents and falls. The external cause status codes are not applicable to poisonings, adverse effects, misadventures or late effects.

Do not assign a code from category Y99 if no other external cause codes (cause, activity) are applicable for the encounter.

An external cause status code is used only once, at the initial encounter for treatment. Only one code from Y99 should be recorded on a medical record.

Do not assign code Y99.9, Unspecified external cause status, if the status is not stated.

(See Appendix A, Section I, C20, b-k.)

Courtesy of the Centers for Medicare & Medicaid Services, www.cms.gov

Summary

- Chapter 20 of ICD-10-CM classifies environmental events and circumstances as the cause of injury, and other adverse effects.
- Use the appropriate seventh character for categories within Chapter 20 of ICD-10-CM, where appropriate.
- Codes from Chapter 20 of ICD-10-CM are never used as the primary diagnosis code.
- More than one code may be assigned from Chapter 20 of ICD-10-CM, though sequencing of the codes is important, as outlined in the Official Coding Guidelines.
- Sequela are indicated by use of the seventh character S.

Chapter Review

Multiple Choice

Select the best answer that completes the statement or answers the question.

1. The external causes of morbidity codes are codes used to:
    a. code an acute medical condition such as pharyngitis.
    b. code the environmental event or circumstances as the cause of injury, or the adverse effect.
    c. code an evaluation and management service to report the service rendered.
    d. code the injury that occurred.

2. The codes from Chapter 20 capture the _____, the _____, and the _____ of the event that brought the patient to the facility.
    a. complication, location, duration
    b. location, functioning, injury
    c. intent, location, complication
    d. cause, intent, location

3. Other land transport accidents are reported using:
    a. V98–V99
    b. V90–V94
    c. V80–V89
    d. V70–V79

4. Another way of saying "diseased state" is to use the term:
    a. morbidity
    b. mortality
    c. toxic effect
    d. external cause

5. Which of the following reflects the proper sequencing if more than one code from Chapter 20 is necessary for reporting an encounter?
    a. W45.2-, Y04.1-, Y92.215
    b. W45.2-, Y92.215, Y04.1-
    c. Y04.1-, Y92.215, W45.2-
    d. Y04.1-, W45.2-, Y92.215

6. Which of the following reflects the proper sequencing if more than one code from Chapter 20 is necessary for reporting an encounter?
   a. V96.01-, X36.1-, Y38.892-
   b. X36.1-, V96.01-, Y38.892-
   c. Y38.892-, V96.01-, X36.1-
   d. Y38.892-, X36.1-, V96.01-

7. A _____ is defined as any person involved in an accident who was not at the time of the accident riding in or on a motor vehicle, railway train, streetcar, or animal-drawn or other vehicle, or on a pedal cycle or animal.
   a. passenger
   b. driver
   c. pedestrian
   d. rider

8. In ICD-10-CM, sequela are indicated by the seventh character:
   a. A
   b. B
   c. D
   d. S

9. Complications of medical and surgical care are classified to code block:
   a. V40–V49
   b. Y62–Y84
   c. Y90–Y99
   d. X30–X39

10. Injuries inflicted by another person with intent to injure or kill, by any means is:
    a. assault
    b. battery
    c. liable
    d. slander

Coding Guidelines True/False

Review the ICD-10-CM Official Guidelines for Coding and Reporting and indicate if the statement(s) is true or false.

11. _____ The external causes of morbidity codes should always be sequenced as the first-listed or principal diagnosis.

12. _____ There is no national requirement for mandatory ICD-10-CM external cause code reporting. Unless a provider is subject to a state-based external cause code reporting mandate or these codes are required by a particular payer, reporting of ICD-10-CM codes in Chapter 20, External Causes of Morbidity, is not required.

13. _____ Assign the external cause code, with the appropriate 7th character (initial encounter, subsequent encounter or sequela) for each encounter for which the injury or condition is being treated.

14. _____ The selection of the appropriate external cause code is guided by the Alphabetic Index of External Causes and by Inclusion and Exclusion notes in the Alphabetic Index of External Causes.

15. _____ Certain of the external cause codes are combination codes that identify sequential events that result in an injury, such as a fall which results in striking against an object.

Coding Assignments

Instructions: Using an ICD-10-CM code book, assign the proper external cause code to the following statements. (Assume initial encounter unless otherwise specified.)

1. exposure to sound waves

2. bitten by an alligator

3. explosion of aerosol can

4. fall into well

5. fall from bed

6. contact with a nonvenomous toad

7. subsequent encounter for injury due to fall into a well

8. driver of a fire engine injured in a nontraffic accident

9. walked into a coffee table

10. fell into empty swimming pool

11. accidental discharge of a paintball gun

12. fall due to collision between two fishing boats

13. fall from a nonmotorized scooter

14. contact with sharp glass, undetermined intent

15. hypodermic needle stick

16. civilian injured in terrorist attack involving firearms

17. fall on escalator

18. contact with running hot tap water

19. subsequent visit after being struck by a brick from a collapsing building

20. drowning after fall in bath tub

21. subsequent visit after contact injury with a chisel

22. fall from grocery cart

23. exposure to a broken power line

24. fall from scaffolding, subsequent encounter

25. dog bite

26. initial encounter for pedestrian on foot injured in collision with rider of standing electric scooter

27. subsequent encounter for pedestrian on standing electric scooter injured in collision with pedal cycle in traffic accident

28. sequela, pedestrian on standing electric scooter injured in collision with three wheeled motor vehicle in traffic accident

29. initial encounter for a pedestrian that was injured while on a standing electric scooter and collided with a car in a traffic accident

30. subsequent encounter for contact with hot toaster

Case Studies

Instructions: Review each case study and select the correct ICD-10-CM diagnostic code. Do not assign place of occurrence, activity code, or external cause status code unless instructed to do so for the case.

Case 1

Emergency Department Note

Justin was brought to the emergency room with a broken left tibia. Justin was sky diving and, due to a wind shift, he landed in a tree. After a complete examination and scans, the broken tibia is the only injury found. The final diagnosis is a displaced fracture of lateral condyle of left tibia due to a parachutist landing in a tree.

ICD-10-CM Code Assignment: _____

Case 2

Emergency Department Note

This is a 3-year-old patient who was playing outside and received a cut by slipping and falling on an icy sidewalk and landing on a piece of broken glass on the ground.

EXAM: There is a 1-cm laceration of the right hand. The wound was cleaned and searched for any remaining pieces of glass. No foreign body was found.

PROCEDURE: Dermabond glue was used to repair the laceration

PLAN: Patient will follow up with her pediatrician in 1 week to check on healing.

ICD-10-CM Code Assignment: _____

Case 3

Physician Office Note

This is a 27-year-old male who is here for a follow-up visit after falling into the bathtub full of water, causing a contusion of the right shoulder. He said the pain level is down to a level 2 from a 10 on his last visit. There was a follow-up x-ray done and no fracture or other irregularities are noted. He will continue with ibuprofen as needed.

ICD-10-CM Code Assignment: _____

Case 4

Physician Office Visit

This 4-year-old male patient burned his left forearm last week and sustained a first-degree burn from a hot drink. He presents to the office today so I can examine the healing process. Today I changed the dressing and the burn is healing. I instructed his mother to change the dressing each day for the next week and to return to my office at that time.

ICD-10-CM Code Assignment: _____

Case 5

Emergency Department Note

This 6-year-old male patient sustained a second-degree burn of right index finger when he was playing with the candles on his birthday cake while having his party at his home in the dining room. I am requesting a dermatology consult.

For this case, assign a diagnostic code, external cause code, place of occurrence code, activity code, and external cause status code.

ICD-10-CM Code Assignment: _____

Case 6

Emergency Department Note

This 29-year-old male was riding his motorcycle with other cyclists on a recreational ride and hit a deer when he was driving on the highway. He sustained a fracture of his right femur. An orthopedic surgeon has been called in for this case.

For this case, assign a diagnostic code, external cause code, place of occurrence code, activity code, and external cause status code.

ICD-10-CM Code Assignment: _____

Case 7

Emergency Department Case

This 39-year-old male was working on his single-family home when he fell from a ladder. He is complaining of pain in his left shoulder area. X-rays confirm a displaced fracture of the left acromial process of the scapula. Orthopedic consult to occur.

(continues)

(*continued*)

For this case, assign a diagnostic code, external cause code, place of occurrence code, activity code, and external cause status code.

ICD-10-CM Code Assignment: _____

Case 8

Physician Office Visit

This 10-year-old patient was bitten by a dog while he was feeding his dog in the backyard of his parent's single-family home and sustained an open bite wound on his upper left arm.

For this case, assign a diagnosis code, external cause code, place of occurrence code, activity code, and external cause status code.

ICD-10-CM Code Assignment: _____

Case 9

Emergency Department Note

This 40-year-old male patient presents today coming directly from work at Southside restaurant. He is the head chef and was using the fryer and was accidentally burned by the hot oil from the fryer.

For this case, assign an external cause code, place of occurrence code, activity code, and external cause status code.

ICD-10-CM Code Assignment: _____

Case 10

Emergency Department Note

This 20-year-old female was using her cell phone to send a text message while driving on Interstate 81 to a family activity. Her car hit another car.

For this case, assign an external cause code, place of occurrence code, activity code, and external cause status code.

ICD-10-CM Code Assignment: _____

Factors Influencing Health Status and Contact with Health Services, and Codes for Special Purposes

Chapter Outline

Chapter Objectives

At the conclusion of this chapter, you should be able to:

1. Explain the purpose of Z and U codes.
2. Identify key terms that are used to locate Z and U codes in the Alphabetic Index.
3. Describe and identify encounters for which Z and U codes are used.
4. Explain the differences between the blocks and categories outlined in Chapter 21 of the ICD-10-CM code book.
5. Apply ICD-10-CM coding guidelines to factors influencing health status and contact with health services (Z codes) and special purposes (U codes).
6. Select the appropriate Z and U codes for case studies.

Key Terms

Body mass index	Resuscitation	U codes
Diagnostic examinations	Screening examinations	Z codes

REMINDER: As you work through this chapter, you will need to have a copy of the ICD-10-CM coding book to reference. For this chapter, you will also need to reference the ICD-10-CM Official Guidelines for Coding and Reporting. These guidelines can be found in Appendix A which are now available on the Student Companion site and MINDTAP From Cengage.

Introduction

Z codes are to be used to report the reason for the encounter when the circumstances surrounding the encounter are for something other than disease or injury. At the start of the Z code chapter in the code manual, the purpose of the Z codes is stated as follows:

"Z codes represent reasons for encounters. A corresponding procedure code must accompany a Z code if a procedure is performed. Categories Z00–Z99 are provided for occasions when circumstances other than a disease, injury, or external cause classifiable to categories A00–Y89 are recorded as 'diagnoses' or 'problems'. This can arise in two main ways:

(a) When a person who may or may not be sick encounters the health services for some specific purpose, such as to receive limited care or service for a current condition, to donate an organ or tissue, to receive prophylactic vaccination (immunization), or to discuss a problem which in itself is not a disease or injury.

(b) When some circumstance or problem is present which influences the person's health status but is not in itself a current illness or injury."

The Z codes apply to any health care setting and may be used as either a first-listed diagnosis code or as a secondary code depending on the circumstances of the visit.

Introduction to Z Codes

Z codes are located in the Alphabetic Index by referencing a main term.

Main terms that are used to locate Z codes include:

- Admission
- Aftercare
- Attention to
- Chemotherapy
- Counseling
- Encounter for
- Examination
- Fitting
- History of
- Maintenance
- Observation
- Problem
- Replacement
- Resistance
- Screening
- Vaccination

EXAMPLE: Kate was coding the diagnostic statement of "presence of cochlear implant device." At first, she was confused as to where to find this diagnosis because the patient did not have an implant procedure performed in the office at this time. Kate referenced the word *presence* in the Alphabetic Index. She then referenced the sub-term cochlear implant (functional) and found code Z96.21 for the presence of a cochlear implant device. She then reverified the code in the Tabular.

This chapter contains the following blocks:

- Z00–Z13, Persons encountering health services for examinations
- Z14–Z15, Genetic carrier and genetic susceptibility to disease
- Z16, Resistance to antimicrobial drugs
- Z17, Estrogen receptor status
- Z18, Retained foreign body fragments
- Z19, Hormone Sensitivity Malignancy Status
- Z20–Z29, Persons with potential health hazards related to communicable diseases
- Z30–Z39, Persons encountering health services in circumstances related to reproduction
- Z40–Z53, Encounters for other specific health care
- Z55–Z65, Persons with potential health hazards related to socioeconomic and psychosocial circumstances
- Z66, Do not resuscitate status
- Z67, Blood type
- Z68, Body mass index (BMI)
- Z69–Z76, Persons encountering health services in other circumstances
- Z77–Z99, Persons with potential health hazards related to family and personal history of certain conditions influencing health status

Each of these blocks is discussed in this chapter. However, prior to code selection, coders need to be familiar with the following coding guidelines:

ICD-10-CM Official Coding Guideline

Chapter 21: Factors influencing health status and contact with health services (Z00–Z99)

Note: The chapter specific guidelines provide additional information about the use of Z codes for specified encounters.

a. Use of Z codes in any health care setting

Z codes are for use in any healthcare setting. Z codes may be used as either a first-listed (principal diagnosis code in the inpatient setting) or secondary code, depending on the circumstances of the encounter. Certain Z codes may only be used as first-listed or principal diagnosis.

b. Z codes indicate a reason for an encounter

Z codes are not procedure codes. A corresponding procedure code must accompany a Z code to describe any procedure performed.

(See Appendix A, Section I, C 21, a–b.)

Persons Encountering Health Services for Examinations (Category Codes Z00–Z13)

Notes throughout this code block need to be referenced before code assignment is completed. At the start of this block of codes, a note appears that states "nonspecific abnormal findings disclosed at the time of these examinations are classified to categories R70–R94." An Excludes1 instructional note also appears providing information about examinations related to pregnancy and reproduction.

Routine physicals in ICD-10-CM are distinguished by an encounter with or without abnormal findings. If an abnormal finding is identified during this encounter, the code for general medical examination with abnormal findings is coded first; then a secondary code that identifies the abnormal finding is second.

EXAMPLE: Jackson was brought to the doctor by his mother for a well-baby check. Jackson is a 2-year-old male who appears to be healthy. After his vitals were checked, Jackson was examined, and it was determined that he is a very healthy, well-developed 2-year-old. No abnormalities were found.

Code Z00.129, Encounter for routine child health examination without abnormal findings, is used to report this encounter because the code reflects a routine exam for a child without abnormal findings. If an abnormal finding had been identified, code Z00.121, Encounter for routine child health examination with abnormal findings, would have been assigned, along with a code to identify the abnormal finding. It should be noted that code Z00.121 contains an instructional notation to "Use additional code to identify abnormal findings."

The Z codes/categories for routine and administrative examinations are:

- Z00, Encounter for general examination without complaint, suspected or reported diagnosis
- Z01, Encounter for other special examination without complaint, suspected or reported diagnosis
- Z02, Encounter for administrative examination, Except: Z02.9, Encounter for administrative examinations, unspecified
- Z32.0, Encounter for pregnancy test

These codes/categories are governed by the following coding guidelines:

ICD-10-CM Official Coding Guideline

13) Routine and administrative examinations

The Z codes allow for the description of encounters for routine examinations, such as, a general check-up, or examinations for administrative purposes, such as, a pre-employment physical. The codes are not to be used if the examination is for diagnosis of a suspected condition or for treatment purposes. In such cases the diagnosis code is used. During a routine exam, should a diagnosis or condition be discovered, it should be coded as an additional code. Pre-existing and chronic conditions and history codes may also be included as additional codes as long as the examination is for administrative purposes and not focused on any particular condition.

Some of the codes for routine health examinations distinguish between "with" and "without" abnormal findings. Code assignment depends on the information that is known at the time the encounter is being coded. For example, if no abnormal findings were found during the examination, but the encounter is being coded before test results are back, it is acceptable to assign the code for "without abnormal findings." When assigning a code for "with abnormal findings," additional code(s) should be assigned to identify the specific abnormal finding(s).

Pre-operative examination and pre-procedural laboratory examination Z codes are for use only in those situations when a patient is being cleared for a procedure or surgery and no treatment is given.

The Z codes/categories for routine and administrative examinations:

Z00 Encounter for general examination without complaint, suspected or reported diagnosis

Z01 Encounter for other special examination without complaint, suspected or reported diagnosis

Z02 Encounter for administrative examination

Except: Z02.9, Encounter for administrative examinations, unspecified

Z32.0- Encounter for pregnancy test

(See Appendix A, Section I, C21, c13.)

Courtesy of the Centers for Medicare & Medicaid Services, www.cms.gov

Within this code block screening examinations are classified. **Screening examinations** are used to "screen" or to detect a disease. These codes are listed first on a claim form when the screening examination is completed. **Diagnostic examinations** are used to confirm or rule out a suspected diagnosis due to signs and symptoms that the patient has experienced and is therefore not considered a screening examination because a sign or symptom is present. When screenings occur, an additional diagnosis may be assigned if a condition is discovered as a result of the screening. Chapter 21 of ICD-10-CM provides codes for encounters for screenings such as infectious and parasitic diseases, malignant neoplasms, eye disorders, and diseases of the blood and blood-forming organs, among others.

Routine gynecological examinations are coded to the Z01.4 category. Subcategory Z01.41 has instructional notations regarding additional screenings such as the following:

Use additional code:
For screening for human papillomavirus, if applicable, (Z11.51)
For screening vaginal pap smear, if applicable (Z12.72)
To identify acquired absence of uterus, if applicable (Z90.71-)

Attention to detail in the documentation is critical because many of the encounter codes distinguish among those where problems were encountered and those where the findings were within normal limits.

Also classified in this code block are codes for observation encounters that are reported when a person is being observed for a suspected condition that is ruled out after observation. The observation codes are used as a principal diagnosis only.

The following coding guidelines govern the coding of screening and observation encounters:

ICD-10-CM Official Coding Guidelines

5) Screening

Screening is the testing for disease or disease precursors in seemingly well individuals so that early detection and treatment can be provided for those who test positive for the disease (e.g., screening mammogram).

The testing of a person to rule out or confirm a suspected diagnosis because the patient has some sign or symptom is a diagnostic examination, not a screening. In these cases, the sign or symptom is used to explain the reason for the test.

A screening code may be a first-listed code if the reason for the visit is specifically the screening exam. It may also be used as an additional code if the screening is done during an office visit for other health problems. A screening code is not necessary if the screening is inherent to a routine examination, such as a pap smear done during a routine pelvic examination.

Should a condition be discovered during the screening then the code for the condition may be assigned as an additional diagnosis.

The Z code indicates that a screening exam is planned. A procedure code is required to confirm that the screening was performed.

The screening Z codes/categories are:

Z11 Encounter for screening for infectious and parasitic diseases

Z12 Encounter for screening for malignant neoplasms

Z13 Encounter for screening for other diseases and disorders, Except: Z13.9, Encounter for screening, unspecified

Z36 Encounter for antenatal screening for mother

6) Observation

There are three observation Z code categories. They are for use in very limited circumstances when a person is being observed for a suspected condition that is ruled out. The observation codes are not for use if an injury or illness or any signs or symptoms related to the suspected condition are present. In such cases the diagnosis/symptom code is used with the corresponding external cause code.

The observation codes are primarily to be used as a principal/first-listed diagnosis. An observation code may be assigned as a secondary diagnosis code when the patient is being observed for a condition that is ruled out and is unrelated to the principal/first-listed diagnosis (e.g., patient presents for treatment following injuries sustained in a motor vehicle accident and is also observed for suspected COVID-19 infection that is subsequently ruled out). Also, when the principal diagnosis is required to be a code from category Z38, Liveborn infants according to place of birth and type of delivery, then a code from category Z05, Encounter for observation and evaluation of newborn for suspected diseases and conditions ruled out, is sequenced after the Z38 code. Additional codes may be used in addition to the observation code, but only if they are unrelated to the suspected condition being observed.

Codes from subcategory Z03.7, Encounter for suspected maternal and fetal conditions ruled out, may either be used as a first-listed or as an additional code assignment depending on the case. They are for use in very limited circumstances on a maternal record when an encounter is for a suspected maternal or fetal condition that is ruled out during that encounter (for example, a maternal or fetal condition may be suspected due to an abnormal test result). These codes should not be used when the condition is confirmed. In those cases, the confirmed condition should be coded. In addition, these codes are not for use if an illness or any signs or symptoms related to the suspected condition or problem are present. In such cases the diagnosis/symptom code is used.

Additional codes may be used in addition to the code from subcategory Z03.7, but only if they are unrelated to the suspected condition being evaluated.

Codes from subcategory Z03.7 may not be used for encounters for antenatal screening of mother. See Section I.C.21. Screening.

For encounters for suspected fetal condition that are inconclusive following testing and evaluation, assign the appropriate code from category O35, O36, O40 or O41.

The observation Z code categories:

Z03 Encounter for medical observation for suspected diseases and conditions ruled out

Z04 Encounter for examination and observation for other reasons

Except: Z04.9, Encounter for examination and observation for unspecified reason

Z05 Encounter for observation and evaluation of newborn for suspected disease and conditions ruled out

(See Appendix A, Section I, C21, c 5–6.)

Courtesy of the Centers for Medicare & Medicaid Services, www.cms.gov

Also represented within ICD-10-CM are follow-up codes. The follow-up code categories are:

- Z08, Encounter for follow-up examination after completed treatment for malignant neoplasm
- Z09, Encounter for follow-up examination after completed treatment for conditions other than malignant neoplasm
- Z39, Encounter for maternal postpartum care and examination

These categories are governed by the following coding guidelines:

ICD-10-CM Official Coding Guideline

8) Follow-up

The follow-up codes are used to explain continuing surveillance following completed treatment of a disease, condition, or injury. They imply that the condition has been fully treated and no longer exists. They should not be confused with aftercare codes, or injury codes with a 7th character for subsequent encounter, that explain ongoing care of a healing condition or its sequelae. Follow-up codes may be used in conjunction with history codes to provide the full picture of the healed condition and its treatment. The follow-up code is sequenced first, followed by the history code.

A follow-up code may be used to explain multiple visits. Should a condition be found to have recurred on the follow-up visit, then the diagnosis code for the condition should be assigned in place of the follow-up code.

The follow-up Z code categories:

Z08 Encounter for follow-up examination after completed treatment for malignant neoplasm

Z09 Encounter for follow-up examination after completed treatment for conditions other than malignant neoplasm

Z39 Encounter for maternal postpartum care and examination.

(See Appendix A, Section I, C21, c 8.)

Courtesy of the Centers for Medicare & Medicaid Services, www.cms.gov

Genetic Carrier and Genetic Susceptibility to Disease (Category Codes Z14–Z15)

This block of codes classifies genetic carrier and genetic susceptibility to disease. Certain diseases can be identified through testing or family history that may be indicative of a carrier of a gene associated with a specific disease. The knowledge that a person may be a carrier of a disease allows the person to know whether his or her offspring may be at risk or susceptible to the disease.

If a patient is presenting for genetic counseling, code Z31.5, Encounter for procreative genetic counseling, is sequenced first; the code from category Z15, Genetic susceptibility, is the secondary code. If there are applicable codes for family history of a certain disease, they are also listed after the Z31.5 code.

If the patient is being seen for treatment of a specific disease or birth defect, the code for the specific disease or birth defect is assigned instead of a code from this category.

Category Z14 and Z15 are considered status codes. There are also other status codes that are contained in ICD-10-CM. The ICD-10-CM Official Guidelines for Coding and Reporting explain status codes.

ICD-10-CM Official Coding Guideline

3) Status

Status codes indicate that a patient is either a carrier of a disease or has the sequelae or residual of a past disease or condition. This includes such things as the presence of prosthetic or mechanical devices resulting from past treatment. A status code is informative, because the status may affect the course of treatment and its outcome. A status code is distinct from a history code. The history code indicates that the patient no longer has the condition.

A status code should not be used with a diagnosis code from one of the body system chapters, if the diagnosis code includes the information provided by the status code. For example, code Z94.1, Heart transplant status, should not be used with a code from subcategory T86.2, Complications of heart transplant. The status code does not provide additional information. The complication code indicates that the patient is a heart transplant patient.

For encounters for weaning from a mechanical ventilator, assign a code from subcategory J96.1, Chronic respiratory failure, followed by code Z99.11, Dependence on respirator [ventilator] status.

The status Z codes/categories are:

Z14 Genetic carrier

Genetic carrier status indicates that a person carries a gene, associated with a particular disease, which may be passed to offspring who may develop that disease. The person does not have the disease and is not at risk of developing the disease.

Z15 Genetic susceptibility to disease

Genetic susceptibility indicates that a person has a gene that increases the risk of that person developing the disease.

Codes from category Z15 should not be used as principal or first-listed codes. If the patient has the condition to which he/she is susceptible, and that condition is the reason for the encounter, the code for the current condition should be sequenced first. If the patient is being seen for follow-up after completed treatment for this condition, and the condition no longer exists, a follow-up code should be sequenced first, followed by the appropriate personal history and genetic susceptibility codes. If the purpose of the encounter is genetic counseling associated with procreative management, code Z31.5, Encounter for genetic counseling, should be assigned as the first-listed code, followed by a code from category Z15. Additional codes should be assigned for any applicable family or personal history.

Z16 Resistance to antimicrobial drugs

This code indicates that a patient has a condition that is resistant to antimicrobial drug treatment. Sequence the infection code first.

Z17 Estrogen receptor status

Z18 Retained foreign body fragments

Z19 Hormone sensitivity malignancy status

Z21 Asymptomatic HIV infection status

This code indicates that a patient has tested positive for HIV but has manifested no signs or symptoms of the disease.

Z22 Carrier of infectious disease

Carrier status indicates that a person harbors the specific organisms of a disease without manifest symptoms and is capable of transmitting the infection.

Z28.3 Underimmunization status

Z33.1 Pregnant state, incidental

This code is a secondary code only for use when the pregnancy is in no way complicating the reason for visit. Otherwise, a code from the obstetric chapter is required.

Z66 Do not resuscitate

This code may be used when it is documented by the provider that a patient is on do not resuscitate status at any time during the stay.

Z67 Blood type

Z68 Body mass index (BMI)

BMI codes should only be assigned when there is an associated, reportable diagnosis (such as obesity). Do not assign BMI codes during pregnancy.

See Section I.B.14 for BMI documentation by clinicians other than the patient's provider.

Z74.01 Bed confinement status

Z76.82 Awaiting organ transplant status

Z78 Other specified health status

Code Z78.1, Physical restraint status, may be used when it is documented by the provider that a patient has been put in restraints during the current encounter. Please note that this code should not be reported when it is documented by the provider that a patient is temporarily restrained during a procedure.

Z79 Long-term (current) drug therapy

Codes from this category indicate a patient's continuous use of a prescribed drug (including such things as aspirin therapy) for the long-term treatment of a condition or for prophylactic use. It is not for use for patients who have addictions to drugs. This subcategory is not for use of medications for detoxification or maintenance programs to prevent withdrawal symptoms (e.g., methadone maintenance for opiate dependence). Assign the appropriate code for the drug use, abuse, or dependence instead.

Assign a code from Z79 if the patient is receiving a medication for an extended period as a prophylactic measure (such as for the prevention of deep vein thrombosis) or as treatment of a chronic condition (such as arthritis) or a disease requiring a lengthy course of treatment (such as cancer). Do not assign a code from category Z79 for medication being administered for a brief period of time to treat an acute illness or injury (such as a course of antibiotics to treat acute bronchitis).

Z88 Allergy status to drugs, medicaments and biological substances

Except: Z88.9, Allergy status to unspecified drugs, medicaments and biological substances status

Z89 Acquired absence of limb

Z90 Acquired absence of organs, not elsewhere classified

Z91.0- Allergy status, other than to drugs and biological substances

Z92.82 Status post administration of tPA (rtPA) in a different facility within the last 24 hours prior to admission to a current facility

Assign code Z92.82, Status post administration of tPA (rtPA) in a different facility within the last 24 hours prior to admission to current facility, as a secondary diagnosis when a patient is received by transfer into a facility and documentation indicates they were administered tissue plasminogen activator (tPA) within the last 24 hours prior to admission to the current facility.

This guideline applies even if the patient is still receiving the tPA at the time they are received into the current facility.

The appropriate code for the condition for which the tPA was administered (such as cerebrovascular disease or myocardial infarction) should be assigned first.

Code Z92.82 is only applicable to the receiving facility record and not to the transferring facility record.

Z93 Artificial opening status

Z94 Transplanted organ and tissue status

Z95 Presence of cardiac and vascular implants and grafts

Z96 Presence of other functional implants

Z97 Presence of other devices

Z98 Other postprocedural states

Assign code Z98.85, Transplanted organ removal status, to indicate that a transplanted organ has been previously removed. This code should not be assigned for the encounter in which the transplanted organ is removed. The complication necessitating removal of the transplant organ should be assigned for that encounter.

See section I.C19. for information on the coding of organ transplant complications.

Z99 Dependence on enabling machines and devices, not elsewhere classified

Note: Categories Z89–Z90 and Z93–Z99 are for use only if there are no complications or malfunctions of the organ or tissue replaced, the amputation site or the equipment on which the patient is dependent.

(See Appendix A, Section I, C21, c 3.)

Some of the guidelines listed above will be reviewed in this chapter in more detail as they relate to specific code descriptions.

Resistance to Antimicrobial Drugs (Category Code Z16)

This category is used to classify resistance to antimicrobial drugs. Category Z16 indicates that a patient has a condition that is resistant to antimicrobial drug treatment. When reporting these cases, the code for the infection is sequenced prior to the code from category Z16. The instructional notation following the category heading reads:

> The codes in this category are provided for use as additional codes to identify the resistance and non-responsiveness of a condition to antimicrobial drugs.
>
> Code first the infection

Estrogen Receptor Status (Category Code Z17)

The two codes in this category are used to report positive and negative estrogen receptor status. An instructional notation appears for these codes that instructs the coder to "Code first malignant neoplasm of breast (C50.-)."

Persons with Potential Health Hazards Related to Communicable Diseases (Category Codes Z20–Z29)

This code block represents codes that indicate exposure to or contact with communicable diseases. No signs or symptoms of disease are evident at the time of the visit, but exposure to or contact with an infected individual has caused concern for the patient. These codes might also be referenced if the patient presents for an encounter after living in a disease epidemic area. The codes from the Z20 category might be reported first or, in some cases, second to identify a potential risk.

> **EXAMPLE:** Sylvia, a nurse, presented because she was concerned about a fingerstick she received from a needle that was used by an HIV-infected person. Because the needlestick caused direct exposure, we did a blood test to check for HIV exposure. The doctor assigns code Z20.6, Contact with and exposure to human immunodeficiency virus (HIV).

Category Z21 classifies asymptomatic HIV infection status. This code indicates that a patient has tested positive for HIV but has manifested no signs or symptoms of the disease.

Category Z22 classifies a carrier of an infectious disease. Carrier status indicates that a person harbors the specific organisms of a disease without manifest symptoms and is capable of transmitting the infection.

Category Z23 reports an encounter for immunization. If the prophylactic immunization is given during a routine health exam, a Z23 code is assigned as a secondary code as part of the visit. A procedure code is necessary to accurately identify the actual type of immunization given.

The Z28 code category represents codes for encounters for immunizations not carried and underimmunization status. For proper code selection, the documentation must reflect the reason that the immunization was not given. Reference the Z28 category to identify the specific reasons for why the immunization was not carried out. For example code Z28.1 is used when an immunization is not carried out because of a person's religious belief or other group pressure.

Category Z29 reports encounters for prophylactic measures that includes: prophylactic immunotherapy, prophylactic fluoride administration, other specified prophylactic measures and unspecified prophylactic measures. Review category Z29 in the ICD-10-CM for the specific codes and descriptions used for this category.

The following coding guidelines govern the coding of categories Z20–Z29:

ICD-10-CM Official Coding Guidelines

1) Contact/Exposure

Category Z20 indicates contact with, and suspected exposure to, communicable diseases. These codes are for patients who do not show any sign or symptom of a disease but are suspected to have been exposed to it by close personal contact with an infected individual or are in an area where a disease is epidemic.

Category Z77, Other contact with and (suspected) exposures hazardous to health, indicates contact with and suspected exposures hazardous to health.

Contact/exposure codes may be used as a first-listed code to explain an encounter for testing, or, more commonly, as a secondary code to identify a potential risk.

2) Inoculations and vaccinations

Code Z23 is for encounters for inoculations and vaccinations. It indicates that a patient is being seen to receive a prophylactic inoculation against a disease. Procedure codes are required to identify the actual administration of the injection and the type(s) of immunizations given. Code Z23 may be used as a secondary code if the inoculation is given as a routine part of preventive health care, such as a well-baby visit.

(See Section I, c21, c 1–2.)

Persons Encountering Health Services in Circumstances Related to Reproduction (Category Codes Z30–Z39)

This code block is reported when a patient presents for an encounter related to contraceptive management. This includes Z30, encounters for contraceptive management; Z31, encounters for procreative management; and Z32, encounters for pregnancy test and childbirth and childcare instruction.

Also found within this code block are codes related to pregnancy. Category Z33 classifies pregnant state, and category Z34 is used to report encounters for supervision of normal pregnancies. Code Z33.1 is used as a secondary code when the pregnancy is in no way complicating the reason for the visit. The number of weeks of gestation is reported with category Z3A and is used only on the maternal record to indicate the weeks of gestation of the pregnancy. The outcome of delivery, category Z37, is used on the maternal record to identify the number of children born or stillbirths. Category Z38 is used as the principal code on the initial infant's record to identify the place of birth and type of delivery. Encounters for maternal postpartum care and examination are classified to category Z39.

The following guidelines govern encounters for counseling, obstetrical and reproductive services, and newborns and infants:

ICD-10-CM Official Coding Guideline

10) Counseling

Counseling Z codes are used when a patient or family member receives assistance in the aftermath of an illness or injury, or when support is required in coping with family or social problems.

The counseling Z codes/categories:

Z30.0- Encounter for general counseling and advice on contraception

Z31.5 Encounter for procreative genetic counseling

Z31.6- Encounter for general counseling and advice on procreation

Z32.2 Encounter for childbirth instruction

Z32.3 Encounter for childcare instruction

Z69 Encounter for mental health services for victim and perpetrator of abuse

Z70 Counseling related to sexual attitude, behavior and orientation

Z71 Persons encountering health services for other counseling and medical advice, not elsewhere classified

Note: Code Z71.84, Encounter for health counseling related to travel, is to be used for health risk and safety counseling for future travel purposes.

Z76.81 Expectant mother prebirth pediatrician visit

11) Encounters for Obstetrical and Reproductive Services

See Section I.C.15. Pregnancy, Childbirth, and the Puerperium, for further instruction on the use of these codes.

Z codes for pregnancy are for use in those circumstances when none of the problems or complications included in the codes from the Obstetrics chapter exist (a routine prenatal visit or postpartum care). Codes in category Z34, Encounter for supervision of normal pregnancy, are always first-listed and are not to be used with any other code from the OB chapter.

Codes in category Z3A, Weeks of gestation, may be assigned to provide additional information about the pregnancy. Category Z3A codes should not be assigned for pregnancies with abortive outcomes (categories O00–O08), elective termination of pregnancy (code Z33.2), nor for postpartum conditions, as category Z3A is not applicable to these conditions. The date of the admission should be used to determine weeks of gestation for inpatient admissions that encompass more than one gestational week.

The outcome of delivery, category Z37, should be included on all maternal delivery records. It is always a secondary code. Codes in category Z37 should not be used on the newborn record.

Z codes for family planning (contraceptive) or procreative management and counseling should be included on an obstetric record either during the pregnancy or the postpartum stage, if applicable.

Z codes/categories for obstetrical and reproductive services:

Z30 Encounter for contraceptive management

Z31 Encounter for procreative management

Z32.2 Encounter for childbirth instruction

Z32.3 Encounter for childcare instruction

Z33 Pregnant state

Z34 Encounter for supervision of normal pregnancy

Z36 Encounter for antenatal screening of mother

Z3A Weeks of gestation

Z37 Outcome of delivery

Z39 Encounter for maternal postpartum care and examination

Z76.81 Expectant mother prebirth pediatrician visit

12) Newborns and Infants

See Section I.C.16. Newborn (Perinatal) Guidelines, for further instruction on the use of these codes.

Newborn Z codes/categories:

Z76.1 Encounter for health supervision and care of foundling

Z00.1- Encounter for routine child health examination

Z38 Liveborn infants according to place of birth and type of delivery

(See Appendix A, Section I, C21, c 11–12.)

Encounters for Other Specific Health Care (Category Codes Z40–Z53)

Category codes Z40 to Z53 report encounters for other specific health care. At the start of the code block the following note appears: "Categories Z40–Z53 are intended for use to indicate a reason for care. They may be used for patients who have already been treated for a disease or injury, but who are receiving aftercare or prophylactic care, or care to consolidate the treatment, or to deal with a residual state."

Z40—Encounter for Prophylactic Surgery

Category Z40 classifies encounters for prophylactic organ removal and is governed by the following coding guidelines:

Z41—Encounters for Procedures for Purposes Other Than Remedying Health State

Category Z41 classifies encounters for cosmetic surgery (such as breast implants), routine and ritual male circumcision, ear piercing, and other procedures for purposes other than remedying a health state.

Z42—Encounters for Plastic and Reconstructive Surgery Following Medical Procedure or Healed Injury

Category Z42 reports encounters for surgery that follow a previous medical procedure or healed injury. For example, if breast reconstruction following a previous mastectomy occurred, code Z42.1 would be reported.

Z43—Encounter for Attention to Artificial Opening

Category Z43 is used to report encounters for attention to artificial openings such as tracheostomy, gastrostomy, ileostomy, colostomy, cystostomy, and other artificial openings. Reference category Z43 to identify the specific codes.

Z44—Encounters for Fitting and Adjustment of External Prosthetic Device

Category Z44 reports encounters for the fitting and adjustment of artificial limbs, artificial eyes, artificial breasts, and other external prosthetic devices. This category includes removal or replacement of external prosthetic devices.

Z45—Encounter for Adjustment and Management of Implanted Device

Category Z45 reports encounters for the adjustment and management of implanted devices and includes the removal or replacement of the implanted device. This includes such devices as cardiac pacemakers, pulse generators, infusion pumps, and cerebrospinal fluid drainage devices, to name a few. The category provides much detail as to the type of device.

Z46—Encounter for the Fitting and Adjustment of Other Devices

Category Z46 reports the fitting and adjustment of other devices that are not reported in categories Z44 and Z45.

Z47—Orthopedic Aftercare

Category Z47 reports aftercare for orthopedic surgery. It does not report aftercare for healing fractures, as these cases are reported with the appropriate fracture code and a seventh-character code for subsequent encounter.

Z48—Encounter for Other Postprocedural Aftercare

Category Z48 reports encounters for attention to dressings, sutures and drains, aftercare following organ transplant, and other postprocedural aftercare.

Z49—Encounter for Care Involving Renal Dialysis

Category Z49 reports preparatory care for renal dialysis and adequacy testing for dialysis. Coders need also to code any associated end-stage renal disease.

Z51—Encounter for Other Aftercare and Medical Care

Category Z51 classifies encounters for antineoplastic radiation therapy, chemotherapy and immunotherapy, palliative care, and therapeutic drug-level monitoring. An instructional notation appears at the start of the category that instructs coders to "Code also condition requiring care." An instructional notation also appears at code Z51.81 that states: "Code also any long-term (current) drug therapy (Z79.-)."

Z52—Donors of Organs and Tissues

Category Z52 classifies donors of organs and tissues and includes autologous and other living donors.

The coding guideline that governs category Z52 states the following:

ICD-10-CM Official Coding Guideline

9) Donor

Codes in category Z52, Donors of organs and tissues, are used for living individuals who are donating blood or other body tissue. These codes are only for individuals donating for others, not for self-donations. They are not used to identify cadaveric donations.

(See Appendix A, Section I, C21, c 9.)

Z53—Persons Encountering Health Services for Specific Procedures and Treatment, Not Carried Out

Category Z53 is used to report encounters in which a specific procedure or treatment was not carried out because of contraindication, a patient's decision, or for other reasons.

The following coding guidelines govern codes in categories Z40 to Z53:

ICD-10-CM Official Coding Guideline

7) Aftercare

Aftercare visit codes cover situations when the initial treatment of a disease has been performed and the patient requires continued care during the healing or recovery phase, or for the long-term consequences of the disease. The aftercare Z code should not be used if treatment is directed at a current, acute disease. The diagnosis code is to be used in these cases. Exceptions to this rule are codes Z51.0, Encounter for antineoplastic radiation therapy, and codes from subcategory Z51.1, Encounter for antineoplastic chemotherapy and immunotherapy. These codes are to be first-listed, followed by the diagnosis code when a patient's encounter is solely to receive radiation therapy, chemotherapy, or immunotherapy for the treatment of a neoplasm. If the reason for the encounter is more than one type of antineoplastic therapy, code Z51.0 and a code from subcategory Z51.1 may be assigned together, in which case one of these codes would be reported as a secondary diagnosis.

The aftercare Z codes should also not be used for aftercare for injuries. For aftercare of an injury, assign the acute injury code with the appropriate 7th character (for subsequent encounter).

The aftercare codes are generally first-listed to explain the specific reason for the encounter. An aftercare code may be used as an additional code when some type of aftercare is provided in addition to the reason for admission and no diagnosis code is applicable. An example of this would be the closure of a colostomy during an encounter for treatment of another condition.

Aftercare codes should be used in conjunction with other aftercare codes or diagnosis codes to provide better detail on the specifics of an aftercare encounter visit, unless otherwise directed by the classification. The sequencing of multiple aftercare codes depends on the circumstances of the encounter.

Certain aftercare Z code categories need a secondary diagnosis code to describe the resolving condition or sequelae. For others, the condition is included in the code title.

Additional Z code aftercare category terms include fitting and adjustment, and attention to artificial openings.

Status Z codes may be used with aftercare Z codes to indicate the nature of the aftercare. For example code Z95.1, Presence of aortocoronary bypass graft, may be used with code Z48.812, Encounter for surgical aftercare following surgery on the circulatory system, to indicate the surgery for which the aftercare is being performed. A status code should not be used when the aftercare code indicates the type of status, such as using Z43.0, Encounter for attention to tracheostomy, with Z93.0, Tracheostomy status.

The aftercare Z category/codes:

Z42 Encounter for plastic and reconstructive surgery following medical procedure or healed injury

Z43 Encounter for attention to artificial openings

Z44 Encounter for fitting and adjustment of external prosthetic device

Z45 Encounter for adjustment and management of implanted device

Z46 Encounter for fitting and adjustment of other devices

Z47 Orthopedic aftercare

Z48 Encounter for other postprocedural aftercare

Z49 Encounter for care involving renal dialysis

Z51 Encounter for other aftercare and medical care

(See Appendix A, Section I, C21, c 7.)

Exercise 26.1—Category Codes Z00–Z53

Using an ICD-10-CM code book, assign the proper code for the diagnostic statements given.

Diagnosis	Code
1. encounter for allergy test	_____
2. encounter for examination of potential donor of organ tissue	_____
3. encounter for screening for osteoporosis	_____
4. encounter for screening for respiratory tuberculosis	_____

(continues)

Exercise 26.1—*continued*

5. contact with exposure to rabies _____

6. encounter for Rh incompatibility status _____

7. immunization not carried out because of immune-compromised state of the patient _____

8. carrier of typhoid _____

9. encounter for ear piercing _____

10. encounter for fitting and adjustment of an orthodontic device _____

Persons with Potential Health Hazards Related to Socioeconomic and Psychosocial Circumstances (Category Codes Z55–Z65)

This code block identifies problems related to education (Z55), such as problems with literacy and maladjustment with teachers and classmates.

The code block also allows for coding for an encounter related to problems with employment and unemployment (Z56), occupational exposure to risk factors (Z57), housing and economic circumstances (Z59), and social environment (Z60).

The problems related to negative life events in childhood are classified to category Z62. Specific code assignment depends on documentation. The provider's documentation must support code assignments from this code range. Category Z63 reports problems related to the primary support group, including family circumstances. Categories Z64 and Z65 report problems related to psychosocial circumstances.

Do Not Resuscitate Status (Category Code Z66)

The medical procedure performed to restore cardiac and/or respiratory function is known as **resuscitation**. When a patient makes the decision not to have this procedure performed and puts the decision in writing, it is known as a "Do Not Resuscitate (DNR)" order. The only code in this category is Z66, which indicates a DNR status.

Blood Type (Category Code Z67)

This category is referenced when the indication needs to be made as to the patient's blood type. Types A, B, O, and AB are coded from this category. The code selection is based on blood type and if the patient is Rh negative or Rh positive.

Body Mass Index (BMI) (Category Code Z68)

Body mass index is calculated by taking a person's weight and height and then calculating the index value. A BMI for an adult is calculated differently than a BMI for a child. The code selection is based on age. The adult codes reflect the BMI of patients 20 years and older. Pediatric BMI codes are for patients between 2 and 19 years of age.

Persons Encountering Health Services in Other Circumstances (Category Codes Z69–Z76)

This block of codes classifies encounters for services relating to mental health issues and counseling services (Z69–Z71). The counseling services include codes for drug, alcohol, and tobacco abuse counseling (Z71). Problems related to lifestyle are reported with category Z72, and problems related to life management difficulty are reported with category Z73. Category Z74 reports problems related to care provider dependency. Problems related to medical facilities are reported with category Z75. Category Z76 reports persons encountering health services in circumstances such as a healthy person accompanying a sick person (Z76.3), and encounters for issue of repeat prescription (Z76.0).

Persons with Potential Health Hazards Related to Family and Personal History and Certain Conditions Influencing Health Status (Category Codes Z77–Z99)

The first category in this block of codes, Z77, reports contact with and (suspected) exposures hazardous to health. Category Z77 is differentiated according to the chemical, environmental pollutant, or hazardous substance that the individual was in contact with or exposed to.

Category Z78 reports asymptomatic menopausal state (Z78.0) and physical restraint status (Z78.1). Code Z78.1 is used when physical restraints are documented by the provider and used during the current encounter. It should be noted that this code should not be reported when it is documented by the provider that a patient is temporarily restrained during a procedure.

Category Z79 reports long-term (current) drug therapy. This category reports the long-term use of anticoagulants, antibiotics, steroids, and aspirin, to name a few. These codes are referenced when a patient is on Coumadin, steroids, or insulin. These codes are necessary, in some instances, to support medical necessity for lab testing. The coding guidelines state the following in relation to code Z79:

ICD-10-CM Official Coding Guideline

Z79 Long-term (current) drug therapy

Codes from this category indicate a patient's continuous use of a prescribed drug (including such things as aspirin therapy) for the long-term treatment of a condition or for prophylactic use. It is not for use for patients who have addictions to drugs. This subcategory is not for use of medications for detoxification or maintenance programs to prevent withdrawal symptoms (e.g., methadone maintenance for opiate dependence). Assign the appropriate code for the drug use, abuse, or dependence instead.

Assign a code from Z79 if the patient is receiving a medication for an extended period as a prophylactic measure (such as for the prevention of deep vein thrombosis) or as treatment of a chronic condition (such as arthritis) or a disease requiring a lengthy course of treatment (such as cancer). Do not assign a code from category Z79 for medication being administered for a brief period of time to treat an acute illness or injury (such as a course of antibiotics to treat acute bronchitis).

(See Appendix A, Section I, C21, c 3.)

Categories Z80 to Z92 report family and personal history.

The history Z code categories are:

- Z80, Family history of primary malignant neoplasm
- Z81, Family history of mental and behavioral disorders
- Z82, Family history of certain disabilities and chronic diseases (leading to disablement)
- Z83, Family history of other specific disorders
- Z84, Family history of other conditions
- Z85, Personal history of malignant neoplasm
- Z86, Personal history of certain other diseases
- Z87, Personal history of other diseases and conditions
- Z91.4, Personal history of psychological trauma, not elsewhere classified
- Z91.5, Personal history of self-harm
- Z91.8, Other specified personal risk factors, not elsewhere classified,
  - Exception: Z91.83, Wandering in diseases classified elsewhere

- Z92, Personal history of medical treatment,
  - Except: Z92.0, Personal history of contraception
  - Except: Z92.82, Status post administration of tPA (rtPA) in a different facility within the last 24 hours prior to admission to a current facility

Categories Z80 to Z84 report family history of diseases. Family history codes are used to support medical necessity for certain tests that might be ordered.

EXAMPLE: Jack presented to the doctor's office for a routine physical exam. His doctor was obtaining a medical history and found out that Jack's father had died at age 57 from prostate cancer. Even though Jack is only 35 years old, he is at high risk for prostate cancer, so the doctor orders a screening PSA for prostate cancer. The code Z80.42, Family history of malignant neoplasm of the prostate, is assigned to the order for the lab test for the prostate screening. This supports the medical necessity for a PSA even though Jack is only 35 years old.

In addition to family history codes, personal history codes are also found in ICD-10-CM. The personal history codes not only include personal history of cancer but also personal history of different types of medical conditions and treatments, such as surgery.

The history codes are governed by the following coding guidelines:

ICD-10-CM Official Coding Guidelines

4) History (of)

There are two types of history Z codes, personal and family. Personal history codes explain a patient's past medical condition that no longer exists and is not receiving any treatment, but that has the potential for recurrence, and therefore may require continued monitoring.

Family history codes are for use when a patient has a family member(s) who has had a particular disease that causes the patient to be at higher risk of also contracting the disease.

Personal history codes may be used in conjunction with follow-up codes and family history codes may be used in conjunction with screening codes to explain the need for a test or procedure. History codes are also acceptable on any medical record regardless of the reason for visit. A history of an illness, even if no longer present, is important information that may alter the type of treatment ordered.

The history Z code categories are:

Z80 Family history of primary malignant neoplasm

Z81 Family history of mental and behavioral disorders

Z82 Family history of certain disabilities and chronic diseases (leading to disablement)

Z83 Family history of other specific disorders

Z84 Family history of other conditions

Z85 Personal history of malignant neoplasm

Z86 Personal history of certain other diseases

Z87 Personal history of other diseases and conditions

Z91.4- Personal history of psychological trauma, not elsewhere classified

Z91.5 Personal history of self-harm

Z91.81 History of falling

Z91.82 Personal history of military deployment

Z92 Personal history of medical treatment

Except: Z92.0, Personal history of contraception

Except: Z92.82, Status post administration of tPA (rtPA) in a different facility within the last 24 hours prior to admission to a current facility

(See Appendix A, Section I, C21, c 4.)

Category Z88 reports allergy status to drugs, medicaments, and biological substances. The category is differentiated by the type of substance.

Category Z89 reports acquired absence of limb and includes amputation status, postprocedural loss of limb, and post-traumatic loss of limb. Category Z90 reports acquired absence of organs. For example, code Z90.13, acquired absence of breasts and nipples, would be reported following a bilateral mastectomy. Category Z91 reports personal risk factors, and category Z92 reports personal history of medical treatment. Code Z92.82 and category codes Z93–Z98 are governed by the following coding guideline:

ICD-10-CM Official Coding Guideline

Z92.82 Status post administration of tPA (rtPA) in a different facility within the last 24 hours prior to admission to a current facility

Assign code Z92.82, Status post administration of tPA (rtPA) in a different facility within the last 24 hours prior to admission to current facility, as a secondary diagnosis when a patient is received by transfer into a facility and documentation indicates they were administered tissue plasminogen activator (tPA) within the last 24 hours prior to admission to the current facility.

This guideline applies even if the patient is still receiving the tPA at the time they are received into the current facility.

The appropriate code for the condition for which the tPA was administered (such as cerebrovascular disease or myocardial infarction) should be assigned first.

Code Z92.82 is only applicable to the receiving facility record and not to the transferring facility record.

Z93 Artificial opening status

Z94 Transplanted organ and tissue status

Z95 Presence of cardiac and vascular implants and grafts

Z96 Presence of other functional implants

Z97 Presence of other devices

Z98 Other postprocedural states

Assign code Z98.85, Transplanted organ removal status, to indicate that a transplanted organ has been previously removed. This code should not be assigned for the encounter in which the transplanted organ is removed. The complication necessitating removal of the transplant organ should be assigned for that encounter. *See section I.C19. for information on the coding of organ transplant complications*.

Z99 Dependence on enabling machines and devices, not elsewhere classified

Note: Categories Z89–Z90 and Z93–Z99 are for use only if there are no complications or malfunctions of of the organ or tissue replaced, the amputation site or the equipment on which the patient is dependent.

(See Appendix A, Section C21, c 3.)

Category Z99 reports dependence on enabling machines and devices such as dependence on aspirator (Z99.0), dependence on respirator (Z99.11 and Z99.12), dependence on renal dialysis (Z99.2), and wheelchair dependence (Z99.3).

Additional Guidelines

There are three additional guidelines that coders must consider when selecting Z codes. They discuss the use of miscellaneous Z codes, nonspecific Z codes and Z codes that may only be principal/first listed diagnoses. The guideline for prophylactic organ removal was discussed earlier in this chapter but it is also listed here in the guideline for miscellaneous Z codes as it is an example of a miscellaneous Z code.

ICD-10-CM Official Coding Guidelines

14) Miscellaneous Z Codes

The miscellaneous Z codes capture a number of other health care encounters that do not fall into one of the other categories. Certain of these codes identify the reason for the encounter; others are for use as additional codes that provide useful information on circumstances that may affect a patient's care and treatment.

Prophylactic Organ Removal

For encounters specifically for prophylactic removal of an organ (such as prophylactic removal of breasts due to a genetic susceptibility to cancer or a family history of cancer), the principal or first-listed code should be a code from category Z40, Encounter for prophylactic surgery, followed by the appropriate codes to identify the associated risk factor (such as genetic susceptibility or family history).

If the patient has a malignancy of one site and is having prophylactic removal at another site to prevent either a new primary malignancy or metastatic disease, a code for the malignancy should also be assigned in addition to a code from subcategory Z40.0, Encounter for prophylactic surgery for risk factors related to malignant neoplasms. A Z40.0 code should not be assigned if the patient is having organ removal for treatment of a malignancy, such as the removal of the testes for the treatment of prostate cancer.

Miscellaneous Z codes/categories:

Z28 Immunization not carried out

Except: Z28.3, Underimmunization status

Z29 Encounter for other prophylactic measures

Z40 Encounter for prophylactic surgery

Z41 Encounter for procedures for purposes other than remedying health state

Except: Z41.9, Encounter for procedure for purposes other than remedying health state, unspecified

Z53 Persons encountering health services for specific procedures and treatment, not carried out

Z55 Problems related to education and literacy

Z56 Problems related to employment and unemployment

Z57 Occupational exposure to risk factors

Z58 Problems related to physical environment

Z59 Problems related to housing and economic circumstances

Z60 Problems related to social environment

Z62 Problems related to upbringing

Z63 Other problems related to primary support group, including family circumstances

Z64 Problems related to certain psychosocial circumstances

Z65 Problems related to other psychosocial circumstances

Z72 Problems related to lifestyle

Note: These codes should be assigned only when the documentation specifies that the patient has an an associated problem

Z73 Problems related to life management difficulty

Z74 Problems related to care provider dependency

Except: Z74.01, Bed confinement status

Z75 Problems related to medical facilities and other health care

Z76.0 Encounter for issue of repeat prescription

Z76.3 Healthy person accompanying sick person

Z76.4 Other boarder to healthcare facility

Z76.5 Malingerer [conscious simulation]

Z91.1- Patient's noncompliance with medical treatment and regimen

Z91.83 Wandering in diseases classified elsewhere

Z91.84 - Oral health risk factors

Z91.89 Other specified personal risk factors, not elsewhere classified

See Section I.B.14 for Z55–Z65 Persons with potential health hazards related to socioeconomic and psychosocial circumstances, documentation by clinicians other than the patient's provider.

15) Nonspecific Z codes

Certain Z codes are so non-specific, or potentially redundant with other codes in the classification, that there can be little justification for their use in the inpatient setting. Their use in the outpatient setting should be limited to those instances when there is no further documentation to permit more precise coding. Otherwise, any sign or symptom or any other reason for visit that is captured in another code should be used.

Nonspecific Z codes/categories:

Z02.9 Encounter for administrative examinations, unspecified

Z04.9 Encounter for examination and observation for unspecified reason

Z13.9 Encounter for screening, unspecified

Z41.9 Encounter for procedure for purposes other than remedying health state, unspecified

Z52.9 Donor of unspecified organ or tissue

Z86.59 Personal history of other mental and behavioral disorders

Z88.9 Allergy status to unspecified drugs, medicaments and biological substances status

Z92.0 Personal history of contraception

16) Z Codes That May Only be Principal/First-Listed Diagnosis

The following Z codes/categories may only be reported as the principal/first-listed diagnosis, except when there are multiple encounters on the same day and the medical records for the encounters are combined:

Z00 Encounter for general examination without complaint, suspected or reported diagnosis

Except: Z00.6

Z01 Encounter for other special examination without complaint, suspected or reported diagnosis

Z02 Encounter for administrative examination

Z04 Encounter for examination and observation for other reasons

Z33.2 Encounter for elective termination of pregnancy

Z31.81 Encounter for male factor infertility in female patient

Z31.83 Encounter for assisted reproductive fertility procedure cycle

Z31.84 Encounter for fertility preservation procedure

Z34 Encounter for supervision of normal pregnancy

Z39 Encounter for maternal postpartum care and examination

Z38 Liveborn infants according to place of birth and type of delivery

Z40 Encounter for prophylactic surgery

Z42 Encounter for plastic and reconstructive surgery following medical procedure or healed injury

Z51.0 Encounter for antineoplastic radiation therapy

Z51.1- Encounter for antineoplastic chemotherapy and immunotherapy

Z52 Donors of organs and tissues

Except: Z52.9, Donor of unspecified organ or tissue

Z76.1 Encounter for health supervision and care of foundling

Z76.2 Encounter for health supervision and care of other healthy infant and child

Z99.12 Encounter for respirator [ventilator] dependence during power failure

(See Appendix A, Section I, C21, 14–16.)

Courtesy of the Centers for Medicare & Medicaid Services, www.cms.gov

Introduction to Chapter 22 of ICD-10-CM—Codes for Special Purposes

On October 1, 2020, Chapter 22, entitled Codes for Special Purposes, was added to ICD-10-CM. This chapter contains one block of codes:

- U00–U49 Provisional assignment of new diseases of uncertain etiology or emergency use.

Effective on October 1, 2020 there is only one category for this chapter of ICD-10-CM, entitled U07 Emergency Use of U07. There are only two valid codes for this chapter of ICD-10-CM. Code U07.0 reports vaping-related disorder and code U07.1 reports COVID-19.

Vaping-related Disorder

A number of individuals have experienced disorders and illnesses related to the use of battery powered vaping devices such as vapes, electronic pipes, electronic cigarettes, and other electronic nicotine delivery systems (ENDS). The uses of these products have caused symptoms in various body systems and include the following:

- Respiratory symptoms—cough, chest pain and shortness of breath
- Gastrointestinal symptoms—abdominal pain, diarrhea, nausea, and vomiting
- Additional symptoms—fever, chills and weight loss.

Patients have developed lung injury due to the use of these systems known as E-cigarette, or vaping, product use associated lung injury (EVALI). The development of the lung injuries has caused the death of an increasing number of patients.

For more information about E-cigarettes and vaping review the following website: https://www.cdc.gov/tobacco/basic_information/e-cigarettes/index.htm.

Code U07.0

Code U07.0 reports Vaping-related disorder. Locate code U07.0 in the tabular listing of the ICD-10-CM coding manual and note that the following disorders appear under the code heading:

- Dabbing related lung damage
- Dabbing related lung injury
- E-cigarette, or vaping, product use associated lung injury [EVALI]
- Electronic cigarette related lung damage
- Electronic cigarette related lung injury

This is signaling to the coder a list of alternative terms that are used.

Code U07.0 also contains the following instructional notation:

Use additional code to identify manifestations, such as:

- abdominal pain (R10.84)
- acute respiratory distress syndrome (J80)
- diarrhea (R19.7)
- drug-induced interstitial lung disorder (J70.4)
- lipoid pneumonia (J69.1)
- weight loss (R63.4)

This notation alerts the coder to add additional codes if the patient is experiencing these manifestations of the disease process.

The following coding guideline also needs to be considered when assigning additional codes for patients with vaping-related disorders.

ICD-10-CM Official Coding Guidelines

e. Vaping-related disorders

For patients presenting with condition(s) related to vaping, assign code U07.0, Vaping-related disorder, as the principal diagnosis. For lung injury due to vaping, assign only code U07.0. Assign additional codes for other manifestations, such as acute respiratory failure (subcategory J96.0-) or pneumonitis (code J68.0).

Associated respiratory signs and symptoms due to vaping, such as cough, shortness of breath, etc., are not coded separately, when a definitive diagnosis has been established. However, it would be appropriate to code separately any gastrointestinal symptoms, such as diarrhea and abdominal pain. (See Section I, 10, e.)

Courtesy of the Centers for Medicare & Medicaid Services, www.cms.gov

EXAMPLE:

Patient 1 is diagnosed with the following:

EVALI with diarrhea

This case is coded with code U07.0 for the EVALI and code R19.7 for the diarrhea. The instructional note found in the ICD-10-CM coding manual instructs the coder to report the code for the diarrhea and the coding guidelines also states the need for the code assignment for diarrhea.

Patient 2 is diagnosed with the following:

Vaping-related lung damage with shortness of breath.

This case is coded with just code U07.0 as per the ICD-10-CM Official Coding Guidelines.

COVID-19

In March of 2020 the World Health Organization declared a worldwide pandemic of SARA-CoV-2 commonly known as COVID-19. **COVID-19** is a contagious viral respiratory infection. As the illness is spreading across the world new information is being learned about the illness and the complications that occur.

Individuals experiencing COVID-19 have a mixed variety of symptoms and varying degrees of symptoms. Some individuals experience mild symptoms while others experience severe symptoms and have to be hospitalized and placed on ventilators and other supportive medical devices. Symptoms typically appear two to fourteen days after exposure to the virus. Symptoms include:

- Cough
- Diarrhea
- Fever or chills
- Fatigue
- Muscle or body aches
- Headache
- New loss of taste or smell
- Sore throat
- Shortness of breath or difficulty breathing
- Congestion or runny nose
- Nausea and/or vomiting

As the spread of the disease occurs more is being understood about the possibility of other symptoms.

Some individuals that have COVID-19 are not experiencing symptoms and are known as asymptomatic patients.

Older individuals and individuals with underlying medical conditions are at higher risk of developing serious and severe complications from COVID-19. The Centers for Disease Control and Prevention (CDC) has reviewed the current healthcare data and has determined that as a person's age increases the risk of experiencing severe complications increases. Individuals that are in their 70s and 80s are at higher risk than individuals that are younger. However all ages groups are affected by COVID-19. Besides age there are other risk factors that contribute to the severity of complications of the disease in adults. Other groups that are at risk of developing serious complications include individuals with the following underlying medical conditions, which are considered risk factors:

- Cancer
- Heart disease—such as heart failure, coronary artery disease and cardiomyopathies
- Lung disease—such as COPD
- Kidney disease
- Type 2 Diabetes
- Obesity—BMI of 30 or over
- Sickle cell disease
- Weakened immune system from solid organ transplant

The CDC is also reviewing data that suggest that there may be other risk factors that include:

- Moderate to severe asthma
- Type 1 Diabetes
- Cerebrovascular diseases
- Cystic fibrosis
- Hypertension
- Liver disease
- Pregnancy
- Smoking
- Thalassemia
- Pulmonary disorders—such as damage or scarred lung tissue
- Immunocompromised state caused by blood or bone marrow transplant, immune deficiencies, HIV, use of corticosteroids and other immune weakening medicines

The impact of the disease on children is also under review and analysis by the CDC. Data has shown that children who are medically complex have an increased risk. Children who have genetic, neurological, metabolic and congenital heart disease might be at increased risk for developing severe illness from COVID-19. Risk for children is also increased if a child is obese, has diabetes, asthma, chronic lung disease or has immunosuppression. The CDC is also reviewing the data to determine the relationship of children who have COVID-19 and the development of Multisystem Inflammatory Syndrome in Children (MIS-C). MIS-C is a rare but very serious complication.

As a coder it is important to review information that is being published by the CDC about COVID-19.

Current information can be found at: https://www.cdc.gov/coronavirus/2019-ncov/index.html

It is also important to understand how COVID-19 is being diagnosed and treated. Currently various types of diagnostic tests are being developed. Some of the tests that are being developed can test for COVID-19, and influenza A and B viruses at the same time. Testing for multiple viruses can help providers determine a more definitive treatment protocol. Information about the development of diagnostic testing for COVID-19 is also available on the CDC website at https://www.cdc.gov/coronavirus/2019-ncov/lab/testing.html.

Currently there is no cure for COVID-19 but as more and more patients are being treated research is showing some treatments that increase the survival rate of patients. In the United States the National Institutes of Health are overseeing clinical trials related to COVID-19. Information about clinical trials, treatments and other related information about COVID-19 can be found at: https://www.nih.gov/coronavirus.

Code U07.1

Code U07.1 reports COVID-19. Locate code U07.1 in the tabular listing of the ICD-10-CM coding manual and note that the following instructional notations appear under the code heading:

Use additional code to identify pneumonia or other manifestations.

Additional information for reporting COVID-19 cases is detailed in the ICD-10-CM Official Guidelines for Coding and Reporting. Effective October 1, 2020 the following 2021 ICD-10-CM Official Guidelines for Coding and Reporting cases related to COVID-19 are to be used. Please note that these guidelines may be updated during the upcoming year.

ICD-10-CM Official Coding Guidelines from Section I.C.1.g

Chapter 1: Certain Infectious and Parasitic Diseases (A00-B99), U07.1

g. Coronavirus infections

1) COVID-19 infection (infection due to SARS-CoV-2)

(a) Code only confirmed cases

Code only a confirmed diagnosis of the 2019 novel coronavirus disease (COVID-19) as documented by the provider or documentation of a positive COVID-19 test result. For a confirmed diagnosis, assign code U07.1, COVID-19. This is an exception to the hospital inpatient guideline Section II, H. In this context, "confirmation" does not require documentation of a positive test result for COVID-19; the provider's documentation that the individual has COVID-19 is sufficient.

If the provider documents "suspected," "possible," "probable," or "inconclusive" COVID-19, do not assign code U07.1. Instead, code the signs and symptoms reported. See guideline I.C.1.g.1.g.

(b) Sequencing of codes

When COVID-19 meets the definition of principal diagnosis, code U07.1, COVID-19, should be sequenced first, followed by the appropriate codes for associated manifestations, except when another guideline requires that certain codes be sequenced first, such as obstetrics, sepsis, or transplant complications.

For a COVID-19 infection that progresses to sepsis, see Section I.C.1.d. Sepsis, Severe Sepsis, and Septic Shock

See Section I.C.15.s. for COVID-19 infection in pregnancy, childbirth, and the puerperium

See Section I.C.16.h. for COVID-19 infection in newborn

For a COVID-19 infection in a lung transplant patient, see Section I.C.19.g.3.a. Transplant complications other than kidney.

(c) Acute respiratory manifestations of COVID-19

When the reason for the encounter/admission is a respiratory manifestation of COVID-19, assign code U07.1, COVID-19, as the principal/first-listed diagnosis and assign code(s) for the respiratory manifestation(s) as additional diagnoses.

The following conditions are examples of common respiratory manifestations of COVID-19.

(i) Pneumonia

For a patient with pneumonia confirmed as due to COVID-19, assign codes U07.1, COVID-19, and J12.89, Other viral pneumonia.

(ii) Acute bronchitis

For a patient with acute bronchitis confirmed as due to COVID-19, assign codes U07.1, and J20.8, Acute bronchitis due to other specified organisms.

Bronchitis not otherwise specified (NOS) due to COVID-19 should be coded using code U07.1 and J40, Bronchitis, not specified as acute or chronic.

(iii) Lower respiratory infection

If the COVID-19 is documented as being associated with a lower respiratory infection, not otherwise specified (NOS), or an acute respiratory infection, NOS, codes U07.1 and J22, Unspecified acute lower respiratory infection, should be assigned.

If the COVID-19 is documented as being associated with a respiratory infection, NOS, codes U07.1 and J98.8, Other specified respiratory disorders, should be assigned.

(iv) Acute respiratory distress syndrome

For acute respiratory distress syndrome (ARDS) due to COVID-19, assign codes U07.1, and J80, Acute respiratory distress syndrome.

(v) Acute respiratory failure

For acute respiratory failure due to COVID-19, assign code U07.1, and code J96.0-, Acute respiratory failure.

(d) Non-respiratory manifestations of COVID-19

When the reason for the encounter/admission is a non-respiratory manifestation (e.g., viral enteritis) of COVID-19, assign code U07.1, COVID-19, as the principal/first-listed diagnosis and assign code(s) for the manifestation(s) as additional diagnoses.

(e) Exposure to COVID-19

For asymptomatic individuals with actual or suspected exposure to COVID-19, assign code Z20.828, Contact with and (suspected) exposure to other viral communicable diseases.

For symptomatic individuals with actual or suspected exposure to COVID-19 and the infection has been ruled out, or test results are inconclusive or unknown, assign code Z20.828, Contact with and (suspected) exposure to other viral communicable diseases. See guideline I.C.21.c.1, Contact/Exposure, for additional guidance regarding the use of category Z20 codes.

If COVID-19 is confirmed, see guideline I.C.1.g.1.a.

(f) Screening for COVID-19

During the COVID-19 pandemic, a screening code is generally not appropriate. For encounters for COVID-19 testing, including preoperative testing, code as exposure to COVID-19 (guideline I.C.1.g.1.e).

Coding guidance will be updated as new information concerning any changes in the pandemic status becomes available.

(g) Signs and symptoms without definitive diagnosis of COVID-19

For patients presenting with any signs/symptoms associated with COVID-19 (such as fever, etc.) but a definitive diagnosis has not been established, assign the appropriate code(s) for each of the presenting signs and symptoms such as:

- R05 Cough
- R06.02 Shortness of breath
- R50.9 Fever, unspecified

If a patient with signs/symptoms associated with COVID-19 also has an actual or suspected contact with or exposure to COVID-19, assign Z20.828, Contact with and (suspected) exposure to other viral communicable diseases, as an additional code.

(h) Asymptomatic individuals who test positive for COVID-19

For asymptomatic individuals who test positive for COVID-19, see guideline I.C.1.g.1.a. Although the individual is asymptomatic, the individual has tested positive and is considered to have the COVID-19 infection.

Courtesy of the Centers for Medicare & Medicaid Services, www.cms.gov

(i) Personal history of COVID-19

For patients with a history of COVID-19, assign code Z86.19, Personal history of other infectious and parasitic diseases.

(j) Follow-up visits after COVID-19 infection has resolved

For individuals who previously had COVID-19 and are being seen for follow-up evaluation, and COVID-19 test results are negative, assign codes Z09, Encounter for follow-up examination after completed treatment for conditions other than malignant neoplasm, and Z86.19, Personal history of other infectious and parasitic diseases.

(k) Encounter for antibody testing

For an encounter for antibody testing that is not being performed to confirm a current COVID-19 infection, nor is a follow-up test after resolution of COVID-19, assign Z01.84, Encounter for antibody response examination.

Follow the applicable guidelines above if the individual is being tested to confirm a current COVID-19 infection.

For follow-up testing after a COVID-19 infection, see guideline I.C.1.g.1.j.

EXAMPLE:

Examples of cases when patient has exposure to covid-19

1. Patient is asymptomatic and has been exposed to COVID-19– Assign code Z20.828.
2. Patient is symptomatic with exposure to COVID-19 and the infection has been ruled out– Assign code Z20.828.
3. Patient presents with cough and has been exposed to COVID-19 but a definitive diagnosis has not been established– Code R05 for the cough and Z20.828 for the exposure to COVID-19.

EXAMPLE:

Examples of cases when the patient has COVID-19 and there are manifestations of the disease.

1. Patient with pneumonia due to COVID-19. Assign code U07.1 for the COVID-19 and assign an additional code of J12.89 for other viral pneumonia.
2. Patient with acute bronchitis due to COVID-19. For this case code U07.1 is used to report the COVID-19 and code J20.8 is used to report the acute bronchitis.
3. Patient with bronchitis due to COVID-19. When the bronchitis is not specified as acute or chronic report code U07.1, COVID-19, and code J40, Bronchitis not specified as acute or chronic as the secondary code.
4. Patient with COVID-19 and an associated lower respiratory infection not otherwise specified or an acute respiratory infection, not otherwise specified. For this case U07.1 is used to report the COVID-19 and code J22 reports the unspecified acute lower respiratory infection.
5. Patient with COVID-19 and an associated respiratory infection not otherwise specified– In this case the respiratory infection is not otherwise specified therefore code U07.1 reports the COVID-19 and code J98.8 reports the other specified respiratory disorders per the guideline.
6. Patient with acute respiratory distress syndrome due to COVID-19– For this case report code U07.1 for the COVID-19 and code J80 for the acute respiratory distress syndrome.
7. Patient with COVID-19 and acute respiratory failure– The COVID-19 is reported with code U07.1 and the acute respiratory failure is reported with code J96.00.

ICD-10-CM Official Coding Guidelines from Section I.C.15.s.

Chapter 15: Pregnancy, Childbirth, and the Puerperium (O00-O9A)

s. COVID-19 infection in pregnancy, childbirth, and the puerperium

During pregnancy, childbirth or the puerperium, when COVID-19 is the reason for admission/encounter, code O98.5-, Other viral diseases complicating pregnancy, childbirth and the puerperium, should be sequenced as the principal/first-listed diagnosis, and code U07.1, COVID-19, and the appropriate codes for associated manifestation(s) should be assigned as additional diagnoses. Codes from Chapter 15 always take sequencing priority.

If the reason for admission/encounter is unrelated to COVID-19 but the patient tests positive for COVID-19 during the admission/encounter, the appropriate code for the reason for admission/encounter should be sequenced as the principal/first-listed diagnosis, and codes O98.5- and U07.1, as well as the appropriate codes for associated COVID-19 manifestations, should be assigned as additional diagnoses.

Courtesy of the Centers for Medicare & Medicaid Services, www.cms.gov

EXAMPLE: Mary Lou, who is in her first trimester at 9 weeks, is seen for cough and she has been exposed to COVID-19. The rapid COVID-19 test is positive.

Assign code O98.511 for other viral disease complicating pregnancy, first trimester.

U07.1 for the COVID-19

Z3A.09 for the 9th week of pregnancy

ICD-10-CM Official Coding Guidelines from Section I.C.16.h

Chapter 16: Certain Conditions Originating in the Perinatal Period (P00-P96)

h. COVID-19 Infection in Newborn

For a newborn that tests positive for COVID-19, assign code U07.1, COVID-19, and the appropriate codes for associated manifestation(s) in neonates/newborns in the absence of documentation indicating a specific type of transmission.

For a newborn that tests positive for COVID-19 and the provider documents the condition was contracted in utero or during the birth process, assign codes P35.8, Other congenital viral diseases, and U07.1, COVID-19.

When coding the birth episode in a newborn record, the appropriate code from category Z38, Liveborn infants according to place of birth and type of delivery, should be assigned as the principal diagnosis.

Courtesy of the Centers for Medicare & Medicaid Services, www.cms.gov

EXAMPLE: Dija, a newborn, tests positive for COVID-19 and the provider documents "Dija contracted COVID-19 in utero." This is not the birth episode. The following codes should be assigned:

P35.8, Other congenital viral diseases

U07.1, COVID-19

Exercise 26.2—Codes for Special Purposes

Using an ICD-10-CM coding manual, assign the proper code for the diagnostic statements given.

Diagnosis	Code
1. personal history of COVID-19	_____
2. confirmed COVID-19 positive patient	_____
3. suspected COVID-19 patient with fever	_____
4. ARDS due to COVID-19	_____
5. acute bronchitis due to COVID-19	_____

Summary

- Diagnostic examinations are used to confirm or rule out a suspected diagnosis due to signs and symptoms that the patient has experienced.
- Z codes represent reasons for encounters whereas U codes represent codes for special purposes.
- Screening examinations are used to screen for a disease when no signs or symptoms are present.
- Z codes reports family and personal histories of diseases.
- Acquired absence of organs is reported with Z codes.
- DNR orders, blood type, and body mass index are also reported using Z codes.

Internet Links

For more information on cancer, visit **www.cancer.gov/about-cancer/screening** and **www.cancer.gov**.

Chapter Review

Fill-in-the-Blank

Enter the appropriate term(s) to complete each statement.

1. Codes that might indicate an influence on care but that are not themselves a current illness or injury are called _____.

2. To locate a code for a person suffering from a psychosocial problem, the coder references the _____ code range.

3. In determining the proper code for a routine physical exam, the coder must know whether there were or were not _____.

4. When coding for a patient who presents for an annual gynecological exam, including pap, the code assignment is _____.

5. When coding for genetic counseling, _____ is sequenced first, and a code from the _____ category is next if the purpose of the encounter is associated with procreative management.

6. A patient presents for a vasectomy. This would be coded with Z code _____.

7. Diagnostic _____ are used to confirm or rule out a suspected diagnosis due to signs and symptoms.

8. The code needed to reflect a patient who has blood type AB+ is _____.

9. A BMI, or _____, for an adult is calculated _____ than for a child.

10. Leslie suffered from breast cancer 5 years ago. At her annual physical she noted this as a part of her past medical history. Code _____ is assigned in addition to a code for her physical exam.

Coding Guidelines True/False

Review the ICD-10-CM Official Guidelines for Coding and Reporting and indicate if the statement(s) is true or false.

11. _____ Z codes for pregnancy are for use in those circumstances when none of the problems or complications included in the codes from the Obstetrics chapter exist (a routine prenatal visit or postpartum care).

12. _____ The Z codes allow for the description of encounters for routine examinations, such as a general check-up, or examinations for administrative purposes, such as a pre-employment physical. The codes are not to be used if the examination is for diagnosis of a suspected condition or for treatment purposes. In such cases the diagnosis code is used. During a routine exam, should a diagnosis or condition be discovered, it should not be coded as an additional code.

13. _____ For encounters specifically for prophylactic removal of an organ (such as prophylactic removal of breasts due to a genetic susceptibility to cancer or a family history of cancer), the principal or first-listed code should be a code from category Z40, Encounter for prophylactic surgery, followed by the appropriate codes to identify the associated risk factor (such as genetic susceptibility or family history).

14. _____ The follow-up codes are used to explain continuing surveillance following completed treatment of a disease, condition, or injury. They imply that the condition has been fully treated and no longer exists.

15. _____ There are two types of history Z codes: personal and generational.

Coding Assignments

Instructions: Using an ICD-10-CM code book, assign the proper diagnosis code to the following diagnostic statements. (Assume initial encounter unless otherwise specified.)

1. status post ileostomy _____

2. adjustment and fitting of prosthetic leg _____

3. encounter for Rh typing _____

4. presence of an IUD _____

5. immunization not done because of patient's religious belief _____

6. status post cholecystectomy _____

7. cervical pap smear (not part of a GYN exam) _____

8. encounter of disability determination _____

9.   dietary counseling for colitis _____

10. presence of prosthetic heart valve _____

11. suspected carrier of diphtheria _____

12. removal of right breast implant _____

13. blood type O– _____

14. counseling for medical advice _____

15. genetic susceptibility to malignant neoplasm of ovary _____

16. encounter for testing of male partner of habitual aborter _____

17. positive status for estrogen receptor _____

18. examination for summer camp _____

19. burnout _____

20. counseling for tobacco abuse without nicotine dependence _____

21. bad sleep habits _____

22. victim of torture _____

23. family history of arthritis _____

24. healthy person accompanying sick person _____

25. presence of right artificial wrist joint _____

26. dabbing related lung injury with lipoid pneumonia _____

27. COVID-19 patient with shortness of breath _____

28. COVID-19 patient with fever _____

29. encounter for COVID-19 antibody test _____

30. vaping-related lung damage with acute respiratory distress syndrome _____

Case Studies

Instructions: Review each case study and select the correct ICD-10-CM diagnostic code. Assign only the appropriate Z code in the studies given.

Case 1

This is a 28-year-old patient who presents today expressing anxiety over the fact that his father was just diagnosed with Crohn's disease. His father is 60 years old and has had GI problems for many years. The patient says that he is experiencing some of the same problems his father had prior to this diagnosis, and he would like a complete physical exam to rule out Crohn's disease. A complete physical was performed with no abnormal findings.

ICD-10-CM Code Assignment: _____

Case 2

While traveling out of state, Joan was injured after a fall down six concrete steps. She went to the emergency room at the local hospital and received 13 sutures in her left thigh. Joan now presents to her PCP, who will remove the sutures. After exam of the area, which was without infection, redness, or oozing, the stitches were successfully removed.

ICD-10-CM Code Assignment: _____

Case 3

Joe is an 82-year-old male who presents today for a fitting and adjustment of his hearing aid. He has had marked hearing loss in the left ear, and his doctor prescribed a hearing aid. We ordered the aid, and now Joe will try it to see if we need to make any adjustments to the way it fits.

ICD-10-CM Code Assignment: _____

Case 4

Physician Office Note

CHIEF COMPLAINT: This patient presents for a physical exam and to rule out any disease process.

General status reveals an alert 80-year-old woman who is pleasant and cooperative.

VITAL SIGNS: BP: 128/67, Pulse: 72, Respirations: 24, weight, 125 pounds. Routine lab work completed last week was all within normal ranges.

See personal history record for details of personal history.

FAMILY HISTORY: mother died of breast cancer.

PHYSICAL EXAM:

HEAD: Normocephalic

EYES: Cornea: clear; conjunctivae: pale pink; sclerae: nonicteric; pupils: react to light.

EARS: TMS are clear.

NECK: Supple, no JVD or bruit. Trachea midline. No lymphadenopathy or thyromegaly.

HEART: Regular rhythm, no murmurs. No peripheral cyanosis, pallor, or edema. She has very good distal pulses.

(continues)

(continued)

BREASTS: No masses palpated.

LUNGS: Good air entry, no adventitious sounds.

ABDOMEN: Soft, nondistended. Bowel sounds active.

EXTERNAL GENITALIA: Normal female.

MUSCULOSKELETAL: Functional range of motion of her joints.

NEUROLOGICAL: Cranial nerves 2–12 grossly intact bilaterally.

IMPRESSION: No findings

PLAN: Patient to follow-up in 1 year or sooner if problems develop.

ICD-10-CM Code Assignment: _____

Case 5

Marcy presents today 6 months status postovarian cancer for a follow-up examination. She has been living a healthy lifestyle and taking all medications as directed. She finished her chemotherapy and radiation therapy 6 months ago. All lab work completed a week ago was within normal limits. A CT scan completed 3 days ago is showing no signs of recurrence or any new masses. I instructed her to follow up with me in 4 months.

ICD-10-CM Code Assignment: _____

Case 6

Blood Pressure Clinic

This 74-year-old patient presents to the clinic today for a blood pressure reading. Her BP is 120/75 and I told her this is within normal limits. This will be reported to her primary care provider.

ICD-10-CM Code Assignment: _____

Case 7

Outpatient Lab Testing

This 73-year-old patient presents to the lab today for therapeutic drug-level monitoring. The patient is on long-term anticoagulant therapy.

ICD-10-CM Code Assignment: _____

Case 8

Physician Office Note

This patient is seen today to screen for osteoporosis. Family history is significant for the disease.

ICD-10-CM Code Assignment: _____

Case 9

Physician Office Visit

This 16-year-old basketball player presents to the office today for a sports physical.

VITAL SIGNS: BP: 125/80, Weight: 160 pounds, Height: 5 feet 11 inches.

HEENT: Normal

LUNGS: Clear

HEART: Normal rate and rhythm

ABDOMEN: Soft, no masses noted.

EXTREMITIES: Normal range of motion.

SKIN: Intact.

ASSESSMENT: Patient approved for sports participation.

ICD-10-CM Code Assignment: _____

Case 10

Pediatrician Office Note

This 1-year-old female child presents today for her 1-year physical. Her weight and height are within the 80th percentile for her age. I can observe no developmental concerns at this time.

HEENT: Normal

HEART: Rate and rhythm normal

LUNGS: Clear

ABDOMEN: Soft, active bowel sounds

EXTREMITIES: Well developed, the child is walking.

FINDINGS: Well-developed female with no health concerns at this time.

ICD-10-CM Code Assignment: _____

Introduction to ICD-10-PCS

Chapter Outline

Chapter Objectives

At the conclusion of this chapter, you should be able to:

1. Explain the development of ICD-10-PCS.
2. Explain the purpose of ICD-10-PCS and how it is used.
3. Summarize the format used in ICD-10-PCS.
4. Explain the different sections contained within ICD-10-PCS.
5. Summarize how to build an ICD-10-PCS procedure code.
6. Interpret the ICD-10-PCS Coding Guidelines.

Key Terms

Device

International Classification of Diseases, Tenth Revision, Procedure Coding System (ICD-10-PCS)

Procedure

Qualifier

Root operation

REMINDER: As you work through this chapter, you will need to have a copy of the ICD-10-PCS coding book to reference. For this chapter, you will also need to reference the ICD-10-PCS Official Guidelines for Coding and Reporting. These guidelines can be found in Appendix B which are now available on the Student Companion site and MINDTAP From Cengage.

Introduction

ICD-10-PCS, or the ***International Classification of Diseases, Tenth Revision, Procedure Coding System***, has been developed as a replacement for ICD-9-CM volume 3–Procedure codes. ICD-9-CM volume 3 has been used for facility reporting since January 1979, with the first revision taking place in 1986. ICD-9-CM procedure codes were a four-digit system, and it became apparent that with the constant evolution in the procedural forum, the code system would not be able to support these changes for long. A newer, larger, more comprehensive procedural coding system was devised by 3M Health Information Systems, and that system is ICD-10-PCS.

One of the goals set forth by the Centers for Medicare and Medicaid Services (CMS), which funded the 3-year contract with 3M, was to develop a new coding system that would improve accuracy. The uniqueness of the latest procedures needed to be reflected with unique codes, and the new procedure codes needed to be able to be expanded. Because new procedures are always being developed, new codes need to be developed to reflect the evolution of newer technology.

It was determined that the ICD-10-PCS codes also needed to be consistent, and each of the individual character positions needed to retain its meaning across broad ranges of codes. Therefore, a seven-character axis was developed, which is explained further in this chapter. The terminology used in ICD-10-PCS is, therefore, standardized. Definitions are included in ICD-10-PCS codes for this reason. Understanding these definitions is key in selecting the correct code assignment for procedures performed in a facility.

In development of ICD-10-PCS, the following general principles were followed:

- Procedure descriptions do not contain any diagnostic information. A disease or disorder is reflected in the diagnosis coding, not in the procedure coding.
- Explicit NOS (not otherwise specified) options are not provided in ICD-10-PCS.
- NEC (not elsewhere classified) has limited options in ICD-10-PCS. NEC codes may need to be referenced when a new procedure is performed that has not yet been assigned a proper ICD-10-PCS code.
- Procedures currently in use and being performed can be specified in the ICD-10-PCS code book with the use of a seven-character code.

Code Structure

Seven is the lucky number when it comes to ICD-10-PCS codes. The ICD-10-PCS codes contain seven characters, which can be letters or numbers. Each alphanumeric character has a specific meaning or value depending on its place in the lineup. Each code is made up of any one of the 10 digits 0–9 and any one of 24 letters A–H, J–N, and P–Z. The letters *O* and *I* are not used so as not to be confused with the numbers *0* and *1*. Therefore it is important that when entering codes into electronic systems that the codes are entered using the numbers 0 and 1 not the letters O and I. Entering letters when numbers should be used will cause problems with the processing and billing of claims and cause denials in payments to facilities.

ICD-10-PCS defines the term **procedure** to mean the complete specification of the seven characters. Each procedure is divided into specific sections that identify the general type of procedure with the first character, either a number or letter, designating the section. The sections and their corresponding section identifier (number or letter) are as follows:

Section	Section Identifier
Medical and Surgical	0
Obstetrics	1
Placement	2
Administration	3
Measurement and Monitoring	4

(continues)

(continued)

Section	Section Identifier
Extracorporeal or Systemic Assistance and Performance	5
Extracorporeal or Systemic Therapies	6
Osteopathic	7
Other Procedures	8
Chiropractic	9
Imaging	B
Nuclear Medicine	C
Radiation Therapy	D
Physical Rehabilitation and Diagnostic Audiology	F
Mental Health	G
Substance Abuse Treatment	H
New Technology	X

Exercise 27.1—ICD-10-PCS Sections

Match the identifier to its corresponding section.

_____ **1.** D
_____ **2.** 1
_____ **3.** 9
_____ **4.** 7
_____ **5.** H
_____ **6.** 8
_____ **7.** 4
_____ **8.** 0
_____ **9.** G
_____ **10.** B

a. Chiropractic
b. Mental Health
c. Obstetrics
d. Imaging
e. Radiation Therapy
f. Measurement and Monitoring
g. Substance Abuse Treatment
h. Other Procedures
i. Medical and Surgical
j. Osteopathic

Format

To locate a code in ICD-10-PCS, the coder needs to understand the overall format of the PCS manual. ICD-10-PCS is divided into the following parts: Introduction, Index, Tables, and Appendices.

Introduction

In ICD-10-PCS an Introduction appears. The Introduction details the history of ICD-10-PCS, the number of codes in ICD-10-PCS, and the ICD-10-PCS Manual. It is essential that coders become familiar with the information contained in the Introduction. The Introduction provides specific information about the various sections of PCS outlining the character meanings for each section as well as specific definitions for the various character values. Prior to selecting codes, coders need to read the Introduction. I would suggest that you now take the time to locate and read the Introduction found in the ICD-10-PCS coding manual. Read this multiple times to understand and retain the information.

Index

The Index is a starting point when selecting a code. The Index is a guide to the Tables, which contain the specific characters needed to formulate the code. Main terms are listed alphabetically in the Index, which supplies at a minimum the first three characters of a code. The main terms listed in the Index for the Medical and Surgical and related sections are root operations. An example would be the main term of excision. The main terms listed for the other sections of ICD-10-PCS are the general type of procedure performed. An example would be the main term of fluoroscopy. By referencing the main term, a minimum of three characters will appear in the Index. These three characters will denote the table that is to be used to build a code. Using the characters identified in the Index, the coder should then reference the correct PCS Table.

It should be noted that each character position in the Table has a specific meaning. The meanings for the character positions vary at times from section to section in ICD-10-PCS. The specific character meanings found in each section are discussed in the Introduction of the PCS manual. This will be further discussed in later chapters of this textbook. For example, the specific character positions and meanings for the Medical and Surgical Section of ICD-10-PCS are as follows:

Character Position	Meaning
1	Section
2	Body system
3	**Root operation**—the objective of the procedure, such as bypass, drainage, fluoroscopy, MRI, etc.
4	Body part
5	Approach
6	**Device**—a device that remains in the body after completion of a procedure, such as an IUD, a skin graft, a pacemaker, or radioactive implant.
7	**Qualifier**—additional information unique to the individual procedure being performed, such as full or partial thickness, diagnostic, etc.

Courtesy of the Centers for Medicare & Medicaid Services, www.cms.gov

EXAMPLE: The patient is undergoing open extraction of the bursa in the right elbow. If you reference the term *extraction* in the Index, you find:

Extraction
Bursae and Ligaments
Elbow
Left 0MD4
Right 0MD3

Extraction of the bursa of the right elbow is found in Table 0MD. Once you locate this table, you can finish constructing your code selection: 0MD30ZZ. The character meanings are as follows:

- 0—Medical and surgical section
- M—The body system, the bursae and ligaments
- D—The root operation, the extraction
- 3—The body part, in this case, elbow bursa and ligament, right
- 0—The approach, in this case, the procedure was done as an open procedure
- ZZ—(the sixth and seventh spaces), no device or qualifier needed

Tables

When coding in ICD-10-PCS, the Tables are used to identify groups of codes and to organize them in a way that make it easy to select a code. ICD-10-PCS also uses the Tables to allow coders to build their codes.

The specific Tables in the sections in ICD-10-PCS (e.g., Medical and Surgical, Obstetrics) are identified by the first characters just above the Table.

> **EXAMPLE:** Locate Table 03L in the ICD-10-PCS Manual. Here you will find the following above the Table:
>
> - 0, Medical and Surgical
> - 3, Upper Arteries
> - L, Occlusion: Completely closing an orifice or lumen of a tubular body part

> **EXAMPLE:** In the preceding example, the character 0 identifies the Medical and Surgical section of ICD-10-PCS. The 3 in the second character identifies the body system of upper arteries. The third character L identifies that the root operation is occlusion. The lower portion of the Table offers the options for the remaining characters in positions four through seven.

In some Tables, the coder will notice that the Table contains multiple rows. When selecting characters from a given Table, characters can only be selected from a single row.

> **EXAMPLE:** Review Table 02L in ICD-10-PCS. Here you will find the following:
>
> - 0, Medical and Surgical
> - 2, Heart and Great Vessels
> - L, Occlusion: Completely closing an orifice or the lumen of a tubular body part

Body Part Character 4	Approach Character 5	Device Character 6	Qualifier Character 7
7 Atrium, Left	0 Open 3 Percutaneous 4 Percutaneous Endoscopic	C Extraluminal Device D Intraluminal Device Z No Device	K Left Artial Appendage
R Pulmonary Artery, Left	0 Open 3 Percutaneous 4 Percutaneous Endoscopic	C Extraluminal Device D Intraluminal Device Z No Device	T Ductus Arteriosus Z No qualifier
S Pulmonary Vein, Right T Pulmonary Vein, Left V Superior Vena Cava	0 Open 3 Percutaneous 4 Percutaneous Endoscopic	C Extraluminal Device D Intraluminal Device Z No Device	Z No qualifier

Courtesy of the Centers for Medicare & Medicaid Services, www.cms.gov

When selecting characters from Tables, the coder must select the characters straight across in a given row. Therefore, the body part character 4 value of 7, Atrium, Left, can only be reported with:

approach character 5 values of 0, 3, and 4

device character 6 values of C, D, and Z

qualifier character 7 value of K

ICD-10-PCS Coding Guidelines

ICD-10-PCS Coding Guidelines have been developed to standardize ICD-10-PCS code selection. The guidelines address:

- Conventions
- Medical and Surgical Section Guidelines
- Obstetrics Section Guidelines
- Radiation Therapy Guidelines
- New Technology Section Guidelines
- Selection of Principal Procedure

The introduction to the ICD-10-PCS Guidelines for Coding and Reporting 2021 state the following:

The Centers for Medicare and Medicaid Services (CMS) and the National Center for Health Statistics (NCHS), two departments within the U.S. Federal Government's Department of Health and Human Services (DHHS) provide the following guidelines for coding and reporting using the International Classification of Diseases, 10th Revision, Procedure Coding System (ICD-10-PCS). These guidelines should be used as a companion document to the official version of the ICD-10-PCS as published on the CMS website. The ICD-10-PCS is a procedure classification published by the United States for classifying procedures performed in hospital inpatient health care settings.

These guidelines have been approved by the four organizations that make up the Cooperating Parties for the ICD-10-PCS: the American Hospital Association (AHA), the American Health Information Management Association (AHIMA), CMS, and NCHS.

These guidelines are a set of rules that have been developed to accompany and complement the official conventions and instructions provided within the ICD-10-PCS itself. They are intended to provide direction that is applicable in most circumstances. However, there may be unique circumstances where exceptions are applied. The instructions and conventions of the classification take precedence over guidelines. These guidelines are based on the coding and sequencing instructions in the Tables, Index and Definitions of ICD-10-PCS, but provide additional instruction. Adherence to these guidelines when assigning ICD-10-PCS procedure codes is required under the Health Insurance Portability and Accountability Act (HIPAA). The procedure codes have been adopted under HIPAA for hospital inpatient healthcare settings. A joint effort between the healthcare provider and the coder is essential to achieve complete and accurate documentation, code assignment, and reporting of diagnoses and procedures. These guidelines have been developed to assist both the healthcare provider and the coder in identifying those procedures that are to be reported. The importance of consistent, complete documentation in the medical record cannot be overemphasized. Without such documentation accurate coding cannot be achieved.

In this chapter, we will review the guidelines for conventions. All sections of ICD-10-PCS are governed by the following guidelines that relate to the conventions used in ICD-10-PCS.

ICD-10-PCS Coding Guidelines

ICD-10-PCS Coding Guidelines—Conventions

Conventions

A1

ICD-10-PCS codes are composed of seven characters. Each character is an axis of classification that specifies information about the procedure performed. Within a defined code range, a character specifies the same type of information in that axis of classification.

Example: The fifth axis of classification specifies the approach in sections 0 through 4 and 7 through 9 of the system.

A2

One of 34 possible values can be assigned to each axis of classification in the seven-character code: they are the numbers 0 through 9 and the alphabet (except I and O because they are easily confused with the numbers 1 and 0). The number of unique values used in an axis of classification differs as needed.

Example: Where the fifth axis of classification specifies the approach, seven different approach values are currently used to specify the approach.

A3

The valid values for an axis of classification can be added to as needed.

Example: If a significantly distinct type of device is used in a new procedure, a new device value can be added to the system.

A4

As with words in their context, the meaning of any single value is a combination of its axis of classification and any preceding values on which it may be dependent.

Example: The meaning of a body part value in the Medical and Surgical section is always dependent on the body system value. The body part value 0 in the Central Nervous body system specifies Brain and the body part value 0 in the Peripheral Nervous body system specifies Cervical Plexus.

A5

As the system is expanded to become increasingly detailed, over time more values will depend on preceding values for their meaning.

Example: In the Lower Joints body system, the device value 3 in the root operation Insertion specifies Infusion Device and the device value 3 in the root operation Replacement specifies Ceramic Synthetic Substitute.

A6

The purpose of the alphabetic index is to locate the appropriate table that contains all information necessary to construct a procedure code. The PCS Tables should always be consulted to find the most appropriate valid code.

A7

It is not required to consult the index first before proceeding to the tables to complete the code. A valid code may be chosen directly from the tables.

A8

All seven characters must be specified to be a valid code. If the documentation is incomplete for coding purposes, the physician should be queried for the necessary information.

A9

Within a PCS table, valid codes include all combinations of choices in characters 4 through 7 contained in the same row of the table. In the example below, 0JHT3VZ is a valid code, and 0JHW3VZ is not a valid code.

Section: 0 Medical and Surgical

Body System: J Subcutaneous Tissue and Fascia

Operation: H Insertion: Putting in a nonbiological appliance that monitors, assists, performs, or prevents a physiological function but does not physically take the place of a body part

Body Part	Approach	Device	Qualifier
S Subcutaneous Tissue and Fascia, Head and Neck V Subcutaneous Tissue and Fascia, Upper Extremity W Subcutaneous Tissue and Fascia, Lower Extremity	0 Open 3 Percutaneous	1 Radioactive Element 3 Infusion Device Y Other Device	Z No Qualifier
T Subcutaneous Tissue and Fascia, Trunk	0 Open 3 Percutaneous	1 Radioactive Element 3 Infusion Device V Infusion Pump Y Other Device	Z No Qualifier

A10

"And," when used in a code description, means "and/or," except when used to describe a combination of multiple body parts for which separate values exist for each body part (e.g., Skin and Subcutaneous Tissue used as a qualifier, where there are separate body part values for "Skin" and "Subcutaneous Tissue").

Example: Lower Arm and Wrist Muscle means lower arm and/or wrist muscle.

A11

Many of the terms used to construct PCS codes are defined within the system. It is the coder's responsibility to determine what the documentation in the medical record equates to in the PCS definitions. The physician is not expected to use the terms used in PCS code descriptions, nor is the coder required to query the physician when the correlation between the documentation and the defined PCS terms is clear.

Example: When the physician documents "partial resection" the coder can independently correlate "partial resection" to the root operation Excision without querying the physician for clarification.

Selection of Principal Procedure

When sequencing procedures, coders need to apply the following guideline:

ICD-10-PCS Coding Guidelines

F. Selection of Principal Procedure

The following instructions should be applied in the selection of principal procedure and clarification on the importance of the relation to the principal diagnosis when more than one procedure is performed:

1. Procedure performed for definitive treatment of both principal diagnosis and secondary diagnosis.

a. Sequence procedure performed for definitive treatment most related to principal diagnosis as principal procedure.

2. Procedure performed for definitive treatment and diagnostic procedures performed for both principal diagnosis and secondary diagnosis.

a. Sequence procedure performed for definitive treatment most related to principal diagnosis as principal procedure.

3. A diagnostic procedure was performed for the principal diagnosis and a procedure is performed for definitive treatment of a secondary diagnosis.

a. Sequence diagnostic procedure as principal procedure, since the procedure most related to the principal diagnosis takes precedence.

4. No procedures performed that are related to principal diagnosis; procedures performed for definitive treatment and diagnostic procedures were performed for secondary diagnosis.

a. Sequence procedure performed for definitive treatment of secondary diagnosis as principal procedure, since there are no procedures (definitive or nondefinitive treatment) related to principal diagnosis.

For accurate procedural code selection, the guidelines must be applied when selecting ICD-10-PCS codes. To become familiar with the guidelines, read them multiple times as they provide you guidance in code selection.

Summary

- Diagnostic information is not included in the description of ICD-10-PCS procedures.
- ICD-10-PCS codes contain seven alphanumeric characters. The letters *O* and *I* have been excluded so as not to cause confusion with the numbers *0* and *1*.
- In ICD-10-PCS, sections instead of chapters are used, and each section is identified with either a number or letter.
- Specific ICD-10-PCS Coding Guidelines have been developed to standardize ICD-10-PCS code selection.

Chapter Review

Multiple Choice

Select the best answer that completes the statement or answers the question.

1. ICD-9-CM volume 3 was replaced with ICD-10-PCS because:
   a. it is newer but harder to use.
   b. it contains too many codes.
   c. it was an antiquated, four-digit system that needed to be updated.
   d. it contained diagnoses as well as procedures that were too confusing.

2. It was _____ that actually funded the new ICD-10-PCS program.
   a. 3M
   b. CMS
   c. WHO
   d. AMA

3. One of the goals of ICD-10-PCS is to:
   a. introduce new terminology.
   b. improve accuracy.
   c. include enhanced diagnostic information within ICD-10-PCS.
   d. standardize a new six-digit code set.

4. The section identifier for Radiation Therapy is:
   a. B.
   b. C.
   c. D.
   d. F.

5. The body system on which a procedure is performed is reported in which character position in the code?
   a. 1
   b. 2
   c. 3
   d. 4

Fill-in-the-Blank

Enter the appropriate term(s) to complete each statement.

6. The first character of an ICD-10-PCS code represents a(n) _____.

7. ICD-10-PCS defines _____ to mean the complete specification of the seven characters.

8. The letters _____ and _____ were excluded from ICD-10-PCS so that they would not be confused with _____ and _____.

9. The objective of the procedure is known as the _____.

10. The description of procedures does not include _____ information.

In the following codes given, identify the underlined character as either the Section (S), Body System (BS), Root Operation (RO), Body Part (BP), Approach (A), Device (D), or Qualifier (Q). Then identify the procedure. The first two are done for you.

Code	Character Identification	Code Description
11. 01N33ZZ	RO	Percutaneous release of brachial plexus
12. 07WM00Z	BP	Open revision of drainage device of thymus
13. 05LY0ZZ	_____	_____
14. 0CTN0ZZ	_____	_____
15. 09QF0ZZ	_____	_____
16. BL42ZZZ	_____	_____
17. 0RPWX0Z	_____	_____
18. 0WJ8XZZ	_____	_____
19. 0WW833Z	_____	_____
20. 0UWM00Z	_____	_____

True/False

Indicate whether each statement is true (T) or false (F).

21. _____ An ICD-10-PCS code is composed of four to seven characters.

22. _____ The PCS Tables should always be consulted to find the most appropriate valid code.

23. _____ It is the provider's responsibility to determine what the documentation in the medical record equates to in the PCS definition.

24. _____ The letters I and O are not used in ICD-10-PCS.

25. _____ If the documentation is incomplete for coding purposes, a character value of Z should be assigned.

26. _____ When both a diagnostic procedure and a definitive procedure are performed and the diagnostic procedure relates to the principal diagnosis and the definitive procedure relates to the secondary diagnosis, the diagnostic procedure is sequenced as the principal procedure.

Short Answer

27. Reference the ICD-10-PCS Official Coding Guidelines for Coding and Reporting 2021. Locate the section entitled Conventions. Identify which coding guideline states the purpose of the ICD-10-PCS Alphabetic Index and state the purpose of the Alphabetic Index.

28. Reference the ICD-10-PCS Official Coding Guidelines for Coding and Reporting 2021. Locate guideline A8. List the two components of code selection discussed in guideline A8.

29. Reference the ICD-10-PCS Official Coding Guidelines for Coding and Reporting 2021. Locate the guideline entitled F- Selection of Principal Procedure. Describe how to sequence procedure codes when no procedures performed are related to the principal diagnosis and the procedures performed for definitive treatment and the diagnostic procedures were performed for the secondary diagnosis.

30. Define the term root operation and the term device.

Medical and Surgical Section

Chapter Outline

Chapter Objectives

At the conclusion of this chapter, you should be able to:

1. Define key terms found in this chapter.
2. Explain the code arrangement of the Medical and Surgical Section of ICD-10-PCS.
3. Select PCS descriptions from the ICD-10-PCS manual appendix entitled: Body Part Key.
4. Select PCS descriptions from the ICD-10-PCS manual appendix entitled: Device Key and Aggregation Table.
5. Interpret ICD-10-PCS coding guidelines for the Medical and Surgery Section of ICD-10-PCS.
6. Select a code from the Medical and Surgical Section of ICD-10-PCS.
7. Select ICD-10-PCS codes for case studies.

Key Terms

Access location	Detachment	Fragmentation	Open
Alteration	Dilation	Fusion	Percutaneous
Approach	Division	Insertion	Percutaneous endoscopic
Bypass	Drainage	Inspection	Qualifier
Change	Excision	Instrumentation	Reattachment
Control	External	Map	Release
Creation	Extirpation	Method	Removal
Destruction	Extraction	Occlusion	Repair

Replacement	Revision	Tubular body parts	Via natural or artificial opening with percutaneous endoscopic assistance
Reposition	Supplement	Via natural or artificial opening	
Resection	Transfer		
Restriction	Transplantation	Via natural or artificial opening endoscopic	

REMINDER: As you work through this chapter, you will need to have a copy of the ICD-10-PCS coding book to reference. For this chapter, you will also need to reference the ICD-10-PCS Official Guidelines for Coding and Reporting. These guidelines can be found in Appendix B which are available on the Student Companion site and MINDTAP From Cengage.

Introduction

The medical and surgical codes constitute the bulk of codes reported in an inpatient setting. Each surgical procedure is associated with a specific definition.

Medical and Surgical Section Character Meanings

Section

The first character for the codes reported from the Medical and Surgical section is 0. All Tables from which codes are reported that begin with the number 0 identify that the code is from the Medical and Surgical section of ICD-10-PCS.

EXAMPLE:

- 089, Drainage of the eye
- 08B, Excision of the eye

The second character indicates the body system. The third character references the root operation, and the fourth character indicates the specific body part on which the procedure is performed. The fifth character identifies the approach used to perform the procedure. The sixth character represents any device that was used and remains at the end of the procedure. The seventh character is a qualifier that may have meaning specific to the limited range of the procedure being reported. Not all procedures require a device or qualifier, so the value of Z is used to represent no device or qualifier.

Body Systems

The second character represents body system. The Medical and Surgical section of ICD-10-PCS contains 31 possible characters for the second position. The possible character assignments for the second position are as follows:

Character	Body System
0	Central nervous system and cranial nerves
1	Peripheral nervous system
2	Heart and great vessels
3	Upper arteries
4	Lower arteries
5	Upper veins

(continues)

(continued)

Character	Body System
6	Lower veins
7	Lymphatic and hemic systems
8	Eye
9	Ear, nose, sinus
B	Respiratory system
C	Mouth and throat
D	Gastrointestinal system
F	Hepatobiliary system and pancreas
G	Endocrine system
H	Skin and breast
J	Subcutaneous tissue and fascia
K	Muscles
L	Tendons
M	Bursae and ligaments
N	Head and facial bones
P	Upper bones
Q	Lower bones
R	Upper joints
S	Lower joints
T	Urinary system
U	Female reproductive system
V	Male reproductive system
W	Anatomical regions, general
X	Anatomical regions, upper extremities
Y	Anatomical regions, lower extremities

Courtesy of the Centers for Medicare & Medicaid Services, www.cms.gov

With so many characters available, coders can now formulate more detailed codes than ever before. Seven character positions allow for countless possibilities and leave room for additional descriptors to be added as new techniques evolve.

ICD-10-PCS Official Coding Guidelines Relating to Body System

The selection of ICD-10-PCS codes for the Medical and Surgical section is governed by the following coding guidelines that relate to body systems:

ICD-10-PCS Official Coding Guidelines

B2. Body System

General guidelines

B2.1a

The procedure codes in Anatomical Regions, General, Anatomical Regions, Upper Extremities and Anatomical Regions, Lower Extremities can be used when the procedure is performed on an anatomical region rather than a specific body part or on the rare occasion when no information is available to support assignment of a code to a specific body part.

Courtesy of the Centers for Medicare & Medicaid Services, www.cms.gov

Examples: Chest tube drainage of the pleural cavity is coded to the root operation Drainage found in the body system Anatomical Regions, General.

Suture repair of the abdominal wall is coded to the root operation Repair in the body system Anatomical Regions, General.

Amputation of the foot is coded to the root operation Detachment in the body system Anatomical Regions, Lower Extremities.

B2.1b

Where the general body part values "upper" and "lower" are provided as an option in the Upper Arteries, Lower Arteries, Upper Veins, Lower Veins, Muscles and Tendons body systems, "upper" or "lower" specifies body parts located above or below the diaphragm respectively.

Example: Vein body parts above the diaphragm are found in the Upper Veins body system; vein body parts below the diaphragm are found in the Lower Veins body system.

Root Operations

Root operations reflect the objective of the procedure and are specified in the third character position. Each root operation has an exact definition that is defined in the Introduction of the ICD-10-PCS Manual and is also located next to the term in the Table section of ICD-10-PCS.

The root operations for the Medical and Surgical Section are as follows:

- **Alteration**—Modifying the natural anatomical structure of a body part without affecting the function of the body part. The purpose of this type of procedure is to change and improve appearance, such as a face-lift. (value of 0)

- **Bypass**—Altering the route of passage of the contents of a tubular body part. During these procedures, the rerouting of the contents of a body part occurs, such as when a colostomy formation or cystostomy is completed or when coronary bypass surgery is performed. Figure 28-1 illustrates a cystostomy. (value of 1)

- **Change**—Taking out or off a device from a body part and putting back an identical or similar device in or on the same body part without cutting or puncturing the skin or a mucous membrane. An example is a urinary catheter change. (value of 2)

- **Control**—Stopping or attempting to stop postprocedural or other acute bleeding. An example is the completion of a procedure to control a posthysterectomy hemorrhage. (value of 3)

- **Creation**—Putting in or on biological or synthetic material to form a new body part that to the extent possible replicates the anatomic structure or function of an absent body part. These procedures are used only for sex-change operations. (value of 4)

- **Destruction**—Physical eradication of all or a portion of a body part by the direct use of energy, force, or a destructive agent. An example is cautery of a benign skin lesion. (value of 5)

- **Detachment**—Cutting off all or a portion of the upper or lower extremities. An example is a left leg below-the-knee amputation. (value of 6)

- **Dilation**—Expanding an orifice or the lumen of a tubular body part. A dilation of the esophagus using an intraluminal device is an example. (value of 7)

- **Division**—Cutting into a body part without draining fluids and/or gases from the body part in order to separate or transect a body part. All or a portion of the body part is separated into two or more portions, such as when an osteotomy is performed. (value of 8)

- **Drainage**—Taking or letting out fluids and/or gases from a body part. An incision and drainage of an abscess is an example. (value of 9)

- **Excision**—Cutting out or off, without replacement, a portion of a body part. A partial nephrectomy or a biopsy of the lung is an example. (value of B)

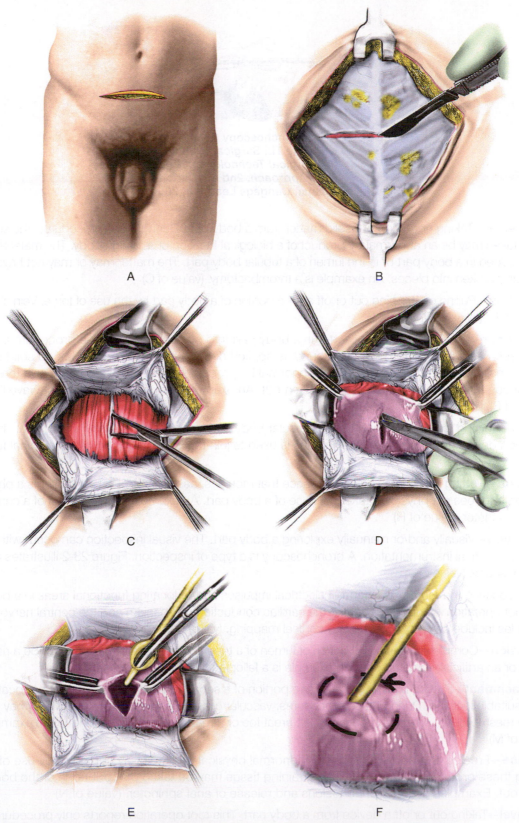

FIGURE 28-1 Open cystostomy: (A) incision site; (B) fascia incised; (C) muscle split; (D) bladder incised; (E) cystostomy tube inserted; (F) cystostomy tube secured with pursestring suture (From Price P, Frey KB, Jung TL. *Surgical Technology fro the Surgical Technologist: A Positive Care Approach,* 2nd ed. Clifton Park, NY: Delmar, Cengage Learning, 2004, p. 766.).

FIGURE 28-2 Rigid bronchoscopy (From Price P, Frey KB, Jung TL. *Surgical Technology fro the Surgical Technologist: A Positive Care Approach,* 2nd ed. Clifton Park, NY: Delmar, Cengage Learning, 2004, p. 887.).

- **Extirpation**—Taking or cutting out solid matter from a body part. During these procedures, the solid matter that is taken may be an abnormal by-product of a biological function or a foreign body. The material can be imbedded in a body part or in the lumen of a tubular body part. The matter may or may not have been previously broken into pieces. An example is a thrombectomy. (value of C)

- **Extraction**—Pulling or stripping out or off all or a portion of a body part by the use of force. Vein stripping is an example. (value of D)

- **Fragmentation**—Breaking solid matter in a body part into pieces. During these procedures, physical force, such as a manual force or ultrasound, is applied directly or indirectly to break up solid matter into pieces. The solid matter may be an abnormal by-product of a biological function or a foreign body. The pieces that are fragmented are not taken out. An example is extracorporeal shockwave lithotripsy. (value of F)

- **Fusion**—Joining together portions of an articular body part, rendering the articular body part immobile. A fixation device, bone graft, or other means is used to join the body part, such as in a spinal fusion. (value of G)

- **Insertion**—Putting in a nonbiological appliance that monitors, assists, performs, or prevents a physiological function but does not physically take the place of a body part. An example is an insertion of a central venous catheter. (value of H)

- **Inspection**—Visually and/or manually exploring a body part. The visual inspection can occur with or without optical instrumentation. A bronchoscopy is a type of inspection. Figure 28-2 illustrates a bronchoscopy. (value of J)

- **Map**—Locating the route of passage of electrical impulses and/or locating functional areas in a body part. This root operation is applicable only to the cardiac conduction mechanism and the central nervous system. Examples include cardiac mapping and cortical mapping. (value of K)

- **Occlusion**—Completely closing an orifice or lumen of a tubular body part. The orifice can be a natural orifice or an artificially created one. An example is a fallopian tube ligation. (value of L)

- **Reattachment**—Putting back in or on all or a portion of a separated body part to its normal location or other suitable location. During these procedures, vascular circulation and nervous pathways may or may not be reestablished. A reattachment of a left great toe or a reattachment of the tongue are examples. (value of M)

- **Release**—Freeing of a body part from an abnormal physical constraint by cutting or by use of force. During these procedures, some of the restraining tissue may be taken out, but none of the body part is taken out. Examples are lysis of adhesions and release of anal sphincter. (value of N)

- **Removal**—Taking out or off a device from a body part. This root operation reports only procedures for taking out a device. If a device is taken out and a similar device is put in without cutting or puncturing the skin or mucous membrane, the procedure is coded to the root operation of change. Examples of removal procedures include cardiac pacemaker removal and removal of an esophageal airway device. (value of P)

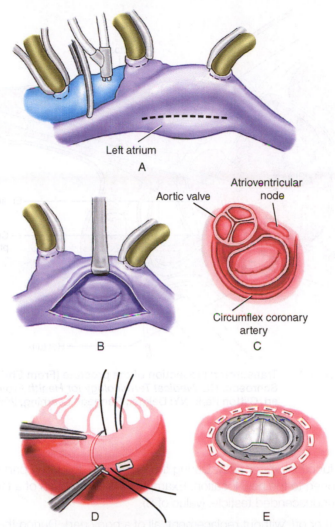

FIGURE 28-3 Mitral valve replacement: (A) atrial incision site; (B) mitral valve exposed; (C) cross section showing related anatomical structures; (D) sutures placed in the annulus; (E) prosthesis in place (From Price P, Frey KB, Jung TL. *Surgical Technology for the Surgical Technologist: A Positive Care Approach*, 2nd ed. Clifton Park, NY: Delmar, Cengage Learning, 2004, p. 917.).

- **Repair**—Restoring, to the extent possible, a body part to its normal anatomic structure and function. This root operation is used only when the method to accomplish the repair is not part of the other root operations. Examples of repair operations are the suturing of a laceration of the right upper arm or a herniorraphy. (value of Q)

- **Replacement**—Putting in or on biological or synthetic material that physically takes the place and/or function of all or a portion of a body part. The body part may have been taken out or replaced, or it may be taken out, physically eradicated, or rendered nonfunctional during the Replacement procedure. Examples include a total knee replacement, mitral valve replacement, or a free skin graft. Figure 28-3 illustrates a mitral valve replacement. (value of R)

- **Reposition**—Moving to its normal location, or other suitable location, all or a portion of a body part. During these procedures, the body part is moved to a new location from an abnormal location or from a normal

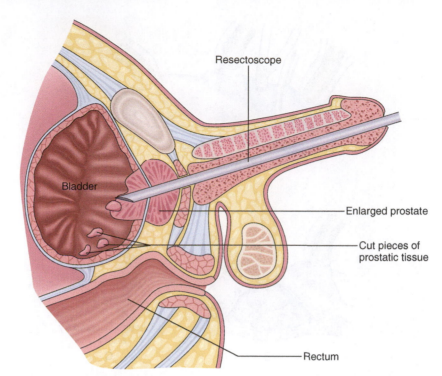

Resectoscope

Bladder

Enlarged prostate

Cut pieces of prostatic tissue

Rectum

FIGURE 28-4 Transurethral resection of the prostate (From Ehrlich A, Schroeder CL. *Medical Terminology for Health Professions*, 4th ed. Clifton Park, NY: Delmar, Cengage Learning, 2001, p. 299.).

location where it is not functioning correctly. During the procedure, the body part may or may not be cut out or off to be repositioned to the new location. Examples are a reduction of a fracture of the left tibia and the repositioning of an undescended testicle. (value of S)

- **Resection**—Cutting out or off, without replacement, all of a body part. During these procedures, the entire body part is removed, such as a complete cholecystectomy, a complete appendectomy, or a total transurethral resection of the prostate. Figure 28-4 illustrates a transurethral resection of the prostate. (value of T)

- **Restriction**—Partially closing an orifice or lumen of a tubular body part. The orifice can be a natural orifice or an artificially created one. An example is a restriction of the thoracic duct with a intraluminal stent or a trans-vaginal intraluminal cervical cerclage. (value of V)

- **Revision**—Correcting, to the extent possible, a portion of a malfunctioning device or the position of a displaced device. The revision can include the correcting of a malfunctioning or displaced device by taking out and/or putting in part of the device. Adjustment of a pacemaker lead or the external repositioning of a Foley catheter to the bladder are examples. (value of W)

- **Supplement**—Putting in or on biological or synthetic material that physically reinforces and/or augments the function of a portion of a body part. The biological material is nonliving or living and from the same individual. The Supplement procedure is performed to physically reinforce and/or augment the function of the replaced body part. The body part may have been previously replaced. A herniorrhaphy using mesh and a free nerve graft are examples. (value of U)

- **Transfer**—Moving, without taking out, all or a portion of a body part to another location to take over the function of all or a portion of a body part. During the Transfer procedure, the body part transferred remains connected to its vascular and nervous supply, such as in a tendon transfer or skin pedicle flap transfer. (value of X)

● **Transplantation**—Putting in or on all or a portion of a living body part taken from another individual or animal to physically take the place and/or function of all or a portion of a similar body part. An example is a heart–lung transplant or a kidney transplant. (value of Y)

 NOTE:

The root operation is used to define the objective of the procedure. The terms are defined, allowing for very precise coding assignments. Appendices A and B in ICD-10-PCS provide more explanation and examples of the Medical and Surgical root operations and approaches.

For example it is essential for the coder to understand the objective of the procedure and the definitions of the root operations as both impact code assignment.

When coding an open tenotomy of the left hand the coder would reference the term Tenotomy in the ICD-10-PCS Index. In the Index, under the main term of Tenotomy the following appears: see Division, Tendons 0L8 and see Drainage, Tendons 0L9.

The coder must know the definitions of division (cutting into a body part without draining fluids and/or gases from the body part in order to separate or transect a body part) and the definition of drainage (taking or letting out fluids and/or gases from a body part) to determine which ICD-10-PCS Table to reference . When coding the open tenotomy of the left hand the coder would reference the Table for Division, Tendons 0L8 as the procedural statement does not state that the procedure is being completed to drain fluids or gases.

However if the coder was to code an open tenotomy to drain fluid from a tendon of the left hand the coder would reference the ICD-10-PCS Table for Drainage, Tendons 0L9.

Therefore the two procedures would be coded as follows:

Tenotomy of left hand, open   0L880ZZ

Tenotomy, open, to drain fluid from tendon of left hand   0L980ZZ

Exercise 28.1—Root Operations

Match the root operation with the corresponding value.

_____	1.	transplantation	**a.** L
_____	2.	occlusion	**b.** 7
_____	3.	detachment	**c.** D
_____	4.	restriction	**d.** J
_____	5.	dilation	**e.** 3
_____	6.	extraction	**f.** Y
_____	7.	map	**g.** 6
_____	8.	control	**h.** N
_____	9.	release	**i.** K
_____	10.	inspection	**j.** V

ICD-10-PCS Official Coding Guidelines Relating to Root Operation

The selection of ICD-10-PCS codes for the Medical and Surgical section is governed by the following coding guidelines that relate to root operations. As you read through the guidelines make note of the examples that are listed for the guidelines. The examples provide information that will help you perfect your coding knowledge.

ICD-10-PCS Official Coding Guidelines

B3. Root Operation

General guidelines

B3.1a

In order to determine the appropriate root operation, the full definition of the root operation as contained in the PCS Tables must be applied.

B3.1b

Components of a procedure specified in the root operation definition or explanation as integral to that root operation are not coded separately. Procedural steps necessary to reach the operative site and close the operative site, including anastomosis of a tubular body part, are also not coded separately.

Example: Resection of a joint as part of a joint replacement procedure is included in the root operation definition of Replacement and is not coded separately.

Laparotomy performed to reach the site of an open liver biopsy is not coded separately.

In a resection of sigmoid colon with anastomosis of descending colon to rectum, the anastomosis is not coded separately.

Multiple procedures

B3.2

During the same operative episode, multiple procedures are coded if:

a. The same root operation is performed on different body parts as defined by distinct values of the body part character.

Example: Diagnostic excision of liver and pancreas are coded separately.

Excision of lesion in the ascending colon and excision of lesion in the transverse colon are coded separately.

b. The same root operation is repeated in multiple body parts, and those body parts are separate and distinct body parts classified to a single ICD-10-PCS body part value.

Example: Excision of the sartorius muscle and excision of the gracilis muscle are both included in the upper leg muscle body part value, and multiple procedures are coded.

Extraction of multiple toenails are coded separately.

c. Multiple root operations with distinct objectives are performed on the same body part.

Example: Destruction of sigmoid lesion and bypass of sigmoid colon are coded separately.

d. The intended root operation is attempted using one approach, but is converted to a different approach.

Example: Laparoscopic cholecystectomy converted to an open cholecystectomy is coded as percutaneous endoscopic Inspection and open Resection.

Discontinued or incomplete procedures

B3.3

If the intended procedure is discontinued or otherwise not completed, code the procedure to the root operation performed. If a procedure is discontinued before any other root operation is performed, code the root operation Inspection of the body part or anatomical region inspected.

Example: A planned aortic valve replacement procedure is discontinued after the initial thoracotomy and before any incision is made in the heart muscle, when the patient becomes hemodynamically unstable. This procedure is coded as an open Inspection of the mediastinum.

Biopsy procedures

B3.4a.

Biopsy procedures are coded using the root operations Excision, Extraction, or Drainage and the qualifier Diagnostic.

Examples: Fine needle aspiration biopsy of fluid in the lung is coded to the root operation Drainage with the qualifier Diagnostic. Biopsy of bone marrow is coded to the root operation Extraction with the qualifier Diagnostic.

Lymph node sampling for biopsy is coded to the root operation Excision with the qualifier Diagnostic.

Biopsy followed by more definitive treatment

B3.4b.

If a diagnostic Excision, Extraction, or Drainage procedure (biopsy) is followed by a more definitive procedure, such as Destruction, Excision or Resection at the same procedure site, both the biopsy and the more definitive treatment are coded.

Example: Biopsy of breast followed by partial mastectomy at the same procedure site, both the biopsy and the partial mastectomy procedure are coded.

Overlapping body layers

B3.5

If the root operations such as Excision, Extraction, Repair or Inspection are performed on overlapping layers of the musculoskeletal system, the body part specifying the deepest layer is coded.

Example: Excisional debridement that includes skin and subcutaneous tissue and muscle is coded to the muscle body part.

Bypass procedures

B3.6a

Bypass procedures are coded by identifying the body part bypassed "from" and the body part bypassed "to." The fourth character body part specifies the body part bypassed from, and the qualifier specifies the body part bypassed to.

Example: Bypass from stomach to jejunum, stomach is the body part and jejunum is the qualifier.

B3.6b

Coronary artery bypass procedures are coded differently than other bypass procedures as described in the previous guideline. Rather than identifying the body part bypassed from, the body part identifies the number of coronary arteries bypassed to, and the qualifier specifies the vessel bypassed from.

Example: Aortocoronary artery bypass of the left anterior descending coronary artery and the obtuse marginal coronary artery is classified in the body part axis of classification as two coronary arteries, and the qualifier specifies the aorta as the body part bypassed from.

B3.6c

If multiple coronary arteries are bypassed, a separate procedure is coded for each coronary artery site that uses a different device and/or qualifier.

Example: Aortocoronary artery bypass and internal mammary coronary artery bypass are coded separately.

Control vs. more definitive root operations

B3.7

The root operation Control is defined as, "Stopping, or attempting to stop, postprocedural or other acute bleeding." If an attempt to stop postprocedural or other acute bleeding is unsuccessful, and to stop the bleeding requires performing a more definitive root operation Bypass, Detachment, Excision, Extraction, Reposition, Replacement, or Resection, then the more definitive root operation is coded instead of Control.

Example: Resection of spleen to stop bleeding is coded to Resection instead of Control.

Excision vs. Resection

B3.8

PCS contains specific body parts for anatomical subdivisions of a body part, such as lobes of the lungs or liver and regions of the intestine. Resection of the specific body part is coded whenever all of the body part is cut out or off, rather than coding Excision of a less specific body part.

Example: Left upper lung lobectomy is coded to Resection of Upper Lung Lobe, Left rather than Excision of Lung, Left.

Excision for graft

B3.9

If an autograft is obtained from a different procedure site in order to complete the objective of the procedure, a separate procedure is coded, except when the seventh character qualifier value in the ICD-10-PCS table fully specifies the site from which the autograft was obtained.

Examples: Coronary bypass with excision of saphenous vein graft, excision of saphenous vein is coded separately.

Replacement of breast with autologous deep inferior epigastric artery perforator (DIEP) flap, excision of the DIEP flap is not code separately. The seventh character qualifier value Deep Inferior Epigastric Artery Perforator Flap in the Replacement table fully specifies the site of the autograft harvest.

Fusion procedures of the spine

B3.10a

The body part coded for a spinal vertebral joint(s) rendered immobile by a spinal fusion procedure is classified by the level of the spine (e.g. thoracic). There are distinct body part values for a single vertebral joint and for multiple vertebral joints at each spinal level.

Example: Body part values specify Lumbar Vertebral Joint, Lumbar Vertebral Joints, 2 or More and Lumbosacral Vertebral Joint.

B3.10b

If multiple vertebral joints are fused, a separate procedure is coded for each vertebral joint that uses a different device and/or qualifier.

Example: Fusion of lumbar vertebral joint, posterior approach, anterior column and fusion of lumbar vertebral joint, posterior approach, posterior column are coded separately.

B3.10c

Combinations of devices and materials are often used on a vertebral joint to render the joint immobile. When combinations of devices are used on the same vertebral joint, the device value coded for the procedure is as follows:

- If an interbody fusion device is used to render the joint immobile (containing bone graft or bone graft substitute), the procedure is coded with the device value Interbody Fusion Device
- If bone graft is the only device used to render the joint immobile, the procedure is coded with the device value Non-autologous Tissue Substitute or Autologous Tissue Substitute
- If a mixture of autologous and nonautologous bone graft (with or without biological or synthetic extenders or binders) is used to render the joint immobile, code the procedure with the device value Autologous Tissue Substitute

Examples: Fusion of a vertebral joint using a cage style interbody fusion device containing morsellized bone graft is coded to the device Interbody Fusion Device.

Fusion of a vertebral joint using a bone dowel interbody fusion device made of cadaver bone and packed with a mixture of local morsellized bone and demineralized bone matrix is coded to the device Interbody Fusion Device.

Fusion of a vertebral joint using both autologous bone graft and bone bank bone graft is coded to the device Autologous Tissue Substitute.

Inspection procedures

B3.11a

Inspection of a body part(s) performed in order to achieve the objective of a procedure is not coded separately.

Example: Fiberoptic bronchoscopy performed for irrigation of bronchus, only the irrigation procedure is coded.

B3.11b

If multiple tubular body parts are inspected, the most distal body part (the body part furthest from the starting point of the inspection) is coded. If multiple non-tubular body parts in a region are inspected, the body part that specifies the entire area inspected is coded.

Examples: Cystoureteroscopy with inspection of bladder and ureters is coded to the ureter body part value.

Exploratory laparotomy with general inspection of abdominal contents is coded to the peritoneal cavity body part value.

B3.11c

When both an Inspection procedure and another procedure are performed on the same body part during the same episode, if the Inspection procedure is performed using a different approach than the other procedure, the Inspection procedure is coded separately.

Example: Endoscopic Inspection of the duodenum is coded separately when open Excision of the duodenum is performed during the same procedural episode.

Occlusion vs. Restriction for vessel embolization procedures

B3.12

If the objective of an embolization procedure is to completely close a vessel, the root operation Occlusion is coded. If the objective of an embolization procedure is to narrow the lumen of a vessel, the root operation Restriction is coded.

Examples: Tumor embolization is coded to the root operation Occlusion because the objective of the procedure is to cut off the blood supply to the vessel.

Embolization of a cerebral aneurysm is coded to the root operation Restriction, because the objective of the procedure is not to close off the vessel entirely, but to narrow the lumen of the vessel at the site of the aneurysm where it is abnormally wide.

Release procedures

B3.13

In the root operation Release, the body part value coded is the body part being freed and not the tissue being manipulated or cut to free the body part.

Example: Lysis of intestinal adhesions is coded to the specific intestine body part value.

Release vs. Division

B3.14

If the sole objective of the procedure is freeing a body part without cutting the body part, the root operation is Release. If the sole objective of the procedure is separating or transecting a body part, the root operation is Division.

Examples: Freeing a nerve root from surrounding scar tissue to relieve pain is coded to the root operation Release.

Severing a nerve root to relieve pain is coded to the root operation Division.

Reposition for fracture treatment

B3.15

Reduction of a displaced fracture is coded to the root operation Reposition and the application of a cast or splint in conjunction with the Reposition procedure is not coded separately. Treatment of a nondisplaced fracture is coded to the procedure performed.

Examples:

Casting of a nondisplaced fracture is coded to the root operation Immobilization in the Placement section.
Putting a pin in a nondisplaced fracture is coded to the root operation Insertion.

Transplantation vs. Administration

B3.16

Putting in a mature and functioning living body part taken from another individual or animal is coded to the root operation Transplantation. Putting in autologous or nonautologous cells is coded to the Administration section.

Example: Putting in autologous or nonautologous bone marrow, pancreatic islet cells or stem cells is coded to the Administration section.

Transfer procedures using multiple tissue layers

B3.17

The root operation Transfer contains qualifiers that can be used to specify when a transfer flap is composed of more than one tissue layer, such as a musculocutaneous flap. For procedures involving transfer of multiple tissue layers including skin, subcutaneous tissue, fascia or muscle, the procedure is coded to the body part value that describes the deepest tissue layer in the flap, and the qualifier can be used to describe the other tissue layer(s) in the transfer flap.

Example: A musculocutaneous flap transfer is coded to the appropriate body part value in the body system Muscles, and the qualifier is used to describe the additional tissue layer(s) in the transfer flap.

Excision/Resection followed by replacement

B3.18

If an excision or resection of a body part is followed by a replacement procedure, code both procedures to identify each distinct objective, except when the excision or resection is considered integral and preparatory for the replacement procedure.

Examples: Mastectomy followed by reconstruction, both resection and replacement of the breast are coded to fully capture the distinct objectives of the procedures performed.

Maxillectomy with obturator reconstruction, both excision and replacement of the maxilla are coded to fully capture the distinct objectives of the procedures performed.

Excisional debridement of tendon with skin graft, both the excision of the tendon and the replacement of the skin with a graft are coded to fully capture the distinct objectives of the procedures performed.

Esophagectomy followed by reconstruction with colonic interposition, both the resection and the transfer of the large intestine to function as the esophagus are coded to fully capture the distinct objectives of the procedures performed.

Examples: Resection of a joint as part of a joint replacement procedure is considered integral and preparatory for the replacement of the joint and the resection is not coded separately.

Resection of a valve as part of a valve replacement procedure is considered integral and preparatory for the valve replacement and the resection is not coded separately.

All of the above coding guidelines are essential and must be followed when selecting codes. The following are some key concepts to keep in mind as you start to select ICD-10-PCS codes.

Take some time to read the ICD-10-PCS guidelines B3 to B18 a number of times as they provide the foundation for understanding ICD-10-PCS coding. It is best for new coders to take time to understand and recall the definitions for all root operations and be guided by the coding guidelines when selecting codes.

As stated in ICD-10-PCS guideline B3.1a you must have an understanding of the definitions of the root operations. For example it is essential that you understand the meaning of Excision versus the meaning of Resection as both involve the cutting out or off of a body part. The difference is that Excision is the cutting out or off, without replacement, a portion of a body part, while Resection is the cutting out or off, without replacement all of a body part. A physician completes an abdominal incision for the removal of the entire sigmoid colon. This is considered a resection and is coded to code 0DTN0ZZ.

As stated in ICD-10-PCS guideline B3.1b, coders must also understand the components of procedures that relate to specific root operations such as the opening of a surgical site or steps necessary to close the site as they are not coded separately. When an incision, such as a laparotomy, is completed to reach the surgical site to complete a biopsy of pancreas the laparotomy is not coded.

ICD-10-PCS guidelines B3.2a to B3.2d provides direction in coding multiple procedures that are completed during the same operative session. Coders need to make sure that all procedures are coded as per the guidelines to completely reflect the work that occurred during the operative session.

ICD-10-PCS guideline B3.2a provides guidance for coding the following situation: If percutaneous endoscopic biopsies are performed on both the common hepatic duct and the common bile duct both would be coded as diagnostic excisions as the body parts have distinct values in ICD-10-PCS Table 0FB. The body part value for the common hepatic duct is 7 and the value for the common bile duct is 9. Therefore code 0FB74ZX, for the biopsy of the common hepatic duct and code 0FB94ZX, for the biopsy of the common bile duct, is reported.

To better help you understand and organize the types of procedures use the following grouping of procedures.

The various root operations can be grouped into the following types of procedures which have similar intent:

1. Procedures that take out some or all of a body part—This includes the root operations of destruction, detachment, excision, extraction and resection.

2. Procedures that put in/put back or move some/all of a body part—This includes the root operations of reattachment, reposition, transfer and transplantation.

3. Procedures the take out or eliminate solid matter, fluids, or gases from a body part—This includes the root operations of drainage, extirpation and fragmentation.

4. Procedures that involve only examination of body parts and regions—This includes the root operations of inspection and map.

5. Procedures that alter the diameter/route of a tubular body part—This includes the root operations of bypass, dilation, occlusion and restriction.

6. Procedures that always involve devices—This includes the root operations of change, insertion, removal, replacement, revision and supplement.

7. Procedures that involve cutting or separation only—This includes the root operations of division and release.

8. Procedures that define other repairs—This includes the root operations of control and repair.

9. Procedures that define other objectives—This includes the root operations of alternation, creation and fusion.

Body Part

The fourth character for the Medical and Surgical codes represents the body part, the specific part of the body system on which the procedure is performed (e.g., pancreas, colic artery, auditory ossicle). The fourth-character assignments in this section get as detailed as auditory ossicle, right, or auditory ossicle, left. The coder will notice in some Tables the term *tubular body parts*. **Tubular body parts** are defined in ICD-10-PCS as hollow body parts that provide a route of passage for solids, liquids, or gases. Vessels for blood flow, the intestines for the flow of waste, and the respiratory tract for the flow of oxygen are examples. (See Figure 28-5 for an illustration of the tubular structures of the lungs.)

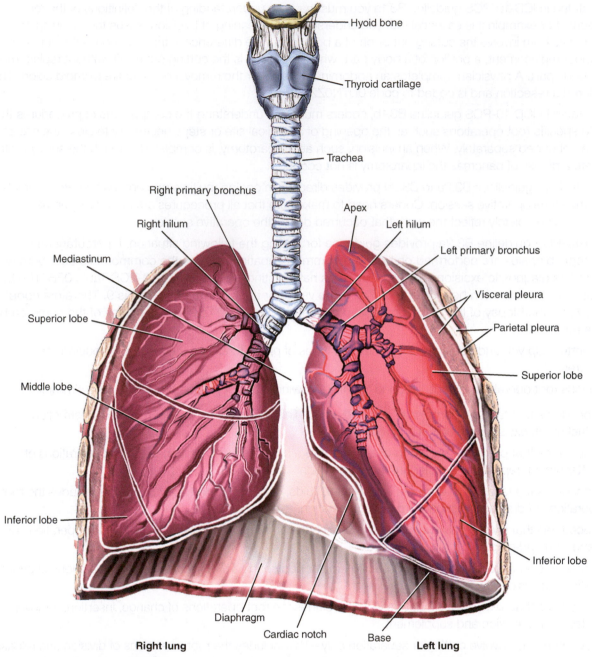

Hyoid bone

Thyroid cartilage

Trachea

Right primary bronchus

Right hilum

Apex

Left hilum

Mediastinum

Left primary bronchus

Superior lobe

Visceral pleura

Parietal pleura

Middle lobe

Superior lobe

Inferior lobe

Inferior lobe

Diaphragm

Cardiac notch

Base

Right lung

Left lung

FIGURE 28-5 Anterior view of lungs (From Lazo DL. *Fundamentals of Sectional Anatomy: An Imaging Approach*. Clifton Park, NY: Delmar, Cengage Learning, 2005, p. 125.).

ICD-10-PCS Official Coding Guidelines Relating to Body Part

The selection of ICD-10-PCS codes for the Medical and Surgical section is governed by the following coding guidelines that relate to body part:

ICD-10-PCS Official Coding Guidelines

B4. Body Part

General guidelines

B4.1a

If a procedure is performed on a portion of a body part that does not have a separate body part value, code the body part value corresponding to the whole body part.

Example: A procedure performed on the alveolar process of the mandible is coded to the mandible body part.

B4.1b

If the prefix "peri" is combined with a body part to identify the site of the procedure, and the site of the procedure is not further specified, then the procedure is coded to the body part named. This guideline applies only when a more specific body part value is not available.

Example: A procedure site identified as perirenal is coded to the kidney body part when the site of the procedure is not further specified.

A procedure site described in the documentation as peri-urethral, and the documentation also indicates that it is the vulvar tissue and not the urethral tissue that is the site of the procedure, then the procedure is coded to the vulva body part.

A procedure site documented as involving the periosteum is coded to the corresponding bone body part.

B4.1c

If a procedure is performed on a continuous section of a tubular body part, code the body part value corresponding to the furthest anatomical site from the point of entry.

Example: A procedure performed on a continuous section of artery from the femoral artery to the external iliac artery with the point of entry at the femoral artery is coded to the external iliac body part.

Branches of body parts

B4.2

Where a specific branch of a body part does not have its own body part value in PCS, the body part is typically coded to the closest proximal branch that has a specific body part value. In the cardiovascular body systems, if a general body part is available in the correct root operation table, and coding to a proximal branch would require assigning a code in a different body system, the procedure is coded using the general body part value.

Example: A procedure performed on the mandibular branch of the trigeminal nerve is coded to the trigeminal nerve body part value.

Occlusion of the bronchial artery is coded to the body part value Upper Artery in the body system Upper Arteries, and not to the body part value Thoracic Aorta, Descending in the body system Heart and Great Vessels.

Bilateral body part values

B4.3

Bilateral body part values are available for a limited number of body parts. If the identical procedure is performed on contralateral body parts, and a bilateral body part value exists for that body part, a single procedure is coded using the bilateral body part value. If no bilateral body part value exists, each procedure is coded separately using the appropriate body part value.

Example: The identical procedure performed on both fallopian tubes is coded once using the body part value Fallopian Tube, Bilateral. The identical procedure performed on both knee joints is coded twice using the body part values Knee Joint, Right and Knee Joint, Left.

Coronary arteries

B4.4

The coronary arteries are classified as a single body part that is further specified by number of arteries treated. One procedure code specifying multiple arteries is used when the same procedure is performed, including the same device and qualifier values.

Examples: Angioplasty of two distinct coronary arteries with placement of two stents is coded as Dilation of Coronary Artery, Two Arteries, with Two Intraluminal Devices.

Angioplasty of two distinct coronary arteries, one with stent placed and one without, is coded separately as Dilation of Coronary Artery, One Artery with Intraluminal Device, and Dilation of Coronary Artery, One Artery with no device.

Tendons, ligaments, bursae and fascia near a joint

B4.5

Procedures performed on tendons, ligaments, bursae and fascia supporting a joint are coded to the body part in the respective body system that is the focus of the procedure. Procedures performed on joint structures themselves are coded to the body part in the joint body systems.

Example: Repair of the anterior cruciate ligament of the knee is coded to the knee bursae and ligament body part in the bursae and ligaments body system.

Knee arthroscopy with shaving of articular cartilage is coded to the knee joint body part in the Lower Joints body system.

Skin, subcutaneous tissue and fascia overlying a joint

B4.6

If a procedure is performed on the skin, subcutaneous tissue or fascia overlying a joint, the procedure is coded to the following body part:

- Shoulder is coded to Upper Arm
- Elbow is coded to Lower Arm
- Wrist is coded to Lower Arm
- Hip is coded to Upper Leg
- Knee is coded to Lower Leg
- Ankle is coded to Foot

Fingers and toes

B4.7

If a body system does not contain a separate body part value for fingers, procedures performed on the fingers are coded to the body part value for the hand. If a body system does not contain a separate body part value for toes, procedures performed on the toes are coded to the body part value for the foot.

Example: Excision of finger muscle is coded to one of the hand muscle body part values in the Muscles body system.

Upper and lower intestinal tract

B4.8

In the Gastrointestinal body system, the general body part values Upper Intestinal Tract and Lower Intestinal Tract are provided as an option for the root operations Change, Inspection, Removal and Revision. Upper Intestinal Tract includes the portion of the gastrointestinal tract from the esophagus down to and including the duodenum, and Lower Intestinal Tract includes the portion of the gastrointestinal tract from the jejunum down to and including the rectum and anus.

Example: In the root operation Change table, change of a device in the jejunum is coded using the body part Lower Intestinal Tract.

Approach

The fifth-character place for Medical and Surgical codes is for the identification of the approach used in the procedure. An **approach** is the way in which the surgeon, physician, or provider performs a procedure. The following approaches are used in ICD-10-PCS for the Medical and Surgical section:

- **External**—Procedures performed directly on the skin or mucous membrane and procedures performed indirectly by the application of external force through the skin or mucous membrane (value of X). Figure 28-6 illustrates an external approach for a closed reduction of a fracture.

- **Open**—Cutting through the skin or mucous membrane and any other body layers necessary to expose the site of the procedure (value of 0). Figure 28-7 illustrates an open approach. An incision is made to remove the appendix.

- **Percutaneous**—Entry, by puncture or minor incision, of instrumentation through the skin or mucous membrane and any other body layers necessary to reach the site of the procedure (value of 3). Figure 28-8 illustrates a percutaneous approach to complete a percutaneous thoracentesis.

- **Percutaneous endoscopic**—Entry, by puncture or minor incision, of instrumentation through the skin or mucous membrane and any other body layers necessary to reach and *visualize* the site of the procedure (value of 4). Figure 28-9 illustrates a percutaneous endoscopic approach to complete a laparoscopic cholecystectomy.

- **Via natural or artificial opening**—Entry of instrumentation through a natural or artificial external opening to reach the site of the procedure (value of 7). Figure 28-10 illustrates an approach of inserting a nasogastric tube via a natural or artificial opening.

- **Via natural or artificial opening endoscopic**—Entry of instrumentation through a natural or artificial external opening to reach and *visualize* the site of the procedure (value of 8). Figure 28-11 illustrates an approach via a natural or artificial opening using an endoscope.

- **Via natural or artificial opening with percutaneous endoscopic assistance**—Entry of instrumentation through a natural or artificial external opening and entry, by puncture or minor incision, of instrumentation through the skin or mucous membrane and any other body layers necessary to aid in the performance of the procedure (value of F). Figure 28-12 illustrates an approach via a natural or artificial opening with percutaneous endoscopic assistance.

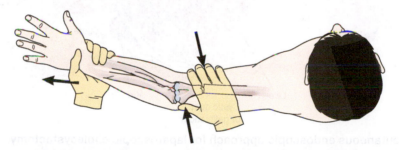

FIGURE 28-6 External approach for closed reduction of fracture.

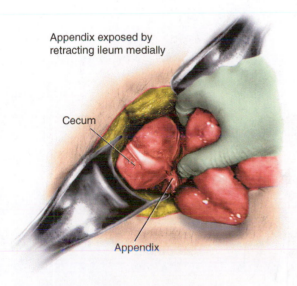

Appendix exposed by retracting ileum medially

Cecum

Appendix

FIGURE 28-7 Open approach for open appendectomy.

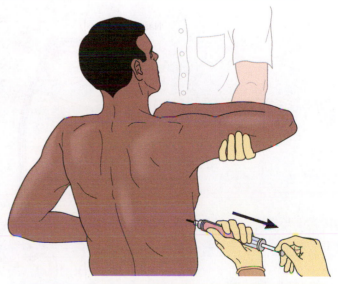

FIGURE 28-8 Percutaneous approach for percutaneous thoracentesis.

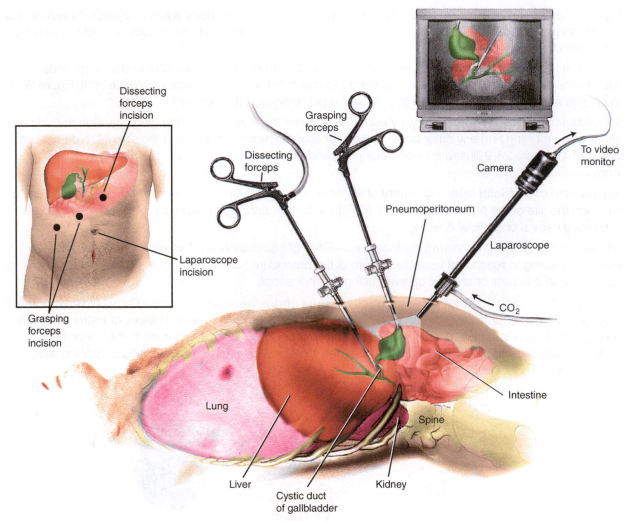

Dissecting
forceps
incision

Grasping
forceps

Dissecting
forceps

Camera

To video
monitor

Pneumoperitoneum

Laparoscope
incision

Laparoscope

Grasping
forceps
incision

CO_2

Lung

Intestine

Spine

Liver

Kidney

Cystic duct
of gallbladder

FIGURE 28-9 Percutaneous endoscopic approach for laparoscopic cholecystectomy.

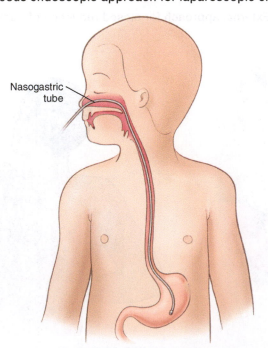

Nasogastric
tube

FIGURE 28-10 Insertion of nasogastric tube
via natural or artificial opening.

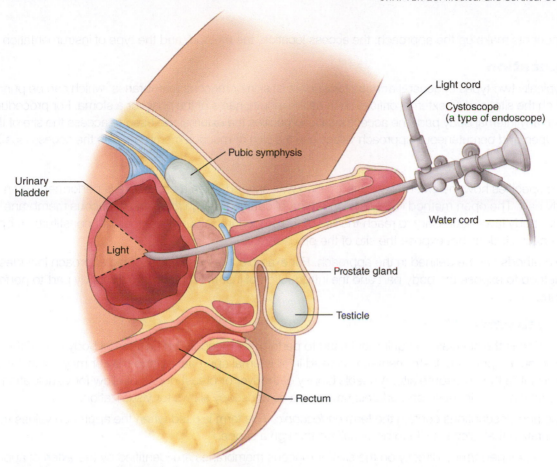

Light cord

Cystoscope
(a type of endoscope)

Pubic symphysis

Urinary
bladder

Water cord

Light

Prostate gland

Testicle

Rectum

FIGURE 28-11 Approach is via natural or artificial opening endoscopic for a cystoscopy, male. Endoscope is inserted via a natural opening.

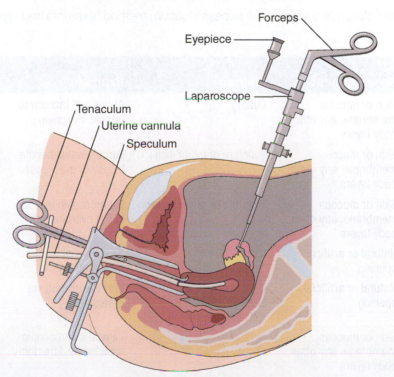

Forceps

Eyepiece

Laparoscope

Tenaculum

Uterine cannula

Speculum

FIGURE 28-12 Approach is via natural or artificial opening with percutaneous endoscopic assistance. Instrumentation is placed in vaginal canal and laparoscope is used for percutaneous endoscopic assistance.

Three components make up the approach: the access location, the method, and the type of instrumentation used.

Access Location

There are typically two types of general **access locations**: (1) skin or mucous membranes, which can be punctured or cut to reach the site, and (2) external orifices such as the mouth, nares of the nose, or a stoma. For procedures performed on any internal body part, the access location specifies the external site used to access the site of the procedure. Open and percutaneous approach values use the skin or mucous membranes as the access location.

Method

The **method** specifies how the external access location was entered when a procedure is performed on an internal body part. The open method identifies some type of cutting through the skin or mucous membrane and any other body layer necessary to reach the site of the procedure. A puncture does not constitute an open approach because it does not expose the site of the procedure.

Multiple methods can be defined in the approach. For example, the open endoscopic approach includes both the open method to expose the body part and the introduction of instrumentation into the body part to perform the procedure.

Type of Instrumentation

Instrumentation is the specialized equipment used to perform a procedure on an internal body part. Other than the basic open approach, instrumentation is used in all internal approaches and may or may not include the capacity to visualize the procedure site. A needle biopsy of the liver or breast does not allow for visualization with the instrumentation used in these procedures; however, a colonoscopy allows for visualization.

Some method descriptions contain the term *endoscopic*. This term is used when the approach values refer to the instrumentation that allows a site to be visualized through a scope.

The procedures performed directly on the skin or mucous membranes are identified by the external approach (e.g., skin excision). Procedures performed indirectly by the application of external force are also identified by the external approach (e.g., closed reduction of a fracture).

The following table will help coders identify the access location, method, example and type of instrumentation for each approach:

Approach	Access Location	Method	Example	Type of Instrumentation
Open	Skin or mucous membrane, any other body layers	Cutting	Abdominal incision to remove the colon	None
Percutaneous	Skin or mucous membrane, any other body layers	Puncture or minor incision	Percutaneous needle biopsy of the breast	Without visualization
Percutaneous endoscopic	Skin or mucous membrane, any other body layers	Puncture or minor incision	Laparoscopic excision of left ovarian cyst	With visualization
Via natural or artificial opening	Natural or artificial opening	Direct entry	Total vaginal hysterectomy	Without visualization
Via natural or artificial opening endoscopic	Natural or artificial opening	Direct entry with puncture or minor incision for instrumentation only	Urethral dilation via cystoscope	With visualization
Via natural or artificial opening with percutaneous endoscopic assistance	Skin or mucous membrane, any other body layers	Cutting	Vaginal laparoscopic-assisted hysterectomy	With visualization
External	Skin or mucous membrane	Direct or indirect application	Excision of scar on the skin of the right hand	None

ICD-10-PCS Official Coding Guidelines Relating to Approach

The selection of ICD-10-PCS codes for the Medical and Surgical section is governed by the following coding guidelines that relate to approach:

ICD-10-PCS Official Coding Guidelines

B5. Approach

Open approach with percutaneous endoscopic assistance

B5.2a

Procedures performed using the open approach with percutaneous endoscopic assistance are coded to the approach Open.

Example: Laparoscopic-assisted sigmoidectomy is coded to the approach Open.

Percutaneous endoscopic approach with extension of incision

B5.2b

Procedures performed using the percutaneous endoscopic approach, with incision or extension of an incision to assist in the removal of all or a portion of a body part or to anastomose a tubular body part to complete the procedure, are coded to the approach value Percutaneous Endoscopic.

Examples: Laparoscopic sigmoid colectomy with extension of stapling port for removal of specimen and direct anastomosis is coded to the approach value percutaneous endoscopic.

Laparoscopic nephrectomy with midline incision for removing the resected kidney is coded to the approach value percutaneous endoscopic.

Robotic-assisted laparoscopic prostatectomy with extension of incision for removal of the resected prostate is coded to the approach value percutaneous endoscopic.

External approach

B5.3a

Procedures performed within an orifice on structures that are visible without the aid of any instrumentation are coded to the approach External.

Example: Resection of tonsils is coded to the approach External.

B5.3b

Procedures performed indirectly by the application of external force through the intervening body layers are coded to the approach External.

Example: Closed reduction of fracture is coded to the approach External.

Percutaneous procedure via device

B5.4

Procedures performed percutaneously via a device placed for the procedure are coded to the approach Percutaneous.

Example: Fragmentation of kidney stone performed via percutaneous nephrostomy is coded to the approach Percutaneous.

Courtesy of the Centers for Medicare & Medicaid Services, www.cms.gov

Exercise 28.2—Approach

Using an ICD-10-PCS code book, identify the approach used and the procedure performed for each of the following examples. The first one is done for you.

Code	Approach	Description
1. 0SS00ZZ	Open	Open reposition of lumbar vertebral joint
2. 07JK0ZZ	_____	_____
3. 0UJ33ZZ	_____	_____
4. 00K83ZZ	_____	_____
5. 0UVC7DZ	_____	_____

Device

The sixth-character position indicates the device. This character is used only to specify devices that remain after a procedure is completed. There are four general types of devices:

- Grafts and Prostheses—This category includes joint prosthesis or skin grafts.
- Implants—An example of this is an IUD or a stent.
- Simple or Mechanical Appliances—An example would be an orthopedic pin.
- Electronic Appliances—Such as a cardiac pacemaker.

All devices can be removed; however, some devices cannot be removed unless another device replaces it. Scopes or other instruments used in visualization are not specified in the device value because they are specified in the approach. Figure 28-13 illustrates an internal fixation device that will remain in place.

Keep in mind the objective of the procedure. If the objective of a procedure is to insert a device, then the root operation is Insertion. If a device is put in to meet an objective other than Insertion, then the root operation defining the underlying objective of the procedure is used. If a joint replacement occurs, the root operation is Replacement, and the prosthetic device is specified in the device character.

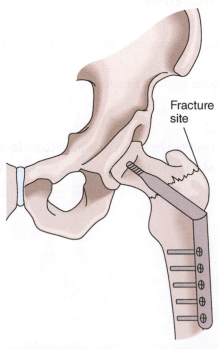

Fracture
site

FIGURE 28-13 Internal fixation device.

ICD-10-PCS contains a PCS Device Aggregation Table as an appendix in the ICD-10-PCS Manual. This table is used to assist the coder in determining the PCS description for specific devices. For example, this table can be utilized to determine that the term "Autograft" device is described in PCS as an Autologous Tissue Substitute.

ICD-10-PCS Official Coding Guidelines Relating to Device

The selection of ICD-10-PCS codes for the Medical and Surgical section is governed by the following coding guidelines that relate to devices:

ICD-10-PCS Official Coding Guidelines

B6. Device

General guidelines

B6.1a

A device is coded only if a device remains after the procedure is completed. If no device remains, the device value No Device is coded. In limited root operations, the classification provides the qualifier values Temporary and Intraoperative, for specific procedures involving clinically significant devices, where the purpose of the device is to be utilized for a brief duration during the procedure or current inpatient stay. If a device that is intended to remain after the procedure is completed requires removal before the end of the operative episode in which it was inserted (for example, the device size is inadequate or a complication occurs), both the insertion and removal of the device should be coded.

B6.1b

Materials such as sutures, ligatures, radiological markers and temporary post-operative wound drains are considered integral to the performance of a procedure and are not coded as devices.

B6.1c

Procedures performed on a device only and not on a body part are specified in the root operations Change, Irrigation, Removal and Revision, and are coded to the procedure performed.

Example: Irrigation of percutaneous nephrostomy tube is coded to the root operation Irrigation of indwelling device in the Administration section.

Drainage device

B6.2

A separate procedure to put in a drainage device is coded to the root operation Drainage with the device value Drainage Device.

Courtesy of the Centers for Medicare & Medicaid Services, www.cms.gov

The ICD-10-PCS guideline B6, entitled Device, provides specific examples that provide the coder guidance. Guideline B6.1a clearly states that a device is coded only if the device remains in place at the conclusion of the procedure. An example of such a procedure is an open reduction with internal fixation of a displaced right lateral ankle fracture. The code for this procedure is 0SSF04Z. The internal fixation device is the device that remains at the end of the procedure. In the sixth character position the 4 is used to indicate the device that remains. Reference ICD-10-PCS Table 0SS to locate the full code description.

When reading procedural notes it is important to note the materials and devices that are used during the procedures. It is important to not code materials that are integral to the performance of the procedure. As stated in guideline B6.1b materials such as sutures, ligatures, radiological markers and temporary post-operative wound drains are not coded as devices. So if a procedural note states "The subcutaneous tissue was reapproximated with an interrupted 5-0 undyed Vicryl suture and the skin was closed with Steri-Strips" even though the suture remains in place it is not coded as a device.

It is essential that coders have a clear understanding of how devices impact ICD-10-PCS coding.

Qualifier

The seventh character in a Medical and Surgical code is the qualifier. The **qualifier** is the information that identifies a unique value being reported for the individual procedure. If a qualifier is not needed in a code, the Table indicates that a *Z* is to be added as a placeholder to make the seven-character code.

Principles for the Medical and Surgical Section

The Medical and Surgical section was developed around four basic principles.

- *Composite terms are not root operations*—The objective of the procedure is the only component of the procedure specified in the root operation. Terms such as *tonsillectomy* and *laryngoscopy* are not root operations because they are specifying many components of a procedure.
  - Laryngoscopy is the *inspection* of the *larynx* using a scope to visualize through a natural or artificial opening endoscopic. The root operation is the inspection, identified by character 3 in the code. Character 4 of the same code would identify the body part, the larynx, and the approach is identified by character 5.
  - Tonsillectomy is the *removal* of the *tonsils*. The root operation is identified as an excision or a resection of the tonsils.

If these terms are referenced in the Index, the coder is then sent to the Tables with the first three characters of the code leading the coder to select the correct root operation and body system from within the Tables.

- *Root operations are based on the objective of the procedure*—As explained, the root operation is based on the objective of the procedure. The root operation is selected based on the procedure that the physician or provider actually performed. The intent of the service might or might not be the procedure performed, but for any number of reasons might need to be modified.
  - For example, the intended procedure might have been a femoral artery bypass. Once the bypass is performed, the blood flow is not producing the desired results, so an arterectomy is performed instead. The arterectomy is now reported because it is the procedure actually performed.
- *Combination procedures are coded separately*—In some cases multiple procedures are defined by distinct objectives. These multiple procedures may be performed during one operative session. If this is the case, multiple codes are used.
  - Endoscopy of bilateral stripping of maxillary sinus, codes 09DQ4ZZ and 09DR4ZZ. Because the procedure was performed bilaterally and the fourth character indicates the body part, we need to use Q for the right maxillary sinus and R for the left maxillary sinus to reflect the bilateral procedure.
- *The redo of procedures is necessary*—Procedures that need to be performed again, whether partially or completely, are coded to the root operation performed, *not* to the root operation *revision*. Revision is referenced if the procedure was being done to correct a malfunctioning or displaced device.
  - A patient may need to have a total knee replacement for the second time. The new prosthetic knee replacement is coded to the root operation replacement.
  - A patient might have trouble with the timing of a cardiac pacemaker. The doctor needs to go in and reset the pacemaker. In this case, revision is the correct place to reference because the cardiac pacemaker is malfunctioning.

Appendices in ICD-10-PCS

In the ICD-10-PCS Coding Manual, various appendices appear that assist the coder in code selection. The appendices provide further definition and comparisons of various root operations, devices, body parts, and qualifiers that are relevant to the Medical and Surgical section as well as other sections of ICD-10-PCS. Coders need to become familiar with the various appendices.

Exercise 28.3—Comparing Root Operations

Locate the appendices in the ICD-10-PCS Coding Manual. Locate the appendix entitled: Comparison of Medical and Surgical Root Operations. Use this to answer the following questions.

1. Name the root operations that take out some or all of a body part. _____
2. Name the root operations that put in/put back or move some/all of a body part. _____
3. Name the root operations that take out or eliminate solid matter, fluids, or gases from a body part.

_____

4. Name the root operations that involve only examination of body parts and regions. _____
5. Name the root operations that alter the diameter/route of a tubular body part. _____
6. Name the root operations that always involve devices. _____
7. Name the root operations that involve cutting or separation only. _____
8. Name the root operations that define other repairs. _____
9. Name the root operations that define objectives. _____

Exercise 28.4—Body Part Key

At times medical documentation will describe a specific body part. In order to select the appropriate body part value, the coder needs to be able to determine the PCS description of the body part. Locate the appendix in the ICD-10-PCS coding manual entitled: Body Part Key. This appendix can be used by the coder to identify the PCS description for specific anatomical terms. Use this appendix to list the PCS description for the anatomical term listed below or use the Alphabetic Index for ICD-10-PCS, as these anatomical terms are also listed in the Alphabetic Index.

Anatomical Term	PCS Description
1. Anterior vagal trunk	_____
2. Cricoid cartilage	_____
3. Bundle of His	_____
4. Renal plexus	_____
5. Precava	_____
6. Spinal dura mater	_____
7. Zygomaticus muscle	_____
8. Thyroid cartilage	_____
9. Xiphoid process	_____
10. Sweat gland	_____
11. Superior turbinate	_____
12. Sixth cranial nerve	_____
13. Right testicular vein	_____
14. Plantar metatarsal vein	_____
15. Optic chiasma	_____

Exercise 28.5—Device Key and Aggregation Table.

Numerous devices are used that remain in the body after a procedure. Locate the appendix in the ICD-10-PCS manual entitled: Device Key and Aggregation Table. This appendix can be used by the coder to identify the PCS description for specific device terms. Use this appendix to list the PCS description for the device term listed below or use the Alphabetic Index for ICD-10-PCS as these device terms are also listed in the Alphabetic Index.

Device Term   **PCS Description**

1. CoAxia NeuroFlo catheter   _____
2. Zenith Flex AAA Endovascular Graft   _____
3. Knee (implant) insert   _____
4. Nitinol framed polymer mesh   _____
5. REALIZE Adjustable Gastric Band   _____
6. Cystostomy tube   _____
7. Bovine pericardial valve   _____
8. Blood glucose monitoring system   _____
9. Ex-PRESS mini glaucoma shunt   _____
10. Deep brain neurostimulator lead   _____

Summary

- The Medical and Surgical section of ICD-10-PCS contains the majority of the codes used in procedure reporting.
- The ICD-10-PCS codes are made up of seven characters.
- The *0* is used to identify the Medical and Surgical section of ICD-10-PCS.
- The third-character position in the codes for Medical and Surgical indicates the root operation, such as detachment, division, excision, removal, and replacement.
- The different types of approaches are specified by the fifth character in the Medical and Surgical section code.
- In developing the Medical and Surgical section of ICD-10-PCS, four specific principles were followed.

Internet Links

To learn more about surgical coding, visit **www.aafp.org**.

To learn more about surgical coding relating to ICD-10-PCS, visit **www.cms.hhs.gov/ICD10**.

Chapter Review

True/False

Indicate whether each statement is true (T) or false (F).

1. _____ The third character in a Medical and Surgical code specifies the objective of the procedure.

2. _____ Completely closing an orifice or lumen of a tubular body part is extirpation.

3. _____ Making a new structure that does not physically take the place of a body part is fragmentation.

4. _____ The root operation of Control is the stopping or attempting to stop postprocedural bleeding.

5. _____ A percutaneous procedure is a puncture or small incision of instrumentation through the skin to reach the site of the procedure.

Coding Guidelines True/False

Review the ICD-10-PCS Official Guidelines for Coding and Reporting and indicate if the statement(s) is true or false.

6. _____ Procedures performed on tendons, ligaments, bursae, and fascia supporting a joint are coded to the body part in the respective body system that is the focus of the procedure.

7. _____ If a procedure is performed on the skin, subcutaneous tissue, or fascia overlying a joint, the procedure is coded to the following body part:
   - Shoulder is coded to Upper Arm
   - Elbow is coded to Upper Arm
   - Wrist is coded to Lower Arm

8. _____ Procedures performed using the open approach with percutaneous endoscopic assistance are coded to the approach Open.

9. _____ Materials such as sutures, ligatures, radiological markers, and temporary postoperative wound drains are coded as devices.

10. _____ A separate procedure to put in a drainage device is coded to the root operation Drainage with the device value Drainage Device.

Coding Assignments

Instructions: Using an ICD-10-PCS code book, assign the proper procedure code to the following procedural statements.

1. exploratory arthrotomy of left knee (open)   _____

2. incision with removal of K-wire fixation, right first metatarsal   _____

3. open bilateral breast augmentation with silicone implants   _____

4. intraoperative cardiac mapping during open heart surgery   _____

5. DIP, low joint amputation of right thumb   _____

6. excision of basal cell carcinoma of lower lip   _____

7. open resection of papillary muscle   _____

8. percutaneous division of right foot tendon   _____

9. percutaneous destruction of right retina   _____

10. percutaneous biopsy of right gastrocnemius muscle   _____

11. closure of open wound of neck   _____

12. incision and removal of right lacrimal duct stone   _____

13. open adrenalorrhaphy of left adrenal gland   _____

14. release of scar contracture, skin of right ear   _____

15. reattachment of severed right ear   _____

16. percutaneous ligation of right renal vein   _____

17. open resection of ventricular septum   _____

18. open division of anal sphincter   _____

19. open dilation of old anastomosis, splenic artery   _____

20. digital rectal exam   _____

21. mechanical percutaneous thrombectomy of right ulnar artery   _____

22. reduction, closed, for dislocation of the left knee joint   _____

23. open right kidney total nephrectomy   _____

24. total, open bladder cystectomy   _____

25. open transposition of median nerve   _____

Case Studies

Instructions: Review each case study and select the correct ICD-10-PCS code.

Case 1

Patient is a 10-year-old male who presents today with right wrist pain. Patient was riding his skateboard when he hit a crack in the sidewalk and fell forward. His arms were outstretched when he hit the concrete. He denies loss of consciousness, which was confirmed by witnesses. He has not had any vomiting, abdominal pain, or dizziness.

X-ray of the right arm and wrist reveals a dislocation of the right wrist. A closed reduction of the distal radioulnar joint was performed. Follow-up x-ray revealed that the bones are now in place. The child was fitted for a splint and shoulder immobilizer, which are to be worn for the next 10 days. We will see him back at the end of the 10 days to reevaluate the injury.

ICD-10-PCS Code Assignment: _____

Case 2

This is a healthy 21-year-old female who presents today for removal of an impacted molar, lower left side. The panoramic radiograph shows the tooth to be in a good position now, but due to the pain it is causing the patient and the slight movement of the existing teeth, surgical intervention is needed to get the tooth out before any further movement can occur.

PROCEDURE: The patient was given Versed and conscious sedation was achieved. The lower jaw area was also injected with 2% Lidocaine. The gingiva was removed from the surface

(continues)

(*continued*)

with an elevator. A #15 blade was used to incise the gum line. The soft tissue was dissected to expose the impacted tooth and the tooth was removed in whole. The area was then rinsed and all debris removed before two sutures were placed with 4-0 silk. The patient was in good condition when returned to the recovery suite.

ICD-10-PCS Code Assignment: _____

Case 3

This 30-year-old patient with a complaint of ear pain was placed in supine position and the left ear was examined using an operating microscope. The tympanic membrane was assessed after all debris was removed from the area. There was also noted to be a small, dark-colored foreign object, almost resembling a bead. The object was removed and antibiotic solution was placed in the ear canal. The patient was awoken and transferred to the recovery room in excellent condition.

ICD-10-PCS Code Assignment: _____

Case 4

Operative Report

PRE- AND POSTOPERATIVE DIAGNOSIS: Hydrocele

ANESTHESIA: General

Under general anesthesia, this 36-year-old male was prepped and draped in the usual fashion. After placing the patient in the lithotomy position, a 3.5-cm incision was made in the left scrotum and a hydrocele was visualized. Hemostasis was achieved. The hydrocele was located in the tunica vaginalis and was dissected and brought through the incision site. The hydrocele was surgically excised, and a drain was placed. The wound was closed in layers using 3-0 chromic sutures. The patient was sent to the recovery room in stable condition and tolerated the procedure well.

ICD-10-PCS Code Assignment: _____

Case 5

Pre- and Postoperative Diagnosis

ANESTHESIA: General

This 64-year-old female patient was taken to the OR and placed in the supine position. An upper midline incision was made and retractors were placed. The LUQ was explored

(*continues*)

(*continued*)

and splenic ligaments and the gastric veins were identified and divided. Dissection at the splenic hilum occurred and the splenic vessels were identified. The splenic artery and vein were double ligated, suture ligated, and divided. The entire spleen was removed and hemostasis was achieved. Blood loss was minimal. A drain was placed and the wound was closed in layers with #3-0 Vicryl for the deep layers and #4-0 Vicryl for the skin. The patient tolerated the procedure well and was taken to the postop recovery room in satisfactory condition. Procedure: Splenectomy with no complications.

ICD-10-PCS Code Assignment: _____

Case 6

DIAGNOSIS: Adenotonsillar hyperplasia

INDICATIONS: This 24-year-old female has had an extensive history of tonsillitis and strep throat. This surgery is a last resort to end this cycle. She is aware of the risks and benefits of this surgery and has given written consent.

PROCEDURE: Patient presented to the operating room and was placed on the operating table in the supine position. She was induced with general anesthesia and then prepped and draped in the usual fashion. Attention was directed to the right tonsil. The tonsil was clutched near the superior pole, retracted medially and inferiorly. The anterior pillar was dissected from the superior to inferior and then anterior to posterior. The tonsil was freed and removed. The left tonsil was removed in the same manner. Attention was then directed to the adenoids through the nares. The soft palate was retracted superiorly and the adenoid tissue was identified. An adenoid curette was used to remove the adenoids. Gauze packing was used and then all points were cauterized. The procedure was completed and the patient was sent to the recovery room in stable condition.

ICD-10-PCS Code Assignment: _____

Case 7

PRE-OPERATIVE DIAGNOSIS: Orbital lesion, OS-left eye

POSTOPERATIVE DIAGNOSIS: Orbital lesion, pathology pending

PROCEDURE: Patient was prepped with proparacaine instilled in the left eye and 2% Lidocaine with 1:200,000 epinephrine injected in the superior aspect of the left orbit.

The upper lid was everted and a herniated lesion was located and measured at 0.50 cm in diameter. The herniated lesion was clamped and excised. Cauterization was then used to stop the bleeding. The mass was sent to pathology. The superior fornix was repaired and antibiotic ointment was applied to the eye. An eye pad was placed over the eye. The patient tolerated the procedure well and was in good condition when sent to the operating area.

ICD-10-PCS Code Assignment: _____

Case 8

PRE- AND POSTOPERATIVE PROCEDURE: Impacted upper molar

Patient was given conscious sedation using Versed. The site was also injected with 2% Lidocaine. The gingiva was removed from the surface with an elevator and then a #15 blade was used to incise the gum line. The soft tissue was dissected to expose the impacted tooth and it was able to be removed in whole. The area was then rinsed and all debris removed before two sutures were placed with 4-0 silk. The patient was in good condition and returned to the recovery suite.

ICD-10-PCS Code Assignment: _____

Case 9

This patient presents today after a nonproductive cough for the last 4 weeks. Last week he had a chest x-ray and it was felt that further diagnostic testing is necessary. Today he underwent a fiberoptic bronchoscopy of the tracheobroncial tree. The images were sent to radiology for interpretation. A plan of care will be determined after the radiology report is read.

ICD-10-PCS Code Assignment: _____

Case 10

PRE-OPERATIVE DIAGNOSIS: Left breast mass

POSTOPERATIVE DIAGNOSIS: Pending pathology

This 45-year-old female patient found a suspicious lump in her left breast. Mammogram completed last week revealed a suspicious area in the left breast. There were no other findings from the mammogram.

PROCEDURE: General anesthesia was administered. The left breast was prepped and draped in the normal sterile fashion. A 3-cm-long incision was made in the upper portion of the breast. Cautery dissection was used to elevate the skin flaps. Hemostasis was achieved and the dissection was carried down to remove the tissue and a biopsy was taken. The specimen was sent to pathology. The wounds were carefully closed and dressed. There were no complications and there was minimal blood loss.

ICD-10-PCS Code Assignment: _____

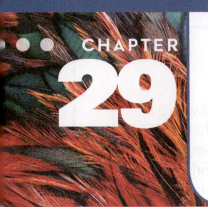

Obstetrics Section

Chapter Outline

Chapter Objectives

At the conclusion of this chapter, you should be able to:

1. Identify the character meanings used for the ICD-10-PCS Obstetrics section.
2. Discuss the root operations used for the ICD-10-PCS Obstetrics section.
3. Identify the purpose of the ICD-10-PCS Obstetrics Section.
4. Identify the approach, device, and qualifiers used the ICD-10-PCS Obstetrics section.
5. Code procedures in the ICD-10-PCS Obstetrics section.
6. Select ICD-10-PCS codes from the Obstetrics Section for case studies.

Key Terms

Abortion	Drainage	Inspection	Repair
Amniocentesis	Extraction	Obstetrics	Reposition
Change	Forceps delivery	Products of conception	Resection
Delivery	Insertion	Removal	Transplantation

REMINDER: As you work through this chapter, you will need to have a copy of the ICD-10-PCS coding book to reference. For this chapter, you will also need to reference the ICD-10-PCS Official Guidelines for Coding and Reporting. These guidelines can be found in Appendix B which are now available on the Student Companion site and MINDTAP From Cengage.

Introduction

The second section found in ICD-10-PCS is "Obstetrics." **Obstetrics** is the specialty that treats women during pregnancy, childbirth, and the period immediately after childbirth. This section of ICD-10-PCS is used to build codes for procedures performed on the products of conception. The term **products of conception** is defined as all the physical components of a pregnancy and includes the fetus, embryo, amnion, umbilical cord, and the placenta. The codes do not differentiate the gestational age of the products of conception, which is defined in the selection of an ICD-10-CM diagnostic code.

ICD-10-PCS Official Coding Guidelines for Obstetric Section

The following coding guidelines govern the Obstetric Section of ICD-10-PCS:

ICD-10-PCS Official Coding Guidelines

C. Obstetrics Section

Products of conception

C1

Procedures performed on the products of conception are coded to the Obstetrics section. Procedures performed on the pregnant female other than the products of conception are coded to the appropriate root operation in the Medical and Surgical section.

Example: Amniocentesis is coded to the products of conception body part in the Obstetrics section. Repair of obstetric urethral laceration is coded to the urethra body part in the Medical and Surgical section.

Procedures following delivery or abortion

C2

Procedures performed following a delivery or abortion for curettage of the endometrium or evacuation of retained products of conception are all coded in the Obstetrics section, to the root operation Extraction and the body part Products of Conception, Retained. Diagnostic or therapeutic dilation and curettage performed during times other than the postpartum or post-abortion period are all coded in the Medical and Surgical section, to the root operation Extraction and the body part Endometrium.

Courtesy of the Centers for Medicare & Medicaid Services, www.cms.gov

Obstetrics Section of the ICD-10-PCS

The seven characters in this section have the same meaning as they do in the Medical and Surgical section.

1	2	3	4	5	6	7
Section	Body system	Root operation	Body part	Approach	Device	Qualifier

Section

The first-character value indicating obstetric procedure codes is 1. Any codes that relate to obstetrics can be identified with the use of this character value.

Body System

The second-character value in this chapter indicating the body system is always going to be 0, Pregnancy.

Root Operation

One of 12 root operations is used for the Obstetrics section of ICD-10-PCS to select a value for the third-character position. The root operations include the following:

- **Abortion**—Artificially terminating a pregnancy. This value is only used in the Obstetrics section of PCS. (value of A) This root operation is unique to the Obstetrics Section of ICD-10-PCS.
- **Change**—Taking out or off a device from a body part and putting back an identical or similar device in or on the same body part without cutting or puncturing the skin or mucous membrane (value of 2)
- **Delivery**—Assisting the passage of the products of conception from the genital canal (value of E). This root operation is unique to the Obstetrics Section of ICD-10-PCS.
- **Drainage**—Taking or letting out fluids and/or gases from a body part (value of 9)
- **Extraction**—Pulling or stripping out or off all or a portion of a body part by the use of force (value of D)
- **Insertion**—Putting in a nonbiological appliance that monitors, assists, performs, or prevents a physiological function but does not physically take the place of a body part (value of H)
- **Inspection**—Visually and/or manually exploring a body part (value of J)
- **Removal**—Taking out or off a device from a body part region or orifice (value of P)
- **Repair**—Restoring, to the extent possible, a body part to its normal anatomic structure and function (value of Q)
- **Reposition**—Moving to its normal location or other suitable location all or a portion of a body part (value of S)
- **Resection**—Cutting out or off, without replacement, all of a body part (value of T)
- **Transplantation**—Putting in or on all or a portion of a living body part taken from another individual or animal to physically take the place and/or function of all or a portion of a similar body part (value of Y)

It should be noted that cesarean section is not a separate root operation in ICD-10-PCS. When a cesarean section occurs, the root operation is Extraction because the objective of the procedure is the pulling out of all or a portion of a body part.

Body Part

The fourth-character values in the Obstetrics section are:

- Products of conception (value of 0)
- Products of conception, retained (value of 1)
- Products of conception, ectopic (value of 2)

Approach

There are six approach values for the fifth character for the Obstetrics section:

- Open (value of 0)
- Percutaneous (value of 3)
- Percutaneous endoscopic (value of 4)
- Via natural or artificial opening (value of 7)
- Via natural or artificial opening endoscopic (value of 8)
- External (value of X)

These approach definitions are the same as in the Medical and Surgical section. It should be noted that for an abortion procedure that uses a laminaria or an abortifacient, the approach is via natural or artificial opening.

Device

The sixth character represents the device. The device values for Obstetrics are:

- Monitoring electrode (value of 3)
- Other device (value of Y)
- No device (value of Z)

An example of a device that would be used in this section is a fetal monitoring electrode.

Qualifier

The seventh character represents the qualifier. There are numerous qualifier values for Obstetrics, as shown in Figure 29-1, which are selected to further define the values for the fifth and sixth characters. The qualifiers are

1: OBSTETRICS
0: PREGNANCY

Approach Character 5		Device Character 6		Qualifier Character 7	
0	Open	3	Monitoring Electrode	0	High
3	Percutaneous	Y	Other Device	1	Low
4	Percutaneous Endoscopic	Z	No Device	2	Extraperitoneal
7	Via Natural of Artificial Opening			3	Low Forceps
8	Via Natural or Artificial Opening Endoscopic			4	Mid Forceps
X	External			5	High Forceps
				6	Vacuum
				7	Internal Version
				8	Other
				9	Fetal Blood OR Manual
				A	Fetal Cerebrospinal Fluid
				B	Fetal Fluid, Other
				C	Amniotic Fluid, Therapeutic
				D	Fluid, Other
				E	Nervous System
				F	Cardiovascular System
				G	Lymphatics and Hermic
				H	Eye
				J	Ear, Nose, and Sinus
				K	Respiratory System
				L	Mouth and Throat
				M	Gastrointestinal System
				N	Hepatobiliary and Pancreas
				P	Endocrine System
				Q	Skin
				R	Musculoskeletal System
				S	Urinary System
				T	Female Reproductive System
				U	Amniotic Fluid, Diagnostic
				V	Male Reproductive System
				W	Laminaria
				X	Abortifacient
				Y	Other Body System
				Z	No Qualifier

FIGURE 29-1 Qualifier values for the Obstetrics section.

used to identify the specific aspect of a root operation. For example, for an extraction involving the use of forceps, one of the following qualifier values would be used: low forceps (value of 3), mid forceps (value of 4), high forceps (value of 5).

Not all of the seventh-character values are used for each root operation. Coders must reference the Obstetric tables to determine the seventh-character values that are applicable to each root operation. Figure 29-2 shows the tables for the following root operations: Change, Drainage, and Abortion. Note that each operation has its own set of qualifiers. The root operation of Change, for instance, has only the qualifier of Z, whereas the root operation of Drainage has a number of qualifier values: 9, A, B, C, D, and U.

1: OBSTETRICS
0: PREGNANCY
2: CHANGE: Taking out or off a device from a body part and putting back an identical or similar device in or on the same body part without cutting or puncturing the skin or a mucous membrane

Body Part Character 4	Approach Character 5	Device Character 6	Qualifier Character 7
0 Products of Conception	7 Via Natural or Artificial Opening	3 Monitoring Electrode Y Other Device	Z No Qualifier

1: OBSTETRICS
0: PREGNANCY
9: DRAINAGE: Taking or letting out fluids and/or gases from a body part

Body Part Character 4	Approach Character 5	Device Character 6	Qualifier Character 7
0 Products of Conception	0 Open 3 Percutaneous 4 Percutaneous Endoscopic 7 Via Natural or Artificial Opening 8 Via Natural or Artificial Opening Endoscopic	Z No Device	9 Fetal Blood A Fetal Cerebrospinal Fluid B Fetal Fluid, Other C Amniotic Fluid, Therapeutic D Fluid, Other U Amniotic Fluid, Diagnostic

1: OBSTETRICS
0: PREGNANCY
A: ABORTION: Artificially terminating a pregnancy

Body Part Character 4	Approach Character 5	Device Character 6	Qualifier Character 7
0 Products of Conception	0 Open 3 Percutaneous 4 Percutaneous Endoscopic 8 Via Natural or Artificial Opening Endoscopic	Z No Device	Z No Qualifier
0 Products of Conception	7 Via Natural or Artificial Opening	Z No Device	6 Vacuum W Laminaria X Abortifacient Z No Qualifier

FIGURE 29-2 Tables for Change, Drainage, and Abortion.

Exercise 29.1—Identifying Qualifiers

Using an ICD-10-PCS coding manual, for each of the root operations listed, identify the qualifiers that are applicable to the root operation in the Obstetrics section. The first one is completed for you.

Root Operation	Qualifiers
1. Change	Z
2. Abortion	_____
3. Insertion	_____
4. Repair	_____
5. Transplantation	_____

Procedure Highlights

The following are some of the common procedures coded to this section of ICD-10-PCS.

Abortion

When an artificial termination of pregnancy occurs, Table 10A is used to select a code. In the seventh-character position the table identifies if a laminaria or abortifacient was used or if the procedure was completed by mechanical means. If an abortifacient or laminaria is used the approach is then Via Natural or Artificial Opening. For all mechanical means of abortion when instrumentation is used, a device value of Z, no device, is used.

Amniocentesis

Amniocentesis is a procedure in which a needle is inserted into the amniotic sac to withdraw fluid for examination. Figure 29-3 illustrates an amniocentesis and the preparation of a specimen for analysis.

> **EXAMPLE:** To code the statement "endoscopic percutaneous amniocentesis for drainage of amniotic fluid for diagnostic purposes," the coder references the term *amniocentesis* in the Index of ICD-10-PCS. Here the coder finds 1090. Referring to this table, the coder then selects the following values: 10904ZU. Note that an amniocentesis is a type of drainage.

Delivery

A normal delivery includes the stages of labor, as illustrated in Figure 29-4.

> **EXAMPLE:** To code a delivery, the coder references the term *delivery* in the Index. Here coder finds "delivery," then "products of conception." The Index then lists 10E0XZZ. This table is then referenced. ICD-10-PCS codes a delivery as 10E0XZZ. The term *delivery* applies to a manually assisted, vaginal delivery in which there is assistance of the passage of the fetus from the genital canal.

Cesarean Deliveries

A cesarean delivery is coded in ICD-10-PCS from the Obstetrics Section. The coder would first reference the main term Cesarean Section or the main term of Extraction to construct a code from Table 10D.

Forceps Extraction

During some deliveries, the use of forceps is necessary. A **forceps delivery** occurs when an instrument is used to grasp the fetus to assist in delivery. When forceps are used during a delivery, the procedure is considered a type of extraction because the baby is being pulled through the birth canal.

> **EXAMPLE:** The coder references the term *extraction* in the Index, then "products of conception." Here the coder finds the various types of extractions listed. The following code should be selected for a low forceps delivery: 10D07Z3.

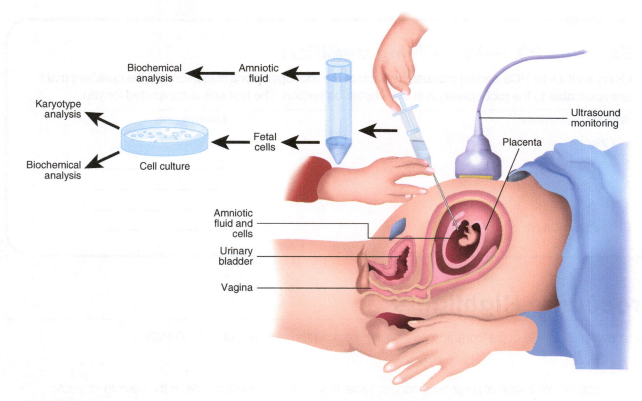

FIGURE 29-3 Amniocentesis and preparation of specimen for amniotic fluid analysis.

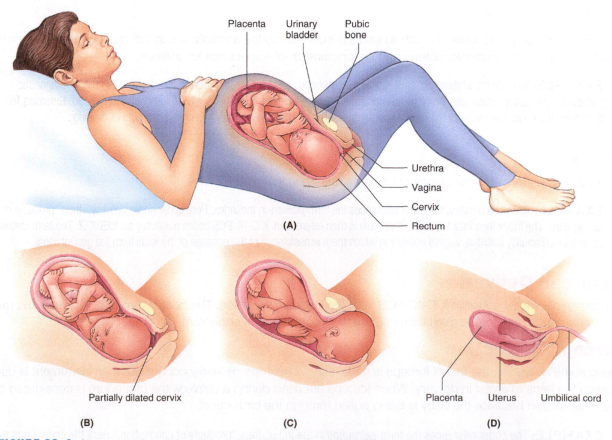

FIGURE 29-4 Stages of labor: (A) position of the fetus before labor; (B) first stage of labor, cervical dilation; (C) second stage of labor, fetal delivery; (D) third stage of labor, delivery of placenta.

Summary

- The first-character value for obstetric procedure codes is 1.
- The second-character value for the body system is pregnancy, with a value of 0.
- Represented in the third-character position is one of 12 root operations for the Obstetrics section of ICD-10-PCS.
- The fourth-character values in the Obstetrics section are 0, 1, and 2 for the body parts.
- The fifth character represents the approach, and there are six different approach values.
- The sixth character represents the device, with three possible values.
- The seventh character represents the qualifiers.

Internet Links

To learn more about types of deliveries, visit the National Women's Health Resource Center at **www.healthywomen.org**.

To learn more about procedures that pertain to obstetrics, visit **www.mayoclinic.org/obstetrics**.

Chapter Review

True/False

Indicate whether each statement is true (T) or false (F).

1. _____ The Obstetric section of ICD-10-PCS is used to build codes for procedures performed on the products of conception.
2. _____ The Obstetric section codes differentiate the gestational age of the products of conception.
3. _____ A forceps delivery occurs when an instrument is used to grasp the fetus to assist in delivery.
4. _____ In the third character for root operation, the letter K is used to represent Inspection.
5. _____ When amniotic fluid is extracted for a therapeutic reason, the correct qualifier to report is C.

Coding Assignments

Instructions: For each procedure, select the correct ICD-10-PCS code.

1. open approach to drain fetal blood from fetus _____
2. removal of retained placenta via birth canal _____
3. delivery with high forceps _____
4. drainage of fetal cerebrospinal fluid, open approach _____
5. induced abortion, percutaneous endoscopic approach _____
6. open incision to inspect fetal development _____
7. drainage of amniotic fluid for diagnostic review via open approach _____
8. vacuum extraction of fetus for delivery _____
9. extraperitoneal extraction of fetus, open approach _____
10. drainage of fetal blood from fetus at 21-week gestation, percutaneous approach _____
11. therapeutic drainage of amniotic fluid, via incision _____
12. resection of ectopic pregnancy, open approach _____
13. open insertion of monitoring electrode into fetus _____
14. diagnostic percutaneous endoscopic drainage of amniotic fluid _____

15. endoscopic extraction of retained products of conception via birth canal _____

16. percutaneous fetal spinal tap _____

17. removal of fetal monitoring electrode via the vagina _____

18. percutaneous fetal blood drainage _____

19. abortion by laminaria insertion _____

20. fetal eye transplant, laparoscopic _____

21. amniocentesis for diagnostic review of fluid _____

22. internal version for vaginal delivery _____

23. change of monitoring electrodes that were previously placed on fetal scalp _____

24. delivery with low forceps _____

25. percutaneous fetal blood draw from fetus _____

Case Studies

Instructions: Review each case study and select the correct ICD-10-PCS code.

Case 1

INDICATIONS FOR PROCEDURE: This is a 29-year-old gravida 1, para 0, who is 37 weeks' gestational age by dates and ultrasound. She has presented with elevated blood pressure of 151/103. Lab values showed platelet count of 54,000, normal liver function test, a hematocrit of 35.0, and normal PT and PTT. It was felt that the patient was suffering from preeclampsia when examination revealed intrauterine growth retardation and hematemesis. Contractions were occurring but not regularly. Patient was dilated 3 cm, but due to the problems presented, we felt delivery could not wait. Patient was advised that an emergency cesarean was needed, and she agreed.

PROCEDURE: This 29-year-old female was brought to the OR, after which epidural anesthesia was administered. Once patient showed no response to sensitivity, we proceeded. Patient was supine and right hip was slightly elevated to keep pressure off the vena cava. A low transverse incision with a #10 blade was carried to the level of the fascia. Mayo scissors were used to open the incision laterally. The posterior fascia was dissected bluntly from the rectus abdominus muscle. The aponeurosis was cut superiorly near the umbilicus and inferiorly to the symphysis pubis. Clamps were placed, and Metzenbaum scissors were then used to make a longitudinal peritoneal incision and extend the fascial opening. At this point, we were able to palpate the uterus, and fetal position was good. The bladder was freed from the uterus and retracted, a small transverse incision was made in the lower uterine segment, and the amniotic sac was exposed and incised. I then manipulated the fetus from the uterus. The infant female was drawn out, and the mouth and nose were immediately suctioned. The umbilical cord was clamped and cut, and cord samples were sent for pathology. The placenta was then recovered, and then a laparotomy sponge was used to clean the interior before a layered closure was performed: 2-0 absorbable sutures were used when closing the uterus. 3-0 Vicryl was used to close the bladder. The skin was closed with staples. Patient tolerated procedure well; mother and baby were fine.

ICD-10-PCS Code Assignment: _____

Case 2

INDICATIONS FOR SURGERY: A 34-year-old female presents with severe abdominal pain. After examination was completed and ultrasound results were reviewed, it was determined that patient had an ectopic pregnancy and surgical intervention was needed.

PROCEDURE: Patient was taken to the operating room, and after general anesthesia was induced, she was prepped and draped in the usual sterile fashion. Examination was performed after anesthesia, which showed a normal-sized, nontender uterus, a left adnexal mass, and a fullness in the vagina, all consistent with hyperperitoneum. A 10-mm trocar was inserted directly into the abdomen through a small incision in the umbilicus. Using 3.5 liters of carbon dioxide, a pneumoperitoneum was created. The hemoperitoneum was noticed, and another 10-mm trocar was placed in a small suprapubic incision. Two 5-mm ports were also placed under direct visualization in both the right and left lower quadrants. With an irrigator and aspirator, the hemoperitoneum was reduced. The left fallopian tube was noted to be almost to the point of rupture due to a mass in the tube. The fallopian tube was distended beyond repair; so this needed to be removed. The tube was tied off and removed with its contents through an Endo Catch bag through the 10-mm port. Inspection of the abdomen noted no other problems; adequate hemostasis was noted, and ports were removed. Defects were closed with 0 Vicryl, and the skin was closed with 4-0 Dexon. She was sent to the recovery room in stable condition.

ICD-10-PCS Code Assignment: _____

Case 3

DIAGNOSIS: False labor without delivery, antepartum complication

This patient is a 20-year-old female who presents today dilated 7 cm with contractions occurring every 3–4 minutes lasting 30–40 seconds. This mother is also an admitted cocaine addict who is worried about how her baby will be when born. At this time we are going to try to obtain a blood sample of the fetus to determine whether we need to have any special services on standby in the NICU.

The fetal monitor is showing a stable heart rate at this time. The amniotic sac is broken, and the amnioscope is inserted through the vagina. A 0.05-mm incision is made in the scalp, and a blood sample is aspirated into a tube for a STAT to the lab. Contractions stopped, and the baby was not delivered at this time.

Procedure completed was an endoscopic drainage via the vagina for fetal blood sample.

ICD-10-PCS Code Assignment: _____

Case 4

Discharge Summary

ADMISSION DATE: 5/6/xx

DISCHARGE DATE: 5/8/xx

HISTORY: This patient is gravida 2, para 1 and was seen in my office for her prenatal visits, which were uneventful. She was admitted with a history of contractions every 3 to 5 minutes. Cervix was 100% effaced and 9 cm dilated.

HOSPITAL COURSE: The patient's water broke at 2 am and after 3 hours the patient delivered a baby girl with an Apgar score of 8 at 1 minute and 10 at 5 minutes. Postpartum care was uneventful. The patient was discharged 2 days later.

INSTRUCTIONS TO PATIENT: Diet as tolerated. Tylenol as needed for pain. She is to follow up in my office in 2 weeks.

ICD-10-PCS Code Assignment: _____

Case 5

Admission Note

This 29-week-pregnant patient is experiencing eclampsia. She is being admitted today so the fetus can be monitored closely.

WEIGHT: 160 pounds. This is a 15-pound weight gain for the patient since the start of her pregnancy. Blood pressure is 140/80. Lab: Urinalysis showed protein present.

Patient is complaining of increased headaches and dizziness.

VAGINAL EXAM: Normal

HEENT: Face appears swollen

EXREMITIES: Edema of feet and hands

PLAN: Patient placed on low-salt diet. Vaginally inserted fetal monitoring electrodes were placed.

ICD-10-PCS Code Assignment: _____

Placement Section

Chapter Outline

Chapter Objectives

At the conclusion of this chapter, you should be able to:

1. Identify the purpose of the ICD-10-PCS Placement Section.
2. Identify the character meanings used for the ICD-10-PCS Placement Section.
3. Discuss the root operations used for the ICD-10-PCS Placement Section.
4. Identify the approach, device, and qualifiers used in the ICD-10-PCS Placement Section.
5. Code procedures in the ICD-10-PCS Placement Section.
6. Select ICD-10-PCS codes from the Placement Section for case studies.

Key Terms

Change
Compression

Dressing
Immobilization

Packing
Removal

Traction

REMINDER: As you work through this chapter, you will need to have a copy of the ICD-10-PCS coding book to reference. For this chapter, you will also need to reference the ICD-10-PCS Official Guidelines for Coding and Reporting. These guidelines can be found in Appendix B which are now available on the Student Companion site and MINDTAP From Cengage.

Introduction

The third section found in ICD-10-PCS is "Placement." Placement procedures include those in which a device is put on or into a body region. The devices are placed to pack, immobilize, stretch, or compress an area.

Placement Section of the ICD-10-PCS

The seven characters in this section have the same meanings as in the Medical and Surgical Section:

1	2	3	4	5	6	7
Section	Body system	Root operation	Body region	Approach	Device	Qualifier

Section

The first-character value for placement procedure codes is 2.

Body System: Anatomical Regions and Anatomical Orifices

The second-character value for the body system has two values: anatomical regions with a value of W and anatomical orifices with a value of Y.

Root Operation

There are seven root operations for the Placement section of ICD-10-PCS. Root operations for the Placement section include only those procedures that are performed without making an incision or a puncture:

- **Change**—Taking out or off a device from a body part and putting back an identical or similar device in or on the same body part without cutting or puncturing the skin or mucous membrane (value of 0)
- **Compression**—Putting pressure on a body region (value of 1)
- **Dressing**—Putting material on a body region for protection (value of 2)
- **Immobilization**—Limiting or preventing motion of a body region (value of 3)
- **Packing**—Putting material in a body region or orifice (value of 4)
- **Removal**—Taking out or off a device from a body part (value of 5)
- **Traction**—Exerting a pulling force on a body region in a distal direction (value of 6)

Body Regions and Orifices

The fourth-character values in the Placement section are:

- Body regions—30 values, are used only with the body system character of W, Anatomical regions.
- Natural orifices—6 values, are used only with the body system character of Y, Anatomical orifices.

See Figure 30-1 for the list of the values for the fourth character, the body system character W. Figure 30-2 contains a list of the values for the body system character of Y. Note that the fourth-character values are different depending on whether you are coding for the body system character of W or Y.

Approach

There is only one approach value: X, External. This is because all placement procedures are performed in one of two manners:

- By direct application on the skin or mucous membrane
- By indirectly applying external force through the skin or mucous membrane

2: PLACEMENT

W: ANATOMICAL REGIONS

Operation—Character 3	Body Region—Character 4
0 Change	0 Head
1 Compression	1 Face
2 Dressing	2 Neck
3 Immobilization	3 Abdominal Wall
4 Packing	4 Chest Wall
5 Removal	5 Back
6 Traction	6 Inguinal Region, Right
	7 Inguinal Region, Left
	8 Upper Extremity, Right
	9 Upper Extremity, Left
	A Upper Arm, Right
	B Upper Arm, Left
	C Lower Arm, Right
	D Lower Arm, Left
	E Hand, Right
	F Hand, Left
	G Thumb, Right
	H Thumb, Left
	J Finger, Right
	K Finger, Left
	L Lower Extremity, Right
	M Lower Extremity, Left
	N Upper Leg, Right
	P Upper Leg, Left
	Q Lower Leg, Right
	R Lower Leg, Left
	S Foot, Right
	T Foot, Left
	U Toe, Right
	V Toe, Left

FIGURE 30-1 Values for the body system character W.

2: PLACEMENT

Y: ANATOMICAL ORIFICES

Operation—Character 3	Body Region—Character 4
0 Change	0 Mouth and Pharynx
4 Packing	1 Nasal
5 Removal	2 Ear
	3 Anorectal
	4 Female Genital Tract
	5 Urethra

FIGURE 30-2 Values for the body system character Y.

Device

The devices placed during the procedure are specified by the sixth character.

The device values for Placement are different for the anatomical region value of W and the anatomical orifice value of Y. The device characters for the anatomical region value of W are:

- 0, Traction apparatus
- 1, Splint
- 2, Cast
- 3, Brace
- 4, Bandage
- 5, Packing material
- 6, Pressure dressing
- 7, Intermittent pressure device
- 9, Wire
- Y, Other device

For the anatomical orifice value of Y, there is only one value: 5, Packing material.

Coders must carefully reference the Tables to review the assignment of the sixth character because there is differentiation among the Tables.

Qualifier

The seventh character represents the qualifier. For the Placement section of ICD-10-CM, there is only one value used: Z, No qualifier.

Exercise 30.1—Identifying Device Characters

Using an ICD-10-PCS coding manual, for each of the operation blocks, identify the device characters from the Placement Section that are applicable. The first one is completed for you.

Operation Block	Possible Device Characters
1. 2W00X	0, 1, 2, 3, 4, 5, 6, 7, Y
2. 2W02X	_____
3. 2W14X	_____
4. 2W44X	_____
5. 2W33X	_____

Procedure Highlights

Here are of the some common procedures that are coded to this section of the code book.

Cast Application

When a bone is broken or when a body part needs to be immobilized, various devices can be applied to immobilize the area. Body regions can be immobilized by splints, cast, braces, traction apparatus/devices, and other devices. The placement of these devices is coded by using Table 2W3 in the Placement section.

To select codes, the coder first locates the term *immobilization* in the Index. This Index entry is then further divided by body region.

> **EXAMPLE:** A cast application on the upper right leg is coded to 2W3NX2Z.

Dressing Application

At times wounds have to be dressed, that is, covered. When dressings are applied, Table 2W2 is used. To locate *dressing application* in the Index, reference the term *dressing*. The Index is then further divided by body region.

> **EXAMPLE:** The code for a dressing application on the left foot is 2W2TX4Z.

Packing

When an area is bleeding, it may need to be packed with packing material. Table 2W4 is used to report the packing of body regions, and Table 2Y4 is used to report the packing of a body orifice. To report packing, the term to reference in the Index is *packing*. The entry is then subdivided into the various body regions or orifice.

> **EXAMPLE:** To code a packing of the nose, assign the code 2Y41X5Z.

Summary

- The first-character value for placement procedure codes is 2.
- The second-character value for the body system has two values: W and Y.
- There are seven root operations for the Placement Section of ICD-10-PCS.
- The fourth character has 30 values for the W anatomical regions and 6 values for the Y anatomical orifices.
- There is only one approach value for the fifth character: X, External.
- The sixth character specifies the devices placed.
- The seventh character always means "no qualifier," represented by the character Z.

Internet Link

To learn about the placement of casts, splints, braces, and the like, visit ***https://www.urmc.rochester.edu/encyclopedia*** and search on the type of device such as casts. There is very detailed information about casts and splints on the site from the university. The site and encyclopedia can also be used for procedures in other body systems and other diseases.

Chapter Review

True/False

Indicate whether each statement is true (T) or false (F).

1. _____ The Placement Section of ICD-10-PCS is used to build codes for procedures performed only on the bones.

2. _____ Compression is exerting a pulling force on a body region in a distal direction.

3. _____ Packing is putting material in a body region or orifice.

4. _____ In the third character for root operation, for anatomical region, the number 2 is used for dressing.

5. _____ When a pressure dressing is used during compression, the sixth-character value is 6.

Coding Assignments

Instructions: Review each case study and select the correct ICD-10-PCS code.

1. splint change, head   _____
2. bandage change for open wound on neck   _____
3. replacement of packing material on right chest wall   _____
4. replacement cast applied on left upper extremity   _____
5. brace change on left lower extremity due to patient growth _____
6. pressure dressing applied for compression of left foot   _____
7. bandage dressing application on left inguinal region   _____
8. brace immobilization of head due to skull fracture   _____
9. compression of right toe using intermittent pressure device _____
10. splint immobilization of right foot due to sprain   _____
11. cast application right foot   _____
12. splint applied to left toe for immobilization   _____
13. abdominal wall packing using sterile packing material _____
14. removal of traction apparatus on head   _____
15. removal of packing material from wound on head   _____
16. traction apparatus removal of device on face   _____
17. placement of traction apparatus on left toe   _____
18. packing of anorectal region using packing material   _____
19. removal of urethra packing material   _____
20. packing of ear with sterile packing   _____
21. application of intermittent pressure device dressing to the upper left leg _____
22. placement of cast on left upper leg   _____
23. placement of brace on right thumb   _____
24. packing of back with sterile packing material   _____
25. dressing of left hand   _____

Case Studies

Instructions: Review each case study and select the correct ICD-10-PCS code.

Case 1

Patient is a 9-year-old male who presents today with pain in his right arm after falling off his bike. He was not unconscious at any time. His right arm is swollen, and the pain is increased when his arm is moved. X-ray of the right arm showed a fracture in the upper extremity. The fracture is well aligned and no alignment is necessary. A cast was placed on the right upper extremity.

ICD-10-PCS Code Assignment: _____

Case 2

Mrs. Smith was admitted to the nursing home on Thursday, and the nursing staff noted that she has a 2-by-3-cm wound on her back on the left side. Today I applied a sterile dressing to the area to protect it from infection.

ICD-10-PCS Code Assignment: _____

Case 3

Emergency Room Note

This 78-year-old male patient presents with a nose bleed for the last 4 hours. The bleeding has increased over the last hour. He has a platelet disorder, which is treated by Dr. Young. I packed the nasal area to stop the bleeding. I instructed him to follow up with Dr. Young in 1 day.

ICD-10-PCS Code Assignment: _____

Case 4

This 16-year-old female presents today following a soccer game in which she injured her right index finger. The finger is not broken but it is swollen. I placed a splint on the right index finger and instructed the patient to wear the splint for the next 5 days and then to return to my office.

ICD-10-PCS Code Assignment: _____

Case 5

This 39-year-old male patient was using a sharp knife and cut his left thumb. He refused to have it sutured closed. I explained to him the advantages of sutures but he still refused. The wound was dressed and I instructed him to change the dressing each day. He is to return to my office if the site becomes swollen and red.

ICD-10-PCS Code Assignment: _____

Administration Section

Chapter Outline

Chapter Objectives

At the conclusion of this chapter, you should be able to:

1. Identify the character meanings used for the ICD-10-PCS Administration Section.
2. Describe the root operations used for the ICD-10-PCS Administration Section.
3. List the body/system region values in the ICD-10-PCS Administration Section.
4. Identify the approach, device, and qualifiers used in the ICD-10-PCS Administration Section.
5. Code procedures in the ICD-10-PCS Administration Section.
6. Select ICD-10-PCS codes from the Administration Section for case studies.

Key Terms

Introduction	Irrigation	Transfusion

> **REMINDER:** As you work through this chapter, you will need to have a copy of the ICD-10-PCS coding book to reference. For this chapter, you will also need to reference the ICD-10-PCS Official Guidelines for Coding and Reporting. These guidelines can be found in Appendix B which are now available on the Student Companion site and MINDTAP From Cengage.

Introduction

The section titled "Administration" is the fourth section found in ICD-10-PCS. This section reports procedures in which a therapeutic, prophylactic, protective, diagnostic, nutritional, or physiological substance is put into or on the body.

Administration Section of the ICD-10-PCS

The seven characters in this section have the following meanings:

1	2	3	4	5	6	7
Section	Body system: Physiological systems and anatomical regions	Root operation	Body/system region	Approach	Substance	Qualifier

Section

The first-character value used to identify the Administration Section is 3.

Body System: Physiological Systems and Anatomical Regions

The second character for the physiological systems and anatomical regions has three values:

- Circulatory system—used for reporting transfusion procedures (value of 0)
- Indwelling device—(value of C)
- Physiological systems and anatomical regions—(value of E)

Root Operation

There are three root operations for the Administration Section of ICD-10-PCS:

- **Introduction**—Putting in or on a therapeutic, diagnostic, nutritional, physiological, or prophylactic substance except blood or blood products, with a character representation of 0
- **Irrigation**—Putting in or on a cleansing substance, with a character representation of 1
- **Transfusion**—Putting in blood or blood products, with a character representation of 2

Body/System Region

The fourth-character value in the Administration Section defines the site where the substance is administered. The character values vary according to the physiological system and anatomical regions. The fourth-character values are as follows:

- Circulatory body system:
  - Peripheral vein (value of 3)
  - Central vein (value of 4)
  - Products of conception, circulatory (value of 7)
  - Vein (value of 8)
- For indwelling devices, there is only one value of Z.
- For physiological systems and anatomical regions, there are 33 values. See Figure 31-1 for the list of the values.

Remember that the fourth character identifies the site in which the substance is administered, not the site where the substance administered takes effect.

3: ADMINISTRATION
E: PHYSIOLOGICAL SYSTEMS AND ANATOMICAL REGIONS

Operation—Character 3	Body System/Region—Character 4
0 Introduction 1 Irrigation	0 Skin and Mucous Membranes 1 Subcutaneous Tissue 2 Muscle 3 Peripheral Vein 4 Central Vein 5 Peripheral Artery 6 Central Artery 7 Coronary Artery 8 Heart 9 Nose A Bone Marrow B Ear C Eye D Mouth and Pharynx E Products of Conception F Respiratory Tract G Upper GI H Lower GI J Biliary and Pancreatic Tract K Genitourinary Tract L Pleural Cavity M Peritoneal Cavity N Male Reproductive P Female Reproductive Q Cranial Cavity and Brain R Spinal Canal S Epidural Space T Peripheral Nerves and Plexi U Joints V Bones W Lymphatics X Cranial Nerves Y Pericardial Cavity

FIGURE 31-1 List of the values for physiological systems and anatomical regions.

Approach

The fifth character identifies the approach. The approaches of intradermal, subcutaneous, and intramuscular injections or introductions are all considered percutaneous approaches. The placement of a catheter into an internal site is also considered a type of percutaneous approach. The approach values are as follows:

- Open (value of 0)
- Percutaneous (value of 3)
- Percutaneous Endoscopic (value of 4)
- Via natural or artificial opening (value of 7)

- Via natural or artificial opening endoscopic (value of 8)
- External (value of X)

The Tables need to be referenced to locate the value that is valid for each physiological system and anatomical region based on the documentation.

Substance

The sixth character identifies the substance (instead of device) being introduced into the body. The values vary according to the physiological system and anatomical region. See Figure 31-2 for the sixth-character values used for the circulatory system associated with Table 302. This table needs to be referenced to determine which substance character is relevant for circulatory transfusion into the peripheral veins and arteries, as well as for products of conception as they relate to the circulatory system. The documentation needs to be referenced to determine which substance character is relevant for each body system character.

Figure 31-3 lists the sixth-character values for physiological systems and anatomical regions. Tables 3E0 and 3E1 need to be referenced for character assignment based on the documentation and the procedure performed.

Coders must carefully reference the tables to review the assignment of the sixth character because there is differentiation among the tables. Attention to the procedure being performed and to the body area involved is essential to proper code assignment.

Qualifier

The seventh character represents the qualifier. For the Administration section of ICD-10-PCS, the values for this character vary according to the table being used. For Table 302, the following qualifiers are used: Z, No qualifier; 0, Autologous; 1, Nonautologous; 2, Allogeneic, Related; 3, Allogeneic, Unrelated; and 4, Allogeneic, Unspecified. For Table 3C1, the only qualifier is Z. See Figure 31-4 for a list of the values for Table 3E1.

Exercise 31.1—Identifying Qualifier Characters

Using an ICD-10-PCS coding manual, for each of the operation blocks, identify the qualifier(s) that are applicable in the Administration Section. The first one is completed for you.

Operation Block	Possible Qualifier Characters
1. 3E1CX8	X, Z
2. 3E0E30	
3. 30233A	
4. 3C1ZX8	
5. 3E0130	

Section	3	Administration
Body System	0	Circulatory
Operation	2	Transfusion: Putting in blood or blood products

Body System/Region	Approach	Substance	Qualifier
3 Peripheral Vein 4 Central Vein	0 Open 3 Percutaneous	A Stem Cells, Embryonic	Z No Qualifier
3 Peripheral Vein 4 Central Vein	0 Open 3 Percutaneous	C Hematopoietic Stem/Progenitor Cells, Genetically Modified	0 Autologous
3 Peripheral Vein 4 Central Vein	0 Open 3 Percutaneous	G Bone Marrow X Stem Cells, Cord Blood Y Stem Cells, Hematopoietic	0 Autologous 2 Allogeneic, Related 3 Allogeneic, Unrelated 4 Allogeneic, Unspecified
3 Peripheral Vein 4 Central Vein	0 Open 3 Percutaneous	H Whole Blood J Serum Albumin K Frozen Plasma L Fresh Plasma M Plasma Cryoprecipitate N Red Blood Cells P Frozen Red Cells Q White Cells R Platelets S Globulin T Fibrinogen V Antihemophilic Factors W Factor IX	0 Autologous 1 Nonautologous
3 Peripheral Vein 4 Central Vein	0 Open 3 Percutaneous	U Stem Cells, T-cell Depleted Hematopoietic	2 Allogeneic, Related 3 Allogeneic, Unrelated 4 Allogeneic, Unspecified
7 Products of Conception, Circulatory	3 Percutaneous 7 Via Natural or Artificial Opening	H Whole Blood J Serum Albumin K Frozen Plasma L Fresh Plasma M Plasma Cryoprecipitate N Red Blood Cells P Frozen Red Cells Q White Cells R Platelets S Globulin T Fibrinogen V Antihemophilic Factors W Factor IX	1 Nonautologous
8 Vein	0 Open 3 Percutaneous	B 4-Factor Prothrombin Complex Concentrate	1 Nonautologous

FIGURE 31-2 Sixth-character values used for the circulatory system associated with Table 302.

3: ADMINISTRATION
E: PHYSIOLOGICAL SYSTEMS AND ANATOMICAL REGIONS

Approach Character 5	Substance Character 6	Qualifier Character 7
0 Open	0 Antineoplastic	0 Autologous
3 Percutaneous	1 Thrombolytic	1 Nonautologous
4 Percutaneous Endoscopic	2 Anti-infective	2 High-dose Interleukin-2
7 Via Natural or Artificial Opening	3 Anti-inflammatory	3 Low-dose Interleukin-2
8 Via Natural or Artificial Opening Endoscopic	4 Serum, Toxoid and Vaccine	4 Liquid Brachytherapy Radioisotope
X External	5 Adhesion Barrier	5 Other Antineoplastic
	6 Nutritional Substance	6 Recombinant Human-activated Protein C
	7 Electrolytic and Water Balance Substance	7 Other Thrombolytic
	8 Irrigating Substance	8 Oxazolidinones
	9 Dialysate	9 Other Anti-infective
	A Stem Cells, Embryonic	A Anti-Infective Envelope
	B Anesthetic Agent	B Recombinant Bone Morphogenetic Protein
	E Stem Cells, Somatic	C Other Substance
	F Intracirculatory Anesthetic	D Nitric Oxide
	G Other Therapeutic Substance	F Other Gas
	H Radioactive Substance	G Insulin
	K Other Diagnostic Substance	H Human B-type Natriuretic Peptide
	L Sperm	J Other Hormone
	M Pigment	K Immunostimulator
	N Analgesics, Hypnotics, Sedatives	L Immunosuppressive
	P Platelet Inhibitor	M Monoclonal Antibody
	Q Fertilized Ovum	N Blood Brain Barrier Disruption
	R Antiarrhythmic	P Clofarabine
	S Gas	Q Glucarpidase
	T Destructive Agent	X Diagnostic
	U Pancreatic Islet Cells	Z No Qualifier
	V Hormone	
	W Immunotherapeutic	
	X Vasopressor	

FIGURE 31-3 Sixth-character values for physiological systems and anatomical regions.

3: ADMINISTRATION
E: PHYSIOLOGICAL SYSTEMS AND ANATOMICAL REGIONS
1: IRRIGATION: Putting in or on a cleansing substance

Body System/Region Character 4	Approach Character 5	Substance Character 6	Qualifier Character 7
0 Skin and Mucous Membranes C Eye	3 Percutaneous X External	8 Irrigating Substance	X Diagnostic Z No Qualifier

9 Nose
B Ear
F Respiratory Tract
G Upper GI
H Lower GI
J Biliary and Pancreatic
      Tract
K Genitourinary Tract
N Male Reproductive
P Female Reproductive
	3 Percutaneous
	7 Via Natural or
	      Artificial
	      Opening
	8 Via Natural or
	      Artificial Open-
	      ing Endoscopic
		8 Irrigating Substance	X Diagnostic
			Z No Qualifier

L Pleural Cavity Q Cranial Cavity and Brain R Spinal Canal S Epidural Space Y Pericardial Cavity	3 Percutaneous	8 Irrigating Substance	X Diagnostic Z No Qualifier
M Peritoneal Cavity	3 Percutaneous	8 Irrigating Substance	X Diagnostic Z No Qualifier
M Peritoneal Cavity	3 Percutaneous	9 Dialysate	Z No Qualifier
U Joints	3 Percutaneous 4 Percutaneous Endoscopic	8 Irrigating Substance	X Diagnostic Z No Qualifier

FIGURE 31-4 Seventh-character values for Table 3E1.

Summary

- The first-character value for Administration procedure codes is 3.
- The second-character value for the body system has three values: 0, C, or E.
- There are three root operations for the Administration section of ICD-10-PCS.
- The fourth-character values in the Administration section vary according to the physiological system and anatomical regions.
- The fifth character identifies the approach and includes values of 0, 3, 4, 7, 8, and X.
- The sixth character identifies the substance being introduced into the body.
- The seventh character is a qualifier and the values vary according to the table used.

Chapter Review

True/False

Indicate whether each statement is true (T) or false (F).

1. _____ There are three root operations for the Administration section of ICD-10-PCS.

2. _____ The sixth character identifies the device being used to introduce the substance into the body.

3. _____ Intradermal, subcutaneous, and intramuscular injections or introductions are all considered percutaneous approaches.

4. _____ The first-character value for the Administration section is 3.

5. _____ For indwelling devices, there is only one value of Z.

Coding Assignments

Instructions: For each procedure, select the correct ICD-10-PCS code.

1. transfusion of embryonic stem cells into peripheral vein, open approach

    _____

2. transfusion of nonautologous frozen plasma into peripheral vein, open approach

    _____

3. transfusion of nonautologous platelets into peripheral vein, open approach

    _____

4. transfusion of autologous hematopoietic stem cells into peripheral vein, open approach

    _____

5. transfusion of nonautologous frozen red cells into peripheral vein, percutaneous approach

    _____

6. transfusion of autologous bone marrow into central vein, open approach

    _____

7. introduction of insulin into central artery, open approach

    _____

8. introduction of serum, toxoid, and vaccine into central artery, percutaneous approach

    _____

9. introduction of platelet inhibitor into central artery, percutaneous approach

    _____

10. introduction of blood brain barrier disruption substance into central vein, percutaneous approach

    _____

11. transfusion of nonautologous antihemophiliac factors into products of conception, circulatory, via natural or artificial opening

    _____

12. irrigation of indwelling device using irrigating substance, external approach _____

13. introduction of oxazolidinones into skin and mucous membranes, external approach _____

14. introduction of anti-inflammatory into ear, external approach _____

15. introduction of analgesics into ear, external approach _____

16. introduction of liquid brachytherapy radioisotope antineoplastic into eye, percutaneous approach _____

17. introduction of monoclonal antibody into eye via natural opening _____

18. introduction of liquid brachytherapy radioisotope into pharynx, external approach _____

19. introduction of serum, toxoid, and vaccine into mouth, percutaneous approach _____

20. introduction of monoclonal antibody into products of conception, via artificial opening _____

21. injection of anti-inflammatory substance into left shoulder joint _____

22. injection of anesthetic agent into epidural space _____

23. percutaneous irrigation of peritoneal cavity with Dialysate _____

24. IM administration of influenza vaccine _____

25. autologous bone marrow transplant via peripheral vein _____

Case Studies

Instructions: Review each case study and select the correct ICD-10-PCS code.

Case 1

Transfusion Unit Note

This 67-year-old female is diagnosed with leukemia and presents today for a nonautologous transfusion of platelets due to a low platelet count. The transfusion was completed in the left arm in a peripheral vein percutaneously. The patient tolerated the procedure well and was told to follow up with her physician in 4 days.

ICD-10-PCS Code Assignment: _____

Case 2

Skilled Nursing Care Note

This 79-year-old male patient has an indwelling catheter, and today it was irrigated per standard nursing protocol. The catheter was cleansed with an irrigating substance.

ICD-10-PCS Code Assignment: _____

Case 3

This 9-year-old patient presents with an inflamed left eye. His mother states that he has gotten "something" in this eye and it has become irritated. His left eye is red and the conjunctiva is inflamed. I felt it best to irrigate the eye with ophthalmic irrigating solution. I also gave the patient a prescription for ophthalmic antibiotics. He is to follow up with me in 10 days or call if the eye becomes worse.

ICD-10-PCS Code Assignment: _____

Case 4

This 20-year-old patient is a competitive college gymnast who has ongoing pain in her lower back due to inflammation. She presents today for an epidural injection of an anti-inflammatory in the sacral area.

ICD-10-PCS Code Assignment: _____

Case 5

Ambulatory Surgery Note

This patient has had ongoing concerns in her left elbow joint. This patient presents today for a percutaneous irrigation of the left elbow joint. The joint was irrigated, there were no complications, and the patient was instructed to return to my office in 1 week.

ICD-10-PCS Code Assignment: _____

Measurement and Monitoring Section

Chapter Outline

Chapter Objectives

Key Terms

Introduction

Measurement and Monitoring Section
  of the ICD-10-PCS

Summary

Chapter Review

Coding Assignments

Case Studies

Chapter Objectives

At the conclusion of this chapter, you should be able to:

1. Identify the character meanings used for the ICD-10-PCS Measurement and Monitoring Section.
2. Describe the root operations used for the ICD-10-PCS Measurement and Monitoring Section.
3. List the body system values in the ICD-10-PCS Measurement and Monitoring Section.
4. Identify the approach, function, and qualifiers used for the ICD-10-PCS Measurement and Monitoring Section.
5. Code procedures in the ICD-10-PCS Measurement and Monitoring Section.
6. Select ICD-10-PCS codes from the Measurement and Monitoring Section for case studies.

Key Terms

Measurement   Monitoring

REMINDER: As you work through this chapter, you will need to have a copy of the ICD-10-PCS coding book to reference. For this chapter, you will also need to reference the ICD-10-PCS Official Guidelines for Coding and Reporting. These guidelines can be found in Appendix B which are now available on the Student Companion site and MINDTAP From Cengage.

Introduction

"Measurement and Monitoring" is the fifth section found in ICD-10-PCS. This section is referenced to report procedures in which a physiological or physical function is measured or monitored.

Measurement and Monitoring Section of the ICD-10-PCS

The seven characters in this section have the following meanings:

1	2	3	4	5	6	7
Section	Body system	Root operation	Body system	Approach	Function	Qualifier

Section

The first-character value for Measurement and Monitoring procedure codes is 4. All tables in this section begin with this character value.

Body System

The second-character value for the Measurement and Monitoring section is either A, Physiological systems, or B, Physiological devices.

Root Operation

Two root operations are identified for the Measurement and Monitoring Section of ICD-10-PCS:

- **Measurement**—Determining the level of a physiological or physical function at a point in time (value of 0)

- **Monitoring**—Determining the level of a physiological or physical function repetitively over a period of time (value of 1)

Body System

The fourth-character values in the Measurement and Monitoring Section identify the body system that is measured or monitored. The values vary according to the table used for the root operation. See Figure 32-1 for the appropriate value of the fourth character for physiological systems and Figure 32-2 for the fourth-character values for physiological devices.

Approach

The fifth character identifies the approach used for the procedure and is similar to those used in the Medical and Surgical Section. The approaches are external, open, percutaneous, percutaneous endoscopic, via natural or artificial opening, and via natural or artificial opening endoscopic.

The tables need to be referenced to locate the values that are valid for each body system. Figure 32-3 lists the fifth, sixth, and seventh characters for physiological systems, and Figure 32-4 lists the fifth, sixth, and seventh characters for physiological devices.

4: MEASUREMENT AND MONITORING
A: PHYSIOLOGICAL SYSTEMS

Operation—Character 3	Body System—Character 4
0 Measurement 1 Monitoring	0 Central Nervous 1 Peripheral Nervous 2 Cardiac 3 Arterial 4 Venous 5 Circulatory 6 Lymphatic 7 Visual 8 Olfactory 9 Respiratory B Gastrointestinal C Biliary D Urinary F Musculoskeletal G Skin and Breast H Products of Conception, Cardiac J Products of Conception, Nervous Z None

Courtesy of the Centers for Medicare & Medicaid Services, www.cms.gov

FIGURE 32-1 Fourth-character values for physiological systems.

4: MEASUREMENT AND MONITORING
B: PHYSIOLOGICAL DEVICES

Operation—Character 3	Body System—Character 4
0 Measurement	0 Central Nervous 1 Peripheral Nervous 2 Cardiac 9 Respiratory F Musculoskeletal

Courtesy of the Centers for Medicare & Medicaid Services, www.cms.gov

FIGURE 32-2 Fourth-character values for physiological devices.

Function

The sixth character identifies the physiological or physical function being measured or monitored. The character values can be obtained from Figures 32-3 and 32-4. Note that not all characters are valid for all tables in the Measurement and Monitoring Section, so the tables need to be referenced for the correct character assignments.

4: MEASUREMENT AND MONITORING
A: PHYSIOLOGICAL SYSTEMS

Approach Character 5	Function/Device Character 6	Qualifier Character 7
0 Open	0 Acuity	0 Central
3 Percutaneous	1 Capacity	1 Peripheral
4 Percutaneous Endoscopic	2 Conductivity	2 Portal
7 Via Natural or Artificial Opening	3 Contractility	3 Pulmonary
8 Via Natural or Artificial Opening Endoscopic	4 Electrical Activity	4 Stress
X External	5 Flow	5 Ambulatory
	6 Metabolism	6 Right Heart
	7 Mobility	7 Left Heart
	8 Motility	8 Bilateral
	9 Output	9 Sensory
	B Pressure	A Guidance
	C Rate	B Motor
	D Resistance	C Coronary
	F Rhythm	D Intracranial
	G Secretion	E Compartment
	H Sound	F Other Thoracic
	J Pulse	G Intraoperative
	K Temperature	H Indocyanine Green Dye
	L Volume	Z No Qualifier
	M Total Activity	
	N Sampling and Pressure	
	P Action Currents	
	Q Sleep	
	R Saturation	
	S Vascular Perfusion	

FIGURE 32-3 Fifth, sixth, and seventh characters for physiological systems.

4: MEASUREMENT AND MONITORING
B: PHYSIOLOGICAL DEVICES

Approach Character 5	Function/Device Character 6	Qualifier Character 7
X External	S Pacemaker	Z No Qualifier
	T Defibrillator	
	V Stimulator	

FIGURE 32-4 Fifth, sixth, and seventh characters for physiological devices.

Qualifier

The seventh character represents the qualifier. See Figures 32-3 and 32-4 for the seventh-character values, which identify the specific body part or a variation of the procedure performed.

Summary

- The first-character value for Measurement and Monitoring procedure codes is 4.
- The second-character value for the body system has two values: A or B.
- There are two root operations for this section of ICD-10-PCS: Measurement and Monitoring.
- The fourth-character values in the Measurement and Monitoring Section vary according to the physiological system or physiological device.
- The fifth character identifies the approach.
- The sixth character identifies the physiological or physical function being measured or monitored.
- The seventh character is a qualifier, and its values vary according to the table being used.

Chapter Review

True/False

Indicate whether each statement is true (T) or false (F).

1. _____ There are three root operations for the Measurement and Monitoring Section of ICD-10-PCS.

2. _____ The third character identifies the root operation.

3. _____ The second-character value represents either the physiological system or the physiological device.

4. _____ *Measurement* is defined as determining the level of physiological or physical function over a period of time.

5. _____ Conductivity is a type of physiological function.

Coding Assignments

Instructions: For each procedure, select the correct ICD-10-PCS code.

1. monitoring of arterial pressure, peripheral, external approach _____

2. monitoring of pulmonary venous pressure, open approach _____

3. monitoring of portal venous flow, percutaneously _____

4. monitoring of venous saturation, portal, open approach _____

5. monitoring of lymphatic flow, open approach _____

6. monitoring of respiratory flow, via nose _____

7. monitoring of gastrointestinal secretion, via artificial opening _____

8. endoscopic monitoring of gastrointestinal pressure _____

9. monitoring of urinary flow _____

10. fetal monitoring of cardiac electrical activity via natural opening _____

11. endoscopic monitoring of fetal cardiac rhythm   _____

12. external measurement of cardiac pacemaker   _____

13. measurement of cardiac defibrillator, external approach   _____

14. measurement of respiratory pacemaker, external approach   _____

15. monitoring of cardiac stress, external approach   _____

16. single measurement cardiac stress test   _____

17. monitoring of heart rate of fetus transvaginally   _____

18. single measurement of external respiratory volume   _____

19. visual pressure test, single measurement   _____

20. EGD with biliary pressure measurement   _____

21. endoscopic urinary manometry to measure urinary pressure   _____

22. measurement of arterial intracranial flow   _____

23. visual acuity measurement   _____

24. measurement of temperature, external   _____

25. transvaginal fetal heart rhythm monitoring   _____

Case Studies

Instructions: Review each case study and select the correct ICD-10-PCS code.

Case 1

Cardiac Unit Note

This 75-year-old female is diagnosed with cardiac abnormalities. She is brought to the cardiac unit to monitor her cardiac output using an external monitor. Full report to follow.

ICD-10-PCS Code Assignment: _____

Case 2

Respiratory Care Unit

This 80-year-old female patient is having difficulty breathing, and her respiratory rate varies. She is brought to this unit to externally monitor her respiratory rate. She is to follow up for results with Dr. Kana.

ICD-10-PCS Code Assignment: _____

Case 3

This 23-week-pregnant female is brought to the unit to monitor the cardiac sounds of her child. The sounds were monitored using an endoscopic vaginal monitor.

ICD-10-PCS Code Assignment: _____

Case 4

This 59-year-old male has been experiencing cardiac symptoms. Today he is receiving a Holter monitor for the next 24 hours. He was instructed to leave the monitor on for the next 24 hours while he is conducting his normal activities. He is also to keep an activity diary of his daily events so his activities can be compared to the electrocardiographic tracings. He is to return to me in 2 days.

ICD-10-PCS Code Assignment: _____

Case 5

Hospital Note

This 62-year-old female had a stress test 2 days ago and it was slightly abnormal. There is a family history of heart attacks with both parents. Today she presented for a cardiac catheterization, bilaterally, with sampling and pressure measurements. The procedure was completed and there are positive findings. See procedure note for details. Cardiac surgeon contacted for consultation.

ICD-10-PCS Code Assignment: _____

Extracorporeal or Systemic Assistance and Performance and Extracorporeal or Systemic Therapies Sections

Chapter Outline

Chapter Objectives

Key Terms

Introduction

Extracorporeal or Systemic Assistance and
   Performance Section of ICD-10-PCS

Extracorporeal or Systemic Therapies Section
   of ICD-10-PCS

Summary

Chapter Review

Coding Assignments

Case Studies

Chapter Objectives

At the conclusion of this chapter, you should be able to:

1. Identify the character meanings used for Section 6, Extracorporeal or Systemic Assistance and Performance, and for Section 7, Extracorporeal or Systemic Therapies, of ICD-10-PCS.
2. Describe the root operations used for these two sections of ICD-10-PCS.
3. List the body system values in these sections of ICD-10-PCS.
4. Identify the duration, function, and qualifiers used in these sections.
5. Code procedures from these ICD-10-PCS sections.
6. Select procedure codes for case studies.

Key Terms

Assistance	Decompression	Extracorporeal	Hypothermia
Atmospheric control	Electromagnetic therapy	Hyperthermia	Performance

| Perfusion | Phototherapy | Shock wave therapy | Ultraviolet light therapy |
| Pheresis | Restoration | Ultrasound therapy | |

REMINDER: As you work through this chapter, you will need to have a copy of the ICD-10-PCS coding book to reference. For this chapter, you will also need to reference the ICD-10-PCS Official Guidelines for Coding and Reporting. These guidelines can be found in Appendix B which are now available on the Student Companion site and MINDTAP From Cengage.

Introduction

The sections titled "Extracorporeal or Systemic Assistance and Performance" and "Extracorporeal or Systemic Therapies" are the sixth and seventh sections found in ICD-10-PCS. Codes in the Extracorporeal or Systemic Assistance and Performance Section report procedures in which a physiological or physical function is performed by equipment outside the body. Codes in the Extracorporeal or Systemic Therapies Section report procedures in which equipment is used for therapy. The term **extracorporeal** means something that is outside of the body.

Extracorporeal or Systemic Assistance and Performance Section of ICD-10-PCS

The seven characters in this section have the following meanings:

1	2	3	4	5	6	7
Section	Body system	Root operation	Body system	Duration	Function	Qualifier

Procedures that will be coded to this section of ICD-10-PCS include cardioversion and mechanical ventilation as well as hemodialysis.

Section

The first-character value for the codes on the Extracorporeal or Systemic Assistance and Performance section tables is 5.

Body System/Physiological System

The second-character value, for body system, in the Extracorporeal or Systemic Assistance and Performance section is A for physiological systems—the only second-position value for these tables.

Root Operation

There are three root operations for the Extracorporeal or Systemic Assistance and Performance Section of ICD-10-PCS:

- **Assistance**—Taking over a portion of a physiological function by extracorporeal means (value of 0)
- **Performance**—Completely taking over a physiological function by extracorporeal means (value of 1)
- **Restoration**—Returning or attempting to return a physiological function to its original state by extracorporeal means (value of 2)

In the Extracorporeal or Systemic Therapies section, the tables have similar characters (explained later in this chapter), but the root operations have different values.

5: EXTRACORPOREAL OR SYSTEMIC ASSISTANCE AND PERFORMANCE
A: PHYSIOLOGICAL SYSTEMS

Duration Character 5	Function Character 6	Qualifier Character 7
0 Single	0 Filtration	0 Balloon Pump
1 Intermittent	1 Output	1 Hyperbaric
2 Continuous	2 Oxygenation	2 Manual
3 Less than 24 Consecutive Hours	3 Pacing	4 Nonmechanical
	4 Rhythm	5 Pulsatile Compression
4 24–96 Consecutive Hours	5 Ventilation	6 Other Pump
5 Greater than 96 Consecutive Hours		7 Continuous Positive Airway Pressure
		8 Intermittent Positive Airway Pressure
6 Multiple		9 Continuous Negative Airway Pressure
7 Intermittent, Less than 6 Hours per Day		A High Nasal Flow/Velocity
		B Intermittent Negative Airway Pressure
8 Prolonged Intermittent, 6–18 hours per Day		C Supersaturated
		D Impellar Pump
9 Continuous, Greater than 18 hours per Day		F Membrane, Central
A Intraoperative		G Membrane, Peripheral Veno-arterial
		H Membrane, Peripheral Veno-venous
		Z No Qualifier

Courtesy of the Centers for Medicare & Medicaid Services, www.cms.gov

FIGURE 33-1 Values for the fifth, sixth and seventh characters in the Extracorporeal or Systemic Assistance and Performance Section.

Body System

The fourth-character values in the Extracorporeal or Systemic Assistance and Performance Section identify the body system in which the assistance is occurring:

- Cardiac (value of 2)
- Circulatory (value of 5)
- Respiratory (value of 9)
- Biliary (value of C)
- Urinary (value of D)

Reference Tables 5A0, 5A1, and 5A2 in ICD-10-PCS to determine the values that are relevant to each table and to each situation.

Duration

The fifth character identifies the duration of the procedure. Figure 33-1 lists the values for the fifth character.

Exercise 33.1—Duration Characters

For each table, identify the fifth character. Reference the Extracorporeal or Systemic Assistance and Performance tables. The first one is done for you.

Table	Fifth Characters
1. 5A0	1, 2, 3, 4, 5
2. 5A2	_____
3. 5A1	_____

Function

The sixth character identifies the physiological function being assisted or performed. See Figure 33-1 for the values.

Qualifier

The seventh character represents the qualifier that specifies the type of equipment used. Figure 33-1 lists the values for the seventh character.

Extracorporeal or Systemic Therapies Section of ICD-10-PCS

The seven characters in this section have the following meanings:

1	2	3	4	5	6	7
Section	Body system	Root operation	Body system	Duration	Function	Qualifier

Section

The first-character value for Extracorporeal or Systemic Therapies procedure codes is 6. This character value distinguishes therapies from assistance and performance.

Body System/Physiological System

The second-character value, for physiological systems, in the Extracorporeal or Systemic Therapies Section is A. As in the assistance and performance tables, the *A* is the only second-position value used.

Root Operation

There are 11 root operations for the Extracorporeal or Systemic Therapies section of ICD-10-PCS:

- **Atmospheric control**—Extracorporeal control of atmospheric pressure and composition (value of 0)

- **Decompression**—Extracorporeal elimination of undissolved gas from body fluids (value of 1). This root operation involves only one type of procedure: treatment for decompression sickness in a hyperbaric chamber.

- **Electromagnetic therapy**—Extracorporeal treatment by electromagnetic rays (value of 2)

- **Hyperthermia**—Extracorporeal raising of body temperature (value of 3). This is used to describe both a temperature imbalance treatment and also an adjunct radiation treatment for cancer. When treating the temperature imbalance, it is coded to this section. For cancer treatment, it is coded in section D, Radiation Therapy.

- **Hypothermia**—Extracorporeal lowering of body temperature (value of 4)

- **Perfusion**—Extracorporeal treatment by diffusion of therapeutic fluid (value of B)

- **Pheresis**—Extracorporeal separation of blood products (value of 5). This procedure occurs for two main purposes: to treat diseases when too much of a blood component is produced (e.g., leukemia) and to remove a blood product, such as platelets from a donor, for transfusion into another patient.

- **Phototherapy**—Extracorporeal treatment by light rays (value of 6). Phototherapy involves using a machine that exposes the blood to light rays outside the body, recirculates it, and then returns it to the body.

- **Ultrasound therapy**—Extracorporeal treatment by ultrasound (value of 7)

- **Ultraviolet light therapy**—Extracorporeal treatment by ultraviolet light (value of 8)

- **Shock wave therapy**—Extracorporeal treatment by shock waves (value of 9)

Body System

The fourth-character values in the Extracorporeal or Systemic Therapies Section identify the body system in which the therapy is performed:

- Skin (value of 0)
- Urinary (value of 1)
- Central nervous (value of 2)
- Musculoskeletal (value of 3)
- Circulatory (value of 5)
- Respiratory System (value of B)
- Hepatobiliary System and Pancreas (value of F)
- Urinary System (value of T)
- None (value of Z)

Reference Tables 6A0 through 6AB in the ICD-10-PCS to determine the values relevant to each situation. Attention to documentation is essential for proper character value assignment.

Duration

The fifth character identifies the duration of the procedure. The two values are 0 for single and 1 for multiple.

Function

The sixth character for Extracorporeal or Systemic Therapies has a value of Z or B.

Qualifier

The seventh character is Z for all the tables in this section except for the root operation of pheresis and ultrasound therapy. Here the seventh character is used to specify the blood component on which pheresis is performed or the anatomical structure on which the ultrasound therapy is performed. See Figure 33-2 for the values of the seventh character.

6: EXTRACORPOREAL OR SYSTEMIC THERAPIES
A: PHYSIOLOGICAL SYSTEMS

Duration Character 5	Function Character 6	Qualifier Character 7
0 Single 1 Multiple	Z No Qualifier B Donor Organ	0 Erythrocytes 1 Leukocytes 2 Platelets 3 Plasma 4 Head and Neck Vessels 5 Heart 6 Peripheral Vessels 7 Other Vessels T Stem Cells, Cord Blood V Stem Cells, Hematopoietic Z No Qualifier

FIGURE 33-2 Values of the seventh character in the Extracorporeal or Systemic Therapies section.

Summary

- The first-character value for Extracorporeal or Systemic Assistance and Performance procedure codes is 5.
- The second-character value for the body system is A.
- There are three root operations for the Extracorporeal or Systemic Assistance and Performance Section of the ICD-10-PCS: Assistance, Performance, and Restoration.
- The fourth-character values in the Extracorporeal or Systemic Assistance and Performance Section identify the body system.
- The fifth character in the Extracorporeal or Systemic Assistance and Performance Section identifies the duration of the procedure.
- The sixth character in the Extracorporeal or Systemic Assistance and Performance Section identifies the physiological function assisted or performed.
- The seventh character in the Extracorporeal or Systemic Assistance and Performance Section is a qualifier, and the values vary according to the table used.
- The first character for Extracorporeal or Systemic Therapies is 6.
- The second character for Extracorporeal or Systemic Therapies is A.
- The third character for Extracorporeal or Systemic Therapies identifies one of 11 root operations.
- The fourth character for Extracorporeal or Systemic Therapies specifies the body system.
- The fifth character for Extracorporeal or Systemic Therapies specifies the duration.
- The sixth character for Extracorporeal or Systemic Therapies is Z or B.
- The seventh character for Extracorporeal or Systemic Therapies is always Z except for pheresis and ultrasound therapy.

Chapter Review

True/False

Indicate whether each statement is true (T) or false (F).

1. _____ There are three root operations for the Extracorporeal or Systemic Assistance and Performance Section of the ICD-10-PCS.

2. _____ The fifth character in the Extracorporeal or Systemic Assistance and Performance Section identifies the root operation.

3. _____ The second character in the Extracorporeal or Systemic Assistance and Performance Section is for the duration of the procedure.

4. _____ *Atmospheric control* is defined as the extracorporeal control of atmospheric pressure and composition.

5. _____ Hyperthermia is the extracorporeal lowering of body temperature.

6. _____ The fourth character in the Extracorporeal or Systemic Therapies Section is to report the body system in which the therapy is performed.

7. _____ In the Extracorporeal or Systemic Therapies Section, the seventh-character value is always Z.

8. _____ Pheresis is the extracorporeal separation of blood products.

9. _____ In Table 6A7, the following values can represent the fifth character: 0, 1, and 2.

10. _____ In Table 6A5, the only fourth-character value is 5, Skin.

Coding Assignments

Instructions: For each procedure, select the correct ICD-10-PCS code.

1. atmospheric control of whole body single therapy

2. electromagnetic therapy of urinary system, single treatment

3. multiple electromagnetic therapy of central nervous system

4. hyperthermia of whole body, single treatment

5. multiple treatments for hypothermia of whole body

6. pheresis of platelets, single duration

7. multiple pheresis of erythrocytes

8. pheresis of cord blood stem cells, multiple

9. multiple treatment of phototherapy of skin

10. single ultrasound therapy of heart

11. single treatment of ultraviolet light therapy of skin

12. single shock wave therapy for musculoskeletal system

13. continuous assistance with cardiac output using pulsatile compression

14. extracorporeal membrane oxygenation assistance, intermittent, hyperbaric

15. assistance with respiratory ventilation, less than 24 consecutive hours, intermittent positive airway pressure

16. assistance with respiratory ventilation, for 48 consecutive hours, with continuous positive airway pressure

17. assistance with respiratory ventilation, for 110 consecutive hours with continuous negative airway pressure

18. manual, single performance of cardiac output

19. respiratory ventilation for 10 consecutive hours

20. urinary filtration for 4 hours

21. continuous positive airway pressure assistance for 8 hours

22. continuous cardiac balloon pump assistance

23. multiple shock wave therapy of leg muscles

24. hyperbaric oxygenation, continuous

25. hemodialysis performed for 19 hours

Case Studies

Instructions: Review each case study and select the correct ICD-10-PCS code.

Case 1

This 40-year-old patient is diagnosed with psoriasis. The left middle and lower back area have numerous red and raised lesions at this time. The patient presented today for ultraviolet treatment. The treatment was completed and the patient was instructed to return in 1 week for examination of the area.

ICD-10-PCS Code Assignment: _____

Case 2

This leukemia patient presents today for extracorporeal separation of blood to remove leukocytes. The patient tolerated the procedure with no complications and was instructed to return to my office in 7 days.

ICD-10-PCS Code Assignment: _____

Case 3

This 2-day-old neonate is jaundiced. I have instructed the nurses to treat her with a single-treatment exposure to fluorescent lights with her eyes and genitalia covered. After 24 hours I want serial tests for the bilirubin level in the blood.

ICD-10-PCS Code Assignment: _____

Case 4

Procedure Note

This 35-year-old male was hiking in the mountains and he was lost for 3 days. The temperature was 10 to 20 degrees. His body temperature is 94 degrees and it was determined that he should undergo an extracorporeal whole-body hyperthermic treatment. The treatment was given and the patient's temperature rose to within normal limits. See temperature records for specific details.

ICD-10-PCS Code Assignment: _____

Case 5

Hemodialysis Unit Note

This 74-year-old male patient presents today for his dialysis treatment due to chronic kidney disease. The patient tolerated the treatment and will return on Wednesday.

ICD-10-PCS Code Assignment: _____

Osteopathic, Other Procedures, and Chiropractic Sections

Chapter Outline

Chapter Objectives

At the conclusion of this chapter, you should be able to:

1. Describe the root operations used for the Osteopathic, Other Procedures, and Chiropractic Sections of ICD-10-PCS.
2. Identify the character meanings used for the Osteopathic, Other Procedures, and Chiropractic Sections of ICD-10-PCS.
3. Identify the approach, devices, and qualifiers used in the Osteopathic, Other Procedures, and Chiropractic Sections of ICD-10-PCS.
4. Code procedures from the Osteopathic, Other Procedures, and Chiropractic Sections of ICD-10-PCS.
5. Select procedure codes for case studies.

Key Terms

Chiropractor	Osteopathic manipulation therapy (OMT)	Other Procedures	Treatment

REMINDER: As you work through this chapter, you will need to have a copy of the ICD-10-PCS coding book to reference. For this chapter, you will also need to reference the ICD-10-PCS Official Guidelines for Coding and Reporting. These guidelines can be found in Appendix B which are now available on the Student Companion site and MINDTAP From Cengage.

Introduction

The Osteopathic, Other Procedures, and Chiropractic sections of ICD-10-PCS are discussed here as a group due to the size of the sections and the nature of the procedures. Each section is discussed individually.

Osteopathic Section

Osteopathic services are sometimes referred to as **osteopathic manipulation therapy (OMT)**. OMT is manually guided therapy that is performed by a doctor of osteopathic medicine (DO) to improve physiological function.

The Osteopathic Section of ICD-10-PCS is made up of one table. Osteopathic procedures are valued with the number 7 as the first character, the section identifier, for this group of codes.

Anatomical Region and Root Operation

The second position is identified as anatomical region and has a value of W. The third position is the root operation, of which there is only one: Treatment. **Treatment** is defined by ICD-10-PCS in the Osteopathic Table as manual treatment to eliminate or alleviate somatic dysfunction and related disorders. The treatment has a value of 0.

Body Region

For osteopathic manipulation, the body region or body area needs to be identified in the fourth-character position. The following notes the body regions and their values for this particular section:

- Head (value of 0)
- Cervical (value of 1)
- Thoracic (value of 2)
- Lumbar (value of 3)
- Sacrum (value of 4)
- Pelvis (value of 5)
- Lower extremities (value of 6)
- Upper extremities (value of 7)
- Rib cage (value of 8)
- Abdomen (value of 9)

Approach, Method, and Qualifier

For the fifth-character position, the approach is always external because osteopathic services are noninvasive. The value is X in the fifth-character position.

The sixth character denotes the method. The method varies depending on the service rendered and appears in the table as follows:

- Articulatory—raising (value of 0)
- Fascial release (value of 1)
- General mobilization (value of 2)
- High velocity—low amplitude (value of 3)

- Indirect (value of 4)
- Low velocity—high amplitude (value of 5)
- Lymphatic pump (value of 6)
- Muscle energy—isometric (value of 7)
- Muscle energy—isotonic (value of 8)
- Other method (value of 9)

Any DO performing OMT services should clearly document the method used. Query the physician before assigning a character from the table if you have any doubt about which method was used.

The seventh-character position is not specified in the Osteopathic Section of ICD-10-PCS, so the value for this position is Z, None.

Exercise 34.1—Body Region/Method

For each code, identify the body region and the method of treatment. The first one is done for you.

Code	Body Region	Method
1. 7W00X1Z	head	fascial release
2. 7W08X2Z	_____	_____
3. 7W03X8Z	_____	_____
4. 7W05X6Z	_____	_____
5. 7W01X4Z	_____	_____

Other Procedures

In the section titled "Other Procedures," there are two tables. The first character, identifying the section, is 8. The second characters have a value of C for indwelling device or E for physiological systems and anatomical regions.

Root Operation

In the tables for other procedures, the third-character position value is 0. The definition given in ICD-10-PCS for **Other Procedures** is methodologies which attempt to remediate or cure a disorder or disease.

Body Region

In the tables for other procedures, the body region character is in the fourth position. Tables 8C0 and 8E0 include values that are unique to each table.

Approach

The fifth-character value represents the approach. For Table 8C0, there is only one option for the fifth character, value X for external. For Table 8E0, the following approach values are used:

- X, External
- 0, Open

- 3, Percutaneous
- 4, Percutaneous endoscopic
- 7, Via natural or artificial opening
- 8, Via natural or artificial opening endoscopic

Method

The tables for other procedures contain various methods not seen in other sections. For Table 8C0, in the sixth-character position, there is only one value used: 6, meaning collection. For Table 8E0, the following values are used in the sixth position:

- 0, Acupuncture. Acupuncture is completed by inserting fine needles into the skin to produce an analgesic effort to relieve pain or to alter the function of a body system. Note in table 8E0 the seventh character identifies the purpose of the acupuncture procedure completed.

- 1, Therapeutic massage. The goal of therapeutic massage is to prevent or relieve pain, increase circulation, reduce stress, and improve muscle tone and to create balance of the soft tissues within the body.

- 6, Collection. Reference table 8C0 and note that this table is for indwelling devices. Also note character 6 is entitled method and is used to denote collection. Here collection denotes that fluid was taken from an indwelling device. Reference table 8E0, in this table in the 6th character position the value of 6 denotes collection of breast milk and sperm. In these two cases drainage of an organ is not required.

- B, Computer assisted procedure. Coders need to select the value of B for the sixth character position in table 8E0 when computer technology is used during the preoperative or operative procedure to assist with the performance and navigation of the procedure.

- C, Robotic assisted procedure. During robotic assisted procedures the surgeon uses a robotic device that allow for increased magnification of the operative field and precision.

- D, Near infrared spectroscopy. NIRS is an non-invasive procedure that is performed by use of a spectroscope to monitor the oxygen availability in the body and to analyze the use of oxygen.

- E, Fluorescence Guided Procedure. A fluorescence guided procedure is an imaging procedure in which a substance is ingested by a patient that helps to detect fluorescently identified structures, such as tumors when they are viewed under blue light.

- Y, Other method. In table 8E0 the sixth character value of Y denotes other methods as they relate to the seventh character values of examination, in vitro fertilization, isolation, meditation, piercing, suture removal, and yoga therapy. Reference table 8E0 and note the use of Y in the sixth character position as they relate to the seventh character position values.

The use of these values is dependent on the procedure completed, and applicable values vary according to body region.

Qualifier

Character position 7 is the qualifier position. These alphanumeric character values identify additional information that clarifies the service rendered. For Table 8C0, the following values are used:

- J, Cerebrospinal fluid
- K, Blood
- L, Other fluid

For Table 8E0, many different values are used depending on the procedures completed.

Exercise 34.2—Other Procedures

Define the code. The first one is done for you.

Code	Description
1. 8E09XY8	suture removal, head and neck region
2. 8E0VX63	_____
3. 8C01X6J	_____
4. 8E0HXY9	_____
5. 8E0YXY8	_____

Chiropractic Section

A **chiropractor**, a doctor of chiropractic medicine, believes that all body functions are connected. For this reason, healing involves the entire body. Like the Osteopathic and Other Procedure Tables, the Chiropractic Table is very small. Chiropractic services are recognized by the first-character value of 9. The second-character position is identified by a W, Anatomical region.

Root Operation

There is only one root operation in the Chiropractic Table: Manipulation. This is identified in the third-character position with a value of B. Manipulation is a manual procedure that involves a directed thrust to move a joint past the physiological range of motion, without exceeding the anatomical limit.

Body Region

The fourth character indicates the body region on which the chiropractic manipulation is performed. The following body regions are noted in the Chiropractic Table:

- Head (value of 0)
- Cervical (value of 1)
- Thoracic (value of 2)
- Lumbar (value of 3)
- Sacrum (value of 4)
- Pelvis (value of 5)
- Lower extremities (value of 6)
- Upper extremities (value of 7)
- Rib cage (value of 8)
- Abdomen (value of 9)

Approach, Method, Qualifier

The approach in the Chiropractic Table in ICD-10-PCS always has a value of X because the approach is always external. The approach is located in the fifth position.

The method of manipulation is identified in the sixth-character position. Several methods coded from this table are categorized as nonmanual, indirect visceral, extra-articular, direct visceral, long lever specific contact, short lever specific contact, long and short lever specific contact, mechanically assisted, and other method. The documentation should clearly state the method of manipulation.

The qualifier for the seventh position is always represented by *Z*, denoting no qualifier.

Summary

- Osteopathic services are sometimes referred to as osteopathic manipulation therapy (OMT).
- Osteopathic and chiropractic treatment services are defined differently in ICD-10-PCS.
- For osteopathic manipulation, the body region needs to be identified in the fourth-character position.
- The Other Procedures Section is identified by the first-character value of 8.
- Suture removal, piercings, and therapeutic massage are coded from the Other Procedures Tables.
- A chiropractor, or doctor of chiropractic medicine, believes that all body functions are connected. For this reason, healing involves the entire body.
- The method of chiropractic manipulation is identified in the sixth-character position.

Internet Links

For definitions of osteopathic procedures and a better understanding of OMT, visit **www.osteopathic.org**.

For more information on chiropractic medicine, visit **www.spineuniverse.com**.

To learn more about near infrared spectroscopy visit **https://www.nih.gov** and search on the words near infrared spectroscopy.

Chapter Review

True/False

Indicate whether each statement is true (T) or false (F).

1. _____ A value of 8 is used to denote the Osteopathic Section of ICD-10-PCS.

2. _____ There are two tables for the Osteopathic Section.

3. _____ A value of 9 denotes the Chiropractic Section of ICD-10-PCS.

4. _____ In Table 9WB, many values are used for the seventh-character position.

5. _____ In code 8E0XXY8, the seventh character of 8 denotes suture removal.

Coding Assignments

Instructions: For each procedure, select the correct ICD-10-PCS code.

1. low velocity-high amplitude for osteopathic treatment of the pelvis _____

2. examination of female reproductive system _____

3. lymphatic pump, osteopathic treatment of the left arm _____

4. fascial release using osteopathic manipulation of the wrist   _____

5. ear piercing (ear lobe)   _____

6. chiropractic extra-articular treatment of shoulder region   _____

7. acupuncture   _____

8. suture removal, left eyebrow   _____

9. chiropractic treatment of lumbar region using long lever
    specific contact   _____

10. osteopathic manipulation of the lumbar spine using general
    mobilization   _____

11. chiropractic manipulation of the pelvic region, indirect visceral   _____

12. therapeutic massage   _____

13. nonmanual chiropractic manipulation of the head   _____

14. suture removal, right thigh   _____

15. indirect OMT of sacrum   _____

16. examination of the nervous system   _____

17. suture removal, back   _____

18. open fluorescence guided procedure, arm   _____

19. fascial release osteopathic treatment of pelvis   _____

20. chiropractic long lever manipulation of lumbar spine   _____

Case Studies

Instructions: Review each case study and select the correct ICD-10-PCS code.

Case 1

Lucy is a 40-year-old female who has been suffering with severe headaches and low back pain for the past month. She has tried ibuprophen and acetominophin without success. Her doctor prescribed medication for migraine headaches, but she still has much pain. She has decided to try acupuncture.

No contraindications are noted, so we proceeded.

Procedure: 20 needles with electrical stimulation for 30 minutes

ICD-10-PCS Code Assignment: _____

Case 2

Chris is a 5-year-old male who presents today to have four stitches removed from his forehead. Ten days ago he was playing on his swing set and fell off the slide, hitting his head on the side of the slide and lacerating the site. He was taken to the emergency room, where four stitches were placed. He is here in the office now to have the wound checked and sutures removed.

The wound is 2.5 cm long and healed nicely. No redness, infection, or drainage is noticed. The 4 sutures were removed without a problem.

ICD-10-PCS Code Assignment: _____

Case 3

Chiropractic Office Note

This 48-year-old female was in an automobile accident and she returns to the office today for treatment for the ongoing pain she is experiencing. Indirect visceral chiropractic manipulation was performed in the pelvic area. She is to return to the office in 2 weeks.

ICD-10-PCS Code Assignment: _____

Case 4

Cardiac Support Note

This 63-year-old male patient attended the meditation group. Prior to the session he stated that he felt stressed and after the session he felt more relaxed.

ICD-10-PCS Code Assignment: _____

Case 5

Ms. Smart is the coding supervisor for Sunny Valley Hospital. She is organizing a coding training on ICD-10-PCS. She is reviewing the ICD-10-PCS Code Manual for a code for a robotic-assisted procedure completed on the arm via an open incision. The code she should use in addition to the code for the procedure being coded is code

_____.

Imaging, Nuclear Medicine, and Radiation Therapy Sections

Chapter Outline

Chapter Objectives

Key Terms

Introduction

Imaging Section

Nuclear Medicine Section

Radiation Therapy Section

Summary

Internet Links

Chapter Review

Coding Assignments

Case Studies

Chapter Objectives

At the conclusion of this chapter, you should be able to:

1. Define the key terms presented in this chapter.
2. Describe the characters and codes associated with the Imaging, Nuclear Medicine, and Radiation Therapy sections of the ICD-10-PCS.
3. Identify the seven-character codes and the differences among the sections of radiology.
4. List the types of radiology procedures classified in ICD-10-PCS.
5. Code procedures from the Imaging, Nuclear Medicine, and Radiation Therapy sections of ICD-10-PCS.
6. Select procedure codes for case studies.

Key Terms

Computed tomography (CT scan)

Contrast material

Fluoroscopy

High osmolar contrast material (HOCM)

Isotope

Low osmolar contrast material (LOCM)

Magnetic resonance imaging (MRI)

Modality

Nonimaging nuclear medicine assay

Nonimaging nuclear medicine probe

Nonimaging nuclear medicine uptake

Nuclear medicine

Plain radiography

Planar nuclear medicine imaging

Positron emission tomographic imaging (PET)

Radiation oncology (rad onc)

Radioactive isotopes

Radiologic technician

Radiologist

Radiology

Radionuclide

Radiopharmaceutical

Systemic nuclear medicine therapy

Tomographic nuclear medicine imaging (tomo)

Ultrasonography

> **REMINDER:** As you work through this chapter, you will need to have a copy of the ICD-10-PCS coding book to reference. For this chapter, you will also need to reference the ICD-10-PCS Official Guidelines for Coding and Reporting. These guidelines can be found in Appendix B which are now available on the Student Companion site and MINDTAP From Cengage.

Introduction

Radiology is the study of x-rays, high-frequency sound waves, and high-strength magnetic fields, and it sometimes includes the use of radioactive compounds to diagnose and/or treat disease or injuries. A **radiologist** is a doctor whose specialty is radiology. The person who is specially trained to use the equipment that generates the pictures or studies is known as a **radiologic technician**.

ICD-10-PCS has broken down the radiology services into three distinct sections with their own tables: the Imaging section, the Nuclear Medicine section, and the Radiation Therapy section. We discuss each section separately in this chapter.

Imaging Section

The imaging procedure codes include codes for plain x-ray services, ultrasounds, fluoroscopy, CT scans, and MRI scans. The ICD-10-PCS Imaging section codes begin with the letter B in the first-character position to identify imaging codes.

Body System and Type

The second character for the Imaging codes identifies the body system on which the service is performed.

The third character is the type or the root type of imaging procedure. The types of imaging procedures are as follows:

- **Plain radiography**—Standard x-ray, planar display of an image developed from the capture of external ionizing radiation on photographic or photoconductive plate (value of 0)

- **Computed tomography (CT scan)**—Computer reformatted digital display of multiplanar images developed from the capture of multiple exposures of external ionizing radiation (value of 2)

- **Ultrasonography**—A real-time display of images of anatomy or flow information developed from the capture of reflected and attenuated high-frequency sound waves (value of 4)

- **Fluoroscopy**—Single-plane or biplane real-time display of an image developed from the capture of external ionizing radiation on a fluorescent screen. The image may also be stored by either digital or analog means. (value of 1)

- **Magnetic resonance imaging (MRI)**—Computer-formatted digital display of multiplanar images developed from the capture of radio-frequency signals emitted by nuclei in a body site excited with a magnetic field (value of 3)

- **Other imaging**—Other specified modality for visualizing a body part.

The various types are referenced in the ICD-10-PCS Index to locate the appropriate table to be referenced for a code selection.

Body Part

The fourth-character position identifies the body part imaged. Attention to detail is important in this value choice because very specific sites are noted in this column of the tables for the Imaging section.

Exercise 35.1—Tables

From the Imaging section, identify the table to be referenced. The first one is done for you.

Imaging Section	Table
1. CT scan of the heart	B22, Reference CT scan
2. fluoroscopy of the veins	_____
3. ultrasound of the CNS	_____
4. plain radiography of the skull and facial bones	_____
5. MRI of the urinary system	_____

Contrast

Contrast material might be injected when some of the imaging services are performed. The use of **contrast material** in the imaging facilitates the identification of abnormalities in the body due to image density. The fifth character identifies whether contrast material is used and whether the material was **high osmolar contrast material (HOCM)** or **low osmolar contrast material (LOCM)**. The high osmolar contrast material has a higher level of particle concentration than normal body fluids. The low osmolar contrast material has a lower level particle concentration than normal body fluids.

Qualifier

The sixth and seventh character values identify further detail as needed. Character value 6 may identify unenhanced followed by enhanced, or laser. Typically for this section, the value is Z, None.

Exercise 35.2—Imaging

Match the item in column 1 with the definition or description in column 2.

_____	1. radiologist	a.	single or biplane real-time images that can be stored digitally or by analog means
_____	2. Imaging section	b.	Imaging section is denoted with this
_____	3. CT scans	c.	always Z
_____	4. character 4 in the Imaging section	d.	multiplanar images that have been computer reformatted to capture multiple images
_____	5. Value of B	e.	lower levels of particle concentration than normal body fluids
_____	6. HOCM	f.	doctor who specializes in radiology
_____	7. LOCM	g.	might be injected at the time an imaging service is performed
_____	8. fluoroscopy	h.	body part being imaged
_____	9. contrast material	i.	codes for ultrasounds are found here
_____	10. character 7 in the Imaging section	j.	higher levels of particle concentration than in normal body fluids

Nuclear Medicine Section

Nuclear medicine treats and diagnoses diseases using small amounts of radioactive material called **radioactive isotopes**, which create an image. The value identifying the Nuclear Medicine section is the letter C.

Body System

The body system on which a nuclear medicine procedure is performed is identified by the second-character position. The value depends on the part of the body being tested and the table being referenced.

Type

The third character in the code identifies the type of procedure being performed. The following identifies the types used in the Nuclear Medicine section, along with their values:

- **Planar nuclear medicine imaging**—Introduction of radioactive materials into the body for single-plane display of images, developed from the capture of radioactive emissions (value of 1)

- **Tomographic (tomo) nuclear medicine imaging**—Introduction of radioactive materials into the body for three-dimensional display of images, developed from the capture of radioactive emissions (value of 2)

- **Positron emission tomographic (PET) imaging**—Introduction of radioactive materials into the body for three-dimensional display of images, developed from the simultaneous capture, 180 degrees apart, of radioactive emissions (value of 3)

- **Nonimaging nuclear medicine uptake**—Introduction of radioactive material into the body for measurements of organ function, from the detection of radioactive emissions (value of 4)

- **Nonimaging nuclear medicine probe**—Introduction of radioactive materials into the body for the study of distribution and fate of certain substances by the detection of radioactive emissions; or alternatively, measurement of absorption of radioactive emissions from an external source (value of 5)

- **Nonimaging nuclear medicine assay**—Introduction of radioactive materials into the body for the study of body fluids and blood elements, by the detection of radioactive emissions (value of 6)

- **Systemic nuclear medicine therapy**—Introduction of unsealed radioactive material into the body for treatment (value of 7)

Body Part or Region

The fourth character in the Nuclear Medicine section identifies the body part or region being studied. The values for each body part or region vary depending on the table being referenced, but they are the same within one body system or region.

EXAMPLE: In the cardiovascular system, the heart is valued in the fourth position as a 6.

C, Nuclear medicine

2, Heart

1, Planar nuclear medicine imaging

Body Part: Character 4	Radionuclide: Character 5	Qualifier: Character 6	Qualifier: Character 7
6, Heart, right and left	1, Technetium 99m (Tc-99m)	Z, None	Z, None
	Y, Other radionuclide		

In the gastrointestinal system, a value of 6 in the fourth-character position identifies the liver and spleen.

C, Nuclear medicine

F, Hepatobiliary system and pancreas

1, Planar nuclear medicine imaging

Body Part: Character 4	Radionuclide: Character 5	Qualifier: Character 6	Qualifier: Character 7
4, Gallbladder	1, Technetium 99m (Tc-99m)	Z, None	Z, None
5, Liver	Y, Other radionuclide		
6, Liver and spleen			
C, Hepatobiliary system, all			

Radionuclide

A **radionuclide**, also called a radioactive isotope or **radiopharmaceutical**, is a radioactive substance that can either be found in nature or human-made and that is the source of the radiation causing the emissions so that an image can be produced. These radionuclides indicate the location, size, or function of organs, tissues, or vessels. Radioactive material is used to aid in the determinations made with regard to the patient's condition. The radionuclides are represented in the fifth-character position in the Nuclear Medicine Tables. Some of the radionuclides currently being used are:

- Technetium 99m (Tc-99m, value of 1)
- Cobalt 58 (Co-58, value of 7)
- Indium 111 (In-111, value of D)
- Iodine 125 (I-125, value of H)
- Chromium (Cr-51, value of W)

The Y value in the tables presented in the Nuclear Medicine section indicates "Other radionuclide." This value is provided for the newly approved radionuclides that have not yet been assigned a value. Reference the tables for the specific character values applicable to each table.

Qualifier

The sixth- and seventh-character positions are both qualifiers. For the Nuclear Medicine section of ICD-10-PCS, a Z value is always in these positions because there are no specified qualifiers for this section at this time.

Exercise 35.3—Nuclear Medicine

Indicate whether each statement is true (T) or false (F).

1. _____ Images found in a nuclear medicine test can also be treated by nuclear medicine.
2. _____ The body system being treated with nuclear medicine is valued at Z as a placeholder.
3. _____ A nonimaging uptake introduces radioactive materials into the body so that simultaneous images can be captured.
4. _____ PET stands for positron emission testing.

(*continues*)

Exercise 35.3—*continued*

5. _____ Radioactive seeds planted in the prostate to treat prostate cancer are considered systemic therapy and are coded to the Nuclear Medicine section of ICD-10-PCS.

6. _____ Character 4 in a nuclear medicine code indicates the body system or region being treated.

7. _____ The value of each body part or region varies depending on the table being referenced.

8. _____ In-111 is a radiopharmaceutical.

9. _____ Code CB221ZZ indicates a PET scan of the chest.

10. _____ Code C72YYZX indicates that Tc-99 was used in a tomo of the spleen.

Radiation Therapy Section

Radiation oncology (rad onc), also known as radiation therapy, is a form of radiology that is therapeutic as opposed to diagnostic in nature. The patient is typically undergoing treatment for a malignant neoplasm; the aim is for the radiation to eradicate or shrink the neoplasm or obstruction, relieving pain.

Coding for radiation therapy is to be completed according to the following guidelines.

Radiation Therapy Section Guidelines (section D)

D. Radiation Therapy Section

Brachytherapy

D1.a Brachytherapy is coded to the modality Brachytherapy in the Radiation Therapy section. When a radioactive brachytherapy source is left in the body at the end of the procedure, it is coded separately to the root operation Insertion with the device value Radioactive Element.

Example: Brachytherapy with implantation of a low dose rate brachytherapy source left in the body at the end of the procedure is coded to the applicable treatment site in section D, Radiation Therapy, with the modality Brachytherapy, the modality qualifier value Low Dose Rate, and the applicable isotope value and qualifier value. The implantation of the brachytherapy source is coded separately to the device value Radioactive Element in the appropriate Insertion table of the Medical and Surgical section. The Radiation Therapy section code identifies the specific modality and isotope of the brachytherapy, and the root operation Insertion code identifies the implantation of the brachytherapy source that remains in the body at the end of the procedure.

Exception: Implantation of Cesium-131 brachytherapy seeds embedded in a collagen matrix to the treatment site after resection of brain tumor is coded to the root operation Insertion with the device value Radioactive Element, Cesium-131 Collagen Implant. The procedure is coded to the root operation Insertion only, because the device value identifies both the implantation of the radioactive element and a specific brachytherapy isotope that is not included in the Radiation Therapy section tables.

D1.b A separate procedure to place a temporary applicator for delivering the brachytherapy is coded to the root operation Insertion and the device value Other Device.

Examples: Intrauterine brachytherapy applicator placed as a separate procedure from the brachytherapy procedure is coded to Insertion of Other Device, and the brachytherapy is coded separately using the modality Brachytherapy in the Radiation Therapy section.

Intrauterine brachytherapy applicator placed concomitantly with delivery of the brachytherapy dose is coded with a single code using the modality Brachytherapy in the Radiation Therapy section.

Radiation therapy codes begin with section value of D. The character positions are then divided further as follows:

Character Position	Description
2	Body System
3	Modality
4	Treatment Site
5	Modality Qualifier
6	Isotope
7	Qualifier

Body System

The second character identifies the body system being treated:

- Central and peripheral nervous system (value of 0)
- Lymphatic and hematologic system (value of 7)
- Eye (value of 8)
- Ear, nose, mouth, and throat (value of 9)
- Respiratory system (value of B)
- Gastrointestinal system (value of D)
- Hepatobiliary system and pancreas (value of F)
- Endocrine system (value of G)
- Skin (value of H)
- Breast (value of M)
- Musculoskeletal system (value of P)
- Urinary system (value of T)
- Female reproductive system (value of U)
- Male reproductive system (value of V)
- Anatomical regions (value of W)

Modality

Modality in medicine means a certain protocol, therapeutic method, or agent, such as chemotherapy, brachytherapy, or stereotactic radiosurgery. Modalities are valued in the third-character position.

Treatment Site

The fourth character identifies the specific treatment site that is the target of the radiation therapy.

EXAMPLE:

Body System: Character 2	Treatment Site: Character 4
0, Central and peripheral nervous system	0, Brain
	1, Brain stem
	6, Spinal cord
	7, Peripheral nerve

7, Lymphatic and hematologic system	0, Bone marrow
	1, Thymus
	2, Spleen
	3, Lymphatics, neck
	4, Lymphatics, axillary
	5, Lymphatics, thorax
	6, Lymphatics, abdomen
	7, Lymphatics, pelvis
	8, Lymphatics, inguinal

The fourth-character value changes as the body system changes.

EXAMPLE: The value of 0 in the central and peripheral nervous system indicates the brain, whereas in the lymphatic and hematologic system, the value of 0 indicates bone marrow.

Modality Qualifier

The fifth position is for the modality qualifier. This position further clarifies the radiation modality, as identified in the third character. Examples include the following:

EXAMPLE: SEE TABLE D00 IN ICD-10-PCS MANUAL.

Modality Qualifier: Character 5
0, Photons < 1 MeV (mega-electron volt)
1, Photons 1–10 MeV
2, Photons > 10 MeV
3, Electrons
4, Heavy particles (protons, ions)
5, Neutrons
6, Neutron Capture

Isotope

Character 6 identifies the isotope. An **isotope** is one of two or more atoms that contain the same atomic number (protons) but have different mass numbers (neutrons) in the nucleus. The same radioactive isotopes discussed in the Nuclear Medicine section are found in the Radiation Therapy section, and they are identified in the sixth-character position.

Qualifier

Character 7 is a qualifier position that has three possible values, 0 for intraoperative, 1 for unidirectional source or Z for none.

Summary

- A radiologist is a medical doctor whose specialty is radiology.
- The imaging procedure codes include codes for plain x-ray services, ultrasounds, fluoroscopy, CT scans, and MRI scans.

- The use of contrast material in the imaging facilitates the identification of abnormalities in the body due to image density.
- Nuclear medicine treats and diagnoses diseases using small amounts of radioactive material called radioactive isotopes.
- Radiation oncology/therapy is a form of radiology that is therapeutic as opposed to diagnostic in nature.
- The patient is typically undergoing treatment for a malignant neoplasm; the aim of the radiation therapy is to eradicate or shrink the neoplasm or obstruction, relieving pain.

Internet Links

For more information on nuclear medicine, diagnostic radiology, or interventional radiology, visit **www.radiologyinfo.org**.

For more information on radiation oncology, visit **www.cancercenter.com** and search the term radiation oncology.

Chapter Review

Multiple Choice

Select the best answer that completes the statement or answers the question.

1. Which of the following is the study of x-rays, high-frequency sound waves, and high-strength magnetic fields that sometimes involves the use of radioactive compounds to diagnose and/or treat disease or injuries?
    a. Nuclear medicine
    b. Radiotherapy
    c. Radiology
    d. Radiation therapy

2. The character value B indicates which section of ICD-10-PCS?
    a. Radiation Therapy
    b. Nuclear Medicine
    c. Imaging
    d. Radiotherapy

3. A(n) _____ is a real-time display of images of anatomy developed from the capture of reflected and attenuated high-frequency sound waves.
    a. CT scan
    b. ultrasonography
    c. fluoroscopy
    d. MRI scan

4. _____ treat(s) and diagnose(s) diseases using small amounts of radioactive material called _____, which create(s) an image.
    a. Radiopharmaceuticals, radiation
    b. Radioactive isotopes, radiation
    c. Radiopharmaceuticals, nuclear medicine
    d. Nuclear medicine, radioactive isotopes

5. Which of the following is a single-plane display of images, developed from the capture of radioactive emissions after the introduction of radioactive materials?
   a. Planar imaging
   b. Tomo
   c. PET
   d. Nonimaging assay

6. A _____ is a three-dimensional display of images produced after introduction of radioactive materials. The radioactive materials allow the capture of radioactive emissions to produce these images.
   a. nonimaging probe
   b. tomo
   c. PET
   d. nonimaging assay

7. Which of the following is a form of radiology that is therapeutic as opposed to diagnostic in nature?
   a. Oncology
   b. Chemotherapy
   c. Radiation therapy
   d. Isotope therapy

8. In a patient being treated with stereotactic other photon radiosurgery of the ovaries, the modality qualifier is:
   a. C.
   b. D.
   c. F.
   d. G.

9. Brachytherapy is a type of:
   a. isotope.
   b. qualifier.
   c. modifier.
   d. modality.

10. In the Radiation Therapy section of ICD-10-PCS, the respiratory system is represented by the character value _____, and the diaphragm is represented by the character value _____.
    a. 9, B
    b. B, 9
    c. D, 8
    d. B, 8

Coding Assignments

Instructions: For each procedure, select the correct ICD-10-PCS code.

1. routine fetal ultrasound, first trimester, single fetus   _____

2. CT scan of the lumbar spine, no contrast   _____

3. MRI of the pelvis, no contrast   _____

4. portable x-ray study of the right radius/ulna shaft, standard series   _____

5. upper GI scan with Tc-99m   _____

6. nonimaging assay of blood using I-125   _____

7. beam radiation of the brain stem, photons 1–10 MeV   _____

8. stereotactic gamma beam radiosurgery of the larynx   _____

9. ultrasound of the scrotum   _____

10. x-ray of the lumbosacral joint   _____

11. fluoroscopy of the upper GI tract and small bowel with contrast   _____

12. bilateral CT scan of the lungs with densitometry and high osmolar contrast   _____

13. uniplanar scan of the spine using technetium 99m   _____

14. tomo scan of parathyroid gland using T1-201   _____

15. hyperthermia radiation treatment of the pelvic region   _____

16. carbon 11 PET scan of the brain with qualification   _____

17. nonimaging probe of lower extremities   _____

18. PET scan of the brain using technetium 99m   _____

19. whole body phosphorus 32 administration with risk to hematopoetic system   _____

20. MRI of the thyroid, no contrast   _____

21. MRI of right ankle, no contrast   _____

22. CT of bilateral adrenal glands, no contrast   _____

23. high osmolar plain radiography of multiple mammary ducts, right breast   _____

24. intraoperative beam electron radiation therapy of brain   _____

25. brachy therapy of eye, using low dose rate iodine 125   _____

Case Studies

Instructions: Review each case study and select the correct ICD-10-PCS code.

Case 1

This is a 38-year-old-male who presents with a diagnosis of Kaposi's sarcoma, lungs, and the diaphragm. The patient will be receiving two separate treatments today.

TREATMENT: Radiation therapy

PROCEDURE PERFORMED: Radiation treatment delivery

INDICATIONS FOR PROCEDURE: Kaposi's sarcoma, lung, with mets to diaphragm

PROCEDURE: Two separate treatment areas, right lung and the diaphragm. Each area was properly marked, and beam radiation of 20-MeV photons was delivered to each area, first the lungs, then the diaphragm. Patient tolerated his treatment well and will return in 2 days for the next treatment.

ICD-10-PCS Code Assignment: _____

Case 2

Mr. Afina presents today with a very painful, barky cough. He said this has been going on for the last 2 days and he feels terrible. He has been running a fever and is feeling weak. After a physical exam, Dr. Divine ordered a chest x-ray with AP/PA and lateral views. This x-ray confirmed the diagnosis of pneumonia, and Mr. Afina was sent to the hospital immediately.

ICD-10-PCS Code Assignment: _____

Case 3

Caryn is a 40-year-old female who presented to the doctor's office with a recent change in her mental status. Her doctor wants an MRI of the brain with and without contrast—STAT.

Multiplanar, multisequence imaging of the brain was performed. There is an abnormality of the right frontal region. Postadministration of gadolinium contrast, there is an increased signal on T2 weighted images within the left basal ganglia. The appearance is typical of a focal basal ganglionic infarct on the left.

IMPRESSION: 2-cm lesion of right frontal area

Basal ganglia, likely ischemic in nature, left

ICD-10-PCS Code Assignment: _____

Case 4

Two weeks ago this patient had a mammogram with a suspicious area on her left breast.

This patient presents today for an MRI of the left breast. She was informed that she will be contacted by her physician to discuss the findings.

ICD-10-PCS Code Assignment: _____

Case 5

This 49-year-old female patient is complaining of abdominal pain for the last 5 weeks. Today she presents for an abdominal ultrasound. Her physician will contact her with the findings.

ICD-10-PCS Code Assignment: _____

Physical Rehabilitation and Diagnostic Audiology Section

Chapter Outline

Chapter Objectives

At the conclusion of this chapter, you should be able to:

1. Identify the character meanings used in the Physical Rehabilitation and Diagnostic Audiology section.
2. Describe the root types used in the Physical Rehabilitation and Diagnostic Audiology section of ICD-10-PCS.
3. Identify the body system and body region to which the Physical Rehabilitation and Diagnostic Audiology codes apply.
4. Code procedures found in the ICD-10-PCS Physical Rehabilitation and Diagnostic Audiology section.
5. Select procedure codes for case studies.

Key Terms

Assessment

Caregiver training

Fittings

Treatment

Type

REMINDER: As you work through this chapter, you will need to have a copy of the ICD-10-PCS coding book to reference. For this chapter, you will also need to reference the ICD-10-PCS Official Guidelines for Coding and Reporting. These guidelines can be found in Appendix B which are now available on the Student Companion site and MINDTAP From Cengage.

Introduction

Physical rehabilitation encompasses physical therapy, occupational therapy, and speech-language pathology. The focuses of these rehabilitation areas are different, but they are grouped under the physical rehabilitation title. Because different specialties are involved, the codes reflect different forms of treatment. Diagnostic audiology is included in this section because of the nature of the services provided, such as device fitting and rehabilitative treatment for cochlear implant patients. Careful attention to detail when coding from this section is critical.

 NOTE:

> Osteopathic and chiropractic procedures are located in separate sections and are not contained in the Physical Rehabilitation and Diagnostic Audiology section of ICD-10-PCS.

Physical Rehabilitation and Diagnostic Audiology Section

All codes found in the ICD-10-PCS Physical Rehabilitation and Diagnostic Audiology section begin with the first character of F. To locate a table in the Index, the coder references either *rehabilitation* or *diagnostic audiology*.

Section Qualifier

The section qualifier, the second character in the coding for this section, is the value that determines whether one is coding for rehabilitation or for diagnostic audiology. At this time, the value 0 indicates rehabilitation, and the diagnostic audiology value is 1.

Type

The third character in this section designates type. The **type** is similar to the root operation in the Medicine and Surgery section.

There are 14 type values in the Physical Rehabilitation and Diagnostic Audiology section, and they can be classified into four basic categories:

- **Treatment**—The use of specific activities or methods to develop, improve, and/or restore the performance of necessary functions, compensate for dysfunction, and/or minimize debilitating conditions
- **Caregiver training**—Educating caregiver with the skills and knowledge used to interact with and properly assist the patient
- **Fittings**—Design, fabrication, modification, selection, and/or application of splint, orthosis, prosthesis, hearing aids, and/or other rehabilitation device
- **Assessment**—Includes a determination of the patient's diagnosis when appropriate, need for treatment, planning for treatment, periodic assessment, and documentation related to those activities

Some of the 14 types include motor and/or nerve function assessment, activities of daily living assessment, motor treatment, device fitting, and hearing aid assessment. As with other sections in ICD-10-PCS, the definitions for this character position are given next to each of the types and should be referenced before a code is assigned.

Body System and Region

The fourth-character number identifies the body region and/or system on which the procedure is performed. This character position of the ICD-10-PCS must always be valued. A specific body part may not be identified within the table, but the character place still needs to be identified. The character Z is used if this is the case. The body part or region is identified, if applicable. However, in some cases the code description does not single out just one body system or region but encompasses the body as a whole.

EXAMPLE: A person is going through occupational therapy to be able to go back to work after an injury. The coder references this table:

F, Physical rehabilitation and diagnostic audiology

0, Rehabilitation

8, Activities of daily living treatment: Exercise or activities to facilitate functional competence for activities of daily living.

Body System and Region: Character 4	Type Qualifier: Character 5	Equipment: Character 6	Qualifier: Character 7
Z, None	7, Vocational activities and functional community or work reintegration skills	B, Physical agents C, Mechanical D, Electrotherapeutic E, Orthosis F, Assistive, adaptive, supportive, or protective G, Aerobic endurance and conditioning U, Prosthesis Y, Other equipment Z, None	Z, None

The code assignment for the patient is F08Z7ZZ. Character 4 for the body system or region does not apply because the therapist is treating the whole body.

Type Qualifier

The fifth character denotes the type qualifier and identifies the procedure performed in more detail.

EXAMPLE: Code F13ZHZZ indicates:

- F, Physical rehabilitation and diagnostic audiology
- 1, Diagnostic audiology
- 3, Hearing assessment—measurement of hearing and related functions
- Z, Body system and region—no character identified because it is inferred that the ear is the region being evaluated
- H, Acoustic reflex threshold—the procedure being performed
- Z, No equipment
- Z, No further qualifier needed

Equipment and Qualifier

Character 6 identifies the equipment used in the therapy performed. There is no defined value for the equipment used, but broad categories are specified.

EXAMPLE: In Table F06, the value M indicates augmentative/alternative communication, whereas P indicates computer and K, audiovisual. This is the same in Table F01. The tables need to be referenced for additional values.

Character 7 is always Z in the Rehabilitative and Diagnostic Audiology section because the qualifier always has a value of none.

Summary

- Physical, occupational, and speech-language pathology are coded to this section of ICD-10-PCS.
- The coder needs to reference *rehabilitation* or *diagnostic audiology* to locate the appropriate table for code assignment.
- The section value for the Physical Rehabilitation and Diagnostic Audiology section is F.
- Section qualifier, type, body system and region, type qualifier, equipment, and qualifier are the remaining values identified in the seven-digit code.
- There are four basic categories of rehabilitation and diagnostic audiology procedures.
- The seventh character for the codes in this section is always Z.

Internet Links

For more information on physical therapy, visit **www.physicaltherapy.about.com**.

Chapter Review

Completion: For the <u>underlined</u> character in each code, identify the character type and state the meaning. The first one is done for you.

Code	Character Type	Meaning
1. F14Z<u>3</u>PZ	Type qualifier	Binaural hearing aid
2. F0<u>D</u>Z3MZ	_____	_____
3. F09Z<u>1</u>KZ	_____	_____
4. F06Z4<u>Q</u>Z	_____	_____
5. F07<u>B</u>6CZ	_____	_____
6. F00Z0<u>2</u>Z	_____	_____
7. F02<u>6</u>GYZ	_____	_____
8. F01G<u>0</u>UZ	_____	_____
9. F<u>0</u>DZ05Z	_____	_____
10. F14<u>Z</u>65Z	_____	_____

Coding Assignments

Instructions: For each procedure, select the correct ICD-10-PCS code.

1. pure tone audiometry, air and bone _____
2. Bekesy audiometry assessment using audiometer _____
3. cerumen management _____
4. voice analysis of voice prosthetic _____
5. verbal assessment of patient pain level _____
6. treatment of motor speech using voice analysis _____

7. motor treatment of shoulders and upper back using weights (therapeutic exercise)   _____

8. individual fitting of the left eye prosthesis   _____

9. speech assessment, distorted speech   _____

10. electrophysiologic facial nerve function assessment   _____

11. physical therapy for range of motion and mobility of right hip, no equipment used   _____

12. biosensory feedback, perpetual processing assessment   _____

13. voice analysis   _____

14. auditory processing treatment using computer   _____

15. speech word recognition assessment   _____

16. assessment of electrophysiologic auditory evoked potentials   _____

17. vestibular treatment for musculoskeletal system, postural control   _____

18. tone decay hearing assessment using tympanometer   _____

19. electrotherapeutic wheelchair mobility, motor treatment   _____

20. mechanical gait training   _____

21. motor therapy treatment of lower back muscles using manual therapy   _____

22. therapy using adaptive techniques for wheelchair mobility   _____

23. hearing counseling   _____

24. ADL treatment for dressing using prosthesis   _____

25. caregiver training for patient transfer   _____

Case Studies

Instructions: Review each case study and select the correct ICD-10-PCS code.

Case 1

This is an 81-year-old female who had a CVA 3 weeks ago. She is here for a speech assessment.

ASSESSMENT: Patient underwent testing for receptive/expressive language function. Levels were evaluated. She is showing vast improvement from our last testing, done 12 days ago. Formal report to follow.

Total time with this patient was 60 minutes.

ICD-10-PCS Code Assignment: _____

Case 2

This 78-year-old male is status post hip replacement 6 days ago. He is now at the Sunny Hill Rehabilitation Center, to assess if he will be able to live at home and function normally.

This patient's goal is to be able to groom and dress himself. He is very anxious to able to use the shower but would be unable to get into his tub unassisted. Today we worked on walking to the closet/dresser, walking back to the bed, and assessing his ability to get his clothes on unassisted. He did very well, though he tired easily, and we did not get to the bathroom to brush teeth or wash up. The assessment took 60 minutes.

ICD-10-PCS Code Assignment: _____

Case 3

Patient presents today for therapy for medial meniscus tear, left knee.

Therapy at today's visit included gait and functional ambulation training.

Total time of visit, 35 minutes. Patient tolerated well and was given exercises to perform at home. Looking for increase in strength and ROM at next visit in 2 days.

ICD-10-PCS Code Assignment: _____

Case 4

Audiology Service Note

This 3-year-old twin was born at 27 weeks' gestation. At the time of birth her weight was 2 pounds, 5 ounces. At birth the child failed the Universal Infant Hearing Screen and was then seen by me for auditory brainstem response evaluation. At 2 years old the child was fit with binaural Oticon Tego post-auricular hearing aids. The child presents today for a hearing aid assessment. At this time her canals and TM are clear.

RESULTS:

Testing at an intensity level of 70 dB nHl indicated absolute and interwave latencies that were within normative values. Responses to air-conducted clicks were obtained at intensities down to 30 dB nHl in the right ear and 40 dB nHl in the left ear.

Results are consistent with mild bilateral high-frequency hearing loss. Continued binaural hearing aid use is indicated. Schedule for reevaluation in 3 months.

ICD-10-PCS Code Assignment: _____

Case 5

This 11-year-old male had a hearing screening at school and was then referred to me for further evaluation. History includes middle ear pathology 2 years ago due to ear infections. At this time the left canal and TM are clear. The right TM is obscured due to cerumen.

A tympanometry was conducted using a tympanometer and found to be consistent with normal middle ear pressure and mobility. Hearing is adequate. No further evaluation at this time.

ICD-10-PCS Code Assignment: _____

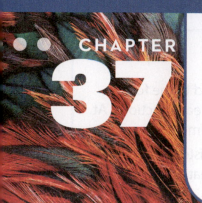

Mental Health and Substance Abuse Treatment

Chapter Outline

Chapter Objectives

Key Terms

Introduction

Mental Health Section

Substance Abuse Treatment Section

Summary

Internet Links

Chapter Review

Coding Assignments

Case Studies

Chapter Objectives

At the conclusion of this chapter, you should be able to:

1. Define key terms presented in this chapter.
2. Discuss the types of services/procedures used for the Mental Health and Substance Abuse Sections of ICD-10-PCS.
3. Identify the character meanings used for the Mental Health and Substance Abuse Sections.
4. Code procedures from these sections.
5. Select procedure codes for case studies.

Key Terms

Abuse

Addiction

Diagnostic and Statistical Manual of Mental Disorders (DSM-5)

Mental disorders

Psychiatrist

Psychiatry

REMINDER: As you work through this chapter, you will need to have a copy of the ICD-10-PCS coding book to reference. For this chapter, you will also need to reference the ICD-10-PCS Official Guidelines for Coding and Reporting. These guidelines can be found in Appendix B which are now available on the Student Companion site and MINDTAP From Cengage.

Introduction

Mental disorders are disorders that affect the ability of a person to function in a healthy, socially acceptable way. **Psychiatry** is the branch of medicine that treats individuals with mental disorders, which include emotional and behavioral disorders. The **psychiatrist** is a medical doctor who administers treatment for patients with mental, emotional, and behavioral disorders. Psychologists and social workers also counsel and treat individuals with mental disorders in a variety of health care settings.

The *Diagnostic and Statistical Manual of Mental Disorders* **(DSM-5)** is the main reference guide for mental health professionals when assigning a diagnosis code to a patient encounter. A mental disorder can manifest itself at different levels of severity in different patients. The DSM-5 helps define conditions for health care professionals to appropriately identify a disorder.

Both the Mental Health Section and the Substance Abuse Treatment Section of ICD-10-PCS are presented in this chapter, and they are discussed separately.

Mental Health Section

The Mental Health Section of ICD-10-PCS is identified with the first-character value of G. All services coded from this section begin with this letter.

In other sections of ICD-10-PCS, the second character position represents body system, anatomical region, physiological system, or section qualifier. According to the Introduction of ICD-10-PCS, the meaning of the second-character position in the Mental Health section is body system. However, in the Mental Health section the second-character position always has a value of Z, None.

> **EXAMPLE:**
>
> G, Mental health
>
> Z, None
>
> 1, Psychological tests: The administration and interpretation of standardized psychological tests and measurement instruments for the assessment of psychological function.

Type

The third character position in the Mental Health section specifies the procedure type. In the case of mental health, the type is the specific service or procedure provided, such as psychological tests, counseling, family psychotherapy, individual psychotherapy, crisis intervention, electroconvulsive therapy, biofeedback, and other mental health procedures. Each of these types has a character value, and the definition is provided next to the type listed in both the Introduction and at the start of the Tables.

> **EXAMPLE:**
>
> G, Mental health
>
> Z, None
>
> 3, Medication management: Monitoring and adjusting the use of medications for the treatment of a mental health disorder.

The value 3, Medication management, is the type, and the description that follows it is the definition assigned to the type medication management in ICD-10-PCS.

The types for mental health are:

- **Psychological tests (value of 1)**—The administration and interpretation of standardized psychological tests and measurement instruments for the assessment of psychological function

- **Crisis intervention (value of 2)**—Treatment of a traumatized, acutely disturbed, or distressed individual for the purpose of short-term stabilization

- **Medication management (value of 3)**—Monitoring and adjusting the use of medications for the treatment of a mental health disorder

- **Individual psychotherapy (value of 5)**—Treatment of an individual with a mental health disorder by behavioral, cognitive, psychoanalytic, psychodynamic, or psychophysiological means to improve functioning or well-being

- **Counseling (value of 6)**—The application of psychological methods to treat an individual with normal developmental issues and psychological problems in order to increase function, improve well-being, alleviate distress, maladjustment, or resolve crises

- **Family psychotherapy (value of 7)**—Treatment that includes one or more family members of an individual with a mental health disorder by behavioral, cognitive, psychoanalytic, psychodynamic, or psychophysiological means to improve functioning or well-being

- **Electroconvulsive therapy (value of B)**—The application of controlled electrical voltages to treat a mental health disorder

- **Biofeedback (value of C)**—Provision of information from the monitoring and regulating of physiological processes in conjunction with cognitive-behavioral techniques to improve patient functioning or well-being

- **Hypnosis (value of F)**—Induction of a state of heightened suggestibility by auditory, visual, and tactile techniques to elicit an emotional or behavioral response

- **Narcosynthesis (value of G)**—Administration of intravenous barbiturates in order to release suppressed or repressed thoughts

- **Group psychotherapy (value of H)**—Treatment of two or more individuals with a mental health disorder by behavioral, cognitive, psychoanalytic, psychodynamic, or psychophysiological means to improve functioning or well-being

- **Light therapy (value of J)**—Application of specialized light treatments to improve functioning or well-being

Qualifier

The fourth character in the Mental Health Section of ICD-10-PCS is a qualifier. The qualifier, the fourth character of a code, is used to indicate more information about the type, the third character of a code.

EXAMPLE: Stan came in today for vocational counseling, which lasted 30 minutes.

G, Mental health

Z, None

6, Counseling: The application of psychological methods to treat an individual with normal developmental issues and psychological problems in order to increase function, improve well-being, alleviate distress, maladjustment, or resolve crises.

Type Qualifier: Character 4	Qualifier: Character 5	Qualifier: Character 6	Qualifier: Character 7
0, Educational			
1, Vocational	Z None	Z None	Z None
3, Other counseling			

Reference the main term *counseling* in the Index, then *Mental Health Services*, then *vocational*, which guides you to code GZ61ZZZ. In the Table, character 4 lists the options: 0, Educational; 1, Vocational; 3, Other Counseling. Stan is receiving vocational counseling, so you identify the type of counseling with the type qualifier of 1 for vocational counseling.

Qualifier

Characters 5, 6, and 7 are qualifiers in the Mental Health Section, and have a value of Z, None. The Z must be used as a placeholder because all codes are reported with seven characters.

 NOTE:

The qualifier character 4 is different for each table. In Table GZ1, for instance, the qualifier of 0 identifies developmental psychological tests. In Table GZ5, the qualifier of 0 identifies interactive individual psychotherapy.

Exercise 37.1—Mental Health Coding

Match the ICD-10-PCS code in column one with the code description given in column two.

ICD-10-PCS Code	*Code Description*
_____ 1. GZ60ZZZ	**a.** bilateral electroconvulsive therapy for single seizure
_____ 2. GZFZZZZ	**b.** hypnosis
_____ 3. GZGZZZZ	**c.** medication management for depression
_____ 4. GZ3ZZZZ	**d.** educational counseling
_____ 5. GZB2ZZZ	**e.** narcosynthesis

Substance Abuse Treatment Section

In general, **abuse** is described as the use of a substance (e.g., alcohol, drugs, or tobacco) in excess without having a physical dependence. The abuse may or may not be to the point where it is having an impact on the patient's daily life. **Addiction** is described as abuse to the point where a person cannot get by without the substance of choice (e.g., alcohol, drugs, or tobacco); the body has become physically dependent on the substance. Patients seek care for both abuse and addiction.

The section identifier for the Substance Abuse Treatment Section is H. This means that the H is located in the first character position.

The second character value is for body system. Because this value does not apply in this section, the value of none is indicated by Z.

Type

Like the third-character position in the Mental Health Section, the type in the Substance Abuse Treatment Section identifies the service performed. These services include:

- Detoxification Services: Detoxification from alcohol and/or drugs.
- Individual Counseling: The application of psychological methods to treat an individual with addictive behavior.
- Group Counseling: The application of psychological methods to treat two or more individuals with addictive behavior.

- Individual Psychotherapy: Treatment of an individual with addictive behavior by behavioral, cognitive, psychoanalytic, psychodynamic, or psychophysiological means.
- Family Counseling: The application of psychological methods that includes one or more family members to treat an individual with addictive behavior.
- Medical Management: Monitoring and adjusting the use of replacement medications for the treatment of addiction.
- Pharmacotherapy: The use of replacement medications for the treatment of addiction.

Qualifier

The fourth character qualifier, further explains the type, the third character.

EXAMPLE: Carrie has been coming in for the past 2 months to take part in our behavioral group counseling session. The group addresses tobacco abuse. This would be reported using the following:

H, Substance abuse treatment

Z, None

4, Group counseling: The application of psychological methods to treat two or more individuals with addictive behavior

Type Qualifier: Character 4	Qualifier: Character 5	Qualifier: Character 6	Qualifier: Character 7
0, Cognitive	Z None	Z None	Z None
1, Behavioral			
2, Cognitive-behavioral			
3, 12-Step			
4, Interpersonal			
5, Vocational			
6, Psychoeducation			
7, Motivational enhancement			
8, Confrontational			
9, Continuing care			
B, Spiritual			
C, Pre/Post-test infectious disease			

The service provided to Carrie is coded as HZ41ZZZ to reflect behavioral group counseling.

Qualifiers

Characters 5, 6, and 7 are qualifiers in the Substance Abuse Treatment Section and have a value of Z, None. The Z must be used as a placeholder because all codes are reported with seven characters.

Summary

- Mental disorders are disorders that affect the ability of a person to function in a healthy, socially acceptable way.
- The Mental Health section of ICD-10-PCS is identified with the first-character value of G.
- Characters 5, 6, and 7 are qualifiers in the Mental Health and Substance Abuse Treatment sections. The place values have a value of Z, None. The Z must be used as a placeholder because all codes are reported with seven characters.

- Abuse is described as the use of a substance (e.g., alcohol, drugs, or tobacco) in excess without physical dependency.
- Addiction is described as abuse to the point where a person cannot get by without the substance of choice (e.g., alcohol, drugs, or tobacco). The body has become physically dependent on the substance.
- The section identifier for the Substance Abuse Treatment Section is H.

Internet Links

For information on different types of abuse, visit **www.nlm.nih.gov** and then use the site's search feature to search on the words *substance abuse*.

For more information on mental disorders, visit **www.apa.org**, the homepage of the American Psychological Association.

Chapter Review

Multiple Choice

Select the best answer that completes the statement or answers the question.

1. _____ are disorders that impact the ability of a person to function in a healthy, socially acceptable way.
   a. Diagnostic disorders
   b. Mental disorders
   c. Health care disorders
   d. Medical disorders

2. A _____ is able to treat patients and prescribe medication in a psychiatric facility.
   a. psychologist
   b. psychiatrist
   c. social worker
   d. nurse

3. The application of controlled electrical voltages to treat mental health disorders is the ICD-10-PCS definition of:
   a. narcosynthesis.
   b. light therapy.
   c. pharmacotherapy.
   d. electroconvulsive therapy.

4. The use of replacement medications for the treatment of addiction is the ICD-10-PCS definition of:
   a. narcosynthesis.
   b. light therapy.
   c. pharmacotherapy.
   d. electroconvulsive therapy.

5. The third-character position in the Substance Abuse section of ICD-10-PCS represents the:
   a. type qualifier.
   b. type.
   c. mental disorder.
   d. body system.

6. Of the following, which identifies a type of substance abuse treatment as identified in ICD-10-PCS?
   a. Biofeedback
   b. Light therapy
   c. Hypnosis
   d. Pharmacotherapy

7. As part of the rehab program at the abuse and addiction center, John was offered vocational training to help him find a job after he finished the program. Which type qualifier is assigned for this type of counseling?
   a. 1
   b. 3
   c. 5
   d. 7

8. Of the following tables, which is referenced if the patient is reporting for methadone maintenance?
   a. HZ2
   b. HZ4
   c. HZ6
   d. HZ8

9. Sam was concerned that he may have been exposed to an STD prior to going to rehab and wanted to get tested to be sure this was not the case. The doctor explained that the counseling performed at this time was the pretest counseling. However, there would also be post-test counseling when he received the results of the test. The counseling is reported from which table?
   a. HZ3
   b. HZ4
   c. HZ5
   d. HZ6

10. Jenny's family had been worried about her state of mind. She was depressed and sad for the past week, but she would not talk about why or what had happened to get her to this point. They decided to have an intervention done before she did something drastic. Which code best describes a crisis intervention?
    a. GZJZZZZ
    b. HZ2ZZZZ
    c. GZ60ZZZ
    d. GZ2ZZZZ

Coding Assignments

Instructions: For each procedure, select the correct ICD-10-PCS code.

1. light therapy _____

2. interactive individual psychotherapy, mental health _____

3. twelve-step group counseling _____

4. individual spiritual counseling for substance abuse _____

5. narcosynthesis _____

6. neurobehavioral and cognitive testing _____

7. clonidine management for substance abuse _____

8. substance abuse detoxification services _____

9. family counseling due to substance abuse _____

10. psychophysiological psychotherapy, individual _____

11. vocational counseling, mental health   _____

12. cognitive-behavioral substance abuse counseling, individual   _____

13. individual interpersonal psychotherapy for drug abuse   _____

14. hypnosis   _____

15. developmental psychological testing   _____

16. pharmacotherapy treatment, bupropion   _____

17. electroconvulsive therapy, bilateral multiple seizures   _____

18. family psychotherapy   _____

19. motivational group counseling for substance abuse   _____

20. psychodynamic psychotherapy for drug-dependent patient   _____

21. group psychotherapy   _____

22. biofeedback   _____

23. substance abuse medication management using Naloxone   _____

24. pharmacotherapy using methadone maintenance   _____

25. confrontational individual psychotherapy for substance abuse   _____

Case Studies

Instructions: Review each case study and select the correct ICD-10-PCS code.

Case 1

Detox Care Unit Discharge Summary

Patient: Zack J. Johns

Age: 42

Zack was brought in by ambulance. He was at a party and had been drinking vodka for 4 hours and then passed out. He began to vomit, and witnesses said that it looked like "he might have had a seizure" but they were not sure. Zack's wife accompanied him to the emergency room and said that Zack does have a drinking problem and thinks he should be admitted for detoxification. Zack was admitted for detox and was moved to the detox unit. Detox was completed.

ICD-10-PCS Code Assignment: _____

Case 2

Counseling Note

This is a 68-year-old female who is being seen today because she feels "tired and very depressed." She states that she has lost her appetite for the past month and has not been

(continues)

(continued)

able to sleep well. Her medical doctor requested she see a counselor so that we can do some counseling, see if we can get her back on track, and make life more pleasurable for her again.

At this time, she denies any substance abuse. She denies any suicidal thoughts or tendencies. She is oriented to time, person, and surroundings with no confusion. She cannot, at this time, identify any situation that might have triggered this state, but she does state that her youngest child just moved out of the area. When asked if this might be the trigger, she did affirm that the timing would be right and it was possible.

She has agreed to meet with me twice a week to talk and see if we can get her back on track.

ICD-10-PCS Code Assignment: _____

Case 3

Counseling Note

This family of five presents today to discuss the eldest son's addiction to cocaine. The patient states that he has been a user for 3 years and the addictive behaviors have increased over the last 3 months. He has been treated for the last 2 months on an outpatient basis due to his cocaine addiction. The parents want to discuss inpatient treatment. I spent 1 hour with the family discussing the best options for the patient and educating them about substance abuse.

ICD-10-PCS Code Assignment: _____

Case 4

This 3-year-old female presents today due to possible developmental delays. The parents state that they feel she is not developing at the same rate that the child's older siblings did. Today I am administering a series of developmental tests.

ICD-10-PCS Code Assignment: _____

Case 5

Outpatient Counseling Note

This 39-year-old male patient presents today due to ongoing treatment for alcohol addiction using a 12-step approach. He has made significant gains in identifying situations that trigger addictive cravings and techniques to prevent relapse. He has not used in 30 days and is encouraged to attend daily AA meetings and to see me in 4 days.

ICD-10-PCS Code Assignment: _____

New Technology Section

Chapter Outline

Chapter Objectives

At the conclusion of this chapter, you should be able to:

1. Identify the characters and meanings used to build a code from the New Technology Section of ICD-10-PCS.
2. Intrepret the ICD-10-PCS guidelines that apply to the New Technology Section.
3. Code procedures from the New Technology Section of ICD-10-PCS.

Key Terms

New Technology   Section X

> **REMINDER:** As you work through this chapter, you will need to have a copy of the ICD-10-PCS coding book to reference. For this chapter, you will also need to reference the ICD-10-PCS Official Guidelines for Coding and Reporting. These guidelines can be found in Appendix B which are now available on the Student Companion site and MINDTAP From Cengage.

Introduction

The **New Technology** section starts with the first character value of X. This section of ICD-10-PCS, also known as **Section X**, will be used to capture new technologies that are requested by the New Technology Application Process and that are not part of another section of ICD-10-PCS.

During various ICD-10 Coordination and Maintenance Committee Meetings, and from public comments, it was decided that codes for new technologies were needed. Because there was opposition to adding new codes to the existing ICD-10-PCS sections, the New Technology Section was created, in a manner that uses the same root operation and body part values as the closest counterparts that appear in the other sections of ICD-10-PCS.

New Technology Section Character Meanings

Section Organization

The first-character value in the New Technology Section is X. The second character indicates the body system. The root operation is indicated in the third-character position, while in the fourth-character position the body part is denoted. The fifth-character position denotes the approach of the root operation. The sixth-character position denotes the device/substance/technology that relates to the procedure performed. The seventh character denotes the new technology group of the procedure, which indicates the year in which the code was added to ICD-10-PCS.

Body System

The second-character position in Section X of ICD-10-PCS denotes the body system. Within Section X this denotes the body system, body region, or the physiological system of the procedure. The values for the second character are:

2—denotes Cardiovascular

H—denotes Skin, Subcutaneous Tissue, Fascia, and Breast

K—denotes Muscles, Tendons, Bursae, and Ligaments

N—denotes Bones

R—denotes Joints

T—denotes Urinary System

V— denotes Male Reproductive System

W—denotes Anatomical Regions

X—denotes Physiological Systems

Y—denotes Extracorporeal

Review Tables X2C, XR2, and XW0 in the ICD-10-PCS manual., and note the display of the second character values.

Root Operation

In Section X of ICD-10-PCS, the third-character position represents the root operation. The root operations are:

- **Assistance (value of A)**—Taking over a portion of a physiological function by extracorporeal means
- **Extirpation (value of C)**—Taking or cutting out solid matter from a body part
- **Fusion (value of G)**—Joining together portions of an articular body part rendering the articular body part immobile
- **Destruction (value of 5)**—Physical eradication of all or a portion of a body part by the direct use of energy, force, or a destructive agent.
- **Dilation (value of 7)**—Expanding an orifice or the lumen of a tubular body part.
- **Introduction (value of 0)**—Putting in or on a therapeutic, diagnostic, nutritional, physiological, or prophylactic substance, excepting blood or blood products
- **Measurement (value of E)**—Determining the level of a physiological or physical function at a point in time.
- **Monitoring (value of 2)**—Determining the level of a physiological or physical function repetitively over a period of time
- **Replacement (value of R)**—Putting in or on biological or synthetic material that physically takes the place and/or function of all or a portion of a body part
- **Reposition (value of S)**—Moving to its normal location, or other suitable location, all or a portion of a body part
- **Supplement (value of U)**—Putting in or on a biological or synthetic material that physically reinforces and/or augments the function of a portion of a body part
- **Transfusion (value of 2)**—Putting in blood or blood products

Section	X New Technology
Body System	R Joints
Operation	2 Monitoring: Determining the level of a physiological or physical function repetitively over a period of time

Body Part Character 4	Approach Character 5	Device Character 6	Qualifier Character 7
G Knee Joint, Right H Knee Joint, Left	0 Open	2 Intraoperative Knee Replacement Sensor	1 New Technology Group 1

Courtesy of the Centers for Medicare & Medicaid Services. www.cms.gov

FIGURE 38-1 Table XR2 of ICD-10-PCS.

Body Part

The body part values in the New Technology Section of ICD-10-PCS specify the same body part values as are found in their closest counterparts in the other sections of ICD-10-PCS. For example, the body part values displayed in Table XR2 include G for right knee joint and H for left knee joint (see Figure 38-1). These are similar to other body part listings in other sections of ICD-10-PCS.

Approach

Character 5 in the New Technology Section of ICD-10-PCS specifies the approach of the procedure as defined in the Medical and Surgical Section of ICD-10-PCS. The values are as follows:

Approach Title	Definition
External	Procedures performed directly on the skin or mucous membrane and procedures performed indirectly by the application of external force through the skin or mucous membrane.
Percutaneous Endoscopic	Entry, by puncture or minor incision, of instrumentation through the skin or mucous membrane and any other body layers necessary to reach and visualize the site of the procedure.
Open	Cutting through the skin or mucous membrane and any other body layers necessary to expose the site of the procedure
Percutaneous	Entry, by puncture or minor incision, of instrumentation through the skin or mucous membrane and any other body layers necessary to reach the site of the procedure
Via Natural or Artificial Opening Endoscopic	Entry of instrumentation through a natural or artificial external opening to reach and visualize the site of the procedure
Via Natural or Artificial Opening	Entry of instrumentation through a natural or artificial external opening to reach the site of the procedure.

Device/Substance/Technology

The sixth-character position of Section X of ICD-10-PCS denotes the new device, substance, or technology being employed during the procedure. This is considered the key feature of the codes from Section X. An example of a new technology that is reported with a code from Section X of ICD-10-PCS is intraoperative knee replacement sensor monitoring of the right knee. This code is built from Table XR2. Review Figure 38-1 to build the code for this procedure.

The code for this procedure would be XR2G021.

Qualifier

The seventh character in Section X of ICD-10-PCS denotes the new technology group. The character is a number or letter that changes each year when new technology codes are added. Using this approach of changing the seventh character allows the values in the third, fourth, and sixth characters to be reused as needed.

Coding Guidelines for Section X of ICD-10-PCS

The New Technology Section of ICD-10-PCS is governed by the following coding guidelines.

ICD-10-PCS Official Coding Guidelines

E. New Technology Section

General guidelines

E1.a

Section X codes fully represent the specific procedure described in the code title, and do not require additional codes from other sections of ICD-10-PCS. When section X contains a code title which fully describes a specific new technology procedure, and it is the only procedure performed, only the section X code is reported for the procedure. There is no need to report an additional code in another section of ICD-10-PCS.

Example: XW04321 Introduction of Ceftazidime-Avibactam Anti-infective into Central Vein, Percutaneous Approach, New Technology Group 1, can be coded to indicate that Ceftazidime-Avibactam Anti-infective was administered via a central vein. A separate code from table 3E0 in the Administration section of ICD-10-PCS is not coded in addition to this code.

E1.b

When multiple procedures are performed, New Technology section X codes are coded following the multiple procedures guideline.

Examples: Dual filter cerebral embolic filtration used during transcatheter aortic valve replacement (TAVR), X2A5312 Cerebral Embolic Filtration, Dual Filter in Innominate Artery and Left Common Carotid Artery, Percutaneous Approach, New Technology Group 2, is coded for the cerebral embolic filtration, along with an ICD-10-PCS code for the TAVR procedure.

Magnetically controlled growth rod (MCGR) placed during a spinal fusion procedure, a code from table XNS, Reposition of the Bones is coded for the MCGR, along with an ICD-10-PCS code for the spinal fusion procedure.

Summary

- The seven characters in the New Technology Section have the following meaning:
  - Character 1   Section
  - Character 2   Body system
  - Character 3   Root operation
  - Character 4   Body part
  - Character 5   Approach
  - Character 6   Device/Substance/Technology
  - Character 7   Qualifier

Internet Links

To learn more about orbital atherectomy, visit ***https://www.cathlabdigest.com/articles/Orbital-Atherectomy-A-new-treatment-complex-peripheral-arterial-disease***.

Chapter Review

True/False

Indicate whether each statement is true (T) or false (F).

1. _____ The New Technology Section of ICD-10-PCS is also known as Section Z.

2. _____ The third-character position in the New Technology Section denotes the body part.

3. _____ Section X codes fully represent the specific procedure described in the code title and do not require additional code from other sections of ICD-10-PCS.

4. _____ Monitoring in Section X of ICD-10-PCS is defined as putting in a therapeutic, diagnostic, nutritional, physiological, or prophylactic substance.

5. _____ The fourth character in the New Technology Section of ICD-10-PCS identifies the approach.

Coding Assignments

Instructions: Using an ICD-10-PCS code book, assign the proper procedure code to the following procedural statements.

1. percutaneous introduction of isavuconazole in central vein, new technology group 1   _____

2. percutaneous introduction of idarucizumab in peripheral vein, new technology group 1   _____

3. orbital atherectomy technology for the extirpation of matter from one coronary artery, percutaneous approach, new technology group 1   _____

4. monitoring of right knee joint using intraoperative knee replacement sensor, open approach, new technology group 1   _____

5. percutaneous introduction of blinatumomab in central vein, new technology group 1   _____

6. introduction of Ceftazidime-Avibactam, percutaneous approach into peripheral vein, new technology group 1   _____

7. extirpation of three coronary arteries using orbital atherectomy, percutaneous approach, new technology group 1   _____

8. monitoring of left knee, open approach, using intraoperative knee replacement sensor, new technology group 1   _____

9. peripheral vein percutaneous introduction of isavuconazole, new technology group 1   _____

10. percutaneous introduction of idarucizumab, dabigatran reversal agent into central vein, new technology group 1   _____

11. Transfusion of Brexucabtagene Autoleucel Immunotherapy via central vein   _____

12. Lumbar vertebral joint fusion, Interbody fusion device, Radiolucent Porous, open   _____

13. Percutaneous dilation of Left Posterior Tibial Artery inserting a Sustained Release Drug-eluting intraluminal Device   _____

14. Endoscopic transurethral Robotic Waterjet Ablation of Prostate   _____

15. Percutaneous reinforcement of Thoracic Vertebra with a mechanically expandable Synthetic substitute   _____

16. Replacement of skin using Porcine Liver Derived, skin substitute   _____

17. Open Reposition Lumbar Vertebra utilizing a Magnetically Controlled Growth Rod   _____

18. Percutaneous dilation of Left Proximal Popliteal Artery inserting 2 Sustained Release Drug-eluting intraluminal Devices   _____

19. New Technology, Introduction of Omadacycline Anti-infective in peripheral vein, percutaneous   _____

20. Introduction of Caplacizumab into subcutaneous tissue   _____

A

abortion artificially terminating a pregnancy.

abruptio placentae a premature sudden separation of the placenta from the uterus prior to or during labor.

abscess a localized collection of pus; indicates tissue destruction.

abuse use of a substance in excess without having a physical dependence.

acariasis being run over or infested with mites or acariads.

access locations skin or mucous membranes that can be punctured or cut to reach the site; external orifices such as the mouth, nares of the nose, or a stoma.

accessory organs secondary organs.

Accrediting Bureau of Health Education Schools (ABHES) accredits graduates of an accredited medical assisting program.

acquired conditions conditions that occur during a person's life.

Acquired Immunodeficiency Syndrome (AIDS) a condition in which the body's immune system deteriorates.

acute bronchitis inflammation of the bronchus that lasts for a short period of time.

acute kidney failure the sudden interruption of kidney function.

addiction abuse to the point that a person cannot get by without the substance of choice.

administrative simplification aspect of the Health Insurance Portability and Accountability Act of 1996 that developed standards for the electronic exchange of health care data by administrative and financial transactions.

adnexa a term for the accessory or appendage of an organ.

adult onset diabetes the body is unable to produce sufficient amounts of insulin within the pancreas; patient might be insulin dependent or not; also known as Type II diabetes.

adverse effect hypersensitivity or reaction to a correct substance properly administered.

aftercare visits services provided during healing or recovery.

agammaglobulinemia a hereditary disorder in which the immunoglobulin (immune proteins) are extremely low, leaving the person open to infection.

agranulocytes cells that do not have a granular appearance.

alcohol abuse drinking alcohol to excess but not having a physical dependence on it.

alcohol dependence a person becomes dependent on alcohol and is unable to stop drinking even though the alcoholism has negative effects on the person's health, social relationships, and normal daily activities such as work; also known as alcoholism.

alcoholism a person becomes dependent on alcohol and is unable to stop drinking even though the alcoholism has negative effects on the person's health, social relationships, and normal daily activities such as work; also known as alcohol dependence.

alimentary canal another name for the digestive system.

alopecia hair loss.

alpha thalassemia condition in which there is a deficiency in the alpha protein being produced.

alteration modifying the anatomical structure of a body part without affecting its function.

altered state of consciousness transient alteration of awareness; altered loss of awareness.

Alzheimer's disease a disease in which brain structure changes lead to memory loss, personality changes, and ultimately impaired ability to function.

American Academy of Professional Coders (AAPC) organization founded in an effort to elevate the standards of medical coding.

American Association of Medical Assistants (AAMA) association that represents individuals trained in performing routine administrative and clinical jobs that keep medical offices and clinics running efficiently and smoothly.

American Health Information Management Association (AHIMA) organization that represents the health information professionals who manage, organize, process, and manipulate patient data.

American Medical Billing Association (AMBA) provides education and networking opportunities for medical billers; offers the Certified Medical Reimbursement Specialist credential (CMRS) and also provides continuing education and ongoing research related to medical billing.

American Medical Technologists (AMT) professional association for medical technicians.

amniocentesis a procedure in which a needle is inserted into the amniotic sac to withdraw fluid for examination.

angina pectoris severe chest pain caused by an insufficient amount of blood reaching the heart.

angiohemophilia a deficiency in the clotting factor and platelet function; also known as von Willebrand disease.

animate object an object capable of moving on its own.

ankylosing spondylitis form of rheumatoid arthritis in which there is a chronic inflammation of the spine and sacroiliac joints that leads to the stiffening of the spine.

ankylosis complete fusion of the vertebrae.

anomaly a deviation from what is normal in the development of a structure or organ.

antepartum the time before childbirth.

anterior forward or front.

anterior chamber a chamber located in front of the lens of the eye.

anxiolytic   sedative that relieves anxiety.

aplastic anemia   failure of bone marrow to produce blood components.

aporosity   Swiss-cheese appearance of the bones, creating a decrease in bone mass.

appendicitis   inflammation of the appendix.

appendix   a wormlike structure that is found at the blind end of the cecum.

approach   the technique or manner in which the surgeon, physician, or provider performs a procedure.

aqueous humor   fluid that fills the two cavities of the interior of the eye.

arteries   vessels that carry oxygen-rich blood from the heart to the body.

arthritis   inflammation of a joint.

arthropods   organisms that include insects, ticks, spiders, and mites.

aspiration pneumonia   occurs when a solid or liquid is inhaled into the lung.

assault   a violent crime committed against another.

assessment   initial and follow-up evaluations of the patient's diagnosis, care plan, need for treatment, and documentation related to the patient's care.

assistance   taking over a portion of a physiological function by extracorporeal means.

atmospheric control   control of atmospheric pressure and composition.

auditory ossicles   the three small bones that transmit sound waves.

auditory tube   connects the bony structures of the middle ear to the pharynx; also known as eustachian tube.

auricle   known as the pinna or earlobe.

autonomic nervous system   the part of the nervous system that regulates the activities of the cardiac muscle, smooth muscle, and glands.

avulsion   a ripping or tearing away.

B

bacteria   one-celled organisms named according to their shapes and arrangements.

bed wetting   incontinence of urine that occurs at night; also known as nocturnal enuresis.

bedsore   a sore resulting from continuous pressure in an area that eventually limits or stops circulation and oxygen flow to an area; also known as decubitus ulcer, pressure ulcer, or pressure sore.

benign prostatic hypertrophy (BPH)   an abnormal enlargement of the prostate.

benign tumors   caused by noncancerous growth of cells.

beta thalassemia   condition in which there is a lack of beta protein being produced.

bile   chemical secreted by the liver to help in digestion.

biopsy   removal of tissue or cells for pathological examination.

birth defect   a deviation from what is normal in the development of a structure or organ; also called an anomaly.

blepharitis   inflammation of the eyelids.

blepharochalasis   atrophy of the intercellular tissue that causes relaxation of the skin of the eyelid.

body mass index (BMI)   figured by taking a person's weight and height and figuring the index of fat in relation to these elements.

bones   dense, porous, calcified connective tissue that protect the internal organs and form the framework of the body.

bony labyrinth   consists of bones that make up the inner ear.

brackets   used in the Tabular Listing and Alphabetic Index to enclose synonyms, alternative wording, abbreviations, or explanatory phrases.

bronchi   formed when the trachea branches off in the chest.

bronchitis   inflammation of the bronchus.

burn   an injury to body tissue as a result of heat, flame, sun, and/or chemicals, radiation, or electricity.

bursa   synovial-fluid-filled sac that works as a cushion to assist in movement.

bursitis   an inflammation of the bursa.

bypass   altering the route of passage of the contents of a tubular body part.

C

ca in situ (CIS)   neoplastic cells that are undergoing malignant changes confined to the original epithelium site without invading surrounding tissues; also called transitional cell carcinoma, noninfiltrating carcinoma, noninvasive carcinoma, and preinvasive carcinoma.

calculus   a stone in the kidney or ureter.

cancer   condition that is characterized by malignant neoplasm.

cancerous growth   a condition in which cancer cells multiply; also called a malignant neoplasm.

candidiasis   fungal infections caused by the *Candida* fungus; also known as moniliasis.

canthus   inner edge of the eye.

carbuncles   furuncles cluster and form a puslike sac.

carcinoma   cancer of epithelial cells of connective tissue.

carcinoma in situ (CIS)   neoplastic cells that are undergoing malignant changes confined to the original epithelium site without invading surrounding tissues; also called transitional cell carcinoma, noninfiltrating carcinoma, noninvasive carcinoma, and preinvasive carcinoma.

cardiomyopathy   diseases of the heart muscle.

caregiver training   educational in nature, teaching the caregiver skills and knowledge necessary to interact with and properly assist the patient.

cartilage   smooth, nonvascular connective tissue that comprises the more flexible parts of the skeleton.

cataracts   the abnormal loss of transparency of the lens of the eye.

cecum   the end of the ileum and the start of the large intestine.

cellulitis   a type of infection that develops in the layers of the skin.

Centers for Medicare and Medicaid Services (CMS)   a government agency responsible for maintaining the procedure codes of ICD-10-PCS.

central nervous system (CNS) the part of the nervous system made up of the brain and spinal cord.

cerebral hemorrhage bleeding in the brain or layers of brain lining.

cerebral palsy a disorder in which the motor function of the brain is impaired; present at birth, chronic, and nonprogressive.

cerebrovascular accident (CVA) disruption in the normal blood supply to the brain; also called a stroke.

cerebrovascular disease abnormal nontraumatic conditions that affect the cerebral arteries.

Certified Coding Associate (CCA) certification offered by the AHIMA.

Certified Coding Specialist (CCS) certification offered by the AHIMA.

Certified Coding Specialist, Physician-Based (CCS-P) certification offered by the AHIMA.

Certified Documentation Improvement Practitioner (CDIP) certification offered by AHIMA.

Certified Health Data Analyst (CHDA) certification offered by the AHIMA.

Certified in Healthcare Privacy and Security (CHPS) certification offered by the AHIMA.

Certified Inpatient Coder (CIC) certification offered by the AAPC.

Certified Outpatient Coder (COC) certification offered by the AAPC.

Certified Professional Coder (CPC) certification for coders offered by the AAPC.

Certified Professional Coder, Hospital Based (CPC-H) certification for coders in a hospital setting.

Certified Risk Adjustment Coder (CRC) certification offered by the AAPC.

cerumen honey-colored, thick, waxy substance; also known as earwax.

ceruminous gland sweat glands found in the external auditory canal.

chalazion a small tumor of the eyelid caused by the retention of secretions of the meibomian gland.

change taking out or taking off a device from a body part and putting back an identical or similar device in or on the same body part without cutting or puncturing the skin or a mucous membrane.

childbirth the delivery of one or more infants.

chiropractor a doctor who practices chiropractic medicine.

chlamydiae a type of bacteria that lives inside a host cell and is usually dormant but at some point can become active in a disease process.

choclear duct a membranous structure that is found in the inner ear and aids in the hearing process.

cholecystitis inflammation of the gallbladder.

cholelithiasis formation or presence of gallstones.

choroids layer just beneath the sclera containing capillaries that provide the blood supply and nutrients to the eye.

chronic bronchitis prolonged inflammation lasting for more than 3 months and occurring for two consecutive years.

chronic kidney disease (CKD) progressive disease in which renal failure increases, causing multisystem problems.

chronic renal failure progressive disease in which renal failure increases, causing multisystem problems.

chronic sinusitis prolonged inflammation of one or more of the sinus cavities.

cilia tiny hairs along the external auditory canal.

ciliary body muscles responsible for adjusting the lens.

cleft lip congenital defect that results in a deep groove or opening of the lip running upward to the nose; also called a harelip.

cleft palate a congenital groove or opening of the palate that involves the hard palate, soft palate, or both, as well as the upper lip.

closed fracture a fracture in which the bone is broken but the skin has not been broken; also known as a complete or simple fracture.

coagulation process of blood clotting.

cochlea snail-shaped, bony structure in the ear that transmits sound.

cochlear duct a membranous structure that aids in the hearing process.

Code Also instructs the coder that two codes may be needed to fully code the diagnostic phrase being coded; no sequencing directions are provided.

Code First notes appearing in the Tabular section of ICD-10-CM and identifying for the coder the sequence of the code assignment.

coding the assignment of numerical or alphanumerical characters to specify diagnostic and procedural phrases.

colitis an inflammation of the colon.

Colles' fracture a wrist fracture that typically occurs when a person tries to break a fall by extending the arm.

colon used in the Tabular listing after a term that is modified by one or more terms following the colon.

coma a deep state of unconsciousness.

combination code a single code used to classify two diagnoses, a diagnosis with an associated secondary process, or a diagnosis with an associated complication.

comminuted fracture the bone is crushed and may be splintered.

Commission on Accreditation of Allied Health Education Programs (CAAHEP) accredits medical assisting programs in both public and private postsecondary institutions throughout the United States.

complete fracture a fracture in which the bone is broken but the skin has not been broken; also known as a closed or simple fracture.

complete placenta previa occurs when the placenta entirely covers the cervical os.

complete prolapse entire uterus descends and protrudes beyond the introitus, and the vagina becomes inverted.

complicated fracture an internal organ injured as a direct result of the fracture.

compound fracture a fracture that has broken through the skin at the fracture site; also known as an open fracture.

compression putting pressure on a body region.

compression fracture   the bone is pressed on itself.

compression fractures of the spine   the vertebrae in the spine become weak and collapse under low stress.

computed tomography (CT scan)   multiplanar images that have been computer reformatted.

concussion   a violent shaking or jarring of the brain.

congenital anomaly   a disorder that exists at the time of birth and may be a result of genetic factors, agents causing defects in the embryo, or both.

conjunctiva   colorless mucous membrane that lines the anterior part of the eye.

constitutional aplastic anemia   congenital or hereditary anemia.

contrast material   material injected into the patient to allow for quicker identification of abnormalities in the body due to image density.

control   stopping, or attempting to stop, postprocedural bleeding.

conventions   a group of instructional notes, punctuation marks, abbreviations, and symbols.

conversion disorders   conditions occurring when a patient represses emotional conflicts; sensory, motor, or visceral symptoms occur.

cornea   a transparent nonvascular structure located on the anterior portion of the sclera.

corrosion   a burn due to chemicals.

creation   making a new genital structure that does not take over the function of a body part.

Crohn's disease   a form of inflammatory bowel disease that can cause the thickening and scarring of the abdominal wall; also known as regional enteritis.

culture and sensitivity (C&S)   a test that identifies the type of organism causing the infection (the culture), and the sensitivity identifies the antibiotic that should be used to treat the infection.

Cushing's syndrome   condition that results from the excessive and chronic production of cortisol by the adrenal cortex or by the administration of glucocorticoids in large doses for a period of several weeks or longer.

cutane   skin.

cystitis   an inflammation of the bladder.

D

dacryoadenitis   inflammation of the lacrimal gland.

decompression   extracorporeal elimination of undissolved gas from body fluids.

decubitus ulcer   sore resulting from continuous pressure in an area that eventually limits or stops circulation and oxygen flow to an area; also known as pressure sore, pressure ulcer, or bedsore.

deformity   a problem in the structure or form that may or may not be disfiguring.

degenerative joint disease   a type of osteoarthritis.

delivery   assisting the passage of the products of conception from the genital canal.

delusional disorders   include the feeling of paranoia in which the patient has a constant distrust and suspicion of others.

dementia   a loss of brain function that impacts memory, language, judgment, and the ability to think logically.

depressed fracture   the skull bone is broken and pushed inward.

dermatitis   an inflammation of the upper layer of the skin.

dermis   the thick layer of tissue located directly below the epidermis.

destruction   eradicating all or a portion of a body part.

detachment   cutting off of all or a portion of an extremity.

developmental dyspraxia   an impaired ability to perform coordinated movements in the absence of any defect in sensory or motor functions.

device   an object that is supposed to remain in the body after the completion of a procedure, such as a pacemaker.

diabetes mellitus   chronic problem resulting from problems with the pancreas.

Diagnostic and Statistical Manual of Mental Disorders, Fifth Revision (DSM-5)   psychiatric disorders diagnosed by psychiatrists most commonly are recorded using the nomenclature established by the American Psychiatric Association and set forth in the DSM-5.

diagnostic examinations   used to confirm or rule out a suspected diagnosis due to signs and symptoms that the patient has experienced.

diastolic blood pressure   the pressure on the arterial walls during relaxation of the heart muscle.

dilation   expanding an orifice or the lumen of a tubular body part.

direct inguinal hernia   a protrusion in the groin area.

dislocation   a body part has moved out of place; also known as luxation.

dissociative disorders   characterized by emotional conflicts in which the patient represses the emotions in such a manner that a separation in the personality occurs.

diverticula   pouches or sacs in the lining of the intestine that cause diverticulitis if the sacs become inflamed.

diverticulitis   inflammation of the diverticula.

diverticulosis   abnormal condition of the pouches or sacs in the lining of the intestine known as diverticula.

division   separating, without taking out, a body part.

dorsopathies   disorders of the back.

Dowager's hump   an abnormal curvature in the upper thoracic spine.

drainage   taking or letting out fluids and/or gases from a body part.

dressing   putting material on a body region for protection.

drug abuse   taking drugs to excess but not having a dependence on them.

drug dependence   the chronic use of drugs that creates a compulsion to take them in order to experience their effects.

dual-code assignment   occurs when two codes are needed to code a diagnostic statement.

duodenal ulcer   an ulcer that occurs in the upper part of the small intestine.

duodenum   the start of the small intestine at the end of the stomach.

dysplasia   an abnormal development or growth of cells.

E

ear lobe   the flexible cartilaginous flap that has a bottom portion known as the pinna.

ectopic pregnancy   a pregnancy that occurs outside the uterus.

electromagnetic therapy   extracorporeal treatment by electromagnetic rays.

embryo   the developing child from conception through the eighth week of pregnancy.

emphysema   the loss of lung function due to progressive decrease in the number of alveoli in the bronchus of the lung.

encapsulated   surrounded by a capsule; confined to an area within a capsule; not able to metastasize.

encephalitis   an inflammation of the brain.

encephalomyelitis   inflammation of both the brain and spinal cord.

encopresis   the involuntary passage of feces.

endocarditis   the inflammation of the inner layer of the heart.

endocrine system   consists of several different internal groups of glands and structures that produce or secrete hormones.

endolymph   one of the auditory fluids found in the cochlea that aid in hearing.

endometriosis   an abnormal growth of the endometrium outside the uterus.

end-stage renal disease (ESRD)   the late stage of chronic renal failure.

enteritis   an inflammation of the intestines.

entropion   the turning inward of the border of the eyelid against the eyeball.

enuresis   incontinence of urine.

eosinophilia   a condition in which the eosinophil white blood cell is found in excess in the blood or body tissues.

epidermis   the outermost layer of the skin.

epilepsy   a transient disturbance of cerebral function that is recurrent and characterized by episodes of seizures.

epiphora   tearing of the eyes.

erythrocytes   red blood cells that are formed in the bone marrow.

Escherichia coli (E. coli)   rod-shaped bacillus found in the large intestine of humans.

esophagitis   an inflammation of the esophagus.

esophagus   structure that connects the throat to the stomach.

eustachian tube   connects the bony structures of the middle ear to the pharynx; also known as the auditory tube.

excision   cutting out or off, without replacement, a portion of a body part.

Excludes   notes used to signify that the conditions listed are not assigned to the category or block of category codes.

Excludes1   used to signify that the diagnostic terms listed are not coded to the category or subcategory; therefore, the two conditions are mutually exclusive.

Excludes2   used to signify that the diagnostic terms listed after the note are not part of the condition(s) represented by the code or code block.

external   outside of the body.

external auditory canal   the canal that allows sound waves to travel to the inner part of the ear; also known as the external auditory meatus.

external auditory meatus   the canal that allows sound waves to travel to the inner part of the ear; also known as the external auditory canal.

external ear   the visible part of the ear, not within the structure of the skull.

extirpation   the taking or cutting out of solid matter from a body part.

extracorporeal   something that is outside of the body.

extraction   pulling or stripping out or off all or a portion of a body part.

eyelashes   located along the edge of the eyelids to protect the eye from foreign material.

eyelids, upper and lower   the lids that protect the eyes and help to keep the surface of the eyeball lubricated.

F

factitious disorders   characterized by a patient exhibiting disease symptoms caused by the patient's deliberate actions to gain attention.

fascia   connective tissue that not only covers but supports and separates muscle.

female genitalia   the female reproductive organs.

female genital prolapse   downward displacement of the genital organs.

fetus   the developing child from the ninth week until birth.

first-degree burns   burns that do not present a danger to the patient because they are limited to the outer layer of the epidermis.

fissured fracture   the bone has a narrow split that does not go through to the other side.

fitting(s)   necessary to fabricate, modify, and/or design a splint, orthosis, prosthesis, hearing aid, or other rehabilitative device for application.

fluoroscopy   external ionizing radiation on a fluorescent screen captures a single-plane or biplane real-time image, which can also be stored by digital or analog means.

folate   a water-soluble B vitamin most commonly found in food.

folate deficient anemia   insufficient amounts of folic acid, which is needed for proper cell reproduction and growth.

forceps delivery   an instrument is used to grasp the fetus to assist in the delivery.

fracture (fx)   broken bones resulting from undue force or pathological changes.

fragmentation breaking solid matter in a body part into pieces.

fungi microscopic plant life that lack chlorophyll and are not able to manufacture their own food.

fusion the joining of portions of an articular body part, rendering the part immobile.

G

gallbladder stores bile secreted by the liver.

gastric ulcer an ulcer that occurs in the stomach.

gastroesophageal reflux disease (GERD) the reflux of stomach acid and pepsin into the esophagus, causing inflammation.

gastrointestinal (GI) tract of the digestive system.

gastrojejunal ulcer an ulcer that occurs in the stomach and the jejunum.

geographic tongue on the tongue, irregularly shaped patches that resemble landforms on a map.

glaucoma disease of the eye marked by increased pressure in the eyeball that may result in damage to the optic nerve, causing the gradual loss of vision.

glomerulonephritis inflammation of the glomeruli of the kidneys.

glucose needed for the cells to properly supply energy for the body's metabolic functions.

goiter a condition in which the thyroid becomes enlarged even though hormone secretions fall within normal limits.

grand mal severe seizure.

granularity the level of detail.

granulocytes cells with a granular appearance.

greenstick fracture as with a greenstick of a tree, the bone bends as well as breaks.

H

hair a form of protection used by the body to keep foreign material from entering through the skin.

hallucinogens substances that induce a perception of visual image or a sound that is not present.

harelip a congenital defect that results in a deep groove or opening of the lip running upward to the nose; also called a cleft lip.

healed myocardial infarction identifies a history of a heart attack in the past.

Health Insurance Portability and Accountability Act of 1996 (HIPAA), Public Law 104-191 law passed by Congress in 1996 that mandates how paper and electronic health information is cared for and monitored.

heart a muscular organ that pumps blood throughout the body.

heart attack occurs when there is inadequate blood supply to a section or sections of the heart; also known as myocardial infarction.

heart failure a decreased ability of the heart to pump a sufficient amount of blood to the body's tissue.

helminths organisms that include flatworms, roundworms, and flukes.

hemiparesis a condition in which one side of the body is paralyzed due to brain hemorrhage, cerebral thrombosis, embolism, or a tumor of the cerebrum; a synonym for hemiplegia.

hemiplegia a condition in which one side of the body is paralyzed due to brain hemorrhage, cerebral thrombosis, embolism, or a tumor of the cerebrum; a synonym for hemiparesis.

hemolytic anemia occurs when red blood cells are broken down at a faster rate than bone marrow can produce them.

hemorrhoids enlarged veins in or near the anus.

hepatic pertaining to the liver.

hereditary factor VIII deficiency a form of hemophilia.

hernia a protrusion or bulge through the tissue that normally contains the structure.

herniated disc the result of the rupture of the nucleus pulposus, or the material in the center of the disc.

hiatal hernia the sliding of part of the stomach into the chest cavity.

high osmolar contrast material (HOCM) material that has a higher level of particle concentration than normal body fluids.

hirsutism excessive hair growth.

hives urticaria.

hordeolum commonly known as a sty.

hormones chemical substances produced by the body to keep organs and tissues functioning properly.

host supports a parasite.

Human Immunodeficiency Virus (HIV) the virus that leads to AIDS.

hydrocephalus an accumulation of fluid in the cranial meninges.

hyperparathyroidism an abnormal condition of the parathyroid glands in which there is an excessive secretion of parathyroid hormone.

hypertension an increase in systolic pressure, diastolic pressure, or both.

hyperthermia the raising of body temperature.

hyperthyroidism the thyroid is producing excessive amounts of thyroid hormones.

hypnotics sleep-inducing agents.

hypoparathyroidism the abnormal or insufficient secretion of parathyroid hormone by the parathyroid glands, caused by a primary parathyroid dysfunction or elevated serum calcium level.

hypotension low blood pressure.

hypothermia the lowering of body temperature.

hypothyroidism the thyroid is not operating as efficiently as it could be due to a deficiency of hormone secretion.

I

ICD-10-CM abbreviation for the *International Classification of Diseases*, Tenth Revision, Clinical Modification; an arrangement of classes or groups of diagnoses and procedures by systemic division.

ICD-10-PCS abbreviation for the ICD-10 Procedure Coding System; the most recent version of the ICD coding system set up to replace volume 3 of the ICD-9-CM system.

ICD-10 Procedure Coding System   the most recent version of the ICD coding system set up to replace volume 3 of the ICD-9-CM system.

idiopathic aplastic anemia   a condition in which the bone marrow is not able, for unknown reasons, to produce cells properly.

ileum   the last part of the small intestine, starting at the end of the jejunum.

immobilization   limiting or preventing motion of a body region.

immune system   the body's defense mechanism against disease and other foreign materials.

impacted fracture   one end of the broken bone is wedged into the other bone.

impulse disorders   characterized by a sudden desire or urge to act without consideration of consequences that may result.

inanimate object   object that is not alive or able to move (animate) on its own power.

Includes   note used to define and/or give examples of the content of a particular category or a block of category codes.

incomplete prolapse   the uterus descends into the introitus.

incus   anvil-shaped bone of the middle ear; one of the auditory ossicles.

Index to Diseases and Injuries   alphabetic listing of terms and corresponding codes in the ICD-10-CM.

Index to External Causes of Injuries   alphabetic listing of terms and corresponding codes in the ICD-10-CM.

indirect inguinal hernia   a protrusion that has moved to the scrotum.

In Diseases Classified Elsewhere   applies to the etiology/manifestation conventions.

infectious arthropathies   disorders of the joints that are caused by an infectious agent.

infectious diseases   diseases that occur when a microorganism invades the body and causes disease.

influenza   highly contagious respiratory disease.

inguinal hernia   part of the intestine passes through a weak point or tear in the abdominal wall.

inhalants   substances that are inhaled for their euphoric effect.

insertion   putting in a nonbiological appliance that monitors, assists, performs, or prevents a physiological function but does not physically take the place of a body part.

in situ neoplasms   neoplastic cells that are undergoing malignant changes confined to the original epithelium site without invading surrounding tissues; also known as carcinoma in situ, ca in situ, or CIS.

inspection   visually and/or manually exploring a body part.

instructional notes   appear in both the Tabular List and Alphabetic Index of ICD-10-CM and provide further instruction for the coder.

instrumentation   the specialized equipment used to perform a procedure on an internal body part.

insulin   used by the body to process glucose.

insulin-dependent diabetes mellitus (IDDM)   a form of diabetes in which the patient requires insulin injections to survive; patient may be a type I or a type II diabetic.

integumentary   covering or outer layer.

intellectual disabilities   classified as mild, moderate, severe, or profound based on the person's current level of functioning.

International Classification of Diseases, Tenth Revision (ICD-10)   produced by the World Health Organization and used as a basis for the ICD-10-CM.

International Classification of Diseases, Tenth Revision, Clinical Modification (ICD-10-CM)   an arrangement of classes or groups of diagnoses and procedures by systemic division.

International Classification of Diseases, Tenth Revision, Procedure Coding System (ICD-10-PCS)   developed as a replacement for ICD-9-CM volume 3–Procedure codes; a newer, larger, more comprehensive procedural coding system devised by 3M Health Information Systems.

introduction   putting in or on a therapeutic, diagnostic, nutritional, physiological, or prophylactic substance other than blood or blood products.

iris   the colored portion of the eye.

irrigation   putting in or on a cleansing substance.

ischemic heart disease   an inadequate supply of blood to the heart caused by an occlusion.

isotope   one of two or more atoms that contain the same atomic number but have different mass numbers in the nucleus.

J

jejunum   starts at the end of the duodenum and is the middle section of the small intestine.

joints   allow for bending and rotating movements.

juvenile diabetes, IDDM   form of diabetes in which the patient has an insufficient amount of insulin secretions, requiring insulin injections; also known as type I diabetes mellitus.

K

kidneys   bilateral organs located against the dorsal wall that filter blood to constantly to remove waste.

kleptomania   pathological stealing.

L

labor and delivery   process of childbirth.

labyrinth   bony and membranous structures of the inner ear.

lacrimal duct   the duct that drains the tears from the eye through the eye and that is located at the inner edge of the eye.

lacrimal gland   the gland that produces tears.

lagophthalmos   the inability of the eye to close completely.

larynx   made up of cartilage and ligaments that compose the vocal cords or voice box.

late effect a condition produced after the acute phase of an illness or injury has terminated.

lateral away from the midline toward the side.

laterality for bilateral sites ICD-10-CM indicates the specific site.

legally induced abortion termination of a pregnancy that is done by medical personnel working within the law.

lens a colorless structure that allows the eye to focus on images.

leukemia cancer of the blood-forming organs.

leukocytes white blood cells that protect the body from disease.

ligaments bands of connective tissue that connect the joints.

lipoma a benign neoplasm of adipose tissue.

liver considered an accessory organ of the digestive system that filters red blood cells, produces glycogen, and secretes bile.

low osmolar contrast material (LOCM) · material with a lower level of particle concentration than normal body fluids.

lungs the main organs of the respiratory system.

lupus a disease in which the body produces too many antibodies, which begin to turn against the patient's own body, attacking body organs, joints, and muscles.

luxation a body part has moved out of place; also known as dislocation.

lymphadenitis inflammation of the lymph nodes.

lymphoma cancer of the lymph nodes and immune system.

M

magnetic resonance imaging (MRI) multiplanar images developed from the capture of radio frequency signals emitted by nuclei in a particular body site excited within a magnetic field that can produce a computer-formatted digital display of the images.

male genitalia made up of the scrotum, testicles, and the penis.

malignant neoplasm cancerous growth.

malignant primary refers to the originating site of a malignant tumor.

malignant secondary refers to the site of tumor metastasis.

malleus hammer-shaped bone found in the middle ear; one of the auditory ossicles.

malunion fracture the fracture site is misaligned.

map locating the route of passage of electrical impulses and/or the functional areas in a body part.

measurement determining the level of something at a point in time.

medial closest or nearest to the midline of a structure.

Medical Association of Billers (MAB) founded in 1995 and approved and licensed by the Commission for Post Secondary Education; offers the CMBS, CMBS-CA, CMBS-H, and CMBSI credentials.

medicaments term for medicine.

melanocytes cells that produce dark pigment.

melanoma fast-growing cancer of melanin-producing cells.

membranous labyrinth a term used to describe the structures in the inner ear that are not bony structures.

meningitis the inflammation of the membranes, or meninges, of the spinal cord or brain.

menopause the time in a woman's life when her menstrual cycle ceases.

mental disorders disorders that affect the ability of a person to function in a healthy, socially acceptable way.

metabolism the rate at which energy is used by the body and at which body functions occur.

metastasize the growing and spreading of cancer to other body parts.

methemoglobinemia a disorder of the hemoglobin in which oxygen is not able to be transported by the cells.

method specifies how the external access location was entered when a procedure is performed on an internal body part.

micturate voiding or urinating.

middle ear also known as the tympanic cavity; found in the temporal bone and houses the auditory ossicles.

mild intellectual disabilities an IQ of 50–55 to approximately 70; also referred to as mild mental subnormality or mild mental retardation.

missed abortion the fetus has died before the completion of 22 weeks of gestation, with the retention of the dead fetus or products of conception for up to 4 weeks after demise.

modality in medicine, a certain protocol, therapeutic method, or agent.

moderate intellectual disability an IQ of 35–40 to 50–55; also referred to as moderate mental subnormality or moderate mental retardation.

molar pregnancy a blighted ovum in the uterus that develops into a mole or benign tumor.

mold caused by long filament-shaped fungi.

moniliasis a fungal infection that can affect various sites; also called candidiasis.

monitoring determining the level of something over a period of time.

morbidity the rate or frequency of disease; diseased state.

morphology the form and structure of neoplastic growth of cells.

mortality the rate or frequency of death.

multiple sclerosis a demyelinating disorder in which patches of hardened tissue form in the brain or spinal cord and cause partial or complete paralysis and muscle tremors.

muscle holds the body erect and allows movement.

myelitis an inflammation of the spinal cord.

myelopathy any disorder of the spinal cord.

myelophthisis severe form of anemia in which certain bone marrow material shows up in the peripheral blood.

myocardial infarction (MI) occurs when there is inadequate blood supply to a section or sections of the heart; also called a heart attack.

myocarditis inflammation of the heart muscle.

myositis inflammation of the muscle.

N

nails hardened cells of the epidermis.

National Center for Health Statistics (NCHS) organization responsible for maintaining the diagnostic codes that are found in volume 1 and 2 of the ICD-CM manual.

NEC (not elsewhere classified) used to signal coders that the term being coded is considered a general term.

neoplasms uncontrolled abnormal growth of cells; also called tumors.

neoplasms of uncertain behavior neoplasms in which cells are not histologically confirmed even after pathological investigation.

neoplasms of unspecified behavior tumors in which the morphology and behavior of the neoplasm are not specified in the patient's medical record.

nephritis the inflammation of the kidneys.

nephrons found in the kidneys and used to filter, reabsorb, and secrete urine.

nephropathy a disease or disorder of the kidney.

nephrosis a disease or disorder of the kidney.

nervous system system that controls all bodily activities and is made up of the central nervous system and the peripheral nervous system.

neutropenia an abnormal decrease of granular leukocytes in the blood.

New Technology a section in the ICD-10-PCS manual that was added in October 2015 to code procedures that relate to new technologies that are not coded in other sections of ICD-10-PCS.

nicotine a poisonous alkaloid found in tobacco.

nocturnal enuresis incontinence of urine that occurs at night; also known as bed wetting.

nonessential modifiers the terms found in the parentheses that do not change code assignment.

nonimaging nuclear medicine assay after the introduction of radioactive materials, radioactive emissions are detected, identified, and measured in the body fluids and blood elements.

nonimaging nuclear medicine probe after the introduction of radioactive materials into the body, there is a study of the distribution and fate of certain substances by the detection of the radioactive emissions.

nonimaging nuclear medicine uptake after the introduction of radioactive materials into the body, organ function can be determined from the detection of radioactive emissions.

noninfiltrating carcinoma neoplastic cells that are undergoing malignant changes confined to the original epithelium site without invading surrounding tissues; also known as transitional cell carcinoma, carcinoma in situ, noninvasive carcinoma, and preinvasive carcinoma in situ.

noninsulin-dependent diabetes mellitus (NIDDM) a type of diabetes in which the patient does not require insulin injections to survive; the diabetic patient might be controlled by diet, exercise, or other medications outside of insulin, and is usually a type II diabetic.

noninvasive carcinoma neoplastic cells undergoing malignant changes that are confined to the original epithelium site without invading surrounding tissues; also called transitional cell carcinoma, noninfiltrating carcinoma, carcinoma in situ, and preinvasive carcinoma.

nonmalignant tumor not life-threatening, benign.

nonunion fracture fracture fragments fail to unite.

NOS (not otherwise specified) codes are not specific and should be used only after the coder has clarified with the physician that a more specific code is not available.

nuclear medicine treats and diagnoses diseases using small amounts of radioactive material to create an image.

O

obsessive-compulsive disorder a psychoneurotic disorder where the patient has obsessions or compulsions and suffers extreme anxiety or depression that can interfere with the patient's ability to function occupationally, interpersonally, or socially.

obstetrical care medical care that occurs during pregnancy and childbirth.

obstetrics medical care that occurs during pregnancy and childbirth.

occlusion complete closure of an orifice or lumen of a tubular body part, such as a vessel.

occlusion of cerebral and precerebral arteries the blocking of arteries.

old myocardial infarction identifies a history of a heart attack in the past.

omphalitis the inflammation of the navel.

open cutting through the skin or mucous membrane and any other body layers necessary to expose the site of the procedure.

open fracture a fracture that has broken through the skin at the fracture site; also known as a compound fracture.

open with percutaneous endoscopic assistance cutting through the skin or mucous membrane and any other body layers necessary to expose the site of the procedure, along with entry by puncture or minor incision of instrumentation through the skin or mucous membrane and any other body layers necessary to aid in the performance of the procedure.

optic disc the blind spot on the optic nerve that is the point of entry for the artery supplying blood to the retina.

optic nerve the nerve that transmits impulses to the brain from the eye.

organ of corti the true organ of hearing found in the cochlea.

osteoarthritis (OA) most common form of arthritis; causes the degeneration of the articular cartilage.

osteopathic manipulation therapy (OMT) manually guided therapy that is performed to improve physiological function.

osteoporosis the reduction in bone mass that is responsible for different conditions affecting a person's health.

otalgia earache.

other procedures a methodology that attempts to remediate or cure a disorder or disease.

otitis externa the inflammation of the external auditory canal.

otorrhagia   hemorrhage from the ear.

otorrhea   a discharge from the external ear.

otosclerosis   a growth of spongy bone in the inner ear.

oval window   what separates the middle ear and inner ear.

ovarian cyst   an encapsulated sac of the ovary that is filled with semisolid or liquid material.

P

packing   putting material in a body region.

pancreas   anatomically located under the stomach in the upper abdomen; performs various physiological functions.

pancytopenia   a decrease in the number of platelets, white blood cells, and red blood cells.

paralysis   the loss of sensation or voluntary motion.

paraphilias   sexual perversions or deviations.

parasite   lives within another organism and may or may not cause disease.

parasitic disease   a disease caused by an organism that lives within another organism and that can cause illness.

parentheses   used in both Tabular List and Alphabetic Index around terms providing additional information about the main diagnostic term.

Parkinson's disease   a progressive disease characterized by a masklike facial expression, weakened muscles, tremors, and involuntary movement.

partial placenta previa   occurs when the placenta covers part of the cervical os.

pathogen   a microorganism that can cause disease in humans.

pathologic fracture   a break of diseased bone that occurs from a minor stress or injury that would not normally occur in healthy bone.

pedal cycle   type of transportation operated by a person without the help of a motor.

pedestrian   any person who is not riding in or on any type of motor or wheeled form of transportation.

pediculosis   an infestation of lice.

penis   the male organ that functions in both the urinary and reproductive systems.

peptic ulcer   an ulcer that occurs in an unspecified site of the GI tract.

percutaneous   entry, by puncture or minor incision, of instrumentation through the skin or mucous membrane and/or any other body layers necessary to reach the site of the procedure.

percutaneous endoscopic   entry, by puncture or minor incision, of instrumentation through the skin our mucous membrane and/or any other body layers necessary to reach and visualize the site of the procedure.

performance   completely taking over a physiological function by extracorporeal means.

perfusion   extracorporeal treatment by diffusion of therapeutic fluid.

periapical abscess   an infection of the pulp and surrounding tissue.

pericarditis   the inflammation of the outer layers of the heart.

perilymph   one of two auditory fluids found in the inner ear that aid in the transmission of sound.

perimenopausal   when symptoms of menopause begin.

perinatal period   the time surrounding the birth of the child and up to 28 days after birth.

peripheral nervous system (PNS)   the part of the nervous system that directly branches off the central nervous system.

peritonitis   inflammation of the lining of the abdominal cavity.

pernicious anemia   an autoimmune disorder in which the stomach is unable to produce intrinsic factor needed to absorb vitamin B_{12}.

petit mal   a seizure, less severe than a grand mal.

pharyngitis   a sore throat.

pharyngotympanic tube   connects the bony structures of the middle ear to the pharynx; also known as the eustachian tube.

pharynx   the throat.

pheresis   the separation of blood products.

phlebitis   the inflammation of a vein.

phototherapy   treatment by light rays.

pica   a person has an abnormal craving and eating of substances that are not normally eaten by humans.

pinna   flexible cartilaginous flap that has a bottom portion known as the ear lobe.

placenta previa   the abnormal positioning of the placenta in the lower uterus so that the cervical os is partially or completely covered.

plain radiography   standard x-ray, with planar display of an image.

planar nuclear medicine imaging   single-plane display of images after the introduction of radioactive materials.

plasma   the liquid portion of the blood, without its cellular elements.

platelets   ovoid-shaped structures that initiate blood clotting.

pneumonia   a condition in which liquid, known as exudates, and pus infiltrate the lung and cause inflammation.

point dash   a signal to the coder that the code contains a list of options at a level of specificity past the three-character category.

poisoning   an overdose of a substance or the intake of a wrong substance given or taken in error.

polycystic kidney disease   an inherited disorder in which the kidneys gradually lose the ability to function due to the grapelike clusters of cysts that form.

polymorphonuclear neutrophils   white blood cells found in the peripheral blood.

polysubstance drug use   indiscriminate use of multiple drugs.

portal vein thrombosis   a blood clot in the main vein of the liver.

positron emission tomographic imaging (PET)   a three-dimensional image is produced after the introduction of radioactive materials but the images are simultaneously captured 180 degrees apart.

posterior   back or behind.

posterior chamber   a chamber located behind the lens of the eye.

postmenopausal   when a woman has not had a period for at least 1 year until the time she celebrates her 100th birthday.

postpartum   from birth until 6 weeks after the birth.

preinvasive carcinoma   neoplastic cells undergoing malignant changes that are confined to the original epithelium site without invading surrounding tissues; also called transitional cell carcinoma, noninfiltrating carcinoma, noninvasive carcinoma, and carcinoma in situ.

premenopausal   the time right before menopause.

pressure sore   sore resulting from continuous pressure in an area that eventually limits or stops circulation and oxygen flow to an area; also known as decubitus ulcer, pressure ulcer, or bedsore.

pressure ulcer   sore resulting from continuous pressure in an area that eventually limits or stops circulation and oxygen flow to an area; also known as decubitus ulcer, pressure sore, or bedsore.

principal diagnosis   the condition defined after study as the main reason for admission of a patient to the hospital.

procedure   the complete specification of the seven characters to identify what service was performed.

products of conception   all of the physical components of a pregnancy, including the fetus, amnion, umbilical cord, and the placenta.

profound intellectual disability   IQ below 20–25; also referred to as profound mental subnormality or profound mental retardation.

prostate gland   secretes fluid that is part of the semen and also aids in the motility of the sperm in the male.

protozoa   one-celled organisms that live on living matter and are classified by the way they move.

psychiatrist   a medical doctor who administers treatment for patients with mental, emotional, and behavioral disorders.

psychiatry   the branch of medicine that deals with mental disorders.

pterygium   a benign growth over the conjunctiva of the eye.

puerperium   the postpartum period beginning from birth until 6 weeks after birth.

pulp   the center of a tooth.

pulpitis   an abscess of the pulp.

pupil   the center of the iris that controls the amount of light entering the eye.

pure red cell aplasia   a condition in which precursors to the red blood cells are affected in the bone marrow and eventually cease to be produced.

purpura   the accumulation of blood under the skin that forms multiple pinpoint hemorrhages.

pyromania   an impulse disorder characterized by the desire to set fires.

 Q

qualifier   additional information unique to the individual procedure being performed.

 R

radiation oncology (rad onc)   a form of radiology that is therapeutic as opposed to diagnostic.

radioactive isotopes   radioactive material used to create an image.

radiologic technician   a person specially trained to use the equipment unique to the radiology department.

radiologist   a doctor whose specialty is radiology.

radiology   the study of x-rays, high-frequency sound waves, and high-strength magnetic fields, which sometimes includes the use of radioactive compounds to diagnose and/or treat disease or injuries.

radionuclide   a radioactive substance that can be found in nature, that can be human-made, and that is the source of the radiation causing the emissions for the image to be produced; also called a radioactive isotope or radiopharmaceutical.

radiopharmaceutical   a radioactive substance that can be found in nature, that can be human-made, and that is the source of the radiation causing the emissions for the image to be produced; also called a radioactive isotope or radionuclide.

reattachment   putting back in or on all or a portion of a separated body part in its normal location or other suitable locations.

red blood cells (RBCs)   disc-shaped cells formed in the bone marrow that contain hemoglobin.

reduction   the act of putting something back into its proper place.

regional enteritis   a form of inflammatory bowel disease that can cause the thickening and scarring of the abdominal wall; also known as Crohn's disease.

Registered Health Information Administrator (RHIA)   certification offered by AHIMA to members who have obtained their bachelor's degree from an accredited program.

Registered Health Information Technician (RHIT)   certification offered by AHIMA to members who have obtained their associate's degree from an accredited program.

Registered Medical Assistant (RMA)   professional credentials for a medical technician.

release   the freeing of a body part.

removal   taking out or off a device from a body part.

renal colic   acute pain caused by the passage of a kidney stone from the kidney through the ureter.

repair   restoring, to the extent possible, a body part to its normal anatomic structure and function.

replacement   putting in or on a biological or synthetic material that physically takes the place of all or a portion of a body part.

reposition   moving to its normal location or other suitable location all or a portion of a body part.

resection   cutting out or off, without replacement, all of a body part.

respiratory system   the system containing structures that exchange oxygen and carbon dioxide in the body.

restoration   the return or the attempt to return a physiological function to its natural state by extracorporeal means.

restriction   partially closing an orifice or lumen of a tubular body part.

resuscitation   procedure performed to restore cardiac and/or respiratory function.

retina   the nerve cell layer of the eye that changes light rays into nerve impulses.

revision   correcting, to the extent possible, a malfunctioning or displaced device.

rheumatism   the general term for the deterioration and inflammation of connective tissue, including muscles, tendons, synovium, and bursa.

rheumatoid arthritis (RA)   an autoimmune disease in which the synovial membranes are inflamed and thickened.

root operation   the objective of the procedure, such as bypass, drainage, fluoroscopy, and the like.

rumination disorder of infancy   when a person regurgitates and chews previously swallowed food.

S

saccule   membranous sac that aids in maintaining balance.

sarcoma   cancer of supportive tissue, such as blood vessels, bones, cartilage, and muscles.

schizophrenia   a psychotic disorder characterized by disruptive behavior, hallucinations, delusions, and disorganized speech.

sclera   the white portion of the eye that maintains the shape of the eyeball.

screening examinations   examinations used to screen, or look, for diseases.

sebaceous glands   glands of the skin that produce an oily secretion to condition the skin.

secondary diagnoses   conditions that are not responsible for admission but that exist at the time of treatment.

secondary hypertension   high arterial blood pressure due to another disease, such as vascular disease.

second-degree burn   a partial-thickness burn that forms blisters.

Section X   also known as the New Technology Section in ICD-10-PCS, this section was added to ICD-10-PCS in October of 2015.

sedatives   drugs that induce a relaxed state and calm or tranquilize a patient.

See   used in the Alphabetic Index and instructs the coder to cross-reference the term or diagnosis following the notation.

See Also   refers the coder to another location in the Alphabetic Index when the initial listing does not contain all the necessary information to select an accurate code.

semicircular canals   bony structures filled with fluid that help maintain balance.

semicircular ducts   found in the middle ear; aid in balance.

sepsis   a life-threatening bacterial infection that causes clots to form, which block blood flow to vital organs.

septicemia   bacteremia with sepsis.

sequela (late effect)   the residual effect (condition produced) after the acute phase of an illness or injury has terminated.

severe intellectual disability   IQ of 20–25 to 35–40; also referred to as severe mental subnormality or severe mental retardation.

severe sepsis   a septic infection with associated acute organ dysfunction or failure.

shock wave therapy   treatment by shock waves.

sickle-cell anemia   genetic disorder in which the development of an abnormal type of hemoglobin in red blood cells causes decreased oxygenation in the tissues.

sickle-cell trait   an asymptomatic condition in which the patient receives the genetic trait from only one parent.

sideropenic dysphagia   a type of iron-deficiency anemia that becomes so severe that the patient has difficulty swallowing in addition to the other symptoms of anemia; also known as Plummer-Vinson syndrome.

sign   observed by the physician/provider and objective evidence of disease.

simple fracture   a fracture in which the bone is broken but not the skin; also known as a closed or complete fracture.

single-code assignment   occurs when only one code is needed to code the diagnostic statement.

somatoform disorders   characterized by symptoms that suggest a physical illness or disease but for which there are no organic causes or physiologic dysfunctions.

spina bifida   a congenital condition in which the spinal canal fails to close around the spinal cord.

spiral fracture   a severe twisting motion causes the bone to twist apart.

spirochetal   a gram-negative bacteria made up of spiral-shaped cells.

spleen   located in the upper-left quadrant of the abdomen; the site of lymphocyte and monocyte formation and erythrocyte storage.

spondylitis   an inflammation of the vertebrae.

sprain   an injury to a joint, specifically the ligament of the joint that becomes stretched.

stapes   stirrup-shaped bone that is part of the middle ear; one of the auditory ossicles.

stenosis   narrowing of the cerebral arteries that supply blood to the brain.

stomach   pouchlike structure at the end of the esophagus.

strain   an injury at the joint site to a muscle or tendon.

stress fracture   excessive impact on the bone causes small hairline crack.

stroke   the disruption in the normal blood supply to the brain; also called a cerebrovascular accident.

subcutaneous   the layer of skin that connects to the muscle surface.

subluxation   part of the joint surface has moved away from where it should be; also called a partial dislocation.

supplement   putting in or on biological or synthetic material that physically reinforces and/or augments the function of a portion of a body part.

suspensory ligaments   ligaments that attach to the lens and hold it in place.

symptom   the reason that brings a patient to seek medical attention; the subjective information.

syncope a condition in which there is a brief loss of consciousness due to lack of oxygen to the brain; also known as fainting.

synovia the fluid that acts as a lubricant for joints, tendon sheath, or bursa.

systemic nuclear medicine therapy the introduction of unsealed radioactive material into the body for treatment; does not include the encapsulated radioactive material used in cancer treatment.

systolic blood pressure the pressure on the arterial walls during heart muscle contraction.

T

Tabular List of Diseases and Injuries an alphanumerical list of codes, commonly referred to as the *Tabular*; divided into chapters based on body system (anatomical site) or condition (etiology).

tendons connect muscle to bone.

teratogens agents that cause defects in an embryo.

terrorism the unlawful use of force or violence against persons or property to intimidate or coerce a government, the civilian population, or any segment thereof in the furtherance of political or social objectives.

thalassemia red blood cells are not formed or functioning properly, and the globulin gene arrangement is affected.

third-degree burn full-thickness burn affecting the epidermis, dermis, and subcutaneous layers.

thrombocytes one of the cellular elements of blood; also known as platelets.

thrombocytopenia an abnormal decrease in platelet count that causes purpural hemorrhages.

thrombolytic therapy the intravenous administration of thrombolytic agents, often completed to open the coronary artery occlusion and to restore blood flow to the cardiac tissue.

thrombophilia a condition in which the patient is predisposed to develop thromboses.

thrombophlebitis the inflammation of a vein with the formation of a thrombus.

thyroid gland secretes hormones that regulate growth and metabolism.

thyrotoxic crisis symptoms of hyperthyroidism that are so severe as to threaten the patient's life; also known as thyrotoxic storm.

thyrotoxic storm symptoms of hyperthyroidism that are so severe as to threaten the patient's life; also known as thyrotoxic crisis.

tic disorder a repetitive involuntary muscle spasm that is usually psychogenic and that can increase due to stress or anxiety.

tomographic nuclear medicine imaging (tomo) a three-dimensional display of images, developed from the capture of radioactive emissions.

tonsils protect the entrance to the respiratory system.

trachea the windpipe.

traction exerting a pulling force on a body region in a distal direction.

transcobalamin II necessary to transport vitamin B_{12}.

transfer moving, without taking out, all or a portion of a body part.

transfusion putting in blood or blood products.

transitional cell carcinoma neoplastic cells undergoing malignant changes and confined to the original epithelium site without invading surrounding tissues; also called carcinoma in situ, noninfiltrating carcinoma, noninvasive carcinoma, and preinvasive carcinoma.

transplantation putting in or on all or a portion of a living body part taken from another individual or animal to physically take the place and/or function of all or portion of a similar body part.

treatment manual treatment to eliminate or alleviate somatic dysfunction and related disorders.

trichiasis the turning inward of the eyelashes.

trichotillomania an impulse disorder characterized by the desire to pluck hair.

tuberculosis an infection caused by *Mycobacterium tuberculosis* that spreads throughout the body via lymph and blood vessels and that most commonly localizes in the lungs.

tubular body parts hollow body parts that provide a route of passage for solids, liquids, or gases.

tumor the uncontrolled abnormal growth of cells; also called a neoplasm.

tympanic cavity the middle ear found in the temporal bone and housing the auditory ossicles and the eustachian tube.

tympanic membrane the eardrum.

type similar to root operation.

type I diabetes mellitus type of diabetes with insufficient amount of insulin secretion, so that the patient requires insulin injections; also known as juvenile diabetes.

type II diabetes mellitus type of diabetes in which the body is unable to produce sufficient amounts of insulin in the pancreas; patient might be insulin dependent or not; also known as adult-onset diabetes.

U

U codes represent codes for special purposes in ICD-10-CM.

ulcerative colitis the colon becomes inflamed, and ulcers develop in the lining of the intestine.

ulcers erosions of the skin in which tissue becomes inflamed and then lost.

ultrasonography the real-time display of images of anatomy, developed from the capture of reflected and attenuated high-frequency sound waves.

ultrasound therapy treatment by ultrasound.

ultraviolet light therapy treatment by ultraviolet light.

underdosing taking less of a medication than what is prescribed or instructed by the physician or the manufacturer, whether deliberately or inadvertently.

unstable angina an accelerating, or crescendo, pattern of chest pain that occurs at rest or during mild exertion, typically lasting longer than angina pectoris and not responsive to medication.

ureters very narrow tubes that conduct urine from the kidneys to the bladder.

urethra a small tube extending from the bladder to outside the body.

urethral stricture a narrowing of the urethra.

urethritis an inflammation of the urethra.

urinary bladder holds urine until it moves to the urethra.

urinary system the system that maintains the balance of the contents of the fluids in the body.

urinary tract infection (UTI) the abnormal presence of microorganisms in the urine.

urine fluid waste.

urticaria hives.

Use Additional Code instructs the coder to use an additional code to identify the manifestation that is present.

uterus the organ that sits above the cervix and houses a fetus until birth.

utricle the structure of the inner ear that aids in maintaining balance.

V

valgus deformity of feet congenital outward turning of the feet.

varicose veins dilated superficial veins of the legs.

varus deformity of feet congenital inward turning of the feet.

Vault of the skull made up of the two parietal bones and the frontal bone.

veins vessels that carry deoxygenated blood from the body back to the heart.

vertebral column shields the spinal column and is made up of cervical, thoracic, and lumbar vertebra.

vestibule the central portion of the inner ear.

via natural or artificial opening the entry of instrumentation through a natural or artificial external opening to reach the site of the procedure.

via natural or artificial opening endoscopic the entry of instrumentation through a natural or artificial external opening to reach and *visualize* the site of the procedure.

via natural or artificial opening with percutaneous endoscopic assistance the entry of instrumentation through a natural or artificial external opening and entry, by puncture or minor incision, of instrumentation through the skin or mucous membrane and any other body layers necessary to aid in the performance of the procedure.

virus the smallest of infectious pathogens.

vitamin B$_{12}$ deficiency anemia anemia due to an insufficient dietary intake of vitamin B$_{12}$ or the inability of the body to absorb vitamin B$_{12}$ appropriately.

vitreous humor a clear, jellylike fluid that fills the posterior chamber of the eye and that helps to shape the eye.

vocal cords ligaments that produce sound or speech when air passes through them.

voiding urination or micturating.

Volkmann's deformity congenital dislocation of the tibiotarsal.

von Willebrand disease the most common of the hereditary bleeding disorders, in which the clotting process is not working properly.

W

white blood cells (WBCs) protect the body from disease; also called leukocytes.

World Health Organization (WHO) responsible for preparing and publishing the revisions to ICD system; based in Geneva, Switzerland.

Y

yeast infection caused by unicellular fungi that reproduce by budding.

Z

Z codes used to report encounters when the circumstances surrounding the encounter are for something other than disease or injury.

INDEX

E

J

K